INNOVATIONS IN ADOLESCENT
SUBSTANCE ABUSE INTERVENTIONS

INNOVATIONS IN ADOLESCENT SUBSTANCE ABUSE INTERVENTIONS

EDITED BY

ERIC F. WAGNER

Florida International University, Florida, USA

HOLLY B. WALDRON

University of New Mexico, New Mexico, USA

2001

Pergamon
An Imprint of Elsevier Science

Amsterdam – London – New York – Oxford – Paris – Shannon – Tokyo

ELSEVIER SCIENCE Ltd
The Boulevard, Langford Lane
Kidlington, Oxford OX5 1GB, UK

First edition 2001

Library of Congress Cataloging in Publication Data
A catalog record from the Library of Congress has been applied for.

British Library Cataloguing in Publication Data
A catalog record from the Library of Congress has been applied for.

ISBN 0-08-043577-7

∞ The paper used in this publication meets the requirements of ANSI/NISO Z39.48-1992 (Permanence of Paper).
Printed in The Netherlands.

Contents

Contributors

Nicole M. Attaway
Alcohol Studies
Department of Psychology
Rutgers University
Piscataway, NJ

Nate Azrin, Ph.D.
Center for Psychological Studies
Nova Southeastern University
Fort Lauderdale, FL

Nancy P. Barnett, Ph.D.
Center for Alcohol and Addiction Studies
Brown University
Providence, RI

Gilbert J. Botvin, Ph.D.
Institute for Prevention Research
Cornell University Medical College
New York, NY

Sandra A. Brown, Ph.D.
Departments of Psychology and Psychiatry
University of California San Diego
La Jolla, CA

Brenna Hafer Bry, Ph.D.
Department of Psychology
Rutgers University
Piscataway, NJ

Michael L. Dennis, Ph.D.
Chestnut Health Systems
Bloomington, IL

Thomas J. Dishion, Ph.D.
Child and Family Center
Department of Psychology
University of Oregon
Eugene, OR

Brad Donohue, Ph.D.
Department of Psychology
University of Nevada
Las Vegas, NV

Leona L. Eggert,
Ph.D., RN, FAAN
University of Washington School of Nursing
Seattle, WA

Andres G. Gil, Ph.D.

College of Health and Urban Affairs
Florida International University
Miami, FL

Mark D. Godley, Ph.D.

Chestnut Health Systems
Bloomington, IL

Kenneth W. Griffin, Ph.D.
M.P.H.

Institute for Prevention Research
Cornell University Medical College
New York, NY

William B. Hansen, Ph.D.

Tanglewood Research
Greensboro, NC

Susan Harrington Godley,
Ph.D.

Chestnut Health Systems
Bloomington, IL

Jerald R. Herting, Ph.D.

Psychosocial and Community Health
Sociology Department
University of Washington
Seattle, WA

Aaron Hogue, Ph.D.

Department of Psychology
Fordham University
New York, NY

Shannon I. Jackson, M.A.

Department of Clinical and Health Psychology
University of Florida
Gainesville, FL

Yifrah Kaminer, M.D.

Alcohol Research Center
Department of Psychiatry
University of Connecticut Health Center
Farmington, CT

Jon D. Kassel, Ph.D.

Department of Psychology
University of Illinois at Chicago
Chicago, IL

Kathryn Kavanagh, Ph.D.

Child and Family Center
Department of Psychology
University of Oregon
Eugene, OR

Elizabeth Kortlander, Ph.D.

Teen Intervention Project
Florida International University
Miami, FL

William W. Latimer, Ph.D.

Community Integration
University of Minnesota
Minneapolis, MN

Howard A. Liddle, Ph.D.   Center for Treatment Research on Adolescent Drug Abuse
Department of Epidemiology and Public Health
University of Miami School of Medicine
Miami, FL

Peter M. Monti, Ph.D.   Providence VA Medical Center and Center for Alcohol and
Addiction Studies
Brown University
Providence, RI

Staci Leon Morris, Psy. D.   Teen Intervention Project
Florida International University
Miami, FL

Mark G. Myers, Ph.D.   Department of Psychiatry
University of California San Diego
Veterans Affairs
V.A. Medical Center
San Diego, CA

Brooke P. Randell,   University of Washington School of Nursing
DNSc, CNS   Seattle, WA

Randy Stinchfield, Ph.D.   Department of Psychiatry
University of Minnesota
Minneapolis, MN

Elaine A. Thompson,   University of Washington School of Nursing
Ph.D., RN   Seattle, WA

Jonathan G. Tubman, Ph.D.   Department of Psychology
Florida International University
Miami, FL

Eric F. Wagner, Ph.D.   College of Health and Urban Affairs
Florida International University
Miami, FL

Holly B. Waldron, Ph.D.   Department of Psychology
University of New Mexico
Albuquerque, NM

Ken C. Winters, Ph.D.   Department of Psychiatry
University of Minnesota
Minneapolis, MN

Mark D. Wood, Ph.D.   Center for Alcohol and Addiction Studies
Brown University
Providence, RI

Preface

The idea for this volume began with a symposium that took place in 1998 at the annual meeting of the Research Society on Alcoholism. I had assembled a group of NIH-funded investigators who shared an interest in the development and empirical validation of developmentally sensitive intervention approaches for adolescents with substance use problems. The speakers in this symposium included Sandra Brown, Peter Monti, Mark Myers, Holly Waldron, and myself, and we received a warm reception from the members of RSA who attended the session. One of the things that became quite apparent during this symposium was the absence of any single book that researchers, students, and practitioners could turn to for guidance about appropriate interventions for teens with alcohol or other drug problems. Recognition of this void motivated Holly Waldron and me to put together a book proposal, which I shopped to David Hoole at Elsevier Science. David was enthusiastic about our idea, and a book contract soon followed. In retrospect, this may have been the easiest part of putting this volume together.

Three years later, I finally am sending this volume to press. I will spare you the details about what it took to bring this book to fruition, but suffice it to say that we were more than a little bit naïve about how much work it would take to put an edited volume like this together. However, I am convinced that it was worth the effort—I certainly learned a great deal, and I think we have ended up with a unique and important contribution to the literature.

While probably not news to readers of this book, knowledge about effective assessment and intervention approaches for teen substance use and abuse remains limited. While certain approaches have demonstrated effectiveness, many currently used instruments and programs do not. Until very recently, approaches used with substance abusing adolescents have mirrored those used with adult clients. While this was a good place to start, clinicians and researchers have increasingly recognized that adolescent specific developmental issues need to be taken into account for assessment, prevention, and treatment programs to be effective with teens.

For this book, we sought out contributors who have actively pursued research agendas concerned with developmentally appropriate approaches to the assessment, prevention, or treatment of substance use problems among adolescents. We recruited some of the best researchers in the field to write chapters for this volume, and, in my estimation, they produced excellent pieces. The chapters are loosely arranged along a continuum of care beginning with assessment, progressing to substance use prevention, moving next to early intervention, and concluding with treatment and aftercare. We also have included two "special topics" chapters particularly relevant to addressing substance use problems among teenagers.

I would like to briefly acknowledge those persons who helped make this volume a reality. Holly Waldron, the book's co-editor, worked diligently to recruit authors and edit chapters. Her enthusiasm and dedication were especially appreciated given the personal tumult she has endured over the past three years. Diana Jones, who inherited from David Hoole the unenviable job of making sure we came through on our promises to Elsevier, was a gentle and patient publishing editor. She demonstrated particular skill and insight in using behavioral and motivational techniques to help move us along in bringing this book to press. Sandy Brown, Mark and Linda Sobell, Michel Hersen, Dick Longabaugh, Ellen Frank, and Saul Shiffman, who through their teaching, mentoring, and friendship, provided guidance and inspiration for pursuing this kind of work. Edwin and Carol Wagner, who as parents, psychologists, and book authors, contributed both genetically and environmentally to my life and work. Susan Tarolla, who through her good humor, sharp intellect, and ability to spot a typo at 50 paces, was an incredibly helpful editors' assistant. The National Institute on Alcohol Abuse and Alcoholism, and especially Joanne Fertig and Cherry Lowman, supported my training and research in the treatment of addictions, and thus indirectly this book. Finally, Sady Reyes, who through her love, encouragement, and faith, inspired me to get the book done so I could spend more time with her.

Eric F. Wagner
Coconut Grove, Florida

Chapter 1

Assessing Adolescent Substance Use

Ken C. Winters, William W. Latimer, and Randy Stinchfield*

Introduction

Although no large-scale national epidemiological surveys exist of diagnosable substance use disorder rates in general adolescent populations, estimates based on limited community surveys have been recently published. Cohen and colleagues (Cohen *et al.*, 1993) found in a representative household sample of 676 New York State youths alcohol abuse disorder prevalence rates of 3.5 percent for 14- to 16-year-olds and 14.6 percent for 17- to 20-year-olds. Perhaps the largest investigation of its kind, Harrison and colleagues (Harrison, Fulkerson & Beebe, 1998) surveyed 74,000 Minnesota high school students and found among 9th graders seven percent met criteria for substance abuse and four percent for substance dependence, and among 12th graders 16 per cent for substance abuse and seven percent for substance dependence.

Whereas there is preliminary evidence that various treatment approaches can reduce drug use and the related consequences among clinic-referred adolescents (Winters, 1999), there is a need for a meaningful effort to identify youth having few but significant substance use problems and to address them efficiently outside the context of specialized treatment. Suitable methods of identification require conceptual agreement on which assessment variables are relevant and what measures of such variables are appropriate. Because drug involvement and related problems occur along a continuum of severity, and given the potential relevance of diagnostic boundaries in determining referral criteria, both dimensional and categorical measurement strategies are needed in the field.

To provide a framework for this chapter, we begin with a discussion of the substance use problem severity continuum and its heterogeneity, followed by a discussion of the abuse threshold. The chapter then discusses core variables and domains relevant to adolescent substance abuse assessment, and several issues related to the assessment process, including developmental considerations and the validity of self-report. Finally, the chapter provides an overview of prominent screening and comprehensive assessment instruments.

*This study was supported in part by National Institute on Drug Abuse grants 04434 and 05104 to the first author and by National Institute on Drug Abuse grant 00254 (Scientist Development Award) to the second author. The authors acknowledge Nikki Anderson for assisting with the manuscript. Correspondence concerning this chapter should be addressed to Ken C. Winters, Department of Psychiatry, University of Minnesota, F282/2A West, 2450 Riverside Avenue, Minneapolis, MN 55454 (winte001@umn.edu).

Issues of Definition

Given the heterogeneity of adolescent drug involvement, a broad definition of adolescent substance abuse is warranted. Clearly, few teenagers who use drugs, even regularly, are or will become drug dependent. Yet when problems associated with drug involvement are severe and when frequency of use is habitual and long standing, a substance dependence disorder may emerge. At the other end of the spectrum is the more common pattern in which use is infrequent and consequences are minimal and transient. If we take a traditional "diagnostic" view of drug involvement, abuse is defined as use of psychoactive substances that increases risk of harmful and hazardous consequence and dependence is defined as a pattern of compulsive seeking and using substances despite the presence of severe personal and negative consequences. However, these distinctions often do not consider the special case of adolescents (Martin & Winters, 1998). The abuse term is often used to refer to any use by adolescents because on legal grounds alone, any use of substances is illegal; or some believe that use of any substance contributes to the "abuse" of a developing body and personality. Several other limitations of traditional diagnostic criteria for adolescents have been noted, including that 1) diagnostic symptoms ignore reasons for drug use; 2) excessive heterogeneity is produced by the one symptom threshold for a substance abuse diagnosis, 3) abuse symptoms do not always precede the onset of dependence symptoms in youth, which is contrary to expectations about the progression of substance use involvement, and 4) an appreciable percentage of regular users display one or two dependence symptoms but no abuse symptoms (Kaczynski & Martin, 1995; Martin, Kaczynski, Maisto, Bukstein & Moss, 1996; Winters *et al.*, 1999).

Regardless of the suitability of traditional nomenclature for adolescents, it is useful to take a developmental perspective when considering how youth progress to severe involvement with drugs. Drug use problem severity may be conceptualized along the following continuum (Center for Substance Abuse Treatment, 1999b): 1) Abstinence; 2) Experimental Use: Minimal use, typically associated with recreational activities; often limited to alcohol use; 3) Early Abuse: More established use, often involving more than one drug; greater frequency; adverse consequences begin to emerge; 4) Abuse: Regular and frequent use over an extended period; several adverse consequences emerge; 5) Dependence: Continued regular use despite repeated severe consequences; signs of tolerance; adjustment of activities to accommodate drug seeking and drug use.

The problem severity of drug use is also determined, in part, by the age of the child. Research has consistently revealed frequent alcohol use among a majority of high school age students (Johnston, O'Malley & Bachman, 1999). Any level of alcohol use or other drug experimentation during pre-adolescence is not normative and has been shown to predict a variety of adverse outcomes, including later substance abuse, deviant behavior, and school failure. Experimental use during later adolescence may reflect non-problem behavior if it desists on its own after a time-limited period. However, a comparable level of experimental use is a definite risk factor if exhibited by a younger adolescent. Thus, experimental use exhibited by a ten-year-old is cause for much greater concern than the same level of use exhibited by a 16-year-old. A general rule regarding the relationship between age and problem severity is that signs of early abuse reflect danger and a need, at minimum, for secondary prevention.

The progression from substance abuse or dependence to recovery has been researched extensively by Prochaska and colleagues. Five stages of change in addictive behaviors have been identified across a substantial number of studies (Prochaska & DiClemente, 1992). Precontemplation is when there is no intention to change behavior in the foreseeable future. Contemplation refers to individuals who are seriously thinking about overcoming drug use, but have yet to make a commitment to take action. Preparation refers to individuals who are intending to take action to change their behavior. Action refers to individuals who are modifying their behavior to overcome drug use. Maintenance involves work to prevent relapse and consolidate gains attained during action. Research spanning approximately 15 years suggests that therapeutic techniques have an optimal effect when coordinated with the client's stage of change (Prochaska, DiClemente & Norcross, 1992).

Naturally, any response to an adolescent who is using substances should be consistent with the severity of involvement and their level of motivation for behavior change. These considerations should be addressed within the broad range of treatment interventions that exist, ranging from preventive and brief intervention strategies (e.g., abstinence contract, risk elimination, risk reduction, pattern normalization) to minimal interventions to long-term residential treatment. While no explicit guidelines exist, the most intensive treatment services should be devoted to youth who show signs of dependency, that is, a history of regular and chronic use, with the presence of multiple personal and social consequences and evidence of an inability to control or stop using substances. Of course, any system that matches client problem severity with an appropriate level of care is irrelevant if such a continuum of treatment does not exist.

The Abuse Threshold

The idea that any use of psychoactive substances constitutes abuse is widely accepted at present, at least in part because of the use by adolescents of almost all psychoactive substances including alcohol and tobacco is illegal. It is therefore asserted by some authorities that there is no meaningful distinction between use and abuse.

There are problems with the simplest forms of this claim. Because the majority of adolescents experiment with alcohol and many experiment with other substances, to define abuse as use implies that virtually every adolescent requires some sort of drug abuse intervention. This creates a definition of abuse that is too broad to be meaningful. Many of those who use alcohol or other drugs when they are young, particularly those who use does not reach a regular use pattern or lead to serious adverse consequences, do not reveal serious substance abuse problems as they make the transition into young adulthood (Shedler & Block, 1990). Given the scarcity of treatment services, equating use and abuse seems impractical because it hinders the identification of those who should receive early intervention or more intensive treatment.

One alternative is to conceptualize the abuse threshold and the stages that precede and follow it in terms of a combination of use patterns that place the individual at unacceptable levels of health risk, as well as in terms of negative consequences resulting from such use. This conceptualization further assumes that it is important to identify several stages that precede the severe, dependent, end of the continuum. Thus, the single heterogeneous "abuse category" would be replaced by more specificity. The "early abuse" and "abuse" distinction noted above is one such example. It is further recommended that the delineation of stages should be sensitive to identifying those users who are most appropriate targets for a given level of treatment (Newcomb & Bentler, 1989).

Several considerations should be included and factored into the linking of drug use behaviors and assignment to intensity of intervention. First, the use of some drugs (e.g., crack cocaine) is sufficiently dangerous that, by itself and in the absence of any other personal consequences or diagnostic symptoms, is a cause for intervention. Second, an age distinction is important in that any regular use (apart from other considerations) by a child or very young adolescent is sufficient criteria for early intervention or treatment. Third, prolonged use of intermediate quantities of drugs or acute ingestion of large quantities of drugs at any age is sufficiently risky that such behavior probably justifies intervention. Fourth, use in particularly inappropriate settings (e.g., prior to driving, or during school hours) may be considered "abuse" even in the absence of the overtly negative consequences of such use; it makes no sense to delay intervention until the person advances to more serious consequences such as getting arrested or involved in a disastrous automobile accident. Fifth, in the event that an ambiguous pattern of risky substance use exists, intervention is warranted when the individual has experienced negative social or psychological effects of use. Because the major purpose of any drug abuse intervention is to prevent or reverse the negative effects of drug use problems, concern for consequences legitimately preempts concern for specific patterns of use. Sixth, and perhaps the most controversial, would be the instance in which there is an absence of drug use and consequences, but the presence of several drug use risk factors, such as history of family of drug addiction or alcoholism, drug involvement by older siblings, presence of conduct disorder or ADHD, positive expectancy effects for future drug use, etc. Whether targeted intervention strategies for such individuals is effective in preventing future drug abuse or escalation to dependence remains an empirical question.

Problems with the DSM-IV

The discussion of the abuse threshold would be incomplete without considering the DSM-IV criteria for substance use disorders. The applicability of the criteria for adolescents has been called into question (Martin & Winters, 1998). For example, some DSM-IV criteria appear to have limited diagnostic utility because they have a very low prevalence, even in clinical samples. This appears to be the case for withdrawal and drug related medical problems that likely emerge in most persons only after years of continued drinking or drug use. Relatedly, tolerance appears to have low specificity because the development of tolerance for alcohol in particular is likely a normal developmental phenomenon that happens to most adolescent drinkers. Martin and colleagues (Martin, Kaczynski, Maist, Bukstein & Moss, 1995) found that tolerance was highly prevalent among the adolescents with and without alcohol dependence even when symptom assignment required an average quantity per drinking occasion of five or more standard drinks. There appear to be other limitations of DSM-IV criteria when applied to adolescence. The broad range of problems covered by the DSM-IV abuse symptoms, plus the one symptom threshold, produces a great deal of heterogeneity among those with an abuse diagnosis. There is evidence that symptoms of alcohol abuse do not precede symptoms of alcohol dependence, contrary to the notion that abuse should be a prodromal category compared to dependence (Martin, Kaczynski, Maisto & Tarter, 1996).

Furthermore, there is the problem of "diagnostic orphans." This term is used to describe individuals who reveal one or two dependence symptoms, and no abuse symptoms, and therefore do not quality for any diagnosis. Several investigations have found that diagnostic orphans are common among adolescents; reported rates range from ten and 30 percent (Lewinsohn, Rohde & Seeley, 1996; Harrison *et al.*, 1998; Kaczynski & Martin, 1995). Kaczynski and Martin (1995) found that orphans had levels of drinking and drug use that were similar to adolescents with alcohol abuse and significantly higher than other adolescent regular drinkers without an alcohol diagnosis. These findings suggest that these individuals have "fallen through the cracks" of the DSM-IV system. While research is needed to address the meaning of diagnostic orphans, this group may also be appropriate for early intervention strategies.

Normative Considerations

An important factor in the assessment of drug involvement among adolescents is the need to separate out the normative and developmental roles played by drug use in this age group. It is difficult to determine when adolescent drug use has negative long-term implications versus short-term effects and perceived social payoff. In a strict sense, a "normal" trajectory for adolescents is to experiment with the use of psychoactive substances. As described in the seminal work by Kandel and colleagues (Kandel, 1975; Yagamuchi & Kandel, 1984), experiences by adolescents with substance use most often first take place in a social context which the use of "gateway" substances such as alcohol and cigarettes, which are legal for adults and readily available to minors. While almost all adolescents experiment with gateway drugs, progressively fewer of them advance to later and more serious levels of substance use, including the use of marijuana and other illicit drugs (Kandel, 1975). Moreover, the presence of some abuse symptoms is not all that rare among adolescents who use substances, even if not at heavy levels. A further finding from the Minnesota student survey (Harrison *et al.*, 1998) was that among youth who reported any recent substance use, 14 percent of 9th graders and 23 percent of 12th graders reported at least one abuse symptom. Also, it has been observed that even moderate alcohol users reveal relatively high rates of personal consequences associated with such use (Kaczynski & Martin, 1995).

Core Constructs for Assessment

Any meaningful assessment of adolescent substance abuse requires attention toward a wide range of variables. Two major sets of assessment variables are considered here. One set of measures has been traditionally included in standardized screening and comprehensive assessment tools and are viewed as essential to the identification, referral and treatment of problems associated with adolescent drug involvement. These variables serve to assist the clinician to determine the extent of the problem, what factors may underlie it, and what intervention response is the most appropriate. The second set of variables represents cognitive variables which traditionally are not included in existing adolescent substance abuse assessment instruments. Nevertheless, these variables not only have a role in helping to determine motivation to change and level of treatment, particularly brief intervention strategies, but they also may mediate and moderate change behaviors and, thus, are relevant to outcome research.

Traditional Variables for Determining Level and Nature of Intervention

- *Drug Abuse Problem Severity.* Several pretreatment factors pertinent to drug abuse problem severity have been identified as important to treatment referral, planning and outcome.
  - Onset of any drug use;
  - Onset of weekly or daily drug use;
  - Lifetime and recent frequency, quantity, and duration for specific drugs;
  - Preferred drug or drugs;
  - DSM symptoms and additional consequences associated with substance abuse and dependence;
- *Biopsychosocial Risk and Protective Factors.* Biopsychosocial factors refer to the range of personal, environmental and biological factors that influence the onset, development and maintenance of drug use behaviors. Because many of these factors work together to increase or decrease an individual's propensity to use drugs, these factors have been integrated into various etiological models of adolescent drug use (Petraitis, Flay & Miller, 1995). Identification of these risk and protective factors is important because addressing them in treatment may maximize effectiveness. The risk factors provide "points of entry" for treatment goals, and the protective factors offer areas of strength upon which the plan for relapse prevention can be based. Even if an individual does not use drugs currently, the presence of certain factors may reflect an increased risk for future drug involvement. The factors delineated below, which are organized as risk or protective based on the weight of extant literature, are considered important in the assessment process.
- Risk factors
  - History of familial drug abuse or dependence;
  - History of familial drug abuse or dependence treatment;
  - Deviant behavior/legal problems;
  - Co-morbid psychiatric disorders (e.g., conduct disorders, ADHD, affective disorders, learning disorders; see Kaminer, 1994);
  - School failure;
  - Peer drug use/delinquency;
  - Poor impulse control or frustration tolerance; (i.e., disinhibition)

- Parental substance use or abuse;
- Sibling substance use or abuse;
- Community population density and level of crime.
- Protective factors
  - Psychological well-being;
  - Social connectedness to caring adults and institutions;
  - Goal directedness in school or vocation;
  - Association with abstinent peers;
  - School connection;
  - Academic achievement;
  - Problem-solving and coping skills;
  - Involvement in religion.
  - Function of use (e.g., relieve anxiety or depression, social benefits).

Cognitive Domains: Possible Mediators and Moderators of Change

A growing body of research highlights the importance of substance related beliefs in medi-ating and moderating early drug use (Christenson & Goldman, 1983; Christenson, Smith, Roehling & Goldman, 1989, Zucker, Kincaid, Fizgerald & Bingham, 1995). Research on the cognitive precursors of drug use behaviors has been directed at demonstrating either that groups with different behaviors such as alcohol consumption possess different cogni-tions (Johnson & Gurin, 1994) or, conversely the groups with different cognitions show increased likelihood of future drug use behaviors (Christenson, Smith, Roehling & Goldman, 1989).

Naturally, developmental issues are important with respect to assessing cognitive factors with adolescents. Cognitive capacities for abstract thinking begin to take a prominent role during early adolescence, yet older adolescents are better equipped to consider the future consequences of their actions (Keating & Clark, 1980). Another consideration is that environmental and personal adjustment variables interact with cognitive variables to influence and promote behavioral change. For example, social support from peers and family members will likely facilitate feelings of self-accomplishment.

Four cognitive variables related to behavioral change have been prominently discussed in the substance abuse literature: reasons for drug use, expectancies about behavioral outcomes (and the related construct of risk perception), readiness to change, and confi-dence in personal ability (or self-efficacy).

- *Reasons for Drug Use.* Research suggests that drug use by adolescents may be associ-ated with several reasons, including social and recreational, social conformity, mood enhancement, and coping with stress (Petraitis, Flay & Miller, 1995). There is some evidence that substance dependent youth place a greater emphasis on mood enhance-ment as a reason for drug involvement compared to adolescents in general (Henly & Winters, 1988) which is not surprising given that the former group is more likely to suffer from co-existing psychological distress compared to the latter group.

- *Expectancies*. For adolescents, it is relevant to measure drug use-related expectancies related to negative physical effects, negative psychosocial effects, future health concerns, positive social effects, and reduction of negative affect (e.g., Brown, Christianson & Goldman, 1980). Similar concepts discussed in the literature are risk perception or perceived cost versus benefit of the behavior. Individuals who lack knowledge about a hazard and its risk show a consistent tendency to deny that they, personally, are at risk. This denial can lead to two cognitive processes 1) belief perseverance in which individuals selectively attend to messages that support their belief (Festinger, 1957) and exhibit counter arguments when faced with disconfirming evidence (Nisbit & Ross, 1980) and 2) optimistic bias or erroneous beliefs that personal risk is less than the risk faced by others (Janis & Mann, 1977). Some variables relevant for measurement of expectancies and risk perception include perceived vulnerability to, and knowledge about, the health risk of drug use, perceived personal vulnerability to drug related consequences, the person's belief that quitting drug use will reduce their personal risk for such consequences, and the way the individual communicates susceptibility to risk. Also, there may be merit in measuring what has been referred to as "optimistic bias" for personal risk. Subjects can be asked to rate their chances of developing certain consequences of drug use behaviors (e.g., much lower than average, lower than average, above average, etc.) and their responses can be compared to estimates of actual consequences obtained from national data (Weinstein, 1984).
- *Readiness for Behavior Change*. This domain involves problem recognition, readiness for action, treatment suitability (availability and accessibility), and coercion variables, such as perceptions about being respectfully included in a fair decision-making process, whether there were legal pressures applied to the situation, and whether there were perceived negative pressures, such as force and threats. These motivational factors may affect an adolescent's attitude toward subsequent treatment, including their inclination to adhere to treatment plans (Prochaska, DiClemente & Norcross, 1992). We know very little about the determinants of motivational variables that promote positive change in adolescents.
- *Self-efficacy*. Self-efficacy, or the confidence in personal ability, has a central role in many conceptualizations about behavioral control and change (e.g., Bandura, 1977). Self-efficacy has been shown to predict a variety of health behavior outcomes (O'Leary, 1985; Grimbowski *et al.*, 1993). Self-efficacy judgment not only determines one's choice of activities, such as behavior change goals, but also how much effort is expended in such activities, and how long one will persist in the face of adversity. Because levels of self-efficacy have predicted goal achievement (Borrelli & Mermelstein, 1994), it may be that self-efficacy influences outcome by impacting attention to achieving goals. Thus, self-efficacy measures should be accompanied by measures of goal setting and achievement.

Critical Measurement Issues

Developmental Considerations

The measurement process is affected by developmental factors. Substance-abusing youth have been characterized as developmentally delayed in terms of their cognitive, social and ego functioning (Noam & Houlihan, 1990). These delays may affect perception of problems, the willingness to report them, and how such problems are disclosed, if they are disclosed at all, and receptivity to treatment. It stands to reason that admitting to a serious drug problem requires considerable self-insight. Many youth may not be emotionally prepared to take an open view of their behavior and recognize the negative effects that continued drug use may elicit. Also, a genuine commitment to engage in treatment most necessarily requires a fairly advanced level of maturity on the part of the individual.

Also, it has been clinically observed that immaturity may contribute to the tendency of some youth to overstate problems. (Obviously, such "faking bad" tendences could be due to other factors, such as an intentional effort to manipulate the assessment process.) In addition, the selection of assessment questionnaires and interviews requires that the assessor consider the developmental appropriateness of the instrument. Some tools have been primarily normed and validated on older adolescents, and there is the issue that the reading and comprehension level may not be appropriate for younger adolescents. To determine the suitability of an instrument, it is important to review its manual.

Validity of Self-Report

The use of assessment measures assumes that self-reports are valid, although the validity of self-report of drug use behavior has been the subject of considerable debate (Babor Stephens & Marlatt, 1987; Watson, Tilleskjor, Hoodecheck-Show, Pucel & Jacobs, 1984). In addition to purposely distorting the truth, clients' responses can be distorted due to lack of insight, inattentiveness, misunderstanding of a question, or as noted above, to immaturity.

The adolescent clinical literature is relatively sparse in terms of the extent to which compromised self-report occurs and what factors contribute to it. However, an examination of the instrumentation literature provides findings in support of the validity of self-report: 1) a large proportion of respondents in clinic-referred settings admitting to illicit drug use; 2) low rates of endorsements of items indicative of faking bad; 3) higher rates of drug use and accompanying psychosocial problems in clinical samples compared to community or school samples; 4) a pattern of convergence when self-report is compared to other informants (e.g., parents and teachers) and archival records; and 5) a general consistency of disclosures across time (e.g., Brown *et al.*, 1998; Maisto, Connors & Allen, 1995; Shaffer, Schwab-Stne, Fisher & Cohen, 1993; Winters, Stinchfield, Henly & Schwartz, 1991).

Inconsistent self-reports, nevertheless, have been noted by investigators. When adolescents are asked about past drug use that was sporadic or infrequent (Single, Kandel & Johnson, 1975) and when queried over a one year period about the reported age of first use for alcohol and marijuana (Bailey, Flewelling & Rachal, 1992), significant inconsistencies have been observed. Relatedly, there have been discrepancies noted when intake data are compared to similar data collected at treatment completion. This issue was investigated by Stinchfield (1997), and addresses the potential problem often noted from clinical experience that drug abusers tend to minimize the extent or level of their drug use. Stinchfield compared self-reports of drug use problems obtained from adolescents at two points in time: at drug assessment intake and after completion of treatment one month later. In both instances, subjects were instructed to base their self-reports on the same historical time frame, namely, one year prior to treatment. When test scores were compared the scores at discharge were significantly higher than the scores at intake.

The lower intake scores may have been the result of a self-report dampening effect caused by denial and the general reluctance of individuals to fully self-disclose under difficult situations. Test effects can impact relative levels of self-reported drug use. Does the study suggest that self-report data is useless? Even given the lower levels of reported drug use at intake, the clinic-referred adolescents indicated levels of drug use much higher than those of a nonclinical, community comparison sample. Thus, the impact of the so-called "intake–discharge" effect, whatever its causes, does not appear to disregard self-report data. This effect can be extended to diagnostic data. In a comparison of admission and discharge diagnoses, the frequency of substance use disorders (and other disorders) were found to be greater at discharge (Aronen, Noam & Weinstein, 1993). The authors speculate that more complete data may have been reported by the patient at the time of discharge, as well as additional information from other sources.

Both the use of standardized questionnaires and structured interviews serve as vehicles for proving the validity of self-report. Standardized instruments have several advantages, including minimized bias, tendency for clients to feel less threatened by this testing process, and inclusion of scales to designed to assess response bias. Interviews, particularly structured ones, can promote validity of self-report in three ways. First, the interviewer has an opportunity to express concern about the client's situation. When a client feels intimidated by the assessment or is resistant to questioning expressions of empathy may improve his or her willingness to self-disclose. Second, general information may be gained by observing nonverbal clues such as emotional and physical characteristics. Finally, follow-up questioning may elicit information that would have been difficult to obtain through the forced choice format of a questionnaire.

Parents' report. A related validity issue is the value of parents' reports to corroborate youth report. Whereas the adolescent psychopathology literature suggests that parents and adolescents' reports are fairly congruent with each other for some problem areas, particularly externalizing behaviors (Ivens & Rehm, 1988), the adolescent drug abuse literature provides a mixed picture. Clinical experience has long suggested that parents generally do not provide meaningful details about their child's alcohol and other drug use behaviors. Empirically, diagnostic agreement between mothers' and children's reports of substance use disorders have shown a considerable range. Edelbrock (1986) reported an average mother–child agreement of 63 percent for substance use disorder symptoms, whereas Weissman's research team reported an average agreement between mothers' and sons' reports of only 17 percent (Weissman *et al.*, 1987). A recent agreement study examined drug clinic adolescents' and mothers' reports on a wide range of drug use behaviors and consequences (Winters, Anderson, Bengston, Stinchfield & Latimer, 2000). They found that mothers concurred at a 70 percent level with their child in terms of reporting general frequency of substance use. However, when mothers were asked about specific details about the child's substance involvement, nearly one-third responded "do not know," and concordance with child data was only moderate for mothers that did respond to the specific questions. A related study also examined agreement between mother and child with respect to drug use consequences; here agreement was modest ($r = .35$) (Winters, Stinchfield & Henly, 1996).

Urinalysis as validation of drug use self-report. Urinalysis is a method widely used by clinicians and researchers alike to validate self-report of substance use by youth. While urinalysis has some utility as a validity criterion, particularly for THC (i.e., marijuana and hashish), research findings generally suggest a low association between substance use self-report and drug test findings (McLaney, Del-Boca & Babor, 1994). Interestingly, this is not due to low rates of admitting to drug use, but rather to the discordant pattern of negative drug screens in the face of self-reports of drug use. Drug test results are influenced by several factors, including the amount and frequency of drug use. Additional factors include drug test sensitivity and the amount of time between use and sample collection. Moreover, false positive conclusions (i.e., when screen results are positive yet screened substance was not used) may result from the use of common diet pills and decongestants that mimic, for example, opiate use. Conversely, there are concerns that false-negative readings (i.e., screen results are negative yet the substance used) can be produced by the youth using diuretics, diluting the sample, or adding large quantities of salt to the sample.

What interpretations can be inferred from urinalysis? A *positive* result on a urinalysis indicates that the identified drug was in the adolescent's urine. A positive result, however, does not provide any specific information about the client's use, including how much the indicated substance was used or the pattern or method of use. In addition, a positive finding alone does not suggest abuse or dependence. Thus, incorporating random drug screens during treatment or research is only suggestive of the adolescent's pattern of use. Three plausible conclusions have been suggested when a drug screen is *negative* (Manno, 1986). First, the adolescent may not be using drugs. Second, the urinalysis may not be sensitive enough to detect the drug in question. The best example of this problem in relation to drug testing among youth is the length of time a urinalysis can successfully detect alcohol use. Specifically, alcohol generally can only be detected if consumed within six to ten hours prior to when the urine sample is taken. Thus, urinalysis could reveal a negative finding for youth who use alcohol on a near-daily basis. The length of the urinalysis detection period is fairly limited across a variety of drugs, including eight hours for LSD, between one and two days for amphetamines and heroin, two to four days for cocaine, and two to ten days for barbiturates. Urinalysis is better at detecting THC (marijuana and hashish) and benzodiazepines for periods up to six weeks after use. Finally, a negative drug test finding may also result if a given drug is used too little or too infrequently or if the adolescent has tampered with the sample.

Although research examining the utility of drug testing is needed, perhaps the greatest advantage of the drug test is not so much in its ability to accurately indicate an adolescent's substance use, but rather in the message it conveys to a prospective client or study participant that a method is being employed to check the honesty of their answers. This message could possibly alienate the adolescent by suggesting mistrust or just as easily promote honesty by virtue of the adolescent's assumption that the drug test will reveal the truth.

Selecting Appropriate Assessment Instruments

Psychometric Considerations

There are two standard psychometric attributes upon which assessment instruments are evaluated: reliability and validity. Reliability refers to the capacity of an instrument to measure a relatively enduring trait with some level of consistency over time, across settings, and between raters. If a given instrument consistently measures a phenomenon it is said to be reliable. A standard measure of reliability is stability (or test-retest reliability), which refers to the expectation that the person's responses differ little, if at all over a short time period (e.g., from day to day, or week to week). Thus if the instrument is administered a second time to the respondent a short time after the first administration, the data for the two administrations should be quite consistent. Because we have theoretical support for viewing symptoms as relatively stable, changes in scores can be interpreted as random measurement error. Other measures of reliability include internal consistency, which reflects the extent items within a given scale are responded to in a consistent manner, and inter-rater agreement, which is the degree to which two different examiners will tend to collect the same scores from the same respondent (an index of reliability pertinent only to interviews). Reliability coefficients of .70 or greater are usually considered adequate, although lower values are sometimes acceptable whereas higher values are sometimes necessary (such coefficients can range in size from -1.00 to $+1.00$).

Validity on the other hand, pertains to actually measuring that which is sought to be measured, as opposed to something else. That is, validity refers to the accuracy of the test in measuring what it intends to measure (Goldstein & Simpson, 1995). Face validity is the most basic. As commonly understood, face validity means that "on the face of it" the instrument appears to measure what it purports to measure. Other types of validity include criterion, convergent, and construct. Evidence for criterion validity would be present if an instrument distinguishes, for example, those with a definite substance dependence use disorder from those with a substance abuse disorder, and individuals who are almost totally free of substance use. Convergent validity, as the name implies, compares the scores of the test with independent measures of the same behaviors being evaluated. The results of the target instrument should have a relatively high correlation with the results of the independent measure. Finally, construct validity exists only after the other levels of validity have been achieved, and the explanation for produced findings (i.e., the existence or prevalence of a phenomenon, such as pathological gambling) reflects widely supported theories about the phenomenon measured by the instrument.

Validity is neither a static nor an inherent characteristic of a psychological instrument. Determining the validity of an instrument or a construct is an unending and dynamic investigative process. For example, we cannot simply conclude that an instrument has been shown to be valid for all purposes and all settings. "An indicator (e.g., an instrument, such as a test, a rating, or an interview) can be valid for one purpose, but not for another" (Goldstein & Simpson, 1995, p. 230).

Assessment Practices

Based on the advice from a panel of testing experts (Eyde, Moreland, Robertson, Primoff & Most, 1988), the following test practices can serve as a guide for appropriate use of questionnaires and interviews:

1. *Proper Test Use*. Responsible and competent use of a test includes making sure the test actually measures what it is supposed to be measuring. The test's manual should describe the traits and characteristics that the test is intended to measure, the types of patients, and in what settings the use of the test is appropriate.
2. *Psychometric Knowledge*. Test users need to have some knowledge about the test's reliability and validity. The psychometric data should be relevant for the intended use of the test. Test results must be interpreted with caution if its use does not match the conditions under which the test was psychometrically evaluated. If scales are to be used as part of a pre-post comparison, it is especially important to consider their standard error of measurement.
3. *Appropriate Use of Norms and Criterion Data*. When using norm-based tests, the norms associated with the test must be appropriate for the given sample being tested. For criterion-based tests (e.g., diagnostic interviews), it is important to make sure that all criterion measures that were established in the development of the test are appropriate for the patients being tested. It also is important to ensure that the condition and setting under which the norms and criterion data were collected are similar to the present application of the test.
4. *Scoring Accuracy*. The test administrator must take responsibility for checking scoring accuracy when the test is hand-scored. Computerized score reports that provide narrative summaries and recommendations for treatment should be interpreted cautiously because they are based on generalities.
5. *Interpretative Feedback*. The user must have the skills to give interpretation and provide appropriate services and referrals to the individual being tested.

Review of Existing Instruments

It is quite cost-effective to take advantage of the assessment work of others given the considerable amount of technical expertise, time and resources that are required to develop sound instruments. While there are several instruments available to researchers and clinicians, locating and reviewing appropriate tools can be challenging. Sorting through them to determine their accuracy and utility can also be a time-consuming task. Fortunately, many of the more recent instruments have been well-studied and have favorable psychometric properties, and the process of reviewing them is simplified because several handbooks and review articles can serve as a reference guide (Allen & Columbus, 1995; Farrow, Smith & Hurst, 1993; Leccese & Waldron, 1994; Center for Substance Abuse Treatment, 1999a). Brief summaries of the more prominent screening and comprehensive tools (interview and paper-and-pencil formats) are provided below.

Screening Instruments

Several adolescent substance abuse screening instruments are available. These tools are useful because they can briefly estimate a youth's position along the problem severity continuum. Screening measures typically yield conservative scoring decisions (e.g., "probable substance abuser" or "needs a comprehensive assessment") in an effort to guard against the mistake of claiming there is no substance use problem when in fact one exists (i.e., a false negative). A screening tool's full value is appreciated when it is used to determine the appropriateness of a more complete assessment.

Adolescent Alcohol Involvement Scale (AAIS). The AAIS is a 14-item self-report (Mayer & Filstead, 1979) that examines the type and frequency of alcohol use. Questions address such aspects as the last drinking episode, reasons for the onset of drinking behavior, drinking context, short- and long-term effects of drinking, the adolescent's perception about drinking, and how others perceive his/her drinking. An overall score, ranging from 0–79, labels the adolescent's severity of alcohol abuse (i.e., nonuser/normal user, misuser, abuser/dependent). Test scores are significantly related to substance use diagnosis and ratings from other sources, such as independent clinical assessments and parents, and estimates of internal consistency range from .55 in a clinical sample to .76 in a general sample (Moberg, 1983). Norms for both clinical and nonclinical samples are available in the 13- to 19-year old range.

Adolescent Drinking Index (ADI). The ADI (Harrell & Wirtz, 1989) is a 24-item self-administered test that examines adolescent problem drinking by measuring psychological symptoms, physical symptoms, social symptoms, and loss of control. Written at a 5th grade reading level, it yields a single score with cutoffs, as well as two subscale scores (self-medicating drinking and rebellious drinking) intended as research scales. The ADI yields high internal consistency reliability (coefficient alpha, .93–.95), and has demonstrated validity in measuring the severity of adolescent drinking problems. Studies show a moderate correlation with alcohol consumption level, as well as significant differences between criterion groups with different levels of alcohol problem severity. In addition, studies have revealed a quite favorable hit rate of 82 percent in classification accuracy of the ADI (Harrell & Wirtz, 1989).

Adolescent Drug Involvement Scale (ADIS). Moberg and Hahn (1991) modified the AAIS (described above) to address drug use problem severity. Psychometric studies on the 13-item questionnaire reveal favorable internal consistency (.85). Validity evidence indicates that the ADIS correlates .72 with drug use frequency and .75 with independent ratings by clinical staff. The scale is written at an 8th grade reading level.

Client Substance Index (CSI). This 113-item instrument (Moore, 1983) is based on Jellinek's 28 symptoms of drug dependence. Scores on the CSI reflect the degree of drug dependence, ranging from no problem, to misuse of substances and abuse of substances, to chemical dependency. CSI scores have been shown to discriminate normal from drug treatment samples (Moore 1983).

Client Substance Index — Short (CSI-S). The CSI-S (Thomas, 1990) was developed and evaluated as part of a larger Substance Abuse Screening Protocol through the National Center for Juvenile Justice. This tool is a 15-item, yes/no self-report instrument that was adapted from Moore's (1983) multi-scale Client Substance Index. The objective of this brief screen is to identify juveniles within the court system who are in need of additional drug abuse assessment. Reliability data are favorable (coefficient alpha = .84–.87). Its validity is supported by convergence of the total score with established measures of adolescent substance abuse, as well as its ability to discriminate groups defined according to the severity of their criminal offense (Thomas, 1990).

Drug and Alcohol Problem (DAP) Quick Screen. This 30-item screening questionnaire utilizes a yes/no/uncertain format. The DAP was tested in a pediatric practice setting (Schwartz & Wirtz, 1990), in which the authors report that about 15 percent of the respondents endorsed six or more items, considered by the authors to be a cut score for "problem" drug use. Item analysis indicates that the items contribute to the single dimension score, but no reliability or criterion validity evidence is available.

Drug Use Screening Inventory — Revised (DUSI-R). The DUSI-R is a 159-item instrument that documents the level of involvement with a range of drugs, and additionally describes the severity of consequences related to such involvement. The measure yields scores on ten problem density subscales (e.g., substance use, behavior problems, psychiatric disorder) and one lie scale. Domain scores were related to DSM-III-R substance use disorder criteria in a sample of adolescent substance abusers (Tarter, Laird, Bukstein & Kaminer, 1992). An additional psychometric report provides norms and evidence of scale sensitivity (Kirisci, Mezich & Tarter, 1995).

Personal Experience Screening Questionnaire (PESQ). The PESQ (Winters, 1992) is a brief 40-item screening instrument that consists of a problem severity scale (coefficient alpha, .91–.95), drug use history, select psychosocial problems, and response distortion tendencies ("faking good" and "faking bad"). Norms for normal, juvenile offender and drug abusing populations are available. The test is estimated to have an accuracy rate of 87 percent in predicting need for further drug abuse assessment (Winters, 1992).

Problem Oriented Screening Instrument for Teenagers (POSIT). This 139-item self-administered yes/no instrument is part of the Adolescent Assessment and Referral System developed by the National Institute on Drug Abuse (Rahdert, 1991). Similar to the DUSI-R, the POSIT addresses ten functional adolescent problem areas: substance use, physical health, mental health, family relations, peer relationships, educational status, vocational status, social skills, leisure and recreation, and aggressive behavior/delinquency. Cut scores for determining need for further assessment have been rationally established, and some have been confirmed with empirical procedures (Latimer, Winters & Stinchfield, 1997). Convergent and discriminant evidence for the POSIT has been reported by several investigators (e.g., Dembo, Schmeidler, Borden, Chin Sue & Manning, 1997; McLaney, Del-Boca & Babor, 1994).

Rutgers Alcohol Problem Index (RAPI). The RAPI (White & Labouvie, 1989) is a 23-item questionnaire that focuses on consequences of alcohol use pertaining to family life, social relations, psychological functioning, delinquency, physical problems and neuropsychological functioning. Based on a large general population sample, the RAPI was found to have high internal consistency (.92), and, among heavy alcohol users, a strong correlation with DSM-III-R criteria for substance use disorders (.75–.95) (White & Labouvie, 1989).

Substance Abuse Subtle Screening Inventory (SASSI). Miller's (1985) 81-item adolescent version of the SASSI yields scores for several scales, including face valid alcohol, face valid other drug, obvious attributes, subtle attributes, and defensiveness. Validity data indicate that SASSI scale scores are highly correlated with MMPI scales and that its cut score for "chemical dependency" corresponds highly with intake diagnoses of substance use disorders (Risberg, Stevens & Graybill, 1995).

Psychiatric Interviews

Diagnostic Interview for Children and Adolescents (DICA). The DICA (Herjanic & Campbell, 1977; Reich, Herjanic, Welner & Gandhy, 1982) is a 416-item structured interview that currently has a DSM-IV version available (Reich, Shayla & Taibelson, 1992). Psychometric evidence specific to substance use disorders has not been published on the DICA, but some of the other sections have been evaluated for reliability and validity (Welner, Reich Herjanic, Jung & Amado, 1987).

Diagnostic Interview Schedule for Children (DISC-C). This instrument has undergone several adaptations (e.g., Costello, Edelbrock & Costello, 1985; Shaffer, Fisher & Dulcan, 1993), and now features a DSM-IV version (Shaffer, Fisher & Dulcan, 1996). Separate forms of the interview exist for the child and the parent. As part of larger study focusing on several diagnoses, Fisher and colleagues (1993) found the DISC-C to be highly sensitive in correctly identifying youth who had received a hospital diagnosis of any substance use disorder (n = 8). Both interview forms (parent and child) had a sensitivity of 75 percent. For the single case in which a parent–child disagreement occurred, the parent indicated that they did not know any details about their child's substance use. Also, the DISC-C is associated with moderate test–retest stability for substance use disorders (kappa = .46) (Roberts, Solovitz, Chen & Casat, 1996).

Kiddie SADS (K-SADS). This well-known semi-structured interview is organized around Research Diagnostic Criteria and adapted for young clients of the Schedule for Affective Disorders and Schizophrenia (SADS) (Endicott & Spitzer, 1978). The multisource data obtained from the interview is then integrated into the most appropriate diagnosis. The alcohol and drug questions are contained in the lifetime version of the interview (K-SADS-E) (Orvaschel, 1985), and a DSM-IV version also exists (K-SADS-E-5) (Orvaschel, 1995). The newest version incorporates changes from the results from a test–retest reliability study (Puig-Antich & Ryan, 1986). However, no psychometric data on the substance use disorder section have been reported.

Structured Clinical Interview for the DSM (SCID). The SCID features a guided, deci-sion-free structure, in which interviewers present questions verbatim. Specific operational definitions and severity criteria are presented for each symptom. Interviewers rate each symptom as absent, subclinical, or clinically present. The SCID is widely used to assess substance use disorders among adults, and has shown good reliability in field trials (e.g., Williams, Gibbon, First & Spizer, 1992). Martin, Kaczynski, Maist, Bukstein & Moss (1995) modified the DSM-III-R version of the SCID (Spitzer, Williams & Gibbon, 1987) to assess DSM-IV substance use disorders among adolescents. Symptoms and diagnoses showed good concurrent validity, and preliminary analyses suggested moderate to good inter-rater reliability for this interview (Martin *et al.*, 1995).

Substance-Use Disorder Interviews

Adolescent Diagnostic Interview (ADI). The ADI (Winters & Henly, 1993) assesses the symptoms associated with psychoactive substance use disorders as described in DSM-III-R and DSM-IV. The instrument's structured interview also measures sociodemographic information, substance use consumption history, and psychosocial functioning, including mental health. Evidence for the interview's inter-rater agreement (kappa = .66–.96), test–retest reliability (kappa = .53–.79), concurrent validity (i.e., concordance to alternate measures of problem severity), and criterion validity (i.e., concordance to independent diagnoses) have been reported (Winters & Henly, 1993; Winters, Stinchfield, Fulkerson & Henly, 1993).

Customary Drinking and Drug Use Record (CDDR). The CDDR (Brown *et al.*, 1998) is a research-focused, structured interview that measures alcohol and other drug use consumption for both recent (under three months) and lifetime periods. The interview assesses DSM-III-R and DSM-IV substance dependence symptoms (including a detailed assessment of withdrawal symptoms) and several types of consequences of alcohol and other drug involvement. Psychometric studies provide evidence that the CDDR is reliable over time and across interviewers (average one-week test–retest coefficients for all major content domains is .91), discriminates community youths from substance-abusing youths, and converges with alternate measures (Brown *et al.*, 1998).

Substance Use Disorders Diagnostic Schedule (SUDDS). This instrument is a diagnostic checklist that is keyed to DSM-III-R criteria (Hoffmann & Harrison, 1989). Its use among adolescents should proceed cautiously; several items are not appropriate for young people's experiences and content coverage is weak in regards to school consequences and peer-use issues. The SUDDS is accompanied by other measures to assist in determining the level of client treatment care based on client placement criteria from the American Society of Addiction Medicine (Level of Care Index, and Recovery Attitude and Treatment Evaluator; Mee-Lee & Hoffmann, 1992). The SUDDS current and lifetime ratings have been shown to be highly congruent with independent clinical diagnoses in an adult sample (overall agreement, 71–100 percent) (Davis, Hoffmann, Morse & Luehr, 1992), although there have been no psychometric evaluations of the interview with adolescents.

Interviews Modeled after the Addiction Severity Index

Several interviews for adolescents are adaptations of a well-known adult tool, the Addiction Severity Index (ASI) (McLellan, Luborsky, Woody & O'Brien, 1980).

Adolescent Drug Abuse Diagnosis (ADAD). The ADAD is a 150-item structured interview that addresses the following content areas: medical status, drug and alcohol use, legal status, family background and problems, school/employment, social activities and peer relations, and psychological status. The interviewer uses a ten-point scale to rate the patient's need for additional treatment in each content area. These severity ratings translate to a problem severity dimension (no problem, slight, moderate, considerable, and extreme problem). The drug use section includes a detailed drug use frequency checklist and a brief set of items that address aspects of drug involvement (e.g., poly-drug use, attempts at abstinence, withdrawal symptoms, and use in school). Psychometric studies on the ADAD, using a broad sample of clinic-referred adolescents, provide favorable evidence for its reliability and validity (Friedman & Utada, 1989). A shorter form (83 items) of the ADAD intended for treatment outcome evaluation is also available.

Adolescent Problem Severity Index (APSI). The APSI was developed by Metzger and colleagues (Metzger, Kushner & McLellan, 1991) of the University of Pennsylvania/VA Medical Center. The APSI provides a general information section that addresses the reason for the assessment and the referral source, as well as the adolescent's understanding of the reason for the interview. Additional sections of the APSI include drug/alcohol use, family relationships, education/work, legal, medical, psycho/social adjustment, and personal relationships. Some concurrent validity for the alcohol/drug section has been empirically demonstrated (Metzger, Kushner & McLellan, 1991) and predictive validity evaluations are underway.

Comprehensive Addiction Severity Index for Adolescents (CASI-A). The CASI-A is a structured interview developed by Meyers (1991). It covers several domains, including the following: education, substance use, use of free time, leisure activities, peer relationships, family (including family history and intrafamilial abuse), psychiatric status, and legal history. At the end of several major topics, space is provided for the assessor's comments, severity ratings, and ratings of the quality of the respondent's answers. An interesting feature of this interview is that it incorporates results from a urine drug screen and observations from the assessor. Psychometric studies on the CASI-A are being conducted by the author.

Teen Severity Index (T-ASI). Another adolescent version of the ASI was adapted by Kaminer, Bukstein & Tarter (1991). The T-ASI consists of seven content areas: chemical use, school status, employment-support status, family relationships, legal status, peer–social relationships, and psychiatric status. A medical status section was not included because it was deemed to be less relevant to adolescent drug abusers. Patient and interviewer severity ratings are elicited on a five-point scale for each of the content areas.

Psychometric data indicate very favorable inter-rater agreement and validity data (Kaminer, Wagner, Plummer & Seifer, 1993).

Paper-and-Pencil Questionnaires

Adolescent Self-Assessment Profile (ASAP). This self-administered, 225-item, multi-scale inventory (Wanberg, 1992) was developed on the basis of a series of multivariate research studies by Wanberg and colleagues. The instrument provides an in-depth assessment of drug involvement, including drug use frequency and drug use conse-quences and benefits, as well as the major risk factors associated with such involvement (e.g., deviance, peer influence). Supplemental scales, which are based on common factors found within the specific psychosocial and problem severity domains, can be scored as well. Extensive reliability and validity data based on several normative groups are provided in the manual.

Chemical Dependency Assessment Profile (CDAP). This 235-item self-report question-naire assesses eleven dimensions of drug use, including expectations of use (e.g., drugs reduce tension), physiological symptoms, quantity and frequency of use, and attitude toward treatment. A computer-generated report is provided. Limited normative data are available thus far on only 86 subjects (Harrell, Honaker & Davis, 1991).

Hilson Adolescent Profile (HAP). The HAP consists of 310 true–false items that cover 16 scales, two of which measure alcohol and drug use. The other content scales correspond to characteristics found in psychiatric diagnostic categories (e.g., antisocial behavior, depression) and psychosocial problems (e.g., home life conflicts). Normative data have been collected from clinical patients, juvenile offenders, and normal adolescents (Inwald, Brobst & Morissey, 1986).

Juvenile Automated Substance Abuse Evaluation (JASAE). The JASAE (ADE. Inc. 1987) is a computer-assisted, 108-item (T/F) instrument that is based on a similar adult measure, the SALCE. The JASAE produces a five-category score, ranging from no use to drug abuse (including a suggested DSM-IV classification), accompanied by a summary of drug use history. The instrument also includes a measure of life stress and a scale for test-taking attitude. The JASAE has been shown to discriminate clinical groups from nonclin-ical groups.

Personal Experience Inventory (PEI). The PEI is 276-item, multi-scale questionnaire that measures chemical involvement problem severity (ten scales), psychosocial risk (or protective) factors (twelve scales), and response distortion tendencies (five scales). Supplemental problem screens measure eating disorders, suicide potential, physical/ sexual abuse, and parental history of drug abuse. The scoring program provides a compu-terized report that includes narratives and standardized scores for each scale, as well as other various clinical information. Normative and psychometric data (including test–retest reliability and convergent and predictive validity) are available (Winters & Henly, 1989; Winters *et al.*, 1993; Winters *et al.*, 1996).

Prevention Management Evaluation System (PMES). This structured interview and questionnaire is appropriate for treatment planning and follow-up evaluation (Simpson, 1991). The PMES consists of three parts: a client intake form (which includes substance use history), a form that focuses on family and friends, and a follow-up interview. Treatment planning is based upon information on family background, school and legal problems, family relations, peer activity, and self-esteem (Barret, Simpson & Lehman, 1988). Inter-rater agreement for the interview is good (Simpson, 1991), but in-depth validity evidence is lacking.

Expectancies Measures

Alcohol Expectancy Questionnaire — Adolescent Version (AEQ-A). This 90-item questionnaire measures an individual's expected or anticipated effects of alcohol use (marijuana and cocaine versions are available as well) (Brown, Christiansen & Goldman, 1980). Six positive expectancies are measured (global positive effects, social behavior change, improvement of cognitive/motor abilities, sexual enhancement, increased arousal and relaxation/tension reduction), as well as one negative expectancy (deteriorated cognitive/behavioral functioning). Favorable reliability and validity evidence exists for the AEQ-A (Brown Christiansen & Goldman, 1987; Christiansen, Smith, Roehling & Goldman, 1989).

Decisional Balance Scale. This 16-item scale was developed by Migneault, Pallonen & Velicer (1997) in a non-clinical population of adolescent alcohol users and abusers. It measures two factors: advantages of drinking and disadvantages of drinking. Both scales have adequate internal reliability (.81 and .87).

Perceived-Benefit of Drinking and Drug Use Scales. This ten-item scale was constructed to serve as a non-threatening problem severity screen (Petchers & Singer, 1987). It is based on the approach that beliefs about drug use, particularly regarding expected personal benefits of drug use, reflect actual use. Five perceived-benefit questions are asked regarding use of alcohol and then repeated for drug use. The scale has moderate internal reliability (.69–.74) and is related to several key indicators of drug use behavior when tested in school and adolescent inpatient psychiatric samples (Petchers & Singer, 1990).

Readiness for Behavior Change Measures

Unlike the intensive development of instruments to assess motivational variables associated with adult substance use, few similar instruments have been developed specifically for adolescents. Only two tools were located in the literature.

Problem Recognition Questionnaire (PRQ). This 24-item adolescent scale consists of separate factors pertaining to drug use problem recognition and readiness for treatment (i.e., action orientation). The scale was developed with a combination of rational and empirical procedures. The PRQ factors have adequate internal reliability and were shown to modestly predict posttreatment functioning in an adolescent substance-abusing population (Cady, Winters, Jordan & Solheim, 1996).

Circumstances, Motivation, Readiness and Suitability scales (CMRS). The 25-item CMRS, which was originally developed for use with adults in a therapeutic community setting, has also been evaluated for use with drug-abusing adolescents (Jainchill, Bhattacharya & Yagelka, 1995). The questionnaire consists of four scales and a total score designed to predict retention of treatment. The scales include Circumstances (external motivation), Motivation (internal motivation), Readiness (for treatment) and Suitability (perceived appropriateness of the treatment modality). The scales have favorable internal consistency (alpha's ranging from .77 to .80), and they moderately predict short-term (30-day) retention.

Self-Efficacy Measure

Drug Avoidance Self-Efficacy Scale (DASES). The DASES is a self-report measure of self-efficacy for abstinence intended for young drug abusers (Martin, Wilkinson & Paulos, 1995). Subjects are asked to predict whether they would resist or use drugs/alcohol in 16 different high risk situations, and they rate the confidence in their prediction on a scale of one to seven. The DASES has excellent internal reliability (.91), and its predictive validity was supported given that scale scores were shown to predict subsequent drug and alcohol behaviors (greater self-efficacy was associated with lower future drug use).

Laboratory Measures

Drugs may be detected in the blood or urine using several laboratory tests (Schwartz, 1988). Thin Layer Chromatography (TLC) may be used to screen for alcohol or drugs. Colors associated with various substances are generated by the TLC method when chemicals are combined with the sample. Radioimmunoassay (RIA) is a labor-intensive yet sensitive method that identifies drugs in body fluids by utilizing radioactive labels and antibodies. Fluorescence Polarization Immunoassay (FPIA) uses one chemical to identify amphetamines, barbiturates, and cocaine in body fluids. Enzyme Immunoassay (EIA) and Enzyme Multiplied Immunoassay Technique (EMIT) are inexpensive and widely used urinalysis methods. The molecular structure of drugs is detected via spectrometer measurements.

Positive drug test results obtained by any of the above methods should be confirmed by one of three additional techniques (Schwartz, 1988). Gas Chromatography is an expensive and time-consuming procedure that identifies alcohol and inhalants in bodily fluids by using inert gases to separate sample components. High Performance Liquid Chromatography (HPLC) detects substances in body fluids by separating specimen components via propelled liquid. Gas Chromatography with Mass Spectrometry (GC/MS) is an expensive yet highly sensitive test that combines Gas Chromatography with Mass Spectrometry that identifies drugs in bodily fluids at the molecular level.

Summary and Future Directions

Service providers and researchers now have a number of adolescent drug abuse screening and comprehensive tools from which to choose. Many of them are modeled after the adult Addiction Severity Index (McLellan, Luborsky, Woody & O'Brien). Whereas an empirical comparison of the various adolescent instruments has not been conducted, Leccese and Waldron's (1994) provide a critical review and conclude that several of the existing instruments have promising psychometric properties and "that recent progress in this field is encouraging" (p. 561).

In terms of content coverage, the existing instruments provide adequate attention toward drug use problem severity and related biopsychosocial risk and protective factors. Nevertheless, future research should expand into domains that have been promoted by the adult treatment literature. For example, more work is needed regarding measures related to matching adolescent substance abusers to levels of care, such as readiness for change, self-efficacy, risk perception and coercion to seek treatment. Another area for further research attention is the issue of the validity of self-report. Most tools have reported validity data on severe-end cases, and there is reason to expect that measurement error may be greater for moderate or low-end cases. For example, it has been shown that reports of prior drug use are more unreliable when such use is infrequent (Single, Kandel & Johnson, 1975). Moreover, it stands to reason from a clinical perspective that self-report minimization may be more likely when the individual has been a moderate user and not experienced severe consequences yet. There is also a need for more research on the validity of response distortion scales to detect compromised self-report. Many existing adolescent defensiveness measures, for example, are based on adult scales and may not be appropriate for use among adolescents, and it is difficult to judge whether the scales are measuring true denial, or simply reflecting natural impression management tendencies of young people to portray oneself in a favorable light. Finally, the impact of assessment mode on drug use disclosure rates is an understudied area. The comparability of computer versus paper-and-pencil administration has been studied to some degree, but little is known about the differential effect on self-report of paper-and-pencil format compared to interviews (Aquilino, 1994).

References

A.D.E., Incorporated (1987), *Juvenile Automated Substance Abuse Evaluations. (JASAE)*. Clarkston, MI: A.D.E., Incorporated.

Allen, J. P., & Columbus, M. (eds.) (1995), *Assessing alcohol problems: A guide for clinicians and researchers*. NIAAA Treatment Handbook Series 4. Bethesda, MD: National Institute on Alcohol Abuse and Alcoholism.

Aquilino, W. S. (1994), "Interview mode effects in surveys of drug and alcohol use." *Public Opinion Quarterly 58*, 210–240.

Aronen, E. T., Noam, G. G., & Weinstein, S. R. (1993), "Structured diagnostic interviews and clinicians' discharge diagnoses in hospitalized adolescents." *Journal of the American Academy of Child and Adolescent Psychiatry 32*, 674–681.

Babor, T. F., Stephens, R. S., & Marlatt, G. A. (1987), "Verbal report methods in clinical research on alcoholism: Response bias and its minimization." *Journal of Studies on Alcohol 48*, 410–424.

Bailey, S. L., Flewelling, R. L., & Rachal, J. V. (1992), "The characteristics of inconsistencies in self-reports of alcohol and marijuana use in longitudinal study of adolescents." *Journal of Studies on Alcohol 53*, 636–647.

Bandura, A. (1977), *Social learning theory*. Englewood Cliffs, NJ: Prentice-Hall.

Barret, M. E., Simpson, D. D., & Lehman, W. E. (1988), "Behavioral changes among adolescents in drug abuse intervention programs." *Journal of Clinical Psychology 44,* 461–473.

Borrelli, B., & Mermelstein, R. (1994), "Goal setting and behavior change in a smoking cessation program." *Cognitive Therapy and Research 18* (1), 68–83.

Brown, S. A., Christiansen, B. A., & Goldman, M. S. (1987), "The Alcohol Expectancies Questionnaire: An instrument for the assessment of adolescent and adult alcohol expectancies." *Journal of the Studies on Alcohol 48,* 483–491.

Brown, S. A., Creamer, V. A., & Stetson, B. A. (1987), "Adolescent alcohol expectancies in relation to personal and parental drinking patterns." *Journal of Abnormal Psychology 96*, 117–121.

Brown, S. A., Myers, M. G., Lippke, L., Tapert, S. F., Stewart, D. G., & Vik, P. W. (1998), "Psychometric evaluation of the Customary Drinking and Drug Use Record (CDDR): A measure of adolescent alcohol and drug involvement." *Journal of Studies on Alcohol 59,* 427–438.

Cady, M., Winters, K. C., Jordan, D., & Solheim, K. (1996), "Motivation to change as a predictor of treatment outcome for adolescent substance abusers." *Journal of Child and Adolescent Substance Abuse 5*, 73–91.

Center for Substance Abuse Treatment. (1999a). *Screening and assessing adolescents for substance use disorders* (Treatment Improvement Protocol [TIP] Series 3) (eds, K. C. Winters, T. McLellan & R. Dembo). Rockville, MD: Author.

Center for Substance Abuse Treatment. (1999b). *Treatment of substance use disorders among adolescents* (Treatment Improvement Protocol [TIP] Series 3) (ed., K. C. Winters). Rockville, MD: Author.

Children's Defense Fund (1991), *The adolescent and young adult fact book*. Washington, D.C.: Author.

Christiansen, B. A., & Goldman, M. S. (1983), "Alcohol-related expectancies versus demographic background variables in the prediction of adolescent drinking." *Journal of Consulting and Clinical Psychology 51,* 249–257.

Christiansen, B. A., Smith, G. T., Roehling, P. V., & Goldman M. S. (1989), "Using alcohol expectancies to predict adolescent drinking behavior after one year." *Journal of Consulting and Clinical Psychology 57*, 93–99.

Cohen, P., Cohen, J., Kasen, S., Velez, C. M., Hartmark, C., Johnson, J., Rojas, M., Brook, J., & Streuning, E. L. (1993), "An epidemiological study of disorder in late childhood and adolescence I. Age- and gender-specific prevalence." *Journal of Child Psychology and Psychiatry 34*, 851–867.

Costello, E. J., Edelbroch, C., & Costello, A. J. (1985), "Validity of the NIMH Diagnostic Interview Schedule for Children: A comparison between psychiatric and pediatric referrals." *Journal of Abnormal Child Psychology 13*, 570–595.

Davis, L. J., Hoffmann, N. G., Morse, R. M., & Luehr, J. G. (1992), "Substance Use Disorder Diagnostic Schedule (SUDDS): The equivalence and validity of a computer-administered and interviewer-administered format." *Alcoholism: Clinical and Experimental Research 16,* 250–254.

DAWN (Drug Abuse Warning Network) (1996), *1996 DAWN report.* Washington, D.C.: SAMHSA.

Dembo, R., Schmeidler, J., Borden, P., Chin Sue, C., & Manning, D. (1997), "Use of the POSIT among arrested youths entering a juvenile assessment center: A replication and update." *Journal of Child and Adolescent Substance Abuse 6,* 19–42.

Edelbrock, C. S. (1986), "Parent–child agreement on child psychiatric symptoms assessed via structured interview." *Journal of Child Psychology & Psychiatry & Allied Disciplines 27,* 181–190.

Endicott, J., & Spitzer, R. L. (1978), "A diagnostic interview: The schedule for affective disorder and schizophrenia." *Archives of General Psychiatry 35,* 837–844.

Eyde, L. D., Moreland, K. L., Robertson, G. J., Primoff, E. S., & Most, R. B. (1988), Executive summary: Test user qualifications: A data-based approach to promoting good test use. Report of the Test User Qualifications Working Group of the Joint Committee on Testing Practices. Washington, DC, American Psychological Association.

Farrow, F. A., Smith, W. R., & Hurst, M. D. (1993), *Adolescent drug and alcohol assessment instruments in current use: A critical comparison.* Seattle, WA: University of Washington.

Festinger, L. (1957), *A theory of cognitive dissonance.* Stanford, CA: Stanford University Press.

Fisher, P., Shaffer, D., Piacentini, J.C., Lapkin, J., Kafantaris, V., Leonard, H. & Herzog, D. B. (1993), "Sensitivity of the Diagnostic Interview Schedule for Children, 2nd edition (DISC-2.1) for specific diagnoses of children and adolescents." *Journal of the American Academy of Child and Adolescent Psychiatry 32,* 666–673.

Friedman, A. S., & Utada, A. (1989), "A method for diagnosing and planning the treatment of adolescent drug abusers: Adolescent Drug Abuse Diagnosis Instrument." *Journal of drug education 19,* 285–312.

Goldstein, J. M., & Simpson, J. C. (1995), *Validity: definitions and applications to psychiatric research.* In M. T. Tsuang, M. Tohen & G. E. Zahner (Eds.), Textbook in psychiatric epidemiology (pp. 229–242). New York: Wiley-Liss.

Grimbowski, D., Patrick, D., Diehr, P., Durham, M., Beresford, S., Kay, E., & Hecht, J. (1993), "Self-efficacy and health behavior among older adults." *Journal of Health and Social Behavior 34,* 89–104.

Harrel, T. H., Honaker, L. M., & Davis, E. (1991), "Cognitive and behavioral dimensions of dysfunction in alcohol and polydrug abusers." *Journal of Substance Abuse 3,* 415–426.

Harrell, A., & Wirtz, P. M. (1989), "Screening for adolescent problem drinking: Validation of a multidimensional instrument for case identification." *Psychological Assessment 1,* 61–63.

Harrison, P. A., Fulkerson, J. A., & Beebe, T. J. (1998), "DSM-IV substance use disorder criteria for adolescents: A critical examination based on a statewide school survey." *American Journal of Psychiatry 155,* 486–492.

Henly, G. A., & Winters, K. C. (1988), "Development of problem severity scales for the assessment of adolescent alcohol and drug abuse." *The International Journal of the Addictions 23,* 65–85.

Herjanic, B., & Campbell, W. (1977), "Differentiating psychiatrically disturbed children on the basis of a structured interview." *Journal of Abnormal Child Psychology 5,* 127–134.

Hoffmann, N. G., & Harrison, P. A. (1989), *Substance Use Disorders Diagnostic Schedule (SUDDS).* St. Paul, MN: New Standards, Inc.

Inwald, R. E., Brobst, M. A., & Morissey, R. F. (1986), "Identifying and predicting adolescent behavioral problems by using a new profile." *Juvenile Justice Digest 14,* 1–9.

Ivens, C., & Rehm, L. P. (1988), "Assessment of childhood depression: Correspondence between reports by child, mother, and father." *Journal of the American Academy of Child and Adolescent Psychiatry 6*, 738–741.

Jainchill, N., Bhattacharya, G., & Yagelka, J. (1995), "Therapeutic communities for adolescents." In E. Rahdert, & D. Czechowicz (eds), *Adolescent drug abuse: Clinical assessment and therapeutic interventions*. (Research Monograph Series. No. 156, pp. 190–217). Rockville, MD: National Institute on Drug Abuse.

Janis, I. L., & Mann, L. (1977), *Decision making: A psychological analysis of conflict, choice and commitment*. New York: Free Press.

Johnson, P. B., & Gurin, G. (1994), "Negative affect, alcohol expectancies, and alcohol-related problems." *Addiction 89*, 581–586.

Johnston, L. D., O'Malley, P. M., & Bachman, J. G. (1999), "National survey results on drug use from the monitoring the future study, 1975–1998." Rockville: National Institute on Drug Abuse, U.S. Dept. of Health and Human Services, Public Health Service, National Institute of Health.

Kaczynski, N. A., & Martin, C. S. (1995), Diagnostic orphans: Adolescents with clinical alcohol symptomatology who do not qualify for DSM-IV abuse or dependence diagnosis. Paper presented at the annual meeting of the Research Society on Alcoholism, Steamboat Springs, CO, June 1995.

Kaminer, Y. (1994), *Adolescent substance abuse: A comprehensive guide to theory and practice*. New York: Plenum Publishing Corporation.

Kaminer, Y., Bukstein, O. G., & Tarter T. E. (1991), "The Teen Addiction Severity Index (T-ASI): Rationale and reliability." *International Journal of Addiction 26*, 219–226.

Kaminer, Y., Wagner, E., Plummer, B., & Seifer, R. (1993), "Validation of the Teen Addiction Severity Index (T-ASI): Preliminary findings." *American Journal on Addiction 2*, 221–224.

Kandel, D. B. (1975), "Stages in adolescent involvement in drug use." *Science 190*, 912–914.

Keating, D. P., & Clark, C. L. (1980), "Development of physical and social reasoning in adolescence." *Developmental Psychology 16*, 23–30.

Kirisci, L., Mezzich, A., & Tarter, R. (1995), "Norms and sensitivity of the adolescent version of the Drug Use Screening Inventory." *Addictive Behaviors 20*, 149–157.

Kokotailo, P. (1995), "Physical health problems associated with adolescent substance abuse." In E. Rahdert & D. Czechowicz (eds), *Adolescent drug abuse: Clinical assessment and therapeutic interventions* (Research Monograph Series. No. 156, pp. 112–129). Rockville, MD: National Institute on Drug Abuse.

Latimer, W. W., Winters, K. C., & Stinchfield, R. D. (1997), "Screening for drug abuse among adolescents in clinical and correctional settings using the Problem Oriented Screening Instrument for Teenagers." *American Journal of Drug and Alcohol Abuse 23*, 79–98.

Leccese, M., & Waldron, H. B. (1994), "Assessing adolescent substance use: A critique of current measurement instruments." *Journal of Substance Abuse Treatment 11*, 553–563.

Lewinsohn, P. M., Rohde, P., & Seeley, J. R. (1996), "Alcohol consumption in high school adolescents: Frequency of use and dimensional structure of associated problems." *Addiction 91*, 375–390.

Mackenzie, R. G. (1993), "Influence of drug use on adolescent sexual activity." *Adolescent medicine: State of the art reviews* (Vol. 4, No. 2). Philadelphia, PA: Henley & Belfus.

Maisto, S. A., Connors, G. J., & Allen, J. P. (1995), "Contrasting self-report screens for alcohol problems: A review." *Alcoholism: Clinical and Experimental Research 19*, 1510–1516.

Manno, J. E. (1986), "Interpretation of urinalysis results." In R. L. Hawks & C. N. Chiang (eds), *Urine testing for drugs of abuse*. (Research Monograph Series No. 73, pp. 54–61). Rockville, MD: National Institute on Drug Abuse.

Martin, C. S., Kaczynski, N. A., Maisto, S. A., Bukstein, O. M., & Moss, H. B. (1995), "Patterns of DSM-IV alcohol abuse and dependence symptoms in adolescent drinkers." *Journal of Studies on Alcohol 56,* 672–680.

Martin, C. S., Kaczynski, N. A., Maisto, S. A., & Tarter, R. E. (1996), "Polydrug use in adolescent drinkers with and without DSM-IV alcohol abuse and dependence." *Alcoholism: Clinical and Experimental Research 20,* 1099–1108.

Martin, C. S., & Winters, K. C. (1998), "Diagnosis and assessment of alcohol use disorders among adolescents." *Alcohol Health and Research World 22,* 95–105.

Martin, G. N., Wilkinson, D. A., & Paulos, C. X. (1995), "The drug avoidance self-efficacy scale." *Journal of Substance Abuse 7,* 151–163.

Mayer, J., & Filstead, W. J. (1979), "The Adolescent Alcohol Involvement Scale: An instrument for measuring adolescent use and misuse of alcohol." *Journal of Studies on Alcohol 40,* 291–300.

McLaney, M. A., Del-Boca, F., & Babor, T. (1994), "A validation study of the Problem Oriented Screening Instrument for Teenagers (POSIT)." *Journal of Mental Health-United Kingdom 3,* 363–376.

McLellan, A. T., Luborsky, L., Woody, G. E., & O'Brien, C. P. (1980), "An improved diagnostic evaluation instrument for substance abuse patients: The Addiction Severity Index." *Journal of Nervous and Mental Disease 186,* 26–33.

Mee-Lee, D., & Hoffmann, N. G. (1992), *Level of Care Index.* St. Paul, MN: New Standards, Inc.

Mee-Lee, D., & Hoffmann, N. G. (1992), *Recovery Attitude and Treatment Evaluator.* St. Paul, MN: New Standards, Inc.

Metzger, D., Kushner, H., & McLellan, A. T. (1991), *Adolescent Problem Severity Index.* Philadelphia: University of Pennsylvania.

Meyers, K. (1991), *Comprehensive Addiction Severity Index for Adolescents.* Philadelphia: University of Pennsylvania.

Migneault, J., Pallonen, U., & Velicer, W. (1997), "Decisional balance and stage of change for adolescent drinking." *Addictive Behaviors 22,* 339–351.

Miller, G. (1985), *The Substance Abuse Subtle Screening Inventory — Adolescent Version.* Bloomington, IN: SASSI Institute.

Moberg, D. P., & Hahn, L. (1991), "The Adolescent Drug Involvement Scale." *Journal of Adolescent Chemical Dependency 2,* 75–88.

Moberg, D. (1983), "Identifying adolescents with alcohol problems: A field test of the Adolescent Alcohol Involvement Scale." *Journal of Studies on Alcohol 44,* 701–721.

Moore, D. (1983), *Client Substance Index.* Olympia, WA: Olympic Counseling Services.

Newcomb, M. D., & Bentler, P. M. (1989), "Substance use and abuse among children and teenagers." *American Psychologist 44,* 242–248.

Nisbit, R. E., & Ross, L. (1980), *Human inference: Strategies and shortcomings of social judgement.* Englewood Cliffs, NJ: Prentice Hall.

Noam, G. G., & Houlihan, J. (1990), "Developmental dimensions of DSM-III diagnoses in adolescent psychiatric patients." *American Journal of Orthopsychiatry 60,* 371–378.

Orvaschel, H. (1985), "Psychiatric interviews suitable for use in research with children and adolescents." *Psychopharmacology Bulletin 21,* 737–745.

Orvaschel, H. (1995), *Schedule for Affective Disorders and Schizophrenia for School-Age Children-Epidemiologic Version-5 (K-SADS-E-5).* Fort Lauderdale, FL: Nova Southeast University.

O'Leary, A. (1985), "Self-efficacy and health." *Behavior Research and Therapy 23,* 437–451.

Pascale, P. J., & Evans, W. J. (1993), "Gender differences and similarities in patterns of drug use and attitudes of high school students." *Journal of Drug Education 23,* 105–116.

Petchers, M., & Singer, M. (1990), "Clinical applicability of a substance abuse screening instrument." *Journal of Adolescent Chemical Dependency 1*, 47–56.

Petchers, M., & Singer, M. (1987), "Perceived-Benefit-of-Drinking Scale: Approach to screening for adolescent alcohol abuse." *Journal of Pediatrics 110*, 977–981.

Petraitis, J., Flay, B. R., & Miller, T.Q. (1995), "Reviewing theories of adolescent substance use: Organizing pieces in the puzzle." *Psychological Bulletin 117*, 67–86.

Prochaska, J. O., & DiClemente, C. C. (1992), *Stages of change in the modification of problem behaviors.* In M. Hersen, R. M. Eisler & P. M. Miller (eds), Progress in behavior modification (pp. 184–214). Sycamore, IL: Sycamore Press.

Prochaska, J. O., DiClemente, C. C., & Norcross, J. C. (1992), "In search of how people change: Applications to addictive behaviors." *American Psychologist 47*, 1102–1114.

Puig-Antich, J., & Ryan, N. (1986), *Schedule for Affective Disorders and Schizophrenia for School-Age Children (6–19 Years) — Kiddie-SADS-Present Episode (K-SADS-P), 4th Working Draft.* Pittsburgh, PA: Western Psychiatric Institute and Clinic, University of Pittsburgh School of Medicine.

Rahdert, E. (ed.) (1991), *The Adolescent Assessment/Referral System Manual.* Rockville, MD: U.S. Department of Health and Human Services, ADAMHA, National Institute on Drug Abuse, DHHS Pub. No. (ADM) 91-1735.

Reich, W., Herjanic, B., Welner, Z., & Gandhy, P. R. (1982), "Development of a structured psychiatric interview for children: Agreement on diagnosis comparing child and parent interviews." *Journal of Abnormal Child Psychology 10*, 325–336.

Reich, W., Shayla, J. J., & Taibelson, C. (1992), *The Diagnostic Interview for Children and Adolescents — Revised (DICA-R).* St. Louis, MO: Washington University.

Risberg, R. A., Stevens, M. J., & Graybill, D. F. (1995), "Validating the adolescent form of the Substance Abuse Subtle Screening Inventory." *Journal of Child and Adolescent Substance Abuse 4*, 25–41.

Roberts, R. E., Solovitz, B. L., Chen, Y. W., & Casat, C. (1996), "Retest stability of DSM-III-R diagnoses among adolescents using the Diagnostic Interview Schedule for Children (DISC-2.1C)." *Journal of Abnormal Child Psychology 24*, 349–362.

Schwartz, R. H. (1988), "Urine testing in the detection of drugs of abuse." *Archives of Internal Medicine 148*, 2407–2412.

Schwartz, R. H., & Wirtz, P. W. (1990), "Potential substance abuse: Detection among adolescent patients using the Drug and Alcohol Problem (DAP) Quick Screen, a 30-item questionnaire." *Clinical Pediatrics 29*, 38–43.

Shaffer, D., Schwab-Stone, M., Fisher, P. W., & Cohen, P. (1993), "The Diagnostic Interview Schedule for Children — revised version (DISC-R): I. Preparation, field testing, interrater reliability, and acceptability." *Journal of the American Academy of Child and Adolescent Psychiatry 32,* 643–650.

Shaffer, D., Fisher, P., & Dulcan, M. (1996), "The NIMH Diagnostic Interview Schedule for Children (DISC 2.3): Description, acceptability, prevalence, and performance in the MECA study." *Journal of the American Academy of Child and Adolescent Psychiatry 35*, 865–877.

Shedler, J., & Block, J. (1990), "Adolescent drug use and psychological health." *American Psychologist 45*, 612–630.

Simpson, D. D. (1991), *The TCU Prevention Intervention Management and Evaluation System (PMES).* Fort Worth, TX: Institute of Behavioral Research, Texas Christian University.

Single, E., Kandel, D., & Johnson, B. D. (1975), "The reliability and validity of drug use responses in a large scale longitudinal survey." *Journal of Drug Issues 5*, 426–443.

Spitzer, R., Williams, J., & Gibbon, B. (1987), *Instructions Manual for the Structured Clinical Interview for the DSM-III-R*. New York: New York State Psychiatric Institute.

Stinchfield, R. D. (1997), "Reliability of adolescent self-reported pretreatment alcohol and other drug use." *Substance Use and Misuse 32*, 63–76.

Tarter, R. E., Laird, S. B., Bukstein, O., & Kaminer, Y. (1992), "Validation of the adolescent Drug Use Screening Inventory: Preliminary findings." *Psychology of Addictive Behaviors 6*, 322–236.

Thomas, D. W. (1990), *Substance Abuse Screening Protocol for the Juvenile Courts*. Pittsburgh, PA: National Center for Juvenile Justice.

Wanberg K. W. *Adolescent Self Assessment Profile*. Arvada, CO, Center for Alcohol/Drug Abuse Research and Evaluation, 1992.

Watson, C., Tilleskjor, C., Hoodecheck-Show, E., Pucel, J., & Jacobs, L. (1984), "Do alcoholics give valid self-reports?" *Journal of Studies on Alcohol 45*, 344–348.

Weinstein, N. D. (1984), "Why it won't happen to me: Perceptions of risk factors and illness susceptibility." *Health Psychology 3*, 431–457.

Weissman, M. M., Wickramaratne, P., Warner, V., John, K., Prusoff, B. A., Merikangas, K. R., & Gammon, G. D. (1987), "Assessing psychiatric disorders in children: Discrepancies between mothers' and children's reports." *Archives of General Psychiatry 44*, 747–753.

Welner, Z., Reich, W., Herjanic, B., Jung, K., & Amado, K. (1987), "Reliability, validity, and parent-child agreement studies of the Diagnostic Interview for Children and Adolescents (DICA)." *Journal of the American Academy of Child and Adolescent Psychiatry 26*, 649–653.

White, H. R., & Labouvie, E. W. (1989), "Towards the assessment of adolescent problem drinking." *Journal of Studies on Alcohol 50*, 30–37.

Williams, J. B., Gibbon, M., First, M. B., & Spitzer, R. L. (1992), "The Structured Clinical Interview for DSM-III-R (SCID). II. Multisite test-retest reliability." *Archives of General Psychiatry 49*, 630–636.

Winters, K. C. (1992), "Development of an adolescent alcohol and other drug abuse screening scale: Personal Experience Screening Questionnaire." *Addictive Behaviors 17*, 479–490.

Winters, K. C. (1999), "Treating adolescents with subtance use disorders: An overview of practice issues and treatment outcome." *Substance Abuse, 20*, 203–225.

Winters, K. C., Anderson, N., Bengston, P., Stinchfield, R. D., & Latimer, W. (2000), "Development of a parent questionnaire for use in assessing adolescent drug abuse." *Journal of Psychoactive Drugs 32*, 3–13.

Winters, K. C., & Henly, G. A. (1989), *Personal Experience Inventory and manual*. Los Angeles: Western Psychological Services.

Winters, K. C., & Henly, G. A. (1993), *Adolescent Diagnostic Interview schedule and manual*. Los Angeles: Western Psychological Services.

Winters, K. C., Latimer, W., & Stinchfield, R. D. (1999), "The DSM-IV criteria for adolescent alcohol and cannabis use disorders." *Journal of Studies on Alcohol 60*, 337–344.

Winters, K. C., Stinchfield, R. D., Henly, G. A., & Schwartz, R. H. (1991), "Validity of adolescent self-report of alcohol and other drug involvement." *International Journal of Addictions 25*, 1379–1395.

Winters, K. C., Stinchfield, R. D., Fulkerson, J., & Henly, G. A. (1993), "Measuring alcohol and cannabis use disorders in an adolescent clinical sample." *Psychology of Addictive Disorders 7*, 185–196.

Winters, K. C., Stinchfield, R. D., & Henly, G. A. (1996), "Convergent and predictive validity of scales measuring adolescent substance abuse." *Journal of Child and Adolescent Substance Abuse 5*, 37–55.

Yagamuchi, K., & Kandel, D. B. (1984), "Patterns of drug use from adolescence to young adulthood-III: Patterns of progression." *American Journal of Public Health 74,* 673–681.

Zucker, R. A., Kincaid, S. B., Fitzgerald, H. E., & Bingham, C. R. (1995), "Alcohol schema acquisition in preschoolers: Differences between children of alcoholics and children of nonalcoholics." *Alcoholism: Clinical & Experimental Research 19,* 1011–1017.

Chapter 2

Life Skills Training: Theory, Methods, and Effectiveness of a Drug Abuse Prevention Approach

Gilbert J. Botvin and Kenneth W. Griffin*

Introduction

During adolescence, drug use generally progresses both in terms of the frequency and quantity of use as well as in the number of different drugs used (Millman & Botvin, 1992). For any single substance, the amount and frequency of use typically increase as youth transition from non-use to occasional use to more frequent use. There is also a progression in the type of drug or drugs used during this time period. For most youth, tobacco and alcohol are the first substances used, and some youth use inhalants early in the progression due to their wide availability. Later, a proportion of these youth begin to use marijuana, and some will eventually go on to use stimulants, opiates, hallucinogens, cocaine, and other illicit substances. It is now recognized that early experimentation with drugs increases the risk for drug abuse and other drug-related problems in later years. For this reason, adolescent drug abuse prevention programs should focus on preventing the early stages of drug involvement as a method of reducing drug abuse risk. For middle or junior high school students, prevention should involve attempting to prevent the initiation of drug use or the escalation to regular use, with a primary emphasis on the use of tobacco, alcohol, and marijuana.

Fortunately, research findings over the past two decades have provided a firm conceptual foundation for the development of effective approaches to drug abuse prevention. Much of this research has been conducted in school settings and has tested the impact of prevention programs designed to target the psychosocial factors associated with the initiation and early stages of drug use. The earliest of these psychosocial prevention studies focused on cigarette smoking, but more recent research has focused on the impact of drug abuse prevention programs on the use of a range of substances. Recent evaluation studies of psychosocial approaches to prevention have been larger, better designed and more sophisticated than in previous years, and this research has shown that drug abuse prevention approaches can be effective (reviewed in Botvin & Botvin, 1992; Goodstadt, 1986).

*Correspondence concerning this chapter should be addressed to Gilbert J. Botvin or Kenneth W. Griffin, Institute for Prevention Research, Cornell University Medical College, New York, NY.

Innovations in Adolescent Substance Abuse Interventions, pages 31–50.
Copyright © 2001 by Elsevier Science Ltd.
All rights of reproduction in any form reserved.
ISBN: 0-08-043577-7

The goal of this chapter is to describe a drug abuse prevention intervention approach called Life Skills Training (LST), one of the most widely evaluated school-based prevention programs available. The theoretical basis for the LST program is described and the scientific evidence on the effectiveness of the program is reviewed, including data on the effectiveness of the program with different target populations. In addition, some future directions for prevention intervention research are discussed, particularly in terms of the dissemination of programs that have been proven to be effective.

Theoretical Background and Rationale

Etiology research has identified several important risk factors for adolescent drug use, as well as several protective factors that are important in countering the effects of these risks (Hawkins, Catalano & Miller, 1992). An integrated domain model of the most important factors contributing to drug-taking behavior is presented in Figure 1. These variables can be grouped into three broad categories or domains. The *Background/ historical* domain consists of demographic factors (e.g., age, gender, social class), biological and cultural factors (e.g., temperament, acculturation, ethnic identity), and environmental influences (e.g., community disorganization, availability of drugs). The *Social factors* domain includes school factors (e.g., school climate, school bonding), family factors (e.g., family management practices, discipline, monitoring, parental drug use), media influences (e.g., television shows, movies, and advertising that promote drug use), and peer influences (e.g., friends' drug use and pro-drug attitudes). The *Personal factors* domain includes cognitive expectancies (e.g., attitudes, beliefs, and normative expectations regarding drug use), personal competence skills (e.g., decision-making, self-control), social skills (e.g., communication skills, assertiveness), and a set of relevant psychological factors (e.g., self-efficacy, self-esteem, psychological well-being).

A general model of drug use initiation that incorporates each of these key variable domains into an overall conceptual framework is shown in Figure 2. This theoretical framework contains key elements from the most prominent etiological theories of drug use, including social learning theory (Bandura, 1977) and problem behavior theory (Jessor & Jessor, 1977), as well as self-derogation (Kaplan, 1980), persuasive communications (McGuire, 1968), and peer cluster theories (Oetting & Beauvais, 1987). In this model, drug use is conceptualized as the result of a dynamic interaction of environmental and individual factors, in which peers, parents, and other social influences interact with individual psychosocial vulnerabilities to promote drug use. For example, some individuals may be primarily influenced to use drugs by media presentations that normalize or glamorize drug use, while others may be primarily influenced by family members or friends who use drugs or hold attitudes and beliefs supportive of drug use. These social influences are likely to have the strongest impact on those individuals with poor social and personal competence skills, and together these factors may lead to certain psychological vulnerabilities such as low self-esteem, social anxiety, and psychological distress. The more risk factors that an individual has, the greater the likelihood that he or she will become a drug user and/or abuser.

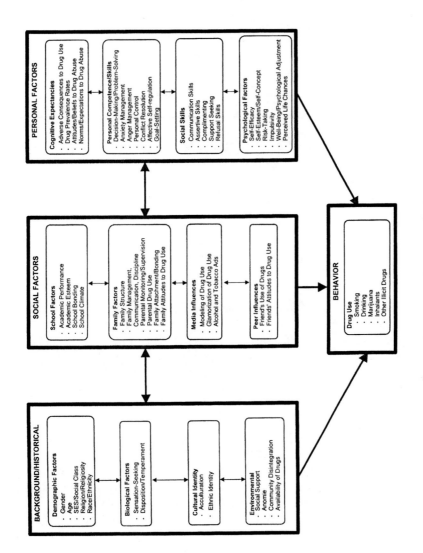

Figure 1: Integrated Domain Model of Drug Use Behavior.

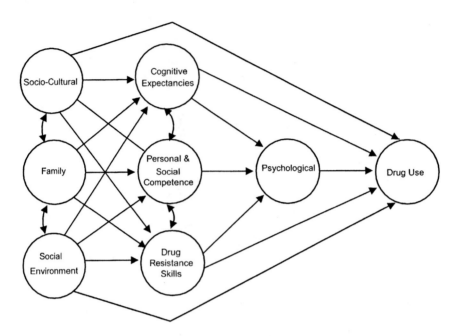

Figure 2: Hypothesized Model of Drug Use Initiation.

In addition to organizing key factors associated with drug use initiation, the hypothe-sized model in Figure 2 is useful for conceptualizing potential points of intervention for drug abuse prevention. For example, a prevention program that improves personal and social competence skills may have a beneficial impact on various psychological factors associated with reduced drug abuse risk. However, this type of model also has some inherent limitations. The model does not capture the dynamic and recursive nature of these mechanisms, nor does it contain an exhaustive list of etiologic factors.

Description of the Life Skills Training Program

The Life Skills Training (LST) program is an adolescent drug abuse prevention program that is typically provided in school classrooms. The LST program was designed to have a major impact on the individual-level *Personal factors* shown in Figure 1. The program is a *primary* prevention program that targets individuals who have not yet developed drug abuse prob-lems, and this is accomplished by impacting on risk factors associated with the early stages of drug use. By intervening with a prevention program with younger populations (e.g., junior high school students), it is presumed that this ultimately will reduce the prevalence of drug abuse among these youth as they become older (e.g., seniors in high school). The LST approach is also a *universal* intervention designed for all individuals in a given setting, rather than a selective or targeted intervention designed only for individuals at "high risk."

Program Overview

The LST prevention program consists of three major components. The first component is designed to teach students a set of general self-management skills, and the second focuses on general social skills. These two components are designed to enhance overall personal and social competence and to decrease motivations to use drugs and vulnerability to pro-drug social influences. The third component of LST includes information and skills that are specifically related to drug use, and these are included to promote drug resistance skills, antidrug attitudes, and antidrug norms. The LST program consists of 15 to 17 class periods (about 45 minutes each) and is intended for middle or junior high school students. In addition to the initial year of intervention in grade seven, the LST approach contains an additional two years of booster intervention designed to reinforce the material covered during the first year. This consists of ten booster sessions in grade eight and five in grade nine. For school districts with a middle school, the LST program can be implemented with students in grades six, seven, and eight. Below is a brief description of the major components of the LST program.

Program Components

Personal self-management skills. The personal skills component of the LST program is designed to impact on a broad array of self-management skills. To accomplish this, the personal skills component contains material to: (1) foster the development of decision-making and problem-solving (e.g., identifying problems, defining goals, generating alternative solutions, considering consequences); (2) teach skills for identifying, analyzing, and resisting media influences; (3) provide students with self-control skills for coping with anxiety (e.g., relaxation training) and anger/frustration (e.g., inhibiting impulsive reactions, reframing, using self-statements); and (4) provide students with the basic principles of personal behavior change and self-improvement (e.g., goal-setting, self-monitoring, self-reinforcement).

Social skills. The social skills component is designed to impact on several important social skills and enhance general social competence. This social skills component contains material designed to help students improve general interpersonal skills such as how to overcome shyness and how to give and receive compliments. This material emphasizes the teaching of: (1) communication skills; (2) general social skills (e.g., initiating social interactions and conversational skills); (3) skills related to dating relationships; and (4) verbal and nonverbal assertive skills.

Drug-related information and skills. This component is designed to impact on knowledge and attitudes concerning drug use, normative expectations, and skills for resisting drug use influences from the media and peers. The material contained in this component is similar to that contained in many psychosocial drug abuse prevention programs which focus on the teaching of social resistance skills. Included is material concerning the: (1) short- and long-term consequences of drug use; (2) knowledge about the actual levels of drug use among adolescents and adults in order to correct normative expectations about drug use; (3) information about the declining social acceptability of cigarette smoking and other drug use; (4) information and class exercises demonstrating the immediate physiological effects of cigarette smoking; (5) material concerning media pressures to smoke, drink, or use drugs; (6) information concerning the techniques used in tobacco and alcohol advertisements to promote the use of these drugs, along with skills for resisting these influences; and (7) techniques for resisting direct peer pressure to smoke, drink or use drugs.

Program Materials

Curriculum materials have been developed to standardize the implementation of the LST program and increase its exportability. These materials consist of a *Teacher's Manual* and *Student Guide* for each year of the program (published by Princeton Health Press). The *Teacher's Manual* contains detailed lesson plans that describe the overall goal and objectives for each session and provide the appropriate content and activities for each intervention session. The *Student Guide* contains class exercises, homework assignments to prepare students for specific sessions and to reinforce the content already covered, as well as reference material for each session. The *Student Guide* also contains goal-setting principles, basic principles of self-directed behavior change, and material for a semester long "self-improvement" project.

Prevention Methods

The LST program is taught using cognitive-behavioral skills training, facilitated group discussion, classroom demonstrations, and traditional didactic teaching methods. Much of the material in the LST program is most effectively taught by facilitating group discussion and through skills training, although lecturing and conventional didactic teaching methods are appropriate for some of the material. Because the major emphasis of the LST program is on the teaching of general personal self-management skills, social skills, and drug resistance skills, the most important intervention method is *skills training*. The cognitive-behavioral skills in the LST program are taught using a combination of instruction, demonstration, behavioral rehearsal, feedback, social reinforcement, and extended practice in the form of behavioral homework assignments.

Instruction and Demonstration

The first step in the skills training process involves instruction and demonstration. *Instruction* involves explaining a particular skill to students in a careful step-by-step fashion, along with a clear explanation of when to use the skill. *Demonstration* involves showing students how to perform a particular skill. This can be done by the program provider, by videotape, or even by a member of the class who has already learned the skill being taught.

Behavioral Rehearsal

Once the skill has been explained and demonstrated by the LST provider, students are given the opportunity to practice the skill themselves through selected behavioral rehearsal scenarios. In order to practice the skills, students can take turns coming to the front of the classroom to participate in a brief role play that requires that they use the skill being taught. The class can also be divided into small groups, with the program provider circulating from group to group to observe the students practicing. The behavioral rehearsal scenarios are first described by the provider or a small-group leader, and the exercises are kept as brief as possible (a minute or less each) so that as many students as possible can have a chance to participate.

Feedback

After students have rehearsed the skills being taught, they are provided with feedback concerning the strengths and weaknesses of their skills performance. The teacher or program provider conveys this information in a supportive manner so students understand what aspects of the skill they performed well and what needs improvement. It is important that students are given specific recommendations concerning how to improve. Emphasis is placed on constructive feedback designed to guide students as they strive to improve and "successively approximate" mastery of the skills being taught.

Social Reinforcement

Since the primary objective of the LST program is to reduce risk for drug abuse, the goal of the skills training is to improve the target skills and self-efficacy of each student. Therefore, students are assessed individually with respect to improvement over their own baseline levels, however low. During and after the behavioral rehearsal exercises, the teacher or LST program provider reinforces each student for one or two positive elements of his or her performance of the skill. Although at times this may be a challenge, the program provider can simply identify the *most positive element* of the student's performance.

Extended Practice

The purpose of extended practice is to provide opportunities for additional practice of the target skills outside of the classroom, in an effort to promote skill development and utilization. This is accomplished through behavioral "homework" assignments, which may include tasks such as practicing a new technique for coping with anxiety once a day, or using an assertive response in three different situations that arise during a particular week. In addition to providing opportunities for practice in general, extended practice is intended to facilitate the use of new skills in situations outside of the classroom and to encourage students to use these skills in their everyday lives.

Intervention Providers, Selection, and Training

A critical element of any effective intervention is the intervention provider. The LST program has been successfully implemented by several different types of intervention providers, including regular classroom teachers (Botvin, Renick & Baker, 1983; Botvin, Baker, Renick, Filazzola & Botvin, 1984; Botvin, Baker, Dusenbury, Tortu & Botvin, 1990), older peer leaders (Botvin & Eng, 1982; Botvin, Baker, Botvin, Filazzola & Millman, 1984), and outside health care professionals (Botvin, Eng & Williams, 1980; Botvin, Schinke, Epstein & Diaz, 1994). There are several reasons why classroom teachers may be the most logical choice as providers for a school-based prevention program such as LST. Teachers are readily available and generally have more teaching experience and better classroom management skills than other potential providers. Peer leaders (same-age or older students) can assist teachers in implementing the curriculum and can also serve an important informal function as positive role models for the kinds of skills and behaviors being taught in the curriculum. In selecting program providers, it is important to choose individuals that have demonstrated interest, experience, enthusiasm, and commitment to drug abuse prevention. In addition to attending the training workshop, providers must also be willing and able to implement the intervention carefully and completely according to the provider's guide, complete the necessary process evaluation forms, and should be interested in serving as a positive role model for students.

Provider training typically consists of a one- or two-day training workshop to familiarize intervention providers with the prevention program and its rationale, and to provide an opportunity for trainees to learn and practice the skills needed to successfully implement the prevention program (Tortu & Botvin, 1989). Training for peer leaders has involved an initial half-day workshop to provide them with a general orientation to the prevention program and their responsibilities as well as the information and skills needed to implement the prevention program. Teachers meet with peer leaders prior to each session to provide them with session-specific preparation for the upcoming session and debrief them regarding the last session.

Evidence of Effectiveness

The most important challenge to the field of drug abuse prevention has been to show that preventive interventions can work, and in particular, can have an impact on drug use *behavior*. While some prevention approaches have been shown to have an impact on knowledge and attitudes in a direction consistent with decreased drug use, this is increasingly viewed as inadequate. Effectiveness should include evidence that participation in the prevention program reduces the incidence of drug use in an intervention group, relative to a control group not receiving the program. Over the past two decades there has been a gradual accumulation of empirical evidence supporting the effectiveness of school-based prevention approaches on drug use behavior.

Begin in the early 1980s, a series of evaluation studies has demonstrated that the Life Skills Training (LST) approach produces behavioral effects on drug use. These studies have demonstrated that the LST approach is effective when implemented by different types of providers, with different populations, and with different problem behaviors. The focus of the early LST evaluation research was on cigarette smoking and involved predominantly white middle-class populations. More recent research has extended this work to other problem behaviors including the use of alcohol, marijuana, and illicit drugs, and has begun to examine its potential for reducing aggressive and violent behaviors. In addition, this research has increasingly focused on the utility of the LST approach when used with inner-city minority populations. Finally, this research has assessed the long-term durability of the LST prevention model and its impact on hypothesized mediating variables.

Preventing Smoking

The LST program was initially developed as a smoking prevention program. Pilot research (Botvin, Eng & Williams, 1980) examined the short-term effectiveness of the LST approach for preventing cigarette smoking. Participants were students in the eighth, ninth, or tenth grades (N = 281) in two comparable suburban schools that were randomly assigned to either the experimental condition (in which students received the ten-session prevention program) or a control group. The prevention program was conducted by health professionals who were members of the project staff. Results of this study found a 75 percent reduction in the number of new cigarette smokers at the initial posttest and a 67 percent reduction in new smoking at the three-month follow-up.

Role of peer leaders. A second study (Botvin & Eng, 1982) tested the effectiveness of the LST approach when implemented by older peer leaders (eleventh and twelfth graders) with seventh-grade students (N = 426). Saliva samples were collected from students prior to the collection of self-report data to enhance the validity of smoking self-report data and to provide an objective measure of smoking status via saliva thiocyanate measures. Post-test results indicated that there was a 58 percent reduction in new smoking in the experimental group relative to controls. These results were corroborated by the results of the saliva thiocyanate analysis that showed a significant increase in smoking for the students in the control group, but no increase for students in the experimental group. There was also a 56 percent reduction in regular (weekly) smoking at the one-year follow-up. Significant program effects were also found on several hypothesized mediating variables including smoking knowledge, advertising knowledge, and social anxiety.

Role of classroom teachers and booster programming. A third study (Botvin, Renick & Baker, 1983) tested the efficacy of the LST prevention approach when implemented by regular classroom teachers and when combined with booster sessions for preserving initial prevention effects. Seventh-grade students (N = 902) from seven suburban New York schools were included in the study, and, as in the previous study, saliva samples were collected to ensure high-quality self-report data. Significant program effects were found at the initial post-test using a measure of monthly cigarette smoking, and at the twelve- and 18-month follow-up there were intervention effects for monthly, weekly, and daily smoking. Students receiving additional booster sessions had half as many regular (weekly or daily) smokers as those not receiving booster sessions. Thus, these findings provided empirical support for the effectiveness of the LST program when conducted by regular classroom teachers, and showed that combining the initial intervention with booster sessions was able to enhance the effects of the prevention program. This study also showed that the intervention was effective when implemented on a regular weekly schedule or as a mini-course taught several times a week.

Preventing Alcohol Use

Following the initial LST evaluation research on smoking prevention, several studies were conducted to determine the efficacy of the LST prevention approach with other types of substance use. The first of these tested the impact of the LST program on alcohol use frequency, episodes of drunkenness, and heavy drinking. The study was conducted with seventh graders from two comparable New York City public schools (N = 239) randomly assigned to experimental and control conditions (Botvin, Baker, Botvin, Filazzola & Millman, 1984). The intervention was modified to include material concerning the potential consequences of alcohol use and, where appropriate, skills were taught in relation to situations that might promote alcohol use. Although no effects were evident at the initial post-test, significant program effects emerged at the six-month follow-up. These findings indicated that significantly fewer (54 percent) experimental students reported drinking in the past month, 73 percent fewer reported heavy drinking, and 79 percent fewer reported getting drunk at least once a month.

Preventing Alcohol and Marijuana Use

A larger study was then conducted to replicate the alcohol results and to test the generalizability of the LST approach to the prevention of marijuana use. This study also examined the relative effectiveness of the LST program when implemented by older (tenth- and eleventh-grade) peer leaders or by regular classroom teachers (Botvin, Baker, Renick, Filazzola & Botvin, 1984). The study included seventh-grade students (N = 1311) from ten suburban New York junior high schools which were randomly assigned to: (1) teacher-led prevention curriculum; (2) peer-led prevention curriculum; (3) teacher-led prevention curriculum and booster sessions; (4) peer-led prevention curriculum and booster sessions; and (5) control group. Results at the end of the first year showed significant prevention effects for tobacco, alcohol, and marijuana use. Adolescents who participated in the LST program drank significantly less alcohol per drinking occasion and drank to the point of intoxication less frequently relative to controls. Furthermore, these effects were stronger for students in the peer-led condition relative to both teacher-led and control conditions. With respect to marijuana, findings indicated that fewer students reported monthly and weekly marijuana use, and the magnitude of these effects was quite substantial. The LST program reduced experimental marijuana use by 71 percent for students in the peer-led condition, and reduced regular (weekly or daily) marijuana use by 83 percent. One-year follow-up results from this study showed that there were up to 82 percent fewer cigarette smokers and up to 78 percent fewer marijuana users in the peer-led booster group, up to 50 percent fewer cigarette smokers, up to 47 percent fewer experimenters with marijuana, and 51 percent fewer drinkers in the high-fidelity teacher-led group (Botvin, Baker, Filazzola & Botvin, 1990).

Results from a Large-Scale Prevention Trial

One of the largest and most methodologically rigorous drug abuse prevention trials ever conducted began in 1985 and included close to 6000 students from 56 junior high schools in New York State (Botvin, Baker, Dusenbury, Tortu & Botvin, 1990). This study evaluated the efficacy of the LST approach in preventing the use of tobacco, alcohol, and marijuana in an adolescent sample that was 52 percent male and 91 percent white. With pre-intervention school smoking rates used as a blocking variable, schools were randomly assigned to one of three conditions: prevention with training and support by project staff; prevention without training and support by project staff; and a control condition. The pretest, intervention, and post-test occurred while students were in the seventh grade. Retention rates based on all available students at the pretest were 93 percent at the initial posttest, 81 percent at the end of the eighth grade, 75 percent at the end of the ninth grade, and 67 percent at the end of the tenth grade, and were virtually identical across prevention conditions.

Using both the *individual* and the *school* as the unit of analysis in two separate series of analyses, prevention effects were found for drug use behavior as well as for several hypothesized mediating variables at the ninth-grade follow-up, and at the tenth-grade follow-up for students who received at least 60 percent of the intervention program. The results of the individual-level analysis at the ninth-grade follow-up found significantly less smoking and marijuana use among the two intervention groups, and less problem drinking in the intervention group without training and support relative to controls. Results of the school-level analysis at the ninth-grade follow-up revealed that schools in both intervention conditions had significantly less cigarette smoking than control schools. At the tenth-grade follow-up, there was significantly less marijuana use in the intervention group with training and support and less excessive drinking in both intervention groups than among controls.

Evidence of Long-Term Effectiveness

While a growing number of evaluation studies of drug abuse prevention programs have demonstrated prevention effects, most of these studies have focused on short-term effectiveness. In order to determine the durability of drug abuse prevention in general and the LST approach in particular, a long-term follow-up study was conducted (Botvin, Baker, Dusenbury, Botvin & Diaz, 1995). Students (N = 3597) from 56 schools in New York State who participated in the drug abuse prevention trial described above were located and data were collected at the end of the twelfth grade either in school, by telephone, or by mail. The average length of follow-up was six years after the initial baseline assessment.

Follow-up results indicated that there were significantly fewer smokers, heavy drinkers, or marijuana users for students who received the LST prevention program during the seventh grade and had booster sessions during the eighth and ninth grades, relative to controls.

In order to assess the impact of the prevention program on more serious levels of drug involvement, prevention and control students also were compared in terms of polydrug use, defined as the monthly or weekly use of tobacco, alcohol, and marijuana. At the end of the twelfth grade, there were 44 percent fewer LST students than controls who were polydrug users within the past month and 66 percent fewer LST students who reported using all three substances within the past week. Prevention effects also were found for several hypothesized mediating variables in the direction of decreased drug abuse risk. The strongest prevention effects were produced for the students who received the most complete implementation of the prevention program.

Preventing Illicit Drug Use

Additional long-term follow-up results from the large-scale prevention trial discussed above provided evidence that the LST prevention program can reduce illicit drug use. An underlying assumption of primary prevention efforts is that if they prevent or reduce the use of tobacco, alcohol, and/or marijuana they will have a corresponding impact on the use of other substances further along the developmental progression. In other words, preventing gateway drug use also will translate into later reductions in the use of illicit drugs such as cocaine or heroin. However, despite the fact that this rationale is commonly used to justify targeting tobacco, alcohol, and marijuana use in primary prevention programs, this assumption has never been explicitly tested.

The impact of the LST program on illicit drug use was addressed by analyzing data collected from an anonymous subsample of students involved in the long-term follow-up study described above. Data were collected by mail from 447 individuals (mean age = 19 years) who were contacted after the end of the twelfth grade, after an average of 6.5 years from the initial baseline assessment. The survey assessed the use of 13 illicit drug categories following those used in the University of Michigan *Monitoring the Future* study (Johnston, O'Malley & Bachman, 1994). Findings indicated that there were significantly lower levels of illicit drug use among the LST students relative to controls on composite measures of illicit drug use and illicit drug use other than marijuana (Botvin *et al.*, 2000). Significantly lower levels of use also were found for hallucinogens, heroin and other narcotics in the prevention group relative to controls.

Target Populations

Several studies have been conducted to test the generalizability of the LST approach to ethnic minority youth. This work is important because it addresses a critical gap in the drug abuse prevention field — high-quality evaluation research with minority populations. In general, the development of preventive interventions for minority populations has followed two strategies. The first strategy involves developing interventions that are population-specific, based on the assumption that the etiology of drug abuse is different for different populations. The second strategy involves developing interventions that are generalizable to a broad range of individuals from different populations. This is based on the assumption that the etiology of drug abuse is more similar than different across populations. Research with the LST program has primarily followed the second course, i.e., attempting to develop a program that is widely generalizable, while at the same time acknowledging that some modifications may be needed to maximize cultural sensitivity, relevance, and acceptability to varied populations. There are several reasons why LST has been developed as a universal program that is appropriate for youth of all backgrounds. First, evidence suggests that there is substantial overlap in the factors promoting drug use among different racial/ethnic groups (Bettes, Dusenbury, Kerner, James-Ortiz & Botvin, 1990; Botvin, Baker, Botvin, *et al.*, 1993; Botvin, Epstein, Schinke & Diaz, 1994; Botvin, Goldberg, Botvin & Dusenbury, 1993; Dusenbury *et al.*, 1992; Epstein, Botvin, Diaz & Schinke, 1995). Second, even if highly tailored programs are successful, it would be extremely difficult to implement separate interventions for different subgroups of students because most urban schools contain individuals from a variety of racial and ethnic backgrounds.

Research testing the generalizability of the LST prevention approach for inner-city, minority youth has progressed through the following sequence: (1) exploratory/qualitative research consisting of focus group testing and key informant interviews; (2) expert review of intervention methods and materials; (3) consumer-based review of intervention materials and methods; (4) small-scale pilot studies; and (5) large-scale randomized field trials. Modifications to intervention materials and methods were made, as necessary, throughout the process of development and testing, although these changes did not modify the underlying prevention methods or strategy. Rather, these changes were related to factors such as the reading level of intervention materials, the inclusion of appropriate graphics (e.g., illustrations or pictures of minority youth), language, skills training scenarios, and the use of examples appropriate to the target population.

Prevention Research with Hispanic Youth

The first study testing the effectiveness of the LST approach with a minority population was designed to test the feasibility, acceptability, and effectiveness of LST as a smoking prevention intervention in a sample of predominantly Hispanic youth (Botvin, Dusenbury, Baker, James-Ortiz & Kerner, 1989). This largely low-income sample was 74 percent Hispanic and eleven percent African-American, and included 471 seventh graders attending eight public schools in the New York metropolitan area. Schools were randomly assigned to an intervention or control condition. Significant post-test differences in smoking were found between the experimental and the control group, controlling for pretest smoking status, gender, friends' smoking, and acculturation. Intervention effects were also found for knowledge concerning the immediate consequences of smoking, smoking prevalence, the social acceptability of smoking, decision-making, and normative expectations concerning adult and peer smoking.

Data from a large-scale randomized trial also demonstrated significant program effects when implemented with a predominately Hispanic sample of urban minority students (Botvin, Dusenbury, Baker *et al.*, 1992). This study involved 3501 students from 47 public and parochial schools in the greater New York City area, and schools were randomly assigned to experimental and control conditions. Using school means as the unit of analysis, significant reductions in cigarette smoking were found for the adolescents who received the LST program when compared to control students at the end of the seventh grade. Adolescents who received the LST program had monthly prevalence and onset rates that were nearly 30 percent lower than those of controls. Follow-up data demonstrated the continued presence of prevention effects through to the end of the tenth grade (Botvin, 1994).

Prevention research with African-American Youth

Before testing the LST approach on African-American youth, the intervention materials and methods were once again subjected to an extensive review to determine their cultural appropriateness for this population. Following this, a small-scale study was conducted with nine urban junior high schools in northern New Jersey (Botvin, Batson, Witts-Vitale *et al.*, 1989). The pretest involved 608 seventh-grade students, and of these, 221 were in the prevention group and 387 in the control group. The sample was 87 percent African-American and ten percent Hispanic. Schools were randomly assigned to prevention and control conditions within each of three participating communities. Students in the prevention schools received the LST program; students in the control schools received the smoking education curriculum normally provided by their school. Throughout the prevention program, classroom observation data and teacher feedback were collected. A series of multivariate statistical analyses with pretest scores, age, grades, and friends smoking as covariates indicated that there were 57 percent fewer monthly smokers at post-test in the LST group relative to the control group. Significant program effects were also found for knowledge of smoking consequences, and normative expectations regarding adult and peer smoking prevalence.

A large-scale prevention trial involving predominantly African-American youth from 46 inner-city schools in northern New Jersey provided additional empirical support for the effectiveness of the LST prevention approach with this population (Botvin & Cardwell, 1992). Schools were randomly assigned to prevention and control conditions after first blocking on school-wide smoking rates. In the prevention condition, all eligible seventh-grade classes in participating schools received the LST intervention, and booster sessions were provided a year later in the eighth grade; in the control group all classes received the health (smoking) education normally provided to its students. The sample (N = 2512) was 78 percent African-American and 13 percent Hispanic. Initial post-test results showed significantly less smoking for students in the prevention group who received the LST program in the seventh grade and booster sessions in the fall of the eighth grade when compared with both the non-booster prevention group and the controls. At the final follow-up, students who received booster sessions and the original intervention had a 92 percent lower rate of smoking during the past month than the controls.

A recent study examined the effectiveness of the LST program in preventing smoking among a sample of predominantly minority inner-city girls from 29 New York City public schools (Botvin, Griffin, Diaz, Miller & Ifill-Williams, in press). The sample consisted primarily of economically disadvantaged youth and was 60 percent African-American and 23 percent Hispanic. Students who received the program (N = 1278) were compared to a control group of girls (N = 931) who did not. One-year follow-up data indicated that those who participated in the LST program were significantly less likely to initiate smoking relative to controls, and 30 percent fewer intervention students escalated to monthly smoking relative to control students. These behavioral effects were partly mediated by significant program effects on smoking intentions, smoking knowledge, perceived peer and adult smoking norms, drug refusal skills, and risk taking.

Tailoring LST to Minority Youth

Although research has demonstrated the generalizability of the LST approach to minority youth, it is often argued that the strongest prevention effects are likely to come from an intervention approach tailored to the specific population being targeted. A recent study tested the relative effectiveness of the LST approach and a prevention approach specifically tailored to African-American and Hispanic youth (Botvin, Schinke, Epstein & Diaz, 1994). Both prevention approaches were similar in that they taught students a combination of generic "life skills" and skills specific to resisting offers to use drugs. However, the tailored or culturally focused approach was designed to embed the skills training material in myths and legends derived from the African-American and Hispanic cultures. Six junior high schools containing predominantly (95 percent) minority students were assigned to receive either (1) the LST program, (2) the culturally focused prevention approach, or (3) information only. The sample was 48 percent African-American and 37 percent Hispanic.

Results indicated that students in both skills training prevention conditions had lower intentions to drink beer or wine relative to the information-only controls, and the students in the LST condition had lower intentions to drink hard liquor and use illicit drugs. Both skills training conditions also impacted on several mediating variables in a direction consistent with non-drug use. According to these results, both prevention approaches were equally effective, producing significant reductions in behavioral intentions to drink and use illicit drugs, and suggesting that a generic drug abuse prevention approach with high generalizability may be as effective as one tailored to individual ethnic populations. These data, therefore, provide support for the hypothesis that a single drug abuse prevention strategy can be used effectively with multi-ethnic populations.

Follow-up data (N = 456) collected two years later at the end of the ninth grade once again found significant prevention effects for both prevention approaches (Botvin, Schinke, Epstein, Diaz & Botvin, 1995). Students in both skills training prevention conditions drank alcohol less often, became drunk less often, drank less alcohol per drinking occasion, and had lower intentions to use alcohol in the future relative to the controls. The magnitude of these effects was reasonably large. For example, there were 50 percent fewer adolescents drinking alcohol during the past month than in the control group. However, these data also showed that the culturally focused intervention produced significantly stronger effects on these variables than the generic LST approach. The findings of the follow-up study are particularly interesting because, while they suggest that it may be possible to develop a preventive intervention that is effective for a relatively broad range of students, they also indicate that tailoring interventions to specific populations can increase effectiveness with inner-city minority populations.

Future Directions

For many years, the challenge to prevention researchers and public health professionals has been to identify promising intervention approaches, carefully test them, and provide evidence that they worked. That challenge has largely been met. A considerable amount of information is now known about the causes of drug abuse and how to prevent it. Although more work is needed to further refine existing approaches and develop new ones, the challenge now facing the field is how best to bridge the gap between research and practice, and how to disseminate research-based effective prevention approaches into real-world settings.

Dissemination is important because prevention programs proven to be successful are unlikely to have any real public health impact unless they are used in a large number of schools. However, many programs with proven effectiveness, such as the LST program, are not widely used. Instead drug abuse prevention programs most commonly used in real-world settings are those that have not shown evidence of effectiveness or have not been evaluated properly (Silvia & Thorne, 1997). Regarding the research-based programs shown to be effective, it is unclear to what extent schools participating in this research have continued to use these prevention programs after the evaluation period has ended. Although schools may be willing and able to implement prevention programs for a time-limited evaluation period, they may not have the motivation or resources to continue such programs after the conclusions of these studies.

Thus, an important area that deserves further attention is how effective school-based drug abuse prevention programs can be widely disseminated, adopted, and institutionalized. There are a number of challenges that interfere with the widespread implementation of effective school-based prevention programs, including the lack of appropriate infrastructures at the school and school district levels (Elias, 1997). A recent U.S. Department of Education study was conducted to evaluate a sample of nineteen "real-world" school-based prevention programs provided to over 10,000 students in 19 school districts that received funding under the drug free schools act (Silvia & Thorne, 1997). In this study, researchers identified several factors that facilitated the implementation of prevention programming. These included: (1) the level of commitment of the program implementers; (2) the leadership provided by the prevention program coordinator and the presence of staff to assist the coordinator; (3) the level of community involvement in the program; and (4) recognition at the district level of the importance of reinforcing a school-level commitment to prevention through prevention coordinators and adequate staff training.

Furthermore, even if the distribution channels and organizational supports are present, schools must be willing to whole-heartedly embrace these programs as their own. For this to happen, prevention programs must be "user-friendly" and appealing to schools, teachers, students, and even parents. Prevention programs developed by university researchers, while more effective and better evaluated than commercial drug abuse prevention programs, are rarely packaged in a way that is competitive with commercial programs. Because the emphasis is on evaluation, the bulk of the money spent relates to evaluation, while commercial drug abuse prevention curricula typically invest more resources in packaging their materials in an appealing and sophisticated way. If the most effective prevention programs are to be successfully disseminated, adopted, and institutionalized by schools across the country, it will be necessary to invest more resources in the packaging and marketing of prevention materials.

Summary

Recent national data indicate that adolescent drug use is once again on the rise. The etiology of drug abuse is complex, involving multiple determinants and developmental pathways. To be effective, prevention approaches must target these determinants as comprehensively as possible. Approaches that focus on drug-related health knowledge or attitudes or the use of scare tactics have failed to produce an impact on drug use behavior. The most effective prevention approaches have focused on teaching social resistance skills either alone or in combination with general life skills.

The Life Skills Training program is currently the most extensively evaluated school-based prevention approach available. More than a decade and a half of research has demonstrated prevention effects with respect to tobacco, alcohol, and marijuana use, gateway polydrug use, and illicit drug use, as well as on hypothesized mediating variables. The magnitude of reported effects of the LST approach has typically been relatively large, with most studies demonstrating initial reductions of 50 percent or more among students receiving the intervention relative to controls. These studies have generally produced reductions in both occasional or experimental drug use as well as in more serious levels of drug involvement. Research with the Life Skills Training approach includes studies testing its short-term effectiveness as well as its long-term durability, studies testing different delivery methods and the effectiveness of booster sessions, studies testing its effectiveness when conducted by different program providers, and studies testing its effectiveness with different populations. These studies have ranged from small-scale pilot studies involving two schools and a few hundred adolescents to large-scale, multi-site, randomized field trials involving over 50 schools and several thousand adolescents.

This chapter described the theoretical basis and intervention methods of the Life Skills Training program, and summarized nearly two decades-worth of evaluation research of this approach. This body of work demonstrates that the LST approach to drug abuse prevention can produce reductions in drug use of up to 80 percent (relative to controls), that booster sessions can help maintain and even enhance prevention effects, that reductions in drug use for individuals exposed to a prevention program during junior high school can last until at least the end of high school, and that reductions in drug use produced during junior high school also translate into reductions in more serious forms of drug involvement (e.g., heavy use, the regular use of multiple substances, and the use of illicit drugs other than marijuana). Finally, prevention effects have been demonstrated for a relatively broad range of students including white, suburban youth and inner-city minority (African-American and Hispanic) youth. However, notwithstanding the body of research demonstrating the effectiveness of this and other similar prevention approaches, additional research is needed both to refine these approaches further and to determine the most effective means of promoting their dissemination, adoption, and institutionalization.

References

Bandura, A. (1977), *Social Learning Theory*. Englewood Cliffs, NJ: Prentice Hall.

Bettes, B. A., Dusenbury, L., Kerner, J., James-Ortiz, S., & Botvin, G. J. (1990), "Ethnicity and psychosocial factors in alcohol and tobacco use in adolescence." *Child Development 61*, 557–565.

Botvin, G. J. (1994), "Smoking Prevention Among New York Hispanic Youth: Results of a Four-Year Evaluation Study." (Unpublished manuscript.)

Botvin, G. J., Baker, E., Botvin, E. M., Filazzola, A. D., & Millman, R. B. (1984), "Alcohol abuse prevention through the development of personal and social competence: A pilot study." *Journal of Studies on Alcohol 45*, 550–552.

Botvin, G. J., Baker, E., Dusenbury, L. D., Botvin, E. M., & Diaz, T. (1995), "Long-term follow-up results of a randomized drug abuse prevention trial." *Journal of American Medical Association 273*, 1106–1112.

Botvin, G. J., Baker, E., Dusenbury, L., Tortu, S., & Botvin, E. M. (1990), "Preventing adolescent drug abuse through a multimodal cognitive-behavioral approach: Results of a 3-year study." *Journal of Consulting & Clinical Psychology 58*, 437–446.

Botvin, G. J., Baker, E., Filazzola, A., & Botvin, E. M. (1990), "A cognitive-behavioral approach to substance abuse prevention: A one-year follow-up." *Addictive Behaviors 15*, 47–63.

Botvin, G. J., Baker, E., Renick, N. L., Filazzola, A. D., & Botvin, E. M. (1984), "A cognitive-behavioral approach to substance abuse prevention." *Addictive Behaviors 9*, 137–147.

Botvin, G. J., & Botvin, E. M. (1992), "Adolescent tobacco, alcohol, and drug abuse: Prevention strategies, empirical findings, and assessment issues." *Developmental & Behavioral Pediatrics 13*, 290–301.

Botvin, G. J., & Cardwell, J. (1992), "Primary prevention (smoking) of cancer in Black populations." Grant contract number N01-CN-6508. Final Report to National Cancer Institute (NCI). Cornell University Medical College.

Botvin, G. J., Dusenbury, L., Baker, E., James-Ortiz, S., & Kerner, J. (1989), "A skills training approach to smoking prevention among Hispanic youth." *Journal of Behavioral Medicine 12*, 279–296.

Botvin, G. J., & Eng, A. (1982), "The efficacy of a multicomponent approach to the prevention of cigarette smoking." *Preventive Medicine 11*, 199–211.

Botvin, G. J., Eng, A., & Williams, C. L. (1980), "Preventing the onset of cigarette smoking through Life Skills Training." *Preventive Medicine 9*, 135–143.

Botvin, G. J., Epstein, J. A., Schinke, S. P., & Diaz, T. (1994), "Correlates and predictors of smoking among inner city youth." *Developmental & Behavioral Pediatrics 15*, 67–73.

Botvin, G. J. *et al.* (1989), "A psychosocial approach to smoking prevention for urban black youth." *Public Health Reports 104*, 573–582.

Botvin, G. J. *et al.* (1992), "Smoking prevention among urban minority youth: Assessing effects on outcome and mediating variables." *Health Psychology 11*, 290–299.

Botvin, G. J. *et al.* (1993), "Factors promoting cigarette smoking among black youth: A causal modeling approach." *Addictive Behaviors 18*, 397–405.

Botvin, G. J., Goldberg, C. J., Botvin, E. M., & Dusenbury, L. (1993), "Smoking behavior of adolescents exposed to cigarette advertising." *Public Health Reports 108*, 217–224.

Botvin, G. J., Griffin, K. W., Diaz, T., Miller, N., & Ifill-Williams, M. (1999), "Smoking initiation and escalation in early adolescent girls: One-year follow-up of a school-based prevention intervention for minority youth." *Journal of the American Medical Women's Association 54*, 139–143, 152.

Botvin, G. J, Griffin, Diaz, Miller & Ifill-Williams (2000), "Preventing illicit drug use in adolescents: Long-term follow-up data from a randomized control trial of a school population." *Addictive Behaviors 5*, 769–774.

Botvin, G. J., Renick, N., & Baker, E. (1983), "The effects of scheduling format and booster sessions on a broad-spectrum psychosocial approach to smoking prevention." *Journal of Behavioral Medicine 6*, 359–379.

Botvin, G. J., Schinke, S. P., Epstein, J. A., & Diaz, T. (1994), "The effectiveness of culturally-focused & generic skills training approaches to alcohol and drug abuse prevention among minority youth." *Psychology of Addictive Behaviors 8*, 116–127.

Botvin, G. J., Schinke, S. P., Epstein, J. A., Diaz, T., & Botvin, E. M. (1995), "Effectiveness of culturally focused and generic skills training approaches to alcohol and drug abuse prevention among minority adolescents: Two-year follow-up results." *Psychology of Addictive Behaviors 9*, 183–194.

Dusenbury, L. *et al.* (1992), "Predictors of smoking prevalence among New York Latino youth." *American Journal of Public Health 82*, 55–58.

Elias, M. J. (1997), "Reinterpreting dissemination of prevention programs as widespread implementation with effectiveness and fidelity." In R. P. Weissberg, T. P. Gullotta *et al.* (eds), *Healthy children 2010: Establishing preventive services. Issues in children's and families' lives.* Thousand Oaks, CA: Sage Publications, 253–289.

Epstein, J. A., Botvin, G. J., Diaz, T., & Schinke, S. P. (1995), "The role of social factors and individual characteristics in promoting alcohol among inner-city minority youth." *Journal of Studies on Alcohol 56*, 39–46.

Goodstadt, M. S. (1986), "Drug education: The prevention issues." *Journal of Drug Education 19*, 197–208.

Hawkins, J. D., Catalano, R. F., & Miller, J. Y. (1992), "Risk and protective factors for alcohol and other drug problems in adolescence and early adulthood: Implications for substance abuse prevention." *Psychological Bulletin 112*, 64–105.

Jessor, R., & Jessor, S. L. (1977), *Problem Behavior and Psychosocial Development: A longitudinal study of youth.* New York: Academic Press.

Johnston, L. D., O'Malley, P. M., & Bachman, J. G. (1994), *National Survey Results on Drug Use from the Monitoring the Future Study, 1975–1993. Volume I Secondary School Students.* Rockville, MD: US Department of Health and Human Services.

Johnston, L. D., O'Malley, P. M., & Bachman, J. G. (1995), *National Survey Results on Drug Use from the Monitoring the Future Study, 1975–1994, Volume I Secondary school students.* Washington, DC: US Department of Health and Human Services.

Kaplan, H. B. (1980), *Deviant Behavior in Defense of Self.* New York: Academic Press.

McGuire, W. J. (1968), "The nature of attitudes and attitude change." In G. Lindzey & E. Aronson (eds), *Handbook of Social Psychology.* Reading, MA: Addison-Wesley, 136–314.

Millman, R. B., & Botvin, G. J. (1992), "Substance use, abuse, and dependence." In M. Levine, N. B. Carey, A. C. Crocker & R. T. Gross (eds), *Developmental-Behavioral Pediatrics* (2nd ed.). New York: W.B. Saunders Company, 451–467.

Oetting, E. R., & Beauvais, F. (1987), "Peer cluster theory, socialization characteristics, and adolescent drug use: A path analysis." *Journal of Consulting & Clinical Psychology 34*, 205–213.

Silvia, E. S., & Thorne, J. (1997), *School-based Drug Prevention Programs: A longitudinal study in selected school districts.* Final Report to US Department of Education. Research Triangle Institute.

Tortu, S., & Botvin, G. J. (1989), "School-based smoking prevention: The teacher training process." *Preventive Medicine 18*, 280–289.

Chapter 3

Reconnecting Youth to Prevent Drug Abuse, School Dropout and Suicidal Behaviors Among High-Risk Youth

Leona L. Eggert, Elaine A. Thompson, Jerald R. Herting, and Brooke P. Randell*

Introduction

Prevention research today is the critical frontier for advancing universal, selective and indicated prevention programs that are effective in reducing adolescent drug involvement and related problem behaviors. Classifying prevention programs as universal, selective or indicated (Gordon, 1987; IOM, 1994) is a recent adoption by the National Institute on Drug Abuse (NIDA, 1997). *Universal* drug use prevention programs are meant to reach everyone in a population. For example, universal school-based programs have the primary goal of keeping a school community drug-free and preventing students from initiating alcohol, tobacco or other drug use (ATOD use). By contrast, *selective* drug use prevention programs are designed to serve groups known to be at greater risk of ATOD use. The goal of a selective drug use prevention program for children of alcoholics, e.g., is to impede the onset of ATOD use by youth in this high-risk group. On the other hand, *indicated* drug abuse prevention programs are intended to benefit specific individuals, those already showing early signs of drug involvement and/or related risk factors. In indicated prevention programs the primary goal is to stem the progression of ATOD use and/or reduce drug involvement among the high-risk individuals.

Unlike universal prevention programs, where all students in a school or classroom receive the preventive intervention, indicated prevention programs are best reserved for

Special thanks to the Co-Developer of the *Reconnecting Youth* school-based prevention program, Liela J. Nicholas, and to the many school personnel and youth who participated in experimental tests of RY. Similarly, our gratitude is extended to the research personnel who helped immensely with the data preparation and analyses. For the dedication of all the Reconnecting Youth Prevention Research team members, we acknowledge their individual roles in advancing the efficacy of RY and prevention science. Without them very little of this would have been possible.

*Correspondence concerning this chapter should be addressed to: Leona L. Eggert, Ph.D., RN, FAAN, Spence Endowed Professor, Principal Investigator, Reconnecting Youth Prevention Research Program, Psychosocial and Community Health Department, University of Washington School of Nursing, Seattle, WA 98195. Elaine A. Thompson, Ph.D., RN, Professor, Co-Principal Investigator; Jerald R. Herting, Ph.D., Research Associate Professor, Co-Principal Investigator; Brooke P. Randell, DNSc, CNS, Research Assistant Professor, Co-Principal Investigator.

Innovations in Adolescent Substance Abuse Interventions, pages 51–84.
Copyright © 2001 by Elsevier Science Ltd.
ISBN: 0-08-043577-7

those in greatest need. This is because indicated prevention programs are more costly per individual and more intensive than needed by most students. Indicated prevention programs are designed to deliver a larger "dose" of the program elements, in sufficient strength to "reverse" problem behaviors. To be most effective, indicated prevention approaches are designed to directly influence the identified risk and protective factors. Thus, indicated prevention programs demand an understanding and assessment of the individual students' risk and protective factors related to drug abuse.

Reconnecting Youth is an indicated prevention program designed for particular high-risk individuals, those on a trajectory toward high school dropout (Eggert, 1998). These intended participants demonstrate a need for a stronger "dose" of preventive interventions as they are at risk for a steady progression toward drug abuse (NIDA, 1994). They are significantly more likely to report alcohol, marijuana, and cocaine use than the typical high school student (Johnson, O'Malley & Bachman, 1996). Our research shows these youth experience other problem behaviors besides drug involvement and school performance problems, such as aggression, depression, and suicidal behaviors (Eggert & Herting, 1993; Eggert & Nicholas, 1992; Thompson, Moody & Eggert, 1994; Thompson, Connelly & Eggert, 2000a).

The purpose of this chapter is to review the Reconnecting Youth (RY) indicated prevention program. The chapter is addressed to practitioners whose charge it is to intervene with potential high school dropouts and youth already engaged in drug involvement. Our message is also intended to speak to policymakers, including legislators, school board members, school district administrators, and principals, whose duty it is to select effective prevention programs for high-risk individuals.

In the first section of the chapter, we describe the theoretic underpinnings of the RY indicated prevention model. We posit the effects of the focused school, peer-support and individual strategies on a set of mediators, arguing that these mediators influence changes in the high-risk youth's drug involvement, school deviance and/or emotional distress and suicidal behaviors. We then describe the specific elements of the RY program as it is implemented in schools, and provide empirical evidence for the efficacy of RY with the youth for whom it is intended. We conclude the chapter with suggested future directions and a general summary.

The RY Program Goals

Before discussing the theoretic framework for RY, an overview of the program goals and objectives is provided as a context for understanding the program's general philosophy and purposes. Reducing risk factors and enhancing resiliency or protective factors (Hawkins, Catalano & Miller, 1992) are key objectives used to achieve the indicated prevention program goals in RY (Eggert & Kumpfer, 1997; Eggert, Nicholas & Owen, 1995a).

RY has three central program goals with specific measurable objectives as follows:

Goal 1: Decreased drug involvement — evidenced by decreased frequency of alcohol and other drug use, decreased drug use control problems, and decreased adverse drug use consequences.

Goal 2: Increased school performance — evidenced by increased attendance and GPA (grade point average) in all the classes taken by a student, as well as increased credits earned toward graduation.

Goal 3: Decreased emotional distress — reflected by decreased aggression, depression and suicidal behaviors.

Risk-reduction objectives in RY that support these goals include: (1) changing personal risk factors such as impulsive decision-making and actions through skills training in personal control strategies and interpersonal communication, and (2) decreasing related interpersonal and school risk factors (chiefly deviant peer bonding) through enhancing positive peer-group support and teacher support in the RY program. One resiliency-enhancing objective in RY that fosters program goal achievement includes increasing *personal resources* known to be protective — i.e., a strong sense of self-worth, a belief in one's ability to handle life's problems, and a positive view of the future (Powell-Cope & Eggert, 1994). A second resiliency-enhancing RY objective is to enhance *social or environmental protective factors* — i.e., a network of supportive friends and family, school bonding through social support from favorite teachers, and support for school from parents (Eggert, Thompson, Herting & Nicholas, 1994b; Powell-Cope & Eggert, 1994). Objectives in the RY prevention approach are directed at reducing risks and enhancing resiliency — not just for the youth, but also in their networks of close friends, family, school, and community (Eggert & Parks, 1987; Hansen, 1992; Hawkins, Catalano & Miller, 1992). Achieving these objectives is known to enhance RY goals.

Achieving the RY indicated prevention program goals means facing major challenges: (1) identifying and serving an elusive and high-risk group of students — potential high school dropouts; (2) integrating the proposed interventions into high schools whose culture is not always friendly toward research; and (3) testing theory-based preventive interventions designed to enhance assets and reduce risks (Eggert, 1996b).

Theoretic Framework for the Reconnecting Youth Indicated Prevention Approach

The framework for Reconnecting Youth (RY) is a social-network-support model (Eggert, 1987, Eggert, Seyl & Nicholas, 1990). This framework explicitly incorporates the idea that individual human behaviors do not exist in a vacuum; rather they occur within a person's social context. This means that a student's drug involvement, emotional well-being, and school performance are developed and maintained within his or her peer network, family, and school contexts. Thus, as an example, if changes in drug involvement behaviors are desired, preventive interventions must occur within the adolescents' social context. In RY, the social context includes:

1. A *social network component*, including key partners within the school community — i.e., the students' parents or guardians, the RY teacher, and the RY peer group. These are the social and interpersonal relationships that exist among people in a typical RY student's social network.

2. The *social support and social learning processes* that include: (a) the exchange of support among the key "partners" in the RY program, and (b) the cognitive and behavioral learning that takes place.

Figure 1 illustrates this social network support framework on which RY is based. Both the social network support structure and processes are essential for fostering cognitive and behavioral changes among the students participating in RY.

At the left side of Figure 1 the social support structure consists of school network connections, family ties, and the teacher-to-student and peer-to-peer interpersonal relationships established in RY. Through these interpersonal ties, social support and learning opportunities are delivered and received by program participants. In the middle of Figure 1, the RY social support processes include the exchange and active facilitation of social support: (1) *expressive support* or bonding (caring, group belonging, positive reinforcement), and (2) *instrumental support* (specific "aid" such as the RY teacher's coaching and skills training). These exchanges of social support provide the essential "medium" required for social learning to take place. The basic premise is that this support is perceived by the RY participants at a cognitive level, which serves to motivate and influence changes in the levels of perceived personal control, actual support received, and personal and social skills acquired. In turn, these immediate outcomes are hypothesized to influence RY program goal achievement, the outcomes shown on the right side of Figure 1.

The benefits of social support are widely acknowledged. Studies of resiliency (Blaney & Ganellen, 1991; Jessor, 1993; Resnick *et al.*, 1997) and social support (Cohen & Syme, 1985; Cutrona & Russell, 1991; Dunkel-Schetter & Bennett, 1991; Sarason, Pierce &

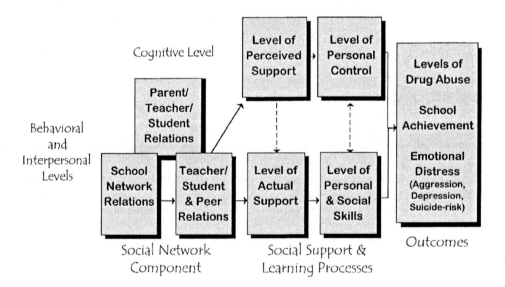

Figure 1: RY prevention program theoretic model of social network and social support processes and outcomes

Sarason, 1991) indicate that people who have greater personal and social resources benefit in many health-promoting ways (Botvin & Dusenbury, 1989; Cauce & Srebnik, 1989; Eggert, 1987; Lin, Dean & Ensel, 1986; Rainer & Slavin, 1992). Thus, social support interventions that simultaneously create an understanding, reinforcing, interpersonal context and assist youth in acquiring essential life skills are crucial for altering the problem behaviors evidenced by high-risk youth.

The next sections provide greater details regarding the specification of social support interventions in RY. Interventions are synthesized into three domains: school, peers, and individual. Prevention strategies for each of these domains are illustrated in Boxes 1–3. For each section, prevention strategies for the domain are described. Then, theoretic premises are advanced for why these interventions should work to decrease drug involvement, emotional distress and high school dropout. Finally, the theoretic mechanisms depicted in Figure 1 are explained in terms of how the interventions are posited to influence the mediating factors of personal control and perceived support, thereby influencing the desired outcomes.

RY School-focused Preventive Interventions

Prevention strategies. Several key interventions in the RY model are at the school-system level and the RY program level. Theoretically these interventions enhance the overall school experience of high-risk youth. They are detailed in Box 1 and include norm setting, enhancing school network support for high-risk youth, and facilitating prosocial school and community bonding experiences.

Theoretic premise. School-system strategies motivate and provide social support from specific adults in the youth's school network. As a result, youth should experience greater *access to help* within their natural school environment. Increasing access to help is thought to reduce barriers and provide greater opportunities for school bonding, thus enhancing the acquisition of self-efficacy skills (Pentz, 1993; Weissberg, Caplan & Sivo, 1989). Youth involved in meaningful connections to school experience opportunities for school bonding and peer-group belonging (a central concern for adolescents); they also experience less loneliness, healthier fun activities and greater purpose in life (Harlow, Newcomb & Bentler, 1986).

Theoretic mechanisms. Enhancing *personal control* and perceived *school support/ bonding*, two known mediating protective factors, is the intent of the school-focused, social support interventions. Theoretically, providing youth with greater amounts of school network support — by shaping and monitoring opportunities to participate in meaningful relationships with caring adults, in prosocial school activities, and in community service — works to directly increase: (1) students' personal competencies and control, thus reinforcing a positive view of school and teachers; and (2) conventional school bonding, enhancing a greater sense of belonging and purpose (Bandura, 1977; Botvin & Dusenbury, 1989; Catalano, Hawkins, Wells, Miller & Brewer, 1991; Schinke & Gilchrist, 1984; Schinke, Botvin & Orlandi, 1991). Enhanced personal control and conventional school bonding should promote the RY

Box 1: RY School System Preventive Intervention.

1. Setting school norms for and monitoring
   (a) Improved attendance in all classes
   (b) Improved achievement in all classes
   (c) No drug involvement at school
2. Improving school network support
   (a) Delivering consistent RY teacher support
   (b) Fostering teacher support in all classes
   (c) Providing for individual case management
3. Facilitating prosocial activities
   (a) Encouraging school bonding in RY class, school clubs, sports and other desired prosocial functions
   (b) Fostering community service involvement

---

outcomes or program goals shown in Figure 1 (Brendtro, Brokenleg & Van Bockern, 1990; Kellam & Rebok, 1992; Kellam *et al.*, 1991).

RY Peer-focused Preventive Interventions

Prevention strategies. For developmental and etiologic reasons, peers represent a critical context for delivering RY prevention strategies. Several key strategies are designed to engage and motivate the youth within an interactive peer group, *and* to counteract negative peer bonding/activities. These strategies, detailed in Box 2, include: (1) setting and main-taining RY group norms for making personal commitments to the program goals of increasing school achievement, decreasing drug involvement and improving mood manage-ment; (2) reinforcing daily the norms of a positive peer group culture while redirecting deviant norms and activities (Brendtro et al., 1990; Eggert *et al.*, 1995a; Vorrath & Brendtro, 1985; Tobler, 1992); and (3) replacing deviant group bonding with prosocial group bonding in the RY class.

Theoretic premise. The RY peer-focused strategies involve developing and maintaining a positive peer group culture (Vorrath & Brendtro, 1985) to counteract key risk factors commonly evidenced in disenfranchised youth. Theoretically this prosocial culture posi-tively influences conventional peer bonding and reduces drug involvement, aggression/ depression and school deviance (Eggert, Thompson, Herting, Nicholas & Dicker, 1994c; Eggert *et al.*, 1990). Fostering prosocial activities and recreational opportunities for high-risk youth is an essential RY strategy. Such daily program activities and multiple booster-group activities across a school year are known to positively influence program outcomes (Brendtro *et al.*, 1990; Eggert, Thompson, Herting & Nicholas, 1995b; Tobler, 1986, 1992).

Theoretic mechanisms. Conventional/prosocial peer bonding is a primary mediator predicted to influence RY outcomes. Positive peer relationships are acknowledged as pivotal for healthy adolescent development (Cauce & Srebnik, 1989; Heller, Price & Hogg, 1991;

Box 2: RY Peer Group Preventive Interventions

1. Developing norms in RY of personal and group commitment to the program goals of:
   (a) "Doing school" — attending and achieving
   (b) Managing moods
   (c) Decreasing drug involvement
2. Reinforcing daily the norms related to a positive peer group culture — i.e.,
   (a) Actively supporting/helping each group member's progress toward goal achievement
   (b) Making it cool to care, perceiving problems as an opportunity for growth and assume responsibility for building and maintaining a positive RY peer group
3. Replacing deviant peer/group belonging with prosocial group belonging
   (a) Promoting group bonding in RY class
   (b) Fostering a climate and culture of care and concern
   (c) Replacing deviant activities and relationships with prosocial RY activities and relationships

---

Moskowitz, 1988). In social influence models (Botvin & Dusenbury, 1989; Dorn, 1984), prosocial bonding counteracts deviant orientation (Elliott, Huizinga & Ageton, 1985). Hence, expressive and instrumental support from RY peers meets the adolescents' needs for group belonging. Also, this support reinforces prosocial norms and provides opportunities for developing new non-drug using friends, thereby, negatively influencing deviant peer bonding (Eggert *et al*, 1994c). Further, the RY peer group reinforces the acquisition of life skills in the daily class, directly influencing personal control and self-efficacy (Bandura, 1977). These outcomes are expected because the RY teacher's role is to actively develop and maintain peer group support in the class by modeling support, positively reinforcing support among group members, while not reinforcing deviant peer bonds and activities (Eggert & Herting, 1991; Vorrath & Brendtro, 1985).

Individual-focused Preventive Interventions

Prevention strategies. Skills training is a primary preventive intervention in the individual-focused domain of RY. Social and life-skills training provides youth with daily opportunities for learning and practicing skills in the four areas indicated in Box 3. Central elements of this strategy include: (1) providing personally relevant information and feedback regarding each youth's acquisition and application of life skills, and (2) coaching students in ways to apply the basic skills to personal barriers hampering achievement of the RY program goals — i.e., improving school performance, mood management, and drug use control.

Theoretic premises. The RY skills units represent a nucleus of personal and interpersonal social skills necessary for effective coping and adaptation. These protective factors function to counteract drug abuse and other problem behaviors (Botvin & Dusenbury, 1989; Botvin &

Box 3: RY Personal & Social Skills Training

1. Self-esteem Enhancement
   Learning to communicate esteem enhancing talk for self and others in the RY class
2. Decision-making
   Learning to use the S.T.E.P.S. decision making process and applying it to making healthy decisions about drug use, school and mood management
3. Personal Control
   Learning stress, anger and depression management skills; practicing coping skills for "triggers" related to drug use, truancy and uncontrolled moods
4. Interpersonal Communication
   Learning to give and receive support with friends, and negotiation skills with teachers and parents

---

Tortu, 1988; Eggert, 1995). RY skills training, based on integrated social learning and control theories (Elliott, Huizinga & Ageton, 1985), provides opportunities for acquiring skills within a supportive interpersonal and valued peer-group context. Social learning is enhanced through teacher modeling, individual practice and group reinforcement for prosocial coping and fun activities. These RY skills training units specifically address key risk and protective factors that influence co-occurring problem behaviors including school dropout, drug involvement, aggression and suicidal behaviors.

Theoretic mechanisms. Personal control (or self-efficacy) is a mediating factor that directly influences adolescent substance use, aggression, depression, and school deviance (Eggert *et al.*, 1994c; Eggert *et al.*, 1995b; Thompson, Eggert & Herting, 2000b). Personally relevant feedback delivered in a nonjudgmental way has been linked with increased motivation (Janis, 1983) and with decreased denial, less resistance, and increased self-help motivation (Miller & Rollnick, 1991; Miller & Sanchez, 1993; Miller & Sovreign, 1989). Thus, RY works through acquiring and practicing specific life skills and reducing uncertainty, thereby increasing self-efficacy and a sense of personal control. These, in turn, decrease negative outcomes (Botvin & Dusenbury, 1989; Eggert & Herting, 1991).

Description of the Reconnecting Youth Prevention Program

How RY is implemented in the field is detailed in this section. Addressed are the program structure, the intended participants, four core program elements, and features of the daily RY class. This description illustrates how our knowledge of high-risk youth guided the overall structure, design, and implementation of RY in many urban high schools.

The Structure of Reconnecting Youth (RY)

The organization of RY is unique in several important ways. First, it is grounded in a partnership model between students, school personnel, parents and prevention practitioners/researchers. RY is also designed to be high school-based; the core component is structured as an elective course that is part of a high-school's curriculum offerings. Second, trained teachers who meet the selection criteria and whose teaching assignment includes RY as just one of their teaching assignments deliver the RY course. Third, the RY school-based team includes an RY coordinator whose responsibility is to oversee the fidelity of the RY program implementation, and to provide collegial support and advice for the RY teacher.

Launching RY in any high school requires effective administrative leadership, community support and talented, school personnel trained in the RY group leader/teacher role. These system-level supports are necessary for RY to be implemented as designed, to reach its full potential of reconnecting youth to school and to achieving the program goals. Program success requires the support and training of all partners. Strong, committed administrative leadership is critical for: (1) developing the partnership model; (2) establishing a community support team; (3) setting up a school-based crisis response team; and (4) preparing for the implementation of RY by selecting appropriate teachers and an RY coordinator, arranging for their training and facilitating student selection according to the model. Full details of these structural issues are provided in *Reconnecting Youth: A Peer Group Approach to Building Life Skills* (Eggert *et al.*, 1995a).

Intended participants. RY is designed to identify and serve potential high school dropouts, in grades 9–12 in regular high schools. We extend a personal invitation to youth to participate in RY because an ethnographic study of these youth revealed that a "personal invitation" was used when they were asked to "skip" or "cut" class and use drugs (Eggert & Nicholas, 1992). The invitation takes the form of a strong appeal to join RY; it is an invitation to "drop into school" as an alternative to dropping out. The invitation includes the promise of being able to "belong," of learning to help oneself and others succeed in school, reduce drug involvement and better manage harmful moods. During this invitation process, students are motivated to take RY by illustrating how others have benefited from the program in specific ways at school, work, home, and with friends.

In our experience, effective RY groups were heterogeneous, multicultural and included males and females in grades nine to twelve. Getting this "mix" of youth occurred through random selection from an available pool of youth who were at risk of school dropout. Less effective was filling the class with only youth who were determined to have the greatest need.

RY Program Components

There are four key components of RY that are integrated into the school environment. These are: (1) the RY daily class; (2) a school bonding/activities component; (3) parent involvement; and (4) a school-based crisis response plan (Eggert *et al.*, 1995a). Each component serves a critical preventive function in enhancing specific protective factors, warranting some detail in terms of how they are implemented in a high school setting.

1. The RY daily class. This is the core element of the RY program. The RY class is structured as a regular high school course, with several key features.

- The RY class is conducted in daily, 50-minute periods during regular school hours for a full semester (typically 90 days); it is taken for elective or required credit.
- The teacher-to-student ratio of 1:10 (or 1:12 at most) is congruent with small-group work models on which RY is based.
- RY is taught by specially selected and trained high school teachers (or other school-based staff such as counselors, nurses, social workers, psychologists, etc.).
- The content of the RY class includes life-skills training; the process involves the development and maintenance of a positive peer-group culture.
- An optional second semester program, RY-II, is currently being tested for its efficacy in preventing relapse and promoting continued growth in personal control and social support resources, and in school bonding activities.

2. The school bonding activities component. This element focuses on prosocial, recreational school bonding activities. Interventions are designed to reconnect students to school and to health-promoting activities. These activities address the students' needs for healthy activities as alternatives to drug involvement, loneliness or depression. The RY program coordinator collaborates with the RY teacher to plan within- and out-of-classroom activities.

Activities that are suggested include: (1) recreational field trips; (2) drug-free weekend activities, (3) projects to encourage school service as an opportunity for growth, (4) school clubs or activities of the student's choice (Weissberg, Caplan & Sivo, 1989). Rewards are linked directly to prosocial behavior — e.g., students may receive community service credit; RY recognition through praise, certificates, related job reference letters; and school-wide recognition (e.g., in the school paper, on special posters). Developing friendships with "nondrug-using" youth through these activities is reinforced (Brendtro *et al.*, 1990; Eggert *et al.*, 1995a).

3. Parent involvement. Parents (including guardians or other adults functioning in this role) are important RY partners and essential for providing support at home for the day-to-day life skills learned in the RY class. Parent involvement begins when the RY teacher contacts parents prior to the start of the RY class to: (1) take the first step in establishing the partnership relationship, (2) seek the parent's consent for their son or daughter to be in the RY program, and (3) enlist the parent's support in helping their son or daughter make important changes by reinforcing the program goals in appropriate ways at home.

Throughout the RY class, students are taught to enlist the help of their parents in supporting their program goal achievement. Parental support and encouragement is reinforced by the RY teacher sending home positive progress notes, offsetting years of "poor work slips" or negative messages from school typically experienced by these parents.

4. A school crisis response system. Establishing a school-based crisis response plan as part of the RY program is important because depression and suicidal behaviors are experienced by many of the targeted high-risk youth. The crisis response plan serves the school community in supporting RY youth; it provides guidelines for classroom teachers and other school personnel for recognizing warning signs of suicide risk and knowing how to help a suicidal youth.

To reiterate, the daily RY class fosters a sense of belonging and life-skills acquisition for the program participants. The school activities component, parent involvement and crisis response plan all foster the development of a school-wide network of support. These elements help high-risk youth sustain desired behavioral changes fostered in RY and apply them in other settings at school and at home.

Critical Features of the RY Daily Class

The RY model integrates group work and life-skills training sub-models. This integration of content and process in RY and its application to the RY program goals is illustrated in Figure 2 and Table 1.

These various program components are sequenced over the course of a school semester. Note that two semesters of RY are detailed. RY-I is the full-semester program covered in the RY leader's manual (Eggert *et al.*, 1995a). RY-II is a recent extension that involves booster sessions, individual work and small group sessions during a second semester. In general RY-I helps youth *develop* necessary life skills within a supportive peer group and RY-II provides youth with opportunities to *reinforce* and *generalize* these skills, preparing youth to apply the skills more fully in their daily life experiences and to prevent relapse.

Integrating group work and skills training. Group work and skills training are vitally linked. Teaching RY is both an *art* and a *science.* The *art* is in the process of integrating the skills training and group work sub-models. "This is a delicate dance," as one of our RY teachers said. The *science* is in the framework, content, and sequencing of the group stages and skills training. Special features of this integration are highlighted in Box 4 and detailed next.

RY group work, skills training and daily monitoring are combined to achieve specific purposes. Group support and caring enhance a feeling of belonging. Life-skills training enhances personal and social skills acquisition. The purpose of monitoring is to help youth

---

Box 4: Integrating skills training within an RY group is unique

- Objectives and key concepts of each lesson are standardized. The lesson activities meet these objectives, but other activities that fit the teacher and students in better ways can be substituted provided they meet the objectives and are congruent with the key concepts.
- The examples and situations used for skills building and application must come from the individual student's experiences, making learning personally relevant and applicable to their culture and values.
- RY is developmentally appropriate for adolescents in grades 9–12 and designed for multicultural groups.

Table 1: Overview of Implementation Schedule of Reconnecting Youth

Fall Semester	RY-I Program Content
Weeks 1–2	Daily Class: *Getting Started Unit* Build a positive peer culture; target program goals **Social Activities:** Drug-free week-end event **School Bonding:** Conduct school involvement assessment
Weeks 3–6	**Daily Class:** *Self-esteem Enhancement Unit* Build skills for appreciating self and others; application of skills to program goals **Social Activities:** Drug Free week-end event; Ropes course **School Bonding:** Support student's involvement with one campus group
Weeks 7–10	**Daily Class:** *Decision-making Unit* Use STEPS decision-making process to set goals; apply STEPS to program goals **Social Activities:** Drug-free week-end event; Volunteer activity (4 hours) **School Bonding:** Select and implement class service project in school
Weeks 11–14	**Daily Class:** *Personal Control Unit* Identify stress and stress responses; use healthy coping strategies to manage stress, application of these strategies to program goals **Social Activities:** Attend school social event; Advanced Ropes course **School Bonding:** Participation in a school club or sport of choice; Group recognition
Weeks 15–18	**Daily Class:** *Interpersonal Communication Unit* Express care and concern; learn helping S.T.E.P.S. and negotiation skills; give and receive constructive criticism, apply communication skills to program goals **Social Activities:** Drug-free week-end event; Volunteer activity (4 hours) **School Bonding:** Participation in a school club or sport of choice
Weeks 19–20	**Daily Class:** Wrap-up — *Graduation* Evaluate skills and progress made toward program goals; celebrate growth **Social Activities:** Drug-free celebration **School Bonding:** RY school-wide recognition/graduation (presentation, media coverage)

Spring Semester	RY-II Program Content
Weeks 1–3	**RY Boosters** Assessment and Goal Setting (individual) Check-in "Monitoring Goal Attainment" **Social Activities:** Drug-free week-end event; Volunteer activity (4 hours) **School Bonding:** Conduct school involvement assessment
Weeks 4–12	**Advanced Group Support and Skills Training** Session 1: Self-Esteem — using affirmations; interrupting automatic thoughts Session 2: Self-Esteem — visualizing + self-images; giving and receiving helpful criticism Session 3: Decision-Making — evaluating decisions; taking S.T.E.P.S. Session 4: Decision-Making — making mini-decisions; managing time Individual assessment, goal setting and monitoring **Social Activities:** Advanced Ropes course; Volunteer activity (4 hours) **School Bonding:** Participation in a school club or sport of choice
Weeks 13–20	**Advanced Group Support and Skills Training** Session 5: Personal Control — identifying stress triggers; getting support Session 6: Personal Control — working out stress; controlling anger and/or depression Session 7: Interpersonal Communication — using "I" messages; listening actively Session 8: Interpersonal Communication — helping vs. enabling; negotiating conflict Individual assessment, goal setting and monitoring **Social Activities:** Attend school social event; Drug-free week-end event **School Bonding:** School-based group activity (RY Service Project, advocacy)

Figure 2: The basic RY class interventional model

to chart their progress toward goal achievement and gain insights from both the personal assessments made and the constructive feedback provided by the RY teacher and peer group (Eggert *et al.*, 1995a).

Group work and life-skills training in RY also follows a specific sequence:

1. *Cognitive/Motivational Preparation* — this means inspiring the students to become involved. It includes the forming stage of the group as a whole during the "getting started" unit of RY, as well as motivating the group to work together during each daily session.
2. *Skills Building* — this involves teaching, demonstrating and role modeling the specific skills. As a team, the group begins developing norms to acquire skills, analogous to learning the specific skills of a team sport.
3. *Skills Practice* — this entails multiple opportunities for each student to become and be judged as competent by the group in the particular skill being taught. This requires a more mature "working" group that is comfortable practicing together, helping each other and encouraging greater competence in the skills being practiced.
4. *Skills Application and Transfer* — this requires the youth to apply the skills in the RY group and in their life at school, with friends and family. As the group reaches "maturity," they work together on applying the behavioral changes both within and outside the group (Eggert *et al.*, 1995a).

After developing a supportive group environment and acquiring basic life skills, the students practice these life skills in addressing their real-life problems. Boosters, activities that reinforce understanding of and competency in the new skills, are promoted both in and beyond the RY group. Cross-cultural understanding and acceptance are prominently featured and promoted. By using the students' real-life problems, beliefs and values, RY promotes cultural sensitivity in multicultural groups.

The daily RY experience. A *Daily Agenda*, like the sample in Box 5, helps to integrate group work and skills training. For example, the teacher starts with *Check In* to monitor progress on the program goals. How are they doing in relation to school? How are drug use control and mood management progressing? "This is like taking the group's temperature," said an RY teacher. It leads nicely into *Check Back*, where students are encouraged to report on successes experienced with the skills learned in yesterday's class. Here the norm of support — praising steps taken toward mini-goals — is exercised. There is celebrating with "high-fives" and other suitable acclamations, expressed praise or reinforcers.

Box 5: RY Agenda Date	Time Needed
Check In/Check Back:	
• Monitoring school, drug use control, mood goals	10 min
• Bring 'n Brag — about yesterday's contract & practice task	
Shared Agenda: Who needs time? Support desired?	10 min
• Trisha: Caught using drugs – willing to fold into today's lesson	
• Marc: Suspended - What now? Wants group to brainstorm options	
• Others?	
Today's Topic/Skills/S.T.E.P.S. to Drug Use Control	25 min
• Evaluating decisions made about drug use	
• Taking S.T.E.P.S. to improve drug use control	
• Supporting drug non-use — what does that look and sound like?	
Contracting to Practice	10 min
	Total 55 min

The teacher then asks if anyone wants time for group support and advice related to a personal issue. This leads into a preview of the training focus for the day. Once the leader has an idea of the students' issues, s/he finesses links between the students' issues and the skills training for the day.

The students help set the agenda and take turns keeping notes of group discussions and decisions on a flipchart. This shares the leadership and focuses the group work and time. In this day's lesson, *S.T.E.P.S. to Drug Use Control*, follows earlier skills training sessions that covered understanding *S.T.E.P.S.* as a decision-making model, including: *Stop*, *Think* of options, *Evaluate* options as being helpful or hurtful, *Perform* or take action on the chosen option and then, *Self-praise* for using steps for making healthy choices.

As an example, here is how an RY leader used a series of bridging communications to incorporate Marc's and Trisha's issues during the skills training topic for the day.

- (The teacher begins.) *In the "Stop" step of our decision-making model, a good strategy is to use self-talk. What kind of self-talk do you all think would be helpful in Marc's situation?* (Group brainstorms, listing on the flipchart self-talk examples they've learned in previous sessions.) (Teacher reinforces.) *Okay, great work! Now let's make a poster of this positive self-talk and give it to Marc.*
- (Having motivated the group, the leader involves Marc by asking,) *Marc, which of these options would you like us to include for you? Ben, would you be the scribe for us?* (Here the leader is coaching the group to help Marc with his issue, while simultaneously reviewing the first step in the RY *S.T.E.P.S.* decision-making model.)
- (Next, the group leader continues the skills training by incorporating Trisha's issue.) *Since our theme this week is taking S.T.E.P.S. to drug-use control, Trisha, would you be willing to have us use your experience in practicing how we apply S.T.E.P.S. to drug use control?* (Trisha agrees.)
- (Teacher reinforces and then coaches.) *Great!* (Pause) *We need you to start by thinking about your decision to use. While you're doing that, each of us is going to think too--to identify a drug-use decision we've made in the last 2 weeks — a decision made to NOT use, or a decision made to use.* (The leader is weaving Trisha's experience into skills training and extending it to the entire group to work on one of the day's objectives — evaluating decisions made about drug use and drug non-use.)

In RY, students disclose their personal problems and related feelings about many issues, including drug use and non-use. Two key principles applied daily are that *problems are an opportunity for growth* and *we can grow and reach our goals with the help of our friends and family.* Many students already understand that their personal and school problems are linked with drug involvement and/or feelings of depression and hopelessness. The RY teacher helps the youth to assess their current school, drug use control, and mood management goals and monitor mini-steps taken toward RY program goal achievement — during *Check In/Check Back.* In this process, and particularly when discussing drug involvement, the RY teacher must stop "war stories," so drug use is never reinforced. At the same time, the teacher supports a leadership role for students who are not using drugs. S/he enlists their help in sharing the reasons for not using, and strategies for maintaining non-use. The leader provides praise and positive reinforcement for these drug non-use behaviors, as well as consistently counteracting any drug use "contagion effect" that may occur in the group. *The point*: drug non-use is rewarded during the group sessions as a healthy decision and worthy goal (Eggert *et al.*, 1995a).

The RY Class Goes Hand in Hand with the Other Program Components

In summary, it is important to bear in mind that the RY class component is only one of four important elements in this indicated prevention program (as discussed previously). Without establishing a bond between the student and school, without the school-based crisis response plan and the parent involvement component, RY is incomplete. As a "stand-alone program" it is unlikely to be sustained. The RY teacher and youth need a "supporting cast" to help reconnect the at-risk youth to school, home and community.

Empirical Studies Supporting the Reconnecting Youth Indicated Prevention Program

RY targets potential high school dropouts who are identified by using a verified sample selection model (Herting, 1990) based on school records and referrals sought from all personnel working in the participating high schools. Our studies show these youth differ significantly from "typical" high school students, evidencing greater drug involvement, emotional distress and likelihood of dropping out of high school. About 30–40 percent of these potential dropouts also evidence suicidal behaviors and higher levels of aggression and depression (Thompson *et al.*, 1994; Thompson *et al.*, 2000a). In short, drug involvement, aggression, depression, and suicidal behaviors are interrelated among this high-risk population of youth. Hence our prevention efforts address these problem behaviors simultaneously — by enhancing common protective factors and reducing risk factors theoretically linked to the outcome behaviors.

Our many studies with high-risk youth have followed a logical sequence of: *(1) conducting an ethnography of "Skippers"* (Eggert & Nicholas, 1992); *(2) assessing their drug involvement* (Eggert & Herting, 1993, Eggert, Herting & Thompson, 1996; Herting, Eggert & Thompson, 1996) *and suicide risk* (Eggert & Nicholas, 1992; Eggert *et al.*, 1994b, Powell-Cope & Eggert, 1994; Thompson *et al.*, 1994; Thompson & Eggert, 1999); *(3) developing and evaluating the original RY model* (Eggert *et al.*, 1990; Eggert & Herting, 1991; Eggert *et al.*, 1994c; Eggert *et al.*, 1995a; Eggert *et al.*, 1995b; Thompson, Horn, Herting & Eggert, 1997; Thompson, *et al.*, 2000b); and *(4) creating extensions of the RY model based on findings from our efficacy studies* (Eggert, 1994b; 1995, 1996a; Eggert, Thompson, Randell & Pike, 2001; Randell, 1999; Randell, Eggert & Pike, 2001).

In this section, we focus on the first two areas of study because they were integral to designing and testing the efficacy of our intervention approaches. Then, addressed in greater detail, are the results of the school-based prevention trials of Reconnecting Youth.

Characteristics of High-Risk Youth

We conducted a series of descriptive studies (both ethnographic and survey) using triangulation and multiple research methods to enhance our understanding of potential high school dropouts. Identifying *causal* risk factors and their linkage to school dropout were critical challenges in the beginning. Accurately identifying the youth at highest risk of school dropout and screening youth for potential risk of suicidal behaviors were other challenges faced.

In repeated studies, the vulnerabilities of high-risk youth that we profiled (Eggert & Herting, 1993; Eggert & Nicholas, 1992; Powell-Cope & Eggert, 1994; Thompson *et al.*, 1994; Thompson *et al.*, 2000a) pointed to significant differences between the high-risk youth and "typical" high school students. High-risk youth had more negative school experiences, greater drug involvement, more emotional distress (anger, depression, stress, suicidal behaviors), more deviant peer bonding, greater family strain, and less social support provided by school people and other special persons in their social networks. For many of these high-risk youth, negative school experiences were long-standing. Drug involvement, by the students' own admission, was out of control. In their own words they linked their drug involvement with poor school experiences, with depression, and with suicidal behaviors. Characteristic of more than two-thirds of the youth, negative peer influences, family distress, and social disorganization were prominent. The factors exerting the greatest negative influences on adolescent drug involvement included school strain, family strain and deviant peer bonding. Key predictors of suicide ideation included depression, drug involvement, family distress and the likelihood of dropout (Thompson *et al.*, 1994).

Studies of Relevant Measures for Testing the Efficacy of the RY Program

From 1985 to the present, members of the RY Prevention Research Team completed major instrumentation studies to establish valid, reliable and *brief* scales of all constructs (antecedent, intervention, mediators and outcomes) in our prevention model. These scales allow for: (1) reduced response burden for high-risk adolescents who typically have short attention spans, (2) suitability for structural equation modeling with multiple indicators; and (3) measurement of the "dosage" of intervention. Included in this process was the development of both the central instrument, the High School Study Questionnaire: Profile of Experiences (HSQ) and alternative HSQ forms, e.g., for telephone use (Eggert, Herting & Thompson, 1989; 1995). We included pre-tests with youth to gauge clarity, reading level, sensitivity to ethnic and gender differences, and developmental appropriateness.

Measuring drug involvement as a multidimensional construct. Also as part of our RY program research, we developed the Drug Involvement Scale for Adolescents (DISA) (Eggert, Herting & Thompson, 1996; Herting, Eggert & Thompson, 1996), a means of assessing alcohol, tobacco, and other drug (ATOD) use/behavior. According to reviewers, this was a major breakthrough in measuring the multidimensional construct of adolescent drug involvement. We posited and tested a five-dimensional structure of drug involvement: *access* (ease of obtaining different types of drugs); *frequency of alcohol use, frequency of other drug use, drug use control problems* (e.g., using more ATOD than intended); and *adverse drug use consequences* (e.g., feeling guilty, getting into fights, failing classes at school). These dimensions were important in distinguishing current drug users from "experimenters" (i.e., those in early stages of use) (Eggert & Herting, 1993). Compared to measures of drug use frequency, using the multidimensional DISA permitted us to explore how the RY prevention program worked. The strongest effects were in decreased illicit (or hard) drug use, decreased adverse drug use consequences and increased drug use control, suggesting a reversal or halting of the typical progression of drug abuse (Eggert & Kumpfer, 1997; Eggert *et al.*, 1994c). The DISA provides a more complete picture of change and helps us understand how an intervention curbs or reverses the progression of drug involvement among high-risk youth. Both total scale ($\alpha = 0.90$) and brief sub-scales ($\alpha = 0.73–0.85$) have high reliability and evidence predictive and construct validity (Eggert *et al.*, 1996; Herting *et al.*, 1996).

Measuring depression and suicide risk. Other instrumentation studies involved developing and testing the psychometric properties of the Suicide Risk Screen (SRS) (Eggert *et al.*, 1994a; Thompson & Eggert, 1999) and a computer-assisted Measure of Adolescent Potential for Suicide (MAPS), a comprehensive psychosocial assessment of risk and protective factors (Eggert *et al.*, 1994a). The SRS is a 15-item index embedded in the High School Questionnaire (Eggert, Herting & Thompson, 1989; 1995) serving to identify those youth at suicide risk, and also serving as a measure of change. It taps suicidal thoughts, direct and indirect suicide threats, and suicide attempts, depressed affect and drug involvement ($\alpha = 0.90$); it has demonstrated criterion and discriminate validity (Thompson & Eggert, 1999). Similarly, studies of the MAPS revealed high reliability coefficients for all scales of suicide risk factors, related risk factors and protective factors (Eggert *et al.*, 1994a). Criterion and construct validity were established, as were high reliability coefficients for all MAPS scales. We also developed a short version of the MAPS interview, called the Screen for Youth Suicide Risk (SYSR), that can be used by school personnel to initially interview RY youth to assess their suicide-risk status.

Efficacy of the Reconnecting Youth (RY) Model

We turn now to a discussion of the studies conducted to demonstrate the efficacy of the RY intervention program. Included are also studies of the mechanisms whereby RY was theoretically hypothesized to achieve its effects of reducing drug involvement, suicide risk, and poor school performance. See Table 2 at the end of this section for a summary of each study — design, sample, program features, analysis and outcomes.

Our early studies revealed that RY was effective for increasing school achievement (attendance, GPA, credits earned/semester) and decreasing school dropout. RY also worked to decrease drug use control problems and adverse drug use consequences (See Study 1, Table 2). Early studies also revealed the importance of the RY leader's support and caring to increase peer support within the RY group and to decrease drug involvement among the high-risk youth participants (see Study 2, Table 2). These two early studies of the RY class led to fuller tests with improved study designs, funded by the National Institutes of Health (Eggert, 1989; 1991).

RY effects on school deviance, drug involvement and deviant peer bonding. A NIDA-funded prevention trial further supported and extended the efficacy of RY. Trend analyses of pre-test to program exit (at five months) to follow-up (at ten months) showed significantly different patterns of change between the RY participants versus controls (Eggert *et al.*, 1994c). Youth in RY had increasing trends in grades (GPA) across all their classes, and in school bonding, a mediator thought to be central to helping youth change. Importantly, participation in RY was associated with decreased drug use control problems and consequences, decreased hard drug use, and a tendency toward decreased drug use progression.

Fostering positive peer bonding in RY also led to significant trend differences in deviant peer bonding. RY youth showed declines in deviant peer bonding, while the controls experienced increases. This latter finding was qualified as the effects held for RY females, but not males. When a structural equation modeling approach was used, "chain model" results revealed that for youth in RY, decreased drug involvement occurred across three time points (baseline, to five-month, to ten-month follow-up). No comparable changes occurred for the controls, $\beta_E=$ -0.267 vs. $\beta_C = -0.049$ (Herting & Eggert, 1992). (See Study 3, Table 2 for further evidence.)

These positive outcomes differ from research reported by Dishion and his colleagues (Dishion, French & Patterson, 1995). They suggest from their findings that grouping high-risk youth may lead to increased drug use. However, building a positive peer culture with group norms that promote program goal achievement of decreased drug involvement is an essential feature of the RY program. Our findings suggest the important benefits of a positive peer group component that is carefully fostered by a well-trained and competent RY group leader. Noteworthy is that Dishion and his colleagues' study was with a sample of middle school-aged boys; the program and training of leaders also differed from that of RY.

Increased efficacy with RY model refinements/enhancements. Careful process evaluation of RY implementation indicated that RY program changes would be necessary to address the underestimated prevalence of depression and suicide risk among both experimental and control groups of high-risk youth. NIMH funding (Eggert, 1991) supported a third prevention trial; this included refinements to the one-semester RY curriculum (RY-I) and the addition of a second semester intervention (RY-II).

Tests of the refined RY-I program (Thompson, Horn, Herting & Eggert, 1997) demonstrated that intervention outcomes were influenced by enhancing RY-I to include depression and anger management (Eggert, 1994a), and increased monitoring of drug use. Comparisons using regression analyses of data from youth in early cohorts (before RY-I refinements) versus later cohorts (after RY-I changes) revealed that the later cohorts showed greater decreases in hard drug use, in levels of depression and perceived stress, and greater increases in levels of self-esteem and anger control (see Study 4, Table 2).

Effects of RY I and II on suicide risk. Study 5 included potential school dropouts who also screened in at suicide risk. We used a three-group, repeated-measures design to compare the efficacy of: (1) the suicide risk assessment protocol plus RY-I; (2) the assessment protocol plus RY-I & II; and (3) the suicide-risk assessment only. All three groups showed significant decreases in suicidal behaviors, depression, anger, hopelessness, and stress as well as increases in self-esteem and social support. Increased personal control was observed only in the RY-I and RY-I & II groups (see Study 5, Table 2 for more specifics).

This study extended the efficacy of the RY program for reducing suicide-risk behaviors and depression, besides reducing drug involvement and increasing school performance. Increases in person control, a key posited mediator, suggest the desired effects of RY life-skills training. The results also support arguments for the extended RY-II program. Providing RY-II to students who were more depressed and hopeless at baseline resulted in enhanced outcomes for these youth. Net of RY-I, RY-II provided added benefits for these youth in four areas: greater school achievement; less likelihood of dropping out of school; and greater decreases in hard drug use and depression. These are important because they show that success in a second semester of RY may reverse the progression to more severe problems and/or prevent relapse. Surprisingly, the results also suggested the potential therapeutic value of targeted, brief assessment and crisis intervention strategies like the MAPS (Eggert *et al.*, 1995a).

Mediating effects of the RY program elements on reducing depression and suicide-risk behaviors. Given the above study results, a follow-up study with the same sample was undertaken. The purpose was to explore the intervention processes of the RY indicated prevention program for youth at suicide risk (Thompson *et al.*, 2000b) We hypothesized that RY program outcomes (reduced depression, suicide risk) were influenced by the direct effects of the RY teacher social support and the mediated effects of teacher support through enhanced peer group support and perceived personal control. A three-wave, longitudinal design was used with the data from pre-intervention, 5-month and 10-month follow-up assessments. Structural equation modeling was used to test the hypotheses for the three study groups: (1) suicide risk assessment protocol plus RY-I; (2) assessment protocol plus RY-I & II; and (3) the suicide-risk assessment only group. As hypothesized, the RY teacher support directly enhanced peer group support with stronger effects evident in both RY intervention groups versus the assessment-only control group. The general hypothesis that depression and suicide-risk behaviors are ameliorated through enhanced personal control received partial support. The RY teacher plays a central role in fostering peer support; in turn, this peer support directly — and indirectly through personal control — influenced reductions in depression and suicidal behaviors (see Study 6, Table 2).

In this section we reviewed select studies completed by the RY prevention research team, highlighting some studies and providing greater detail on those demonstrating the efficacy of RY. In addition, we explored the hypothesized pathways by which RY worked to achieve program outcomes. Next we detail work in progress and address recommendations for future directions.

Recommendations For Future Directions

Shown in the previous section were the cumulative research efforts of the multidisciplinary group of RY investigators. These various descriptive and etiologic studies demonstrate an understanding of the critical risk and protective factors influencing potential high school dropouts. We developed effective sampling and recruiting methods for reaching high-risk youth and retaining them in the RY program in many high schools, and established the reliability and validity of our sample selection model and screening methods for identifying youth at high risk of school dropout, drug use/abuse and suicide risk. We also were able to develop and comprehensively demonstrate the efficacy of the original RY indicated prevention model and its refinements.

Despite these advances, RY is one of very few indicated prevention programs that has been rigorously evaluated. Hence, important future research directions we recommend include: (1) replication studies of RY; (2) testing adaptations and briefer versions of RY; and (3) testing more comprehensive versions of RY including broader school-based and parent intervention approaches. Each of these warrants brief discussion with illustration of testable hypotheses.

Table 2: Summary of *Reconnecting Youth* (RY) efficacy studies for preventing drug abuse, school dropout and suicide risk

Study #, Authors, Study Purpose	Sample/ Targeted Participants	Program Features and Elements	Research Design/ Analysis	Intervention & Mediating Variables	Dependent/ Outcome Measures	Findings/Comments
1. Eggert, Seyl, & Nicholas (1990), *Int. J. of the Addictions 25*, 772–801. Purpose: To test the effects of the initial RY prevention program in deterring school dropout and drug abuse among potential high school dropouts.	264 high-risk youth (E = 124, C = 140); grades 10–12; *M* age = 16.7 yr. Potential school dropouts — identified using school record data and potential drug users identified using referrals from school drug intervention staff.	• 1-semester, 90 days — of an elective daily high school class • Teacher-to-student ratio of 1:10–12 • Content — goal setting/decision making, self-management training, peer tutoring & study skills, resistance skills training • Teacher-facilitated peer-group social support/social influence model	Quasi-experimental design; conducted in one high school using 2 conditions: A. Pretest/post-test, with matched comparison (C) group using trend analyses (2-factor mixed ANOVA) for assessing changes in school performance; B. Pretest/post-test in E group only using paired *t*-tests for assessing changes in drug involvement	A. Expressive and instrumental support from: • Group leader • Program peers. B. Program peer group belonging	A. School performance (official records): • GPA • # credits earned • Truancy (days absent in all classes/ semester B. Drug involvement (self-report): • Drug use control • Drug use consequences	All hypotheses were supported: • Significantly more program youth stayed in school (E vs. C, 74% vs. 61%) • Significant trend differences in daily absences with absenteeism decreasing for E group and increasing for C youth ($F = 25.23$, $p < .0001$) • Significant trend differences in GPA ($F = 21.83$, $p < .0001$) and credits earned/semester ($F = 21.35$, $p < .0001$), with increases for E youth and decreases for C youth • Significant pre/post-test decreases in drug use control problems ($t = 4.27$, $p < .0001$) and consequences ($t = 3.96$, $p < .0001$). Conclusion: Initial program efficacy was demonstrated. Positive results occurred for students in the program but findings did not demonstrate the mechanism by which these results were obtained, leading to Study #2.

Table 2: Continued

Study #, Authors, Study Purpose	Sample/ Targeted Participants	Program Features and Elements	Research Design/ Analysis	Intervention & Mediating Variables	Dependent/ Outcome Measures	Findings/Comments
2. Eggert, & Herting (1991), *Youth & Society 22*, 482–524. *Purpose:* To focus on the process of preventing drug abuse among potential high school dropouts — testing the effects of RY teacher support and peer-group support on drug use control problems and adverse use consequences.	124 E youth who successfully completed the experimental program in #1 above	Same as in #1 above	Pre/post longitudinal design. Structural equation modeling used to analyze the intervention effects from the above quasi-experiment in Study #1.	A. Exogenous factors: • Prior drug use • Prior adverse consequences • Prior school deviance • Family disruption B. Intervention factors: • Teacher support • Peer support	A. Endogenous factors: • Drug use control problems • Adverse drug use consequences	Findings explained 27% of the variance in post-drug control problems and 60% in post drug use consequences. Significant pathways were: • Post-program drug use control problems influenced adverse use consequences ($\beta = 0.44$) • Teacher support influenced decreased drug control problems ($\beta = -0.22$), thereby indirectly affecting post-consequences • Teacher support influenced peer group support ($\beta = 0.34$) showing the intervention altered perceived levels of support from peers; peer support did not influence drug use outcomes • Prior drug use influenced post-drug use ($\beta = 0.51$); prior drug use consequences influenced more program peer support ($\beta = 0.37$) and post-program drug use consequences ($\beta = 0.71$) • Being from a "single mother" home reduced perceived support ($\beta = -0.23$) in the program, and decreased drug use problems ($\beta = -0.23$). Conclusion: Teacher support was a mechanism by which the program worked to reduce drug use control problems and consequences.

Table 2: Continued

Study #, Authors, Study Purpose	Sample/ Targeted Participants	Program Features and Elements	Research Design/ Analysis	Intervention & Mediating Variables	Dependent/ Outcome Measures	Findings/Comments
3. Eggert, Thompson, Herting, Nicholas, & Dicker (1994), *Amer. J. Health Promotion* 8, 202–215; Eggert, & Kumpfer, (1997). *Purpose:* To test the hypothesis that experimental subjects, relative to controls would demonstrate significant increases in school performance and decreases in drug involvement at program exit and 10-month follow-up.	259 students, (E = 101, C = 158); grades 9–12 in 4 schools; 509 typical student comparison group. *M* age, 16 yr. School record data used to create the high-risk pool of potential dropouts. Youth then randomly drawn from the pool and invited to participate.	Experimental intervention was • 1-semester (5-month) RY elective course taken for credit • Teacher-to-student ratio of 1:12 • Integrated social support/life skills training model • Skills training in self-esteem enhancement, decision-making, personal control, interpersonal communication Control condition included a regular school schedule.	A 2-group, repeated-measures design; youth randomized to condition in 4 urban schools. Trend analysis used to assess the predicted shape and direction of change between the experimental (E) and control (C) youth. Pre-test, 5-month post-test and 10-month follow-up assessments used.	A. Intervention variables: • Teacher and peer-group expressive and instrumental support • Exposure to life skills training B. Posited mediators: • Self-esteem • School bonding • Deviant peer bonding	A. School performance (official records): • GPA • Absences in all classes B. Drug involvement Scale (*DISA*): • Drug use control problems & adverse use consequences • Drug use frequency • Drug use progression	As predicted, trend analyses revealed significantly different patterns of change over time between E vs. C groups: • In decreased drug control problems and consequences ($F=4.85$, $p<.03$) • In decreased hard drug use ($F=19.82$, $p<.001$) • In decreased drug use progression ($F=3.41$, $p<.066$) • In increased GPA ($F=5.14$, $p<.02$) but not attendance. Trend analyses also revealed significantly different patterns of change in: • Increased self-esteem ($F=7.89$, $p<.005$) • Increased school bonding ($F=5.79$, $p<.02$) • Decreased deviant peer bonding ($F=6.32$, $p<.01$) Conclusion: Further support for program efficacy shown for decreasing drug involvement and increasing grade point average. Expected changes in posited mediators occurred — i.e., increased self-esteem, school bonding and decreased deviant peer bonding.

Table 2: Continued

Study #, Authors, Study Purpose	Sample/ Targeted Participants	Program Features and Elements	Research Design/ Analysis	Intervention & Mediating Variables	Dependent/ Outcome Measures	Findings/Comments
4. Thompson, Horn, Herting, & Eggert (1997). *J. Drug Ed.*, 27 19–41. *Purpose:* To examine the net effects of refining the RY model, testing if the program changes promoted greater improvements in indicators of emotional distress, drug involvement and school performance among youth exposed to the finalized vs. earlier RY model.	280 high-risk youth — grades 9–12 in 4 schools; from early (n = 140) and late cohorts (n = 140) from Study #3 above; all available youth having pre- and post-intervention data were included here.	Same as in #3 above with program refinements for "later" cohorts including: • Enhanced personal control skills training adding depression & anger management, and • Greater drug use monitoring • Synthesis of skills training units and augmented application of skills to program goals.	Program participants in Study #3 were divided into early vs. later cohorts (pre and post curriculum enhancements). Using multiple regression analysis, later program participation served as the key predictor and specified program outcomes and mediators served as the criterion variables. Pre-intervention and 5-month post-intervention data only.	A. Program refinement B. Personal resources: • Self-esteem • Stress • Personal control	A. School performance (school records): • GPA • Absences B. Drug involvement scale (*DISA*): • Drug use frequency • Drug use control problems • Adverse use consequences C. Emotional distress: • Depression • Anger/ aggressive tendencies	Late cohort predicted significant improvements: • Reduced hard drug use ($F=4.28, p <.05$) • Reduced depression ($F=17.84, p <.0001$) • Reduced anger control problems ($F=19.50, p <.0001$) • Reduced stress ($F=16.05, p <.0001$) • Enhanced self-esteem ($F=23.15, p <.0001$) • Gender effects were observed for depression and stress — being female predicted more depression and stress at post-test controlling for baseline equivalencies. Conclusion: Outcomes for the later cohorts demonstrated greater efficacy of the refined RY indicated prevention program, supporting the curriculum enhancements. Refinements did not further enhance earlier findings of increased school performance and reduced drug involvement (with the exception of enhancing reduced hard drug use).

Table 2: Continued

Study #, Authors, Study Purpose	Sample/ Targeted Participants	Program Features and Elements	Research Design/ Analysis	Intervention & Mediating Variables	Dependent/ Outcome Measures	Findings/Comments
5. Eggert, Thompson, Herting, & Nicholas (1995), *Suicide & Life-Threatening Behavior 25,* 276–296. *Purpose:* To test the efficacy of the experimental RY program for reducing suicide potential (i.e., decreased suicide-risk behaviors, depression, hopelessness, stress and anger; and increased personal control, self-esteem and network support) among high-risk youth.	105 youth from the late cohorts in Study #4 — in grades 9–12 from 4 high schools; 509 typical student comparison group. *M* age, 16 yr. The 105 youth were potential dropouts who also screened in at suicide-risk on base-line survey. They were then assessed with the *Measure of Adolescent Suicide Potential* [MAPS], a comprehensive computer-assisted interview.	Experimental conditions were 1. The MAPS suicide assessment protocol + a 1-semester (5-month) RY-I elective course taken for credit — with refinements tested in #4 above. 2. The MAPS suicide assessment protocol + 2-semester (10-month) RY-I & II electives taken for credit. RY-II included relapse prevention and enhanced social/ school bonding activities. 3. Control condition included the MAPS assessment protocol plus the regular school schedule.	A 3-group, repeated-measures, indicated prevention trial with youth at suicide risk — (an experiment within Study #3 experiment). Study Groups: 1) MAPS + RY-I (n = 36) 2) MAPS+ RY I & II (n = 34) 3) MAPS only control (n = 35) Trend analysis was used to assess the predicted shape and direction of change between the 3 groups; Pre-intervention, 5-month post-intervention and 10-month follow-up assessments were used.	Intervention variables: • Teacher and peer-group expressive and instrumental support • Exposure to life skills training Posited mediators: • Self-esteem • Personal control • Social network support — measured by the *High School Questionnaire: Profile of Experiences*	Suicide risk behaviors — suicide ideation, direct and indirect suicide threats, and suicide attempts Related risk factors: • Depression • Hopelessness • Stress • Anger all measured by the *High School Questionnaire: Profile of Experiences*	Significant findings in major outcomes are detailed below; gender was not a factor unless mentioned. • Suicide risk behaviors declined for all 3 study groups ($F = 104.14$, $p < .001$). Over 85% of youth in Groups 1 & 3 (in 65% in Group 2) showed decreased suicide risk behaviors by ≥25%. • Depression declined for all 3 groups ($F=88.93$, $p <.001$). Over 65% of all youth showed a decline of ≥ 25% with Groups 1 & 3 having the greatest declines. • Hopelessness also declined for all 3 groups ($F=55.81$, $p <.001$) with a gender interaction effect — Group 1 females had the most dramatic declines. Over 60% of all youth reported declines. • Stress declined similarly in all 3 groups ($F=27.70$, $p <.001$) but with only 45% of the youth showing declines of ≥ 25%. • Anger declined differently among the 3 groups ($F=4.13$, $p <.02$) with Groups 1 & 3 declines being the greatest. Over 65% in Groups 1 & 3 vs. 44% in Group 2 showed ≥ 25% reductions.

Table 2: Continued

Study #, Authors, Study Purpose	Sample/ Targeted Participants	Program Features and Elements	Research Design/ Analysis	Intervention & Mediating Variables	Dependent/ Outcome Measures	Findings/Comments
Study #5, continued						Significant findings in posited mediating factors were as follows: • Personal control increased for both RY Groups 1 & 2 but not Group 3 (F=3.76, p <.03). Over 44% of youth in Groups 1 & 2 improved vs. 20% in Group 3. • Self-esteem increased for youth in all 3 groups (F=60.17, p <.001), but Group 2 youth had lower self-esteem at baseline. • Social support changes increased significantly for youth in all 3 groups (F=32.08, p <.001), with "favorite teacher" and "parents" accounting for the increases. Conclusion: This study extends the efficacy of RY in reducing suicide-risk among potential dropouts. Increases in personal control, a key posited mediator, suggested the desired effects of RY life-skills training. The results also suggested the potential therapeutic value of targeted, brief assessments like the MAPS.

Table 2: Continued

Study #, Authors, Study Purpose	Sample/ Targeted Participants	Program Features and Elements	Research Design/ Analysis	Intervention & Mediating Variables	Dependent/ Outcome Measures	Findings/Comments
6. Thomspon, Eggert, & Herting (2000), *Suicide & Life-Threatening Behavior*, 30, 252–271 *Purpose:* To explore the intervention processes of RY: i.e., testing the hypothesis that RY program outcomes (reduced depression, suicide risk) were influenced by the direct effects of RY teacher support and the mediated effects of teacher support through enhanced peer group support and personal control.	Same as in Study #5 above — i.e., potential dropouts also at risk for suicidal behaviors. In grades 9–12 from 4 high schools; 89% were 15–17 yr. of age.	Same program elements delivered as in Study #5 above. By design for clinical reasons, all youth received the MAPS suicide risk assessment and were in one of 3 study groups: 1. RY-I — the 1-semester (5-month) class (n=36) 2. RY I & II — the 2-semester (10-month) classes (n=35) 3. Assessment only controls (n=35)	Structural equation modeling (SEM) was used to assess the posited intervention processes — i.e., that program effects were influenced by the direct and mediating effects of teacher social support on peer group support and on perceived personal control, thereby influencing reductions in the outcomes. A 3-wave, longitudinal design was used with data from pre-intervention, 5-month, and 10-month follow-up assessments.	Intervention variables: • Teacher and peer-group expressive and instrumental support • Exposure to life skills training Posited mediator: • Personal control measured by the *High School Questionnaire: Profile of Experiences*	Suicide risk behaviors — suicide ideation, direct & indirect suicide threats, and suicide attempts Depression (adapted from the CES-D)	As was hypothesized: • Teacher support directly enhanced peer support more strongly in the RY-I (β=.52, p < .001) and RY-II (β=.72, p < .001) groups vs. in the control group (β=.40, p < .05). • Peer support directly enhanced personal control in RY-I (β=.43, p < .05), but not RY-II. This also indicated the indirect effect of teacher support on enhancing personal control (in RY-I only) and, as predicted, not in Group 3. • Personal control had direct ameliorating effects on suicide-risk behaviors for both RY-I (β=−0.30, p < .01) and RY-I&II (β=−0.23, p <.10); and on depression in both RY-I (β=−0.29, p < .05) and RY-I & II (β=−0.49, p < .05). In Group 3, personal control ameliorated suicide-risk behaviors (β=−0.40, p < .05) but not depression. Conclusion: Results further support the RY theory-based intervention processes, especially for the central RY teachers' role in fostering the positive peer group culture and support to enhance personal control. This enhanced personal control and peer support served to decrease depression and suicidal behaviors among the high-risk youth.

RY Replication Studies

In the previous section, we reviewed the findings from several separate studies of RY that, taken together, provide evidence of its efficacy for decreasing drug involvement, suicidal behaviors, depression, school dropout, as well as increasing the posited mediators of personal control, school bonding, and deviant peer bonding. These efficacy trials, however, were limited to a single urban school district. Thus, replication studies are needed to assess the broad effectiveness of RY. In short, testing RY across multiple settings and geographic locations, with other high-risk youth, and ethnically diverse populations is needed. To this end, we are currently testing RY across multiple sites and in multiculturally diverse schools. Hopefully others will join in this work, thereby testing the boundary conditions of RY. Similarly, long-term follow-up studies of youth who participated in RY are needed to assess if the short-term positive effects of RY are sustained into young adulthood. For replication studies it is vital that RY be implemented as designed to assure that the youth participants receive the appropriate dose and all intervention elements. Key to the success of implementation fidelity is selection of the appropriate teachers for implementing RY, as well as the standardized training and supervision. Given their importance in replication studies, these factors are discussed briefly below before making additional recommendations for future studies.

Selection criteria for RY teachers in replication studies. RY teacher selection criteria include: (1) a strong desire to work with high-risk youth and assume the roles and responsibilities for the position; (2) a genuine liking and respect for high-risk youth and their families; (3) competence in the helping relationship process and enthusiasm for advanced learning in this arena; (4) eagerness to cooperate with training and implementation fidelity of RY; and (5) willingness to cooperate fully with RY process and outcome evaluation.

We discovered a simple but important strategy for identifying ideal RY teacher candidates. We ask the school principals, the faculty and staff to nominate those teachers within the school who work well with high-risk youth, genuinely liking and respecting them. Next we ask the high-risk students who their favorite teachers are. Those teachers who are nominated by the administration, staff, their colleagues and high-risk youth are good candidates. With training and support, these candidates have the potential for becoming successful RY teachers.

Initial RY teacher training and continued training/support. RY teachers rarely are able to implement the program without quality initial training from the developers and ongoing support and supervision from a qualified RY Coordinator. Initial RY teacher training includes a five-day standardized training that covers: (1) an introduction to the overall intervention protocol and theoretic framework for RY; (2) dimensions of the group leader's role as skills trainer and support network designer; (3) content of the RY skills training units, (4) use of group strategies/role plays for assessing life skills; (5) drug abuse prevention principles/strategies; and (6) helper limitations, referrals, and self-care. Weekly ongoing training/support through individual supervision and bi-weekly group consultation is necessary to monitor adherence to protocols, provide feedback using videotape reviews and direct observation, and prevent "burnout." Importantly, RY teachers typically require training in how to recognize warning signs of substance abuse and suicide risk, and how to refer as per school district protocols.

In sum, replication studies are necessary to further test the boundary conditions of the RY program. These studies, to be meaningful, need to implement RY as designed, paying careful attention to appropriate RY teacher training and student selection criteria. In addition, however, we recommend studies of briefer versions of RY, detailed next.

Selective and Indicated Studies with Briefer Versions of RY

Somewhat unexpectedly and during the course of our efficacy trials with one- and two-semester versions of RY, we discovered that our brief, individually focused crisis assessment and intervention protocols appeared to be effective for reducing suicidal behaviors and concomitant indicators of emotional distress, such as depression and hopelessness. These findings served as a basis for two ongoing funded studies (from NINR) to evaluate the efficacy of brief interventions derived from the *Reconnecting Youth* model. Essentially, it appears that varying levels of intensity and dosage are needed for the different outcomes — i.e., suicide-risk behaviors versus drug involvement and school deviance. Thus we recommend that the various components of the RY prevention model be investigated to determine the "dosage" requirements, delivery modalities and elements necessary and sufficient to influence the various co-occurring problem behaviors. What works for whom, for which problem behaviors, and in what dose, are all critical questions to be addressed. We are currently in the process of investigating the effects of two brief adaptations of the RY model with potential dropouts who are also at suicide risk: Project CAST (Coping and Support Training) and Counselors-CARE (Eggert, 1995). We hypothesize that these briefer interventions will be more efficacious for reducing emotional distress and suicide risk than for reducing drug involvement. If these brief interventions work, they would be less costly than the longer RY class component. This would have significant benefits for youth by discovering crisis interventions that effectively stem the tide of youth suicidal behaviors.

The above suggests a need to "fit" interventions to youth needs. That is, if a youth is identified as being at suicide risk, a brief indicated prevention program may be sufficient. However, if the youth screens in at suicide risk and is also drug involved, he or she may need a more comprehensive indicated prevention program, such as that described next.

Comprehensive Indicated Prevention Efficacy Trials with an Extended RY Model

Our third set of recommendations for future directions involves testing extensions of the RY model. Extensions could include development of supplemental components, such as a parent or mentor component. Other possibilities could be a summer back-to-school transitions component, a middle-to-high school transition component, tutoring to enhance school study skills, or a school volunteer program or project. One example in progress is the Parents And Youth with Schools (PAYS) program that advances a combined parent and school-based social network support/skills training model. With funding from NIDA (Eggert, 1996a) to test this model, potential high school dropouts will receive a full school year of the program, RY-I and II, and parents will participate in Parents as Partners, a home and school-based program designed to enhance the delivery of support to their RY son/daughter, facilitate reinforcement of the overall RY program goals, and increase parenting effectiveness. The rationale for these extensions is that several factors continued to exert negative influences on the adolescents' drug involvement in our prior studies, counteracting the positive effects to the RY school-based program. Chief among these are family factors, including serious family distress and lack of family support, and school strain such as lack of support in the students' other classes (Eggert *et al.*, 1994b; Eggert, 1998).

We expect that each intervention component, the youth component (Reconnecting Youth) and the parent component (Parents As Partners), will independently influence the outcomes, but that the combined effect of PAYS (Parents And Youth with Schools) will be superior to either Reconnecting Youth or Parents As Partners alone. If these hypotheses are borne out, the indicated PAYS prevention model could also bring us a step closer to matching the needs of various high-risk youth with appropriate intervention approaches. By testing the interventions with potential dropouts, and investigating the efficacy of the program on their cluster of problem behaviors simultaneously, we will advance understanding of the value, program feasibility, and acceptability of such comprehensive interventions, especially for preventing drug abuse. Another value of this research approach is that we can begin to assess the separate benefits of each intervention component. This will be especially useful and informative given the difficulty associated with incorporating parents in an intervention program. Also, by exploring the efficacy of PAYS across gender and ethnic groups, we should be able to establish its generalizability.

Summary and Conclusions

The overall purpose of this chapter was to review the Reconnecting Youth indicated prevention program. In the first section of the chapter, we described the integrated theoretic framework for the RY prevention model. We argued that RY, if implemented as designed, should work to bring about decreases in the high-risk youth's drug involvement, school deviance, emotional distress, and/or suicidal behaviors. The logic was that the focused school, peer-support and individual intervention strategies are designed to enhance both personal and social support protective processes known to counteract drug involvement and other problem behaviors. We also detailed key features of the RY program; we developed and provided specifics for how it is implemented in schools. It was shown how ethnographic studies of "Skippers" informed the overall RY structure, activities and implementation processes. In the section that followed, empirical evidence supporting the efficacy of the RY program was highlighted, illustrating what makes RY a model indicated prevention approach. We concluded the chapter with suggested future research directions, indicating the need for replication efficacy and effectiveness trials of RY, tests of briefer versions, and extensions to create a more comprehensive RY program. Research following these directions promises improved matching of adolescent needs with appropriate preventive interventions, and enhanced and sustained outcomes for high-risk youth.

The problems and needs of high-risk youth in our nation's high schools demand the design and rigorous testing of *indicated* prevention approaches. There is substantial evidence demonstrating that these youth are at greater risk for drug involvement and co-occurring problems such as aggression, depression and suicidal behaviors. Reconnecting Youth represents one evidence-based approach. It can be integrated into high schools as not only a means of curbing the trajectory toward increased drug involvement, but also for reducing high school dropout and suicide risk behaviors (Eggert, 1998). Our hope is that the framework and examples presented in this chapter will stimulate others to join in extending this work or in testing other models of indicated prevention. High-risk youth and their families merit our very best efforts in both prevention research and health promotion.

References

Bandura, A. (1977), "Self-efficacy: Toward a unifying theory of behavioral change." *Psychology Review, 84,* 191–215.

Blaney, P. H., & Ganellen, R. J. (1991), "Hardiness and social support." In B. R. Sarason, I. G. Sarason & G. R. Pierce (eds), *Social support: An interactional view*, NY: Wiley & Sons, 297–318.

Botvin, G. J., & Tortu, S. (1988), "Peer relationships, social competence and substance abuse prevention: Implications for the family." *Journal of Chemical Dependency Treatment, 1,* 145–173.

Botvin, G. J., & Dusenbury, L. (1989), "Substance abuse prevention and the promotion of competence." In L. A. Bond & B. E. Compas (eds), *Primary prevention & promotion in the schools.* Newbury Park, CA: Sage, 146–178.

Brendtro, L. K., Brokenleg, M., & Van Bockern, S. (1990), *Reclaiming Youth at Risk.* Bloomington, IN: National Educational Service.

Catalano, R. F., Hawkins, J. D., Wells, E. A., Miller, J., & Brewer, D. (1991), "Evaluation of the effectiveness of adolescent drug abuse treatment, assessment of risks for relapse & promising approaches for relapse prevention." *International Journal of the Addictions, 25,* 1085–1140.

Cauce, A. M., & Srebnik D. S. (1989), "Peer networks and social support." In L. A. Bond & B. E. Compas (eds), *Primary Prevention & Promotion in the Schools.* Newbury Park: Sage, 235–254.

Cohen, S., & Syme, S. L. (eds) (1985), *Social Support & Health.* NY: Academic Press.

Cutrona, C. E., & Russell, D.W. (1991), "Type of social support and specific stress: Toward a theory of optimal matching." In B. R. Sarason, I.G. Sarason & G. R. Pierce (eds), *Social Support: An interactional view.* NY: Wily & Sons, 319–366.

Dishion, T. J., French, D. C., & Patterson, G. R. (1995), "The development and ecology of antisocial behavior." In D. Cicchetti & D. Cohen (eds), *Manual of Developmental Psychopathology.* New York: Wiley, 421–471.

Dorn, F. J. (1984), "The social influence model: A social psychological approach to counseling." *Personnel and Guidance Journal, 62*(6), 342–345.

Dunkel-Schetter, C., & Bennett, T. L. (1991), "Differentiating the cognitive and behavioral aspects of social support." In B. R. Sarason, I. G. Sarason & G. R. Pierce (eds), *Social Support.* NY: Wiley, 267–296.

Eggert, L. L. (1987), "Social support in family ties: Stress, coping, and adaptation." In T. L. Albrecht, M. B. Adelman & Associates, *Communicating Social Support: Process in context.* Beverly Hills: Sage, 80–104.

Eggert, L. L. (1989), *Reconnecting At-risk Youth: drug users and dropouts.* National Institute on Drug Abuse. Grant R01-DA04530 (with J. R. Herting & L. J. Nicholas).

Eggert, L. L. (1991), *Preventing Suicide Lethality Among Vulnerable Youth*. National Institute of Mental Health. Grant R18-MH48139 (with E. A. Thompson, J. R. Herting & L. J. Nicholas).

Eggert, L. L. (1994a), *Anger Management for Youth: Stemming aggression and violence*. Bloomington, IN: National Educational Service.

Eggert, L. L. (1994b), *A Measure of Adolescent Potential for Suicide*. National Institute of Nursing Research, Grant R01-NR03550 (with E. A. Thompson).

Eggert, L. L. (1995), *Promoting Competence and Support to Prevent Suicide Risk*. National Institute of Nursing Research, Grant R01-NR-MH03548 (with E. A. Thompson).

Eggert, L. L. (1996a), *Preventing Drug Abuse: parents and youth with schools*. National Institute on Drug Abuse, Grant R01-DA10317 (with J. R. Herting, B. P. Randell).

Eggert, L. L. (1996b), "Psychosocial approaches in prevention science: Facing the challenge with high-risk youth." *Communicating Nursing Research, 29*, 73–85.

Eggert, L. L. (1998), "Reconnecting youth: An indicated prevention program." In *National conference on Drug Abuse Prevention Research: Presentations, Papers, and Recommendations*. NIH Publication #98–4293. Rockville, MD: DHHS, National Institutes of Health, National Institute on Drug Abuse.

Eggert, L. L., & Herting, J. R. (1991), "Preventing teenage drug abuse: Exploratory effects of network social support." *Youth and Society, 22,* 482–534. [Reprinted, National Prevention Evaluation Research Collection, Rockville, MD: Aspen, 1993].

Eggert, L. L., & Herting, J. R. (1993), "Drug exposure among potential dropouts and typical youth." *Journal of Drug Education, 23*, 31–55.

Eggert, L. L., Herting, J. R., & Thompson, E. A. (1989; 1995), *High School Questionnaire: Profile of Experiences*. University of Washington School of Nursing, Psychosocial and Community Health.

Eggert, L. L., Herting, J. R., & Thompson, E. A. (1996), "The drug involvement scale for adolescents (DISA)." *Journal of Drug Education, 26*, 101–130.

Eggert, L. L., & Kumpfer, K. L. (1997), *Drug Abuse Prevention for At-risk Individuals*. NIH Publication #97–4115. Rockville, MD: DHHS, National Institutes of Health, National Institute on Drug Abuse, Office of Science Policy and Communications.

Eggert, L. L., & Nicholas, L. J. (1992), "Speaking like a skipper: 'Skippin' an' gettin' high." *Journal of Language & Social Psychology, 11*, 75–100.

Eggert, L. L., Nicholas, L. J., & Owen, L. (1995a), *Reconnecting Youth: A peer group approach to building life skills*. Bloomington, IN: National Educational Service.

Eggert, L. L., & Parks, M. R. (1987), "Communication network involvement in adolescents' friendships and romantic relationships." *Communication Yearbook, 10*, 283–322.

Eggert, L. L., Seyl, C., & Nicholas, L. J. (1990), "Effects of a school-based prevention program for potential high school dropouts and drug abusers." *International Journal of the Addictions, 25*, 772–801.

Eggert, L. L., Thompson, E. A., & Herting, J. R. (1994a), "Measure of adolescent potential for suicide (MAPS): Development and preliminary findings." *Suicide & Life-Threatening Behavior, 24*, 359–381.

Eggert, L. L., Thompson, E. A., Herting, J. R., & Nicholas, L.J. (1994b), "A prevention research program: Reconnecting at-risk youth." *Issues in Mental Health Nursing, 15*, 107–135.

Eggert, L. L., Thompson, E. A., Herting, J. R., & Nicholas, L. J. (1995b), "Reducing suicide potential among high-risk youth: Tests of a school-based prevention program." *Suicide & Life-Threatening Behavior, 25*, 276–296.

Eggert, L. L., Thompson, E. A., Herting, J. R., Nicholas, L. J., & Dicker, B. G. (1994c), "Preventing adolescent drug abuse & high school dropout through an intensive school-based social network development program." *American Journal of Health Promotion, 8*, 202–214.

Elliott, D. S., Huizinga, D., & Ageton, S. S. (1985), *Explaining Delinquency & Drug Use*. Newbury Park: Sage.

Gordon, R. (1987), "An operational classification of disease prevention." In J. A. Steinberg & M. M. Silverman (eds), *Preventing Mental Disorders*. Rockville, MD: DHHS, 20–26.

Hansen, W. B. (1992), "School-based substance abuse prevention: A review of the state of the art in curriculum, 1980–1990." *Health Education Research, 7*, 403–430.

Harlow, L. L., Newcomb, M. D., & Bentler, P. M. (1986), "Depression, self-derogation, substance use & suicide ideation: Lack of purpose in life as a mediational factor." *Journal of Clinical Psychology, 42*, 5–21.

Hawkins, D. H., Catalano, R. F., & Miller, J. Y. (1992), "Risk and protective factors for alcohol and other drug problems in adolescence and early adulthood: Implications for substance abuse prevention." *Psychological Bulletin, 112*, 54–105.

Heller, K., Price, R. H., & Hogg, J. R. (1991), "The role of social support in community and clinical interventions." In B. R. Sarason, I. G. Sarason & G. R. Pierce (eds), *Social Support*. NY: Wiley & Sons, 482–508.

Herting, J. R. (1990), "Predicting at-risk youth: Evaluation of a sample selection model." *Communicating Nursing Research, 23*, 178.

Herting, J. R., & Eggert, L. L. (1992), "Chain model of drug involvement: High-risk intervention youth versus controls." Unpublished manuscript. Stanford University, Department of Sociology.

Herting, J. R., Eggert, L. L., & Thompson, E. A. (1996), "A multidimensional model of adolescent drug involvement." *Journal of Research on Adolescence, 6*, 325–361.

Institute of Medicine (IOM) (1994), *Reducing risks for Mental Disorders: Frontiers for preventive intervention research*. P. J. Mrazek & R. J. Haggerty (eds). Washington, DC: National Academy Press.

Janis, I. L. (1983), *Short Term Counseling: Guidelines based on recent research*. New Haven: Yale University.

Jessor, R. (1993), "Successful adolescent development among youth in high-risk settings." *American Psychologist, 48*, 117–26.

Johnson, L. D., O'Malley, P. M., & Bachman, J. G. (1996), *National Survey Results on Drug Use from the Monitoring the Future Study, 1975–1995: Vol. 1. Secondary school students*. NIH Pub. No. 96–4139, Rockville, MD: US DHHS, NIH, NIDA.

Kellam, S. G., & Rebok, G. W. (1992), "Building developmental and etiological theory through epidemiologically based preventive intervention trials." In J. McCord & R. E. Tremblay (eds), *Preventing Antisocial Behavior: Interventions from birth through adolescence*. NY: Guilford Press.

Kellam, S. G., et al. (1991), "Developmental epidemiologically based preventive trials: Baseline modeling of early target behaviors and depressive symptoms." *American Journal of Community Psychology, 19*, 563–584.

Lin, N., Dean, A., & Ensel, W. (1986), *Social Support, Life Events, & Depression*. Orlando: Acad Press.

Miller, W. R., & Sovereign, R. G. (1989), "The Check-up: A model for early intervention in addictive behaviors." In T. Loberg *et al.* (eds), *Addictive Behaviors*. Amsterdam: Swets & Zeitlinger, 219–231.

Miller, W. R., & Rollnick, S. (1991), *Motivational Interviewing*. NY: Guilford Press.

Miller, W. R., & Sanchez, V. C. (1993), "Motivating young adults for treatment and lifestyle change." In G. Howard (ed.), *Issues in Alcohol Use and Misuse by Young Adults*. Notre Dame, IN: University of Notre Dame Press.

Moskowitz, J. (1988), "Evaluating the effects of parent groups on the correlates of adolescent substance abuse." *Journal of Psychoactive Drugs, 17*(3), 173–178.

National Institute on Drug Abuse (NIDA) (1994), *Coming together on prevention* (Videotape). Rockville MA: DHHS, National Institutes of Health.

National Institute on Drug Abuse (NIDA) (1997), *Drug Abuse Prevention: What works!* NIH Publication #97–4110. Rockville, MD: DHHS, National Institutes of Health, National Institute on Drug Abuse, Office of Science Policy and Communications.

Pentz, M. A. (1993), "Benefits of integrating strategies in different settings." In A. Elster, S. Panzarine & K. Holt (eds), *AMA state-of-the-art conference on adolescent health promotion: Proceedings.* Arlington, VA: Nat Ctr for Ed Mat/Child Health, 15–33.

Powell-Cope, G. M., & Eggert, L. L. (1994), "Psychosocial risk and protective factors: Potential high school dropouts vs. typical youth." *National Dropout Center Yearbook I.* Using what we know about at-risk youth: Lessons from the field. Lancaster, PA: Technomic, 23–51.

Rainer, K. L., & Slavin, L. A. (1992), "Social support networks and stressful events of low-income African-American adolescents and their single mothers." Presented at the Society for Research on Adolescence Meeting, Washington, DC.

Randell, B. P. (1999), *Promoting CARE: Counselors and parents prevent youth suicide risk.* National Institutes on Drug Abuse Grant R01 NR04933. (with L. L. Eggert and J. R. Herting).

Randell, B. P., Eggert, L. L., & Pike, K. (2001), "Immediate post interventions." *Suicide and Life Threatening Behavior, 31*, 41–61.

Resnick, M. D., *et al.* (1997), "Protecting adolescents from harm: Findings from the national longitudinal study on adolescent health." *Journal of the American Medical Association 278*, 823–865.

Sarason B. R., Pierce, G. R., & Sarason, I. G. (1991), "Social support: The sense of acceptance and the role of relationships." In B. R. Sarason, I. G. Sarason & G. R. Pierce (eds), *Social Support.* NY: Wiley & Sons, 97–128.

Schinke, S. P., & Gilchrist L. D. (1984), *Life Skills Counseling with Adolescents.* Austin, TX: Pro-Ed.

Schinke, S. P., Botvin, G. J., & Orlandi, M. A. (1991), *Substance Abuse in Children and Adolescents: Evaluation and intervention.* Newbury Park, CA: Sage.

Thompson, E. A., Connelly, C. D., & Eggert, L. L. (2000a), "Co-occurring problem behaviors among high-risk youth: Suicide risk behaviors, depression, drug involvement and aggression." Manuscript submitted for publication.

Thompson, E. A., & Eggert, L. L. (1999), "Using the Suicide Risk Screen to identify suicidal adolescents among potential high school dropouts." *Journal of Child and Adolescent Psychiatry 38*(12), 1506–1514.

Thompson, E. A., Eggert, L. L., & Herting, J. R. (2000b), "Mediating effects of an indicated prevention program for reducing youth depression and suicide risk behaviors." *Suicide & Life-Threatening Behaviors, 30* (3), 252–271.

Thompson, E. A., Eggert, L. L., Randell, B. P., & Pike, K. C. (2001), "Evaluation of indicated suicide risk prevention approaches for potential high school dropouts." *American Journal of Public Health, 91*(5), 742–752.

Thompson, E. A., Horn, M., Herting, J. R., & Eggert, L. L. (1997), "Enhancing outcomes in an indicated drug prevention program for high-risk youth." *Journal of Drug Education 27*, 19–41.

Thompson, E. A., Mazza, J., & Eggert, L. L. (2000), "The mediating roles of anxiety, depression, and hopelessness on adolescent suicidal behaviors." Manuscript submitted for publication.

Thompson, E. A., Moody, K., & Eggert, L. L. (1994), "Discriminating suicide ideation among high-risk youth." *Journal of School Health, 64*, 361–367.

Tobler, N. (1986), "Meta-analysis of 143 adolescent drug prevention programs: Quantitative outcome results of program participants compared to a control or comparison group." *Journal of Drug Issues, 16*, 537–567.

Tobler, N. S. (1992), "Drug prevention programs can work: Research findings." *Journal of Addictive Diseases, 11*, 1–28.

Vorrath, H., & Brendtro, L. (1985), *Positive Peer Culture* (2nd edition), Chicago: Aldine.

Weissberg, R. P., Caplan, M. Z., & Sivo, P. J. (1989), "A new conceptual framework for establishing school-based social competence promotion programs." In L. A. Bond & B. E. Compas (eds), *Primary Prevention & Promotion in the Schools.* Newbury Park, CA: Sage, 255–296.

Chapter 4

All Stars: Problem Behavior Prevention Programming for Schools and Community Groups

William B. Hansen

Theoretical Background and Rationale

Beginnings: Building a Tradition of Research in Prevention

Early research on the prevention of problem behavior among teenagers was highly academic. That is, researchers viewed themselves as discoverers of truth rather than solvers of public health dilemmas. The goal of prevention, always seen as worthy, was not thought to be imminent. The goal was to learn enough through research to identify promising means of accomplishing meaningful and measurable changes in controlled research studies. Thus, initial prevention projects focused on applying theories of researchers' host disciplines to see what preventive effects might result. Initial projects focused on teen smoking and quickly expanded to include alcohol and marijuana as well.

Early prevention research focused heavily on applying a number of popular social psychological theories to prevention. These included Social learning theory, both as proposed as an explanation of the role of *social modeling* in the expression of aggression in children (Bandura, 1977) and as subsequently revised to include the concept of *self-efficacy* (Bandura, 1984) or one's perception that one can perform a skill that will accomplish what is intended by the one performing it.

After it was published, the *Theory of Reasoned Action* (Azjen & Fishbein, 1980) also became a frequently considered foundational theory for prevention efforts. This theory incorporated such concepts as beliefs about consequences, values, attitudes, normative beliefs, and intentions in a framework that was useful to social scientists working with applied topics such as drug use.

Even early on, there was some evidence for and a general willingness toward accepting the notion that social influence processes were at work in the onset of cigarette smoking. Akin to the idea of social modeling, researchers quickly drew conclusions about the potential role of *peer pressure* as a primary culprit in the onset of drug prevention. There was early evidence (Biglan, Severson, Bavry & McConnell, 1983) that smoking was very likely to occur primarily in a social context and that other youth were the source of obtaining cigarettes and encouraging experimentation. Nonetheless, the specifics of how social influences operated were primarily left to conjecture.

Innovations in Adolescent Substance Abuse Interventions, pages 85–108.
ISBN: 0-08-043577-7

The Tobacco and Alcohol Prevention Program (TAPP)

As part of the effort to apply social learning theory, several programs were developed and tested. TAPP (Hansen, Malotte & Fielding, 1988) was the first program we developed that attempted to go beyond smoking prevention to include another gateway substance. This project included a wide array of program elements including training in resisting peer pressure, an analysis of advertising for cigarettes and alcohol, teaching about the long-term and short-term health and social consequences of tobacco and alcohol use, and teaching and applying skills about the decision-making process to decisions about smoking and drinking. TAPP produced modest long-term outcomes suggesting an impact on smoking and drinking. However, results were far from overwhelming.

Project SMART

Project SMART (Self-Management and Resistance Training; Hansen, Johnson, Flay, Graham & Sobel, 1988) continued the systematic attempt to create an effective program for multiple substance prevention. Indeed, Project SMART stands out as our first attempt to specifically test competing approaches to prevention. This project compared two theory-based approaches to preventing the onset of substance abuse among adolescents. The first approach addressed issues related to social influences. This program included lessons about the nature of peer pressure, skills for resisting peer pressure, correcting exaggerated estimates of peer drug use prevalence, short-term consequences of drug use, media awareness, resisting media influences, finding alternatives to drug use, building positive friendships, and making a commitment to resist peer pressure.

The second approach, self-management, included methods that had been developed by researchers from a different tradition (Schaps, DiBartolo, Moskowitz, Palley & Churgin, 1981) who focused on affective education. This program taught students about stress and stress management, goal setting and achieving skills, the potential for drugs to interfere with personal goals, decision-making skills, self-esteem, assertiveness training, identifying alternatives to drug use, and making a commitment to engage in alternatives instead of using drugs. Three group-based programs were created, and two schools were randomly assigned to receive each program. An additional four schools were assigned to be no treatment controls. The program was delivered during seventh-grade health classes. Students' tobacco, alcohol, and marijuana use were monitored twelve and 24 months later.

Students who received the social influence program generally had lower rates of onset for all three substances. There were strong statistical differences between social influence program students and control students when rates of high use were considered. For example, when the social influence and control groups were compared for the percent of students who reported having two or more drinks during the past month, there were fewer social influence program students (6.8 percent) who reported doing so than control group students (10.3 percent). The social influence group generally had lower marijuana use than the control group. At the twelve-month post-test, 6.8 percent of the social influence program students and 10.9 percent of control students reported any marijuana use. These effects for marijuana became non-significant at the 24-month post-test. The self-management students, in contrast, had higher rates of drug use onset than controls.

Mediating Variables: Keys to Understanding Prevention Effectiveness

Subsequent to these early intervention projects, it became clear that there were many issues to resolve about program content and structure if a truly effective prevention approach was to be developed. A consensus had emerged from many researchers that a social influences approach was the most likely means of accomplishing this goal. Indeed, it became almost doctrinaire that peer pressure resistance training was the cornerstone on which all program effectiveness rested. The federal "Just Say No" campaigns relied on this assumption. It was as if the problem had been solved and what was left for the research community to do was simply wrap up loose ends. Fortunately, bright researchers who had different training and specialized talents were constantly entering the field.

The Adolescent Alcohol Prevention Trial (AAPT)

In the search for clarification about social influence issues, John Graham and I (Hansen & Graham, 1991) began the Adolescent Alcohol Prevention Trial (AAPT). AAPT was intent on answering one question: How did training adolescents in skills for resisting peer pressure and correcting erroneous normative beliefs about the prevalence and acceptability about drugs independently affect program outcomes? The idea for AAPT grew from a presentation about a social influence prevention program in which the investigator stated that teaching students skills for saying "no" to drugs had been so successful that smoking and drinking became observably "uncool" within the group. Was it possible that developing skills to resist pressure also caused a change in normative beliefs? Or, were skills and normative beliefs separately influenced entities that required their own interventions?

The goal of AAPT was to test these issues. AAPT therefore examined two approaches to preventing alcohol, tobacco, and marijuana use among adolescents. The first approach was titled "Normative Education." The goal of this program was to establish beliefs in conventional norms among students. This program taught students that the prevalence of substance use among their peers was lower than they might otherwise expect. It also taught students that their peer group generally did not approve of substance use. The second approach was titled "Resistance Skills Training." The goal of this program was to build skills in students for resisting peer and other forms of social pressure. Students were taught a variety of techniques for identifying and resisting social pressure. They were taught skills for being assertive in peer interactions and practiced these skills through role-played scenarios. Programs that included both elements (Normative Education & Resistance Skills Training), each element alone, and neither element (only information about consequences of using alcohol, tobacco, and marijuana) were compared.

The Normative Education program produced lower rates of increase for all three substances that were measured. The Resistance Skills Training program, in contrast, did not produce lower use rates for any of the substances. Between pretest and post-test, classes that were exposed to either Information Only or Resistance Skills Training (only) demonstrated increases in the percentage of students reporting "ever being drunk" (11 percent). The increase for students in classes exposed to Normative Education was 4 percent. Only 1.4 percent of students reported having problems that could be associated with alcohol use in the seventh grade. By eighth grade, problems associated with alcohol among students who were not enrolled in a Normative Education class increased 2.4 percent. Problem alcohol use among students in Normative Education classes increased 0.3 percent.

Initial use of alcohol among students in Normative Education classes increased eleven percent. Among students in classes that did not receive Normative Education, the increase was 14 percent. At pretest, five percent of students overall reported drinking during the past week. This increased by five percent among no Normative Education classes, but increased less than three percent among students who were exposed to Normative Education. The onset of marijuana use was lower among students exposed to the Normative Education program. Reports of ever having used marijuana increased 2.2 percent among students exposed to Normative Education; the rate increased 6.2 percent among students who did not receive Normative Education. Normative Education students reported lower smoking in the past 30 days (4.8 percent) than students not enrolled in Normative Education (6.5 percent).

We further modeled the outcomes of the AAPT interventions looking at the role-specific mediators played in changing substance use onset (Donaldson, Graham & Hansen, 1994). What we discovered was that both programs changed their primary targeted mediating variables. The Resistance Skills Training program significantly improved the resistance skills of students who received our instruction. Similarly, students who were exposed to Normative Education had significantly improved, meaning more conventional, perceptions of alcohol, tobacco, and marijuana use norms within the peer group. Of significant interest was our finding that the reported presence of offers to use drugs were actually reduced among those who participated in the Normative Education program. Our analyses showed no relationship between changing resistance skills and reducing drug use. In contrast, improved normative beliefs and reduced offers for drug use were significantly predictive of a reduction in the onset of drug use.

The Midwest Prevention Project and Project STAR

These findings actually corroborated earlier findings presented by MacKinnon and colleagues (MacKinnon *et al.*, 1991) on the mediators that accounted for the effects of Project STAR in the Midwest Prevention Project. The Midwestern Prevention Project (Pentz *et al.*, 1989a; 1989b) was a school- and community-based project designed to prevent or delay the onset of gateway drug use (tobacco, alcohol, and marijuana) in adolescents. Project STAR, the school curriculum, was developed using many of the activities from AAPT and was based on the social influences approach to prevention. The Project STAR program attempted to change eight mediators. These included: improved commitments to avoid drug use; increased beliefs about negative consequences of drug use; decreased beliefs about positive consequences of drug use; increased knowledge of social influences on drug use (such as peer pressure and media messages); improved skills for resisting social pressures; improved communication skills; corrections of erroneous beliefs about drug use prevalence among peers; and developing beliefs that friends do not approve of drug use.

Fewer students who received Project STAR reported smoking cigarettes, drinking alcohol, and using marijuana than did the control students at the post-test. Project STAR students reported significant improvements in their intentions and commitment to not smoke cigarettes, to not drink alcohol, and to not use marijuana. Students who received Project STAR became less likely to believe in the positive consequences of cigarette, alcohol, and marijuana use than did the control students. Students enrolled in Project STAR classes were more likely to think it would be easy to talk to a friend about a school or drug problem. At post-test, Project STAR students were more likely to report that their friends would be unfriendly towards their drug use. In contrast, students in the control schools were less likely to care about their friends' reactions regarding drug use. The program did not change beliefs about negative consequences of drug use, knowledge of social influences to use drugs, reported ability to resist social influences or perceived peer norms related to drug use.

Only the four variables that were statistically different for Project STAR and control students were included in mediating variable analyses. The mediator, friends' reactions to drug use, was largely responsible for the program effect on alcohol use. This variable explained approximately 66 percent of the reduction of alcohol use. About 31 percent of the reductions in alcohol use were also explained by changed intentions and commitment. Cigarette smoking was also predicted primarily by changes in one mediator. Changes in expected friends' reactions to smoking explained 45 percent of the reduction of cigarette smoking. The changes in beliefs about positive consequences and in intentions to use were too small to account for the reductions observed in cigarette smoking.

Effect "Laws" and the Search for Mediators

From this research, the expected reactions of friends (i.e., the belief that drug use is unacceptable to the friendship group) emerged as a clearly superior focus of intervention to teaching students to "Just Say No." This finding was disconcerting to many. To us, it suggested that the way to identify promising methods for intervention was to focus more closely on the issue of mediating variables.

A NIDA-sponsored review of school-based prevention programs (Hansen, 1992) and a subsequent survey project yielded a means of focusing attention on the issue of defining which mediating variables and what kinds of program components held the greatest promise for prevention research. As AAPT and the mediating variables results from the Midwestern Prevention Project hint, targeting and changing the appropriate mediating variables is central to the process of achieving preventive effects.

Those who design prevention programs often target changing characteristics of the individual or of the individual's social environment. These characteristics are known as mediators. The essential idea of a mediator is that it represents the more immediate outcome that is changed by the program. Thus, it is the mediator — not the program — that accounts for the effectiveness of a prevention program in terms of changes in behavior. A program that is designed to prevent drug use does so by first changing some characteristic that accounts for the onset of drug use in the natural course of things.

The statistical methods that are used to analyze mediators hold important lessons for designing and implementing effective programs. Two laws emerge from a consideration of mediating variable analysis methods (Hansen & McNeal, 1996). First, changes produced in behaviors (such as drug use) are the result of changes that are produced in mediators. Therefore, programs never directly change behavior. They always work by changing some other quality. This suggests the first law of prevention, "The Law of Indirect Effect." This law states that changes in target behaviors can only be accomplished by changing mediators.

The second law is called "The Law of Maximum Expected Potential Effect." As we can gather from AAPT and Project STAR results, programs can be more or less effective depending on two qualities related to mediators that act together. First, programs that produce a large change in a mediator have bigger effects in terms of changing behavior than programs that produce a small change in the same mediator. Second, programs that produce changes in mediators that have strong predictive power have the potential to produce larger behavioral changes that programs that change weak mediators. This is because all mediators have upper limits in their potential to cause effects. The upper limit for weaker mediators is lower than the upper limit for stronger mediators.

Translated into slightly more concrete language, program developers would be well advised to identify mediators that have the strongest possible natural statistical relationship with the behavior that is being changed. Once identified, the job of the program developer is to design a program that allows the intervention to change the mediator in a positive direction as much as possible. It becomes the job of the program implementer to maximize the potential of the program by understanding the mediator and working directly towards changing the quality it represents in the young people who are enrolled.

From the NIDA review, twelve strategies that had been used in drug prevention in the past were identified. These included

- Normative education programs that attempted to develop conventional normative beliefs about substance use prevalence and acceptability
- Values clarification programs that attempted to build psychological dissonance between desired lifestyles and high-risk behaviors
- Knowledge programs addressing beliefs and expectations about consequences
- Commitment-building programs
- Social pressure resistance skills training programs
- Stress management training programs
- Self-esteem-building programs
- Alternatives programs that attempted to show young people how to find alternatives to meeting the needs fulfilled by drugs
- Decision-making skills training programs
- Goal-setting skills training programs
- Social skills training programs that addressed such topics as assertiveness, communication and interpersonal problem-solving skills
- Assistance skills training programs that focused on providing information and skills for assisting peers resolve conflict and deal with their problems.

Each program is associated with a specific mediating variable. For example, normative education programs are uniquely associated with normative beliefs and values clarification programs are uniquely associated with lifestyle incongruence. Beginning in 1991, we surveyed students in local schools. The surveys assessed mediating variable measures that represented what each of these twelve programs was attempting to change. We also measured alcohol, tobacco, marijuana, inhalant, and other drugs used by students. The goal was to compare the natural potential of each measure to act as a mediator. The rule for selection becomes relatively simple. The mediators that are the strongest predictors of drug use are those that represent the best hope for preventing drug use when changed. Programs should therefore focus their attention on the limited set of mediators that have the strongest potential for affecting drug use outcomes.

The results of this study (Hansen, Uebersax & Rose, unpublished; McNeal & Hansen, 1999) revealed three measures to have superior potential as mediators (see Table 1). These were normative beliefs, commitment, and lifestyle incongruence. Holding appropriate beliefs about consequences, primarily beliefs about social and psychological — not health — consequences was a close fourth. Having skills for resisting peer pressure — the focus of so much of the social influences prevention programming in the past — was fifth in order.

Table 1: Cross-lagged correlations and standardized regression (path) coefficients between postulated mediating variables in Year 1 and substance use in Year 2 (N = 2639).

Postulated mediating variable	Alcohol r_{m1s2}	Path Coeff.	Tobacco r_{m1s2}	Path Coeff.	Other drugs r_{m1s2}	Path Coeff.
Normative beliefs	−0.445†	−0.196†	−0.390†	−0.134†	−0.197†	−0.145†
Commitment	−0.398†	−0.185†	−0.369†	−0.129†	−0.187†	−0.155†
Lifestyle incongruence	−0.400†	−0.170†	−0.376†	−0.123†	−0.198†	−0.151†
Consequence beliefs	−0.318†	−0.085†	−0.293†	−0.071†	−0.176†	−0.121†
Resistance skills	−0.270†	−0.093†	−0.208†	−0.033‡	−0.134†	−0.093†
Self-esteem	−0.151†	−0.071†	−0.169†	−0.059†	−0.079†	−0.059†
Goal-setting skills	−0.146†	−0.064†	−0.141†	−0.043‡	−0.064†	−0.043‡
Decision skills	−0.115†	−0.036‡	−0.113†	−0.027‡	−0.076†	−0.055‡
Alternatives	−0.104†	−0.019	−0.120†	−0.024	−0.066†	−0.040‡
Stress management	−0.079†	−0.021	−0.089†	−0.033‡	−0.032‡	−0.012
Assistance skills	0.080*b*	0.021	0.033	0.011	0.018	0.008
Social skills	0.073*b*	0.045*a*	0.024	0.013	0.030	0.031
Average	−0.189	−0.073	−0.184	−0.054	−0.097	−0.070

† Significant (one-tailed) at p < .001.
‡ Significant (one-tailed) at p < .05.
a Significant (two-tailed) at p < .05.
b Significant (two-tailed) at p < .001.

These analyses, coupled with a variety of other studies, suggested that an effective prevention program should primarily attend to three topics: normative education, commitment building, and values clarification. Normative education and commitment building had long been associated with social influence programs because of their relationship to the Theory of Reasoned Action.

Values clarification programs were largely associated affective education approaches, although this concept, too, is associated with the Theory of Reasoned Action. In part, its disassociation with the social influences model primarily had to do with the fact that values clarification as an approach in education was under serious attack during the decade in which social influences programs were developing. These were fostered by methodological failures — values clarification programs failed to change the targeted mediators — as well as political failures — values clarification programs often openly stated assumptions that parents did not agree with, such as *there is no right or wrong*. Nonetheless, the quantitative support for lifestyle incongruence as a mediator appeared solid.

The results of these analyses thus served as the basis for the development of All Stars. It was clear that we had experience with interventions designed to change normative beliefs. We had dabbled with commitment-building activities. Values clarification had received minimal attention and clearly needed to be transformed both methodologically and politically so that in attempting to accomplish a worthwhile goal, there would be the possibility of both methodological success and political acceptance.

Other Research of Note

Much of the story told so far is highly personal. However, significant independent lines of research ultimately came to be incorporated in All Stars that deserve attention. For example, Susan Ennett and Karl Bauman (1993) identified social isolates as a group at particular risk for drug use. Similar findings for aggression were found by John Coie and his colleagues (Terry & Coie, 1991; Coie, Dodge & Coppotelli, 1982; Coie & Koeppl, 1990) and by Shep Kellam and his colleagues (Kellam, Ensminger & Simon, 1980). Reviews of the literature have also demonstrated the potential usefulness of peer opinion leaders (Rooney & Murray, 1996). All this research underscores the need for addressing general issues of social group structure, social acceptance, and prosocial bonding (Hawkins, Catalano & Miller, 1992).

There has also been significant research on the role of parents in prevention. Much of this work has focused on the parents of high-risk youth (Dishion & Andrews, 1995). However, other work has focused on the role of parents in the etiology of drug use (e.g., Brook, Nomura & Cohen, 1989a; 1989b; Hansen *et al.*, 1987; Richardson *et al.*, 1989). Results of these studies and others indicate that parents play an important role in protecting students from influences to use drugs. Important considerations include parents' monitoring, standard setting, and role modeling. At the same time it has become clear that there are challenges involving parents as active agents in prevention programs. Attendance at special events is often low. Parents have radically different styles for addressing problems faced by their children. Nonetheless, this research suggests that, at a minimum, prevention programs benefit to the extent to which parental involvement can be encouraged and supported.

Theory: Explaining Data

The data from mediating variable analyses and from field trials speak about variables and relationships. However, to be useful each of the mediators needs to be defined in a human context. Each mediator reflects an underlying process of socialization that involves both psychological and sociological processes. Psychological processes occur within the individual and include perceptions, beliefs, thoughts, and emotions. Sociological processes occur primarily within the peer group and include a characterization of how the group responds. In fact, measuring the group has remained elusive. The influence of the group is known primarily because of observed differences between individuals when alone and when in a group. There are things individuals do only when they are in a group. However, because the science needed to define the nature of group influence does not exist, the theory must present it as a hypothesis.

Prosocial ideals refers to an individual's or a group's perception that the qualities they hold to be important do not fit with a lifestyle that includes substance use, violence, and premature sexual activity. There is a sociological component to this: what is important and has priority is often defined by the reference group as much as by the individual. Note that prosocial ideals do not simply refer to having high ideals or aspirations. They do not necessarily refer to holding religious or traditional family values. The concept is very practical. No matter what is important, if that value is in conflict with engaging in problem behaviors, it has a long-term suppressing effect on developing the behavior. Young people start with ideals that do not fit with drug use; those who start using drugs lose this perspective as they grow older. The goal of intervention is to help the young person develop and maintain a vision of a future life that would be perceived to be seriously compromised if drug use and other high-risk behaviors were engaged in.

Group norms and **normative beliefs** technically reflect two different phenomena. Group norms define what the group does and finds acceptable. Normative beliefs, meanwhile, reflect a given individual's *perceptions* of the group's behavior and what they *expect* the group to find acceptable and unacceptable. Group norms refer to an unseen, but apparently real, phenomenon that must be understood as group behavior. It is as if a human social group, friends or family or classroom, has a life that is definably distinct from the lives of the individuals who make up that group. Groups are relatively transient in many senses. Friends apparently act as a group only when they are together. When the individuals have gone their separate ways, the group disappears. The friendship shared by the individuals may still exist, but the group itself becomes dormant. Groups also change over time. It is rare for the same group of friends to remain intact without either the addition of new people or the deletion of those once a part of the group. This makes it a bit difficult to define such a quality as a group norm, but the concept is important. Conventional beliefs about norms "erode" as students mature; students who use drugs are more likely to have poor normative beliefs than students who do not use drugs. The goal of intervention is to develop a belief that the norm within the peer group is conventional with regard to drug use, violence, and premature sexual activity. That is, young people need to have conventional beliefs reinforced. Exaggerated and erroneous beliefs that high-risk behaviors are common and widely accepted need to be challenged and corrected. The eventual goal of intervention is to transform the peer group as much as the individual.

Prosocial bonding refers to the attachments that form between individuals and the social institutions to which they belong. Bonding is a two-way street. Not only must the individual feel an attachment to the institution, but the institution must provide some reciprocal allegiance to the individual. Bonding is not necessarily prosocial or positive. Gang members have bonded to their gang. They have a place where they belong and that claims them. Yet, the bond brings with it many negative behaviors that reflect high-risk norms. The quality that defines positive bonding is the normative standard of the group with which bonding is made. Churches and schools often have the most clearly defined positive norms. Sports teams may or may not have positive normative standards. Gangs have clearly defined negative standards. Once bonds are established, they can be difficult to sever. The goal of intervention is to develop attachments between young people and the prosocial institutions with which they interact. Students need to feel wanted and accepted at school. Young people need to have access and belong to adult-led groups, such as churches and recreation centers, where they feel accepted. It is important that the norms of such groups regarding drug use, violence, and other high-risk behaviors be clearly integrated into the code of conduct of these groups.

Commitment is thought of as internalized intentions. However, it can also be thought of as a public and social expression of one's intentions. In many respects, being committed implies having considered the alternatives and having then made a voluntary determination about what to do. People often refer to this as *decision-making*. Clearly commitments should reflect the endpoint of a process, but making a commitment means more than that. Commitments reflect one's self-image as well as the expected image that is transmitted to others. Both psychological and sociological elements of making commitments provide protection for high-risk behaviors. The ability to defend commitments when challenged is evidence that a commitment exists. Students start with naturally strong commitments to not use drugs or engage in high-risk behaviors, and even among students who do not use drugs, there is some erosion of commitment. However, among those who start using drugs, the erosion is marked. The goal of intervention is to strengthen existing positive commitments and intentions. Youths need to have the opportunity to think deeply about personal commitments. Because of the tendency of commitment to erode, this topic needs to be revisited, reassessed, and revised periodically.

Parental attentiveness has to do with interactional qualities between youth and their parents. Adolescence is a period of increased independence from parental control, even in the most congenial of children. Parents who are most successful at contributing to the prevention of high-risk behaviors are those who have the following characteristics. Parents are effective when they nurture a close, involved, loving relationship with their children. They are more effective when they supervise and monitor their child's whereabouts, activities, and companions. They are more effective when they provide clear and consistent rules and expectations for their child's behavior. Parents should teach values and skills that encourage bonding to positive peers and social institutions. They should establish clear rules and expectations regarding alcohol and drug use, intimacy and violence. Finally, parents are more effective when they model appropriate behaviors, including low-risk alcohol use, abstinence from tobacco and illegal drugs, and appropriate personal relationships. The goal of parental involvement in All Stars is to increase and maintain high levels of parental involvement with their children.

Description of the Intervention

All Stars is a relatively recent program. The first version (1.0) was prepared in 1994. The second (1.1), third (1.2), and fourth (1.3) versions were pilot tested in 1995 and 1996. The fifth version (1.4) was field tested beginning in 1996 and has since been revised twice (versions 1.5 and 1.6), the last in 1998. Yet the beginnings of All Stars extend back to 1975 with the first federally funded prevention research on tobacco prevention (Evans *et al.*, 1978). As such, All Stars is viewed best as the cumulative result of years of research that we anticipate will extend into the future. All Stars is an interim product that will continue to change and evolve in the future, incorporating the best available research, changing form, expanding size, emphasis, and adapting to new settings.

Key Concepts and Objectives

Teachers who deliver All Stars — or any other prevention program — ultimately need to understand what these concepts look like. To the scientist and program developer, mediators are quantities, as volts, watts, and amperes are to electrical engineers. However, there needs to be a real-world embodiment. Much as wires and transistors and batteries are the real-world embodiment of electrical concepts, it is words, facial expressions, reactions, attentiveness, and other human thoughts and actions that become the embodiment of targeted mediating variables.

All Stars addresses the concept of **norms** and **normative beliefs** by altering students' perceptions of what their group thinks of as commonplace and acceptable. The primary strategy for doing this is through revealing unassailable information that defines non-participation as normal and demonstrates that the prevalence of participation in high-risk behaviors is low.

The focus of All Stars programming is on drawing from an individual's lifestyle, aspirations, social background, and other existing features to strengthen existing ideals that are likely to be incongruent with high-risk behaviors and build or strengthen that perception in the student.

All Stars builds commitments in students by making commitments a naturally valued outcome of growing up. The process within the curriculum allows students to make voluntary private and public commitments, then rewards them and gives them reinforcement for having done so. The fact that students make commitments as a group reinforces the social side of commitments.

All Stars addresses prosocial bonding by allowing individual time between the teacher and the student to find and build on elements that can serve as the basis for finding positive attachments. The program also builds relationships among students who have poor histories of social attachment by helping them understand the norms of the class and placing them in social situations where they can become attached to other students. Peer opinion leaders, students who influence how norms within the peer group are formed, are specifically targeted for inclusion in the program.

Core Program

There are three current versions of the program. One is designed to be delivered by specialists who come into schools with sponsorship from outside agencies. The second version of the curriculum is designed to be delivered by regular teachers as part of a health or social studies class. For both of these versions, the curriculum consists of 21 core sessions (including a celebration at the conclusion of the program). The final version of the program is designed specifically for community group settings. This version of the curriculum consists of 15 core sessions. Session content includes the following:

- Session 1: Friendship and Opinion Surveys (Class/Paper Analysis): In this session, data about friendship groups and participant opinions about high-risk behaviors are collected.
- Session 2: The World of the Future (Class): This class introduces key concepts related to idealism.
- Session 3: Meeting Opinion Leaders (One-on-one): The instructor meets participants who are likely to wield social influence and establishes rapport with them.
- Session 4: Understanding What Is Important (Class): This session focuses on prioritizing ideals and demonstrating group cohesion about positive life goals.
- Session 5: Talent Search (One-on-one or Small Group): This session helps prepare students with recognized artistic talent to assist with a future class activity and helps the instructor build rapport with these participants.
- Session 6: Make Your Mark (Class): This is an art project in which participants translate their ideals into personal symbols.
- Session 7: Only the Lonely (One-on-one): This session helps participants who may be social isolates build rapport with the instructor. Specific needs of these students are understood.
- Session 8: Ideals-Based Reputations (Class): The group works towards understanding how high-risk behaviors will interfere with achieving a desired lifestyle.
- Session 9: Opinion Poll Game (Class): This session consists of a game in which participants attempt to guess indicators of social norms collected earlier and analyzed by the instructor.
- Session 10: Getting to Know Students (One-on-one): One-on-one meetings between the instructor and students continue. Ideals and normative beliefs are assessed.
- Session 11: Norms About Drugs, Violence, & Sex (Class): Conventional normative beliefs are revealed through class discussion.
- Session 12: More Norms About Drugs, Violence, & Sex (Class): Participants debate social norm issues.

- Session 13: Norms: Unwritten Rules of Behavior (Class): Participants establish standards for judging behavior in the court of public opinion with an emphasis on establishing group norms regarding high-risk behaviors.
- Session 14: Opinion Poll Game Rematch (Class): The game begun in Session nine continues.
- Session 15: Great Expectations (Opinion Leader Group — optional): Peer opinion leaders are challenged to work towards establishing conventional norms within their group.
- Session 16: Hypocrisy or Commitment (Class): The topic of adulthood is discussed in the context of commitment and responsibility. Participants label individuals who cannot make commitments as immature and those who make but do not keep commitments as hypocrites.
- Session 17: Commitment Game (Class): This is a group-centered activity that requires groups to identify and keep commitments for a period of time outside of class.
- Session 18: Defending Commitments (Class): In this class, the commitment game is concluded and lessons about how to keep commitments are reviewed.
- Session 19: Personal Commitment (One-on-one): The instructor assesses commitments from participants in nine areas. Parents are asked to co-sign commitments as sponsors. Those with parental approval of commitments are eligible to receive All Stars commitment rings.
- Session 20: Proclaiming Commitments (Class): Personal commitments are scripted and videotaped.
- Session 21: Celebration (Class): Individual certificates and commitment rings are awarded. The videotape is watched. Participants are encouraged to keep commitments.

Booster Program

For all three versions of the program, there is a booster program. The booster consists of seven sessions, each of which is designed to reiterate one of the targeted mediators of the program. The booster recognizes the need for novelty in programming — not the same old stuff — and the growing independence of youths as they mature. Booster sessions include the following:

- Session 1: Group Ideals: This session focuses on establishing group standards that embody incongruence between high-risk behaviors and group ideals through the development of a group crest.
- Session 2: Free Speech: This session encourages debate about current issues, including addressing issues related to high-risk behavior in a talk-show format.
- Session 3: Community Improvement Part I: This session encourages the development of an activist role in improving the world. Participants identify and make plans to complete doable group projects.
- Session 4: Community Improvement Part II: Participants return and report about their group projects and are challenged to make voluntary social activism a part of their character.

- Session 5: Renewed Commitment: Participants are interviewed about success and challenges in keeping prior All Stars commitments. They are challenged to renew or revise their commitments.
- Session 6: Advanced Commitment Defense Skills: Participants understand that commitments are proven when an individual overcomes challenges to keeping their commitments. Participants learn skills needed to overcome challenges they may face to keeping their commitments.
- Session 7: Video Review: Participants review previously videotaped public commitments to engage in prosocial behaviors and avoid high-risk behaviors. Participants reiterate public commitments to engage in prosocial behaviors and avoid high-risk behaviors.

Parent Program and Infusion Training

The program includes a parent program as well as homework assignments that involve parent–child discussions about topics discussed in class. The program is linked with an infusion training program for increasing teachers' understanding of the program and encouraging them to be actively involved in its implementation.

Methods

All Stars focuses on interactive teaching approaches. The primary goals of the program are not dissemination of information but the change of psychological and sociological constructs. Interactive methods are key to accomplishing these goals. The teacher rarely provides information. Instead, participants are repeatedly asked for their opinions. The instructor does not judge specific answers as either correct or incorrect, but uses them as a means of assessing students' attitudes and beliefs. The program provides teachers with opportunities that allow feedback from other students to challenge and correct undesired opinions. The key to success is two-fold. First, questions and situations are predefined and structured so that the preponderance of normal responses will fall within an expected range in which conventional responses will predominate. Second, the instructor provides an indirect source of support to insure that appropriate opinions get aired and supported. This requires the instructor to listen, to be involved, and to react with skill to specific challenges posed by deviant youth. Interactive teaching places a burden on teachers that cannot fully be explained in a curriculum guide.

Empirical Studies

Some elements of All Stars were tested in contexts other than All Stars *per se*. For example, the effects of changing group norms and normative beliefs was studied in AAPT, which was reviewed above (Donaldson, Graham & Hansen, 1994; Hansen & Graham, 1991).

North Carolina Pilot Study

An early version of All Stars (Version 1.1) was pilot tested in Lexington, North Carolina (Hansen, 1996). The purpose of the pilot test was to determine the ability of the program to change each of the four mediators described above. By chance, four of eight Healthful Living classes at the test school had participated in seventh-grade D.A.R.E. in the fall semester. The remaining four spring semester classes were recruited to receive the program in the pilot study. Both sets of classes were pretested prior to the launching of All Stars in January. Classes were again surveyed at the completion of All Stars in May.

All Stars and D.A.R.E. students were equal at pretest in their commitments to avoid high-risk behaviors (see Figure 1). Between the pretest and post-test, D.A.R.E. students' commitments began to erode. All Stars students' commitments significantly improved. Commitment to avoid high-risk behaviors 'erodes' as students grow older. These findings indicate the potential of the program to reverse this trend. The correlation between having received the *All Stars* program and having made commitments at the end of the program was 0.48. In terms of the calculus of prevention discussed earlier, this reflects a strong effect, but one that can be improved.

At pretest, All Stars students were equal to D.A.R.E. students on the measure of school bonding. By post-test, All Stars students increased their bonding to school; D.A.R.E. students' bonding to school decreased. The correlation between bonding to school and having received the All Stars program at posttest was 0.39.

At pretest, All Stars and D.A.R.E. students had similar beliefs about norms regarding high-risk behaviors. At posttest, All Stars students viewed high-risk behaviors to be less common and less accepted. D.A.R.E. students believed high-risk behaviors to be more common and more accepted among their peers. The correlation between having received the All Stars program and students' beliefs about norms at posttest was 0.33.

Finally, All Stars students continued to view their preferred lifestyle to be incongruent with high-risk behaviors. By post-test, D.A.R.E. students started to view high-risk behaviors as fitting with their preferred lifestyles. At post-test, the correlation between having received All Stars and having improved ideals was 0.47.

Improving each of these risk and protective factors is a prerequisite for success at preventing the development of high-risk behaviors.

Kentucky Randomized Field Trial

A randomized field trial to test the effectiveness of the program on changing behavior is currently being conducted in an independent evaluation by researchers at the University of Kentucky. Full results of this trial have not yet been publishemd. However, preliminary findings have been shared by Drs Nancy G. Harrington and Rick Hoyle. Version 1.40 of All Stars was used in this field trial. Two treatment conditions were created. In the first, the program was delivered by outside specialists. In the second, the program was delivered by regular classroom teachers as part of a 30-minute teacher-based guidance class.

Results to date are based only on changes between the pretest and the immediate post-test (see Figure 2). These show that All Stars has had some impact on targeted behaviors.

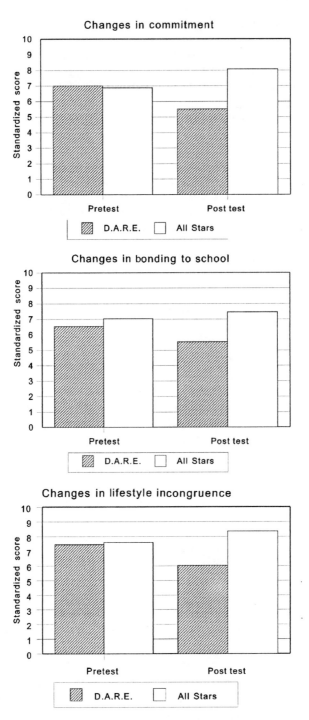

Figure 1: Results of North Carolina pilot study.

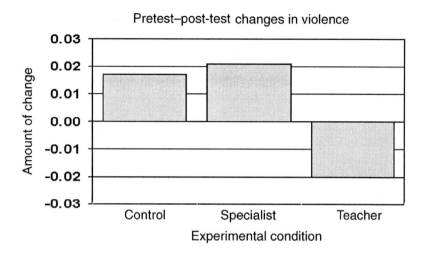

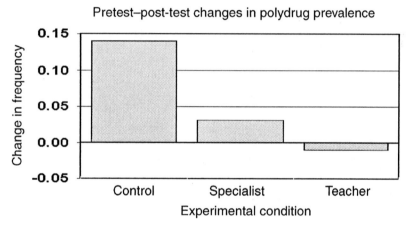

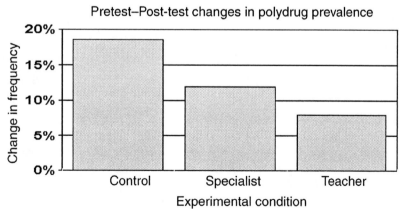

Figure 2: Results of Kentucky Study.

Both specialist-delivered and teacher-delivered versions of the program reduced the onset of sexual activity. All Stars students showed essentially no increase in the frequency of sexual intercourse. Results pictured in the figure are very similar for the number of partners students reported they had. These results were both statistically significant.

There were similar differences in the changes of prevalence of drug use. Figure 2 shows the combined results for alcohol, cigarettes, smokeless tobacco, marijuana, and inhalant use among students. Students in both the specialists and regular teachers' classes had a lower rate of onset than students who were in the control schools. The teacher-led intervention outperformed the specialist led group. Overall, All Stars delivered by regular teachers cut drug use onset by about one-half. When delivered by specialists, onset was cut by about one-third. Regular classroom teachers were also able to reduce the frequency of drug use (not shown). Compared to control students, those who received All Stars from a specialist had a much slower rate of increase in the frequency of drug use, but not the drop that was observed among students in regular classrooms. These results are marginally significant statistically. Before stronger statistical significance can be achieved, more onset among the control group is required.

Rates of violence were also measured from pretest to post-test. Only regular classroom teachers were able to create a drop in violence among students. Students in classes where the program was delivered by specialists were no different than students in control classes regarding the increase observed in violent behavior. This underscores the need to actively involve host teachers in infusing the program when delivered by specialists. Much of this appears to be related to changes in bonding to the school.

Specialists in the field trial were not as effective as regular classroom teachers at promoting bonding. This makes sense given the fact that specialists are outsiders and were often treated as such by teachers and administrators. Building bonds between the school and the student, not the specialist and the student, needs to be a goal of program implementation that should be stressed. It is also possible that some of the effects are due to the fact that violence is often initiated under situation specific circumstances. Having teachers present who can remind students to use information they have learned from All Stars at the moment when such information needs to be used will be more likely to have the desired impact.

Longer-term findings, not yet reported, are said to show a decay in program effects such that treatment and control groups do not differ by the time of the final follow-up. The Kentucky field trial results encouraged the development of the booster program which has not yet been tested.

Pilot Test of the Community Program

The community version of the program was recently tested in eight sites in Nebraska and ten sites in North Carolina in a pretest–immediate post-test evaluation study. There were a number of differences in mediating variables at post-test. Bonding was significantly different for All Stars participants compared to controls. The adoption of conventional norms was higher in the treatment group, but only marginally so. Idealism, as indicated by reported perceived incongruence between desired lifestyle and high-risk behaviors, was not statistically significant, although it was in the desired direction. All Stars youths manifested only slightly more lifestyle incongruence than did controls. Commitment to avoid high-risk behaviors, on the other hand, was statistically different for the two groups. All Stars youths reported higher levels of commitment than did controls. Similarly, there were significant differences reported on parental attentiveness. Following the general pattern of results, All Stars participants' scores on this measure were higher than control subjects' scores.

The general pattern of results demonstrates evidence of program-induced changes in targeted mediating variables (see Figure 3). That is, the program was a mechanism for improving bonding and attachment between individual participants and the parent organization, the adoption of conventional normative beliefs, increased perception that high-risk behaviors did not fit with desired lifestyles, and manifest commitment to avoid high-risk behaviors. The evidence for change in lifestyle incongruence and commitment was stronger for the Nebraska sample than for the North Carolina sample. The program overall appears to have the potential to target and appropriately change mediating variables that are important to deterring the onset of drug use and perhaps for reducing covariant high-risk behaviors as well.

We also examined fidelity of implementation and its relationship to outcomes. There was evidence from each group's pretest-to-post-test changes that there was wide variation in how groups did in terms of changing mediators. For example, eleven of the 18 groups improved the average bonding score within the group by 0.75 or more. However, there were four groups who had worse bonding scores after the program than before it started. The average changes in group scores for normative beliefs were also generally positive.

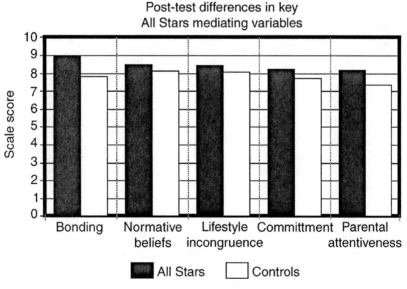

Figure 3: Results of community program study.

There were nine groups who achieved pretest–post-test increases of 0.75 or higher and two groups who improved scores more that 1.75 points on the scale score. At the same time, five groups produced no pretest–post-test change, and several others produced nearly no changes.

Given these patterns, we hoped to find moderators that could account for these variations. To address this, we calculated the correlation between program fidelity and a summary outcome index that included all variables combined. The correlation between program fidelity and the summary program outcome measure was marginally significant (r = 0.35). Group size was not related to overall pretest–post-test changes (r = −0.10). There were only modest, non-significant correlations between group size and changes in lifestyle incongruence (r = −0.27) and commitment (r = −0.24). Both of these relationships suggest that in larger groups, individually focused variables receive less attention, resulting in smaller changes between pretest and posttest. The percent of the participant group that consisted of minority (non-white) participants was the strongest predictor of the summary measure of success (r = 0.50). The results were such that having a group that was primarily minority resulted in better scores. This pattern was most strongly true for the relationship between minority percentage and changes in normative beliefs (r = 0.48) and changes in lifestyle incongruence (r = 0.50). Overall, having a group that was highly ethnic was not correlated with program fidelity (r = −0.18).

We modeled the impact of both fidelity and ethnicity on the summary index of mediating variable outcomes. Both variables together accounted for 44.9 percent of the variance in the outcome. The resulting model included fidelity (standardized beta = 0.45) and percent minority (standardized beta = 0.58). This suggests that both independently contributed as moderators to the success of the program. Overall, these findings are indicative that several important potential moderators are at work during program delivery. Fidelity was predictive of outcomes. We speculate that understanding program concepts, following program materials and being motivated to help participants improve the way they view social norms, lifestyle incongruence, commitment, and their attachment to the organization, are all important factors that contribute to success.

Issues Regarding Matching and Tailoring

All Stars deviates from the traditional idea of quality control. Most programs translate quality control to mean "Stick to the lesson." There are curricula that provide the presenter with a script. For these programs, quality control is judged by comparing what the teacher does with what the curriculum says to do. The goal is to deliver each point precisely and to keep extraneous elements out of the program. This reflects one way of defining teaching: completing the lesson as written.

We have a second way of defining quality teaching: changing the lives of students. Instead of focusing on the teacher's performance as measured by the number of elements correctly delivered, we focus on the degree to which each activity is successful in changing students in the way it was intended.

Each session is designed to accomplish a specific set of objectives. The activities detail steps that will accomplish these objectives if followed. Lessons were originally designed to meet the goal of changing students' lives and need little adaptation to meet this goal. The organization and structure of the program can be followed like other programs that require rigid lock-step adherence. However, there will always need to be some modification and adaptation. The goal is to teach the student, not the lesson. The goal of the program is to change four characteristics that protect students from high-risk behaviors (ideals, the adoption of conventional norms, strong personal commitments, and bonding to prosocial institutions). The lesson is a vehicle to get there.

The curriculum is not a script. Scripting was purposely avoided. The words need to be your own. There is room for variation and interpretation. Indeed, variation and interpretation are needed for delivering the program to different groups based on their cultural heritage, socioeconomic status, religious background, baseline behavior status, temperament, and basic intelligence. Quality control is maintained by following the lesson plan *when the lesson is achieving its goals.* When the lesson plan does not or will not accomplish the goals, the lesson needs to be modified.

To be successful, modifying a lesson requires the instructor to understand thoroughly the goals of the program and to master tactics that can be used to accomplish these goals. Nothing hurts quality control more than substituting other goals for those that exist. The goals of the program are dictated by empirical findings from research. Selecting other goals can only weaken the effect of the program.

Even with correct goals in mind, implementing activities that do not have the potential to achieve appropriate goals also result in program failure. All Star teachers are expected to gain the mastery needed to modify the program when it is warranted. Deviation requires a deep understanding of the principles that underlie the program and have shaped its essence. The teacher should deviate only when the alternative is a clearly superior method for achieving the same goals.

In many places, the lessons as written require invention. For example, during debates or Socratic discussions, the teacher must respond and generate questions spontaneously. Quality control implies that the teacher anticipates the questions that can lead the student to the appropriate end. Each of these activities requires the teacher to understand how to interpret student verbal and non-verbal responses in light of the goals of the program. Such understanding confers freedom on the teacher to maintain quality through appropriate invention.

Future Directions

The research results for All Stars to date suggest that the program has significant promise. Our approach to prevention program design has been different than we have seen with other programs, which will remain unnamed, but some of which have become popular within the recent past. Program developers always want their programs to work. We are no different in this regard. However, our approach to success is not necessarily to be the first to succeed. We do not reanalyze our data until positive results emerge. Rather, our goal is to succeed because we have finally figured out how things work and how to make the intervention do what it is supposed to do. We are striving for a consistent set of findings that make sense given what we know about what factors influence and retard the onset of drug use and how to intervene in those processes. As a consequences, we realize that there are many things yet to be done to produce a reliable, highly effective prevention program. Several specific tasks are in the immediate future.

Teacher Training

It is apparent that a key to success lies in developing program delivery agents — teachers — who can deliver a program like All Stars with high fidelity. We are currently in the process of refining a 30-hour teacher training course that will focus on concept development. Topics like norm setting, building idealism, strengthening commitments, and building prosocial bonds are not the typical emphasis of many university courses that prepare teachers before they venture into the classroom. The more exposure to training teachers can have, the better prepared they will be to either deliver prevention programs or support others when they do so.

We are also aware that teachers begin to gain a depth of understanding as they gain experience with the program. Each of the evaluations conducted to date has tested the skill of a first-time All Stars teacher. Seasoned teachers might be expected to perform better. It has been our experience to date that systematic continuing education and technical support are required to build such skills in teachers. There are, at present, no formal mechanisms or procedures to follow to accomplish these goals.

Program Development

One-shot interventions are not going to be sufficient for preventing behaviors that are highly sensitive to social contexts and psychosocial development. There is a need to develop not only booster programs, but a variety of programmatic efforts of all sorts that can support intervention over a longer period of time. We are in the process of developing two such approaches. The first, we have dubbed All Stars, Jr. and the second, predictably, is referred to as All Stars, Sr. Without specifically trying to replicate or integrate methods, these projects are intended to provide foundation and follow-up to the All Stars approach to prevention with a focus that remains on changing mediators that ultimately account for changes in drug use and other high-risk behaviors that occur over the developmental period of adolescence (from age ten to 19). Pilot projects to accomplish this are currently under way.

Summary

All Stars represents over 20-years of research on prevention program development. The central idea of targeting and changing mediating variables that account for drug use and other high-risk behaviors appears to have a solid foundation in the research literature. Furthermore, there is strong evidence that a handful of variables — normative beliefs, commitment (intentions), bonding to prosocial institutions, parental attentiveness, and life-style incongruence — hold promise as mediators. The goal of All Stars is to provide practitioners with a current state-of-the-art program that, when properly delivered, will have the potential to achieve both long- and short-term reductions in drug use.

References

Ajzen, I., & Fishbein, M. (1980), *Understanding Attitudes and Predicting Behavior.* Englewood Cliffs, NJ: Prentice-Hall.

Bandura, A. (1977), *Social Learning Theory.* Englewood Cliffs, NJ: Prentice-Hall.

Bandura, A. (1989), "Human agency in social cognitive theory." *American Psychologist,* 1175–1184.

Biglan, A., Severson, H., Bavry, J., & McConnell, S. (1983), "Social influence and adolescent smoking: A first look behind the barn." *Health Education,* 14–18.

Brook, J. S., Nomura, C., & Cohen, P. (1989a), "Prenatal, perinatal, and early childhood risk factors and drug involvement in adolescence." *Genetic, Social, and General Psychology Monographs 115,* 223–241.

Brook, J. S., Nomura, C., & Cohen, P. (1989b), "A network of influences on adolescent drug involvement: Neighborhood, school, peer, and family." *Genetic, Social, and General Psychology Monographs 115,* 125–145.

Coie, J. D., Dodge, K. A., & Coppotelli, H. (1982), "Dimensions and types of social status: A cross-age perspective." *Developmental Psychology 18,* 557–570.

Coie, J. D., & Koeppl, G. K. (1990), "Adapting intervention to the problems of aggressive and disruptive rejected children." In S. R. Asher & J. D. Coie (eds), *Cambridge Studies in Social and Emotional Development.* NY: Cambridge University Press, 309–337.

Dishion, T. J., & Andrews, D. W. (1995), "Preventing escalation in problem behaviors with high-risk young adolescents: Immediate and 1-year outcomes." *Journal of Consulting and Clinical Psychology 63*(4), 538–548.

Donaldson, S. I., Graham, J. W., & Hansen, W. B. (1994), "Testing the generalizability of inter-vening mechanism theories: Understanding the effects of adolescent drug use prevention interventions." *Journal of Behavioral Medicine 17,* 195–216.

Evans, R. I. *et al.* (1978), "Deterring the onset of smoking in children: Knowledge of immediate physiological effects and coping with peer pressure, media pressure, and parent modeling." *Journal of Applied Psychology 8*(2), 126–135.

Hansen, W. B. (1992), "School-based substance abuse prevention: A review of the state of the art curriculum 1980–1990." *Health Education Research 7*(3), 403–430.

Hansen, W. B. (1996), "Pilot Test Results Comparing the All Stars Program with Seventh Grade D.A.R.E.: Program Integrity and Mediating Variable Analysis." *Substance Use & Misuse 31*(10), 1359–1377.

Hansen, W. B., & Graham, J. W. (1991), "Preventing alcohol, marijuana, and cigarette use among adolescents: Peer pressure resistance training versus establishing conservative norms." *Preventive Medicine 20,* 414–430.

Hansen, W. B. *et al.* (1987), "The consistency of peer and parent influences on tobacco, alcohol, and marijuana use among young adolescents." *Journal of Behavioral Medicine 10,* 559–579.

Hansen, W. B., Johnson, C. A., Flay, B. R., Graham, J. W., & Sobel, J. L. (1988), "Affective and social influences approaches to the prevention of multiple substance abuse among seventh grade students: results from Project SMART." *Preventive Medicine 17,* 1–20.

Hansen, W. B., Malotte, C. K., & Fielding, J. E. (1988), "Evaluation of a tobacco and alcohol abuse prevention curriculum for adolescents." *Heath Education Quarterly 15*(1), 93–114.

Hansen, W. B., & McNeal, R. B. (1996), "The law of maximum expected potential effect: Constraints placed on program effectiveness by mediator relationships." *Health Education Research 11*(4), 501–507.

Hansen, W. B., Uebersax J. S., & Rose, L. A. (1995), "Comparison of Postulated Mediators of School-Based Substance Use Prevention in Adolescents: A Longitudinal Examination." Accepted for Publication in *Health Psychology* but never published.

MacKinnon, D. P. *et al.* (1991), "How school-based drug prevention works: One year effects of the Midwestern Prevention Project." *Health Psychology 10*, 164–172.

McNeal, R. B., & Hansen, W. B. (1999), "Developmental patterns associated with the onset of drug use: Changes in postulated mediators during adolescence." *Journal of Drug Issues 29*, 381–400.

Pentz, M. A. *et al.* (1989a), "A multi-community trial for primary prevention of adolescent drug abuse: Effects on drug use prevalence." *Journal of the American Medical Association 261*(22), 3259–3266.

Pentz, M. A. *et al.* (1989b), "Longitudinal effects of the Midwestern Prevention Project (MPP) on regular and experimental smoking in adolescents." *Preventive Medicine 18*, 304–321.

Richardson, J. L. *et al.* (1989) "Substance use among eighth graders who take care of themselves after school." *Pediatrics 84*(3), 556–566.

Schaps, E., DiBartolo, R., Moskowitz, J., & Palley, Churgin (1981), "A Review of 127 Drug Abuse Prevention Program Evaluations." *Journal of Drug Issues 11*, 17–43.

Terry, R., & Coie, J. D. (1991), "A comparison of methods for defining sociometric status among children." *Developmental Psychology 27*, 867–880.

Chapter 5

Community-Based Intervention

Brenna Hafer Bry and Nicole M. Attaway*

Theoretical Background and Rationale

Alcohol and other drug use among adolescents living in the United States has remained prevalent over the past 25 years (Johnston, O'Malley & Bachman, 1996). Considering that adolescent substance use has been associated with several specific negative outcomes, teen substance involvement continues to be of great concern for parents, teachers, health and mental health workers, and policy makers. From a developmental perspective, many adolescents have not yet learned important, healthful stress-coping behaviors, and may begin using alcohol and/or drugs as a way to avoid and reduce stress. Early adoption of unhealthful stress-coping behaviors may make it more difficult for substance-using youth to acquire more positive coping behaviors as they mature. Early use also is associated with dangerous health problems such as accidents from drunk driving, unprotected sexual practices and their negative consequences, and later alcohol and/or drug abuse. Finally, cultural values proscribing alcohol use and other drug use by teenagers contribute to societal concern about adolescent substance use (Hawkins, Catalano & Miller, 1992).

Since the 1970s, considerable research has been conducted in order to identify risk factors and precursors of adolescent substance use and abuse, with the goal of understanding the possible etiological nature of these problems (Bry, 1983; Bry, McKeon & Pandina, 1982; Hawkins, Catalano & Miller, 1992; Newcomb, Maddahian & Bentler, 1986). The greater the understanding of the causes and antecedents to youth drinking and drug use, the better these antecedents can be targeted in order to prevent or change drinking and drug use behaviors among adolescents. Although numerous risk factors and precursors have been identified, etiological processes are still unknown (Hawkins, Catalano & Miller, 1992).

Two of the main challenges in creating community-based prevention programs are (a) the targeted behaviors (i.e., alcohol or drug use) have not yet occurred and (b) there is lack of clear knowledge about etiological processes. Bry originated a strategy to address such challenges, described as a risk-focused approach, which has been used subsequently by several other prevention programs (Bry, 1982; Dishion & Andrews, 1995; Harachi, Ayers,

*Correspondence concerning this chapter should be addressed to Brenna Hafer Bry, Rutgers University, GSAPP, 152 Frelinghuysen Rd., Piscataway, NJ 08854-8085.

Innovations in Adolescent Substance Abuse Interventions, pages 109–126.
Copyright © 2001 by Elsevier Science Ltd.
All rights of reproduction in any form reserved.
ISBN: 0-08-043577-7

Hawkins & Catalano, 1996; Spoth, Seongmo, Kahn & Redmond, 1996). A risk-focused approach depends first on having some empirical information about risk factors that are associated with alcohol and drug use behaviors in adolescents. Based on this information about risk factors, the aim of the prevention program becomes to reduce these risk factors in an effort to indirectly change or prevent substance use behaviors. Bry's risk-focused approach also is guided by cognitive behavioral theory, which predicts that one can reduce the occurrence of a targeted behavior by encouraging behaviors that are incompatible with it (Bry, 1983).

Bry and colleagues have developed two levels of secondary prevention programming for adolescents and their families using the risk-focused approach. One is known as the Early Secondary Intervention Program (ESIP), and the other is the Targeted Family Intervention or TFI (Bry, Greene, Schutte & Fishman, 1989). ESIP is based primarily in the schools, whereas TFI combines school- and home-based interventions. These programs are designed to focus on adolescents who have already begun to exhibit some problem behaviors highly correlated with later drug and alcohol use.

During the beginning stages of development in the late 1970s, Bry's prevention programming focused on two risk factors, school failure and conduct problems. Besides being issues of concern in their own right, school failure and conduct problems have been shown to precede the onset of problematic adolescent drug and alcohol use (Bry, 1996). The first series of intervention studies were school-based adolescent intervention programs with a small parental involvement component (Bien & Bry, 1980; Bry, 1982; Bry & George, 1979, 1980). This type of intervention was developed at a time when there were no specific theoretical models or frameworks that could be used directly to guide the creation of secondary prevention programs. Furthermore, there were no guidelines for informing the best strategy to measure successful outcomes or the prevention of a problem.

Description of Intervention and Empirical Studies

School-based Adolescent Intervention with Parental Involvement

Notwithstanding development and measurement challenges, Bry proceeded to develop ESIP, a multi-component, school-based cognitive behavioral group therapy program. This intervention included three components. The first component consisted of weekly conferences with one teacher for each student. During this conference, three types of information were recorded: (a) academic problems or difficulties in need of improvement; (b) teacher's expectations and guidelines for evaluation, and (c) positive course behaviors such as homework completion and class preparation (Stanley, Goldstein & Bry, 1976).

The second component was a cognitive behavioral group meeting involving a small group of students and facilitated by an adult therapist. The facilitator directly addressed any academic or disciplinary problems that students were having, as well as behaviors that the students could work on to increase their grade point averages and/or reduce or avoid getting into trouble. Positive academic and conduct behaviors were reinforced with praise and points that could be exchanged for a reward, which in most cases was a trip at the end of the semester.

The third component addressed parental involvement. Parents were contacted on a regular basis to inform them about the ongoing intervention, update them on their child's progress in the program, and share information about effective strategies of reinforcement that could be used with their child.

The school-based intervention was guided by cognitive behavioral theoretical perspectives, and as such primarily used social reinforcement to increase positive school and conduct behaviors. In an effort to measure the effectiveness of the intervention and to assess which program components were necessary and/or sufficient, Bry and colleagues randomly assigned students to one of three different treatment conditions or to a no-treatment control condition (Bien & Bry, 1980). The first condition consisted of one component — teacher conferences. The second condition consisted of two components — teacher conferences and cognitive behavioral group therapy. The third condition consisted of all three components — teacher conferences, cognitive behavioral group therapy, and parental involvement. In subsequent studies, an intervention group was compared with a no-intervention group (Bry, 1982; Bry & George, 1979, 1980) (see Table 1). In addition, in one of the studies, booster sessions were added for one year after two years of the multi-component intervention had been administered.

Results indicated that all three components were necessary to have a positive impact on school attendance and academic performance. Significant differences between treatment groups and control groups did not occur reliably until the second year of the intervention. After the second year, differences between the control and intervention groups were found in the prevention of further deterioration of school grades and conduct problems. In other words, students receiving the treatment did not show improvements on their pre-intervention grades or disciplinary referrals, but they also did not show the continued deterioration witnessed in the control group of students. These studies were among the first in the literature to suggest that identifying and intervening with students with risk factors could be effective in preventing subsequent problems.

During the development of the intervention, Bry began to consider how these initial positive but modest effects might generalize across time, settings, and behaviors. In order to promote generalization, she incorporated booster sessions into the intervention package. In the first series of studies, booster sessions occurred twice a month for a period of one year in the form of either group meetings or notes mailed home. Booster sessions were conceptualized as brief contacts designed to reinforce and remind students about the positive behaviors they were exhibiting. A five-year follow-up study showed that the multi-component package that included booster sessions significantly reduced delinquency and unemployment. Moreover, some drug use (i.e., the use of hallucinogens, stimulants, glue, tranquilizers, and barbiturates) also was significantly reduced at the end of three years.

It was previously mentioned that reliable outcome differences were not observed between the control and experimental groups until the second year of the intervention. This finding suggests that time may be an important variable in observing outcomes. Several mechanisms might be responsible for this finding, including the developmental stage of adolescents. The intervention was initiated when students were in the seventh grade and continued into the eighth grade; many important developmental changes occur during this period, including puberty. Increasing maturity may contribute to older students being better able to apply the principles of the intervention. The implication here is that length of

Table 1: School-based adolescent intervention with parental involvement.

Author & date	Ss	Research design	TX	Measures
1. Bien and Bry (1980)	40 seventh graders (identified by school due to school and behavioral problems) in urban school; 60% Black; 40% White; 65% boys; 35% girls.	4-group component analysis; randomized blocks within classroom groupings; no intervention vs. 3 different intervention intensities.	Multi-component school-based cognitive behavioral group therapy: weekly teacher conference only (T); T plus twice weekly cognitive behavioral group meeting (TG); or TG plus parent contact (TGP) for one school year.	– Grades in four major subjects – Attendance and promptness – Number of disciplinary referrals records – Frequency of observed classroom behaviors
2. Bry and George (1979)	38 seventh graders (identified by school due to school and behavioral problems) in 2 suburban schools; 20% Black; 80% White; 65% boys; 35% girls.	Random assignment within pairs matched on class group, teachers, attendance, and grades to intervention or no intervention.	Multi-component school-based cognitive behavioral group therapy (twice weekly cognitive behavioral student meetings; weekly teacher interviews; monthly parent contact) for two school years.	– Grades in five major subjects – Attendance and tardiness records – Number of disciplinary referrals – Goal attainment

Table 1: Continued

Author & date	Ss	Research design	TX	Measures
3. Bry and George (1980)	30 seventh graders (identified by school due to school and behavioral problems) in 2 urban schools; 68% Black; 32% White; 60% boys; 40% girls.	Random assignment within pairs matched on class group, teachers, attendance, and grades to intervention or no intervention.	Multi-component school-based cognitive behavioral group therapy (twice weekly cognitive behavioral student meetings; weekly teacher interviews; monthly parent contact) for two school years.	– Grades in four major subjects – Attendance and promptness records – Number of disciplinary referrals
4. Bry (1982)	60 former students in above 2 studies: 32 suburban; 28 urban; 33% Black; 66% White; 66% males; 33% females.	One- and five-year follow-up (seven years from pre-treatment) of randomly assigned groups to intervention or no intervention.	Multi-component school-based cognitive behavioral group therapy for two years plus boosters for one year.	– Grades and discipline records for one year – Interview on incidences of employment, and substance use after one and one half (1.5) years – Number of files in county probation office five years post-intervention.

Table 1: Continued

Data analysis	Results	Conclusions
1. 2 way ANOVA w/randomized blocks (group (meeting time and intervention intensity as factors) on 5 change scores and planned comparisons.	– Intervention intensity had significant effect on grades and disruptive behavior in morning versus afternoon groups. – Grades improved significantly more than control condition only in the TGP condition.	1. TGP was necessary for impact; the other interventions showed no greater effects than the control condition.
2. Comparisons of the two groups on dependent variables using t-tests, in two schools, after one and two years of program.	– In school A, significant improvement in school grades and less attendance deterioration in one year. – In school B, significantly less deterioration in attendance after two years.	1. It took two years to bring improvement in one school; therefore length of intervention plays a role in detection of positive outcomes. 2. Impact of intervention was to prevent the deterioration in school performance that occurs when there was no intervention.
3. Wilcoxon matched pairs signed ranks on first and second year change scores.	– Significant changes in grades and attendance in experimental group vs. control group after two years.	1. It was necessary for the program to continue for two years to show prevention of further deterioration in grades and attendance.
4. Wilcoxn matched pairs signed ranks Chi-square analysis	– Fewer of intervention students had serious school problems, were unemployed, used multiple drugs, and had committed crimes after one year. – Fewer of intervention students had court files than control students after five years.	1. Intervention effects on school, employment drug use and crime lasted for at least one year. 2. Prevention effects on delinquency lasted at least five years.

intervention (e.g., two years) may be less critical than the timing of the intervention (e.g., eighth grade).

A related issue with respect to time of intervention is the duration of intervention effects. Presently, the long-term impact of intervention is unknown, and questions concerning for how long and how many booster sessions are needed to facilitate lasting change remain unanswered. Moreover, although positive outcomes were demonstrated in regard to two risk factors (i.e., school failure and conduct problems), the long-term impact of the intervention on the ultimate target behaviors of drug or alcohol use remains to be studied. Also, the fact that intervention effects were observed only between groups, and not for individual participants within the intervention group, raises questions related to the process and intensity of intervention. Students who received the intervention did not improve over time; however, they did not deteriorate over time. In addition, it is unclear which of each of the components of the intervention is most effective, and how these components may work together or across settings to produce change. Bry examined some of these issues in subsequent studies, which test the intervention in an outpatient clinic.

Clinic-based Family Therapy with School Contacts

The next series of interventions was tested with students who were brought by their families to outpatient counseling for school, conduct and drug use problems (Bry, Conboy & Bisgay, 1986; Bry & Krinsley, 1992) (see Table 2). These studies tested an intervention that focused more intensely on the earlier parent component, and less intensely on the school component (TFI: Bry, Greene, Schutte & Fishman, 1989). They dealt with only a small number of students and their families, but they focused in detail on the effects of the family and parental intervention over time using multiple baseline single-case designs. The intervention again was based on cognitive behavioral principles, as well as the research literature indicating that adolescents with problem behaviors, including substance misuse, tend to come from families with poor child management skills and high degrees of family conflict (Greene & Bry, 1991; Krinsley & Bry, 1991; Whittaker & Bry, 1991). Similar outcome measures were used in these studies as in the previous school-based intervention studies, but these studies added ongoing measures of substance use.

The therapy consisted of weekly sessions for three to twelve months with booster sessions after the end of the treatment, which was determined by the families when their concerns had decreased about their child's problems. Families were taught (a) problem-solving skills to reduce blaming and familial conflict and (b) how to develop and maintain reinforcement contingency plans to increase positive behaviors in their child. Regular feedback from the adolescents' schools to the therapist also was discussed in family therapy sessions. Booster sessions were incorporated to encourage and increase generalization of treatment effects so that gains would not be lost at the end of treatment.

Interestingly, some of the same patterns of findings that were found in the school-based intervention were found for the family therapy intervention. In the short term, adolescents did not exhibit much improvement from baseline measures. Instead, there was a temporary increase in problem behaviors, which then was followed by a decrease. This delayed treatment effect occurred despite the fact the adolescents were older (i.e., 14 years of age, on

Table 2: Clinic-based family therapy with school contacts.

Author & date	Ss	Research design	TX	Measures
5. Bry, Conboy, and Bisgay (1986)	Three adolescents (15–16 years old) identified by parents due to poor grades, drug use, and family conflict. 100% White middle class. Referred to out-patient clinic.	Multiple baseline single case designs.	Cognitive behavioral family therapy (weekly or bi-weekly) for four months.	– Grades – Time-line follow-back interviews to measure daily drug use before, during and after treatment at 1, 2, 3, 6, 9, and 15 months. – Reasons for drug use and non-use. – Perceptions of school contingencies. – Cigarette and alcohol use s non-targeted control behaviors.
6. Bry and Krinsley (1992)	Four adolescents (14–16 years old) 75% boys; 25% girls 75% White; 25% Hispanic. Upper middle-to lower class. Referred to out-patient clinic or school-based intervention.	Multiple baseline single-case designs.	Cognitive behavioral family therapy for five to eight months plus booster sessions at 1, 3, and 6 months following end of treatment.	– Grades point average – Time-line follow-back interviews to measure daily drug and alcohol use

Table 2: Continued

Data analysis	Results	Conclusions
5. Comparison of graphs of ongoing behaviors pre-, during and post-treatment. Contrasting changes in target behaviors with those in non-target behaviors.	– Grade and drug data show improvement from pre-intervention to end of follow-up period. – Non-target behaviors were relatively unaffected. – During follow-up, problem behaviors re-occurred temporarily then improved.	1. Family problem-solving generalized beyond training and decreased drug use and school failure. 2. Delayed responses occurred in all three students in 4 of 6 problem behaviors. 3. Recurrences of problem behaviors occurred temporarily after treatment termination.
6. Comparison of baseline with graphs of ongoing measures during and after intervention.	– All students had fewer drug use and alcohol days at end of intervention. – 1 student w/o booster session increased use at end of follow-up. – 3 students with booster sessions showed temporary increase but eventually decreased use during booster sessions and follow-up to lower than baseline.	1. Academic performance increased and alcohol and drug abuse decreased during follow-up if booster sessions had been provided.

average) in the family therapy study than in the school-based intervention study, suggesting that participant age has less to do with the delayed treatment effects than the actual length of treatment and follow-up. Moreover, for the family intervention, outcome effects were seen in adolescent drug use, with decreases observed during follow-up after treatment. These two studies demonstrate that the effects of an intervention designed to impact family risk factors may generalize to impact adolescents' substance use and school failure, and underscore the importance of a parental component in interventions intended to address school and drug use problems among teens.

The family therapy studies also in part address questions about which processes of the multi-component intervention are likely to be most important. Because these studies focused on the parental and family components, they suggest that increasing parental components may increase preventive effects on adolescent drug and alcohol use. Nonetheless, the appearance of an iatrogenic effect in these studies (i.e., initial increases in problem behaviors) continues to raise questions about what components of the intervention are sufficient for more successful outcomes. In addition, while the impact of family therapy generalized to adolescent substance use, these studies raise questions about what therapeutic processes may best facilitate such generalization. In order to begin to address these questions, Bry and colleagues subsequently conducted two process studies to evaluate the therapists' role in successful family therapy.

Experimental Therapeutic Process Studies

These single-case studies focused on two strategies that can be used to increase family problem solving: (a) reinforcing solution statements that are generated by the family in response to one of their problems; and (b) generating exceptions questions when the family is discussing an instance when the identified adolescent patient is exhibiting negative behaviors (i.e., the therapist asks the family to come up with instances in which the adolescent is exhibiting positive behaviors) (Sternberg & Bry, 1994; Melidonis & Bry, 1995) (see Table 3).

Both of the therapist strategies that were studied resulted in an increase in solution suggestions and/or a decrease in blaming statements. These positive family behaviors ceased to occur, however, as soon as the therapists stopped implementing the experimental strategies. Thus, one of the enduring challenges remains how to promote the generalization of positive family behaviors outside the therapeutic setting so that extinction does not occur quickly after removal of the treatment. Perhaps the explicit repetitions of these therapeutic strategies during booster sessions at the end of treatment could prevent extinction of these positive family problem-solving habits that are negatively correlated with school and drug problems in adolescents.

School- and Family-based Adolescent Intervention

Bry's studies summarized in the foregoing demonstrate that both school-based intervention and clinic-based family intervention can be effective in addressing substance use and

Table 3: Experimental therapeutic process studies.

Author & date	Ss	Research design	TX	Measures
7. Sternberg and Bry (1994)	Three families with parent–adolescent conflict, self-referred to outpatient clinic. 100% White.	ABABA single-case multiple baseline designs	10–12 sessions of cognitive behavioral family therapy during which therapist alternated between verbally reinforcing client solution statements and not reinforcing them.	– Number of solution suggestions each session – (Home) Conflict Behavior Questionnaire each week
8. Melidonis and Bry (1995)	Four families with adolescent school and behavioral problems. Ethnically diverse.	Single-case ABA multiple baseline reversal designs.	The first two sessions of cognitive behavioral family therapy, during which the therapist alternated between asking questions about exceptions to adolescent behavior problems vs not asking them.	– Number of blaming statements made during the session. – Number of positive statements made during the session.

Table 3: Continued

Data analysis	Results	Conclusions
7. Friedman two-way ANOVA on families' mean number of solution suggestions per session during each of five experimental conditions. Significance tests on slopes of weekly Family conflict ratings	– Experimental conditions affected number of solution suggestions made during sessions. – Two of three families had significant reduction in weekly conflict at home during treatment.	1. Therapist reinforcement of solution suggestions during sessions increased solution suggestions by family. 2. Level of conflict at home as revealed by CBQ decreased as treatment progressed for two families.
8. Friedman two-way ANOVA on blaming statements across conditions Friedman two-way ANOVA on positive statements across conditions.	– Mean blaming statements varied significantly across conditions. – Mean positive statements varied significantly across experimental conditions.	1. Exception statements reduced negative communication and increased positive communication in families with adolescent problems during therapy sessions.

related problems among teens. A logical next step was to test an intervention that combined school-based and family-based interventions in an attempt to increase intervention effects.

Two studies were conducted that tested the effectiveness of the combined school- and family-based cognitive behavioral interventions (see Table 4). Krinsley (1991) compared the school-based-only intervention with a combined school-based and family-based intervention. All of the typical components and foci of Bry's interventions were included. In the first condition, weekly conferences were held with each of the students' teachers to monitor students' progress and to collect information about teacher expectations. In addition, students were assigned mentors who worked with them individually in school on a weekly basis towards goals defined in behavioral terms. In the combined school-based and family-based condition, students received all of the benefits of the school intervention, as well as home-based family therapy. The family therapy focused on problem-solving techniques and helping parents to develop contingency plans that could reinforce positive school behaviors and booster sessions. The interventions were conducted over a five-month period, and booster sessions continued during a second school year.

The results of Krinsley's study indicated that prevention of further school failure was effected by the combined interventions, and there were generalization effects on early substance use. No drug use was initiated or increased among adolescents in the combined intervention during their two school years in the study. These results support Bry's risk factor hypothesis (Bry, 1983), which posits that reducing risk factors, such as school failure, decreases the probability of drug use. If such a connection can be replicated, improving school performance could represent an effective strategy for the secondary prevention of drug use among youth who are beginning to exhibit problems with school, conduct, and drug use.

The second study, conducted by Alexander (1997), was a replication of the Krinsley study with African Americans. It compared one year of the combined targeted family and school intervention with no intervention. (An additional component involving parent support groups was planned, but was not attended by parents.) Students in the combined school and family intervention demonstrated significant reductions in serious school outcomes in comparison with the no-intervention comparison group. Some of the substance abuse risk factors that were seen in the no-intervention group and not seen in the combined intervention group were: (a) having to repeat a year in school; (b) being "socially promoted;" (c) being absent from school 35 days more one year than the previous year; and (d) a reduction in grade point average of more than 15 out of 100 points.

Conclusions and Future Directions

Over the past 20 years, Bry, her colleagues, and her students have developed and tested different aspects of a comprehensive intervention designed to prevent or reduce alcohol and substance abuse in adolescents by targeting preliminary academic problems and conduct problems. This strategy has been fruitful for several reasons. First, it is addressing problems with their own direct negative trajectories (e.g., school dropout, subsequent unemployment, delinquency, and criminal behavior). Second, Bry and colleagues have

Table 4: School- and family-based adolescent intervention.

Author & date	Ss	Research design	TX	Measures
9. Krinsley (1991)	29 teens (12–15 years old) 64% boys; 36% girls; 82% White; 18% Black or Latino. Identified by school due to school and behavioral problems. Lower- and working-class backgrounds.	Component design randomly assigned	School versus combined family- and school-based cognitive behavioral interventions for two to five months plus booster sessions.	– Quarterly report cards – Attendance records – Conflict Behavior Questionnaire – Time-line follow-back interviews to measure daily alcohol and drug use
10. Alexander (1997)	40 students (12–15 years old) 47.5% boys; 52.5% girls; 92.5% Black; 5% Latino; 2.5% Asian-American. Low-income backgrounds.	Intervention vs. matched no-intervention comparison	Combined family- and school-based cognitive behavioral intervention for one academic year	– Grades – Attendance and tardiness records – Discipline referral records – Serious school problems

Table 4: Continued

Data analysis	Results	Conclusions
9. Repeated-measures ANOVA, Mann–Whitney U and chi-square tests.	– Significant difference in alcohol and drug use between the groups during 15-month follow-up. – Significant difference between the groups in grades during 15-month follow-up. – No student who received combined family and school intervention initiated or increased alcohol and drug use during the study.	1. Combined school and family intervention can reduce school failure and early adolescent alcohol and drug use.
10. Chi-square and t-test comparisons of treatment group with control group on dependent measures.	– Significant difference in number of serious school problems in combined intervention group compared to no-intervention comparison group.	1. Combined family- and school-based cognitive behavioral intervention reduced serous school problems among minority middle-school youth.

shown addressing these problems prevents (a) increases in drug and alcohol problems for those who have already begun drug and alcohol use and (b) early initiation for those students who have not begun drug and alcohol use. Third, these studies clearly show that a risk-focused approach is useful even in the absence of clear knowledge of the etiology of substance use problems in adolescents. The efforts toward uncovering etiology are no doubt complicated by the hetergeneous nature of multiple substance abuse etiologies that act differently on different individuals (Bry, 1996; Bry, McKeon & Pandina, 1982; Hawkins, Catalano & Miller, 1992). Fourth, Bry's studies also provide support for the importance of intervening at the level of the school, parent, and individual in order for positive effects to be generated for the adolescent in terms of school achievement and appropriate conduct behaviors.

Bry has completed several studies investigating the family and parental components of her intervention. The studies have clearly provided evidence in support of the advantages of combining family and school interventions. However, it remains unclear what components of substance abuse intervention are sufficient for lasting treatment gains. Bry's intervention targets improvement of problem-solving skills and the development of reinforcement contingency programs that are protective against adolescent problem behaviors, but it is still unknown what is the best way to prevent extinction effects at the end of therapy. Including booster sessions is one possible option, and this deserves further investigation.

Another idea that was tested was the addition of parent group meetings that addressed a variety of parenting issues and allowed parents to exchange information and acquire parental allies and supports for the difficult role of parenting. The true effects of such an addition could not be adequately assessed, however, because parents who were used to home-based treatment did not take advantage of the parent meetings, which were held at a venue outside their homes. Potential obstacles could have included access to the meetings, need for child care, overwhelming family responsibilities, or failure to understand the relevancy of parent meetings when one is already receiving family therapy. If these obstacles could be addressed, subsequent tests could be conducted in order to learn if parent group meetings further enhance positive student outcomes.

Finally, the intervention does not directly address drug use issues. It is primarily focused on the risk factors, as well as the cognitive behavioral strategy of promoting alternative positive behaviors that are incompatible with the targeted negative behavior(s). Taken together, the studies indicate that this strategy can yield positive outcomes that are substantial. A remaining question, however, is whether the intervention would be stronger if drug and alcohol use were addressed directly. Further studies are needed.

In conclusion, Bry's intervention represents one of the most effective secondary prevention programs for adolescent alcohol and substance use. It is very comprehensive, including both school-based and family-based interventions. The field still has a long way to go in uncovering all of the mechanisms involved in the etiology of substance abuse, but we cannot wait until we know all of the mechanisms before intervening into the lives of young people whom we know are at risk for substance abuse. The intervention represents one evidence-based way of addressing substance use and abuse among adolescents.

References

Alexander, A. S. (1997), "The impact of behavioral family therapy on early adolescent problems: Replication and an attempt to enhance outcome through neighborhood parent meetings." Unpublished Master's thesis, Graduate School, New Brunswick, Rutgers, the State University of New Jersey.

Bien, N. Z., & Bry, B. H. (1980), "An experimentally designed comparison of four intensities of school-based prevention programs for adolescents with adjustment problems." *Journal of Community Psychology 8*, 110–116.

Bry, B. H. (1982), "Reducing the incidence of adolescent problems through preventive intervention: One- and five-year follow-up." *American Journal of Community Psychology 10*(3), 265–276.

Bry, B. H. (1983), "Empirical foundations of family-based approaches to adolescent substance abuse." In T. J. Glynn, C. G. Leukefeld & J. P. Ludford (eds), *Preventing Adolescent Drug Abuse: Intervention strategies* (Research Monograph No. 47). Rockville, MD: National Institute on Drug Abuse, 154–171.

Bry, B. H. (1996), "Psychological approaches to prevention." In W. K. Bickel & R. J. DeGrandpre (eds), *Drug Policy and Human Nature: Psychological perspectives on prevention, management, and treatment of illicit drug abuse.* New York, NY: Plenum Press, 55–76.

Bry, B. H., Conboy, C., & Bisgay, K. (1986), "Decreasing adolescent drug use and school failure: Long-term effects of targeted family problem-solving training." *Child & Family Behavior Therapy 18*(1), 43–59.

Bry, B. H., & George, F. E. (1979), "Evaluating and improving prevention programs: A strategy from drug abuse." *Evaluation and Program Planning 2*, 127–136.

Bry, B. H., & George, F. E. (1980), "The preventive effects of early intervention on the attendance and grades of urban adolescents." *Professional Psychology 11*, 252–260.

Bry, B. H., Greene, D. M., Schutte, C., & Fishman, C. (1989), *Targeted Family Intervention: Procedures manual* (available from first author, GSAPP, Rutgers University, 152 Frelinghuysen Road, Piscataway, NJ 08854-8085).

Bry, B. H., & Krinsley, K. E. (1990), "Adolescent substance abuse." In E. L. Feindler & G. R. Kalfus (eds), *Casebook in Adolescent Behavior Therapy.* New York: Springer Publishing Company, 275–302.

Bry, B. H., & Krinsley, K. E. (1992), "Booster sessions and long-term effects of behavioral family therapy on adolescent substance use and school performance." *Journal of Behavior & Experimental Psychiatry 23*(3), 183–189.

Bry, B. H., McKeon, P., & Pandina, R. J. (1982), "Extent of drug use as a function of number of risk factors." *Journal of Abnormal Psychology 91*(4), 273–279.

Dishion, T. J., & Andrews, D. W. (1995), "Preventing escalation in problem behaviors with high-risk young adolescents: Immediate and 1-year outcomes." *Journal of Consulting and Clinical Psychology 63*, 538–548.

Greene, D. M., & Bry, B. H. (1991), "A descriptive analysis of family discussions about everyday problems and decisions." *The Analysis of Verbal Behavior 9*, 29–39.

Harachi, T. W., Ayers, C. D., Hawkins, J. D., & Catalano, R. F. (1996), Empowering communities to prevent adolescent substance abuse: Process evaluation results from a risk- and protection-focused community mobilization effort." *The Journal of Primary Prevention 16*(3), 233–254.

Hawkins, J. D., Catalano, R. F., & Miller, J. Y. (1992), "Risk and protective factors for alcohol and other drug problems in adolescence and early adulthood: Implications for substance abuse prevention." *Psychological Bulletin 112*(1), 64–105.

Johnston, L. D., O'Malley, P. M., & Bachman, J. G. (1996), *National Survey Results on Drug Use from the Monitoring the Future Study, 1975–1995, Vol. 1, Secondary school students*. Rockville, MD: National Institute on Drug Abuse.

Krinsley, K. E. (1991), "Behavioral therapy for adolescent school problems: School performance effects and generalization to substance use." *Dissertation Abstracts International 52*, 1725B.

Krinsley, K. E., & Bry, B. H. (1991), "Sequential analysis of adolescent, mother, and father behaviors in distressed and nondistressed families." *Child & Family Behavior Therapy 13*(4), 45–62.

Melidonis, G. G., & Bry, B. H. (1995), "Effects of therapist exceptions questions on blaming and positive statements in families with adolescent behavior problems." *Journal of Family Psychology 9*(4), 451–457.

Newcomb, M. D., Maddahian, E., & Bentler, P. M. (1986), "Risk factors for drug use among adolescents: Concurrent and longitudional analyses." *Journal of Public Health 76*, 525–531.

Spoth, R., Seongmo, Y., Kahn, J. H., & Redmond, C. (1996), "A model of the effects of protective parent and peer factors on young adolescent alcohol refusal skills." *The Journal of Primary Prevention 16*(4), 373–394.

Stanley, H., Goldstein, A., & Bry, B. H. (1976), *Program Manual for the Early Secondary Intervention Prevention* (available from third author, GSAPP, Rutgers University, 152 Frelinghuysen Road, Piscataway, NJ 08854-8085).

Sternberg, J. A., & Bry, B. H. (1994), "Solution generation and family conflict over time in problem-solving therapy with families of Adolescents: The impact of therapist behavior." *Child & Family Behavior Therapy 16*(4), 1–23.

Whittaker, S., & Bry, B. H. (1991). Overt and covert parental conflict and adolescent problems: Observed marital interaction in clinic and nonclinic families. *Adolescence, 26* (104), 865–875.

Chapter 6

An Ecological Approach to Family Intervention for Adolescent Substance Use

Thomas J. Dishion and Kathryn Kavanagh*

Introduction

The Ecological Rationale

The use of substances by young adolescents is associated with heightened risk for drug abuse by young adulthood (Robins & Pryzabeck, 1985), as well as multiple negative consequences, such as marital, work, and educational failures (Kandel, Davies, Karus & Yamaguchi, 1986). Hawkins, Catalano, and Miller (1992) provide a comprehensive review of the variety of risk factors associated with adolescent substance use, including risk at the individual, peer, family, and community levels. The risk factor typology offered by Hawkins et al. suggests that intervention, in order to be most effective, should take into account individual-level factors, as well as the broader social ecology.

Considerable evidence suggests that family management practices are central to multi-level risk identified in previous research (Bry, 1993; Dishion, 1996; DeMarsh & Kumpfer, 1985; Hawkins et al., 1992). The literature on the development of adolescent problem behavior emphasizes the role of parenting as both a direct and indirect effect (see Figure 1). Competent family management skills reduce negative family interactions and improve poor parent-child relationships (Dishion, Capaldi & Yoerger, 1999; Patterson, 1982; Patterson, Reid & Dishion, 1992). In particular, caregiver monitoring and supervision serve as a protective factor against associations with deviant peers, and more seriously, the influences of substance-using peers and siblings (Dishion, Capaldi, Spracklen & Li, 1995; Dishion & Loeber, 1985).

Persistent disruption of family management is associated with children's early display of antisocial behavior (Loeber & Dishion, 1983; McCord, McCord & Howard, 1960). Some hypothesize that antisocial behavior in childhood provides a basis for accumulative risk asso-

*This project was supported by grant DA 07031 from the National Institute on Drug Abuse at the National Institutes of Health to the first author, by grant MH 46690 from the National Institute of Mental Health to John Reid, Ph.D., and by grant MH 37940 from the National Institute of Mental Health to Gerald R. Patterson, Ph.D.

Correspondence regarding this research may be addressed to Thomas J. Dishion, Ph.D., Child and Family Center, Department of Psychology, 195 West 12th Avenue, Eugene, OR 97401–3408; phone (541) 346–4805, fax (541) 346–4858; email tomd@darkwing.uoregon.edu

Innovations in Adolescent Substance Abuse Interventions, pages 127–142.
ISBN: 0-08-043577-7

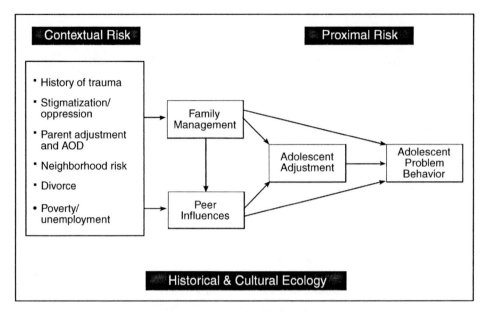

Figure 1: The ecology of parent influence.

ciated with peer rejection, poor academic skills, and eventual involvement in a deviant peer group (Dishion, Patterson, Stoolmiller & Skinner, 1991; Patterson *et al.*, 1992). Consistently, poor monitoring and involvement with deviant peers have been found to be the proximal factors associated with early onset adolescent substance use (Dishion *et al.*, 1995).

An ecological viewpoint also necessitates broadening our lens of understanding to consider the contexts that might impact proximal family and peer effects (Bronfenbrenner, 1989). The literature is replete with evidence on the multiple risk factors that can disrupt parental functioning (see Figure 1). We know that poverty (Conger *et al.*, 1992; Elder, Caspi & Van Nguyen, 1985), marital discord (Hetherington & Clingempeel, 1992), and parental substance use (Chassin, Presson & Sherman, 1990; Dishion, Reid & Patterson, 1988) disrupt family management. Additionally, oppression that results in lack of resources and stigmatization (McLoyd, 1990) can be a major family risk factor.

The role of parenting practices in protecting youth from contextual risks suggests family-centered interventions as a promising prevention target (Dishion, 1996). Intervention outcome literature provides a strong rationale for family-centered interventions. Family-based intervention strategies are effective in reducing the antecedents for adolescent substance use and other problem behavior. They also reduce early oppositional problems in the preschool years (Webster-Stratton, 1984), antisocial behavior in middle childhood (Patterson, 1974; Patterson, Dishion & Chamberlain, 1993), and problem behavior and substance use in early adolescence (Dishion, Andrews, Kavanagh & Soberman, 1996; Henggeler *et al.*, 1986). The empirical literature supports the importance of considering family factors in developing interventions for youth with substance use problems.

The vast majority of children in the United States attend school up to the age 13–14. More-over, schools serve as convenient meeting places for deviant peer groups (Dishion, Duncan,

Eddy, Fagot & Fetrow, 1994; Kellam, 1990; Rutter, 1985). Attending to the school environment, as well as family dynamics, may be necessary to effect comprehensive change in high-risk behavior in children (Patterson, 1974). Following an ecological model, it is critical to embed family interventions within influential social contexts (Biglan, 1995). Preventive intervention programs need to "consider schools as potential sites for service delivery, as well as potential objects of intervention activity" (Trickett & Birman, 1989, p. 361).

Enhancing communication and cooperation between parents and school staff can drastically impact parents' potential for monitoring, limit-setting, and supporting academic progress (Gottfredson, Gottfredson & Hybl, 1993; Reid, 1993). Simply increasing specific information to parents regarding their child's attendance, homework, and class behavior results in improved monitoring and support for at-risk children's academic and social success (Blechman, Taylor & Schrader, 1981; Heller & Fantuzzo, 1993).

Interventions directed at engaging parents in changing their practices should be comprehensive and responsive to the developmental history of the child and family. Two key issues toward this end are: (a) titrating the level of need (the risk status of the child) to the level of support provided to parents; and (b) integrating diverse intervention levels to maximize and support protective parenting practices in a community setting (Dishion & Kavanagh, in press).

Adolescent Transitions Program

The Adolescent Transitions Program (ATP) is a multilevel family-centered intervention delivered in the school setting (Dishion & Kavanagh, in press). This is a multilevel approach, best described as a *tiered* strategy, with each level of intervention building on the previous level. Using traditional nomenclature, the three levels represent "universal," "selected," and "indicated" family interventions. Universal reaches all parents within a school setting, selected addresses the needs of at-risk families, and indicated is best described as family treatment. The model is displayed in Figure 2.

For the remainder of the chapter, we will provide an overview of each intervention level, the ingredients of which address pragmatic, as well as research issues of implementing family-centered interventions within a school setting.

Universal: The Family Resource Room. The first step in establishing family-based services in a school setting is creating a Family Resource Room (FRR). At least one room is needed, preferably with enough space to display a variety of video, audio, and written material. The FRR should provide a comfortable and private meeting place for caregivers and school personnel. Optimally, the FRR should be staffed by a fulltime family counselor, psychologist, or social worker, with training in family-based interventions and school practices.

The goals of the FRR are to: (a) establish an infrastructure for collaboration between school staff and parents; (b) support norms for protective parenting practices; and (c) disseminate information that encourages family management practices that promote school success to prevent the development of early onset alcohol and other drug use. The FRR also provides the vehicle through which a program of multilevel interventions can be

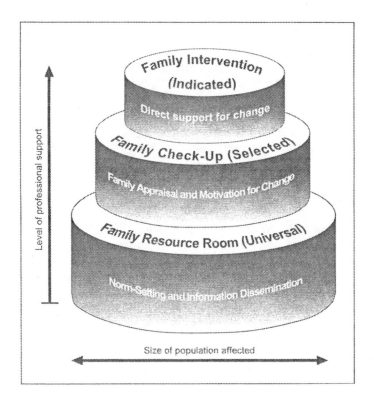

Figure 2: A multilevel model for parenting interventions within a school ecology.

offered throughout the school year. Several strategies can be used to reach out to parents at the universal level.

An effective method for promoting proactive identification of problems is a "Plan for the Coming Year," which can be done in the family home during the summer. The plan includes a review of the previous school year, using checklists to self-assess competencies and problem areas in study skills, peer relations, drug use, attendance, and cooperative and respectful behaviors toward others. This sets the stage for making family change, as well as maintaining successful strategies throughout the school year.

Making the plan is a cooperative meeting between FRR staff and the parents, with each walking away with identified goals. In our ongoing prevention trial, approximately 60 percent of our intervention parents proactively took the opportunity to make a plan. FRR staff report that this collaborative effort sets a good foundation for later work with families.

Another particularly promising tool, also involving parent self-assessment, uses video-tape examples and a simple pencil-and-paper rating form. "Parenting in the Teenage Years" (Dishion & Kavanagh, 1995) was developed to help parents identify observable risk factors in the context of parent-child interaction. The videotape (designed to be viewed by parents during the first week of school) presents examples of teen risk behavior.

It also focuses on the use of effective family management skills (positive reinforcement, monitoring, limit-setting, and relationship skills) to facilitate parents' evaluation of their own level of risk, as well as their child's level of risk.

A third intervention at the universal level, which should occur during the fall term, is a six-week health curriculum (Success, Health, and Peace Curriculum [SHAPe]; see Dishion & Kavanagh, in press) delivered by the FRR staff. The classes include weekly parent–child exercises related to promoting school success, reduced substance use, and reduced conflict (see Figure 3). For maximal engagement, students are graded for completing the assignments with parents. Weekly newsletters summarize information from classes and family activities and provide additional information regarding family norms and practices that promote teenagers' social and academic success. Families may also work through the curriculum exercises on public access television to extend the impact of the program. Underlying this intervention strategy is the use of competent parents within the community to provide and model norms and values of protective parenting practices. This approach is consistent with the basic principle of effective community intervention: build on the strengths within the community (Kelly, 1988).

The FRR may also serve as a nexus of home–school communication by providing parents with weekly information regarding homework, problem situations, and resources within the school. For example, a daily message from school enhances parents' awareness of homework assignments and classroom activities relevant to their child. The FRR can also be a resource to school staff wanting to develop effective strategies for positive collaborative relationships with parents. Figure 4 summarizes the universal services provided by the FRR.

Selected: The Family Check-Up. The Family Check-Up is a selected intervention offering family assessment and professional support and motivation to change. As described by Dishion and Kavanagh (in press), it is an in-depth method that assists parents in accurately appraising their child's risk status and provides parenting resources for reducing risk factors and promoting adjustment. The Family Check-Up, based on motivational interviewing by Miller and Rollnick (1991), is a three-session intervention: (a) the initial interview, (b) a comprehensive multi-agent, multimethod assessment, and (c) a family feedback session, using motivational skills to encourage maintenance of current positive practices and change of disruptive practices.

Focusing on the process of family intervention is an ongoing research problem. Over the years, innovative family intervention researchers have suggested that providing feedback to parents from the findings of psychological assessments is conducive to change (Sanders & Lawton, 1993). The critical feature of such feedback is that it be presented in a supportive and motivating manner.

The optimal condition for building parent motivation is self-identification. This typically occurs when parents come to the FRR because of concerns about their adolescents' adjustment at home or at school. A second motivation-enhancing opportunity occurs when parents are notified of discipline problems in the school. FRR staff should be part of school staffing committees, in order to catch problems early and make recommendations for family intervention, as opposed to child intervention, which is typical of schools.

Lastly, when FRR personnel have become part of a school staff, teachers, counselors, or administrators may proactively refer a child when they begin to have concerns over

The SHAPe* Curriculum

❶ SCHOOL SUCCESS

    Student: Setting goals for school success.

    Parent: Reinforcing homework completion.

❷ HEALTH DECISIONS

    Student: Setting norms for healthy behavior.

    Parent: Limit-setting on tobacco and other drug use.

❸ AVOIDING NEGATIVE PEER PRESSURE

    Student: Discriminating healthy from unhealthy peer activities.

    Parent: Parent monitoring of child activities with peers.

❹ GETTING AND GIVING RESPECT

    Student: Identify the cycle of respect.

    Parent: Promoting respect and handling disrespect in families.

❺ HANDLING STRONG FEELINGS

    Student: Discuss warning signs of anger and strategies for handling anger constructively.

    Parent: Discuss and share positive strategies for dealing with anger in the family.

❻ SOLVING PROBLEMS PEACEFULLY

    Student: Three steps to resolving conflict peacefully.

    Parent: Three steps to resolving family conflict peacefully.

*Success, Health, and Peace

Figure 3: SHAPe Curriculum outline.

Family Resource Room Services

- Parent-focused school orientation (self-check, books, and videos)

- Media on effective parenting and norms

- Classroom-based parent-child exercises that support family management practices

- Communication of specific information to parents about attendance, behavior, and completion of assignments

---

Figure 4: Family Resource Room services.

behavior, peer associations, or emotional adjustment. To promote parent engagement, it is best to have school personnel recommend the Family Check-Up as a way to gather more information about the school's concerns and an opportunity to address any concerns the parents may have about their adolescents' well-being.

In any intervention setting, there are two interrelated issues when working with parents to support family management and change of maladaptive practice—therapeutic process and focus. An extensive literature exists, beginning with the seminal work of Carl Rogers (1957), on key therapist behaviors considered to be the basic ingredients of good process in any helping intervention. During the 1980s, our colleagues at Oregon Social Learning Center began to study client "resistance" in behavior family therapy. In a series of studies, Patterson and colleagues (Chamberlain, Patterson, Reid, Forgatch & Kavanagh, 1984; Patterson & Chamberlain, 1994; Patterson & Forgatch, 1985) found that teaching and confrontation actually *elicited* resistance to change, whereas support, reframing, and questioning were more *conducive* to change. This body of work forms the basis for the motivational interviewing component of the Family Check-Up.

In a preliminary study of factors related to which family, peer, or school factors were predictive of which parents chose feedback, different predictors were found for different levels of child risk (Kavanagh, Dishion, Medici Skaggs & Schneiger, 1998).

At the moderate risk level, children of participants had higher grades and lower teacher-identified risk factors, compared to non-participants in the Family Check-Up. At the high level of child risk, parents who participated in feedback sessions had children with significantly more deviant peer associations. These findings, while preliminary, suggest that the feedback may function as a preventive tool for children within the moderate risk range. For parents of children with more serious risk factors, such as antisocial behavior and substance use, they may be seeking intervention against deviant peers, an area where parents feel the least knowledgeable and effective.

In studying the role of feedback in intervention outcome of the ATP curriculum effectiveness, the authors provided feedback to parents prior to the first ATP intervention session. Weekly parent reports of child behavior problems were examined for those who "responded" to the parent focus intervention, compared with those who did not. Immediate change suggested that the feedback session was a significant factor. Parent reports of child substance use changed dramatically by the fourth session for those who responded (see Figure 5). Patterson (1979) also found a similarly timed effect on the rate of children's observed aggressive behavior in the home. Because of this, we identified the Family Check-Up as the key component of a selected intervention that targets parenting practices.

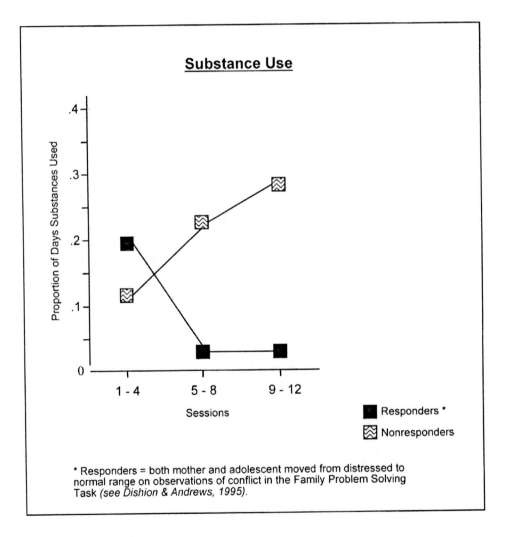

Figure 5: Reductions in substance use during parent group treatment.

Rao (1998) examined the impact of the Family Check-Up in a study involving 40 high-risk families who were randomly assigned to a Family Check-Up intervention or a wait-list control. The analysis revealed that, following the Family Check-Up, parents reported substantial reductions in their child's behavior problems, as well as improvements in their own parenting practices. Similar trends were noted for teacher- and youth-report of behavior problems. The wait-list control group parents, by contrast, did not perceive changes in their children's behavior or their own parenting practices. In addition, parental report of change in parenting was correlated with changes in the child's behavior. These initial findings fit within a body of literature that supports research-based interventions for families (Dishion, in press; Dishion & Patterson, 1992; Patterson *et al.*, 1993).

In addition to finding main effects for the brief Family Check-Up on parent reports of parenting and young adolescent problem behavior, Rao (1998) also documented the process of change. She found therapist adherence to the FRAMES model (Miller & Rollnick, 1991), for therapist–client interaction during the feedback session to be associated with parental reports of improvement, which in turn, correlated with changes in the adolescents' problem behaviors.

Indicated: A Menu of Services. The indicated level of intervention provides direct professional support to parents. These services may include brief family interventions, parent groups, behavioral family therapy, and/or case management services. Following this tiered strategy, families at the indicated level completed the Family Check-Up and received information from the family counselor regarding risk factors for serious problem behaviors and early onset substance use. Additionally, parents were given information regarding the importance of parenting as a protective factor that enhances motivation and collaboration. This level of intervention incorporates approaches described in several protocols by behavioral, structural, and eclectic family therapists working with problematic adolescents (Bry, McGreene, Schuttle & Fishman, 1991; Dishion & Patterson, 1992; Forehand & McMahon, 1981; Henggeler, Melton & Smith, 1992; Patterson, 1982; Szapocznik & Kurtines, 1989)

The Family Check-Up is designed to promote engagement and motivation at the onset of more intensive interventions. However, parents often come to the indicated level of intervention with the attitude that they are seen as deficient. Frequently a teacher, physician, or other extra-familial person recommends getting help, which is usually not conducive to parental engagement. Not surprisingly, in a comparison of self- and agency-referred parents, Chamberlain *et al.* (1984) found a significantly higher level of resistance from agency-referred parents.

Making changes within a family is a highly personal and challenging process. When change is necessary, support is often helpful to maintain the commitment to the change process, to guide parents with the appropriate focus, or to target realistic change goals. The model guiding our work with parents is simplistic: family management practices can protect children against risk, or when improved, can provide a context for child and family healing.

Given this model, our menu of intervention options is grounded in family management practices. However, as discussed in other areas of counseling and clinical psychology (Miller & Rollnick, 1991), it is motivating to the change process to have a variety of

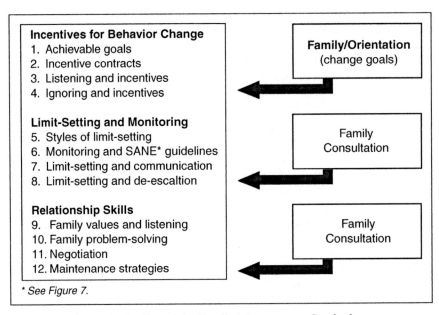

Figure 6: Outline of the Family Management Curriculum.

intervention options. Based on a curriculum for support and skill development in parenting, the Family Management Curriculum (see Figure 6), derived from over 30 years of research, was originally designed to work with individual families (Patterson, Reid, Jones & Conger, 1975) to support parents' efforts to reduce problem behavior (Forehand & McMahon, 1981; Patterson, 1974; Wahler, Winkel, Peterson & Morrison, 1965). We have adapted this content to a curriculum format for group work with parents.

A school monitoring service is a common intervention that parents come to proactively. It is consistent with parents supporting their children in building strong academic and social skills at school, as well as preventing the development of problem behaviors. This service helps develop a strong connection between home and school and provides a weekly telephone summary of attendance, behavior in class, and homework completion. Such telephone contacts have been enhanced by voice-mail technology.

To increase parents' use of family management skills, and to minimize punitive coercive discipline, the home-school monitoring system is made available to parents, contingent upon their attendance at a minimum of two parent-training sessions—one prior to using the system and the second several weeks later to refine and clarify skills. These training sessions focus on teaching parents how to develop good daily practices, provide incentives for positive school weeks, and develop effective communication with school staff about school problems.

There are a number of advantages and disadvantages for working with families in a group format. Most noteworthy of the advantages is cost-effectiveness and social support. We found that group work is especially viable when using videotapes of parenting behavior. These videos provided positive models for parenting, as well as stimulating constructive group discussions of parenting. Single parents and stepfamilies especially enjoyed the group format when other families also shared experiences.

A noteworthy disadvantage of group work is that group process, on occasion, can be difficult. For example, some parents use the group to put forth their personal agenda, resulting in other parents' disengagement. Also, it is difficult to address individual concerns of families, especially if emotions are intense (e.g., a family undergoing divorce, parent–child conflicts, parent recovery issues).

Overall, we recommend group work with parents when possible. The advantages outweigh the disadvantages, especially within school-based models where professional resources are limited and groups can facilitate networking of parents to counter negative peer processes. Brief consultations with families can be used to improve individual focus when doing group work.

The Family Management Curriculum. The Family Management Curriculum provides detailed suggestions of how to conduct a 12-session parent group with a family management focus, including exercises, rationales, role plays, and forms for each session (Dishion, Biglan, Kavanagh, Metzler & Soberman, in press). It also serves as a template for individual work with families, including brief, focused intervention and more extended individual work, such as social interactional family therapy (see Forgatch & Patterson, 1998).

There are three broad foci in the Family Management Curriculum: (a) using incentives to promote positive behavior change; (b) limit-setting and monitoring; and (c) family communication and problem-solving. The first phase utilizes positive reinforcement programs to increase specific behaviors, such as cooperating with parent requests or doing homework. Well-used incentives can have a dramatic effect on reducing problem behavior and result in a more positive family atmosphere. This is also the first step in supporting the parents as leaders in the behavior change process.

Second, we work with parents on limit-setting and monitoring regarding articulation of rules (e.g., "come home directly after school," "avoid unsupervised homes"). Limits are useless unless parents are willing to follow through with consequences. We promote the "SANE" guidelines for limit-setting, which are presented in Figure 7 and described in greater detail in Dishion and Kavanagh (in press) and Dishion and Patterson (1996).

The last, but most important, component of the Family Management Curriculum is relationship skills, which include basic communication skills (e.g., listening), problem-solving, and negotiation. We turn to relationship skills last to avoid regressing into more conflict in families struggling with family management issues. Relationship skills are not as useful when the source of conflict (cooperating with parents, school failure, and so forth) is ongoing.

We offer the Family Management Curriculum as a template for parent interventions. However, flexible adaptation is required to optimize the benefit to parents and families of different educational, economic, and cultural conditions.

There is a body of literature that supports a focus on parenting in interventions to reduce risk factors for early onset substance use (see Dishion, 1996). In our original components analysis of ATP (Dishion & Andrews, 1995), we found immediate effects for parent

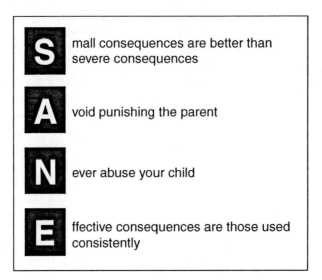

Figure 7: SANE guidelines to limit-setting.

groups guided by the Family Management Curriculum (formerly referred to as Parent Focus). First, as can be seen in Table 1, we found reductions in observations of parent–child conflict in videotaped problem-solving tasks. Second, teachers rated the high-risk boys and girls in the group, who received only family-centered services, as less antisocial at school. Third, Dishion *et al.* (1996) reported reduced substance use within the year following involvement with ATP, in particular, early onset tobacco use.

These findings have recently been replicated by another group of intervention researchers. They, too, document reduced levels of antisocial behavior and improved parenting practices among parents of high-risk adolescents living in rural settings (Irvine, Biglan, Metzler, Ary & Smolkowski, 1999). These findings are consistent with a body of literature on family-centered intervention approaches to preventing or reducing adolescent substance use (for reviews, Dishion, 1996; Henggeler *et al.*, 1986; Patterson *et al.*, 1993).

The data from our program of research, as well as those of others, suggest that family-centered intervention approaches are an important piece of the prevention–intervention armamentarium. We are currently evaluating the multilevel school-based ATP approach within a prevention trial, where 1200 youth are randomly assigned to ATP or middle school, as usual. As of this writing, multimethod data related to youth risk status has been collected over the middle school years from youth, parents, and teachers. This data will allow us to better understand the utility of the FRR model of tiered intervention for affecting reductions in school disaffection and drug use risks.

Summary

The outcome literature consistently supports the use of family intervention to reduce antisocial behavior and adolescent problem behavior (Patterson *et al.*, 1993). A multilevel,

Table 1: Observed Mother and Child Negative Engagement in Family Problem Solving by Intervention Condition and Phase.

Intervention Condition	Baseline		Termination	
	n	M (and SD)	n	M (and SD)
Mother				
Parent only	25	0.63 (0.63)	23	0.39 (0.44)[a]
Teen only	31	0.67 (0.85)	31	0.52 (0.59)[a]
Parent and teen	31	0.56 (0.81)	29	0.46 (0.47)[a]
Self-directed	27	0.49 (0.51)	25	0.56 (0.84)
Control	39	0.62 (0.54)	35	0.90 (0.89)
Child				
Parent only	26	1.27 (1.33)	24	0.81 (0.88)[a]
Teen only	32	1.09 (1.28)	32	0.80 (0.89)[b]
Parent and teen	31	1.33 (1.58)	31	0.93 (1.09)[a]
Self-directed	27	0.78 (0.82)	25	1.06 (1.32)
Control	39	1.22 (1.14)	35	1.36 (1.53)

Note. Scores refer to the rate-per-minute of observed behavior.
[a]Statistically reliable positive intervention effect at termination in contrast to controls.
[b]Statistically marginal ($p < .10$) intervention effect in contrast to controls.

tiered strategy for organizing such services is recommended to parents in school settings. To reach high-risk parents (and maximize effectiveness), intervention services must be embedded within the school context. For the future, we hope that school counselor programs will include intensive training on how to work with parents in academic settings.

Until recently, this intervention has been difficult to integrate within a prevention model, primarily because of the expense of the service, but also due to the issue of reaching families in need. Implementation of family intervention within a school setting, however, addresses these issues. Integration of parent interventions into typical parent–school communications, such as homework assignments, parent–teacher conferences, and discipline contacts, is possible.

Integrating the three intervention levels helps address the related problem of identification and motivation to participate. Parents become more aware of the "resources" coming from the FRR staff at the universal level. In the event of risk, a Family Check-Up offers an informed jump-start to the change process, and treatment can build from the focus and motivation supported in that check-up.

References

Biglan, A. (1995), *Changing cultural practices: A contextualist framework for intervention research*. Reno, NV: Context.

Blechman, E. A., Taylor, C. J., & Schrader, S. M. (1981), "Family problem solving versus home notes as early intervention with high-risk children." *Journal of Consulting and Clinical Psychology 49*, 919–926.

Bronfenbrenner, U. (1989), "Ecological systems theory." In P. Vasta (ed.), *Annals of Child Development, Vol. 6. Six theories of child development: Revised formulations and current issues* (pp. 187–249), London: JAI Press, 187–249.

Bry, B. H. (1993), *Research on Family Setting's Role in Substance Abuse.* Piscataway, NJ: Rutgers, The State University of New Jersey.

Bry B. H., McGreene, D., Schuttle, C., & Fishman, C. A. (1991), "Targeted family intervention manual." Unpublished technical report. Princeton, NJ: Rutgers State University.

Chamberlain, P., Patterson, G. R., Reid, J. B., Forgatch, M. S., & Kavanagh, K. (1984), "Observation of client resistance." *Behavior Therapy 15*, 144–155.

Chassin, L., Presson, C. C., & Sherman, S. J., (1990), "Social psychological contributions to the understanding and prevention of adolescent cigarette smoking." *Personality & Social Psychology Bulletin 16*, 133–151.

Conger, R. D. *et al.* (1992), "A family process model of economic hardship and adjustment of early adolescent boys." *Child Development 63*, 526–541.

DeMarsh, J., & Kumpfer, K. L. (1985), "Family-oriented interventions for the prevention of chemical dependency in children and adolescents." *Journal of Children in a Contemporary Society 18*, 117–151.

Dishion, T. J. (in press), "An ecological approach to child clinical and counseling psychology." Washington, DC: APA Books.

Dishion, T. J. (1996, September), "Advances in family-based interventions to prevent adolescent drug abuse." Paper presented at the National Institute on Drug Abuse conference, Washington, DC.

Dishion, T. J., & Andrews, D. W. (1995), "Preventing escalation in problem behaviors with high-risk young adolescents: Immediate and 1-year outcomes." *Journal of Consulting and Clinical Psychology 63*, 538–548.

Dishion, T. J., Andrews, D. W., Kavanagh, K., & Soberman, L. H. (1996), "Preventive interventions for high-risk youth: The Adolescent Transitions Program." In R. D. Peters & R. J. McMahon (eds), *Preventing Childhood Disorders, Substance Abuse, and Delinquency.* Thousand Oaks, CA: Sage.

Dishion, T. J., Biglan, A., Kavanagh, K., Metzler, C. W., & Soberman, L. H. (in press), "Family Management Curriculum." In T. D. Dishion & K. Kavanagh (eds), *Adolescent Problem Behavior: Family-centered Assessment and Interaction Sourcebook.* New York: Guilford Press.

Dishion, T. J., Capaldi, D., Spracklen, K. M., & Li, F. (1995), "Peer ecology of male adolescent drug use." *Development and Psychopathology 7*, 803–824.

Dishion, T. J., Capaldi, D. M., & Yoerger, K. (1999), "Middle childhood antecedents to progressions in male adolescent substance use: An ecological analysis of risk and protection." *Journal of Adolescent Research, 14* 175–205.

Dishion, T. J., Duncan, T. E., Eddy, J. M., Fagot, B. I., & Fetrow, R. A. (1994), "The world of parents and peers: Coercive exchanges and children's social adaption." *Social Development 3*, 255–268.

Dishion, T. J., & Kavanagh, K. (in press), *Adolescent Problem Behavior: An intervention and assessment sourcebook for working with families in schools.* New York: Guilford Press.

Dishion, T. J., & Kavanagh, K. (1995, July), "Cognitive–behavioral intervention strategies for high-risk young adolescents: A comparative analysis of 1-year outcome effects." Paper presented at the World Congress of Behavioural and Cognitive Therapies, Copenhagen, Denmark.

Dishion, T. J., & Loeber, R. (1985), "Adolescent marijuana and alcohol use: The role of parents and peers revisited." *American Journal of Drug and Alcohol Abuse 11*, 11–25.

Dishion, T. J., & Patterson, G. R. (1992), "Age effects in parent training outcome." *Behavior Therapy 23*, 719-729.

Dishion, T. J., & Patterson, S. G. (1996), *Preventive Parenting with Love, Encouragement, & Limits: The Preschool Years*. Eugene, OR: Castalia.

Dishion, T. J., Patterson, G. R., Stoolmiller, M., & Skinner, M. (1991), "Family, school, and behavioral antecedents to early adolescent involvement with antisocial peers." *Developmental Psychology 27*, 172–180.

Dishion, T. J., Reid, J. B., & Patterson, G. R. (1988), "Empirical guidelines for a family intervention for adolescent drug use." *Journal of Chemical Dependency Treatment 1*, 189–224.

Elder, G. H., Caspi, A., & Van Nguyen, T. (1986), "Resourceful and vulnerable children: Family influences in hard times." In R. K. Silbereisen K. Eyferth, & G. Rudinger (eds), *Development as Action in Context: Problem behavior and normal youth development*. New York: Springer-Verlag.

Forehand, R., & McMahon, R. (1981), *Helping the Noncompliant Child: A clinician's guide to parent training*. New York: Guilford Press.

Forgatch, M. S., & Patterson, G. R. (1998), "Behavioral family therapy." In F. M. Dattilio (ed.), *Case Studies in Couples and Family Therapy: Systematic and cognitive perspectives*. New York: Guilford Press, 85–107.

Gottfredson, D. C., Gottfredson, G. D., & Hybl, L. G. (1993), "Managing adolescent behavior: A multiyear, multischool study." *American Educational Research Journal 30*, 179–215.

Hawkins, J. D., Catalano, R. F., Miller, J. Y. (1992), "Risk and protective factors for alcohol and other drug problems in adolescence and early adulthood: Implications for substance abuse prevention." *Psychological Bulletin 112*, 64–105.

Heller, L. R., & Fantuzzo, J. W. (1993), "Reciprocal peer tutoring and parent partnership: Does parent involvement make a difference?" *School Psychology Review 22*, 517–534.

Henggeler, S. W., Melton, G. B., & Smith, L. A. (1992), "Family preservation using multisystemic treatment: An effective alternative to incarcerating serious juvenile offenders." *Journal of Consulting and Clinical Psychology 60*, 953–961.

Henggeler, S. W. *et al.* (1986), "Multisystemic treatment of juvenile offenders: Effects on adolescent behavior and family interaction." *Developmental Psychology 22*, 132–141.

Hetherington, E. M., & Clingempeel, W. G. (1992), "Coping with marital transitions: A family systems perspective." *Monographs of the Society for Research in Child Development 57*(2–3, Serial No. 227).

Irvine, A. B., Biglan, A., Smolkowski, K., Metzler, C. W., & Ary, D. V. (1999), "The effectiveness of a parenting skills program for parents of middle school students in small communities." *Journal of Consulting and Clinical Psychology 67*, 811–825.

Kandel, D. B., Davies, M., Karus, D., Yamaguchi, K. (1986), "The consequences in young adulthood of adolescent drug involvement." *Archives of General Psychiatry 43*, 746–754.

Kavanagh, K., Dishion, T. J., Medici Skaggs, N., & Schneiger, A. (1998), "Prediction of parent participation in a tiered model of assessment and intervention for early adolescent problem behavior." Paper presented at Sixth Annual Meeting of the Society for Prevention Research, Park City, UT.

Kellam, S. G. (1990), "Developmental epidemiological framework for family research on depression and aggression." In G. R. Patterson (ed.), *Depression and Aggression in Family Interaction*. Hillsdale, NJ: Erlbaum, 11–48.

Kelly, J. G. (1988), *A Guide to Conducting Preventive Research in the Community: First steps*. New York: Haworth.

Loeber, R., & Dishion, T. J. (1983), "Early predictors of male delinquency: A review. *Psychological Bulletin 94*, 68–99.

McCord, W., McCord, J., & Howard, A. (1960), "Familial correlates of aggression in nondelinquent male children." *Journal of Abnormal & Social Psychology 62*, 79–93.

McLoyd, V. (1990), "The impact of economic hardship on black families and children: Psychological distress, parenting, and socio-emotional development." *Child Development 61*, 311–346.

Miller, W. R., & Rollnick, S. (1991), *Motivational Interviewing: Preparing people to change addictive behavior*. New York: Guilford Press.

Patterson, G. R. (1974), "Interventions for boys with conduct problems: Multiple settings, treatments, and criteria." *Journal of Consulting and Clinical Psychology 42*, 471–481.

Patterson, G. R. (1979), "Treatment for children with conduct problems: A review of outcome studies." In S. Feshbach & A. Fraczek (eds), *Aggression and behavior change: Biological and social process* (pp. 83–132), New York: Praeger.

Patterson, G. R. (1982), *A Social Learning Approach: III. Coercive Family Process*. Eugene, OR: Castalia.

Patterson, G. R., & Chamberlain, P. (1994), "A functional analysis of resistance during parent training therapy." *Clinical Psychology: Science and Practice 1*, 53–70.

Patterson, G. R., Dishion, T. J., & Chamberlain, P. (1993), "Outcomes and methodological issues relating to treatment of antisocial children." In T. R. Giles (ed.), *Effective psychotherapy: A handbook of comparative research*. New York: Plenum, 43–88.

Patterson, G. R., & Forgatch, M. S. (1985), "Therapist behavior as a determinant for client resistance: A paradox for the behavior modifier." *Journal of Consulting and Clinical Psychology 53*, 846–851.

Patterson, G. R., Reid, J. B., & Dishion, T. J. (1992), *A Social Learning Approach: IV. Antisocial boys*. Eugene, OR: Castalia.

Patterson, G. R., Reid, J. B., Jones, R. R., & Conger, R. E. (1975), *A Social Learning Approach to Family Intervention: Families with aggressive children (Vol. 1)*. Eugene, OR: Castalia.

Rao, S. A. (1998), "The short-term impact of the Family Check-Up: A brief motivational intervention for at-risk families." Unpublished doctoral dissertation, University of Oregon.

Reid, J. B. (1993), "Prevention of conduct disorder before and after school entry: Relating interventions to development findings." *Journal of Development and Psychopathology 5*, 243–262.

Robins, L. N., & Pryzabeck, T. R. (1985), "Age of onset of drug use as a factor in drug and other disorders." *National Institute on Drug Abuse: Research Monograph Series 56*, 178–192.

Rogers, C. R. (1957), "The necessary and sufficient conditions of therapeutic personality change." *Journal of Consulting Psychology 21*, 95–103.

Rutter, M. (1985), Family and school influences on behavioural development. *Journal of Child Psychology & Psychiatry & Allied Disciplines 26*, 349–368.

Sanders, N. R., & Lawton, J. M. (1993), "Discussing assessment findings with families: A guided participation model of information transfer." *Child and Family Behavior Therapy 15*, 5–33.

Szapocznik, J., & Kurtines, W. M. (1989), *Breakthroughs in Family Therapy with Drug-abusing and Problem Youth*. New York: Springer.

Trickett, E. J., & Birman, D. (1989), "Taking ecology seriously: A community development approach to individually based preventive interventions in schools." In L. A. Bond & B. E. Compas (eds), *Primary Prevention and Promotion in the Schools. Primary prevention of psychopathology, Vol. 12*. Newbury Park, CA: Sage, 361–390.

Wahler, R. G., Winkel, G. H., Peterson, R. F., & Morrison, D. C. (1965), "Mothers as behavior therapists for their own children." *Behaviour Research & Therapy 3*, 113–124.

Webster-Stratton, C. (1984), "Randomized trial of two parent-training programs for families with conduct-disordered children." *Journal of Consulting and Clinical Psychology 52*, 666–678.

Chapter 7

Motivational Interviewing for Alcohol-Involved Adolescents in the Emergency Room

Nancy P. Barnett, Peter M. Monti, and Mark D. Wood*

In recent years clinicians and researchers have been paying greater attention to individuals who do not demonstrate alcohol dependence, but nevertheless are at risk for problems associated with their alcohol use. Adolescents and young adults comprise a large proportion of this at-risk group. Since at-risk adolescents do not typically present for substance abuse treatment, novel approaches for identification and intervention are necessary. Programs that capitalize on developmental transitions such as college entrance, and salient events such as alcohol-related medical treatment, and those that flexibly target motivational and natural change processes, show great promise. This chapter describes the authors' research with alcohol-involved adolescents in an urban trauma center, using motivational interviewing as a brief intervention approach. We set the stage for the presentation of our research program and findings by providing background on alcohol use and misuse among adolescents, including relevant information about alcohol-related injury and risky behavior. The area of brief alcohol intervention with adults and college students also is reviewed, and following the description of our research, we suggest possible future research directions.

Adolescent Alcohol Use, Misuse, and Alcohol-Related Consequences

Monitoring the Future (MTF) data indicate that by their senior year of high school, slightly more than 80 percent of students have consumed alcohol, over 50 percent report being drunk in the past year, and over 30 percent report engaging in heavy episodic drinking within the last two weeks (Johnston, O'Malley & Bachman, 1998a). Ellickson, McGuigan,

*Nancy P. Barnett, Brown University; Peter M. Monti, Providence VA Medical Center and Brown University; Mark D. Wood, Brown University (now at the University of Rhode Island).

This study was supported in part by grants from the National Institute on Alcohol Abuse and Alcoholism (5R01-AA09892 and 5T32-AA07459), by a Department of Veterans Affairs Career Research Scientist Award to Dr Monti, and by a Veterans Affairs Merit Review grant from the Medical Research Office of Research and Development.

Correspondence concerning this chapter should be addressed to Nancy P. Barnett, Ph.D., Center for Alcohol and Addiction Studies, Box G-BH, Brown University, Providence, RI 02912.

Adams, Bell, and Hays (1996) examined high-risk drinking, alcohol-related problems, and high consumption in a large sample of high school seniors and school dropouts. They noted that 64 percent of their late adolescent sample reported having been intoxicated, 52 percent reported having been sick, and 30 percent reported having passed out from alcohol use at least once during the past year. Research also has documented increases in alcohol consumption prevalence rates throughout adolescence and for the first four years after high school; while heavy episodic drinking is high among 18-year-olds (31 percent), it increases to a peak level of 40 percent by the ages of 21–22 (Johnston, O'Malley & Bachman, 1998b).

Alcohol use is associated with various types of risk-taking behaviors, including drinking and driving. It appears drinking and driving typically co-occur with other risky driving behaviors such as speeding, reckless driving (e.g., illegal passing, sudden lane changes, violating traffic signals), and using drugs while driving (Donovan, 1993). Although the percentage of alcohol-related traffic fatalities among 16- to 24-year-olds declined by 30 percent between 1977 and 1993, younger drivers continue to be overrepresented in alcohol-related motor vehicle fatalities. Specifically, 16- to 24-year-olds accounted for 28 percent of all drinking driver deaths in 1993, while comprising only 15 percent of all licensed drivers (National Institute on Alcohol Abuse and Alcoholism, 1997). Drinking and driving also is quite prevalent among college students. For example, in the 1993 and 1997 versions of the Harvard School of Public Health College Alcohol Survey (Wechsler, Dowdall, Maenner, Gledhill-Hoyt & Lee, 1998), 31.6 percent and 35.8 percent of respondents who were current drinkers indicated they had driven after drinking at least once since the beginning of the school year. Finally, motor vehicle crash is one of the most common reasons for medical evaluation of alcohol-positive adolescents treated in emergency settings (Barnett *et al.*, 1998; Hicks, Morris, Bass, Holcomb & Neblett, 1990; Maio, Portnoy, Blow & Hill, 1994).

It is well established that alcohol is associated with the occurrence of non-fatal and fatal injuries in adults. Positive blood alcohol levels are more prevalent in emergency room (ER) patients who are injured than those who are seeking treatment for a non-injury-related medical problem (Cherpitel, 1994b). In a review of the relationship between alcohol use and injury, Cherpitel (1993) found the prevalence of blood alcohol concentration in non-fatal injuries ranged from six to 34 percent. The prevalence of alcohol use in traumatic injury may be even higher; Rivara *et al.* (1993) found 47 percent of patients treated at an ER for blunt or penetrating trauma had a positive blood alcohol concentration (BAC) greater than 0.01 percent, and 36 percent were intoxicated (BAC > 0.10 percent). Although there are only a few studies in adolescent populations, there are parallel findings. In a community sample of nearly 2000 14- to 18-year-olds, Spirito, Rasile, Vinnick, Jelalian and Arrigan (1997) found for injuries requiring medical care, substance use was involved in 70 percent of cases related to weapons, 42 percent of pedestrian injuries, and 38 percent of fights.

Alcohol use also is related to the severity of injury, in that alcohol use is more common in fatal than non-fatal injuries. Cherpitel (1994a) reviewed ER and coroner reports for one county and found 32 percent of recorded fatalities had BACs of 0.10 percent or higher, but only six percent of non-fatally injured ER patients had BACs in this range. Similarly, alcohol is related to injury as the cause of death. Li, Smith, and Baker (1994) reviewed mortality data on adults ages 25–64 and determined those who died as the result of an injury drank more frequently and more heavily than those who died from disease.

Having an alcohol-related injury also places an individual at risk for reinjury. Rivara, Koepsell, Jurkovich, Gurney, and Soderberg (1993) found individuals who were treated for a traumatic injury at an emergency room and who had a BAC greater than 0.10 percent were 2.5 times more likely to be *readmitted* for trauma during the following 28 months than individuals who did not have a positive BAC. Patients who had a positive score on the Michigan Alcoholism Screening Test (i.e., had a history of alcohol abuse), but were not alcohol positive, showed a pattern of reinjury similar to the alcohol-positive patients. In a study of medical care utilization, Blose and Holder (1991) found problem drinkers had almost twice as many injury-related health care events, and had four times as many injury-related hospital days per year when compared to a matched cohort. Together these studies indicate that being a current problem drinker, having a history of alcohol problems, or having an alcohol-related injury increases an individual's risk for future injury.

Alcohol and substance use problems also are associated with suicidal ideation, attempts, and completion in adolescents and young adults. Windle, Miller-Tutzauer, and Domenico (1992) found higher levels of alcohol use were associated with more frequent suicidal ideation and attempts among adolescents interviewed for the National Adolescent Student Health Survey. Rates of substance abuse among adolescent suicide attempters treated in hospitals range from 25 percent (Withers & Kaplan, 1987) to 42 percent (Christoffel, Marcus, Sagerman & Bennett, 1988). Gould *et al.* (1998) found substance abuse/dependence disorders increased the risk of suicide attempts among boys in an adolescent community sample, and substance abuse contributed significantly to the escalation from suicidal ideation to suicide attempts. Another indication that substance abuse is a factor in the severity of suicidality was shown by Brent, Perper, and Allman (1987), who found adolescent suicide victims who used firearms were more likely to have been drinking alcohol than those who used other methods. Clearly, alcohol use and misuse is a major factor in making suicide the leading cause of death among adolescents ages 15–19 (Gould, Shaffer, Fisher, Kleinman & Morishima, 1992).

Like adults, youth who engage in episodes of heavy drinking are especially at risk for experiencing alcohol-related problems. Wechsler *et al.* (1998) found heavy episodic collegiate drinkers were more likely to get hurt or injured, and to drive after drinking, than college students who did not binge-drink. Other problems associated with heavy episodic drinking in this sample were engaging in unplanned sexual activity, not using protection when having sex, missing classes, falling behind in schoolwork, arguing with friends, damaging property, and getting into trouble with police. Similarly, in a study of college students, Werch, Gorman, and Marty (1987) showed successively greater levels of alcohol use resulted in increased probabilities of experiencing adverse alcohol-related consequences.

In sum, data from a wide array of studies consistently point to a pattern of increasing risk for heavy alcohol use and alcohol-related negative consequences from early to late adolescence. These findings underscore the urgency behind developing effective preventive interventions to reduce the negative consequences associated with drinking among this age group. An important component of effectiveness is reaching at-risk adolescents, who do not typically present for help with substance use problems. Medical settings and college campuses are two settings where adolescents with alcohol or other drug problems may be opportunely identified, and are settings where substance problems may be opportunely treated.

Brief Interventions in Medical Settings

In many ways, medical treatment, including primary care routine visits and visits for a problem or injury, provides an optimal time for intervening in alcohol problems. The rate of alcohol problems tends to be higher in populations seeking health care than in the general population (US DHHS, 1997), and problem drinkers are more likely to seek help or advice from a medical practitioner than a substance abuse specialist (Institute of Medicine, 1990).

The first studies of interventions in health care settings were conducted in the early 1960s, and consisted primarily of efforts to facilitate referral of alcoholics to treatment. Approaches included using brief consultation and referrals (Chafetz, 1968; Chafetz *et al.*, 1962), handwritten letters (Koumans & Muller, 1965), telephone calls to the client (Koumans, Muller & Miller, 1967), and making appointments for the client (Kogan, 1957). Clinical trials using no-treatment control groups supported the effectiveness of all of these approaches.

Since the 1980s, a number of studies of brief intervention for alcohol abuse have been conducted in medical settings in Great Britain, Scandinavian countries, and the United States. Brief intervention, which is defined as minimal contact by a medical or mental health professional, was recommended by the Institute of Medicine for reducing alcohol consumption and associated risks in individuals with signs of problems with alcohol, or those who drink in hazardous ways (IOM, 1990; Marlatt, Larimer, Baer & Quigley, 1993). This type of intervention typically includes a brief alcohol assessment followed by a session of advice from a health care practitioner to reduce drinking. Providing referrals for additional services also may be included in brief interventions (Bernstein, Bernstein & Levenson, 1997).

In 1988, Wallace, Cutler, and Haines reported on their research in which primary care patients ($N = 909$) with an excessive drinking profile (men who drank 35 or more drinks per week and women who drank 21 or more drinks per week) were randomized to brief intervention treatment or to a no-treatment control group. The treatment consisted of a session with the patient's general practitioner who assessed alcohol consumption and provided normative feedback and advice, a drinking diary, and an information booklet about sensible drinking limits. Patients were offered one follow-up appointment, and physicians had the discretion of scheduling up to three additional appointments. After one year, the men in the intervention group had reduced their drinking by 18 drinks per week compared to eight in the control group. Proportional reductions were found among women, with those in the intervention group reducing their drinking by eleven drinks versus six in controls. In addition, men in the intervention group showed significant improvements in gamma-glutamyltransferase, a marker associated with liver pathology.

The World Health Organization (WHO) conducted the largest study of a brief intervention in primary care (Babor & Grant, 1992). The WHO study was a cross-national study, with sites in ten countries (due to methodological problems and inconsistencies, data from only eight of the countries were used in the intervention outcome analyses). Patients who were defined as being at risk for chronic health problems were recruited from primary care settings including general hospital wards, primary care clinics, and a health screening agency. Patients were randomly assigned to a control group (20-minute health assessment only), simple advice (assessment and five minutes of advice about the importance of sensible drinking or abstinence, identification of problems, and a take-home pamphlet), or assessment and a 20-minute brief counseling session, which used a problem-solving manual that described the benefits of changing drinking, coping with potentially risky drinking situations, and developing alternatives to drinking. A total of 1119 patients were recruited, with 75 percent successfully followed up approximately nine months after assignment to treatment condition. Men in the intervention conditions showed a reduction in total consumption of alcohol, in number of drinking days, and in the number of drinks per drinking day, but did not show differences in the frequency of dependence symptoms, problems related to alcohol, or concern expressed by others. Interestingly, no group differences were found for female subjects, although all three groups of women showed significant reductions in drinking.

Fleming, Barry, Manwell, Johnson, and London (1997) enrolled 774 problem drinking patients from primary care practices in a brief intervention study. Patients were randomly assigned to receive either two 10- to 15-minute counseling visits with their physicians or a booklet on health issues. After twelve months, patients who had received the counseling intervention showed less alcohol use, including having had fewer drinks in the previous week, fewer episodes of binge-drinking over the previous month, and a lower prevalence of excessive drinking in the past week than patients who had received the booklet.

In sum, studies have consistently shown a positive impact of brief intervention with adult problem drinkers screened in health care settings.[1] Patients in these studies were, on average, in their late 30s to 40s, and at least one study of brief intervention noted the underrepresentation of younger patients (Wallace *et al.*, 1988). This underrepresentation may be due in part to the fact that some studies identified potential participants on the basis alcohol-related health problems (e.g., liver pathology) uncommon among younger problem drinkers. Given the fact that the largest proportion of problem drinkers are young adults (SAMHSA, 1997), it is apparent that a large at-risk group is not receiving potentially effective intervention.

There are a number of reasons why conducting brief alcohol interventions with adolescents in a medical setting could be productive. First, one premise of brief intervention is that it is a way to reach individuals who are at risk for alcohol problems and do not typically present for substance abuse treatment. In a recent study of injured adolescents treated in an ER, only three (four percent) of 73 patients determined at ER presentation to have a diagnosis of alcohol abuse or dependence had received any substance abuse treatment (Chung, *et al.*, 2000). This finding supports the potential

---

[1]In addition to the number of studies that have considered brief intervention in medical settings with problem drinkers, there are also a number of studies that have compared brief intervention to more extensive, traditional substance abuse treatment. A review of those studies is beyond the scope of this chapter; the reader is directed to Bien, Miller & Tonigan (1993) and Babor (1994) for comprehensive reviews.

effectiveness of identifying and treating adolescents with substance use problems in a medical setting. Another reason is that many adolescents and college-age young adults do not have a primary care practitioner, and the only contact they may have with health care providers is for treatment for an emergency medical problem. Additionally, such an approach will reach at least some youth who have dropped out of school and would not be exposed to school-based prevention programs.

As noted above, most brief intervention studies have been conducted with patients who were screened for being *at risk* for alcohol problems. Few published studies have specifically targeted patients who are being medically treated following an alcohol-related event. Nevertheless, the timing of such an intervention could have important implications for its effectiveness. For example, medical treatment for an alcohol-related injury may offer a "teachable moment." In other words, experiencing an alcohol-related injury or aversive event (e.g., medical treatment for extreme intoxication) is likely to make the negative consequences of alcohol use more salient, and promote interest in avoiding another incident, thereby making patients more willing to talking about their experiences with alcohol. It has been observed that negative consequences are most salient following a period of acute intoxication, and that reviewing those circumstances can motivate change attempts (Clancy, 1964; Pediaditakis, 1962). Therefore, conducting an intervention designed to promote discussion about the event, its consequences, and other alcohol-related sequelae may be effective in enhancing the individual's interest in reducing harmful drinking behavior.

It is evident brief interventions can be successful, and they contain important elements for promoting change, even with individuals who are not seeking help for drinking problems. Miller and Sanchez (1993) identified six elements common to effective brief intervention approaches which they describe using the acronym FRAMES. These components include: Feedback of assessment results, an emphasis on personal Responsibility for change, explicit Advice to change, a Menu of change options, therapist Empathy, and encouragement of client Self-efficacy regarding the ability to change behavior. Miller and Rollnick (1991) hypothesized that these elements of brief interventions impact motivation to change. In other words, brief interventions that are characterized by the above elements are thought to set in motion a motivational process whereby the drinker becomes more interested in changing. Indeed, Miller and Rollnick have developed a therapeutic approach, known as Motivational Interviewing (MI), that incorporates the above elements and specifically focuses on reducing problem behaviors by increasing the client's readiness and commitment to change.

Motivational Interviewing

Conceptually, MI integrates client-centered and cognitive-behavioral therapies and is informed by cognitive response approaches from social psychological research on attitude–behavior consistency. MI grew out of the reconceptualization of motivation as a "state" rather than a "trait" variable (Miller, 1985) and from the research on brief intervention discussed earlier (Bien, Miller & Tonigan, 1993; Miller & Rollnick, 1991).

In its focus, MI is a non-confrontational yet directive approach for achieving behavior change. The counselor uses specific strategies to facilitate problem behavior recognition and to suggest avenues for behavior change. Nonetheless, the responsibility for changing behavior rests squarely with the individual. As detailed by Miller and Rollnick (1991), there are five broad clinical principles underlying MI: (1) express empathy; (2) develop discrepancy; (3) avoid argumentation; (4) roll with resistance; and (5) support self-efficacy. An empathic therapeutic style is central to MI and is conveyed to the client through respectful, non-judgmental reflective listening techniques. Regarding the second principle, the counselor actively seeks to increase readiness to change by developing the client's awareness of the discrepancy between their present behavior and broader goals. For example, the counselor might seek to develop discrepancy by promoting discussion of the positive and negative aspects (pros and cons) of the client's alcohol use and/or by providing normative feedback about how an individual's drinking patterns compare to those of his/her peers. The counselor also actively seeks to avoid argumentation by adopting a non-aggressive approach and by avoiding labels (e.g., alcoholic) that may threaten or evoke reactance from the client. When resistance is encountered, it is viewed as a signal to the counselor to alter his or her approach and to utilize a variety of reflective listening strategies with the aim of decreasing client defensiveness. Supporting self-efficacy refers to active attempts by the counselor to increase the client's belief that he or she is capable of changing the targeted behavior. This can be achieved by highlighting relevant abilities and accomplishments in other domains and by reinforcing the client's statements about behavior change. The principles are consistent (and overlap to a degree) with the FRAMES elements described above. Together, they form the foundation for the more specific procedural strategies of MI.

Motivational Interviewing and Adolescents

In addition to the above-described rationale for conducting brief intervention in emergency room settings, there are reasons why motivational interviewing in particular has the potential to be effective with adolescents. First, MI does not assume that the client is interested in changing; instead it emphasizes assessment of the client's motivation through open-ended questioning, followed by the use of strategies that are appropriate to that client's readiness to change (Miller & Rollnick, 1991). Because MI takes the person's level of motivation into consideration, it is particularly applicable to adolescents who may be ambivalent or not ready to make changes in their drinking (Miller, 1994; Miller & Rollnick, 1991). A skills training approach such as those often applied in substance abuse treatment settings may not be appropriate, or effective, with individuals who are not sufficiently interested in changing their behavior. Indeed, Heather, Rollnick, Bell, and Richmond (1996) reported heavy-drinking adult patients who perceived themselves as "not ready to change" reduced their drinking more when provided with a motivational interview than with skills-based counseling. Furthermore, adolescents generally demonstrate lower motivation to change than adults (Melnick, De Leon, Hawke, Jainchill & Kressel, 1997), which suggests motivation needs to be bolstered for behavior change to occur. "The underlying assumption is that if the therapist can help the client to move through precontemplation and ambivalence to decision and commitment, behavior change will often follow" (Miller, 1994, p. 118).

Another reason why MI shows strong potential for use with adolescents is that MI is not confrontational in the way that "confrontation" is often understood and sometimes used in alcohol treatment. For example, some treatment programs include direct confrontation from family, friends, or individuals as one element of treatment. However, this style tends to evoke high levels of resistance in clients and is associated with poor treatment outcome (Miller, 1985; Miller, Benefield & Tonigan, 1993; Miller *et al.*, 1995). With adolescents, the non-aggressive aspect of MI may be especially important, in that adolescents may be defensive about their drinking and may anticipate being scolded or lectured by adults. By avoiding direct confrontation, resistance is reduced, and rapport is enhanced. Nevertheless, motivational interviewing does involve confrontation of a different nature: through the presentation and interpretation of personalized feedback, the client is confronted with the reality of his/her consumption and problems (Miller, 1995). While this confrontation may be direct and intense, it is neither aggressive nor judgmental.

A final reason why MI has great potential for use among adolescents is that it emphasizes the enhancement of self-efficacy. Self-efficacy is an important aspect of problem behavior (Bandura, 1982; Chung & Elias, 1996; Prochaska, Johnson & Lee, 1998) and behavior change (Forsberg, King, Delaronde & Geary, 1996; Lee & Oei, 1993; Marcus, Eaton, Rossi & Harlow, 1994). Schulenberg, Wadsworth, O'Malley, Bachman, and Johnston (1996) studied youth who were transitioning from adolescence to young adulthood and found low self-efficacy was a risk factor for increasing binge-drinking over time. Furthermore, there is evidence that clients' ratings of their ability to control their alcohol intake in challenging situations predicts their later consumption (Kavanagh, Sitharthan & Sayer, 1996). Similarly, when the intervention relies on self-directed behavior change, self-efficacy is likely to be a good predictor of persistence (Bandura, 1982). In MI, the practitioner strives to strengthen the client's sense that he or she can be successful in attempts to change and in coping with the difficulties that arise while attempting to change. This element of MI may be especially important for adolescent problem drinkers who do not have as much experience as adults at attempting personal change.

Motivational Interviewing as a Brief Intervention with Adults

The Motivational Interviewing approach was first developed by Miller, Sovereign, and Krege (1988) in the context of the "Drinker's Check-Up" (DCU), which was designed to provide adult drinkers with a comprehensive assessment of alcohol-related problems and objective feedback from this assessment. The DCU was not a part of a treatment program, and participants did not typically think of themselves as "problem drinkers." Nevertheless, most of the drinkers who referred themselves to the program did indeed have alcohol-related problems (Miller, 1995). Several trials conducted by Miller and colleagues found this approach reduced alcohol consumption in participants. Miller et al. (1988) randomly assigned problem drinkers to either receive an immediate DCU or a DCU six weeks later.

The group that received the immediate DCU showed moderate reductions in alcohol use, as did the delayed group following their intervention. Similar results were found by Miller *et al.* (1993), who reported significant effects of the DCU compared to a wait-list control group, and a 57 percent reduction in alcohol use that was maintained until one year following the intervention.

Two additional studies found the DCU to be effective as a precursor to substance abuse treatment. Brown and Miller (1993) assigned patients who were entering substance abuse treatment at a private psychiatric hospital to receive either two MI sessions or to receive nothing prior to beginning treatment. Patients who had received the pre-treatment MI were perceived by their therapists as being more invested in their subsequent treatment, and showed a greater reduction in drinking three months after discharge than the no-MI control group. Bien, Miller, and Boroughs (1993) found similar results with patients in outpatient treatment at a Veterans Affairs Medical Center.

The largest study to use a motivational approach was a multi-site study of treatment matching in which alcohol treatment clients were randomly assigned to receive either Motivational Enhancement Therapy (MET; a four-session version of MI), Cognitive-Behavioral Therapy (CBT), or Twelve-Step Facilitation (TSF) (Project MATCH Research Group, 1997). Although the primary purpose of the study was to determine which treatments were most effective for which clients, the overall treatment outcome findings are relevant here. Although the MET protocol consisted of one-third the number of sessions of CBT or TSF, there were no major outcome differences among the three treatment groups twelve months following the intervention. This finding indicates that MET, despite its brevity, may be as effective as other standard treatment approaches.

In sum, empirical support for using Motivational Interviewing as a sole outpatient treatment, as a brief intervention with problem drinkers, and as a preparation for intensive inpatient treatment is strong. In fact, in an extensive quantitative evaluation of 211 treatment outcome studies of 43 treatment modalities, Brief Intervention received the best overall rating, followed by Social Skills Training and Motivational Enhancement (Miller *et al.*, 1995).

Motivational Interviewing with Alcohol-involved Adolescents

As described above, the potential for using Motivational Interviewing as an approach with alcohol or substance-involved adolescents is good, and the research in support of it is growing. Recently, Marlatt *et al.* (1998) examined the effectiveness of a brief Motivational Interview (MI) in reducing college student alcohol use and problems. Following an assessment, participants assigned to the MI condition met individually with a counselor for a single 45-minute session. Consistent with MI formulations, the interviewers avoided directive techniques and attempted to engage the students through the use of open-ended questions about their drinking behavior. Students were given individualized summary sheets comparing their alcohol use with other students. Beliefs about the effects of drinking (alcohol expectancies) also were discussed with reference to both "placebo" effects and alcohol's biphasic (i.e., initial stimulant effects followed by depressive effects). Students received a handout that reviewed the alcohol expectancy information and provided risk reduction strategies.[2] One year after their interview, participants in the MI condition were mailed individualized feedback reports based on their assessments at baseline, and at the six- and 12-month follow-up assessments. Individuals ($n = 56$) classified as at "high" or "extreme" risk (based on reported peak drinking levels and alcohol-related problems) were telephoned by project staff to offer assistance and to encourage risk reduction. Thirty-four of these individuals received an additional MI in Year 2.

Results based on data collected through the first two years of the project revealed significant intervention effects at both short- (baseline to six-month) and long-term (baseline, one-year, and two-year) follow-ups on multiple measures of alcohol use and problems. Compared to an assessment-only control group, the MI group demonstrated significantly lower levels of reported alcohol consumption and alcohol-related problems. For example, at the two-year follow-up, eleven percent of students in the MI group met criteria for alcohol dependence, compared to 26.9 percent of those in the assessment-only control condition.[3] Although the intervention effect sizes were characterized as modest for measures of alcohol consumption, they were more substantial for alcohol-related problems.

Marlatt *et al.*'s brief Motivational Interview resulted in significantly lower levels of alcohol use and problems at six-, 12-, and 24-month follow-ups compared to assessment only. These effects are particularly noteworthy when examined in the context of the larger literature on college student preventive interventions. Although the existing literature base of well-controlled studies is quite small, observed effects typically have been very small to nonexistent (Moskowitz, 1989; Wood, 1998). Finally, the finding of larger effects for alcohol-related problems, as compared to alcohol use, is consistent with MI's harm reduction orientation, and provides strong support for the validity of MI as an intervention to reduce risky drinking and alcohol-related problems among college students and young people in general.

Motivational Interviewing in the ER

Our program of research involves conducting brief motivational interviews with alcohol-involved adolescents who are recruited from a Level one trauma center. Adolescents under the age of 18 receive treatment in a pediatric emergency room, and adolescents 18 and older receive treatment in an adult emergency room. Eligible patients (i.e., English speaking, not suicidal or in police custody) between the ages of 13 and 19 are approached during or immediately following their medical treatment. Older (18–19-year-old) adolescents participate without parental involvement, while younger adolescents participate in the study with a parent. Participation in our research studies is voluntary, and approximately 65 percent of eligible patients volunteer.

Assessments. We have compiled an assessment battery that has been computerized for ease of administration and data collection. The counselor serves as the assessor, asks each

---

[2]See Marlatt *et al.* (1998) or Dimeff, Baer, Kivlahan, and Marlatt (1999) for a more complete description of the study and the use of MI with college students.
[3]Based on a cutoff score of eleven on the Alcohol Dependence Scale (see Marlatt *et al.*, 1998).

question aloud, and then enters the patient's answer into a laptop computer program. In addition to demographic information, the assessment consists of measures of alcohol consumption, alcohol problems, drinking and driving, risk-taking behavior and perceptions of risk, injuries and alcohol-related injuries, readiness to change drinking behavior, pros and cons of drinking, and depression.[4] For research purposes, we also conduct a review of the patient's medical record to derive medical information about the nature of the patient's injury. For patients under the age of 18, one parent completes a brief assessment of his/her own history of drinking and family policies with regard to teenage drinking and driving after drinking. The assessment battery used at the follow-up points is similar to that used at baseline, with the addition of questions concerning attempts that were made during the follow-up period to change drinking or to seek treatment for substance problems.

Intervention. Once patients have completed the assessment, they are randomly assigned to receive either MI or standard hospital care (SC). The SC group receives several handouts about the risks of drinking and driving and ways to limit it, and a referral list of local mental health agencies that specialize in adolescents and substance abuse. The MI procedure incorporates the central principles described by Miller and Rollnick (1991). The MI is multi-focused in that it incorporates exploration, feedback, and discussion about both alcohol and alcohol-related behaviors, including injuries and driving after drinking. Consistent with an MI approach, the specific content of the discussion is modified to be appropriate for each individual patient.

The motivational interview that we have designed has five sections: (1) Introduction and review of the alcohol event; (2) Exploration of motivation for change; (3) Personalized feedback and motivational enhancement; (4) Imagining the future; and (5) Establishing goals for change. The counselor introduces the interview as a chance for patients to talk about their thoughts and feelings about the event that led to the patient being treated in the emergency room, and if the patient is interested, to talk about ways to avoid similar events in the future. In order to minimize defensiveness on the part of the patient, the counselor emphasizes their intention not to tell the patient what to do, but rather to discuss the patient's decisions and choices about drinking and things they do while drinking. The purpose of this first component is to present the counselor as empathic, concerned, non-authoritarian, and non-judgmental (Miller, 1995), and for the counselor to learn the circumstances surrounding the event, such as how much the patient had been drinking, and whom the patient was with at the time. Next, level of *motivation for change* is explored by asking questions about the patient's likes and dislikes about drinking (pros and cons), and reasons why they might drive after drinking or avoid drinking and driving. Open-ended questions and reflective listening statements are used to encourage patients to generate as many responses as possible, and to talk about the alcohol effects that matter most to them and the worst things they could imagine happening. Patients also are asked about their parents' and friends' attitudes toward drinking and toward driving after drinking, and the effect of those attitudes on the patient. The goal of this element of the intervention is for

[4]Information about the specific measures can be obtained from the corresponding author.

the counselor to identify the positive and negative aspects of drinking and of driving after drinking most salient to the patients. The counselor can then tailor the MI to these personalized "pros" and "cons," while keeping in mind the patients' stage of readiness for changing their behavior.

During the third portion of the intervention, patients are provided with computer-generated feedback derived from their assessment data. Feedback is provided orally and in written format. The feedback form has three sections. First, information about the patient's pattern of drinking and how he or she compares to peers of the same age and gender is provided. This information includes how often the patient drinks, how much he or she typically drinks on a drinking occasion, and how frequently he or she gets drunk. In addition to providing concrete feedback, this section is designed to correct overestimations common among youth about the prevalence of drinking, heavy drinking, and alcohol problems (Baer & Carney, 1993; Baer, Stacy & Larimer, 1991) and to provide the opportunity to discuss the greater problems that are associated with heavy episodic drinking (Midanik & Clark, 1995). If the patient's BAC was measured at the time of the precipitating event, it is discussed and information about blood alcohol and metabolism is presented. Participants often are surprised by the normative feedback (i.e., they don't realize the extreme levels of their drinking compared to same-age peers), and tend to have a poor understanding of the impact of BAC on behavior, especially driving behavior. Second, information about indices of physical and emotional dependence shown by the patient is provided, including a description of tolerance. This part of the intervention is intended to address misconceptions about tolerance including that tolerance to alcohol is a positive characteristic or something to be proud of. Third, age and gender-based normative information about alcohol-related consequences including problems with family, friends, and school is provided, as is information about the patient's history of injuries and reckless behavior. For each of the feedback topic areas, the counselor reviews the feedback with the patient, asks for the patient's reaction, and provides further information when relevant. Counselors explore which aspect of the feedback raised the most concern with the patient, and clarify the meaning of the information if necessary. After obtaining permission from the patient, counselors express their own concerns as well. Patients are given a copy of the feedback sheet and informational handouts about alcohol and about drinking and driving to take home with them.

Counselors next ask the patients to *imagine the future* by asking them what might happen if their drinking were to stay the same and if their drinking were to decrease. This part of the MI is designed to develop the patients' sense of discrepancy between current behavior and future goals, and presumably serves to increase the patients' ambivalence about their current behavior (Miller & Rollnick, 1991). The final phase of the intervention involves helping patients *identify goals for behavior change*, and explore barriers to these changes. Patients are encouraged to talk about what they would like to do differently, and to devise behavioral strategies for reducing their alcohol use. Counselors provide advice and suggestions as needed and help patients imagine putting the plan into place and coping with difficulties in implementing the plan. This approach is used for a number of reasons, specifically because research shows motivation is enhanced by encouraging participation in all decision-making regarding alcohol use (Cooney, Zweben & Fleming, 1995), using individualized strategies leads to more positive outcomes (Miller & Hester, 1986), and problem drinkers prefer to select their own goals rather than having goals set for them (although a subsample prefer to have goals prescribed [Sobell, Sobell, Bogardis, Leo & Skinner, 1993]). The entire MI session takes approximately 35–40 minutes.

Evaluation of intervention fidelity. In addition to weekly clinical supervision meetings and quarterly assessment review sessions, two manual-guided methods were developed to monitor and evaluate the fidelity of the MI. First, patients and clients complete evaluation forms following each MI. Initial items assess participants' and counselors' perceptions of whether core features of motivational interviewing were present in their session. These core features include perceived rapport (the counselor was easy to talk to), empathy (the counselor was concerned about me), and self-efficacy enhancement (the counselor helped me believe I can change my drinking if I want to). Response options range from *strongly disagree* (1) to *strongly agree* (4). Ten additional items determine whether specific aspects of the protocol were perceived as taking place in the interview, and the perceived utility of these specific facets of the protocol. These include items that assess discussion of pros and cons, normative feedback about drinking, parents' and peers' feelings about drinking and drinking and driving, and strategies to avoid drinking and driving. Response options on these items range from topic not discussed (0) to very useful (3).

Participants gave very high ratings to counselors on rapport (average rating of 3.9), empathy (average rating of 3.7) and self-efficacy enhancement (average rating of 3.7), providing strong support for the fidelity of the intervention with respect to core features of MI. According to patients, essential elements of the protocol were presented to them 88 percent of the time. Counselors reported administering these essential elements 89 percent of the time. Generally speaking, the patients viewed each of the assessed facets as either "somewhat useful" or "very useful" with average ratings of 2.3 to 2.8. The discussion of ways to avoid drinking and driving was rated as the most useful by patients, followed by discussion of drinking cons, and provision of normative feedback.

Given that most of our MIs were conducted bedside in a crowded and noisy ER, it was not possible to videotape or audiotape actual MIs for later coding. Nonetheless, because we wished to augment the feedback sheets with a more objective third-party rating system, we developed a second procedure for evaluating the fidelity of the intervention. This procedure adapted methods used by Project MATCH (Carroll *et al.*, 1998) to rate the delivery of Motivational Enhancement Therapy, and was designed to provide a means by which trained raters could evaluate the implementation of the study protocol *in vivo*. The rater's manual (Behr, Bisighini, Carroll, MacLean & Nuro, 1994) provides explicit criteria both for assessing the extent to which counselors followed the project protocol and evaluating their demonstrated skill level across a number of MI-relevant domains (e.g., expressing empathy, avoiding argumentation).

Counselors conducted videotaped role-play MIs and were rated across eleven MI-relevant categories by three raters trained in MI and familiar with the study protocol. Items assessed counselor's use and skill with regard to core principles of MI (e.g., empathy, reflective listening, non-confrontational style), as well as their adherence and skill in specific aspects of the protocol (e.g., provision of normative feedback). Items were scored with response options ranging from *not at all* (1) to *extensively* (5). Consistent with procedures used by Project MATCH, the scoring criteria were intentionally conservative in that the starting point for each item scale was "1." Raters were instructed to assign ratings greater than "1" only if specific examples of the MI core principles and protocol target behaviors were exhibited. Ratings of "2" generally reflected explicit adherence to the protocol by the counselor with some missed opportunities to use MI-relevant strategies to promote behavior change. A rating of "3" on a particular item indicated that the counselor adhered to the protocol *and* took advantage of some (but not all) additional opportunities to engage in MI-consistent processes. Ratings of "4" and "5" sought to go beyond adherence and assess the skill level of the counselor. A "4" indicated that the counselor took advantage of all opportunities but did not weave them into the MI in a fully optimal fashion. A "5" was assigned when the counselor not only covered the protocol and all additional opportunities, but did so in a flawless manner.

Two primary raters and one secondary rater observed videotaped role plays and completed observer rating forms. Raters observed the videotapes while taking notes on worksheets specifically designed for this purpose. Individual ratings were then assigned to each of the eleven categories assessed. There was consistent evidence for adherence to core features of MI and the treatment protocol across each of the eleven rated behaviors. Average ratings ranged from 2.1 for supporting self-efficacy to 3.8 for use of reflective listening. Mean ratings above "3" were noted for "demonstrating empathy," "avoiding argumentation," "emphasizing personal responsibility for change," and "providing normative feedback." The average total score of the scale was 3, which indicates that the elements of the protocol were administered quite consistently. This score is slightly higher than the average subscale score measured in Project MATCH (Carroll *et al.*, 1998).

In sum, the methods detailed above have provided us with information strongly supportive of the fidelity of our protocol implementation and its conceptual match to the tenets of MI. Ratings from patients, counselors, and trained observers provide converging evidence that we were successful in creating an empathic interaction, and that counselors consistently adhered to specific elements of the intervention protocol. Through this process, we also have gained insight into aspects of the protocol that could be augmented in future studies (e.g., the lowest rated self-efficacy enhancement element). Finally, in addition to their utility as measures of treatment fidelity, these procedures have proved invaluable adjuncts to our routine staff training and supervision processes, as corrective feedback is provided on a regular basis to avoid counselor drift.

Effectiveness of the intervention. Developmental differences within the 13–19 age range, as well as differences in parental involvement and urgent care setting (i.e., pediatric vs. adult emergency rooms), led us to conceptualize our study patients as two distinct samples. The older age group consisted of 18–19-year-old patients, and the younger age group consisted of 13–17-year-old patients.

Analyses conducted on the older age group after the six-month follow-up period were promising (see Monti *et al.*, 1998, for a full report). Ninety-four patients were interviewed three and six months after their emergency room visit. Follow-up rates for the two assessment points averaged 91 percent. Regardless of the intervention received, patients showed a reduction in overall alcohol consumption, with the greatest reduction occurring from baseline to the three-month follow-up interview. The lack of a significant difference in drinking between patients who received a motivational interview and patients who received standard hospital care suggests the alcohol-related event itself, medical treatment in the emergency room, or the subsequent involvement in our project, resulted in a reduction in drinking for both groups.

However, we did find several significant group differences in alcohol-related behaviors and consequences at the six-month follow-up interview. Specifically, adolescents in the MI group reported a significant decrease in drinking and driving whereas adolescents who were provided with standard hospital care did not. At baseline, only six percent of patients in the MI group reported not drinking and driving in the previous six months; six months after the intervention, 38 percent reported they had not driven after drinking since their emergency room visit. By contrast, at baseline, 15 percent of the patients in the SC group reported not drinking and driving; at six-month follow-up, this percentage was unchanged. In addition, patients in the MI group, but not the SC group, showed a significant decrease in traffic violations. Violations reduced from 43 percent to 13 percent in the MI group, and from 36 percent to 29 percent in the SC group. Department of Motor Vehicle records were collected for participants who had driver licenses, and this information indicated both groups of participants were accurately reporting moving violations.

Reports of injuries and alcohol-related injuries also differed significantly by group at the six-month follow-up period. Sixty-four percent of the MI group had experienced an injury compared to 87 percent of the SC group. Over half (51 percent) of the SC group had been injured while under the influence of alcohol, compared to 21 percent of the MI group. Finally, the MI group experienced a significantly lower number of alcohol-related problems (i.e., with parents, friends, police, someone the patient had been dating, or problems at school) in the six months following the ER visit.

Our findings from an emergency room are consistent with Marlatt *et al.*'s (1998) from a college campus. Specifically, Marlatt *et al.* also found decreased consumption at follow-up across the intervention and control groups, but only the MI group showed significant reduction in alcohol-related consequences. Interestingly, at least two studies of brief intervention with adult problem drinkers in medical settings also found reductions in alcohol consumption across both treatment and control groups, but greater harm reduction effects (i.e., decreased alcohol problems) in the intervention group (Chick, Lloyd & Crombie, 1985; Richmond, Heather, Wodak, Kehoe & Webster, 1995).

In order to identify potential mechanisms for the effects of the motivational intervention, we compared the MI and SC groups on the pros and cons of drinking and the experience of additional treatment. We found no treatment group differences on these variables. Because we did not find any group differences on these variables, we cannot identify the processes by which our MI worked to change behavior in the patients who received it. It is possible that the process of MI assists recipients in devising and using strategies that help them to avoid engaging in risky behaviors (such as driving after drinking) and to avoid the dangerous situations that can result in alcohol-related injuries and problems. This and other putative mediators require further study.

We did find youth who received the MI showed a decrease in traffic violations from baseline to follow-up, regardless of their baseline motivation to change. However, for youth in the SC condition, only those adolescents with greater baseline readiness to change showed an improvement in traffic violations. Apparently, the MI influenced those patients whose motivation to change was not impacted by the emergency room visit alone (as indicated by their low level of interest in changing at the baseline assessment).

Younger patients. As in our trial with older adolescents, we found that among younger alcohol-positive patients drinking decreased significantly in the three months following the alcohol-related incident, and no differences between the MI and SC groups were found (Colby, *et al.*, 1999). We have found younger patients to be a more disparate sample than the 18–19-year-olds, in that they span a broader age and developmental range, and demonstrate greater variability at baseline across our measures. One aspect of this variability is that younger patients tended to be in the process of acquiring drinking behavior, so may not have yet reached a pattern of consumption that would show reduction in response to intervention. By the same token, episodes of alcohol-related consequences had occurred at low levels at baseline, creating a "floor effect" such that significant reductions between groups were not demonstrable.

Another possible explanation for the discrepant results between the two age groups may be that the standard hospital care for the younger adolescents was qualitatively different from that of the older adolescents. Specifically, the younger teenagers were treated in a pediatric emergency room whereas patients 18 or older were treated in a busier adult ER. Consequently, it is possible different-aged patients were treated differently by medical staff. For example, younger patients were more likely to be admitted to the hospital for further treatment or observation (vs. discharged home from the ER). The fact that parents were more likely to be involved with the younger patients (by virtue of the patient's age) also may have affected the impact of the MI. Given these circumstances, the MI condition may not have been intensive enough to outperform the hospital standard care. Finally, due to their age and relative inexperience, the younger teens may have had a stronger reaction to the ER experience itself, with little added value for the MI. If this is the case, one solution might be to intervene at some point after the ER visit, at a time when the intensity of the event and the patient's reaction have faded. In sum, we cannot yet say whether the MI as administered in this study is efficacious with younger adolescents.

Nevertheless, one promising finding in our work with younger adolescents is that patients who received MI reduced their frequency of heavy drinking from baseline to follow-up, regardless of their readiness to change. By contrast, patients in the standard care group decreased their number of heavy drinking episodes *only if they were already preparing to change*, whereas those who were not planning to change showed a dramatic increase in heavy drinking (Monti & Colby, 1998). This finding provides evidence that the MI process does indeed promote motivation to change, in that younger adolescents who were not interested in changing responded better to MI than to SC.

Future Directions

Given the dearth of research in the area of brief motivational intervention research with adolescents, there are a number of future directions that could be explored. Although four sessions of Motivational Enhancement Therapy had comparable outcomes to Cognitive-Behavioral Therapy and Twelve-Step Facilitation for alcohol dependent adults (Project

MATCH Research Group, 1997), research on "stand-alone" motivational enhancement interventions for adolescents entering treatment for alcohol use has not been conducted. Alternatively, "front-loading" treatment programs with one or two sessions of motivational enhancement (which has been found to facilitate client compliance and outcomes in treatment for alcohol and cocaine problems in adults [Brown & Miller, 1993; Monti, Rohsenow & O'Leary, 1997]) may complement inpatient or outpatient adolescent substance abuse programs.

"Booster" Sessions

In our research with older adolescents, we found that the greatest reduction in alcohol use was during the three months following the ER visit, and that consumption did not decline significantly after that point. One possibility for intensifying the effect of an opportunistic intervention such as our brief MI might be to provide additional "booster" sessions at target points after the intervention. These sessions could include a discussion of the original injury or intoxication event, and what has transpired in the time since the adolescents' ER visit. These additional sessions may serve to prolong the changes implemented by patients. Indeed, such contact is recommended by clinical guidelines (US DHHS, 1993), although research evidence to date is equivocal (cf., Connors, Tarbox & Faillace, 1992; Richmond, Heather, Wodak, Kehoe & Webster, 1994).

Mechanisms of Change

Identifying the underlying processes that account for behavior change is important for the advancement of prevention and intervention outcome research (MacKinnon, 1994; West, Aiken & Todd, 1993). Our research did not detect changes on the part of the participating adolescents that would explain our behavioral outcomes. We assume that change in patient motivation mediates behavior change, and that the motivational intervention promotes patient motivation (Miller, 1994). However, our evidence did not support this hypothesis, in that we found no group differences on decisional balance as expected. Other studies of brief intervention have not conducted mediational analyses, so this area deserves future attention (Babor, 1994).

Alcohol Risk and Alcohol-related Events. As described above, numerous studies have shown that intervening opportunistically, such as in a primary care office, can be an effective approach for reducing problem drinking. It is possible that individuals are disposed toward considering the issue of their health when in a doctor's office, but may be even more willing to consider modifying behavior if they have had a recent aversive event associated with the behavior. Gentilello *et al.* (1988) have described the "creative use of crisis to weaken denial and bring about treatment" (p. 559) using a Social Network Intervention (SNI) which involves a direct confrontation of the alcoholic by family members and friends. "It is hoped that during an SNI, a point will be reached at which the alcoholic's defenses are overwhelmed and he accepts the need for help" (p. 560). Although the target group for brief intervention is those who have not progressed to alcoholism (IOM, 1990), and the "crisis" experienced by adolescents in our study was receiving medical treatment for an alcohol-related event (i.e., not a social network intervention), the concept of crisis providing a unique opportunity to intervene and potentially promoting interest in change is compelling. It may be that individuals who have had a recent salient event will be more receptive to an intervention than individuals who have not, or may be responsive to a less intensive intervention. In the WHO study, for example, males who had experienced a recent alcohol-related problem had the best outcomes when they received simple advice to cut down on drinking whereas men who had not had a recent problem had better outcomes after receiving the more extensive brief counseling (Babor & Grant, 1994).

In our current work, we have included only youth who had a positive blood alcohol level when brought to the ER, or those who reported having been drinking prior to the injury event. This stands in contrast to the series of studies described earlier that were conducted with adult medical patients who were screened for a signs of drinking problems. These populations may or may not be different, but no study to date has included patients from both groups. Such research would provide information about the most productive way to intervene, be it with those who have an acute sign or those who have a history of alcohol abuse (or both).

Similarly, it is possible that a patient's experience of the injury event and the interpretations an individual makes about the relationship of alcohol use to the injury are associated with intervention outcome and motivation to change. For example, Longabaugh *et al.* (1995) found among a sample of adult patients with subcritical injuries, the aversiveness of the injury and the degree to which the patient believed that alcohol was a factor in the injury occurrence predicted the patient's readiness to change. This is an area that has not been studied with adolescents. The importance of the nature and seriousness of the injury event and the patient's response to it are compelling areas for future work.

Individual Differences and Matching Effects. There is not sufficient information available about the success of brief intervention in general, and motivational interviewing in particular, with different kinds of patients (e.g., levels of alcohol dependence), settings, and circumstances of the intervention. Future work should identify variables that are associated with differential outcomes (e.g., social support or social stability). The brief intervention study conducted by Fleming *et al.* (1997) found reductions in drinking in the intervention group, but found no demographic characteristics or health behaviors that accounted for differences in consumption between the groups, including smoking, age, depression, conduct disorder, and Antisocial Personality Disorder. However, we found some interesting differences in readiness to change in our study, with patients in both the younger and older age groups changing in response to the MI, even when they initially said they were not interested in changing. By contrast, youth in the SC group changed only if they had already been planning to change. The possible application of this finding might be to match only those adolescents who showed no interest in changing to motivational enhancement, since those who already showed interest in changing did indeed change on some variables, regardless of the intervention they received. Although our findings are theoretically consistent with the assumptions of Motivational Interviewing, they await replication and further testing with adolescents.

Gender Differences

Several studies in medical settings have found male patients show greater response to brief intervention than female patients (Babor & Grant, 1992; Elvy, Wells & Baird, 1988; Scott & Anderson, 1991; Wallace *et al.*, 1988). By contrast, Marlatt *et al.*'s (1998) and our studies showed no gender differences in outcomes, and Fleming *et al.* (1997) found a stronger effect for female patients than male patients.

Although our study did not find gender differences in treatment response, we did discover a relationship between depressed mood, gender, and outcome for different ages. In an analysis of the six-month follow-up data, we found interactions between depressed mood and gender significantly predicted drinking outcome, and these results varied by age and gender (Tapert *et al.*, 1998). For younger females (13–17 years), higher depression predicted less frequent drinking at follow-up, perhaps indicating an adaptive distress response to the event that precipitated the ER visit. By contrast, higher depression scores among older females was prognostic of poorer outcome (indicated by more frequent subsequent drinking). For males, depression did not predict subsequent drinking regardless of age group, suggesting depression may be more directly related to drinking among females than males. Our findings for older females and all males are consistent with findings from studies of adult alcoholics, which consistently find higher rates of depression among women than men (Hesselbrock & Hesselbrock, 1993). Gender differences from our study and the inconsistent findings with regard to treatment outcome deserve further exploration.

Ethnic/Racial Differences

Studies of substance use and problems in adolescents have shown important ethnic differences. African American adolescents consistently show lower use of alcohol and drugs than White adolescents, and show lower rates of binge-drinking and heavy drinking than White and Hispanic adolescents (SAMHSA, 1997). Studies that include Native American adolescents find they have the highest prevalence rates of alcohol use and most drugs, followed by Whites (Bachman *et al.*, 1991; Oetting & Beauvais, 1990). However, there is evidence that at younger ages Hispanics show the highest use of cocaine, heroin, and marijuana (Johnston, O'Malley & Bachman, 1998b). There are very few randomized controlled studies of alcohol treatment for youth, and, as a result, little is known about ethnic differences in response to treatment. In a sample of adolescents entering substance abuse treatment, Stewart, Brown & Myers (1997) found conduct-disordered behavior was more highly correlated with substance involvement for Hispanic than for non-Hispanic White youth. Such findings have implications for the development of programs such as the culturally focused approach to prevention with minority adolescents developed by Botvin, Schinke, Epstein, Diaz, and Botvin (1995). Unfortunately, our sample contained too few non-White participants to investigate possible ethnic differences. Further work is needed to identify possible intervention response differences between White and ethnic minority youth, and to determine whether tailoring approaches would be beneficial. Given the higher representation of ethnic minorities in ER populations (Cherpitel, 1995), and the greater potential in a community setting compared to a school-based setting to reach minorities (Yung & Hammond, 1997), emergency or urgent care settings are a suitable place for investigating possible ethnic/racial differences, and for implementing culturally relevant programs.

Implications for Other Problem Behaviors

The application of Motivational Interviewing in medical settings also has been investigated with other problem behaviors including adult smoking (Emmons, 1995; Glynn, 1988; Janz, Becker, Kirscht & Eraker, 1987; Orleans, Rotberg, Quade & Lees, 1990). Unfortunately, the results from these studies have been mixed. Our group recently completed a pilot study of MI with adolescent smokers identified in a hospital settings (Colby *et al.*, 1998). Adolescent smokers aged 14–17 who presented for medical treatment at an urban hospital were recruited and randomly assigned to either MI or brief advice. The study participants were not selected on the basis of being motivated to quit smoking. In the 30-minute MI, adolescents explored their beliefs about the effects of smoking, and discussed four videotaped vignettes related to smoking. The videos were used to stimulate discussion about the various consequences (health, social, financial, addiction) of smoking for adolescents. The adolescents were assisted in setting personal goals for behavior change, with the counselors providing advice about strategies where appropriate. Forty adolescents participated at baseline. After three months, two-thirds of the sample had made a serious (>24-hour) quit attempt, with an average duration of about three weeks, and significant reductions were found in smoking rate and nicotine dependence. Twenty-two percent of those who had received MI were no longer smoking at follow-up, compared with ten percent of those who received brief advice ($h = 0.28$, a small-to-medium effect).

Sufficiently encouraged by the findings from this pilot study, we have recently launched a major clinical trial investigating MI with adolescent daily smokers. With a much larger sample and longer-term follow-up, we hope to be able to identify mediating mechanisms and individual difference factors that may play important roles in our understanding young smokers' response to treatment. Attention to the components of our adolescent intervention have led us to believe that using multiple modalities such as computers and videotapes may interest adolescents in participating, and may convey important messages in an attractive and attention-capturing medium. This conclusion is consistent with the innovative work begin conducted by Prochaska (1998) and colleagues who use computers to conduct brief smoking interventions, and Skinner (1998) who utilizes a computer website to engage adolescents in discussions about health behaviors.

Summary

Brief intervention in general, and Motivational Interviewing (MI) as a specific type of brief intervention, have shown great promise with adults but have been minimally studied with adolescents. Our work suggests a brief MI, when introduced at a "teachable moment," can be particularly effective in reducing a number of dangerous behaviors and consequences, including drinking and driving, injuries, alcohol-related injuries, traffic violations, and other alcohol-related problems for older adolescents. However, less convincing results with younger adolescents and with attempts to identify mediators of treatment effects suggest the need for more systematic work in this area.

References

Babor, T. F. (1994), "Avoiding the horrid and beastly sin of drunkenness: Does dissuasion make a difference?" *Journal of Consulting and Clinical Psychology 62*(6), 1127–1140.

Babor, T. F., & Grant, M. (1992), "Project on identification and management of alcohol-related problems. Report on Phase II: A randomized clinical trial of brief interventions in primary health care." Geneva, Switzerland: World Health Organization.

Babor, T. F., & Grant, M. (1994), "Comments on the WHO report 'Brief Interventions for Alcohol Problems': A summary and some international comments." *Addiction 89*, 657–678.

Bachman, J. G. *et al.* (1991), "Racial/ethnic differences in smoking, drinking, and illicit drug use among American high school seniors, 1976–89. *American Journal of Public Health, 81*(3), 372–377.

Baer, J. S., & Carney, M. M. (1993), "Biases in the perceptions of the consequences of alcohol use among college students." *Journal of Studies on Alcohol 54*, 54–60.

Baer, J. S., Stacy, A., & Larimer, M. (1991), "Biases in the perception of drinking norms among college students. *Journal of Studies on Alcohol 52*(6), 580–586.

Bandura, A. (1982), "Self-efficacy mechanism in human agency." *American Psychologist 37*(2), 122–147.

Barnett, N. P. *et al.* (1998), "Detection of alcohol use in adolescent patients in the Emergency Department." *Academic Emergency Medicine 5*(6), 607–612.

Behr, H. M., Bisighini, R. M., Carroll, K. M., MacLean, R., & Nuro, K. F. (1994), "Rater's manual for Project MATCH Tape Rating Scale, Version 8: 9/94." Unpublished manual.

Bernstein, E., Bernstein, J., & Levenson, S. (1997), "Project ASSERT: An ED-based intervention to increase access to primary care, prevention services, and the substance abuse treatment system." *Annals of Emergency Medicine 30*(2), 181–189.

Bien, T. H., Miller, W. R., & Boroughs, J. M. (1993) "Motivational interviewing with alcohol outpatients." *Behavioral and Cognitive Psychotherapy 21*, 347–356.

Bien, T. H., Miller, W. R., & Tonigan, J. S. (1993). Brief interventions for alcohol problems: A review. *Addiction 88*, 315–336.

Blose, J. O., & Holder, H. D. (1991), "Injury-related medical care utilization in a problem drinking population." *American Journal of Public Health 81*, 1571–1575.

Botvin, G. J., Schinke, S. P., Epstein, J. A., Diaz, T., & Botvin, E. M. (1995), "Effectiveness of culturally focused and generic skills training approaches to alcohol and drug abuse prevention among minority adolescents: Two-year follow-up results." *Psychology of Addictive Behaviors 9*(3), 183–194.

Brent, D. A., Perper, J. A., Allman, C. J. (1987). Alcohol, firearms, and suicide among youth. *Journal of the American Medical Association, 257*(24), 3369–3372.

Brown, J. M., & Miller, W. R. (1993), "Impact of motivational interviewing on participation and outcome in residential alcoholism treatment." *Psychology of Addictive Behaviors 7*(4), 211–218.

Carroll, K. M. *et al.* (1998), "Internal validity of Project MATCH treatments: Discriminability and integrity." *Journal of Consulting and Clinical Psychology 66*(2), 290–303.

Chafetz, M. E. (1968). Research in the alcohol clinic: An around-the-clock psychiatric service of the Massachusetts General Hospital. *American Journal of Psychiatry, 124*, 1674–1679.

Chafetz, M. E. *et al.* (1962), "Establishing treatment relations with alcoholics." *Journal of Nervous and Mental Diseases 134*, 395–409.

Cherpitel, C. J. (1993), "Alcohol and injuries: A review of international emergency room studies." *Addiction 88*, 651–665.

Cherpitel, C. J. (1994a), "Alcohol and casualties: A comparison of emergency room and coroner data." *Alcohol and Alcoholism 29*(2), 211–218.

Cherpitel, C. J. (1994b), "Injury and the role of alcohol: County-wide emergency room data." *Alcoholism: Clinical and Experimental Research 18*(3), 679–684.

Cherpitel, C. J. (1995), "Alcohol and casualties: Comparison of county-wide emergency room data with the county general population." *Addiction 90*(3), 343–350.

Christoffel, K. K., Marcus D., Sagerman, S., & Bennett, S. (1988), Adolescent suicide and suicide attempts: A population study." *Pediatric Emergency Care 4*(1): 32–40.

Chick, J., Lloyd, G., & Crombie, E. (1985), Counseling problem drinkers in medical wards: A controlled study." *British Medical Journal 290,* 965–967.

Chung, H., & Elias, M. (1996), "Patterns of adolescent involvement in problem behaviors: Relationship to self-efficacy, social competence, and life events." *American Journal of Community Psychology 24*(6), 771–784.

Chung, T., Colby, S. M., Barnett, N. P., Rohsenow, D. J., Spirito, A., & Monti, P. M. (2000), "Screening adolescents for problem drinking: Performance of brief screens aginst DSM-IV alcohol diagnoses," *Journal of Studies on Alcohol 61*, 579–587.

Clancy, J. (1964), "Motivation conflicts of the alcohol addict." *Quarterly Journal of Studies on Alcohol 25*, 511–520.

Colby, S. M. *et al.* (1998), "Brief motivational interviewing in a hospital setting for adolescent smoking: A preliminary study." *Journal of Consulting and Clinical Psychology 66,* 574–578.

Colby, S. M., Monti, P. M., Barnett, N. P., Spirito, A., Myers, M., Rohsenow, D. J., Woolard, R. H., & Lewander, W. J. (1999). Effects of a brief motivational interview on alcohol use and consequences: Predictors of response to intervention among 13 to 17 year olds. In R. Longabaugh & P. M. Monti (Chairs), *Brief Motivational Interventions in the Emergency Department for adolescents and adults,* symposium conducted at the Annual Meeting of the Research Society on Alcoholism, Santa Barbara, California, June, 1999.

Connors, G. J., Tarbox, A. R., & Faillace, L. A. (1992), "Achieving and maintaining gains among problem drinkers: Process and outcome results." *Behavior Therapy 23*, 449–474.

Cooney, N. L., Zweben, A., & Fleming, M. F. (1995), "Screening for alcohol problems and at-risk drinking in health-care settings." In R. K. Hester & W. R. Miller (eds), *Handbook of alcoholism treatment approaches: Effective alternatives.* (pp. 45–60). Boston: Allyn & Bacon Inc., 45–60.

Dimeff, L. A., Baer, J. S., Kivlahan, D. R., & Marlatt, G. A. (1999), *"Brief Alcohol Screening and Intervention for College Students: A harm reduction approach."* New York: Guilford Press.

Donovan, J. E. (1993), "Young adult drinking–driving: Behavioral and psychosocial correlates." *Journal of Studies on Alcohol 54,* 600–613.

Ellickson, P. L., McGuigan, K. A., Adams, V., Bell, R. M., & Hays, R. (1996), "Teenagers and alcohol misuse in the United States: By any definition it's a big problem." *Addiction 91,* 1489–1503.

Elvy, G. A., Wells, J. E., & Baird, K. A. (1988), "Attempted referral as intervention for problem drinking in the general hospital." *British Journal of Addiction 83*, 83–89.

Emmons, K. M. (1995), *"Motivation for smoking cessation: To quit or not to quit is not the question."* Paper presented in symposium, K. M. Emmons (Chair), Motivation for change across behavioral risk factors: Conceptual and Clinical Advances. Sixteenth Annual Meeting, Society of Behavioral Medicine, San Diego, CA.

Fleming, M. F., Barry, K. L., Manwell, L. B., Johnson, K., & London, R. (1997), "Brief physician advice for problem alcohol drinkers: A randomized controlled trial in community-based primary care practices." *Journal of the American Medical Association 277*(13), 1039–1045.

Forsberg, A. D., King, G., Delaronde, S. R., & Geary, M. K. (1996), "Maintaining safer sex behaviours in HIV-infected adolescents with haemophilia." *AIDS Care 8*(6), 629–640.

Gentilello, L. M. *et al.* (1988), "Major injury as a unique opportunity to initiate treatment in the alcoholic." *The American Journal of Surgery 156*(6), 558–561.

Glynn, T. J. (1988), "Relative effectiveness of physician-initiated smoking cessation programs." *Cancer Bulletin 40.* 359–364.

Gould, M. S. *et al.* (1998), "Psychopathology associated with suicidal ideation and attempts among children and adolescents." *Journal of the American Academy of Child and Adolescent Psychiatry 37*(9), 915–923.

Gould, M. S., Shaffer, D. S., Fisher, P., Kleinman, M. S., & Morishima, M. S. (1992), "The clinical prediction of adolescent suicide." In R. W. Maris, A. L. Berman, J. T. Maltsberger & R. I. Yulit (eds), *Assessment and Prediction of Suicide.* New York: Guilford Press, 130–143.

Heather, N., Rollnick, S., Bell, A., & Richmond, R. (1996), "Effects of brief counseling among male heavy drinkers identified on general hospital wards." *Drug and Alcohol Review 15*(1), 29–38.

Hesselbrock, M. N., & Hesselbrock, V. M. (1993), "Depression and antisocial personality disorder in alcoholism: Gender comparison." In E. S. Gomberg & T. D. Nirenberg (eds), *Women and Substance Abuse.* Norwood, NJ: Ablex Publishing, 142–161.

Hicks, B., Morris, J., Bass, S., Holcomb, G., & Neblett, W. (1990), "Alcohol and the adolescent trauma population." *Journal of Pediatric Surgery 25*, 944–949.

Institute of Medicine (1990), "*Broadening the Base of Treatment for Alcohol Problems.* Washington, DC: National Academy Press.

Janz, N. K., Becker, M. H., Kirscht, J. P., & Eraker, S. A. (1987), "Evaluation of a minimal-contract smoking cessation intervention in an outpatient setting." *American Journal of Public Health 77* (805–809).

Johnston, L. D., O'Malley, P. M., & Bachman, J. G. (1998a), "Drug use by American young people begins to turn downward." (On-line). Available: www.isr.umich.edu/src/mtf; accessed 03/15/99. To appear in: Johnston, L. D., O'Malley, P. M., & Bachman, J. G. (in preparation), *National Survey Results on Drug Use from the Monitoring the Future Study, 1975–1998. Volume I: Secondary school students.* (NIH Publication No.), Rockville, MD: National Institute on Drug Abuse.

Johnston, L. D., O'Malley, P. M., & Bachman, J. G. (1998b), "*National Survey Results on Drug Use from the Monitoring the Future Study, 1975–1997. Volume II: College students and young adults.*" Rockville, MD: National Institute on Drug Abuse. NIDA Publication No. 98–4346.

Kavanagh, D. J., Sitharthan, T., & Sayer, G. P. (1996), "Prediction of results from correspondence treatment for controlled drinking." *Addiction 91*(10), 1539–1545.

Kogan, L. S. (1957), "The short-term case in a family agency: Part II. Results of study." *Social Casework 38*, 296–302.

Koumans, A. J. R., & Muller, J. J. (1965), "Use of letters to increase motivation in alcoholics." *Psychological Reports 16*, 1152.

Koumans, A. J. R., Muller, J. J., & Miller, C. F. (1967), "Use of telephone calls to increase motivation for treatment in alcoholics." *Psychological Reports 21*, 327–328.

Lee, N. K., & Oei, T. P. (1993), "The importance of alcohol expectancies and drinking refusal self-efficacy in the quantity and frequency of alcohol consumption." *Journal of Substance Abuse 5*(4), 379–390.

Li, G., Smith, G. S., & Baker, S. P. (1994), "Drinking behavior in relation to cause of death among US adults." *American Journal of Public Health 84*(9), 1402–1406.

Longabaugh, R. *et al*. (1995), "Injury as a motivator to reduce drinking." *Academic Emergency Medicine 2*, 817–825.

MacKinnon, D. P. (1994), "Analysis of mediating variables in prevention and intervention research." In A. Cazares & L. A. Beatty (eds), *Scientific Methods for Prevention Intervention* (Vol. NIDA Research Monograph No. 139, pp. 127–153). Rockville, MD: National Institute on Drug Abuse.

Maio, R. F., Portnoy, J., Blow, F. C., & Hill, E. (1994), "Injury type, injury severity, and repeat occurrence of alcohol-related trauma in adolescents." *Alcoholism: Clinical and Experimental Research 18*, 261–264.

Marcus, B. H., Eaton, C. A., Rossi, J. S., & Harlow, L. L. (1994), "Self-efficacy, decision-making, and stages of change: An integrative model of physical exercise." *Journal of Applied Social Psychology 24*(6), 489–508.

Marlatt, G. A. *et al*. (1998), "Screening and brief intervention for high-risk college student drinkers: Results from a two-year follow-up assessment." *Journal of Consulting and Clinical Psychology 66* (4), 604–615.

Marlatt, G. A., Larimer, M. E., Baer, J. S., & Quigley, L. A. (1993), "Harm reduction for alcohol problems: Moving beyond the controlled drinking controversy." *Behavior Therapy 24*, 461–504.

Melnick, G., De Leon, G., Hawke, J., Jainchill, N., & Kressel, D. (1997), "Motivation and readiness for therapeutic community treatment among adolescents and adult substance abusers." *American Journal of Drug and Alcohol Abuse 23*, 485–506.

Midanik, L. T., & Clark, W. B. (1995) "Drinking-related problems in the United States: Descriptions and trends, 1984–1990. *Journal of Studies on Alcohol 56*, 39–402.

Miller, W. R. (1985), "Motivation for treatment: A review with special emphasis on alcoholism." *Psychological Bulletin 98*, 84–107.

Miller, W. R. (1994), "Motivational interviewing: III. On the ethics of motivational intervention." *Behavioural and Cognitive Psychology 22*, 111–123.

Miller, W. R. (1995), "Increasing motivation for change." In R. K. Hester & W. R. Miller (eds), *Handbook of Alcoholism Treatment Approaches* (2nd ed.). Boston: Allyn & Bacon, 89–104.

Miller, W. R., Benefield, R. G., & Tonigan, J. S. (1993), "Enhancing motivation for change in problem drinking: A controlled comparison of two therapist styles." *Journal of Clinical and Counseling Psychology 61*, 455–461.

Miller, W. R. *et al*. (1995), "What works? A methodological analysis of the alcohol treatment outcome literature." In R. K. Hester & W. R. Miller (eds), *Handbook of Alcoholism Treatment Approaches* (2nd ed.). Boston: Allyn & Bacon, 12–44.

Miller, W. R., & Hester, R. K. (1986), "Matching problem drinkers with optimal treatment methods." In W. R. Miller & N. Heather (eds), *Treating Addictive Behaviors: Process of Change*. New York: Plenum, 175–204.

Miller, W. R., & Rollnick, S. (1991), "*Motivational Interviewing: Preparing people to change addictive behavior*." New York: Guilford Press.

Miller, W. R., & Sanchez, V. C. (1993), "Motivating young adults for treatment and lifestyle change." In G. Howard (ed.), *Issues in Alcohol Use and Misuse by Young Adults*. Notre Dame, IN: University of Notre Dame Press, 55–79.

Miller, W. R., Sovereign, R. G., & Krege, B. (1988), "Motivational interviewing with problem drinkers: II. The drinker's check-up as a preventive intervention." *Behavioural Psychotherapy 16*, 251–268.

Monti, P. M. (1998), "Introductory remarks." Presented at Adolescents, Alcohol, and Substance Abuse: Reaching Teens Through Brief Interventions Conference, Newport, RI.

Monti, P. M., Abrams, D. B., Kadden, R. M., & Cooney, N. L. (1989), "*Treating Alcohol Dependence: A Coping Skills Training Guide*." New York: Guilford Press.

Monti, P. M., & Colby, S. M. (1998), "Motivational interviewing in opportunistic settings: Reaching teens through brief interventions." Presented at Adolescents, Alcohol, and Substance Abuse: Reaching Teens Through Brief Interventions Conference, Newport, RI.

Monti, P. M. *et al.* (1998), *"Brief intervention for harm reduction with alcohol-positive older adolescents in a hospital emergency department."* Manuscript under review.

Monti, P. M., Rohsenow, D. J., & O'Leary, T. (1997), "Treating substance abusers with coping skills training and motivational interviewing." Invited institute presented at the Annual Meeting of the Association for Advancement of Behavior Therapy, Miami Beach, FL.

Moskowitz, J. M. (1989), "The primary prevention of alcohol problems: A critical review of the research literature." *Journal of Studies on Alcohol 50,* 54–88.

National Institute on Alcohol Abuse and Alcoholism (1997, June), *"Ninth special report to the U.S. Congress on alcohol and health."* NIH Publication No. 97–4017. Washington DC.

Oetting, E. R., & Beauvais, F. (1990), "Adolescent drug use: Findings of National and local surveys." *Journal of Consulting and Clinical Psychology 58*(4), 385–395.

Orleans, C. T., Rotberg, H., Quade, D., & Lees, P. A. (1990), "Hospital quit-smoking consult service: Clinical report and intervention guidelines." *Preventive Medicine 19*, 198–212.

Pediaditakis, N. (January, 1962), "Motivating the acutely intoxicated alcoholic patient to obtain further treatment." *North Carolina Medical Journal* 11–12.

Prochaska, J. O. (1998), "The transtheoretical model of behavior change: Addressing motivation as part of prevention and treatment." Presented at Adolescents, Alcohol, and Substance Abuse: Reaching Teens Through Brief Interventions Conference, Newport, RI.

Prochaska, J. O., Johnson, S., & Lee, P. (1998), "The transtheoretical model of behavior change." In S. A. Shumaker, E. B. Schron, *et al.* (eds), *The Handbook of Health Behavior Change* (2nd ed.). New York: Springer, 59–84.

Project MATCH Research Group (1997), "Matching alcoholism treatments to client heterogeneity: Project MATCH posttreatment drinking outcomes." *Journal of Studies on Alcohol 58*(1), 7–29.

Richmond, R., Heather, N., Wodak, A., Kehoe, L., & Webster, I. (1994), *A controlled evaluation of a general practice-based brief intervention for excessive alcohol consumption: The Alcohol Screen Project. NDARC Monograph Series.* Sydney: National Drug & Alcohol Research Center, University of New South Wales.

Richmond, R., Heather, N., Wodak, A., Kehoe, L., & Webster, I. (1995), "Controlled evaluation of a general practice-based brief intervention for excessive drinking." *Addiction 90*, 119–132.

Rivara, F. P. *et al.* (1993), "The magnitude of acute and chronic alcohol abuse in trauma patients." *Archives of Surgery 128*, 907–913.

Rivara, F. P., Koepsell, T. D., Jurkovich, G. J., Gurney, J. G., & Soderberg, R. (1993), The effects of alcohol abuse on readmission for trauma." *Journal of the American Medical Association 270*(16), 1962–1964.

Schulenberg, J., Wadsworth, K. N., O'Malley, P. M., Bachman, J. G., & Johnston, L. D. (1996), "Adolescent risk factors for binge drinking during the transition to young adulthood: Variable- and pattern-centered approaches to change." *Developmental Psychology 32*(4), 659–674.

Scott, E., & Anderson, P. (1991), "Randomized controlled trial of general practitioner intervention in women with excessive alcohol consumption." *Drug and Alcohol Review 10*, 313–321.

Skinner, H. A. (1998), "Engaging adolescents using computer-assisted technology." Presented at Adolescents, Alcohol, and Substance Abuse: Reaching Teens Through Brief Interventions Conference, Newport, RI.

Sobell, M. B., Sobell, L. C., Bogardis, J., Leo, G. L., & Skinner, H. A. (1993), "Problem drinkers' perceptions of whether treatment goals should be self-selected or therapist-selected." *Behavior Therapy, 23*(1), 43–52.

Spirito, A., Rasile, D., Vinnick, C., Jelalian, E., & Arrigan, M. E. (1997), "Relationship between substance abuse and self-reported injuries among adolescents." *Journal of Adolescent Health 21*, 221–224.

Stewart, D. G., Brown, S. A., & Myers, M. G. (1997), "Antisocial behavior and psychoactive substance involvement among Hispanic and non-Hispanic Caucasian adolescents in substance abuse treatment." *Journal of Child and Adolescent Substance Abuse 6*(4), 1–22.

Substance Abuse and Mental Health Services Administration (1997), *Preliminary results from the 1996 National Household Survey on Drug Abuse.* Office of Applied Studies, Department of Health and Human Services, Rockville, MD.

Tapert, S. F. *et al.* (November, 1998), "Depressed mood and response to motivational interviewing for adolescent alcohol abuse." Poster presented at the annual meeting of the Association for the Advancement of Behavior Therapy, Washington, DC.

US Department of Health and Human Services (1993), *Guidelines for Treatment of Alcohol and Other Drug-abusing Adolescents.* Center for Substance Abuse Treatment, Treatment Improvement Protocol Series (Publication No. 93–2010).

US Department of Health and Human Services (1997), *Ninth Special Report to the U.S. Congress on Alcohol and Health.* Public Health Service, National Institute of Alcohol Abuse and Alcoholism.

Wallace, P., Cutler, S., & Haines, A. (1988), "Randomized controlled trial of general practitioner intervention in patients with excessive alcohol consumption." *British Medical Journal 297*, 663–668.

Wechsler, H., Dowdall, G. W., Maenner, G., Gledhill-Hoyt, J., & Lee, H. (1998), "Changes in binge drinking and related problems among American college students between 1993 and 1997: Results of the Harvard School of Public Health College Alcohol Study." *Journal of American College Health 47*, 57–68.

Werch, C. E., Gorman, D. R., & Marty, P. J. (1987), "Relationship between alcohol consumption and alcohol problems in young adults." *Journal of Drug Education 17*(3), 261–276.

West, S. G., Aiken, L. S., & Todd, M. (1993), "Probing the effects of individual components in multiple component prevention programs." *American Journal of Community Psychology 21*(3), 571–605.

Windle, M., Miller-Tutzauer, C., & Domenico, D. (1992), "Alcohol use, suicidal behavior, and risky activities among adolescents." *Journal of Research on Adolescence 2*(4), 317–330.

Withers, L. E., & Kaplan, D. W. (1987), Adolescents who attempt suicide: A retrospective clinical chart review of hospitalized patients." *Professional Psychology: Research and Practice 18*(4), 391–393.

Wood, M. D. (1998), "Preventive interventions to reduce alcohol and other drug abuse among college students: Implications from alcohol abuse preventive interventions." Position paper solicited by the Network of Colleges and Universities Committed to the Elimination of Alcohol and Drug Abuse.

Yung, B. R., & Hammond, W. R. (1997), "Community-based interventions." In D. K. Wilson, J. R. Rodrigue, & W.C. Taylor (eds), *Health-Promoting and Health-Compromising Behaviors among Minority Adolescents. Application and Practice in Health Psychology, Vol. 3.* Washington, DC: American Psychological Association, 269–297.

Chapter 8

Facilitating Change for Adolescent Alcohol Problems: A Multiple Options Approach

Sandra A. Brown*

The present chapter describes the development and initial evaluation of an innovative secondary intervention for alcohol use among high school students. The intervention is designed to facilitate personal change efforts of adolescents and to fill the void of services available to youth who have begun drinking but have not been referred to a treatment program. Although designed for youth with alcohol experience, preliminary evidence suggests that this voluntary, multiple option intervention is appealing to at-risk youth prior to personal alcohol experience and to abstaining students with a history of serious alcohol problems.

The initial portion of the chapter focuses on both the theoretical underpinnings and empirical foundation of PROJECT OPTIONS. The description of the intervention is provided along with details of the multi-system developmental approach used to promote program acceptability and enhance community commitment to the project. The third section of the chapter focuses on early findings using the approach in high schools. Service utilization data and preliminary outcomes are provided. Finally, a discussion of future research and potential application of this self-selection approach with various populations of youth concludes the chapter.

Theoretical Underpinnings

Despite expenditure of considerable federal resources toward decreasing drinking among teenagers, alcohol involvement remains a major problem for adolescents in the United States. Alcohol is the most commonly used drug of America's youth, with one-third of high school students reporting hazardous alcohol use (five or more drinks per occasion) within a two-week period (e.g., Johnston, O'Malley & Bachman, 1999). Alcohol use among adolescents produces both immediate risks (e.g., accidents, injuries) and long-term risks (e.g.,

This research was supported by grants from the National Institute of Alcohol Abuse and Alcoholism (5R01 AA07033) and (5R01 AA12171) and The Center for Substance Abuse Treatment.
*Correspondence concerning this chapter should be addressed to Sandra A. Brown, Ph.D., University of California, San Diego, Department of Psychology (0109), La Jolla, CA 92093.

Innovations in Adolescent Substance Abuse Interventions, pages 169–187.

neuropsychological damage). Alcohol involvement among adolescents consistently is associated with such potentially developmentally damaging sequelae as poor school performance and dropout, high-risk sexual behavior, use of other psychoactive substances, and a variety of mental health disorders (e.g., Hussong & Chassin, 1994; Lewinsohn, Hops, Roberts & Seelye, 1993; Newcomb & Bentler, 1988; Tapert, Stewart & Brown, 1999).

Despite the high rates of problematic alcohol involvement by teens, remarkably small proportions of teens currently seek and receive treatment specifically for alcohol problems. In fact, traditional approaches to intervention do not appear to be optimal for adolescents (Brown, 1993). Changes in the health care system, a high threshold for care, and delays in treatment entry result in failure to capitalize on transient high motivational states of youth who want to make changes in their drinking, and result in poor engagement of youth. The vast majority of treated adolescents do not seek treatment (Brown, 1993), in part because of negative social stereotypes associated with traditional approaches to treatment (e.g., Sobell, Sobell, Toneatto & Leo, 1993; Tucker, 1995). Although there are specific exceptions (e.g., Liddle & Dakof, 1994), few forms of alcohol treatment for adolescents have clearly demonstrated efficacy. Finally, even when treated, the high relapse rates common to alcohol dependent adults are paralleled among adolescents (e.g., Brown, Vik & Creamer, 1989; Brown, Myers, Mott & Vik, 1994). Given the remarkable variety of deviant behaviors adolescents display when entering treatment for alcohol and/ or drug problems (e.g., Brown, Mott & Stewart, 1992; Stewart & Brown, 1995), it is not surprising that the tertiary interventions considered most promising for alcohol-abusing adolescents require substantial resources in multiple contexts to provoke and sustain necessary lifestyle changes (e.g., Henggeler, 1993). Clearly, interventions targeted at youth in earlier stages of the development of alcohol problems hold much promise for reaching more adolescents in need, cost savings, and avoiding considerable personal and family hardship (e.g., Institute of Medicine, 1990; Mulford, 1977).

Natural Recovery

It now appears, as with adults, many youth that develop and resolve alcohol problems never receive formal treatment (Fillmore, 1988; Wagner, Brown, Monti, Myers & Waldron, 1999). There is a remarkable discrepancy between national alcohol problem rates of youth and numbers of adolescents who receive treatment for alcohol or drug problems (Johnston, O'Malley & Bachman, 1994). Longitudinal studies suggest that a portion of adolescents mature out of hazardous alcohol use and resultant problems as they transition into adulthood (e.g., Bates & Labouvie, 1994; Donovan & Jessor, 1985; Newcomb & Bentler, 1988). While only recently have studies examined the process of this self-change or natural recovery from alcohol problems among youth (Smart & Stoduto, 1997; Wagner *et al.*, 1999), three-fourths of adults who resolve their alcohol problems do so without formal treatment (e.g., Sobell, Cunningham & Sobell, 1996). Our recent studies suggest that significant proportions of high school students (approximately 25 percent of drinkers) make purposeful attempts to cut down or stop their drinking, and a substantial proportion of high-risk youth who experience alcohol problems resolve their problems without formal treatment (Wagner *et al.*, 1999).

Even youth that receive specific treatment for alcohol and drug abuse appear to improve or maintain behavioral changes through means other than those recommended by treatment programs. Among adolescent alcohol and drug abusers we have studied during and following treatment (e.g., Brown, 1993; Brown *et al.*, 1994), only 53 percent were found to comply with the primary behavioral prescription of alcohol and drug treatment programs - attending Twelve-Step meetings. Approximately one-third of the adolescents who failed to attend the mandated Twelve-Step meetings used other methods to consistently abstain or have minimal alcohol involvement during the first year following treatment (Brown, 1993).

In concert, longitudinal findings from community and clinical samples indicate that substantial portions of adolescents make efforts to reduce or cease their alcohol involvement independent of formalized treatment programs, and that certain self-change efforts result in success maintained over at least a one year time period. Understanding the strategies that adolescents employ in their natural environment to resolve their own alcohol problems can facilitate our understanding of the process of self-change, potentially enhance the effectiveness of all intervention efforts, and allow treatment to reach portions of the adolescent population that do not currently seek treatment (Brown & D'Amico, in press; Sobell *et al.*, 1996; Watson & Sher, 1998).

Self-change Process

The processes whereby individuals successfully change problematic alcohol consumption without formal treatment are not well understood (Watson & Sher, 1998), and remarkably little investigation has been done with the adolescent population despite the considerable theoretical value and practical importance of such information (Smart & Stoduto, 1997; Wagner *et al.*, 1999). Although models of change (e.g., Stages of Change; Prochaska, DiClemente & Norcross, 1992) have been generated and applied to addictive behaviors, few are truly process of change models. Thus far, models apply to motivated or purposeful change and fail to consider other factors such as risk perception or required behavioral change, which may produce youth inaction (Bandura, in press).

Motivated change. Studies examining the self-change process for alcohol problems have focused primarily on intentional change such as those who want to change on their own (e.g., Klingemann, 1991; Sobell *et al.*, 1993) or triggers for change (e.g., Tucker, 1995; Tucker, Vuchinich & Gladsjo, 1994). These studies help clarify: the degree of motivation, the process of purposeful progression through change, types of activities engaged in, and precipitants to self-change efforts. The issue of motivation may be particularly important for adolescents as indicated by difficulties in enrolling adolescents into substance use cessation studies (e.g., Myers, Brown & Kelly, 2000; Peltier, Telch & Coates, 1982). The importance of motivation is highlighted for adolescents in that one of the few interventions to date that has demonstrated preliminary success in effecting smoking cessation among adolescents was based on motivational interviewing principles (Colby *et al.*, 1998). Motivation can be conceptualized as a fluctuating state of readiness to change (Miller & Rollnick, 1991; Prochaska *et al.*, 1992), and as such, fostering and enhancing motivation for changing alcohol use appears critical. Adolescents in general may be less motivated to change their alcohol, cigarette, or drug use since they are less likely than adults to have incurred severe negative consequences (Flay, 1993), particularly health-related effects. Also, problem drinking youths in particular are likely to perceive drinking as normative since they tend to be exposed to high levels of use in their environment (e.g., associating with other regular or heavy drinkers). A motivational approach is likely to be particularly important when intervening for alcohol, as some adolescents may have little initial desire to reduce their alcohol use. Therefore, interventions for alcohol problems among adolescent students will benefit from considering motivational obstacles to initial participation, including techniques to enhance and maintain motivation for change, and targeting adolescents' personal concerns that are linked to alcohol involvement rather than alcohol use levels *per se*.

Incidental change. Few studies have examined what might be considered incidental change; that is, change related to natural transitions which unfold with adolescent development such as role shifts or the socialization process (Watson & Sher, 1998). An exception is Yamaguchi and Kandel (1985), who theorized that developmental changes in life stage and specific roles (social, academic, work, and parenting) influence drinking decisions as part of the process of self-selection, preparation for new roles, and anticipatory socialization. Clear examples of alcohol and drug use behavior change with role and context change are abundant in the adult literature (e.g., heroin cessation with transition out of the Vietnam War; alcohol and drug cessation during pregnancy) and have been suggested for adolescents as well (e.g., Brown, 1993; Windle, 1990). For example, we recently found escalation of both alcohol and drug involvement among youth as they initially move to independent living (Brown, Kypri & Coe, 1998). De-escalation from problem drinking levels has also been reported to follow changes in peer group affiliation among high school students (Stice, Myers & Brown, 1998). Since adolescence is a time of rapid social changes and role transitions, a significant proportion of adolescent change efforts may be incidental to common role and activity changes.

Self-change Model

Cognitive social learning theory (Bandura, 1986) has been applied to models of both the development and treatment of alcohol problems (e.g., Abrams, and Niura, Carey, Monti & Binkoff, 1986; Brownell, Marlatt, Lichtenstein & Wilson, 1986). Our research suggests that this model is equally applicable to de-escalation of alcohol involvement among youth. Within this conceptual framework, alcohol use results from cognitive appraisal and evaluation processes (Klingemann, 1991; Myers & Brown, 1996; Sobell *et al.*, 1993; Tucker, Vuchinich & Gladsjo, 1990–91), which are dependent on intentionality (motivation) and personal risk–resource balance (Vik, Mott & Brown, under review). In particular, the developmental, social information processing model (Coie & Dodge, 1998) postulates that proximal cognitive and emotional states lead to engagement in specific behaviors (drinking) within a social context (e.g., peer drinking). Grounded in cognitive science research on the manner in which individuals store and retrieve information, distribute cognitive processing resources, and ultimately solve problems, this model links distal factors (e.g., biological risks, cultural experiences, family risk and resilience factors) with proximal situations (e.g., peer use, alcohol availability, reinforcement expectancies, emotional and motivational states). Our longitudinal research with adolescents suggests that these factors play a role in both the deliberate (intentional) and automatic (incidental) decisions of youth regarding alcohol use. Thus, external contingencies (e.g., sports drug testing, parental threats, changes in peer group) and/or personal experiences (e.g., alcohol problems such as blackouts, nausea, high-risk sexual behavior) may create perception of a need for change for the adolescent. If personal resources are sufficient to cope, then more automatic processing will ensue (use or no use, depending on personal history). However, when personal resources are limited (e.g., poor coping skills, low self-efficacy) or when personal or situational risks are high (e.g., abusing peers and family, limited financial resources for alternative activities, depression), then more deliberative processing results. Furthermore, dependent on stage of neurocognitive development (e.g., myelination of frontal and prefrontal lobes which occurs throughout puberty), immediate and/or long-term consequences will be incorporated into the social cognitions. Such a decision-making process may result in potentially different strategies for personal change efforts, as well as outcomes, during early and middle adolescence compared to later adolescence (Tapert, Brown, Myers & Granholm, 1999).

The social cognition model posits that factors related to initial action in support of reduction/cessation of alcohol/drug use (e.g., motivation, decisional balance, immediate contingencies) are different from those required to sustain behavior change (e.g., self-monitoring skills, available alternative reinforces, distancing). Thus, motivated youth may make efforts to reduce or stop drinking without success in permanent change. This two-phase process has support in the literature on both adult spontaneous remitters (e.g., Klingemann, 1991) and treated samples (e.g., Cronkite & Moos, 1980; Tucker *et al.*, 1994). To our knowledge, the intervention described in this chapter is the first opportunity to examine this bi-phase model in relation to non-clinical samples of adolescents with alcohol problems.

Developmental context. As has been proposed previously, stage of development is a critical consideration in developing and implementing effective interventions for adolescent alcohol problems (Deas, Riggs, Langenbucher, Goldman & Brown, 2000; Myers & Brown, 1996; Myers, Wagner & Brown, 1998). The rapid biological, social, behavioral, and neurocognitive changes of adolescence (Gottlieb, Wahisten & Licklieter, 1998) and acceleration in stressful life experiences (Vik & Brown, 1998) demand social adjustments and skill development. A number of psychosocial tasks of adolescent development are associated with alcohol use and reduction in alcohol involvement. For example, development of new social roles with same sex and opposite sex peers as well as family (identity), development of social skills related to new social roles, separation and individuation within the family (autonomy), and coping with developmentally specific stressors which vary with age, gender, culture, socioeconomic status, and environment may act to provoke or facilitate changes (e.g., identity as an alcohol or drug user), or in other cases interfere with successful task accomplishment (e.g., successful coping which refines skills and enhances self-esteem) (Tapert, Stewart, *et al.*, 1999; Windle, 1990).

Given the diversity and intensity of developmental demands, it is unlikely that singular interventions are appropriate or optimal for youth. Instead, our experience suggests that optimal strategies to reduce/stop alcohol involvement and maintain change for adolescents must: (1) provide personal choice; (2) fit developmental, stage-specific interests; (3) be consonant with needs to optimize engagement; (4) be perceived as helpful; and (5) be sufficiently diverse to reflect the heterogeneity of adolescents who experience alcohol problems (e.g., social leaders, behaviorally undercontrolled, history of abuse and family problems) and sensitive to alcohol-related and concomitant problems (e.g., depression, anxiety, conduct disorder; Lewinsohn *et al.*, 1993; Kaminer, Wagner, Plummer & Seifer, 1993; LaBouvie, Pandina, White & Johnson, 1990; Henry, Feehan, McGee & Stanton, 1993).

Consequently, traditional paradigms for treatment efficacy which require randomized placement and standard amounts and durations of treatment are one form of intervention; while yielding important information, they tell little of the ecological validity of an approach in relation to normal change processes at different developmental stages or psychosocial contexts (e.g., fluctuating motivation). Instead, low-threshold, multiple-option packages ("Toolbox for potential remitters"), which offer diverse forms of engagement, privacy, self-selected preferences, broad availability and strategies perceived by youth as socially acceptable and helpful, suggest a format and constellation of intervention options which may optimize engagement and utilization by adolescents, and thereby produce better personal change and outcome.

Furthermore, evidence continues to mount demonstrating that there are multiple pathways into (e.g., Sher, 1991) and out of (Brown, 1993; Humphreys, Moos & Finney, 1995) alcohol/drug abuse. Individual difference factors such as family history of alcoholism, personality, comorbid psychopathology, and behavioral disinhibition all influence the developmental trajectory of adolescents' alcohol involvement. Similarly, demographic and sociocultural factors such as gender, socioeconomic status, ethnicity, and age relate to the probability of transitions in alcohol use and resultant problems. In concert, this diversity necessitates multiple options as core for an optimal secondary intervention for adolescent alcohol problems. For example, adolescent males have a higher prevalence of abuse and dependence compared to females, and females have higher remission rates (Fillmore, 1988) and differ in their barriers to treatment (Beckman & Amaro, 1986). Younger adolescents appear more likely to use family support to change their addictive lifestyle, whereas older youth rely more on peer and other influences outside the home (Brown, 1993; Chassin, Presson & Sherman, 1985). Cultural factors also appear critical in understanding use patterns (Windle, 1990), progression of alcohol-related problems (Stewart, Brown & Myers 1997), and likelihood to seek and receive treatment or perceive treatment as helpful (Neighbors, 1985). For example, Asian Americans and Latinos are consistently less likely to seek and obtain treatment than non-Hispanic whites (Bui & Takeuchi, 1992; Hough *et al.*, 1987; Padgett, Ptrick, Burns & Schlesinger, 1994), although short-term adolescent addiction treatment outcomes appear comparable across ethnic groups (Stewart *et al.*, 1997). Consequently, there may be differences in rates and patterns of personal change efforts across ethnic groups. It appears that some ethnic differences in problem rates can be accounted for by socioeconomic status. For example, lower socioeconomic status is associated with high prevalence of alcohol problems for African Americans, whereas higher socioeconomic status is associated with elevation in alcohol diagnoses for non-Hispanic whites (Darrow, Russell, Cooper, Mudar & Frone, 1992; Jones-Webb, Hsiao & Hannan, 1995).

Empirical Studies

We have recently conducted a series of alcohol and drug surveys, which have included questions regarding the self-change efforts of high school students. In the first high school study (Wagner *et al.*, 1999), we found that within an ethnically diverse sample of 1388 students, 15 percent of the total sample (25 percent of current drinkers) reported that they had made personal attempts to cut down or stop their alcohol use. Of these, 69 percent reported one or two attempts to cut down or stop, and 15 percent reported five or more specific attempts (Brown *et al.*, 1998; Wagner *et al.*, 1999). Additionally, comparable portions of the total sample (16–18 percent) reported efforts to reduce or stop use of nicotine and other drugs as well.

More recently, we replicated these findings in a second, distinct high school sample. In a sample of over 620 students, we found that 22 percent of high school students who drank in the last month reported attempts within the last year to limit or reduce their alcohol use, and 13 percent of the students reported a history of specific quit attempts. Similarly, large proportions of these students reported efforts to limit or quit cigarette use (31 percent) and other drug use (27 percent). Of note, rates are slightly higher among the 56 percent of the sample that report having been recently high from alcohol, with reduction and quit attempts reported by 26 percent to 16 percent, respectively. One-quarter to one-third of these high school students also report trying to limit or quit cigarette or other drug use. Rates are substantially higher among students with a history of hazardous alcohol use.

Clearly, substantial portions of adolescents in high school make personal attempts to reduce or stop their substance involvement. In a prospective study, we examined whether teens that develop alcohol-related problems are able to resolve those problems without formal treatment. To do this we studied 122 high-risk community adolescents at five time points over four years. When first studied, these community youth had no history of alcohol abuse or problems, were approximately 16 years of age, and 72 percent had at least one alcohol-dependent biological parent. Of these teens, 42 (34.6 percent) began drinking heavily and reported objective alcohol-related problems that were corroborated by family members within the first four years of study. Youth who developed problems were comparable to the larger high-risk sample with the exception that more boys than girls developed problems (64 percent male), and the vast majority (92 percent) had a parental history of alcohol dependence. Of adolescents who progressed to problem drinking, 69 percent subsequently had at least a one-year period of no heavy drinking or alcohol or drug problems. Two youth were referred for outpatient treatment for alcohol but did not participate in treatment. Thus, using the standard criterion for natural recovery (minimum of one-year abstinence or non-problematic use without formal treatment subsequent to problems), it appears that two-thirds of these high-risk community teens evidenced resolution of their alcohol problems without formal treatment.

Adolescent Self-change Process

The next step in investigating adolescent personal change efforts for alcohol use was to evaluate which types of strategies are helpful to adolescents as they make changes in their alcohol use. As the long-term goal of interventions is sustained behavior change (rather than just quit attempts), several developmentally based assumptions were made regarding prerequisites of adolescent efforts to maintain behavior change for their alcohol/drug use. It was presumed that strategies promoting sustained change among adolescents would need to: (1) be readily available to youth; (2) be perceived as helpful in order to continue implementation; (3) be appropriate for stage of development; and (4) reflect diversity in options associated with multiple avenues to success (Brown, 1993). It seemed unlikely that a single strategy or effort could sustain pronounced behavioral change in alcohol involvement over extended periods and across diverse circumstances.

To explore strategies typically employed by youth seeking to cut down or stop their alcohol and drug involvement, we evaluated 30 adolescents in alcohol and drug treatment and 30 demographically matched high-risk youth from the community using semi-structured interviews. Youth were asked what they found useful or helpful in their efforts to reduce or stop their alcohol or other drug involvement. Verbatim responses were content-analyzed to generate six types of personal change strategies: (1) Independent efforts (e.g., "will power," "tried on my own"); (2) Structured activities (e.g., recreation, volunteer, religious involvement); (3) School/ work; (4) Friends ("friends accepted and supported me"); (5) Family (e.g., emotional support, changed activities); and (6) Support groups (e.g., church, community groups, Twelve Step groups).

The youth who developed alcohol problems then rated these reduction/cessation strategies on a Helpfulness Scale from 1 (not at all) to 100 (extremely) for helpfulness in their personal change efforts. The majority of respondents endorsed two or more strategies as moderately to extremely helpful (rating > 40). Independent efforts (i.e., will power, self-control, forced myself) were rated as most helpful ($M = 63.9$; sd = 35.1), and Twelve-Step/Support groups received the lowest helpfulness rating ($M = 12.8$; sd = 28.0). Activities such as structured recreation, sports, hobbies, church, or volunteer work obtained the second highest mean rating of 48.9(sd = 38.0) Eighty-two percent of the sample rated Twelve-Step/Support groups in the 1 to 10 range (little or no help). The remaining categories of School/work, Friends, and Family received moderate levels of endorsement (M range = 36.8–38.8). Intercorrelations of helpfulness ratings were calculated and examined to evaluate potential patterns of efforts. Significant correlations were obtained between Family, Friends, and Support groups (r = 0.47–0.65). Similarly, Independent efforts and School/work correlations were significant (r = 0.33–0.60). Thus, the majority of adolescents with former problems found multiple strategies useful in their reduction/cessation efforts, with Independent/personal efforts and Structured activities rated as most helpful by youth that had resolved their alcohol problems without treatment.

In a third study, we evaluated which personal change efforts were associated with the maintenance of sustained behavior change for adolescents who have received treatment for problems with alcohol and drugs. For this study, 167 adolescents who had received inpatient treatment for alcohol and drug problems were evaluated one year following treatment. Youth aged 13–18 years ($M = 16.07$) were selected for study if they met lifetime DSM-III-R diagnostic criteria for alcohol abuse or dependence. Ninety-two percent of the sample also met DSM-III-R criteria for a current diagnosis of dependence on one other drug, and 78 percent met such criteria for two or more other drugs. At six and twelve months post treatment, participants and their resource people (e.g., parents, roommates, etc.) were independently interviewed, and completed a series of questionnaires. A ten percent random sample of the youth also completed urinalyses (UAs) to confirm substance use reports. The Customary Drinking and Drug Use Record (Brown, Myers, *et al.*, 1998), resource people reports, UAs, and Helpfulness Ratings Scale (range 1 to 100) were used to assess substance involvement and perceptions of helpfulness of efforts in the maintenance of abstinence from alcohol and other drugs. For this study, helpfulness ratings for Old friends and New friends were separated, and all structured activities (school, work, recreation) were combined. A write-in option also was added to identify new strategies. Youth were classified as Positive Outcome (PO; 35 percent) if they abstained during the year following treatment, or had fewer than 30 use days with no more than two consecutive days of use per episode, no binge-drinking (5 drinks per setting), and no identifiable problems (e.g., arrests, missed school or work) resulting from substance use during the post-treatment period. Youth using alcohol or other drugs more frequently or with problems were classified Negative Outcome (NO; 65 percent). The NO group reported alcohol or drug use an average of 307 days in the year post treatment compared to 16 days of use by the PO group.

When examining sustained addictive behavior change in this way, four different types of efforts were found to be very helpful ($M > 60$): Independent/personal efforts, Family, New friends, and Structured activities such as school, work or recreation. Old friends and Twelve-Step/Support groups were rated as much less helpful. Successful adolescents (PO group) evaluated five of six change strategies as more helpful than youth with poor outcomes (M difference = 25.5). Both groups evaluated Old friends (Pretreatment) as only marginally helpful. Additionally, 8 percent identified an additional mechanism as helpful (e.g., counselor).

Thus, the same strategies identified by community adolescents as helpful in their efforts to make self-changes appear relevant to adolescents with severe alcohol problems who are attempting to maintain abstinence following treatment for such problems. Perceived helpfulness is considered a prerequisite of personal change efforts in this conceptual model of self-change for youth. To the extent that these strategies are perceived as helpful by youth, secondary interventions, including the diversity of strategies youth normally use, may increase the likelihood of youth engagement in treatment and subsequent utilization of the strategies peers use to successfully change their drinking.

De-escalation study. Finally, we completed analyses of 600 Arizona high school students who completed two surveys conducted approximately nine months apart and spanning the academic year (Stice *et al.*, 1998). Using theoretically determined predictors, we compared groups of students who during the course of the year increased their alcohol use (nonuse to use; moderate use to heavy use), maintained stable alcohol use patterns (nonuse, moderate use, heavy use), or decreased their drinking (moderate use to abstention, heavy use to moderate use). Planned comparisons indicated that a change in peer group/peer use predicted a change from heavy use to moderate use, and parent engagement (increased parental control) predicted reductions from moderate use to abstinence (Stice *et al.*, 1998). Thus, factors related to change in peer group/peer use (e.g., activities, fostering new friendships) and parental involvement (e.g., parent/family discussions about alcohol use) may be useful components of intervention.

Adolescent Treatment Outcome: Patterns and Process of Resolution

Through a series of longitudinal studies funded by the National Institute on Alcohol Abuse and Alcoholism (NIAAA) spanning 15 years, we have investigated not only the process and circumstances whereby teens fail following treatment for alcohol problems, but also the means through which they succeed. A striking finding in this regard is that only about half of teens (53 percent) comply with the primary behavioral recommendation of all treatment programs—attendance at Twelve-Step groups. Despite non-attendance at these meetings, one-third (32 percent) of abusing teens are able to abstain or limit their use to low-volume, non-problematic level (Brown, 1993; Wagner *et al.*, 1999). Using different strategies (i.e., changing involvement within and outside their families, cognitive and behavioral strategies) teens inherently develop alternative means to succeed, and these routes vary with age (<16 years; >16 years).

We have also learned about strategies of engagement of youth through a treatment development project (Myers *et al.*, 2000) designed to encourage substance-abusing youth to stop smoking cigarettes. One of the difficulties encountered in the course of intervention delivery is the broad range of motivation for behavior change, with many alcohol-abusing adolescents initially not interested in smoking cessation. Thus, we incorporated a variety of motivational enhancement strategies so as to reduce barriers to participation and engage youth in the treatment process. For example, the initial portion of the intervention focused on motivational enhancement and consisted of exploring perceived benefits and costs to cigarette smoking, eliciting adolescent opinions and perspectives on the role of smoking in their lives using motivational techniques such as rolling with the resistance (Miller & Rollnick, 1991), and providing personally relevant feedback to increase ambivalence regarding smoking. Another important innovation introduced in the course of treatment development was providing adolescents with control over the goals for behavior change. Rather than offering cessation as the sole option (as is typical in smoking cessation interventions), adolescents were given a range with respect to their smoking behavior. From the outset of intervention, it was made clear that each adolescent was responsible for selecting individual goals for change that could range from participation in groups with no active efforts at behavior change (representing one end of the continuum) to working towards smoking cessation (at the other end of the range). We found this approach effective at diminishing barriers to participation and engagement. The majority of teens initially elected to work on reducing their rates of smoking, thus choosing an intermediate goal. The utility of this approach was reflected in short-term post-treatment outcome showing that 50 percent of participants had attempted smoking cessation, and 23 percent reported abstinence from smoking in the week prior to follow-up interview (Myers *et al.*, 2000).

Project Options

Development and Implementations

Based on the theoretical and empirical work described above, an intervention was developed which was designed to facilitate interest in reducing and/or stopping drinking of high school students. The underlying conceptual model is that motivation for change, when coupled with adequate resources and behavioral skills, is sufficient to produce personal change efforts of adolescents. It is assumed that personal cessation efforts of teens can be successful in eliminating alcohol use, hazardous alcohol use, and related problems for many adolescents.

Project Options consists of three formats for intervention: group discussions, individual sessions, and an interactive web site. The content is similar across these formats and is primarily focused on issues and problems that teens at each school have identified as important to them. By using intervention formats based on change patterns of youth and preferred by youth, Project Options is designed to allow maximal control by the teen. Barriers and facilitators to treatment involvement were ascertained through twice-annual surveys conducted at each school. The barriers and facilitating factors were considered logistical requirements in the design of the intervention from two perspectives: (1) without such consideration there would be no engagement in this self-selected intervention, and (2) with incorporation of student ideas youth would develop a sense of ownership and receptivity to the alcohol-focused intervention.

A primary barrier to treatment was concerns about confidentiality, which is stressed at the beginning of each individual and group session and the opening page of the web site. Both the youth and the facilitator make a confidentiality pledge within the limitations of the laws of the state of California. Also, confidentiality is discussed as a trust issue in relationships, since students identified this as an important consideration in self-disclosure. Intervention options are designed to maximize availability. Groups and individual sessions are held at noon and after school, as well as during homeroom or other flexible time at each school. Students can log onto the web site from any site (e.g., school, home) using a code. The efforts designed to ensure confidentiality (security) of the web site are described (e.g., firewalls, encryption, personal passwords) to remind students of these with each use.

The group discussions consist of six distinct sessions that students can rotate into at any point; brief individual intervention covers the same material in four sessions. Although students can log onto the web site an unlimited number of times, rewards are only available for six sessions. The web site is linked to other investigator- and student-reviewed web sites for teens and sponsored by national agencies (e.g., NIAAA, NIDA, MADD).

Each intervention contact is designed to: (1) motivate the youth to personally evaluate his/her drinking, (2) provide personal feedback and information about peer use and successful change efforts employed by students at their school, and (3) reward student participation. Strategies used in motivational interviewing are incorporated throughout the intervention. While each session has a specific goal and topic, information shared by the teen in a non-confrontational discussion is used to highlight common problems and positive solutions reached by peers.

Activities in individual and group sessions and on the web site are designed to engage youth in an age- and gender-appropriate fashion. Normative feedback is provided regarding perceived and actual use rates and actual change efforts and successes of students at the specific schools. The barriers and facilitators of personal change efforts are discussed in the context of the most common "problems" or "issues" students want to discuss at each school. These issues are determined by the biannual surveys conducted at each school. Examples include stress, dating, peer pressure to drink/use, grades, and conflict with parents. The primary topics of sessions include:

1. Prevalence of alcohol use and causes of overestimation.
2. Myths and positive expectancies of alcohol use.
3. Managing stress and temptation without drinking alcohol.
4. Evaluating personal effects of alcohol and weighing the advantages and disadvantages of change.
5. Alternative activities/reinforcers and how to accomplish these without drinking.
6. Enhancing skills and resources though communication.

The prevalent problems and issues that were generated by students are discussed in the context of these six thematic sessions.

The web site option contains comparable information. Following the sign-in procedure, each student completes a brief series of questions (e.g., age, gender, grade, drinking frequency and quantity) used to match participants to biannual survey data to provide feedback regarding personal alcohol use patterns. An informative feedback game is completed which compares perceived alcohol use patterns to actual patterns at the student's school. Games can be selected to test knowledge and expose myths about alcohol effects. The "Top 10 Personal Change Strategies" used by peers at the student's school are presented, as well as resource information. In particular, students have access to other youth-focused web sites with alcohol-related information, meeting and contact information for Project Options groups and individual sessions, and contacts for other school and community resources.

Each student is rewarded for his/her participation by selecting a gift or discount certificate from a local food, music, clothing, or recreation establishment (e.g., theatre). The stores and restaurants are based on student preferences identified in school-wide surveys. Students receive the incentive after completing an information form that provides data necessary to match with their personal survey data obtained in the fall and spring. Through this process, the self-selection patterns and utilization rates of the interventions can be determined. Additionally, use rates and changes in drinking patterns can be determined for youth participating in the survey relative to peers who do not self-select into the brief intervention.

Community establishments provide the gift certificates or discount coupons as part of a community effort to promote healthy youth. Establishments voted as youth-preferred sites for shopping, eating, or entertainment were individually contacted and arrangements were made for their contribution. Thus, at no cost to the school or funding agencies, students can receive preferred incentives for their participation in the project. This procedure enhances the school–community relationship and facilitates communication across agencies.

Prior to implementation of the intervention at each school, several structured developmental tasks were completed. A Youth Advisory Council was established for Project Options. Students representing all grades and all schools were asked to critique individual and group session materials and the web site. Based on student feedback, stylistic changes were made to the protocol to make it more student user friendly. Additionally, students generated new ideas to be added and advertisement suggestions. Second, Project Options staff met with principals, vice principals, counselors, and key teachers at each school to build a working alliance, work out logistical details, and develop strategies to effectively and efficiently implement the intervention at each site.

The third form of structural preparation was informing parents of Project Options opportunity for their sons/daughters. Information was sent from the school to each family, and university and district consent forms also were sent to the homes of all students. Articles describing Project Options and student feedback were included in parent newsletters and at least one presentation was provided to parent organizational meeting (PTSA, School foundation) per semester.

Finally, focus groups and classroom testing of the protocol was completed prior to advertisement and implementation at each school. Student feedback was again used to refine the protocol for student selection and use. Furthermore, student volunteers were enlisted for advertisement. Advertisement of the intervention varies form site to site and includes posters, announcements in student papers, auditory daily announcements, and video commercials. Students and staff participate in the advertisement process with gift/discount certificates provided to student participants.

Utilization and Preliminary Outcomes

This novel secondary intervention is currently being implemented in four schools. Preliminary evidence on utilization rates and patterns is available from one school. In the first semester of implementation, 10 percent of the student body participated in one or more of the Project Options activities. Sixty percent of those who participated voluntarily continued participation in the intervention package.

Self-selection participation in this alcohol intervention varies by gender, grade, and ethnic background. Slightly more girls (60 percent) self-selected into the program than boys (40 percent). High school girls more commonly prefer the group format, whereas a larger proportion of males use the web site. Two-thirds of participants are ninth or tenth graders, and these students are more likely to prefer the group format. By contrast, twelve-grade students are nine times more likely than all other students to use the individual intervention format.

Students from all ethnic and cultural backgrounds have participated in Project Options. Self-selection rates in the intervention were found to parallel the ethnic composition of the school. In general, non-Hispanic White youth were more likely to participate in the group format relative to other formats. Asian and Hispanic youth were more highly represented in the individual sessions. American Indians were found to be greater users of the web site than other intervention formats.

The intervention was targeted at moderately to heavy-drinking youth. The majority of participating youth report multiple alcohol use episodes per month. Of significance, binge drinkers were overrepresented in the Project Options program relative to the entire school. Thus, it appears that this package of intervention opportunities is sufficiently appealing to generate interest of students who are at most risk for alcohol problems.

A portion of students who are not current drinkers also chose to use Project Options. While these students were in the minority, they reported former use concerns, problems with a parent or other family members drinking, and concerns about the drinking of a close friend as reasons for using one of the intervention resources. Thus, incidental benefit may be obtained even among youth who are not current drinkers.

While outcome information is available on only a limited sample, it appears that Project Options may alter perceptions of peer use and modestly arrest the progression to heavier alcohol use. Relative to the study body from an SES and ethnically matched school not receiving Project Options, the student body of the school where Project Options was implemented had reduced expectations of peer use. Specifically, while perceptions of frequency of peer use at the comparison school remained the same from fall to spring surveys, estimates of how often students drank alcohol per month decreased at the experimental school. Furthermore, significantly higher proportions of students from the Project Options school were estimated to be non-drinkers or once or twice per month drinkers, and significantly lower proportions of students were estimated to be three or more times per month drinkers. Although perceptions of peer use remained higher than self-reported use at both schools, these preliminary findings are consistent with the goals and efforts of Projection Options (Brown & D'Amico, 2000).

Similarly, although drinking frequency was not found to change significantly over the course of the academic year at the comparison school, reductions in the average number of drinks students consumed per occasion were identified at the high school receiving the Project Options intervention. Additionally, although alcohol problem rates were similar between the two schools at the beginning of the academic year, students at the school receiving Project Options intervention reported experiencing fewer alcohol-related problems during the school year compared to the control school. Again, although this evidence is preliminary, the patterns of findings are consistent with both goals and activities of Project Options.

Future Directions

Although developmentally appropriate interventions have been advocated for high school students, few interventions have been developed to date affording self-selection of both format of intervention and context, as is the case with the Project Options approach. The preliminary evidence available with this approach demonstrates that a self-selected secondary intervention for alcohol is feasible in the high school setting. While the self-selection patterns parallel the ethnic composition of the school, utilization patterns for specific formats for alcohol intervention were found to vary by gender, grade, and ethnic background. Of significance, preliminary evidence suggests that the intervention was associated with decrements in both perceived use by peers, a variable long considered an important prognosticator of future use, and self-reported intensity of alcohol use.

Clearly, future research is needed to confirm the preliminary evidence of the effectiveness of this intervention. As self-selected formats appear to vary across students, it may be that the optimal intervention for alcohol involvement for high school students would look remarkably different across schools. Additionally, because content examples were based on student concerns, it is anticipated that optimal content may vary across schools over time in order for the intervention to be maximally appealing to students.

Additional research is necessary to examine for whom, for how long, and which components of this intervention are most useful to students. Our preliminary findings suggest that although both males and females self-select all formats, girls in high school may be more likely to use group format, whereas boys may be more likely to engage in alcohol-related change opportunities on the computer. Additionally, the privacy afforded by individual contact or web site may be more appealing to minority students. Furthermore, while the current intervention is based on a two-phase model (i.e., motivational enhancement followed by skills building as needed), it will be important to determine if these or other mechanisms promote change in perception of peer use and reductions in alcohol consumption by high school students.

Summary

Project Options represents a first attempt to develop and test an intervention sufficiently attractive to youth that they would self-select a brief treatment for alcohol use. Preliminary evidence in a high school setting shows the potential of such an approach for both infrequent and heavy-drinking students. Although considerable research is needed to demonstrate the effectiveness and efficacy of such an approach with adolescents, our initial efforts suggest that having youth involved in design aspects and marketing of the intervention, in a fashion appealing to students, may afford an opportunity to intervene with youth earlier in their drinking careers and before the need for more traditional interventions.

References

Abrams, D. B., Niura, R. S., Carey, K. B., Monti, P. M., & Binkoff, J. A. (1986), "Understanding relapse and recovery in alcohol abuse." *Annals of Behavioral Medicine 8*(2–3), 27–32.

Bandura, A. (1986), *Social Foundations of Thought and Action: A social cognitive theory*. Englewood Cliffs, NJ: Prentice Hall.

Bandura, A. (1998), "Health promotion from the perspective of social cognitive theory." *Psychology and Health: An International Journal 13*, 623–649.

Bates, M. E., & Labouvie, E. W. (1994), "Familial alcoholism and personality–environment fit: A developmental study in risk in adolescents." *Annals of the New York Academy of Sciences 708*, 202–213.

Beckman, L. J., & Amaro, H. (1986), "Personal and social difficulties faced by women and men entering alcoholism treatment." *Journal of Studies on Alcohol 47*, 135–145.

Brown, S. A. (1993), "Recovery patterns in adolescent substance abuse." In J. R. Baer, G. A. Marlatt & R. J. McMahan (eds), *Addictive Behaviors Across the Lifespan: Prevention, treatment, and policy issues*. Beverly Hills, CA: Sage Publications, Inc.

Brown, S. A., & D'Amico, E. J. (2000), "Facilitating adolescent self-change for alcohol problems: A multiple brief intervention approach." Presented at the American Psychological Association Convention, Washington, DC.

Brown, S. A., & D'Amico, E. J. (in press). "Outcomes for alcohol treatment for adolescents." In: M. Gallanter (ed.), *Recent Developments in Alcoholism: Services research in the era of managed care*. New York: Plenum.

Brown, S. A., Kypri, K., & Coe, M. T. (1998), "Transition to independent living and substance involvement of high-risk youth." Presented at the New Zealand Psychological Society Annual Conference, Wellington, New Zealand.

Brown, S. A., Mott, M. A., & Stewart, M. A. (1992), "Adolescent alcohol and drug abuse." In C. E. Walker and M. C. Roberts (eds). *Handbook of Clinical Child Psychology (2nd ed.)*. New York: John Wiley & Sons, Inc., 677–693.

Brown, S. A. *et al.* (1998), "Psychometric evaluation of the Customary Drinking and Drug Use Record (CDDR): A measure of adolescent alcohol and drug involvement." *Journal of Studies on Alcohol 59*, 427–438.

Brown, S. A., Myers, M. G., Mott, M. A., & Vik, P. W. (1994), "Correlates of success following treatment for adolescent substance abuse." *Applied and Preventive Psychology 3*, 61–73.

Brown, S. A., Vik, P. W., & Creamer, V. A. (1989), "Characteristics of relapse following adolescent substance abuse treatment." *Addictive Behaviors 14*, 291–300.

Brownell, K. D., Marlatt, G. A., Lichtenstein, E., & Wilson, G. T. (1986), "Understanding and preventing relapse." *American Psychologist 41*(7), 765–782.

Bui, K. T., & Takeuchi, D. T. (1992), "Ethnic minority adolescents and the use of community mental health care services." *American Journal of Community Psychology 20*, 403–417.

Chassin, L. A., Presson, C. C, & Sherman, S. J. (1985), "Stepping backward in order to step forward: An acquisition-oriented approach to primary prevention." *Journal of Consulting and Clinical Psychology 53*, 612–622.

Coie, J. D., & Dodge, K. A. (1998), "Aggression and antisocial behavior." In W. Damon & N. Eisenberg (eds), *Handbook of Child Psychology: Social, emotional, and personality development*. New York: John Wiley & Sons, Inc., 779–862.

Colby, S. M. *et al.* (1998), "Brief motivational interviewing in a hospital setting for adolescent smoking: A preliminary study." *Journal of Clinical and Consulting Psychology 66*, 574–578.

Cronkite, R. C., & Moos, R. H. (1980), "Determinants of the post treatment functioning of alcoholic patients: A conceptual framework." *Journal of Consulting and Clinical Psychology 48*(3), 305–316.

Darrow, S. L., Russell, M., Cooper, M. L., Mudar, P., & Frone, M. R. (1992), "Sociodemographic correlates of alcohol consumption among African-American and white women." *Women & Health 18*, 35–51.

Deas, D., Riggs, P., Langenbucher, J., Goldman, M., & Brown, S. A. (2000), "Adolescents are not adults: Developmental consideration in alcohol users." *Alcoholism: Clinical and Experimental Research 24*(2), 232–237.

Donovan, J., & Jessor, R. (1985), "Structure of problem behavior in adolescence and young adulthood." *Journal of Consulting and Clinical Psychology 53*, 890–904.

Fillmore, K. M. (1988), *Alcohol Use Across the Life Course: A critical review of 70 years of international longitudinal research*. Toronto, Ontario: Addiction Research Foundation.

Flay, B. R. (1993), "Youth tobacco use: Risks, patterns, and control." In C. T. Orleans & J. D. Slade (eds), *Nicotine Addiction: Principles and management*. New York, NY: Oxford University Press, 365–384.

Gottlieb, G., Wahlsten, D., & Lickliter, R. (1998), "The significance of biology for human development: A developmental psychobiological systems view." In W. Damon & R. Lerner (eds), *Handbook of Child Psychology: Theoretical models of human development*. New York: John Wiley & Sons, Inc., 233–274.

Henggeler, S. W. (1993), "Multisystemic treatment of serious juvenile offenders: Implications for the treatment of substance abusing youth." In L. S. Onken, J. D. Blaine & J. J. Boren (eds), *Behavioral Treatments for Drug Abuse and Dependence* (Research Monograph 137). Rockville, MD: National Institute on Drug Abuse, 181–199.

Henry, B., Feehan, M., McGee, R., & Stanton, W. (1993), "The importance of conduct problems and depressive symptoms in predicting adolescent substance use." *Journal of Abnormal Child Psychology 21*, 469–480.

Hough, R. L. *et al.* (1987), "Utilization of health and mental health services by Los Angeles Mexican Americans and non-Hispanic Whites." *Archives of General Psychiatry 44*, 702–709.

Humphreys, K., Moos, R. H., & Finney, J. W. (1995), "Two pathways out of drinking problems without professional treatment." *Addictive Behaviors 20*, 427–441.

Hussong, A. M., & Chassin, L. (1994), "The stress-negative affect model of adolescent alcohol use: Disaggregating negative affect." *Journal of Studies on Alcohol 55*, 707–718.

Institute of Medicine (1990), B*roadening the Base of Treatment for Alcohol Problems: Report of a study by a committee of the Institute of Medicine*, Division of Mental Health and Behavioral Medicine. Washington, DC: National Academy Press.

Johnston, L. D., O'Malley, P. M., & Bachman, J. G. (1994), *National Survey Results on Drug Use from Monitoring the Future Study, 1975–1983. Volume 1: Secondary school students*. Rockville, MD, National Institute on Drug Abuse, DHHS publication no. 94–3809.

Johnston, L. D., O'Malley, P. M., & Bachman, J. G. (1999), Drug trends in 1999 are mixed. Ann Arbor, MI (on-line). Available www.monitoringthefuture.org: accessed 9/1/00: University of Michigan News and Information Services.

Jones-Webb, R. J., Hsiao, C., & Hannan, P. (1995), "Relationships between socioeconomic status and drinking problems among Black and White men." *Alcoholism: Clinical and Experimental Research 19*, 623–627.

Kaminer, Y., Wagner, E., Plummer, B., & Seifer, R. (1993), "Validation of the Teen Addiction Severity Index (T-ASI): Preliminary findings." *American Journal on Addictions 2*, 250–254.

Klingemann, H. K. (1991), "The motivation for change from problem alcohol and heroin use." *British Journal of Addiction 86*, 727–744.

LaBouvie, E. W., Pandina, R. J., White, H. R., & Johnson, V. (1990), "Risk factors of adolescent drug use: An affect-based interpretation." *Journal of Substance Abuse 2*, 265–285.

Lewinsohn, P. M., Hops, H., Roberts, E., & Seeley, J. R. (1993), "Adolescent psychopathology: Prevalence and incidence of depression and other DSM-III-R disorders in high school students." *Journal of Abnormal Psychology 102*, 133–144.

Liddle, H. A., & Dakof, G. A. (1994), "Family-based treatment for adolescent drug use: State of the science." In E. Rahdert *et al.*, *Adolescent Drug Abuse: Assessment and treatment*. National Institute on Drug Abuse Research Monograph, Rockville, MD.

Miller, W. R., & Rollnick, S. (1991), "What motivates people to change?" In W. R. Miller & S. Rollnick (eds), *Motivational Interviewing*. New York, NY: Guilford Press, 14–29.

Mulford, H. A. (1977), "Stages in the alcoholic process: Toward a cumulative, nonsequential index." *Journal of Studies on Alcohol 38*, 563–583.

Myers, M. G., & Brown, S. A. (1996), "The adolescent relapse coping questionnaire: Psychometric validation. *Journal of Studies on Alcohol 57*(1), 40–46.

Myers, M. G., Brown, S. A., Kelly, J. F. (2000), "A cigarette smoking intervention for substance abusing adolescents." *Journal of Cognitive and Behavioral Practice 7*, 64–82.

Myers, M. G., Wagner, E. F., & Brown, S. A. (1998), "Adolescent substance abuse treatment protocol." In Van Hasselt & Hersen (eds), *Handbook of Psychological Treatment Protocols for Children & Adolescents*. Lawrence Erlbaum Associates, 381–411.

Neighbors, H. W. (1985), "Seeking professional help for personal problems: Black Americans use of health and mental health services." *Community Mental Health Journal 21*, 156–166.

Newcomb, M., & Bentler, P. (1988), *Consequences of Adolescent Drug Use: Impact on the Lives of Young Adults*. Newbury Park CA: Sage.

Padgett, D. K., Patrick, C., Burns, B. J., & Schlesinger, H. J. (1994), "Ethnicity and the use of outpatient mental health services in a national insured population." *American Journal of Public Health 84*, 222–226.

Peltier, B., Telch, M. J., & Coates, T. J. (1982), "Smoking cessation with adolescents: A comparison of recruitment strategies." *Addictive Behavior 7*, 71–73.

Prochaska, J. O., DiClemente, C. C., & Norcross, J. C. (1992), "In search of how people change: Applications to addictive behaviors." *American Psychologist 47*, 1102–1114.

Sher, K. (1991), *Children of Alcoholics: A critical appraisal of theory and research*. Chicago: University of Chicago Press.

Smart, R. G., & Stoduto, G. (1997), "Treatment experiences and need for treatment among students with serious alcohol and drug problems." *Journal of Child and Adolescent Substance Abuse 7*(1), 63–72.

Sobell, L. C., Cunningham, J. A., & Sobell, M. B. (1996), "Recovery from alcohol problems with and without treatment: Prevalence in two population surveys." *Journal of Public Health 86*, 966–972.

Sobell, L. C., Sobell, M. B., Toneatto, T., Leo, G. I. (1993), W"hat triggers the resolution of alcohol problems without treatment?" *Alcoholism: Clinical and Experimental Research 17*, 217–224.

Stewart, D. G., & Brown, S. A. (1995), "Withdrawal and dependency symptoms among adolescent alcohol and drug abusers." *Addiction 90*, 627–635.

Stewart, D. G., Brown, S. A., & Myers, M. G. (1997), "Antisocial behavior and psychoactive substance involvement among Hispanic and non-Hispanic Caucasian adolescents in substance abuse treatment." *Journal of Child & Adolescent Substance Abuse 6*(4), 1–22.

Stice, E., Myers, M. G., & Brown, S. A. (1998), "A longitudinal grouping analysis of adolescent substance use escalation and de-escalation." *Psychology of Addictive Behaviors 1*, 12–27.

Tapert, S. F., Brown, S. A., Myers, M. G., & Granholm, E. (1999), "The role of neurocognitive abilities in coping with adolescent relapse to alcohol and drug use." *Journal of Studies on Alcohol*.

Tapert, S. F., Stewart, D. G., & Brown, S. A. (1999), "Drug abuse in adolescence." In A. J. Goreczny & M. Hersen (eds), *Handbook of Pediatrics and Adolescent Health Psychology*. Needham Heights, MA: Allyn & Bacon, 161–178.

Tucker, J. A. (1995), "Predictors of help-seeking and the temporal relationship of help to recovery among treated and untreated recovered problem drinkers." *Addiction 90*, 805–809.

Tucker, J. A., Vuchinich, R. E., & Gladsjo, J. A. (1990–91), "Environmental influences on relapse in substance use disorders." *International Journal of the Addictions 25*(7A-8A), 1017–1050.

Tucker, J. A., Vuchinich, R. E., & Gladsjo, J. A. (1994), "Environmental effects surrounding natural recovery from alcohol-related problems." *Journal of Studies on Alcohol 55*, 401–411.

Vik, P. W., & Brown, S. A. (1998), "Life events and substance abuse during adolescence." In T. W. Miller (ed.), *Children of Trauma: Stressful life events and their effects and adolescents*. International University Press, Inc., 179–205.

Vik, P. W., Mott, M. A., & Brown, S. A. (Submitted), "Outcome following adolescent alcohol and drug treatment: Test of a model." *Journal of Abnormal Psychology*.

Wagner, E. F., Brown, S. A., Monti, P. M., Myers, M. G., & Waldron, H. B. (1999), "Innovations in adolescent substance abuse intervention." *Alcoholism: Clinical and Experimental Research*.

Watson, A. L., & Sher, K. J. (1998), "Resolution of alcohol problems without treatment: Methodological issues and future directions of natural recovery research." *Clinical Psychology: Science and Practice 5*(1), 1–18.

Windle, M. (1990), "A longitudinal study of antisocial behaviors in early adolescence as predictors of late adolescent substance use: Gender and Ethnic group differences." *Journal of Abnormal Psychology 99*, 86–91.

Yamaguchi, K., & Kandel, D. B. (1985), "On the resolution of role incompatibility: A life event history analysis of family roles and marijuana use." *American Journal of Sociology 90*, 1284–1325.

Chapter 9

The Teen Intervention Project: A School-Based Intervention for Adolescents with Substance Use Problems

Eric F. Wagner, Elizabeth Kortlander, and Staci Leon Morris*

Theoretical Background and Rationale

The Teen Intervention Project (TIP) is a controlled clinical trial funded by the National Institute on Alcohol Abuse and Alcoholism to test the efficacy of a standardized Student Assistance Program (SAP) for treating adolescents with alcohol and other drug use problems. Modeled after Employee Assistance Programs (EAPs) (Foote & Erfurt, 1991; Walsh, Hingson, Merrigan *et al.*, 1991), SAPs are the most common type of school-based intervention programs for substance-misusing teens, and they have two main components: (a) mechanisms for early identification of students with alcohol and/or other drug use problems and (b) methods for secondary and tertiary prevention of adverse consequences associated with those problems. As such, SAPs differ from primary prevention programs, which are directed at reducing the likelihood of substance use and abuse among the general population of students (Klitzner, Fisher, Stewart & Gilbert, 1993).

The ubiquity of SAPs is reflected in the fact that there is a large national organization (the National Association of Leadership for Student Assistance Programs, with over 3000 members) and a monthly journal (*The Student Assistance Journal*) devoted entirely to the topic of SAPs. Based on the National Student Assistance Alliance Directory (1997), it is estimated that well over 1500 school systems employ SAPs in the United States. In brief, schools with SAPs number in the thousands, and tens of thousands of students come in contact with SAPs each year.

Given the prevalence of SAPs, it is not surprising that there is variation in how SAPs are run. Generally, there are two primary types of SAPs. "Core Team Model" SAPs identify and assess students using trained school personnel, and refer students to outside treatment providers for intervention. "Westchester County, New York, Model SAPs" introduce into

*The preparation of this chapter was supported by National Institute on Alcohol Abuse and Alcoholism Grant AA10246 to the first author. We thank Susan Tarolla, MSW, for her assistance in the preparation of the manuscript, and the faculty, administrators, and students of the Broward County Public Schools, particularly Dr. Cary Sutton, for their involvement in this project.

Correspondence concerning this chapter should be addressed to Eric F. Wagner, College of Health and Urban and Affairs, Florida International University, Biscayne Bay Campus, AC-1, Suite 200, North Miami, Florida 33181-3600. Electronic mail may be sent to wagnere@fiu.edu.

Innovations in Adolescent Substance Abuse Interventions, pages 189–203.

the school environment SAP specialty counselors, who provide both assessment and intervention services at school. Typically, group counseling is the most common school-based intervention provided to substance-abusing students by Westchester Model SAPs (see Morehouse, 1984). Additionally, SAPs differ in their descriptions, philosophies, staffing arrangements, student processing procedures, and other structural and procedural features (c.f., "the Pennsylvania Model" [Newman, Henry, DiRenzio & Stecher, 1988–89; DiRenzio, 1990]; "the Center of Alcohol Studies, Rutgers University SAP" [Milgram, 1989], "Project SCCOPE" [Forman & Linney, 1987], "Alcohol and Drug Defense Program" [Palmer & Paisley, 1991], "Iowa Connection" [Simmering, 1991], and the "Westcherser County, New York, Model" [Morehouse, 1984]).

With such variation in the types of SAPs and how they are run, it is difficult to ascertain the overall effectiveness of such programs in addressing substance use problems among adolescents, let alone the specific factors that may contribute to treatment success or failure. Compounding the problem is the fact that the literature on SAPs generally has been devoted to reports concerning the specifics of conducting SAPs rather than investigations of their effectiveness. Nonetheless, there are a few studies which have examined treatment effectiveness and provide preliminary evidence that certain SAPs can reduce alcohol and other drug use and improve academic performance among substance abusing teens (Morehouse, 1984; Carlson, 1993; Carlson, Hughes & Deeback, 1996).

As part of an NIAAA project, Morehouse (1984) developed and evaluated the Westchester County, New York, Model Student Assistance Program. Morehouse found that 63 percent of students who reported using alcohol and 94 percent of students who reported using marijuana at initial SAP referral reported being abstinent from these drugs following participation in an SAP that included school-based intervention groups. However, she noted that only 50 percent of those students who reported being drunk while in school prior to the intervention stopped this activity following SAP participation. Morehouse also found a significant increase in school attendance following SAP participation for students who reported alcohol use. Carlson and colleagues (Carlson 1993; Carlson *et al.*, 1996) evaluated a Washington State SAP that included school-based intervention groups. She found that 44 percent of high school students who participated in the SAP were rated by SAP counselors as having shown overall improvement by the end of the school year. Finally, Wagner, Dinklage, Cudworth, and Vyse (1999) conducted a pilot test of the intervention described in this chapter. They found that 86 percent of high school students who participated in the pilot program stopped or significantly decreased their substance use, and 73 percent rated their experience as positive (Wagner *et al.*, 1999). In addition, frequency of pre-intervention alcohol use did not predict the impact of the program or participants' ratings of it.

A particularly striking finding of both Morehouse's (1984) and Carlson and colleagues' (Carlson, 1993; Carlson *et al.*, 1996) evaluations of SAPs was that SAPs were not effective for a large number of students. At least 37 percent of alcohol-abusing teens in Westchester County and 56 percent of substance abusing adolescents in Washington State did not change their substance use in response to SAP participation. Unfortunately, neither investigator considered the question of why SAPs were effective for some adolescents but not for others. Also, although Morehouse's (1984), Carlson and colleagues (Carlson, 1993; Carlson *et al.*, 1996), and Wagner *et al.* (1999) are commendable in their attempts to evaluate the effectiveness of specific SAPs, all three investigations are severely limited by methodological weaknesses. None of these studies included a comparison group, engaged in systematic, repeated follow-up of students who took part in the SAP, or evaluated students on standardized alcohol and/or other drug use measures. Furthermore, none of these studies attempted in any way to (a) identify the "active ingredients" of their intervention (i.e., what components of their multi-component interventions were most related to changes in students' substance use) or (b) ascertain why certain students responded to the intervention while others did not.

Given the importance of SAPs for treating adolescent substance abuse, empirical tests of their effectiveness are clearly needed, both in terms of their overall impact in reducing use as well as investigating the specific "active ingredients" that contribute to change (e.g., improved refusal skills, enhanced knowledge of the potential negative consequences of substance use, etc.). To accomplish this, the Teen Intervention Project (TIP) provides a school-based, group counseling (GC) program in which students receive ten weekly sessions of in-school, manual-based treatment. Our intervention evolved from the group counseling methods widely used in Westchester Model SAPs. A comparison group receives assessment and referral (AR) to outside treatment providers only, which is standard practice with substance-abusing students in the school system in which we work.

Both groups are assessed at referral to the program, immediately after treatment (GC) or twelve weeks after referral (AR), and at four, seven, and twelve months after referral. Assessment includes standardized measures of alcohol and drug use, as well as measures examining the putative mechanisms of change associated with the group counseling condition (i.e., the active ingredients). In order to examine why some students respond to the program while others do not, we also assess the impact of several different amenability to treatment variables (e.g., depression, alcohol expectancies, social support) on response to the intervention.

Participant Recruitment and Assessment

School-based research presents many practical and methodological challenges (see Wagner, Swensen & Henggeler, 2000, for a review), and these challenges begin with participant recruitment and assessment. Several initial steps were necessary before TIP could take place in the schools. First, the project was reviewed by the county school board's research and clinical services departments, both of which ultimately approved the research. Next, individual schools were approached to participate in the project. We began with a mass mailing of brochures to administrative and student services personnel at each middle and high school in the district, followed by telephone contacts. For those schools interested in becoming involved with the project, the project director met with school personnel to discuss implementation of the project, and often made presentations to school staff, students, and/or parents. Once we were established in several schools, a contagion-like effect occurred, with additional schools contacting us to participate. Also, a story about the program in the local newspaper further expanded schools' interest in working with us. In the first year of the project, we were able to recruit six schools; as we approach the fifth year of the project, we have worked with over 20 schools.

We have followed the same basic procedures across schools in implementing the program. With the consultation of the school's principal, a contact person is selected to serve as the liaison between the school and the project. Referral arrangements are negotiated with that individual. Generally, a description of the program and some referral forms are distributed to all school personnel with instructions to forward referrals to the school contact person. The contact person, usually a guidance counselor or assistant principal, is responsible for obtaining telephone numbers for each student referred and submitting them to TIP.

Once a referral reaches TIP, the student is assigned a research interviewer, who telephones the student's parent or legal guardian to explain the program and obtain verbal consent for participation. In this process, we have discovered that school records are not always accurate sources for parent contact information. In such cases, we follow up with the school contact person for updated information. We also rely on directory assistance (411), internet searches, and commercially available tracking software to find parents. Our last resort is to send a letter of introduction via certified mail asking parents to call our toll-free line for more information.

We have found that parental reactions to our initial contact are usually positive, but can range from acceptance to fear to indignation. Our research interviewers are trained to tread gently with parents, and during the first telephone contact emphasize the following: (1) the project is approved by the school board; (2) your daughter/son was recommended because he or she may benefit from the services provided; (3) the project is for students experimenting with substances, and thus at risk for developing future problems; (4) TIP is an intervention designed to address problems as they begin to appear, rather than a treatment program for more chronic, severe problems; (5) all information we collect is confidential (the only exception is when students report behavior that endangers themselves or others; in such cases, we notify parents and take appropriate clinical steps); (6) we provide comprehensive assessment and follow-up services over a one-year period, with outside referral if necessary; and (7) all services are provided free of charge and occur within the school.

Once verbal parental consent is obtained, we mail a written consent form to the parent, which is returned to us via postage-paid mail. The research interviewer next meets with the student at school. Since participation is voluntary, the student has the right to deny consent or to withdraw at any time. Once student consent is obtained, the interviewer proceeds with a comprehensive pre-intervention assessment, which includes background variables, alcohol and other drug use behavior, comorbid psychiatric conditions and symptomatology, process variables related to components of treatment (e.g., refusal skills), and other potential determinants of response to intervention (e.g., social support).

A primary goal of the pre-intervention assessment is to distinguish students who are appropriate for TIP from those who are inappropriate for TIP (e.g., not substance involved, in need of more intensive substance abuse or psychiatric treatment). Pre-intervention assessments may last from 50 to 180 minutes, and may occur in one or more sessions. This variation results from individual differences among participants in comorbid symptomatology, reading level, cognitive ability, concentration, and frustration tolerance. Given the breadth of areas measured in the pre-intervention assessment, this is by far the most comprehensive and time-consuming of our assessment contacts.

Our post-intervention assessment takes place at the completion of the ten-week intervention for the students enrolled in the group counseling condition. Students enrolled in the assessment/referral condition are assessed on a parallel schedule. Post-intervention measures include alcohol and other drug use behavior, process variables related to components of treatment, other potential determinants of response to intervention, and consumer satisfaction measures. The interventionists also complete measures of therapy compliance for the group counseling participants. Follow-up assessments are devoted to alcohol and drug use behavior.

Description of the Intervention

Theoretical Background

The theoretical basis for the standardized group counseling (GC) program includes social learning theory (Bandura, 1977) and problem behavior theory (Jessor & Jessor, 1977). Consistent with these models, we believe multiple domains contribute to the development of substance use problems among adolescents (i.e., the biopsychosocial model), though we emphasize potentially modifiable environmental influences and learned beliefs and behaviors associated with substance misuse throughout the intervention (Wagner, Myers & Brown, 1994).

Within this conceptualization, it is assumed that adolescents develop expectancies about the effects of substance use by observing parental, peer, and, more broadly, societal/cultural modeling of substance use (Christiansen, Goldman & Inn, 1982; Goldman, Brown & Christiansen, 1987). These expectancies often are found to predict later substance abuse (Christiansen *et al.*, 1989). Teens' expectancies about the effects of substance use include beliefs that using alcohol will provide stress relief, facilitate social interaction, or make them feel good (Wagner *et al.*, 1994).

In considering the etiology and treatment of adolescent substance use problems, developmental factors relating to substance use also are taken into consideration. Therefore, we recognize that some experimentation with drugs and/or alcohol may be normative (Shedler & Block, 1990). However, teens who lack coping skills to handle negative moods, to engage in comfortable social interactions, to generate positive feelings in the absence of alcohol and drug use, or to effectively manage social pressures for substance involvement are at a greater risk for developing problems related to their alcohol or other drug use (e.g., Bentler, 1992; Pandina & Schuele, 1983).

The GC program also incorporates material from motivational interventions that recognize the importance of client motivation to change in determining treatment outcome (Miller & Rollnick, 1991). One way to bolster substance abusers' commitment for treatment (i.e., motivation) is to allow them choices in approaches to, and goals for, treatment (Sobell & Sobell, 1995). Given adolescents' concern with the degree to which they, rather than others, are making choices about their lives, such involvement with determining aspects of treatment may be especially important for increasing motivation to change. Thus, group members not only assess where they believe they are in terms of their current readiness to change their substance use behavior, but also set both short- and long-term goals for themselves in regard to changing substance use as well as managing other areas of their lives (e.g., relationships, academics, career goals).

In addition, we provide teens with a session-by-session workbook that is used throughout the intervention. This workbook allows for continuing, active involvement with the program's material. In completing the workbook's material in sessions, group members' ideas are constantly solicited. Such active involvement maintains students' attention and enhances self-esteem, thereby heightening their sense of personally shaping their efforts at behavior change (Wagner, Brown & Myers, 1994). In essence, each group member creates a personal record of what they have learned and achieved which they keep at the end of the program. Thus, the manual provides a good, individualized resource for ways to manage any future substance-related difficulties.

In summary, several sources inform our skills-based, group intervention: social learning theory; motivational interventions; and consideration of adolescent development. The program assumes that modeling of substance use behavior, and the concomitant growth of expectancies regarding use, along with skills deficits, such as poor stress management, put teens at risk for substance use and misuse. Adhering to this framework, the GC program focuses on educating teens about alcohol, drugs, and the development of substance use problems, and provides skills training to strengthen functioning in deficit areas. Therapeutically, a motivational stance is taken which advocates helping group members to ascertain their current desire to make changes in their behavior and to set goals for making these changes. Such an approach is especially well suited for adolescents who may respond well to the sense of increased control in their lives imparted by active involvement in the treatment process (Tober, 1991).

Intervention Components

The ten-week GC program is a structured, manualized treatment which sequentially presents material to educate teens about substance use, to heighten their awareness of the reasons for their use, to set and meet goals for reduction or cessation of use, and to develop coping skills to manage stress and other factors relating to use. Broadly speaking, the program may be conceptualized as having two fundamental stages: (1) educating group members about substance abuse (both in general and in terms of each student's particular use); and (2) helping group members make and sustain specific changes in their substance use behavior.

This skills-based treatment utilizes a number of cognitive-behavioral techniques. Group members learn to heighten their awareness of situational factors, such as thoughts and associated feelings connected with substance use, are reinforced for goal achievement, and partake in role plays to strengthen acquired skills. As the program progresses, newly introduced material is always prefaced by a rationale to explain its significance to the concepts and skills that group members are learning.

From the outset, the program's sequential format and the importance of students' active involvement are stressed. Group members are informed that each session's content builds upon earlier material and is critical for grasping future material. At the beginning of each session, material from the previous session is reviewed. To emphasize the importance of each group member's active involvement in the program, the analogy is made that to be good at anything (e.g. music, sports) one must hone one's abilities through practice. Table 1 provides a summary of the components of the GC program, and Table 2 gives a session-by-session outline of the intervention.

The GC program also emphasizes the importance of group process to create productive and meaningful sessions. In the beginning, group members are asked to consider what guidelines are necessary for making a successful group (e.g., maintaining confidentiality, speaking for oneself, listening to others). Also, a "Pair Interview," in which group members interview one another with a set of predetermined questions (e.g., what are your favorite pastimes? what would you most like to change about yourself?) is conducted to facilitate the growth of group cohesion. These interviews help group members to get to know one another, as well as to start considering what changes they want to achieve in the group.

Initial educational components of the GC program include an exploration of adolescents' reasons for substance use, information about alcohol, and an outline regarding the different stages of substance use problems (i.e., from experimentation to dependency). Incorporating a biopsychosocial perspective on the development of substance use, students

Table 1: Components of the standard group counseling intervention.

- *Substance Abuse Education*: Students are educated about substance use and the development of substance use problems.
- *Recognition and Acknowledgment of Personal Substance Use Problems*: Students learn to connect current difficulties with substance use.
- *Self-Monitoring*: Students monitor their own use of alcohol and other drugs.
- *Assessment of Motivation*: Students assess the degree to which they are ready to make changes in their substance use behavior.
- *Commitment Generation*: Students commit to reducing or eliminating their alcohol and other drug use.
- *Goal Setting*: Students set long- and short-term goals for changing substance abuse and achieving other goals.
- *Identification of High-Risk Situations*: Students identify high-risk situations for substance use.
- *Alternatives to Substance Use*: Students develop alternative behaviors to alcohol use, with emphsis on behaviors in high-risk substance use situations.
- *Coping with Stress*: Students learn to recognize stress and develop non-substance use strategies for coping with stress.
- *Communication Skills*: Students are educated about assertiveness and learn specific methods for communicating effectively.
- *Slip Back Effect*: To prevent relapse, students learn to anticipate and cope with the negative emotional reaction that is likely to follow a slip.
- *Practicing Resistance/Refusal*: Students learn and rehearse ways to manage peer-related substance use situations.
- *Social Support*: Students identify groups and individuals who will support their efforts to change their substance use behavior.

Table 2: Session-by-session outline of intervention.

Session #	Session topic(s)	Session #	Session topic(s)
1	Group Introduction and Guidelines	6	Specific Plan for Change; Long- and Short-Term Goals for Change
2	Substance Abuse Education	7	Coping With Stress
3	Recognition and Acknowledgment of Personal Substance Use Problems; Self-Monitoring of Substance Use	8	Improving Relationships; Communication Skills
4	Identifying High-Risk Situations; Assessing Motivation to Change	9	Slip Back Effect; Practicing Resistance/Refusal
5	Commitment Generation;[a] Identifying Alternatives to Substance Use	10	Final Commitment to Change: Social Support; Closing Exercises

[a]Repeated through the remaining sessions.

begin by considering a variety of reasons that teens might use substances (e.g., experimentation, to feel good, to handle boredom or stress). They then focus on their particular reasons and discuss what they believe to be the main cause(s) of their involvement with substances. Education about use continues in the form of an "Alcohol Awareness Quiz" which contains specific questions regarding alcohol and its use. Although group members vary in their knowledge of alcohol, most are surprised by at least some of the answers to the questions, and constructive discussion generally follows.

Students then are introduced to the concept that substance use problems follow a trajectory that starts with experimentation, moves to problem use/abuse, and may eventuate in dependency (i.e., the "Path to Problems"). Descriptions of each stage include associated behaviors and symptoms, and it is stressed that individuals often are unaware that they are moving down the path, and that it becomes more difficult to reduce or stop using, the further down the path one is. This particular component of the treatment is very useful for helping students focus on the extent to which they may be involved with substances, and to constructively challenge any tendencies to minimize their substance involvement. In short, group members end up judging for themselves where their substance use falls rather then having someone else judge for them. Such an emphasis on group members' self-defining the degree of their substance involvement reduces resistance to change and reflects the program's motivational character.

As the sessions progress, education becomes more fine-tuned to the specifics of each student's substance use. Group members consider their personal substance use history in "My Story," which includes material about when they had their first alcoholic drink, how much they had, the first drug other than alcohol they had, their reasons for trying and continuing to use substances, and the responses of others to their use. At this point, group members also start keeping "Weekly Logs" to track their substance use. Presented with the rationale that understanding one's own substance use patterns is important for defining what needs to change and how to begin changing, these logs promote heightened awareness of the thoughts, feelings, and behaviors connected with substance use.

On a daily basis between group meetings, students complete the weekly logs, which ask what they used, how much they used, the situation in which they used, the reasons for use, and the consequences (both negative and positive) of using. Logs for the previous week are reviewed during each group session. Examining the logs allows for a functional analysis of substance use behavior as adolescents articulate the thoughts and feelings associated with their substance use. Such information helps to clarify the expectancies they may have developed regarding substance use and its effects on stress or other correlates of use. From a behavioral perspective, considering the consequences of their use is especially valuable for challenging the group members' beliefs and expectancies about the benefits of use. While positive immediate consequences are acknowledged (e.g., felt more relaxed), often denied or ignored negative consequences, which may not be so immediate, also are explored (e.g., arguments with parents, poor grades, diminished involvement with constructive activities).

Completing the weekly logs exposes group members to the concept of "triggers" for their substance use. Triggers are defined as a situation, behavior, thought, or feeling that is associated with substance use and may therefore spark the urge to use. By identifying their top "triggers" for use, group members heighten their awareness of the automatic thoughts and related feelings and behaviors connected with their substance use. Thoughts, feelings, and situations frequently connected with substance use are labeled "High-Risk" situations, and students are taught to develop specific ways of coping with these situations that do not involve substance use.

The second half of the counseling program focuses on helping group members reduce their substance use involvement, with abstinence as the ultimate goal. An initial, and integral, step for goal setting is helping group members assess their current motivation for change. Group members complete a questionnaire which provides information regarding the degree to which they are concerned about their substance use, the severity of consequences for their substance use, whether or not they know how to make changes, and the importance of sustaining any changes they might have already made.

In line with the program's motivational underpinnings and in accord with the importance of self-directed goal setting for goal commitment espoused by social learning theory (Sobell & Sobell, 1995), each group member is asked to set weekly goals for changing their substance use behavior. Using the weekly "Agreement to Change," group members write out what type of substance use change they hope to make during the upcoming week. Realistic and specific goals are emphasized, and group members are encouraged to consider these goals as "experiments," thereby reducing resistance to considering alternative behaviors and encouraging flexibility in making future goal adjustments. To strengthen the commitment to the "Agreement to Change," each group member signs their weekly goal statement, and another group member co-signs the statement as a witness.

The weekly logs are used to compare actual substance use behavior with each week's goals for substance use behavior. Critical to this process is reinforcing successes (e.g., group members clap for one another for each day of reported abstinence) and constructively analyzing what might have impeded success. Based on this analysis, students then revise their Agreement to Change for the upcoming week. Weekly reviews of the logs and goal statements provide a springboard for group discussion, as group members not only consider their own behaviors but also provide input for one another. Thus, the program capitalizes on group process and constructive peer influence as facilitators of change.

Once the behavioral change aspect of the program is under way, sessions introduce material necessary for maintaining and furthering behavioral changes. Group members learn to identify alternatives to substance use, develop specific plans for furthering substance use reductions, and set short-term and long-term goals for changes in substance use as well as functioning in other areas (e.g., career, relationships, academic). Specific skills include methods for handling stress, for improving relationships (notably communication skills), and for preventing relapse to earlier substance use levels. Role-play and counselor modeling are utilized to help group members anticipate problem situations and rehearse specific ways of coping with these situations.

To help students hone their skills for changing substance use behavior, they are initially asked to generate a list of alternative responses to substance use triggers. Next, they are introduced to the concept that having a specific plan for achieving desired changes in substance use increases the likelihood of success. Thus, group members identify what specific things they plan to do to reduce or end substance use. They consider such things as how to make drugs unavailable to them, increase substance-free activities, and get support for their agreement to make changes. Also, in addition to developing weekly substance use reduction goals, group members develop one-month, one-year, and five-year goals for both substance use and functioning in other areas.

To handle stress, group members identify the general signs and causes of stress, and then specify those causes particularly pertinent to them. Developmental factors are considered, with attention to the types of stress that teens often experience (e.g., parental pressure to be perfect, academic stresses, peer pressure to use substances). Stress prevention strategies, such as regular exercise, setting realistic goals, and learning how to relax, are explained, and stress-coping strategies, such as problem solving and talking with others, are introduced.

It has been our experience that teens commonly identify interpersonal problems as a key source of stress. Frequently, they respond to these problems with anger, which often functions as a trigger for substance use. The program's emphasis on developing communication skills, notably assertiveness, can be especially relevant for helping students learn to manage interpersonal problems without turning to substance use. When defining communication skill, we stress that it involves expressing yourself to others directly, respectfully, and effectively. Building upon this, assertiveness is presented as the capacity to express your feelings honestly and openly while maintaining respect for yourself and others. Specific examples of effective verses ineffective communication are provided to further clarify the characteristics of skillful interpersonal exchanges (e.g., "Speak from the 'I' perspective"; "Focus only on current issues"). We emphasize that these skills must be practiced if they are to be used successfully, and group members engage in role plays that call for the newly learned communication skills.

In order to buttress group members' capacity to sustain changes, the program addresses how to manage relapse. The "Slip Back Effect" is defined in terms of self-defeating thoughts and behaviors that may be experienced should group members revert to previous substance use behavior. More constructive ways of defining this experience (e.g., realizing the "slip" is a mistake; realizing that one "slip" does not mean total defeat) are introduced. Once again, group members engage in role plays, this time focusing how to handle substance use temptation.

During the final session, group members complete a "Long-Term Goal and Commitment to Change." They review their short- and long-term goals for changes in substance use from earlier sessions, and incorporate these in developing their long-term goals. Group members also generate a list of social supports (e.g., friends, family members, professionals) to help them cope with stresses and maintain the changes they have made. At the end of the final session, group members are given their manuals to keep and receive a diploma-like "Certificate of Completion."

Flexible Implementation

Successful implementation of our GC program requires adherence to the counselor and student manuals. However, we recognize that optimally effective counseling requires sensitivity to each individual's unique constellation of problems. Thus, in applying the program we advocate the "flexible" use of our manualized treatment (Kendall, Chu, Gifford, Hayes & Nauta, 1998). To accomplish this, counselors must weave together basic therapeutic skills, such as accurate empathy and attention to each student's particular clinical needs, with a thorough understanding and application of the specific content areas and techniques of the intervention.

In essence, the challenge of such flexibility is to be receptive to a range of information from students and to understand how to address it via the appropriate program components. For instance, a student may be very upset about a fight with a parent and want to discuss this during group time. In such a situation, possible mistakes the counselor could make include dismissing the student's issue because it appears to diverge from the session's goals, or being derailed from addressing group session material in an effort to provide individual support to the student. To successfully negotiate this situation, the counselor may relate the student's specific experiences to the more general focus of the day's session by asking questions including whether the behavioral responses to the fight included substance use, what thoughts and feelings were related to this particular response, and what consequences resulted from the behavioral response. The counselor also may mention the upcoming session on communication skills training, which would be a good time to re-examine the student's experiences.

Flexible application of the manual also involves recognizing that different students may respond best to different components of the intervention. For example, some students may begin to make changes in response to learning to track substance use behavior and becoming aware of previously automatic behavior, while other students may begin to make changes in response to learning how to identify and avoid high-risk situations. In line with this, counselors should become aware of what components of the intervention individual students appear to be responding best to and emphasize these components when appropriate. For instance, one student who was heavily involved with marijuana became motivated to make changes in his substance use when the "Path to Problems" was reviewed. Initially skeptical about this material, he referred back to this as the intervention progressed and eventually recognized that he was at the point of dependency, which motivated him to begin to make changes. In brief, the GC program is sequential but not rigidly linear; material from earlier sessions not only provides the foundation for future material, but also is often directly woven into the content of later sessions.

Making adjustments to meet specific needs of students, such as addressing symptoms of depression or other psychopathology, reflects a flexible application of the GC program as well. For example, a student with depressive tendencies may have difficulty setting goals due to feelings of hopelessness. Sensitivity to such difficulty in envisioning future possibilities might lead a counselor to particularly help a student with goal setting or other facets of the program that might be especially relevant to addressing depressive feelings (e.g., increasing self-reinforcement for positive changes in substance use). More broadly, group characteristics, such as marked differences across students in the level of substance involvement among students, may call for particular strategies. For instance, emphasizing negative consequences for substance use may lessen the impact of peer modeling on students in the very early stages of substance use by those members of the group who are more substance involved.

Summary and Future Directions

The critical question of why some adolescents respond to SAPs and others do not is beginning to be examined through data obtained by the Teen Intervention Project. While these data are yet to be fully analyzed, we would like to discuss our approach to this question, as we believe this to be an important direction for future research.

It is well known that teenagers with substance use problems are a heterogeneous group, with individual differences on factors such as the anticipated effects and consequences resulting from substance use, the context and motivations in which use occurs, and the factors that contribute to or accompany substance use involvement (Wagner & Kassel, 1995). Certain SAPs may be ineffective for some teenagers because of inadequate attention to individual differences among students in demographic, psychological, and/or social factors related to substance use problems.

Individual difference variables likely to affect treatment response have been labeled "amenability to treatment" (Kazdin, 1995) or "matching" factors (Project MATCH, 1997). Very few studies have examined the differential amenability of adolescents to any type of psychosocial intervention, and treatment matching for substance-abusing teens currently is in its infancy. The variables we currently are examining as possible amenability to treatment factors include psychiatric comorbidity, alcohol expectancies, social support, delinquency, motivation to change, history of abuse or maltreatment, family conflict, and parental substance use. As knowledge develops about amenability to treatment factors in relation to SAPs, algorithms may be able to be developed for referring substance-abusing adolescents to the specific SAP program or program component(s) with the greatest chance of success.

Another important direction for future research is to examine the effectiveness of SAPs with other student populations and their generalizability to other domains of adolescent problem behavior. For example, students who have been placed in alternative schools are more likely to be substance involved and have substance use problems than students enrolled in regular high schools. This population clearly is in need of substance abuse intervention, and may benefit from SAP services, especially if the services are modified to address the greater substance abuse severity likely to be encountered with this group. Regarding other domains of problem behavior, substance-abusing adolescents often demonstrate other types of problem behavior such as aggression, high-risk sexual practices, and recklessness. SAPs, with some modifications, may be effective in reducing these problems as well.

The Teen Intervention Project described in this chapter represents an early step in the development of an effective school-based strategy for treating adolescent substance use problems. While we hope this program will contribute to the empirical literature on adolescent substance abuse intervention, much more work remains to be done. Epidemiological data indicate continuing high rates of alcohol and other drug use among adolescents, a small but significant proportion of whom will develop substance use problems. To address this important public health concern, it is essential to conduct additional research that develops and evaluates a variety of promising interventions for treating adolescent substance use problems. An especially important research area is community-based treatment models (e.g., treatment provided in neighborhood clinics, schools, home), which have greater ecological validity and impact, and fewer barriers to treatment access, than more traditional intervention models for adolescent substance abuse (Wagner *et al.*, 2000). Nonetheless, we hope that this chapter provides inspiration and guidance for researchers and clinicians interested in improving the effectiveness of all substance abuse interventions for adolescents.

References

Bandura, A. (1977), *Social learning theory*. Englewood Cliffs, NJ: Prentice-Hall.

Bentler, P. M. (1992), "Etiologies and consequences of adolescent drug use: Implications for prevention." *Journal of Addictive Diseases 11*, 47–61.

Carlson, K. A. (1993), A summary report on the evaluation of the Student Assistance Program offered by the Olympic Educational Service District. Unpublished report.

Carlson, K. A., Hughes, J. D., & Deebach, F. M. (1996), "Proof positive: A student assistance program evaluation." *Student Assistance Journal 8*, 14–18.

Christiansen, B. A., Goldman, M. S., & Inn, A. (1982), "Development of alcohol-related expectancies in adolescents: Separating pharmacological from social-learning influences." *Journal of Consulting and Clinical Psychology 50*, 336–344.

Christiansen, B. A., Smith, G. T., Roehling, P. V., & Goldman, M. (1989), "Using alcohol expectancies to predict adolescent drinking behavior after one year." *Journal of Consulting and Clinical Psychology 57*, 93–99.

DiRenzio, P. M. (1990), "A success story: SAP Development in Pennsylvania." *Student Assistance Journal 2*, 25–29.

Foote. A., & Erfurt, J. C. (1991), "Effects of EAP follow-up on prevention of relapse among substance abuse clients." *Journal of Studies on Alcohol 52*, 241–248.

Forman, S. G., & Linney, J. A. (1988), "School-based prevention of adolescent substance abuse: Programs, implementation and future directions." *School Psychology Review 17*, 550–558.

Goldman, M. S., Brown, S. A., Christiansen, B. A., & Smith, G. T. (1991), "Alcoholism and memory: Broadening the scope of alcohol-expectancy research." *Psychological Bulletin 110*, 137–146.

Jessor, R., & Jessor, S. L. (1977) *Problem Behavior and Psychosocial Development: A Longitudinal Study of Youth*. New York: Academic Press.

Kazdin, A. E. (1995), "Scope of child and adolescent psychotherapy research: Limited sampling of dysfunctions, treatments, and client characteristics." *Journal of Clinical Child Psychology 24*(2), 125–140.

Kendall, P. C., Chu, B., Gifford, A., Hayes, C., & Nauta, M. (1998), "Breathing life into a manual: Flexibility and creativity with manual-based treatments." *Cognitive & Behavioral Practice 5*, 177–198.

Klitzner, M., Fisher, D., Stewart, K., & Gilbert, S. (1993), *Substance Abuse: Early Intervention for Adolescents*. Princeton, NJ: The Robert Wood Johnson Foundation.

Milgram, G. G. (1989), "Impact of a Student Assistance Program." *Journal of Drug Education 19*, 327–335.

Miller, W. R., & Rollnick, S. (1991), *Motivational Interviewing: Preparing People to Change Addictive Behavior*. New York: Guilford Press.

Morehouse, E. R. (1984), *A Study of Westchester County's Student Assistance Program Participants' Alcohol and Drug Abuse prior to and after Counseling during the School Year 1982–1983* (Tech. Rep. No. MHa s65 15-1). White Plains, NY: Westchester County Department of Community Mental Health.

National Student Assistance Directory (1997), "Special Edition of the Student Assistance Journal." *Student Assistance Journal 9*(4).

Newman, L., Henry, P. B., DiRenzo, P., & Stecher, T. (1988–1989), "Intervention and student assistance: The Pennsylvania Model." *Journal of Chemical Dependency Treatment 2*, 145–162.

Palmer, J. H., & Paisley, P. O. (1991) "Student Assistance Programs: A response to substance abuse." *The School Counselor 38*, 287–293.

Pandina, R. J., & Schuele, J. A. (1983), "Psychosocial correlates of alcohol and drug use of adolescent students and adolescents in treatment." *Journal of Studies on Alcohol 44*, 950–973.

Project MATCH (1997), "Matching alcoholism treatments to client heterogeneity: Project MATCH posttreatment drinking outcomes." *Journal of Studies on Alcoholism 58*, 7–29.

Shedler, J., & Block, J. (1990), "Adolescent drug use and psychological health: A longitudinal inquiry." *American Psychologist 45*, 612–630.

Simmering, K. F. (1991), "A team approach to drug-free schools: The Iowa Connection." *Student Assistance Journal 3*, 26–31.

Sobell, M. B., & Sobell, L. C. (1998), "Guiding Self-Change." In W. R. Miller & N. Heather (eds). *Treating Addictive Behaviors: Processes of Change*, 2nd Ed. New York: Plenum, 189–202.

Tober, G. (1991), "Motivational interviewing with young people." In W. R. Miller & S. Rollnick (eds), *Motivational interviewing: Preparing people to change addictive behavior*. New York: Guilford Press, 248–259.

Wagner, E. F., Dinklage, S., Cudworth, C., & Vyse, J. (1999), "A preliminary evaluation of the effectiveness of a standardized Student Assistance Program." *Substance Use & Misuse 34*, 1571–1584.

Wagner, E. F., Myers, M. G., & Brown, S. A. (1994), "Adolescent substance abuse: Assessment and treatment strategies." In L. VandeCreek (ed.), *Innovations in clinical practice: A source book*. Sarasota, FL: Professional Resource Press.

Wagner, E. F., & Kassel, J. D. (1995), "Substance use and abuse." In R.T. Ammerman & M. Hersen (eds), *Handbook of child behavior therapy in the psychiatric setting.* New York: John Wiley and Sons.

Wagner, E. F., Swensen, C. C., & Henggeler, S. W. (2000), "Practical and methodological challenges in community-based interventions." *Children's Services: Social Policy, Research, and Practice 3*, 211–231.

Walsh, D. A. *et al.* (1991), "A randomized trial of treatment options for alcohol-abusing workers." *The New England Journal of Medicine 325*, 775–782.

Chapter 10

Family Behavior Therapy

Brad Donohue and Nate Azrin*

Theoretical Background and Rationale

The standardized program that we will describe in this chapter initially was developed in outcome studies funded by the National Institute of Drug Abuse (Azrin, Donohue, Besalel, Kogan & Acierno, 1996; Azrin, McMahon, *et al.*, 1996) and National Institute of Mental Health (Azrin *et al.*, in press). The program incorporates multiple interventions that target the adolescent's drug use, conduct, problem-solving skills, family relationships, and communication skills. It conceptualizes drug usage as a strong inherent primary reinforcer, which is often enhanced by imitation, physiological and situational prompts, the absence of sources of reinforcement, and/or remoteness or uncertainty of the usual negative consequences (familial/social/legal/vocational/medical). This conceptualization has been outlined previously as the basis for the community reinforcement treatment (CRT) program for alcoholism with adults (Azrin, 1976; Azrin, Sisson, Meyers & Godley, 1982; Hunt & Azrin, 1973). As applied to youth with severe conduct problems, the present conceptualization views a strong positive parent–youth relationship as central in remediating problem behaviors, including drug use, just as the CRT approach has emphasized a positive marital relation with the adults. This conceptualization of youth conduct problems has been described in the Reciprocity Counseling program for youth (Besalel & Azrin, 1981), which emphasizes contingency management and positive communication training. The current program is designed to address drug use and associated behavioral problems using a number of specific standardized procedures, each of which will be described in detail.

Description of the Intervention Program

Initial Contacts with Program Participants

As substance abusers and their significant others are notorious for poor therapy attendance, we have developed an empirically validated method of improving their session

---

*Correspondence concerning this chapter should be addressed to Brad Donohue, University of Nevada, Las Vegas.

Innovations in Adolescent Substance Abuse Interventions, pages 205–227.

attendance (Donohue, Azrin, *et al.*, 1998). In this procedure, an attendant conducts a phone interview with the youth and parent three days prior to the first scheduled appointment. We have found contact greater than three days prior to the scheduled appointment is too far removed from the scheduled session to act as a "reminder," and calls one or two days before the appointment seem to increase the probability of patients rescheduling the appointment. During this initial contact the interviewer attempts to build rapport with the youth through an eight-step process. The adolescent is asked to (1) describe problems that others (usually parents, judges, teachers) have recently caused him/her, and (2) empathy for elicited concerns is subsequently provided. The interviewer (3) reviews benefits that other youth have reported as a result of participating in the program (e.g., reduced time in jail/probation, better treatment from parents), and attempts to (4) elicit potential benefits from the youth's perspective. The youth is (5) asked to identify what s/he is looking for in a therapist, and then told that the assigned therapist will stress these attributes (the therapist is later instructed to emphasize these attributes during therapy). The youth is told that (6) snacks and sodas will be available for the adolescent's pleasure. The snacks and sodas are offered to assist in establishing the treatment program as a generalized reinforcer for the youth. As succinctly put to a therapist by one of the teens who participated in our program, "Thanks for the candy. It's nice to know at least someone gives a shit about my needs." The interviewer attempts to (7) elicit potential problems that may cause the youth to miss the scheduled appointment (e.g., parents and youth have an argument immediately prior to the appointment time), and subsequently (8) engages the youth in an exercise to identify solutions to problems that may have been generated. After this initial telephone contact with the youth, the interviewer asks to speak with the primary guardian and essentially replicates this eight-step process with the guardian.

Two days after the initial face-to-face intake session with the therapist, the youth and parent are contacted separately once again by telephone. The interviewer tells both persons positive things that the therapist said about them, including, if applicable, the client's punctuality in arriving to the session. The youth and parent are prompted to ask questions about their therapy, and to provide suggestions relevant to program/therapist improvement. These suggestions are transmitted to the therapist prior to the next session. The guardian and youth are asked to verify their next appointment time, and potential problems and solutions related to attending the scheduled appointment are again reviewed, when necessary.

Assessment

Upon arrival at the clinic for the intake session, the youth and legal guardian are offered a snack and beverage, and program consent forms are reviewed and subsequently endorsed by both the youth and guardian. An overview of the program is provided by the therapist that includes the following: (a) assessment will include two outpatient sessions of about 90 minutes each; (b) treatment will include 15 sessions that will fade in duration (90 minutes to 60 minutes) and frequency (once per week to once per month) over six months; (c) post-treatment and six-month follow-up assessment sessions will be implemented to measure progress, (d) treatment builds on patient strengths; (e) program goals are designed to help the youth eliminate problems due to drug use and other undesired behaviors, improve family relationships, and enhance academic/work performance; (f) the youth and parent will determine which interventions are emphasized in treatment; and (g) therapists utilize validated treatment manuals to guide their intervention. The adolescent is then instructed to go to the restroom with an attendant to provide a supervised urine specimen for drug analysis (see Drug Analysis section below for details of this procedure).

Although youth and their parents are scheduled to meet with their therapist together for the first 15 or 20 minutes of their assessment sessions to discuss the youth's presenting problems, we have found it helpful to interview the youth and parent separately during most of the assessment phase. This schedule allows the therapist to briefly observe youth/parent interactions, while having sufficient time to assess the youth and parent in confidence. If the guardian is interviewed first, the counselor provides the youth with self-report questionnaires to complete in the waiting room. These questionnaires include the Youth Self Report to assess the youth's conduct across several dimensions from the youth's perspective (Achenbach, 1991a), the Social Problem Solving Inventory (D'Zurrilla & Nezu, 1990), and the Youth Satisfaction with Parent Scale (DeCato, Donohue, Azrin & Teichner, 2001). While the youth completes these questionnaires, the parent is interviewed using the Parent–Child Assessment Survey to obtain clinical diagnostic information (Hodges, Kline, Stern, Cytryn & McKnew, 1982), and an estimate of the adolescent's drug use frequency is ascertained from the parent, according to the time-line follow-back method (Sobell, Sobell, Klajner, Pavan & Basian, 1986). After the parent interview is concluded, the therapist collects the questionnaires from the youth and carefully checks to make sure the youth has completed all items correctly.

The parent then is instructed to go to the waiting room to complete the parent questionnaires. These questionnaires include the Child Behavior Checklist to obtain the parent's perspective of the youth's conduct (Achenbach, 1991b), and the Parent Satisfaction with Youth Scale (Donohue, Decato, Azrin, Teichner, 2001). While the parent completes these questionnaires, the youth is assessed for substance abuse and dependence, according to the substance disorders section of the Structured Clinical Interview for DSM-III-R (Spitzer, Williams, Gibbon & First, 1992), and the youth's report of his/her drug use frequency is assessed via the time-line follow-back procedure (Sobell *et al.*, 1986). The second assessment session is focused on obtaining a urine drug screen from the youth, and assessing youth relationships with family and friends, youth hobbies and activities, and youth goals for treatment.

Drug analysis. At least during the initial stages of interventions, we believe it is very important to test the youth's urine for illicit drugs during each session to provide an objective measure of substance use. Broad screen assays (testing a variety of drugs; e.g., amphetamines, barbiturates, marijuana, cocaine, PCP, heroin) may be analyzed by professional companies for about $10.00 each. When there is a lack of funding available for extensive drug analysis, broad screen assays may be conducted randomly, the frequency of testing may be tapered with confirmed abstinence, or specific drug screens, rather than broad drug screens, may be conducted. If the youth has difficulty urinating, it helps to run water in the bathroom sink while the youth attempts to urinate, to instruct the youth to put his/her hand in warm water prior to attempting urination, and to provide the youth liquids throughout the session. The latter procedure should be used with caution, as high creatine levels may result from excessive consumption of water and potentially invalidate testing results.

When drug use is indicated in the urine testing, therapists usually disclose results in the presence of the parent(s) and youth, unless extenuating circumstances exist. If the youth denies use, therapists report that the tests are highly valid and the most objective indicator of drug use. Therapists then implement, in a matter-of-fact manner, the consequences that have been established during contingency contracting procedures for positive urine assays (see Contingency Contracting section below). Therapists then express that it is important to "move on" (i.e., proceed to the next intervention), as false positives (testing indicates drug use, when in fact no use has occurred) are extremely rare. Indeed, when therapists express uncertainty as to the validity of urine drug assays (e.g., "It is possible that marijuana may still be in John's system. Let's give him the benefit of a doubt this first time"), youth more times than not will question the validity of future testings. In fact it is far more often the case that testing will indicate no use, when in fact drug use has occurred, since illicit drugs other than marijuana ("hard drugs") are excreted rapidly, making it difficult to detect these drugs. In the case of Marijuana, which although rarely may be detected for up to two or three weeks (particularly when youth are obese, inactive, and have recently consumed a large quantity of marijuana), most drug testing companies will report the level of THC found in the urine. Thus, the recent level may be compared with the previous level (recent use of marijuana would be suggested if the recent test indicates a higher level of marijuana in the youth's system). Youth often argue that positive test results for marijuana are due to breathing marijuana smoke of someone else. In these cases, we instruct therapists to simply tell the youth that the report indicates drug use, and that the youth will need to avoid similar situations in the future, particularly since a goal of treatment is to avoid drug associated stimuli.

Disclosing assessment results and assessing patient expectations for treatment. We believe it is important to disseminate assessment findings, and assess patient expectations, for several reasons. By having a clear understanding of the presenting problems, parents and their youth are more apt to recognize, and take action to prevent, contributing problem behaviors, as well as to perform behaviors that are incompatible with problem behavior. This process also provides therapists opportunities to discount unreasonable expectations which often lead to an overly critical environment.

The therapist initiates the first treatment session with verbal reinforcement, telling the youth and parent something positive about their participation in the assessment sessions (e.g., being candid, cooperative, pleasant). The therapist then privately meets with the parent(s), and then the youth, to disclose the results of the assessment sessions using a standardized checklist as a prompt. With the parent(s), the therapist interprets all significantly elevated subscale and total scale scores, diagnoses obtained from P-CAS and SCID-IV, and the lowest Parent Satisfaction with Youth Scale item scores. Parental feedback is encouraged, and parents are asked to discuss past efforts to reduce their youth's drug use and troublesome behavior (desirable and effective methods are praised). Parents are then asked to state their expectations regarding the youth's use of drugs and troublesome behavior consequent to therapy. The therapist provides statements of hope to increase positive expectations for change, and parents are given feedback as to the appropriateness of their expectations. Parents are told that therapy attendance and completion of therapy assignments are strong determinants of goal attainment. As with all sessions, the parents' report of their youth's frequency of illicit drug use since last contact is obtained using the time-line follow-back method.

The parent is then excused, and the therapist meets individually with the youth. The youth is asked if there is anything that she or he felt uncomfortable discussing in front of the parent. Concerns, if any, are addressed, and results of the Youth Satisfaction with Parent Scale are disclosed. In this endeavor, the youth is requested to briefly elaborate on the areas of greatest dissatisfaction from this scale, and empathy is provided, whenever appropriate. If the youth requests information regarding other test results, this information is revealed. The youth is asked to suggest potential methods to improve her/his "situation," including suggestions to reduce her/his drug use and troublesome behavior. Youth expectancies of drug use and relevant problem behaviors are also examined (e.g., "John, you are currently using cocaine one or two days a week. What do you think is going to happen to the frequency of your cocaine use after we start treatment? ... Why do you think it will be that way?".... You're also skipping half your classes at school. What do you think will happen to your school attendance during the next few months? .... What makes you think that?....").

As with all sessions, youths are asked to report the number of days that they used illicit drugs since the last session, according to the time-line follow-back method. Youth and parent(s) also are encouraged to bring additional significant others who are invested in helping the youth obtain his/her goals (e.g., friends of youth, family members, older siblings) to subsequent therapy sessions. Expanding the number of people involved in treatment occurs only after all therapy procedures have been implemented at least once, which is typically accomplished by the sixth session. Indeed, friends of the youth usually find the therapy sessions enjoyable, and often have fun modeling therapy procedures with the target youth. Younger siblings, usually under 13, are excused from sessions when drug use frequency reports and drug use scenarios are reported by the parents or substance abusing youth. Indeed, the content is often graphic, and promotes a premature understanding of drug use that often results in biases of younger siblings to think of the reinforcing "cool" side of drug use.

Intervention

After assessment results and therapy expectations are discussed, the youth and parent(s) are seen together by the therapist so that interventions may be mutually selected from a list of therapy options. The youth and parent are each provided a handout that depicts treatment options. Two columns are included in the handout: one column consists of easy-to-understand descriptions of the various treatment procedures (e.g., "Getting rewards from my parent(s) for decreasing drug use and staying out of trouble" represents our behavioral contracting therapy; "Reviewing ways to avoid situations that involve drugs and trouble, and planning to spend more time in situations that don't involve drugs and trouble" represents our stimulus control intervention); and the other column provides space for the both the parent and youth to rate the expected efficacy of each of these procedures from 0 to 100 (i.e., 0 = not helpful at all, 100 = completely helpful). With the exception of procedures that both the parent and youth rate at zeros, expected efficacy means are tabulated, and the youth and parent are told that the procedures will be implemented in the order of their rankings, with the expectation that the use of the procedures will be successive and cumulative. That is, once a procedure is implemented for the first time, it is implemented during each subsequent session, albeit to a lesser degree. After all procedures are implemented at least once (usually by the sixth session), the youth and parent(s) rate them again, which determines the degree of emphasis on each procedure for the remainder of therapy.

We will now broadly depict how the interventions are implemented. The empirical literature strongly suggests contingency contracting is one of the most effective therapeutic procedures with delinquent youth, suggesting it should be implemented immediately. However, some families do not like contingency management procedures. Therefore, rather than potentially having these persons drop out of treatment, we feel it is most important to enlist their enthusiasm early in therapy by providing the interventions they perceive are most effective, particularly since all of the interventions we describe have demonstrated efficacy in our controlled treatment outcome studies. Thus, we emphasize that procedures be implemented in the order of the patients' rankings (see above).

The Annoyance Review. The purpose of the Annoyance Review procedure is to elicit initial motivation of the youth to decrease drug use and problem behaviors by making the youth more aware of the negative consequences of these actions. The parent(s) is (are) first asked to view their completed Parent Satisfaction with Youth Scale, and select up to five domains that are of greatest concern. Each elicited target behavior and illicit drug is recorded in a list. The youth then is seen individually, and a rationale is provided. For example, a therapist might say,

> I have been informed about the concerns that others have had regarding your use of drugs, including the trouble that you have experienced with adults. However, I haven't had a chance to speak with you about these concerns. I'm interested in knowing what unpleasant consequences you've experienced, or that you imagine could happen, with these things, if any, so that I may appreciate your concerns more fully.

For substance use, and each problem domain identified by the parent, the youth is asked to rate, on a scale of 0–100, how unpleasant it would be if the youth's current pattern of drug use and conduct continued. Each rating is recorded next to its corresponding domain in a second column. The youth then is instructed to disclose unpleasant consequences associated with each of the domains. Each of the elicited responses should be recorded in a third column next to its respective domain.

After these initial unpleasant consequences are recorded, the therapist should prompt additional consequences by stating, with neutral affect, "Anything else?" When no more consequences are provided for a particular target domain, the therapist proceeds to the next domain, and continues as described above. A typically line of inquiry would resemble the following:

What unpleasant things are associated with your current pattern of drug use? (Youth provides an unpleasant consequence) Anything else? (Youth reports no additional consequences) What are the unpleasant consequences associated with doing things that are against the law? (Youth provides two negative consequences) Anything else? (Youth reports no additional consequences) What unpleasant things might happen if you do poorly in school? (Youth reports no unpleasant consequences) Anything else?

Each of the youth's initial unpleasant consequences rated less than 70 should be repeated to the youth, followed by queries regarding what is especially unpleasant/upsetting about the initial consequence (e.g., "You said that you get in arguments with your mother after you steal things. What is especially unpleasant about arguing with your mother?"). The youth should be encouraged to elaborate, clarify, and/or specify in greater detail the unpleasantnesses that are disclosed. An example vignette for the youth's response "I get upset after I use crack," is as follows:

THERAPIST: What do you get upset about?
YOUTH: Lots of things. Like, I must be a bad son.
THERAPIST: Why is that upsetting to you?
YOUTH: I don't know. I just don't feel good about myself.
THERAPIST: Is it distressing for you to have these thoughts?
YOUTH: Yeah.
THERAPIST: So another unpleasant consequence of drug use for you is that you have thoughts that you are a bad son and don't feel good about yourself.

After all consequences reported by the youth are fully delineated, therapists prompt for additional unpleasant consequences that may not have been mentioned but are common among this age group (e.g., time in jail, health-related problems, negative relationships, hurting/upsetting others, disrespect from others, doing badly in school/work). After the consequences are exhausted, therapists empathize with the youth about how "truly" unpleasant these consequences must be for him/her, particularly the highest-rated consequences, and reinforce the idea that it is normal to feel this way. Contrasting positive consequences resulting from drug abstinence and trouble-free behavior also are reviewed.

A modified annoyance review procedure may be implemented in future sessions, whenever resistance and/or lack of motivation occur in therapy. Briefly, the therapist may review the top-rated unpleasant consequences for substance use and each problem domain of concern, tell the youth that these consequences are likely to occur, and empathize with the youth regarding the undesirability of these consequences. The youth then may be descriptively praised for past efforts in therapy, including a brief review of several positive consequences for maintaining trouble-free behavior and abstinence from drugs.

Communication guidelines for therapy. Prior to implementing the core interventions, we have found it helpful to review communication guidelines for therapy. As with all interventions, an initial rationale is provided to the parents and youth together. Rationales contain: (a) a very brief statement of the problem to be addressed; (b) the treatment to be implemented; (c) information that the intervention has been successful for other families with similar problems; and (d) an individualized explanation as to why the therapy is expected to be particularly effective with the present family. An example rationale for the communication guidelines procedure is as follows:

> We have a lot of material to cover in the upcoming treatment sessions. Therefore, it is important to review some guidelines that will increase positive communication during sessions. Guidelines apply to all family members equally, and if a guideline is broken during the session, I will review the guideline with the person who was not able to comply. I will also ask the person to attempt to correct the violation of communication before moving on. Other families have found this procedure to be very helpful because the key to preventing the escalation of session misconduct is early interruption of undesired behaviors. I think this procedure will be particularly effective with your family because you have all expressed a desire to improve communication in your family.

After the rationale for communication guidelines is stated, each family member is given a brief listing of them to keep. All communication guidelines are read to the family, each family member is prompted to acknowledge that the guidelines are important to communication, and each family member is asked to commit to "attempt" to comply with the guidelines. The guidelines include: (a) no interruptions; (b) not talking for more than a minute without inviting others to comment; (c) disclosing aspects of requests that can be done, instead of using the word "no"; (d) no use of sarcasm in any form, (e) no swearing, spiteful, and hurtful statements; (f) avoiding discussion of past problems or weaknesses and instead suggesting solutions to problems; (g) staying focused on specific actions that are desired, not overall criticisms of what negative attitudes are disliked, and (h) speaking in a soft and audible tone of voice.

It is realistically expected that family members will violate guidelines during sessions. However, in obtaining permission from family members to interrupt negative communication and consequently instruct positive communication, the awkwardness of interrupting family members who are emotionally aroused is somewhat alleviated. Role-playing may be initiated to enhance communication skills. In the very rare event that in-session parent–adolescent communication becomes extremely conflictual, the family is instructed to separate for five to 15 minutes, and the session is resumed once family members are calm. Session duration should subsequently be extended for the number of minutes that was interrupted.

Reciprocity awareness. This procedure is designed to bring about awareness of the pleasant aspects of the existing relationship. Prior to implementing this procedure, the family is given the following rationale:

> "Families often forget the positive things they do for one another. When this happens, it is easy to feel unappreciated. This program will build on

your strengths. The therapy we are going to do now is designed to increase awareness of the positive things that you do for one another, and this awareness will motivate your family to continue these positive things in the future.

The youth and parent(s) then are instructed to record several things that are done for each other (i.e., Things I do for you that you like; Things you do for me that I like). Therapists prompt responses by glancing at the lists and making generic comments (e.g., "Wow, you sure have a lot of great things on your list." "Some things that I have heard other adolescents say their parents do for them include ..."). After a few responses are generated, the parent is instructed to tell something that the youth does for the parent, including a statement of appreciation to the youth. The youth is instructed to say how it felt to be appreciated, and that he/she will make an effort to continue to perform the behavior. The youth then is prompted to disclose something that the parent does for her/him, and to tell the parent that the action is appreciated. The parent is instructed to tell the youth how the appreciation felt, and that the action will continue. If siblings/friends are present, adults may collaborate and then exchange compliments with the youth as a team. This may be expanded to include siblings if they are present. These statements of appreciation are practiced one or two more times, and are revisited briefly during next couple of sessions. Therapy assignments include making statements of appreciation at home.

The youth and parent also are taught to remind each other of the good things that occur in their relationship. In this procedure, the parent tells the youth something that the parent does for the youth (obtained from the "things I do for my child" column), and asks whether the youth likes the way the action is performed. If the youth appreciates the action, the youth is instructed to express that appreciation. If the youth does not appreciate the action, the therapist informs the parent that performing the behavior no longer seems necessary. The youth also may be told to request something that would be similarly desired.

The youth then is instructed to tell the parent something that the youth does for the parent ("things I do for my parent" list), and to ask if the parent likes the way the action is performed. As might be expected, if the parent appreciates the action, the parent is instructed to demonstrate appreciation. If the parent does not appreciate the action, the youth is told by the therapist that it seems no longer necessary to perform the behavior, and the parent is encouraged to request something that would be similarly desired. These appreciation reminders are performed one or two more times in the session, and again during the first few minutes of the subsequent two or three sessions. Homework also may be assigned to practice the appreciation reminders at home, or to add, and subsequently review, new items to the lists.

Annoyance prevention. This procedure is an anger management strategy. The following is an example of the rationale for this procedure presented to the family:

Being upset at others makes it difficult to resolve conflicts. This procedure is designed to redirect anger from the person associated with the upset to the situation in which the upset occurred. This procedure has been shown to be very effective, particularly with families like yours who are interested in eliminating aversive interactions.

After the youth and parent are given a handout that depicts each step of the annoyance prevention procedure, the youth is asked to describe a situation in which the parent did something that was annoying. The therapist then models annoyance prevention in response to the situation (e.g., relaxed breathing, objective description of hypothetical situation, stating a situational cause that is out of the individual's control, statement of personal responsibility). The youth is instructed to rehearse the annoyance prevention in response to a similar situation, and feedback subsequently is provided. The parent is also taught to perform the annoyance prevention procedure in a similar manner. The parent and youth are assigned to practice the procedure at home, whenever appropriate, and both the youth and parent role-play the procedure at least once during the next three sessions, or as needed during sessions.

Positive request procedure. This procedure is designed to teach the youth and her/his parents to make requests for desired actions in a positive manner. The following rationale is offered for the procedure:

> People who ask for things positively and convincingly usually get more of what they want. Therefore, you are all going to learn to positively request things that are important to you. This will probably reduce the frequency and severity of your arguments, because you will be focusing on mutually satisfying solutions.

A form is given to all family members depicting specific steps in making a positive request. The therapist then models the positive request procedure in its entirety for a hypothetical example (elicited from the family), utilizing the following steps: (a) politely request a specific action from the other person specifying when the action is desired; (b) state benefits to recipient; (c) state benefits to self; (d) suggest a statement recognizing that it might be difficult to grant the request; (e) offer to help facilitate the action; (f) offer to reciprocate the action; (g) tell recipient that the action would be appreciated; (h) suggest an alternative behavior; and (i) ask recipient to accept or suggest an alternative action. Family members are informed all steps do not have to be implemented when trying to make a positive request at home, but that in the office they should practice the complete set of steps.

The youth then is instructed to ask the parent for something that is desired using the positive request procedure. After feedback is provided to the youth, the parent is instructed to respond to the youth's request. The parent is then instructed to perform a positive request of the youth for something that is desired by the parent. The parent and youth are subsequently asked to practice the positive request procedure at home, whenever something is especially desired. Across the next three sessions, each family member should be instructed to practice at least one request, while the therapist provides feedback.

Contingency contracting. The level system is utilized, whereby standards of the youth's non-drug using and prosocial conduct increase commensurate with parental rewards. Our level system begins with the presentation of the following rationale to the parent and youth:

> (Insert youth's name) has a history of using drugs and getting into trouble. The following procedure is designed to increase motivation in adolescents to avoid drug use and perform behaviors that will keep them out of trouble. In this procedure, I will attempt to identify some of the things that (insert youth's name) would like to receive from you, (insert parent's name). I will also attempt to identify some of the things that (insert parent's name) would like to see you doing better, (insert youth's name). The demands on (insert youth's name) will increase as his behavior improves, but so to will the quality of the privileges and rewards that he is given. The level system has been shown to be very effective in giving adolescents the motivation to stay drug-free and to avoid things that might lead to trouble. I feel this procedure is going to be especially effective in your relationship because you both want a fair exchange. Does this seem like something that you both would like to try out?

The youth then is seen individually, and asked to identify reinforcers, using a standard list of rewards as a prompt (see Appendix A). If the youth shows interest in a particular domain in this list (e.g., transportation), s/he is asked what is currently being provided by the parent(s) in that area. The youth then is asked to discuss how the domain could be "perfect," and the youth's responses are recorded.

After all items in the list are reviewed, the therapist meets with the parent(s) individually. The parent is shown a generic list of common behavior domains that are associated with trouble-free behavior and drug abstinence (see Appendix B).The parent first is asked to select each domain that needs improvement, and the therapist helps the parent identify three levels of increasing behavioral difficulty (i.e., "slight improvement of current behavior," "moderate improvement," "ideal behavior") that may be monitored on a daily basis. To facilitate rapid identification of appropriate levels, each target behavioral domain includes three hypothetical levels that may be modified to accommodate three levels for the youth. Therapists also provide feedback when levels appear too easy, or too difficult for the youth to accomplish. In many cases, it is easier for parents to identify extreme levels first, and then complete the middle level.

After three levels are identified for each target behavior, the youth's ideal reinforcers are disclosed, and the parent is asked to identify three corresponding levels of increasing value for each reinforcer. For instance, if a youth ideally wanted his parent to buy him a car, the parent might be unwilling to buy the youth a car given a slight improvement in his behavior, but might be willing to let the youth drive the family car on Saturday night if a slight improvement in behavior were demonstrated (i.e., equivalent to first level). Similarly, the parent might be willing to assist in the purchase of a used car if the youth demonstrated significant improvements in behavior (i.e., equivalent to third level). As with the behavioral domains, each reinforcer domain includes three levels of increasing reinforcement to facilitate rapid identification of the three levels for the youth. For money (the most common reinforcer desired by youth), parents are instructed to identify the maximum amount that could be provided to the youth per week if the youth was a "perfect" child. This amount is then divided by seven, which becomes the daily amount for the highest level (third level). The daily amount for the lowest level (fist level) is obtained by dividing the amount of money that is currently given to the youth on average (prior to establishing the contingency program) by seven. The middle level is obtained by subtracting the lower amount (first level) from the higher amount, and dividing the resulting amount by two. It sometimes helps to have parents record an inventory of things that are bought for the youth each week to help them understand the difference between contingent and non-contingent reinforcement. All reinforcers that cannot be provided on a daily basis are included as "bonus" reinforcers. That is, the parent decides how many consecutive days the youth will have to accomplish all behaviors in the respective level before the reinforcer is earned (e.g., 30 consecutive days in which all behaviors are performed will result in a compact disc player for the youth).

The youth is seen again individually to verify daily contingent linkages between level one behaviors and level one reinforcers. Bonus reinforcer contingencies are also reviewed. If reservations in accepting the terms are expressed, an attempt is made to negotiate these concerns, though the parent ultimately decides the appropriateness of revised contingencies. The parent is brought into the room, and level-system procedures are explained and subsequently role-played. The youth and parent are instructed to schedule a regular time each night to review the youth's performance in all target behavioral domains and provide reinforcers if the target domains were performed adequately. The youth and parent are told that if all behaviors in the respective level are performed, all reinforcers in the respective level should be provided, and that if just one target behavior is not performed, no reinforcers in that level will be provided. In the event that the youth accomplishes all target behaviors for seven consecutive days, the youth will advance one level. If illicit drugs are indicated, according to urine testing or reports of parents, the youth must drop one level. The youth can arrange to "make up" or correct behaviors when they are not performed, but only with parental approval, and youths cannot "make up" for drug use or being arrested. After the guidelines are explained, the therapist models the role of a parent in reviewing the behaviors with the youth for a hypothetical situation, including the delivery of reinforcers. The parent engages in guided practice of a similar review with the youth, while the therapist provides feedback, and the procedure concludes with the youth and parent endorsing the contract.

In future sessions, the youth and parent are asked to review pleasant aspects pertaining to the completion of outstanding target behaviors that occurred. The therapist should attempt to determine if the parent monitored targeted behaviors, and if reinforcers were provided as previously agreed. Therapists also should determine that no reinforcers were delivered non-contingently. It should be mentioned that the level system provides a great opportunity to descriptively praise desired behaviors, and that some youth will remain on level one for several weeks before a "breakthrough" is made.

Stimulus control. The stimulus control procedure involves three phases. In the first phase the parent and youth are provided the following rationale:

> In a moment I'm going to ask (insert youth's name) to list people, places and activities that he likes to spend time with the most. Each week (insert

youth's name) and I will review these situations so that I can help him avoid drug use and trouble. Everything we talk about during this time will be between (insert youth's name) and me. Later, when (insert youth's name) thinks that it's OK, I'll invite you to talk with us about things that you can do to make it easier for (insert youth's name) to stay clean and out of trouble. However, we won't talk about situations that may have involved drug use or troublesome behavior during this time together. Later, when (insert youth's name) thinks it's OK, we will invite you, (insert parents' names), to talk with us about situations that may have involved drug use or trouble. Other families have found that by talking about drug use and trouble situations with adolescents only, they can be more up-front about these situations, which helps them ultimately accomplish their goals more effectively. I want to remind you both that confidentiality will be necessary. If neither of you has any questions we can get started.

The youth then is seen individually to obtain a list of persons, places, and situations/ activities that have never been associated with drug use or conduct disturbance. The youth is prompted to list all enjoyable persons with whom s/he has never used drugs, or engaged in activity that has led to trouble, and all enjoyable situations/activities that have not involved trouble or drug use. A list of persons, places, and situations/activities associated with problem behaviors is obtained in a similar manner. Prompts may be used to generate "risky" stimuli (e.g., Do you find yourself getting into trouble, or using drugs during parties or get-togethers? Who is present? What do you do at the parties? Do you get in trouble or use drugs after drinking?). When time allows, the youth is asked to briefly discuss what is liked/disliked about outstanding stimuli. The youth is prompted to discuss strategies relevant to increasing the likelihood of "staying clean" and out of trouble. The youth also plans the next 24 hours with safe activities, and is asked to attempt abstinence during this time.

The youth is told that it is necessary to obtain a similar list of people, places, and situations that have involved drug use or trouble for the youth from the parent, and that the parent must verify that safe stimuli given by youth have not involved trouble or drug use. However, the youth is told that every attempt will be made to keep his list of drug use and troublesome situations confidential. Similarly, the parent is told that in order to be a positive influence on the youth in decreasing drug use, it will be important to keep the youth's reports of interactions with drug use stimuli confidential so that the youth will feel able to disclose this information readily. Of the hundreds of youth who have been served in our program, we have never had a parent petition for these worksheets, although it is the parent's right to do so, first with the therapist, and later in court if the therapist refuses to provide these records because she or he believes it is not in the best interest of the child.

The parent then is seen individually to obtain additional "safe" and "at-risk" stimuli. First, the youth's safe association list is reviewed with the parent to assure that each item is not associated with drug use or trouble. If the youth identifies a stimulus as "safe," and the parent(s) identifies the stimulus as "risk," the stimulus is considered a safe association, but the discrepancy in the reports is recorded. The parent also is asked to disclose people/situations/activities that have, or probably have, involved drug use or trouble for the youth.

The parent the describes methods that s/he will attempt to assist the youth in staying absti-nent from drugs and out of trouble. Finally, the youth and parent are seen together to schedule a pleasant family activity to perform together prior to the next session.

The pleasant aspects of the planned activity are reviewed during the next session. If the youth and parent did not complete the scheduled activity, they discuss what they would have enjoyed most about the activity if they had completed the assignment, and how the scheduled family activity could have been accomplished. Another family activity is planned together, and the youth is seen individually to review stimulus items. Specifically, the youth indicates, on a recording sheet, the stimuli encountered since last contact. For each stimulus, the youth is asked what was done to avoid drug use and trouble. When drug use or trouble is reported, the youth is asked to identify alternatives to, or methods to escape from, the situation. The youth also is asked to review the time that was planned (i.e., 24 hours subsequent to previous session), and activities are scheduled for the next 24 hours with non-drug-using peers. The parent is seen individually to review parental strate-gies relevant to helping the youth spend more time with safe stimuli.

Five or six sessions after the stimulus control procedure is implemented, the family graduates to the second phase. In this phase, the youth and parent review the "safe" items together with the therapist. In the final phase, the parent and youth review both the "safe" and "at-risk" lists together. If the youth indicates any reservations about including the parent in the review of at-risk stimuli, the last phase should not be implemented.

Self-control. The self-control procedure is designed to aid the youth in preventing urges to drink or get into trouble. Youth are provided with the following rationale:

> Earlier you told me that you have done spontaneous things that have resulted in trouble for you, such as using drugs. These activities often start out as casual thoughts or mild feelings. Many adolescents say that this is because they react before they've had a chance to think about how the action will affect themselves or others. Tell me about some things that you've done on the "spur-of-the-moment" and that later led to trouble for you or someone else.... The technique you are about to learn is called Self-Control because you will learn to control impulsive thoughts and feelings that usually lead to trouble. Because you're strong-willed, I think you're going to do particularly well with this technique. Do you have any questions?

The youth then is told that practice sessions will be performed "thinking out loud" so that the therapist may understand the youth's thinking patterns. The youth is taught that recognizing and stopping thoughts associated with drug use or trouble when the thought first occurs will greatly increase the chances of preventing drug use and troublesome behaviors. The youth is instructed to disclose a situation in which drugs were last used, and to identify the first thought to use drugs in that situation. As the following vignette demon-strates, the therapist must sometimes assist the adolescent in determining his or her "first" thought to use drugs.

THERAPIST: Tell me about the last time that you used drugs. I'm especially interested in knowing about the thought that you had before you made plans to use drugs in that situation.

YOUTH: I was in the house and saw a guy smoking from a pipe. I thought a rock would feel good.

THERAPIST: You did a good job of identifying a thought that eventually led to drug use. However, I want you to think hard. I'm sure you had a thought that brought you to the crack house.

YOUTH: I started to think of it while I was driving into the neighborhood, and my stomach was churning.

THERAPIST: Now go back further, before you were driving in the neighborhood.

YOUTH: I was getting paid for mowing a lawn, and I thought I deserved it after working so hard that day.

The therapist then models a self-control trial, and subsequently instructs the youth to rehearse the procedure. The first trial is conducted in response to a drug use situation, and the second trial is conducted in response to a thought to engage in troublesome behavior. Subsequent trials alternate between situations involving drug use and troublesome behavior. The number of trials performed will depend on the youth's extent of drug use and troublesome behavior since last contact. Situations may be generated from desired behaviors that were not performed in the level system. Active drug users and youths who have not performed behaviors targeted in the level-system should be instructed to perform more trials than abstainers who are completing level system target behaviors. Poor performance during trials necessitates additional trials per session.

The first step of the self-control procedure is to catch the thought or image to use drugs or engage in troublesome behavior early in the response chain and consequently terminate this thought or image by firmly stating "stop" while muscles are tensed. In the event that the troublesome behavior was an omission of behavior (e.g., not coming home on time, not informing parent of whereabouts prior to curfew), the youth is instructed to state "stop" when the omission could have been prevented. Background information associated with situation should be stated with enough detail to appreciate the situation ("I'm in front of the mailbox. My friend tells me to give the old man's mailbox a bash with the bat").

The second step is to state at least one negative consequence from drug use or troublesome behavior for self, and at least one negative consequence for friends, loved ones, or others affected by the youth. Negative consequences may be obtained from the annoyance review procedure, and should be stated with affect reflecting sadness, anger, disgust and/or despair. Muscles should remain tense. Consequences may be rotated (or added) as trials progress. Therapists should prompt detail regarding negative consequences.

Stating the last negative consequence should signal the performance of a muscle review to assure that negative feeling states, and tension in muscles, are not present. Major muscles should be reviewed from head to toe. During this review, if a major muscle is relaxed (e.g., shoulders), the youth should describe this state. If a muscle is tense, the youth should use relaxing cue words until the muscle is no longer tense (e.g., "My arms are getting more and more relaxed. I am imagining a band of relaxation around my arms. They feel relaxed, calm, more and more relaxed"). Deep, rhythmic breaths should occur. Body weight should be evenly distributed and positioned in a relaxed state. Statements referring to the relaxed state of the body are acceptable throughout the relaxation period, which should continue until all muscle groups feel relaxed (ideally about five to ten seconds). If no tension or negative feeling states are present, the youth may be instructed only to breathe deeply.

The next step involves stating several behaviors that may be performed instead of drug use and troublesome behavior. These steps may include: (a) stating several alternative actions that do not include drug use or troublesome behaviors; (b) briefly checking to make sure the response is unlikely to bring about drug use or trouble for self or others; or (c) reviewing positive consequences for self and others that may occur because of one's actions. During this exercise, it is important to provide prompts to the youth regarding additional alternative behaviors, how self and others would be positively affected by alternative behaviors, what others would do for youth if alternative behaviors were performed, and how problem behaviors may continue to have negative consequences.

After stating several behaviors that are incompatible with problem behavior, the youth is encouraged to choose one option and describe doing the behavior (e.g., "I think the best thing to do is to tell Bob that I have to go to Jackie's house. I'm telling Bob that I have to go to Jackie's house. As I'm telling him I can see that he is disappointed, so I tell him that we can go to the movies together next Saturday. Bob is telling me that I should go to the movies with Jackie. I'm walking away from Bob, and towards Jackie's house. I walk to her house and I'm now telling her that I would like to take her to the movies, and she is smiling and telling me that she'd love to. She tells me that she's proud of me"). When the youth performs this step, the therapist should provide prompts to elicit detail, including questions as to how the youth will successfully resolve difficult situations that are likely to occur. Sometimes the youth may be instructed to practice getting out of difficult interpersonal situations that may lead to drug use, or trouble (e.g., "Show me how you would tell him that you had to go home. I'll be Bob"). Youths should always be instructed to reward their imagined efforts to engage in drug- and trouble-free alternative behaviors.

The next step is to imagine telling a friend and/or family member about having performed the trouble-free alternative behavior. The recipient should respond in a favorable manner, and positive feelings should be delineated. For example, "I'm telling my mom that I could have gone to the movies with Bob, but instead I went to the movies with my girlfriend because she doesn't use drugs. As I'm telling her this I feel good about myself. My mom looks at me and says that I'm doing a great job, and that she's proud of me. She also tells me that she's been thinking about extending my curfew because of my efforts to stay clean."

The trial concludes by describing several pleasant outcomes and positive character attributes (e.g., "I'm really proud of myself for telling Bob that I had to go out with my girlfriend. I'm going to have a great time with her, and improve our relationship. I liked how I told Bob straight up and didn't beat around the bush. That says a lot about the kind of person I am. I can be direct with people but still not hurt their feelings. If I can keep on doing these kinds of things I'm going to be more motivated to get a part-time job, and get back into school, and my parents said that if I stay clear of drugs, and people who get into trouble, they will give me $400 to help me buy a moped").

When youths practice the self-control procedure for the first time, it may be necessary to state the situation and prompt the youth to subsequently state "stop" (e.g., "You're in the park. Bob comes up to you and asks if you want to smoke reefer. Go ahead and yell, stop"). Similarly, it may be necessary to prompt the youth to perform each component initially, and later fade this assistance.

After the youth completes each trial, the therapist asks the youth to provide his/her rating of desire to engage in problem behavior prior to performing the trial, and after the trial is performed (i.e., pre- and post-trial urge level; 0 = no desire, 100 = complete desire). The youth is prompted to critique her/his performance, and the therapist subsequently praises the youth for making statements during the trial that reflected protocol adherence, including suggestions or prompts to youth regarding improvement of future sessions.

Situations to utilize for drug use trials should be prioritized in the following manner: (1) most recent hard drug use during past month, according to self-reports of youth and parent, and/or urine drug screens; (2) most recent marijuana use during past month, according to self-reports of youth and parent, and/or urine drug screens; and (3) time spent in at-risk situations that are particularly likely to influence drug use. Situations to utilize for troublesome behavior trials may be obtained as follows. In the session review of the level system, ask the parent to disclose a target behavior in the level system that was not performed since the last therapy contact, and that was most desired by the parent. In the event that multiple behaviors were not performed, the behaviors should be ranked according to desirability (no more than three trials regarding troublesome behavior and three trials of drug use, per session). If all level-system target behaviors were performed since the last therapy contact, instruct the youth to perform only one trial in response to time spent in the most recent "at-risk" situation listed in the stimulus control procedure.

Empirical Studies

Several controlled treatment outcome studies, funded by the National Institute of Drug Abuse, have demonstrated efficacy of the program. The first study (n = 82; Azrin, McMahon, Donohue, *et al.*, 1994) included a subsample of adolescents. Subjects identified to be using illicit drugs during the time of admission to an outpatient clinic for drug abuse were randomly assigned to the behavioral program described above or to supportive counseling. Study results indicated that subjects receiving the behavioral intervention demonstrated less alcohol and drug use throughout the year following the initiation of treatment than subjects who received supportive counseling. Subjects in the behavioral condition also were significantly less depressed, demonstrated greater satisfaction in their relationships with significant others (e.g., parents), spent less time in institutions, and attended more days at school. Follow-up results indicated that the treatment effects were maintained for up to nine months after the conclusion of intervention (Azrin, Acierno, Kogan, *et al.* 1996). Another outcome study, focusing exclusively on adolescents (n = 26; Azrin, Donohue, Besalel, Kogan & Acierno, 1994), indicated that 73 percent of subjects who received the behavioral intervention evidenced abstinence from illicit drugs at the conclusion of treatment, as compared to 9 percent of subjects who received supportive counseling. Subjects who received the behavioral intervention also demonstrated significantly less depression, behavioral problems, days using alcohol, and attended school more often throughout the six months of the study compared to subjects who received supportive counseling. Parents of subjects who received the behavioral intervention also were more satisfied with their youth than were parents of subjects who received the supportive intervention. Similar improvements have been found in a recent outcome study funded by the National Institute of Mental Health with dually diagnosed youth (Azrin *et al.*, in press).

Prescriptive/Matching Issues

The program was developed to accommodate diversity issues, such as poly-substance abuse and dependence, various behavior problems, and preferences in therapy due to cultural and other factors. Indeed, the program is relatively comprehensive, and, although standardized, is flexible in response to individual patients' needs and desires. For instance, the self-control procedure includes components that may be used to decrease physiologically based urges to use addictive drugs or impulses to engage in unacceptable behaviors (e.g., vandalism, truancy). However, this procedure also includes components that address social influences, which have greater potential to bring about long-term changes associated with a drug-free lifestyle. Thus, a youth who uses marijuana only during "get-togethers" and parties may choose to emphasize the social components of the self-control procedure, whereas a youth who is abusing crack cocaine may wish to emphasize the initial steps of the self-control procedure, which include urge-control strategies. Similarly, communication procedures might be emphasized for youths who do not wish to spend much time at home due to poor relationships with their family, whereas families who evidence no major problems in their communication with family may wish only to briefly examine these procedures. However, each therapy should be implemented at least a few times, as family members may deny, or be unaware of, problems that need to be addressed in therapy. For example, a parent may claim that contingency management strategies are of little importance prior to its implementation, but later change her/his mind after the therapist helps the parent to become aware of her/his history of failing to comply with established contingencies in the behavioral contract.

Anecdotally, we have found the presence of even the most delinquent of peers improves program compliance of our patients because these peers are almost always on their very best behavior to impress the parents of the identified youth so that the parents will be more inclined to allow the identified youth to spend time with the peer. It is also probable that peers are motivated to impress the therapist with compliance, so the therapist will comment to the parents that the peer is a good influence. Therefore, we recommend that family members and friends of the youth be involved in therapy, but not until all therapies are implemented at least once with the parent(s) and youth. When significant others of the patient are included, we have found the following strategies to be useful: (a) limiting the number of non-adult significant others to one; (b) having patients explain all program rationales and procedures; (c) having patients demonstrate how to perform all program techniques; (d) encouraging significant others to actively participate in the therapies (e.g., role plays, supportive comments); and (d) providing token snacks (candy, cakes) and beverages (sodas, coffee) to visiting significant others to make their visit more enjoyable.

Summary and Future Directions

Our studies provide support for the effectiveness of our program for treating problem behaviors among substance-abusing and conduct-disordered youth. The program includes multiple interventions, with an emphasis on various interventions mutually determined by the youth and her/his parent(s). For several years, we have refined the treatment program in controlled outcome studies. However, the program needs to be evaluated against other therapies with demonstrated success for treating this population. We have recently completed an empirical comparison of the aforementioned program to a standardized problem-solving intervention in a sample of adolescents who have been diagnosed with Conduct Disorder and Substance Dependence (National Institute of Mental Health, 5R01MH53455). Examination of study data indicates significant improvements consequent to both intervention programs across measures of drug use frequency and behavior (Azrin *et al.*, in press). In the future, we plan to compare the program with, and without, contingency management strategies. Indeed, anecdotal information derived from patient and therapist reports suggests that youth who evidence serious behavior problems and high rates of drug use are less responsive to contingency contracting procedures than their younger and less severe peers. Lastly, we are interested in discovering if treatment outcome is enhanced by having patients determine the degree of emphasis placed on each intervention, including the order in which these interventions are implemented during therapy.

References

Achenbach, T. M. (1991a), *Manual for the Youth Self Report and 1991 Profile*. Burlington, VT: University of Vermont Department of Psychiatry.

Achenbach, T. M. (1991b), *Manual for the Child Behavior Checklist/4–18 and 1991 Profile*. Burlington, VT: University of Vermont Department of Psychiatry.

Azrin, N. H. (1976), "Improvement in the community-reinforcement approach to alcoholism." *Behaviour Research & Therapy 14*, 339–348.

Azrin, N. H. *et al.* (1996), "Follow-up results of Supportive versus Behavioral Therapy for illicit drug use." *Behaviour Research & Therapy*, 41–46.

Azrin, N. H., Donohue, B., Besalel, V. A., Kogan, E. S., Acierno, R. (1994), "Youth drug abuse treatment: A controlled outcome study." *Journal of Child & Adolescent Substance Abuse 3*, 1–15.

Azrin, N. H., Donohue, B., Teichner, G., Crum, T., Howell, J., & DeCato, L. (in press). A Controlled evaluation and description of Individual Cognitive Problem-Solving and Family Behavioral Therapies in Conduct-Disordered and Substance dependent youth. *Journal of Child and Adolescent Substance Abuse*.

Azrin, N. H. *et al.* (1994), "Behavior therapy for drug abuse: A controlled treatment outcome study." *Behaviour Research & Therapy 8*, 857–866.

Azrin, N. H., Sisson, R. W., Meyers, R., & Godley, M. (1982), "Outpatient alcoholism treatment by disulfiram and community reinforcement therapy." *Journal of Behavior Therapy and Experiential Psychiatry 13*, 105–112.

Besalel, V. A., & Azrin, N. H. (1981), "The reduction of parent–youth problems by reciprocity counseling." *Behaviour Research & Therapy 19*, 297–301.

DeCato, L., Donohue, B., Azrin, N. H., & Teichner, G. (2001), "Satisfaction of conduct-disordered and substance abusing youth with their parents." *Behavior Modification 25*, 44–61.

Donohue, B. *et al.* (1998), "Improving initial attendance in substance abusing and conduct disordered adolescents." *Journal of Child and Adolescent Substance Abuse 8*, 1–15.

Donohue, B., Decato, L., Azrin, N. H., & Teichner, G. (2001), "Satisfaction of parents with their substance abusing and conduct-disordered youth." *Behavior Modification 25*, 21–43.

D'Zurrilla, T. J., & Nezu, A. M. (1990), "Development and preliminary evaluation of the Social Problem-Solving Inventory (SPSI)." *Psychological Assessment: A Journal of Consulting and Clinical Psychology 2*, 156–163.

Miller, W. R., & Brown, S. A. (1999), "Why psychologists should treat alcohol and drug problems." *American Psychologist 12*, 1269–1279.

Eyberg, S., & Ross, A. W. (1978), "Assessment of child behavior problems: The validation of a new inventory." *Journal of Clinical Child Psychology 7*, 113–116.

Hodges, K., Kline, J., Stern, L., Cytryn, L., & McKnew, D. (1982), "The development of a child assessment schedule for research and clinical use." *Journal of Abnormal Child Psychiatry 10*, 173–189.

Hunt, G. M., & Azrin, N. H. (1973), "A community reinforcement approach to alcoholism." *Behaviour Research & Therapy 11*, 91–104.

Sobell, M. B., Sobell, L. C., Klajner, F., Pavan, D., & Basian, E. (1986), "The reliability of the timeline method of assessing normal drinker college students' recent drinking history: Utility for alcohol research." *Addictive Behaviors 11*, 149–162.

Spitzer, R. L., Williams, J. B., Gibbon, M., & First, M. B. (1992), "The structured clinical interview for the DSM-III-R (SCID): I. History, rationale, and description." *Archives of General Psychiatry 49*, 624–629.

Appendix A: Potential Privileges and Benefits

Money	(1) $____ per day, (2) $____ per day, (3) $____ per day.
Transportation	(1) ___ mile ride per day, (2) ___ mile ride per day, (3) ___ mile ride per day. **or** (1) use of car for __ hours per day (approved place, alone), (2) use of car for __ hours per day (approved place w/ _____), (3) use of car for __ hours per day with _____.
Lunch	(1) caregiver packs lunch, (2) caregiver provides paid school lunch, (3) paid school lunch, and ____.
Dessert/meal	(1) choice of _____, (2) choice of _____, (3) trip to ____restaurant.
Laundry	(1) caregiver helps with wash, (2) caregiver helps with wash & dry, (3) caregiver helps with wash, dry, and ironing _____.
Phone use	(1) use own phone for local calls from ___ to ___. (2) use own phone from __ to ___. (3) unlimited local use of own phones, ____mins of long distance.
Sport/fitness/club membership	(1) $___ membership to _____, (2) $___ membership to ____, (3) $___ membership to ___.
Invite friend(s) for sleepover	(1) invite ____, (2) invite ____ and ____ incentives, (3) invite ___ and ___ incentives.
Non-drug/alc. party/get-together	(1) party with ____ persons, (2) party with _____ persons and ____ incentives, (3) party with ___ persons and ___ incentives.
Trips w/ family and/or friends	(1) family trip to ____, with ____, (2) family trip to _____, with ____, (3) trip to ____, with ____ .
Buy a pet	(1) buy ___ pet, (2) pay for ____ pet supplies per week, (3) pay for ____pet supplies per week.
Privacy time	(1) ___mins privacy time in home by self, (2) ___mins privacy time in home with ___ person, (3) ____mins home with ____ person(s).
Letter to probation officer	(1) slightly improved letter, (2) moderately improved, (3) greatly improved letter.

Appendix B: Target Behavioral Domains

Criminal behavior	(1) no police contacts, (2) no police contacts and school suspensions/detentions, (3) no police contacts, school suspensions/detentions, and neg. school reports.
Drug use	(1) no evidence of hard drug use, (2) no evidence of hard drug use and pot, (3) no evidence of drugs and alcohol.
Conduct in therapy	(1) attended scheduled session, (2) on time for scheduled session, (3) cooperated during session.
School attendance	(1) effort to enroll in school, (2) verification of ____% school attendance, (3) verification of ____% school attendance.
Curfew	(1) curfew till _____, (2) curfew till _____, (3) curfew till _____.
Caregiver informed about whereabouts	(1) tell caregiver where going, (2) tell caregiver where going and 1 call during, (3) ask caregiver permission and give 1 call during.
Calm resolution of disagreements	(1) day without intentionally damaging property, (2) day without raising voice at of caregiver, (3) day without raising voice at caregiver & compromise in disagreements.
Compliance with chores	(1) compliance with _____ chores, (2) compliance with _____chores, (3) compliance with _____chores.
Academic progress	(1) read ___ pages of any literature, (2) show caregiver any test, quiz, or school assignment or discuss day at school for ___ mins (3) do ____ mins of school homework, or show caregiver any test, quiz, or school assignment at least ___ letter grades above current GPA in ____ subject(s).
Pleasant conversation	(1) say hi or how are you?, etc. to caregiver, (2) talk to caregiver for __ mins in calm tone of voice about anything, (3) talk to caregiver for __ mins about anything in calm voice.
Friends	(1) talk about positive aspects of 1 or more friends for up to __ mins if caregiver wants to, (2) talk about things that were done with friends for __ mins if caregiver wants to, (3) discuss a problem regarding friends with the caregiver, if caregiver wants to.
Reviewing day	(1) tell caregiver that day was good/bad, (2) tell caregiver one or two highlights of day, (3) ___ mins reviewing day w/ caregiver.

Appendix C: Example of level system recording form

LEVEL 1

Target goals (check if goal achieved for day)	Mon	Tues.	Wed	Thurs	Fri	Sat	Sun
No police contacts							
No evidence of hard drug use							
Attendance at scheduled therapy session							
Verification of school attendance from principal's office							
Mom informed of whereabouts throughout day and night							
Tell caregiver where going at night							
Day without hitting family, and swearing and raising voice at father							
Come home by 11:30 p.m.							
Mow lawn by Fri., do dishes Thurs., clean room by Sat.							
Talk with either parent about "college life-style"							
Say "hi" or "how are you" to father							
Talk about hobbies and good qualities of Joey's friends for 1 min.							
Check if all the preceding behavioral goals above were achieved.							
Check if the following rewards were made available, if all goals achieved?: $1.00 per day, 5 mile ride, paid school lunch, ice cream after dinner, dad does wash (laundry) by Sun., use phone for local calls, use t.v., invite Bob over for dinner, trip to Keys for fishing trip with dad and Bob during weekend, 1 hour privacy time/day, improved letter to probation officer.							

Chapter 11

Multidimensional Family Therapy for Adolescent Substance Abuse

Howard A. Liddle and Aaron Hogue[1]

Introduction

The ultimate goal of psychotherapy research is specification of intervention models and therapeutic strategies with documented effectiveness in treating a given disorder within a given population. A primary step in pursuing this goal is establishment of treatment efficacy. Treatment efficacy refers to intervention strength in producing an expected positive effect under optimal conditions of participant sampling, treatment setting, and treatment implementation (Hoagwood, Hibbs, Brent & Jensen, 1995; Seligman, 1996). Establishing efficacy is not a simple matter. Recent efforts to establish concrete criteria for judging whether a treatment has been proven efficacious (Chambless, 1996; Chambless & Hollon, 1998; Crits-Christoph, 1996; Task Force on Promotion and Dissemination of Psychological Procedures, 1995) have emphasized the following minimally necessary features: (a) existence of an intervention manual that specifies the hypothesized components of change within the treatment and presents guidelines for therapist training and model implementation; (b) testing of the treatment with well-defined samples from populations for whom the treatment was designed; (c) evaluation of treatment processes and outcomes using assessment instruments with established psychometric quality and clinical utility; and (d) controlled research involving comparison of the treatment with appropriate control groups in randomized clinical trials. While not without its critics (e.g., Garfield, 1996), the movement toward codifying criteria for treatment efficacy is noteworthy at the least for galvanizing intervention researchers to scrutinize their methods, identify gaps in basic scientific knowledge as well as applied efficacy concerns, and consider issues related to transporting and disseminating efficacious models to standard clinical settings (Borkovec & Castonguay, 1998; Chambless & Hollon, 1998).

[1]Preparation of this chapter was supported by grants from the National Institute on Drug Abuse (P50-DA07697, P50-DA11328, R01-DA09424, R03-DA12452). Correspondence concerning this chapter should be addressed to Howard A. Liddle, Professor and Director, Center for Treatment Research on Adolescent Drug Abuse, Department of Epidemiology and Public Health, University of Miami School of Medicine, 1400 NW 10th Ave, Dominion Tower Suite 1108, Miami, FL, 33136. Electronic mail may be sent to hliddle@med.miami.edu.

Innovations in Adolescent Substance Abuse Interventions, pages 229–261.

Over the past two decades, the field of child and adolescent psychotherapy has made great strides in testing the efficacy of empirically based treatments for a diverse range of childhood disorders (Durlak, Wells, Cotten & Johnson, 1995; Kazdin, 1991; Weiss, Weisz, Han, Granger & Morton, 1995). The consensus drawn from several meta-analytic reviews of controlled research is that, overall, child and adolescent psychotherapy produces substantial positive effects (Casey & Berman, 1985; Kazdin, Bass, Ayers & Rodgers, 1990; Weiss, Weisz, Alicke & Klotz, 1987; Weiss et al., 1995). Moreover, Kazdin and Weiss (1998) identify several specific intervention approaches with impressive research portfolios that might be judged as meeting criteria for efficacious therapies. These include cognitive-behavioral therapy for child anxiety, parent management training for oppositional and aggressive behavior, and systemic family therapy for adolescent antisocial behavior.

There is no doubt that controlled efficacy studies have greatly advanced the empirical knowledge base on child and adolescent psychotherapy. However, Kazdin (1994) reminds us that investigating treatment efficacy is but one stage of the multistage process needed to reach the ultimate goal of specifying effective treatments. Kazdin cogently argues that, because research on child and adolescent psychotherapy is still at a relatively early stage, there is much to be gained from adopting a systematic approach to developing and validating effective interventions. That is, the progression of empirical knowledge in the field might be maximally enhanced by adherence to a plan of treatment development. This plan would map out the steps needed for building and testing efficacious treatments according to prevailing scientific standards. In the addictions field, these standards have been articulated in work that has been called the technology model of treatment research (Carroll, Rounsaville, & Keller, 1991; Carroll et al., 2000). Planful treatment development has the compelling virtues of (a) offering a common metric for assessing progress in developing effective interventions of various kinds for various disorders and (b) guiding intervention researchers toward efficient, incremental, prioritized additions to the existing knowledge base.

The steps of treatment development proposed by Kazdin (1994) are reproduced in Table 1. Two aspects of this plan warrant emphasis. First, theory development, which includes conceptualization of the dysfunction being treated and the model being tested, plays a leading role. Productive theory development can contribute at both ends of the treatment development process: it promotes construction of clinically practical and targeted interventions, and it provides the basis for interpreting treatment research findings and utilizing those findings to craft successive improvements in the model being evaluated (Liddle, 1999). Theory development therefore requires attention to the original conceptual structure that supports a given model and to the evolution of that structure over the course of repeated model implementation and testing. Second, treatment efficacy research is integrated into a larger framework of psychotherapy research that also includes investigation of core mechanisms of change and treatment effectiveness across diverse populations and contexts. Efficacy research is but one stage of the treatment development process, and each stage is crucial for informing work in other stages and advancing the enterprise as a whole.

This chapter presents the treatment development history of an outpatient family-based intervention for adolescent drug use and behavior problems, multidimensional family

Table 1: Steps in Developing Effective Treatments.

---

1. **Conceptualization of the Dysfunction**
   Conceptualization of key areas that relate to the development, onset, and escalation of dysfunction, proposal of key processes that are antecedents to some facet of conduct disorder and the mechanisms by which these processes emerge or operate.

2. **Research on Processes Related to Dysfunction**
   Research that examines the relation of processes proposed to be critical to the dysfunction (conduct disorder) to test the model.

3. **Conceptualization of Treatment**
   Conceptualization of the treatment focus, how specific procedures relate to other processes implicated in the dysfunction and to desired treatment outcomes.

4. **Specification of Treatment**
   Concrete operationalization of the treatment, preferably in manual form, so that the integrity of treatment can be evaluated, the material learned from treatment trials can be codified, and the treatment procedures can be replicated.

5. **Tests of Treatment Process**
   Studies to identify whether the intervention techniques, methods, and procedures within treatment actually affect those processes that are critical to the model.

6. **Tests of Treatment Outcome**
   Treatment studies to evaluate the impact of treatment. A wide range of treatment tests (e.g., open [uncontrolled] studies, single-case designs, full-fledged clinical trials) can provide evidence that change is produced. Several types of studies (e.g., dismantling, parametric, and comparative outcome) are relevant.

7. **Tests of the Boundary Conditions and Moderators**
   Examination of the child, parent, family, and contextual factors with which treatment interacts. The boundary conditions or limits of application are identified through interactions of treatment X diverse attributes within empirical tests.

---

therapy (MDFT). Reviews of intervention research programs can illuminate progress in meeting the generic challenges in the complex world of intervention science (Forehand, 1990; O'Leary, in press). MDFT is an ecological, developmentally based psychotherapy that focuses on changing individual behavior, within-family interactions as well as interactions between the family members and relevant social systems (Liddle, 1991). Interventions target the interconnected contexts of adolescent development, and within these contexts, the circumstances and processes known to create and/or continue dysfunction (Bronfenbrenner, 1979; Hawkins, Catalano & Miller, 1992; Jessor, 1993). MDFT incorporates multiple social systems into the therapeutic work (individual family members, various family subgroups, and influential extrafamilial persons and systems) and operates within multiple domains of adolescent and family functioning (affective, behavioral, cognitive, and interpersonal). The approach strives for a consistent and obvious connection among its organizational levels — theory, principles of intervention, intervention strategies and methods, and clinical assessment of family progress. MDFT

has been recognized as one of a new generation of comprehensive, multicomponent, theo-
retically derived and empirically supported treatments for adolescent drug abuse (Center
for Substance Abuse Treatment, 1998; Kazdin, 1999; Lebow & Gurman, 1995; National
Institute on Drug Abuse, 1999; Nichols & Schwartz, 1998; Selekman & Todd, 1991;
Stanton & Shadish, 1997; Waldron, 1997; Weinberg, Rahdert, Colliver & Glantz, 1998;
Winters, Latimer & Stinchfield, 1999).

The present chapter describes how MDFT has been articulated, tested, and refined in
accordance with standards of intervention science and in pursuit of empirical support as an
efficacious treatment for adolescent substance abuse and related behavior problems. In our
view, Kazdin's (1994) plan for treatment development is a constructive framework for organizing the discussion of our ongoing treatment validation efforts. The chapter is therefore
sectioned to correspond with the seven steps outlined by Kazdin's blueprint. Just as importantly, Kazdin's plan is an excellent mission statement for judging the extensiveness and
coherence of our progress to date and charting new work to enhance our interventions
effectiveness.

Steps 1 and 2: Conceptualization of the Dysfunction and Research on Processes Related to Dysfunction

Ideally, presumptions about how dysfunction develops, maintains, and exacerbates are
fundamental to every intervention and to the overall model in which interventions
reside. Theory about the nature of the dysfunction being treated should guide assessment, intervention decision-making and execution, orient therapist training in the
model, and be used to gauge the treatment's results. Furthermore, treatment models
should specify the processes or mechanisms by which therapy techniques are expected
to impact the targets of the intervention. This includes statements about how interventions influence the relevant domains of functioning considered central to the
development of dysfunction.

Theory of Dysfunction

Epidemiological, clinical and basic research studies indicate that adolescent drug use is a
multidimensional problem (Brook, Whiteman, Nomura, Gordon & Cohen, 1988;
Bukstein, 1995). Both experimental substance use by adolescents not yet committed to
continued use (see Petraitis, Flay & Miller, 1995) and the diagnosable disorders, adolescent substance abuse and substance dependence (see Weinberg *et al.*, 1998), result from a
confluence of etiological factors. Contemporary studies on the correlates of drug use and
abuse typically encompass several domains of functioning: individual, family, peer,
school, neighborhood/community and societal (Hawkins, Arthur & Catalano, 1995;
Hawkins *et al.*, 1992). Molar level, distal factors such as extreme economic deprivation
and neighborhood influences can have a role in problem development. Proximal factors
such as family conflict and disruptions in family management (Dishion, Capaldi,
Spracklen & Li, 1995; Jessor, 1993) can also contribute to poor developmental outcomes.

Individual factors pertaining to parents and adolescents, such as parental psychopathology and substance use, adolescent's lack of bonding to and success in school, adolescent problems in emotion regulation, and poor interpersonal skill and peer relations are all additional factors predisposing drug use (Brook *et al.*, 1988; Gottfredson & Koper, 1996; Jessor, Van Den Bos, Vanderryn, Costa & Turbin, 1995; Kandel & Andrews, 1987; Newcomb & Felix-Ortiz, 1992; O'Donnell, Hawkins & Abbott, 1995; Pickens & Svikis, 1991). In addition, substance abuse portends a myriad of negative life events for the individual adolescent, including physical health risks (Achterberg & Shannon, 1993; Anderson, 1991), retarded emotional development and problem-solving experiences (Baumrind & Moselle, 1985; Coombs, Paulson & Palley, 1988), impaired interpersonal relationships (Newcomb & Bentler, 1988), school failure (Steinberg, Elmen & Mounts, 1989), and poor investment in prosocial activities (Shilts, 1991; Steinberg, 1991). In short, there are multiple pathways to, and multiple consequences of, adolescent substance use.

Our own conceptualization of adolescent substance use is grounded in three theoretical frameworks that serve as reference points for incorporating the extensive knowledge base on teen drug use into a concrete, feasible treatment plan for each family. The first framework is *risk and protection theory*. According to risk and protection theory, psychological dysfunction is determined by the interaction between risk factors, which predispose an individual to the development of disorder, and protective factors, which predispose positive outcomes and buffer individuals against disorder (Jessor *et al.*, 1995). Complex behavioral problems such as drug use and conduct disorder do not stem from a single causal variable or a fixed set of specifiable precursors; instead, there are several pathways to developing these disorders, and various contributing risk and protective influences can be identified in the psychological, biological, and environmental realms (Bukoski, 1991). Also, risk factors are thought to have a multiplicative effect, such that overall risk increases exponentially with the addition of each new risk factor. That is, risk factors tend to exacerbate one another in synergistic fashion (Newcomb, Maddahian & Bentler, 1986; Rutter, 1987). Protective factors are thought to exert both a direct, positive influence on behavior and a moderating influence on the relation between risk factors and behavior (Jessor *et al.*, 1995).

Profiles of risk and protective factors are used to identify individuals considered to be at risk for behavioral problems, so that appropriate intervention steps can be taken. In the case of MDFT, we pay special attention to risk and protective factors in the family arena. The list of family factors that create vulnerabilities for adolescent drug abuse is too great to catalogue here, but among the most empirically supported are: deficiencies in parental monitoring and discipline practices (Baumrind, 1991; Steinberg, Fletcher & Darling, 1994); high rates of conflict and low rates of communication and involvement between parents and children (Baumrind, 1991; Newcomb & Felix-Ortiz, 1992); lack of parental investment in and attachment to their children (Brook, Nomura & Cohen, 1989); and parental attitudes about and history of drug use (Hawkins *et al.*, 1992). The quality of the child's relationship with his or her parents is a particularly critical factor. Youths who do not use drugs report that their parents provide more praise and encouragement, are perceived as more trusting and helpful, and set clear and consistent limits; in comparison, adolescent drug users describe their parents as having unclear or inconsistent rules, responding only to negative behaviors, and unavailable to discuss important problems (Baumrind, 1991; Block, Block & Keyes, 1988; Coombs & Paulson, 1988; Dembo,

Farrow, Des Jarlais, Burgos & Schmeidler, 1981). Emotional support from the family and the perceived quality of the affective relationship with parents are also strong predictors of general adolescent well-being that insulate youths from negative environmental influences (Resnick *et al.*, 1997; Wills, 1990).

The second framework is *developmental psychopathology*. The goal of developmental psychopathology is to examine the course of individual adaptation and dysfunction through the lens of normative development, so that truly maladaptive behavior patterns can be distinguished from expectable variations within the normative range (Sroufe & Rutter, 1984). Developmental psychopathology is concerned not so much with specific symptoms in a given youth as with (a) the youth's ability to cope with the developmental tasks at hand and (b) the implications of stressful experiences in one developmental period for (mal)adaptation in future periods. Because multiple pathways of adjustment and deviation may unfold from any given point, emphasis is placed equally on understanding competence and resilience in the face of great risk (Garmezy, Masten & Tellegen, 1984). For adolescents, developmental issues that bear upon the initiation and course of drug abuse include self-regulation and exploratory behavior (Hill & Holmbeck, 1986), increased autonomy seeking and emotional perturbations within the family (Steinberg, 1990), and increased peer group involvement (Brown, 1990). Adolescent substance abuse can be conceptualized as a problem of development — a deviation from the normal developmental pathway, or a failure in negotiating and successfully meeting developmental challenges.

The third framework is *ecological theory*. Ecological theory is concerned with understanding the intersecting web of social influences that form the context of human development (Bronfenbrenner, 1986a; Brook *et al.*, 1989). Ecological theory regards the family as the principal context in which human development takes place, and it takes a keen interest in how intrafamilial processes are affected by extrafamilial systems (Bronfenbrenner, 1986b). This theory coincides with contemporary ideas about reciprocal effects in human relationships (Lerner & Spanier, 1978; Sameroff, 1975) and underscores how problems are nested at different levels and how circumstances in one domain can impact other domains. For example, an adolescent's low commitment to school, learning problems, and academic failure might interact with normal developmental issues at home (e.g., exacerbate tensions about autonomy striving) and thereby precipitate risk-taking behavior such as drug use. Or, a parent's poor family management skills may be related to deteriorated functioning in related domains such as periodic depression, a weak social support network, or family disruption created by unemployment. Family management deficiencies also may relate to intrapersonal cognitive processes (e.g., memories and perceptions about past frustrations in parenting). Family management difficulties and inconsistent parental monitoring can provoke increased frustration and inability to address the normal challenges of parenting teenagers. In interaction, these circumstances may create motivation and opportunity for a drug-involved or delinquent adolescent to affiliate with like-problem peers.

Targets for Developmental–Ecological Intervention

Because of the many factors involved in the initiation and continuation of adolescent drug use and abuse, and the number of functional impairments that exist with drug-abusing adolescents, we conclude, as have others, that broad-based, comprehensive treatment strategies are necessary (Hawkins *et al.*, 1992; Newcomb, 1992). Such strategies target the youth's functioning and relationships across multiple ecological niches. The primary treatment goal is to alter the developmental trajectory of the adolescent and his or her social context in a way that establishes healthy and prosocial socialization. That is to say, if adolescent drug abuse is a manifestation of a particular lifestyle (Newcomb & Bentler, 1989), then it is the lifestyle, in its many manifestations, that needs to change. Therefore, our developmental–ecological treatment model intervenes simultaneously in the multiple social systems that are developmentally salient for the adolescent. This is consistent with recommendations in the field about the needed focus in clinical work with multi-problem teenagers and families (Tolan, Guerra & Kendall, 1995). This commitment results in social spheres outside the individual and family being the subject of assessment and intervention. These social systems include assessment and consideration of the neighborhood in which a family resides, the adolescent's school, the adolescent's peer network, and, for some teenagers, the juvenile justice system. Note that developmental–ecological models do not require practitioners to change schools or neighborhoods *per se*. Instead, interventions attempt to influence how family members relate to (i.e., think about and interact with) these systems (Liddle, 1995).

How do interventions select which risk and protective factors to target? This work involves a complex decision-making process. Generally, however, we act and make decisions on the basis of a principle of greatest jeopardy. That is, we assess which aspects of the case and which areas of functioning are presenting the most harm or potential jeopardy to the lives of the adolescent and family. In cases where there are significant legal problems, and these pose the possibility of the teen being removed from the home, we would act to buy time with the legal/juvenile justice system so that the teen's functioning can be stabilized. In situations with parental dysfunction (e.g., parental psychopathology, parental substance abuse), we address these clinical issues directly and immediately. Family functioning and the parent–teenager relationship are not likely to improve until these aspects of functioning are addressed or at least stabilized.

Thinking in terms of risk and protective factors means understanding how personal characteristics or processes are manifest within and across several interlocking social systems. Our treatment development work aims to establish practiced guidelines by which basic and applied developmental research can enhance our clinical model (e.g., Liddle, Rowe, Dakof & Lyke, 1998; Liddle *et al.*, 2000). MDFT therapists are trained to recognize and take therapeutic action upon risk factors known to be associated with the progression of drug use and antisocial behavior. These actions might be a direct blocking of the continued manifestation of the risk factor, the minimization of the risk factor's influence or impact, or the indirect mitigation of the risk factor's impact by focusing on change in another sphere (e.g., minimizing other, related risk factors or promoting buffering or protective factors). Therapists are practical about not trying to change risk factors that are not malleable. Additionally, because each family with a drug-using adolescent has traveled a unique path to the expression of dysfunction, therapists are also sensitive to the idiosyncratic pitfalls and derailments experienced by their clients. This directive encourages therapists to think in terms of helping adolescents and families get back on an adaptive developmental track, rather than in terms of curing a disorder. Thus, a therapist's challenge is not to simply memorize the list of risk and protective factors and to seize opportunities to discuss them, but rather to assess and intervene into multiple systemic and inter-institutional processes, by means of contextualizing the risk and protection profile of a given adolescent and family.

Step 3: Conceptualization of Treatment

MDFT Core Operating Principles

Treatment development is grounded in the clear articulation, and ongoing re-assessment and re-articulation, of the core operating principles of the psychotherapy model. Core operating principles are defined as conceptually grounded rules of therapeutic practice that guide clinical orientation, decision-making and intervention. Integrative, multicomponent treatments such as MDFT face a formidable challenge in delineating their operating principles. A broadened treatment scope makes for more complex treatments and effectively makes impossible invariant, formulaic implementation protocols (Addis, 1997). Additionally, more complex treatments may be more difficult to teach and to deliver, and so transportability may be compromised (Liddle, 1982). At the same time we know this work, although difficult, is possible. There are now several examples of empirically based, family-oriented treatments with carefully articulated operating principles (Fruzetti & Linehan, in press; Henggeler *et al.*, 1998; Miklowitz & Goldstein, 1998).

There are ten core operating principles of MDFT:

1. Adolescent drug abuse is a multidimensional phenomenon, and its conceptualization and treatment are guided by an ecological and developmental perspective. Developmental knowledge informs interventions; presenting problems are defined multidimensionally. This includes intrapersonal, interpersonal, and contextual perspectives, as well as a dynamic perspective that includes an appreciation of the interaction of multiple systems and levels of influence.

2. Current symptoms of the adolescent or other family members, as well as crises and complaints pertaining to the adolescent, not only provide critical assessment information but important intervention opportunities as well.

3. Change is a multifaceted phenomenon. It emerges out of the synergistic effects of interaction among different systems and levels of systems, different people, domains of functioning, time periods, and intrapersonal and interpersonal processes. Assessment and intervention give indications, but not guarantees, about the timing, routes, or kinds of change that are accessible with a particular case at a specific point in time. A multivariate conception of change commits the therapist to a coordinated and sequential working of multiple change pathways and methods.

4. Motivation to change is not assumed to be present with adolescents or their parents. Treatment receptivity and motivation varies across individuals involved in the treatment. We understand a process sometimes known as "resistance" as normative. Although "resistant" behaviors are barriers to successful treatment implementation, they point to processes of important therapeutic focus. Focusing on this reluctance and difficulty regarding change in a non-judgmental way is

critical. We appreciate the adolescent's and family's difficulties in creating lasting lifestyle change.

5. The therapist makes treatment possible through practically oriented, outcome-focused working relationships with family members and extrafamilial sources of influence, and through the exploration of personally meaningful relationship and life themes. These therapeutic themes are emergent — they become specified as a result of inquiry about generic individual and family developmental tasks and about idiosyncratic aspects of the adolescent's and family's history.

6. Interventions are individualized according to each family and their environmental circumstances. Interventions target etiologic risk factors for drug abuse and problem behaviors, and they promote protective processes associated with positive developmental outcomes.

7. Planning and flexibility are critical and complementary. Case formulations are collaboratively constructed blueprints that guide the beginning of treatment and the course of treatment. Formulations are revised based on new information and in-treatment experiences. In partnership with family members and relevant extrafamilial others, therapists continually evaluate the results of all interventions. Using this feedback, they alter the intervention plan and modify particular interventions on a day-to-day basis.

8. Therapist responsibility is emphasized. Therapists feel responsibility for: promoting participation and enhancing motivation of all relevant persons; creating a workable agenda and clinical focus; devising multidimensional and multisystemic treatment options; providing thematic focus and consistency throughout treatment; prompting behavior change; evaluating with participants the ongoing success of interventions; and revising interventions as necessary.

9. Therapists think in terms of stages of work. Particular therapeutic operations (e.g., adolescent engagement and theme formation), parts of a session, whole sessions, phases of therapy, and therapy overall are conceived and organized phasically.

10. Therapist attitude is fundamental to success. Therapists are advocates of the adolescent and family. They are neither child savers nor proponents of "tough love" who focus exclusively on granting authority and control to parents. Therapists are optimistic but not naïve about change. Their sensitivity to environmental or societal influences stimulates ideas about interventions rather than the offering of reasons for why problems began or excuses for why change is not occurring. As instruments of change, therapists know that their personal functioning can facilitate or handicap their work.

MDFT Treatment Parameters

Psychotherapy research makes a valuable distinction between treatment *parameters* and treatment *techniques*. Treatment parameters are program-delivery aspects of the intervention that dictate its timing, intensity, duration, and intended targets (Clarke, 1995; Kazdin *et al.*, 1990). These factors may influence outcome to a significant degree (Borkovec & Castonguay, 1998; Heinicke, 1990). In contrast, treatment techniques are the "active ingredients" of the model. This includes the essential therapist behaviors utilized during case contacts and counseling sessions (Elkin, Pilkonis, Docherty & Sotsky, 1988; Sechrest, 1994). Treatment techniques connect to the model's hypothesized processes of change — what therapist behaviors, in what combinations and during which treatment phases, are provided in response to given client problems.

Several treatment parameters guide MDFT. Sessions are routinely conducted in the clinic, but on occasion, particularly during a crisis, sessions might be held in the family's home or at other appropriate locales (e.g., school, family court). The location also can vary according to the phase of treatment, the living circumstances and preferences of the youth and family, and the session's objectives. Decisions about session composition are made according to one's therapeutic objective at the time. Thus, who to include in one's next contact is made on a session-by-session basis. Both individual and conjoint sessions are regularly used, and it is common for a single session to contain a mixture of individual and conjoint mini-sessions. Indeed, more recent extensions of the model have redefined the concept of session altogether. Phone contact with individual family members may be extended conversations, "sessions" in an extended sense of the term, that occur during the week in-between face-to-face contact time. Thus, as we have conducted studies with more and more difficult cases over time, we think less in terms of numbers of sessions and more in terms of case contact time. The therapist's role in MDFT is broad, to match the intended scope of the intervention. Therapists function as *de facto* case managers who contact schools, churches, community sites (e.g., job training), and juvenile justice facilities in order to incorporate non-familial adults and institutional resources into treatment activities. These activities also facilitate the therapist's focus on changing family members' behavior relative to these influential extrafamilial social systems.

Multidimensional family therapy is a treatment framework that has been developed and tested with different populations, versions, and settings. We have tested different variations of MDFT treatment duration and intensity. Treatment durations of (1) 16 sessions over five months, (2) 15–25 sessions over six months, and (3) 15–25 sessions over three months have been examined. We have successfully piloted and are currently testing an intensive outpatient version on MDFT intended to work with adolescents who have comorbid diagnoses, are deeply involved in the juvenile system, and who have been referred for residential care. This study is testing the intensive outpatient version of MDFT as a clinical and cost-beneficial alternative to residential treatment. In general, more frequent contact with family members occurs during the initial period of therapy, and in the last month the amount of contact decreases. Face-to-face sessions last between one and two hours. Additionally, frequent phone contact with both parents and the adolescent is used to follow up and extend in-session work and to trouble-shoot within the home environment.

MDFT Focal Treatment Areas

MDFT emphasizes four focal treatment areas, each associated with a core roster of treatment goals and techniques: adolescent; parent(s) and other family members; family interactional patterns; and extrafamilial systems of influence. MDFT therapists rely on training, experience, and accumulating knowledge of the family to coordinate intervention efforts within and among the four focal areas. Depending on the family's profile of risk and protective factors, more time is devoted to some foci than others. Progress in one area tends to potentiate work in others, and critical themes are cycled throughout different areas and sometimes recycled within a given area throughout treatment.

Adolescent focus. In this focal area, therapists concentrate on the role of individual adolescents within the family system, as well as their membership within other social systems, principally school and peer groups. Adolescents with drug and behavior problems approach therapy reluctantly (Liddle, Dakof & Diamond, 1991; Taylor, Adelman & Kaser-Boyd, 1985) and with more negativity than other family members (Robbins, Alexander, Newell & Turner, 1996), making therapist–adolescent working alliances especially difficult to build (DiGiuseppe, Linscott & Jilton, 1996). At the outset of treatment, MDFT therapists spend much time alone with adolescents to engage them in treatment and to craft personally meaningful agendas — reasons for a given adolescent to participate that may or may not coincide with agendas set by others (Diamond, Liddle, Hogue & Dakof, 1999). To accomplish this, the therapist works to discover topics of personal significance to the adolescent and to understand, in detail, the current functioning of the extended social systems in which the teen exists. MDFT therapists help adolescents give detailed pictures of how they make decisions, how they relate to their peer networks, how they are adjusting to achievement and maturity demands, and feelings they have about met and unmet personal goals. In this way therapists gain better access to the everyday world of adolescents and the risk and protective factors found there. This information forms the basis for designing treatment goals that are practical and relevant for the teenager and his or her family.

Gradually in this initial engagement phase, individual sessions with the teenager focus on his or her drug-taking and other problem behaviors. Both intrapersonal and interpersonal aspects of drug-taking and delinquent behaviors are discussed, with considerable therapeutic emphasis placed upon the teenager's relationship orientation. Therapists focus on drug use on the assumption that it both reflects problems in developmental functioning and is itself a stimulus for other behavioral problems and negative relations. That is, substance abuse may be a marker of current or past problems in family functioning, but it may also create disharmony or exacerbate only mildly conflictual family relationships — relationships without a history of dysfunction. The adolescent's relationships outside of the family also are examined. Therapists explore how drug-taking and antisocial behavior delimits the quality of available peer and mentoring relationships, promote prosocial interaction with peers and extrafamilial adults, and discuss and create the motivation, opportunities, rewards, and requisite skills for cultivating prosocial relationships.

Parent and family focus. In this focal area, therapists work with parents in their roles as adults who are often managing difficult life circumstances and parents who have often lost faith in their ability to influence their adolescents. The quality of a teenager's relationship with his or her parents is perhaps the most powerful protector against the development of problem behaviors (e.g., Resnick *et al.*, 1997). Unfortunately, parents of adolescents with drug use problems have typically tried many things over the years to curb these behaviors, often stringing together a succession of defeated attempts to enact more effective parenting practices (Patterson, Reid & Dishion, 1992). At the same time, parents of drug-using adolescents are typically under considerable stress from a variety of sources: poor personal and social support, economic hardships, negative feelings about the parenting in their own families of origin, and history of depression or other psychopathology, to name a few (Luster & Okagaki, 1993; Robinson & Garber, 1995). Therefore, prior to or concurrently with addressing adolescent-related issues therapists may devote a significant portion of the treatment to (a) identifying how personal stressors affect the parenting environment, (b) determining how the adolescent (and other children) can be shielded from their effects, and (c) helping parents access various social (and, if needed, psychiatric) resources for themselves.

MDFT therapists look to implement parent-focused interventions in stages. First, therapists assess the status of the attachment relationship between the parent and adolescent. Failure to maintain both autonomy and relatedness in the parent–adolescent relationship creates significant risk for a variety of developmental outcomes (Allen, Hauser & Borman-Spurrell, 1996; Greenberg, Speltz & DeKlyen, 1993), and emotional disengagement is a signature feature of families with drug-using adolescents (Patterson & Stouthamer-Loeber, 1984; Volk, Edwards, Lewis, Sprenkle and Piercy, 1989). As a first step toward behavioral (parenting practices) change, therapists seek to lessen the emotional distance between parent and adolescent. We do this by: (1) enhancing or rekindling the parent's sense of love and commitment to the teen; (2) validating previous attempts to deal with the teen; (3) acknowledging stressful past and present circumstances in the parent's personal life; and (4) generating hope via an increase in the sense of mastery and control (Liddle *et al.*, 1998). These parent–teen reconnection efforts aim to reinstill belief in the need and the possibility of having corrective influence on the teenager. After accomplishing these shifts in the emotion realm, therapists assess and intervene in parenting style and parenting practices, including monitoring, discipline, and limit-setting, fostering a supportive emotional climate, and modeling coping strategies (Diamond & Liddle, 1996). Parental attitudes about and parenting behaviors in relation to the adolescent's drug use are a major focus of this stage.

Whereas individual and interactional work with the adolescent and her/his primary parent are core to MDFT, other family members can also be instrumental in promoting the adolescent's drug-taking or in fostering adaptive socialization. Siblings, family members living outside the home, and extended family members are included in assessment, case formulation, and interventions. Individuals with a key role in the adolescent's life are invited to participate in family and individual sessions as indicated. Cooperation is achieved by highlighting the current serious circumstances of the youth and the need for all potentially influential others, particularly prosocial adults, to join forces in helping the adolescent.

Family interactional focus. This focal area facilitates change in family relationship patterns by providing an interactional context wherein families develop the motivation, skills, and experience to modify relationship bonds and interact in more adaptive ways. Various kinds of negative family interactions are linked to the development and maintenance of adolescent drug use (Baumrind, 1991; Brook *et al.*, 1989; Hawkins *et al.*, 1992). The renegotiation of the parent–adolescent relationship during this stage of the family life cycle is delicate, is accomplished in subtle ways, and is important to short- and longer-term developmental outcomes (Ferrari & Olivette, 1993; Fuligni & Eccles, 1993; Pardeck & Pardeck, 1990). Critically, family therapy research has shown that changes in family interactional patterns are associated with changes in problem behavior, including adolescent drug use (Mann, Borduin, Henggeler & Blaske, 1990; Robbins *et al.*, 1996; Schmidt, Liddle & Dakof, 1996; Szapocznik, Perez-Vidal, Hervis, Brickman & Kurtines, 1989).

MDFT therapists seek to understand, and ultimately modify, the current context of the parent–adolescent relationship by evaluating and coaching family members' unrehearsed interactions in session via the classic family therapy technique of enactment (Minuchin & Fishman, 1981). Conversations are sometimes prompted by therapists in direct attempts to change interactional patterns and, thus, change the relationship; at other times, the conversations occur spontaneously. Therapists watch how parents and adolescents communicate, how they solve or fail to solve problems, and how the viewpoint of each is validated or thwarted. Therapists then shape interactions in an attempt to provide new experiences of existing relationships and to break new relationship ground, thereby instilling more adaptive and protective relationship habits (Diamond & Liddle, 1999). This may involve the therapist translating or extrapolating a communication from one person to another, interpreting new meaning to an interaction as it unfolds, or pushing the content or intensity of dialogue into new areas (Diamond & Liddle, 1996). The opportunity for families to practice new relationship patterns, and to do so in a context in which new behaviors are supported and refined, is crucial for their acceptability and long-term durability. Moreover, as families practice adaptive relationship behaviors in session, they become more able to recognize what good conversations (which are signs of positive relationships) sound and feel like. This process promotes the generalizability of the interventions.

For in-session discussions to be productive in a problem-solving sense, parents and adolescents must first be able to communicate without excessive blame, defensiveness, or recrimination. Interactional interventions with the parent and adolescent therefore aim to reduce negativity (see Robbins *et al.*, 1996) and position each for more constructive discussion and negotiation. Teenagers and parents may need considerable coaching from the therapist before they can begin productive in-session conversations. This coaching is carried out in joint and one-to-one sessions dedicated to preparing participants individually for later, joint sessions where particular, important conversations are sponsored. The overall objectives of preparatory individual coaching include helping each participant formulate the content of what is to be said, prepare for potential reactions by other participants, and solidify a mini-contract that enables the therapist to challenge the participant to follow through as planned once the interaction begins. Preparatory coaching often centers on encouraging participants to express less extreme, emotionally hardened positions. By pre-processing intensely experienced feelings or entrenched opinions in this manner, family members can take a needed first step toward defusing habitual problems in communication. These activities also acknowledge the difficulty in bringing up difficult but important topics. Critically, this piece of the clinical work breaks down the impasse into workable components, emphasizing the need to approach the problem area systematically and with careful planning.

Extrafamilial focus. MDFT therapists seek to develop a high level of collaboration between the family and all other ecological environments in which the adolescent lives — including school, recreational, and juvenile justice systems. We do not assume that changing family interaction patterns alone is sufficient to eradicate the symptoms of problem behavior in youth. Development is influenced for better or worse by many extra-familial and social forces, and these aspects of the teen's ecology are also assessed and targeted as necessary (and, as possible) for intervention. Intervention objectives for the adolescent and family parallel those in the other focal areas: to introduce new kinds of emotional reactions and processing, new appraisals and attitudes, and new behavioral alternatives for interacting with key extrafamilial influences.

To accomplish these objectives, therapists practice intensive case management with family members directly, and indirectly via systems outside the family. For an overburdened parent, help in negotiating complex bureaucracies or obtaining adjunctive services is crucial. Parents may need assistance to secure fundamental services such as housing, medical care, and transportation to job training or self-help programs. Addressing these concrete needs is instrumental in promoting the family's ability to attend to key therapeutic tasks (Prinz & Miller, 1991). The therapist's multisystems work is important in itself, and it is also facilitative of access to and work in other domains. Therapists routinely work with school personnel to assist in enhancing the adolescent's school attendance and performance, and family sessions focus on devising plans for improving school-related behavior and advocating for the teen's unique educational needs (e.g., transfer to an alternative school). Therapists assist families in locating structured after-school and recreational activities suited to the interests and abilities of the adolescent. Also, close collaboration with juvenile justice systems has been found to be a determinative factor in the success of some adolescent drug treatment programs (Pompi, 1994). When there is legal or court involvement, intensive working relationships are swiftly established with the probation officer or other court staff assigned to the adolescent. These relationships foster partnerships and reciprocity between therapeutic and legal systems and their representatives. Therapists work to include treatment generally, and particular aspects of treatment such as curfew, school or job attendance and drug testing, as coordinated, mutually monitored efforts of the legal and treatment systems (Liddle, 2000).

Steps 4, 5, and 6: Specification of Treatment, Tests of Treatment Process, and Tests of Treatment Outcome

Treatment Adherence Monitoring and Evaluation

Treatment adherence, also known as treatment integrity, refers to the degree to which a given therapy is implemented in accordance with essential theoretical and procedural aspects of the model (Moncher & Prinz, 1991). Treatment adherence has important implications for the strength, replicability, and transportability of therapy models (Moncher &

Prinz, 1991; Yeaton & Sechrest, 1981). In fact, the widespread adoption of psychotherapy treatment manuals can be viewed as an effort to make model implementation more specific and standardized, such that prescribed interventions can be delivered reliably, and conceptually inconsistent interventions can be avoided (Waltz, Addis, Koerner & Jacobson, 1993). For these reasons, treatment adherence procedures are required to verify that interventions are practiced according to model specifications. Treatment adherence procedures operate along two complementary dimensions: adherence monitoring and adherence evaluation (Hogue, Liddle & Rowe, 1996). *Adherence monitoring* refers to "quality control" procedures exercised prior to and concurrently with ongoing treatment provision. Training, supervision, and performance review of therapists, along with documentation of clinical procedures in the form of case notes and treatment plans, are elements of adherence monitoring. *Adherence evaluation* refers to systematic *post-hoc* review of treatment implementation for the purpose of determining the degree of adherence actually obtained. Common evaluation methods include session analysis by experts in the model, therapist self-report measures, and process coding of session audiotapes or videotapes.

As a complex and intensive family therapy model, MDFT devotes great attention to therapist training and supervision (Liddle, Becker & Diamond, 1997). Prior to training, MDFT therapists are required to have at least a master's degree and two years of post-masters experience in family-based intervention. Training in MDFT includes approximately 100 hours of model-related literature review, didactic seminars, review of videotapes with an MDFT supervisor and previously trained therapists, and completion of two to three pilot cases. These sessions are supervised live or by videotape. Following training, MDFT therapists routinely receive one to two hours of face-to-face supervision per week that includes a review of developments and case conceptualization for every case, videotape review of sessions, and live supervision of current cases. Case logs are used to track, among other things, which family members and which ecological systems (e.g., school, recreational, religious, legal) are being included in treatment planning and implementation, the time spent in each area of work week by week, and the therapist's and supervisor's written evaluation of week-by-week, and sometimes daily, outcomes.

A process-based adherence study confirmed that MDFT can be implemented with a high degree of treatment integrity (Hogue *et al.*, 1998). We compared intervention techniques of MDFT therapists to intervention techniques of cognitive-behavioral therapists during a randomized controlled trial for treating adolescent substance abuse. Non-participant coders observed videotapes of randomly selected sessions from the MDFT and cognitive-behavioral conditions using an adherence evaluation instrument designed to identify therapeutic techniques and facilitative interventions associated with the two treatment models. Coders estimated both the frequency and the thoroughness (i.e., depth, complexity, or persistence) with which techniques were delivered. Results demonstrated that MDFT therapists reliably utilized the core systemic interventions prescribed by the model: focusing on individual teen and parent functioning, shaping parenting skills, preparing for and coaching multiparticipant interactions in session, and facilitating change with multiple family members. Moreover, in keeping with MDFT's commitment to working on family attachment bonds and developmental themes, MDFT therapists focused significantly on establishing a supportive therapeutic environment, encouraging discussion and expression of affect, engaging clients in crafting a collaborative treatment agenda, and exploring everyday behavior related to normative adolescent development. This study illustrates how fine-grained process-oriented adherence evaluation can contribute to treatment development and therapist training for well-specified therapy models.

MDFT Process Research

There is a great need for research in child and adolescent psychotherapy and adolescent drug treatment on the processes of change within effective therapy models (Kazdin & Kagan, 1994; Ozechowski & Liddle, 2000). Contemporary treatment process research advocates a research agenda that combines clinical validity with theoretical relevance and treatment model-building (Hayes, Castonguay & Goldfried, 1996; Omer & Dar, 1992), with an emphasis on discovery-oriented investigation of change-producing client–therapist interactions (Diamond & Diamond, in press; Russell, 1994). This research agenda is timely for the field of adolescent substance abuse treatment. Efficacy evidence exists for family-based approaches for adolescent drug problems (Liddle & Dakof, 1995; Waldron, 1997). In fact, some reviewers have concluded that family therapy approaches are the most effective and promising treatments for adolescent substance abuse that are available today (Stanton & Shadish, 1997; Williams & Chang, 2000). At the same time, the mechanisms of change hypothesized to account for successful outcome in these approaches remain unverified and poorly understood (Ozechowski & Liddle, 2000). Theory-driven process research is poised to fill this void, thereby stimulating clinical model-building and facilitating dissemination of effective intervention techniques (Diamond & Diamond, in press).

We have conducted a program of process research on the MDFT approach. This work has attempted to illuminate some key but murky or difficult aspects of therapy with drug-using teenagers. We have addressed core challenges such as how to engage adolescents and parents in treatment, and how to address some fundamental aspects of dysfunction that present with significant regularity across many cases. The process studies have focused both on the description and clarification of the core client processes of dysfunction and healing or improvement as well as on the therapist behaviors that intersect with these client processes. These studies provide a first wave of insights, systematically derived, about mechanisms of change within the model. The process studies have employed both hypothesis-driven (focus on confirming clinical theory) and discovery-oriented (focus on refining or extending existing theory and exploring unspecified phenomena) methodological approaches (Hill, 1994; Shoham-Salomon, 1990). The studies to date have addressed four questions that are fundamental to understanding how MDFT pursues clinical change: (1) Does MDFT produce change in family interactions as the model specifies? (2) Does MDFT improve those parenting behaviors that are linked to adolescent drug use and behavior problems, and are these changes in parenting related to reductions in drug and behavior problems? (3) Can MDFT therapists establish productive working alliances with multi-problem, ethnic minority, inner-city youths? and (4) Can MDFT therapists engender culturally meaningful interventions that enhance treatment engagement of African-American adolescents?

Resolving parent–adolescent impasses. Diamond and Liddle (1996, 1999) used task analysis to identify the combination of clinical interventions and family interactions necessary to resolve in-session impasses. These are clinical situations characterized by negative exchanges, emotional disengagement, and poor problem-solving between parents and adolescents. The sample in this process study was substance-abusing, juvenile-justice-referred teenagers and their families. Therapist behaviors that contributed to defusing these negative interactions included: (a) actively blocking, diverting, or addressing and working through negative affect; (b) implanting, evoking, and amplifying thoughts and feelings that promote constructive dialogue; and (c) creating emotional treaties among family members by alternately working in session with parents alone and adolescents alone — a kind of shuttle diplomacy. In cases with successful resolution of the impasse, the therapist transformed the nature and tone of the conversation in the session. The therapist shifted the parent's blaming and hopelessness to attention to their feelings of regret and loss and perhaps sadness about what was occurring with their child. At the same time, the therapist elicited the adolescent's thoughts and feelings about relationship roadblocks with the parent and others. These in-session shifts of attention and emotion made new conversations between parent and adolescent possible. In the process, the parents developed empathy for the difficult experiences of their teenager and offered support, even admiration, for their teen's coping. These interventions and processes facilitated personal disclosure by the adolescent and created give and take exchanges with a different emotional tone than was previously occurring. Severity of family conflict and pessimism predicted successful resolution of the impasse, with the most conflicted and pessimistic families less likely to move to a new conversational level.

This study yielded clinical insights in four areas. First, we found a theory-based way to reliably define and identify family transactional processes that are known determinants of poor developmental outcomes in children and teenagers. Second, we broke down in behavioral terms the components of the impasse, defining the unfolding sequential contributions of both parent and adolescent. Third, we specified the relation of different therapist actions to the impasse. And fourth, we demonstrated that therapists can change an in-session therapeutic impasse, and thus impact one of the putative mechanisms of developmental dysfunction related to drug abuse.

Changing parenting practices. Schmidt, Liddle, and Dakof (1996) investigated the nature and extent of change in parenting behaviors, as well as the link between parental subsystem change and reduction in adolescent symptomatology. In a sample of parents whose teenagers were juvenile justice referred and showed significant drug and mental health problems, parents showed significant decreases in negative parenting behaviors (e.g., negative affect, verbal aggression) and increases in positive parenting (e.g., monitoring and limit-setting, positive affect and commitment) over the course of therapy. Moreover, these changes in parenting behaviors were associated with reductions in adolescent drug use and problem behaviors. Four different patterns of parent–adolescent tandem change were isolated: 59 percent of families showed improvement in both parenting practices and adolescent symptomatology; 21 percent evidenced improved parenting but no change in adolescent problems; ten percent showed improved adolescent symptoms in the absence of improved parenting; and ten percent showed no improvement in either parenting or adolescent functioning. These results support a tenet of family-based treatments: change in a fundamental aspect of the family system (parenting practices) is related to change at the critical level of interest — reduction of adolescent symptoms, including drug abuse. Furthermore, these data suggest that parenting risk and protective factors for drug use are accessible to intervention within a therapeutic environment. Subsequent work has clarified the theory and empirical basis of interventions in the parenting realm (Liddle *et al.*, 1998).

Building therapist-adolescent alliances. We examined the impact of adolescent engagement interventions on improving initially poor therapist–adolescent alliances (Diamond, Liddle, Hogue & Dakof, 1999). The sample was juvenile-justice-involved, substance-abusing inner city teens, most of whom had a dual diagnosis substance abuse and a mental health disorder (Rowe, Liddle & Dakof, in press). Cases with weak therapist–adolescent alliances in the first treatment session were observed over the course of the first three sessions. Significant gains in working alliance were evident when therapists emphasized the following alliance-building interventions: attending to the adolescent's experience; formulating personally meaningful goals; and presenting one's self as the adolescent's ally. Lack of improvement or deterioration in alliance was associated with the therapist continually socializing the adolescent to the nature of therapy. Moreover, in improved alliance cases therapists increased their use of alliance-building interventions from session two to session three (therapist perseverance), whereas therapists in unimproved cases decreased their use (therapist resignation). These results indicate that although it is an important early-stage therapist method, when therapists overfocus on and become stuck in orienting adolescents to therapy, and thus wait too long to discuss how the therapy can be personally meaningful for the teenager, a productive working relationship is not formed. Details about how to engage teenagers in family-based therapy are described elsewhere (Liddle, 1995; Liddle & Diamond, 1991; Liddle *et al.*, 1992).

Crafting culturally specific interventions. Jackson-Gilfort, Liddle, Dakof & Tejeda (in press) investigated whether therapeutic discussion of culturally specific themes enhanced treatment engagement of African-American male youths with an inner-city sample of juvenile-justice-involved, substance-abusing teenagers. Exploration of particular themes, such as anger and rage, alienation, and the journey from boyhood to manhood (i.e., what it means to become an African-American man), were associated with both increased participation and decreased negativity by adolescents in the very next treatment session. These results suggest that use of certain culturally meaningful themes are directly linked to adolescent investment in the treatment process. Jackson-Gilfort & Liddle (in press) describe how these themes pertaining to African-American development were derived and give illustrations of their clinical use.

MDFT Outcome Research

While surely not without its critics (Persons, 1991; Seligman, 1996), the gold standard for evaluating treatment efficacy remains controlled outcome studies. In this kind of research, two or more clinically viable treatments are evaluated for outcome effects within a single sample of participants who have been randomly assigned to treatment condition. Comparative outcome designs offer several methodological and interpretive virtues (Basham, 1986; Davison & Lazarus, 1994; Kazdin, 1986): they facilitate informative comparisons between models with theoretically distinct, or opposed, mechanisms of change; they allow for control of theoretically shared factors such as clinical attention, therapist facilitative behaviors, and maturational effects; they avoid ethical issues related to delaying treatment and deter compromises to internal validity related to participants seeking alternative treatment options; and outcome effect sizes tend to be smaller when treatments are compared to one another (versus comparison to a no-treatment or placebo group), resulting in a more stringent test of treatment efficacy.

The efficacy of MDFT has been evaluated in three controlled comparative studies, and other large-scale studies continue to test different versions of the MDFT model with different subtypes of drug-abusing adolescents. An early intervention/prevention version of MDFT also has been tested (Hogue, Liddle, Becker, & Johnson-Leckrone, in press; Liddle & Hogue, 2000), and two other controlled studies are in process (see www.med.miami.edu/ctrada). In one of the completed randomized trials, MDFT was tested against two alternative treatments, multifamily educational intervention (MFEI; Barrett, 1990) and adolescent group therapy (AGT; Concannon, McMahon & Parker, 1989). MFEI convenes groups of three to four families with one therapist who leads didactic/interactive sessions that provide stress reduction, a review of family and adolescent risk and protective factors, skills-building exercises to improve family problem-solving and communication, a forum to share family stories, and discussion of weekly homework assignments. AGT convenes six to eight adolescents with two group therapists who direct didactic presentations on drug use consequences, group discussions about shared feelings and values, and skills-building exercises in communication, self-control, self-acceptance, problem-solving, and use of peer social support. These two comparison treatments were selected to accentuate similarities and dissimilarities among the models in hypothesized key therapeutic mechanisms: both MDFT and MFEI are family-based interventions that focus on changing parenting behaviors; both MDFT and AGT work extensively on the motivational set and social skills of the individual adolescent; and both MFEI and AGT utilize group support as a primary change agent. The treatment dose of all three treatment conditions was controlled. Each treatment mandated 14–16 weekly office-based therapy sessions.

The study sample consisted of 95 drug-using adolescents and their families who completed treatment. Study eligibility criteria were marijuana use at least three times per week over the past 30 days, or single use of another drug (except alcohol) during that time. Adolescents averaged 16 years of age; 80 percent were male; 51 percent were white non-Hispanic, 18 percent African-American, 15 percent Hispanic, and 16 percent other; 48 percent came from single-parent households, 31 percent two-parent, and 21 percent step-parent; median yearly family income was $25,000; 51 percent were polydrug users, and 49 percent used only marijuana and alcohol; and 61 percent were involved in the juvenile justice system. Assessments were conducted at intake and at six and twelve months following termination on the following outcome indicators: self-reported adolescent drug use, parent-reported adolescent acting-out behaviors, observationally coded family competence, and adolescent grade point average (GPA) obtained from school records.

The general pattern of results indicates improvement among youth in all three conditions, with MDFT participants showing the largest and most diverse gains. All three conditions experienced significant declines in both drug use and acting-out behaviors. MDFT displayed greater reductions in the teen's drug use than the other two conditions. Forty-five percent of adolescents in MDFT (versus 32 percent in AGT and 26 percent in MFEI) demonstrated clinically significant change in drug use, such that their drug use profiles at follow-up fell below intake eligibility criteria. In addition, only MDFT participants reported significant improvement in family competence and GPA. MDFT, as a family-based treatment, aims to change family functioning because a dysfunctional family environment is one of the known determinants and facilitators of adolescent drug problems. Hence this finding is significant in that it addresses one of the presumed mechanisms of action in the approach.

Another important psychosocial protective factor that is targeted by MDFT is the teen's academic performance — a well-established and important dimension of adolescent functioning (Hawkins *et al.*, 1992). The percentage of adolescents achieving a GPA above 2.0 (passing) rose from 25 percent at intake to 68 percent at follow-up in MDFT, 43 percent at intake to 60 percent at follow-up in AGT, and 33 percent at intake to 41 percent at follow-up in MFEI. Finally, MDFT outperformed AGT but not MFEI in preventing treatment attrition: 33 of 45 MDFT participants completed treatment (73 percent); 34 of 52 in MFEI (65 percent), and 29 of 55 in AGT (52 percent).

In a second treatment efficacy study, MDFT was compared to individual cognitive-behavioral therapy for adolescent drug abuse (CBT; Turner, 1992, 1993). CBT for adolescent drug use is divided into three stages. Stage one, treatment planning and engagement, focuses on identifying and prioritizing adolescent problems and constructing the treatment contract. Stage two begins an intensive cognitive-behavioral treatment program with the goals of increasing coping competence and behavioral control over drug use. Core interventions include: contingency contracting, self-monitoring, problem-solving and communication skills training, training in identifying cognitive distortions, increasing prosocial activities, and homework assignments. Stage three focuses on termination issues and relapse prevention with the goal of enhancing long-term self-management skills. CBT was selected as a comparison treatment condition because it is a commonly practiced, empirically supported therapeutic modality. In both conditions, therapy sessions were held primarily once a week in a clinic office.

Participants in the study sample were 224 drug-using adolescents and their families randomly assigned to treatment. At intake all adolescents met criteria for diagnosis of substance abuse or dependence (70 percent reported initiation of marijuana use prior to age 15), and 78 percent had at least one comorbid diagnosis. Adolescents averaged 15 years of age; 80 percent were male; 72 percent were African-American, 18 percent white non-Hispanic, and ten percent Hispanic; median yearly family income was $11,000–$13,000, and 41 percent of families were on public assistance; most lived in the highest crime rate neighborhoods in Philadelphia; 75 percent of adolescents were referred from the juvenile justice system, and 55 percent were on probation at intake.

Self-reported adolescent drug use, and adolescent-reported and parent-reported externalizing and internalizing symptomatology, were assessed at intake and again at six and twelve months following treatment termination. Although both treatments produced a significant decrease in drug use, externalizing problems, and internalizing problems from intake to termination, only MDFT, perhaps because of its more comprehensive, multiple systems therapeutic focus, was able to maintain the symptomatic gain after termination of treatment. Multidimensional family therapy showed a significantly different slope from cognitive-behavioral therapy, suggesting that youth who received family therapy continued to evidence treatment improvement after termination.

A third completed randomized study tested MDFT in a multisite field effectiveness trial — the CSAT Cannabis Youth Treatment (CYT) study (Dennis *et al.*, 2000). Consistent with previous findings, MDFT had a positive impact on drug use and other problem behaviors, and it also showed the capacity to promote positive gains. In the CYT study, which tested a 12–15-session version of MDFT over a three-month treatment delivery period, MDFT reduced days of marijuana use by 27 percent from baseline to three months. At a three-month follow-up assessment, 42 percent of teens were abstinent and nearly two-thirds (65 percent) had no past-month substance abuse disorder symptoms.

The CYT study was the first project in which cost issues of MDFT were addressed. These data indicate that MDFT compares quite favorably to current cost parameters of outpatient adolescent treatment. The National Treatment Improvement Study (NTIES) (Center for Substance Abuse Treatment, 1998; Gerstein & Johnson, 1999) is one of the few studies to provide formal cost estimates of adolescent outpatient drug treatment. The NTIES study surveyed a nationally representative sample of adolescent treatment program directors who estimated the costs of outpatient adolescent drug treatment. The CYT study (Dennis *et al.*, in press) used NTIES data as a benchmark against which to compare the five tested adolescent marijuana treatments in CYT. The economic cost of each treatment in the CYT was determined using the Drug Abuse Treatment Cost Analysis Program (DATCAP) (French *et al.*, in press). The average weekly cost of MDFT was less than the lower weekly estimate from the program directors. The median weekly cost of outpatient adolescent drug treatment in the NTIES study was $267, and the weekly mean (average) treatment cost was $365. The average weekly cost of providing MDFT per adolescent was $164. Given these treatment cost findings, Dennis *et al.* (in press) concluded that it is affordable and programmatically sustainable at current funding levels.

In sum, three major controlled clinical trials have found MDFT to be an efficacious treatment for adolescent drug problems. The approach also demonstrated the capacity to promote protective factors instrumental to the continuation of changes in drug problems. As Brown (1993) has noted in her discussion of recovery patterns of drug-using teens, treatments must not only show that they can reduce drug taking *per se*, but their efficacy evidence should also include changes in the everyday social ecology in which adolescents live. The evidence that MDFT can change dysfunctional family interaction patterns (Diamond & Liddle, 1996), parenting practices (Schmidt *et al.*, 1996), and impact school performance (Liddle *et al.*, in press) suggest that the MDFT approach addresses theory- and research-based, contextually oriented effectiveness criteria.

Step 7: Tests of the Boundary Conditions and Moderators

Planful treatment development requires not only evaluation of treatment success with targeted populations, but also consideration of how treatment models can be enhanced or adapted to serve populations who have special needs, exhibit different kinds of symptom severity levels, or have proven difficult to treat or resistant to treatment effects. We are in the process of testing modified versions of MDFT in three current studies with samples that have notably different risk profiles from those treated in previous efficacy studies. The first is a prevention strategy for a population of high-risk young adolescents recruited from inner-city community sites (Hogue *et al*., in press; Liddle & Hogue, 2000). The second is a treatment population of adolescents with at least two diagnoses (e.g., substance abuse and conduct disorder) referred for placement in a residential drug treatment facility. The third is an early intervention controlled trial with an equal number of male and female substance-abusing adolescents with minimal juvenile justice involvement (mean age 14–15). We discuss the first of these new studies since it represents movement into the prevention intervention specialty, a sphere that is very different from the treatment research area.

Adapting MDFT to High-Risk Early Adolescent Prevention Populations

We modified MDFT's core operating principles and focal treatment areas to build a developmental–ecological prevention model for young adolescents at high risk for drug use and behavior problems (Liddle & Hogue, 2000). It has been suggested that psychotherapy approaches with antisocial youth yield comparatively little gain in light of the high toll exacted on therapists and treatment systems, so that prevention and early intervention are seen as hopeful alternatives (Reid, 1993). Promisingly, family prevention approaches have demonstrated success in preventing drug use and antisocial behavior (Ashery, Robertson, & Kumpfer, 1998; Hogue & Liddle, 1999; Kumpfer & Alvarado, 1995), with family skills training showing the greatest empirical support (e.g., Dishion & Andrews, 1995; Kumpfer, Molgaard & Spoth, 1996; McMahon, Slough & Conduct Problems Prevention Research Group, 1996; Spoth, Redmond & Shin, 1998).

However, family skills training models typically restrict their focus to stimulating or remediating intrafamilial skills such as problem-solving, communicating, family bonding, and negotiating behavioral limits and contracts. For this reason, the family skills training paradigm may be less suited for intervening into the wider social ecology of the family: dealing with parental psychopathology; strengthening social support systems for families; intervening in multiple social contexts that are sources of youth risk and family stress; and incorporating extrafamilial resources into intervention efforts (Blechman, 1998; Griest & Forehand, 1982; Prinz & Miller, 1996; Tolan & McKay, 1996; Webster-Stratton & Herbert, 1993). A more broad-based, comprehensive prevention strategy may be needed for children and adolescents who belong to the highest-risk groups — when they have incipient behavior problems (Tolan, 1996) and their families experience the greatest levels of stress and symptomatology and maintain the weakest support networks (Miller & Prinz, 1990).

By importing MDFT into the prevention context, we have developed and piloted a family-based prevention model specifically designed for high-risk young adolescents (ages 11–14) (Hogue *et al.*, in press). Our MDFT prevention model differs from standard skills-based family prevention in two ways. First, it is a flexibly delivered intervention that assesses the unique profile of risk and protective factors presented by each family in order to establish an individually tailored prevention agenda. The work is conducted in a one-to-one (individual family) setting, and teaching generic skills is secondary to centralizing the idiosyncratic history, problems, and goals of the individual family and its members. Second, the model takes an ecological approach to prevention that systematically assesses and, when indicated, intervenes into the numerous social contexts in which adolescents participate (e.g., family, school, peer, community). It focuses on both the adolescent's level of functioning within these diverse systems and the parents' knowledge about and direct participation in each system. By working to help parents become developmentally savvy navigators of the extended adolescent ecosystem, the model endeavors to create a more flexible and resilient family environment to protect against the onset of antisocial behavior.

Summary and Conclusions

This chapter has described the development of a developmentally and ecologically oriented and family-based comprehensive treatment for adolescent drug problems. While the developments in MDFT theory have been described elsewhere (Liddle, 1999), this chapter traced the model's evolution from the perspective of Kazdin's (1994) framework for treatment development. This approach has been able to attend to and produce empirical work appropriate to the treatment development framework's stages. The studies have been conducted in diverse treatment settings, addressed different sub-populations of adolescent drug abusers, included male and females, and included racially and ethnically diverse samples. The positive results of significantly reducing teen drug abuse at treatment termination and at follow-up periods occurred without any booster sessions post termination. Additionally, the changes in protective or positive factors in the lives of the teenagers and their parents are significant because they are in accord with the recommendations of the treatment field on the importance of measuring and impacting functioning in these important realms.

Our current and future treatment development work exists in several areas. First, we continue to refine and test the approach in different treatment settings, and with different sub-populations of adolescent substance abusers. Relatedly, we are quite involved in the movement to adapt, transport, and test empirically supported approaches in a diversity of drug treatment settings. One of our current studies is determining the process components and treatment outcomes of adapting and adding the MDFT approach to a day treatment program for drug-abusing teens. We also are interested in adapting the approach to residential care settings. On another but related front, we have been contacted by several state substance abuse organizations to collaborate on projects that would implement and test the MDFT approach within statewide adolescent substance abuse treatment systems. There are many challenges in projects of these types. These are practice research projects, studies that will require a new attention not only to the adaptation of clinical methods but also to issues of therapist supervision and training. New training materials are being developed to meet these diverse, practice-setting-specific needs.

Our work on the basic aspects of the treatment model continues as well. Our clinically focused research is exploring the complex factors of co-occurring disorders with adolescent substance abusers (Rowe *et al.*, in press) and adolescent female-specific processes (Dakof, 2000). This work operates, as is always the case in the MDFT research program, within the treatment development thematic.

Although we have organized the telling of the empirical side of the MDFT story to date within the treatment development perspective and specifically within Kazdin's extraordinary treatment development framework, we feel compelled to close with a caveat. That is, we are quite aware of the role of values in the conduct of the kind of science that we have done and continue to do. The values in our work have to do with many things. Primary among these is our continued assumption about the importance of focusing on families and the immediate social contexts of the adolescent who has lost his or her way in a downward cascade of drug use, delinquency, school and relationship failure, legal troubles, and societal alienation. Additionally, in their discussion of the politics and pressures to disseminate empirically supported therapies, Addis and Hatgis (2000) remind us that researchers' values and practices are not superior to those of other parties. This reminder, as well as the periodic values check about the premises that underpin our research program, seems as fitting a close as any to our summary of our efforts to date to devise an effective treatment for adolescent drug problems.

References

Achterberg, C. L., & Shannon, B. (1993), "Nutrition and adolescence." In R. M. Lerner (ed.), *Early Adolescence: Perspectives on research, policy, and intervention. The Penn State series on child & adolescent development*. Hillsdale, NJ: Lawrence Erlbaum, 261–275.

Addis, M. E. (1997). "Evaluating the treatment manual as a means of disseminating empirically validated psychotherapies." *Clinical Psychology: Science and Practice 4*, 1–11.

Addis, M. E., & Hatgis, C. (2000), "Values, practices, and the utilization of empirical critiques in the clinical trial." *Clinical Psychology: Science and Practice 7*(1), 120–124.

Allen, J. P., Hauser, S. T., & Borman-Spurell, E. (1996). "Attachment theory as a framework for understanding sequelae of severe adolescent psychopathology: An 11-year follow-up study." *Journal of Consulting and Clinical Psychology 64*(2), 254–263.

Anderson, L. P. (1991), "Acculturative stress: A theory of relevance to black Americans." *Clinical Psychology Review 11*, 685–702.

Ashery, R. S., Robertson, E. B., & Kumpfer, K. L. (1998). *Drug Abuse Prevention through Family Interventions*. National Institute on Drug Abuse Research Monograph 177. Rockville, MD: National Institute on Drug Abuse.

Barrett, K. (1990), "Multi-family educational intervention (MFEI) Manual." Unpublished manual, University of Washington.

Basham, R. B. (1986), "Scientific and practical advantages of comparative design in psychotherapy outcome research. *Journal of Consulting and Clinical Psychology 54*(1), 88–94.

Baumrind, D. (1991), "Effective parenting during the early adolescent transition." In P. A. Cowan & E. M. Hetherington (eds), *Family Transitions*. Hillsdale, NJ: Lawrence Erlbaum, 111–164.

Baumrind, D., & Moselle, K. A. (1985), "A developmental perspective on adolescent drug abuse." *Advances in Alcohol and Substance Abuse 4*, 41–67.

Blechman, E. A. (1998). "Parent training in moral context: Prosocial family therapy." In J. M. Briemeister & C. E. Schaefer (eds), *Handbook of Parent Training: Parents as co-therapists for children's behavior problems* 2nd edn. NY: Wiley & Sons, 508–548.

Block, J., Block, J. H., & Keyes, S. (1988), "Longitudinally foretelling drug usage in adolescence: Early childhood personality and environmental precursors." *Child Development 59*, 336–355.

Borkovec, T. D., & Castonguay, L. G. (1998), "What is the scientific meaning of empirically supported therapy?" *Journal of Consulting and Clinical Psychology 66*, 136–142.

Bronfenbrenner, U. (1979), *The Ecology of Human Development: Experiments by nature and design*. Cambridge, MA: Harvard University Press.

Bronfenbrenner, U. (1986a), "Ecology of the family as a context for human development." *American Psychologist 32*, 513–531.

Bronfenbrenner, U. (1986b), "Recent advances in research on the ecology of human development." In R. K. Silbereisan, K. Eyferth & G. Rudlinger (eds), *Development as an Action in Context: Problem behavior and normal youth development*. New York: Springer-Verlag, 287–309.

Brook, J. S., Nomura, C., & Cohen, P. (1989), "A network of influences on adolescent drug involvement: Neighborhood, school, peer, and family." *Genetic, Social, and General Psychology Monographs 115*, 123–145.

Brook, J. S., Whiteman, M., Nomura, C., Gordon, A. S., & Cohen, P. (1988), "Personality, family, and ecological influences on adolescent drug use: A development analysis." In R. H. Coombs (ed.), *The Family Context of Adolescent Drug Use*. New York: Haworth Press, 123–161.

Brown, B. B. (1990), "Peer groups and peer culture." In S. S. Feldman & G. R. Elliott (eds), *At the Threshold: The developing adolescent*. Cambridge, MA: Harvard University Press, 171–196.

Brown, S. A. (1993), "Recovery patterns in adolescent substance abuse." In J. S. Baer, G. A. Marlatt & R. J. McMahon (eds), *Addictive Behaviors across the Life Span: Prevention, treatment, and policy issues*. Newbury Park, CA: Sage Publications, 161–183.

Bukoski, W. J. (1991). "A framework for drug abuse prevention research." In C. Leukefeld & W. Bukoski (eds), *Drug Abuse Prevention Intervention Research: Methodological issues*. Rockville, MD: National Institute on Drug Abuse. NIDA Monograph No. 107, 7–28.

Bukstein, O. G. (1995), *Adolescent Substance Abuse: Assessment, prevention and treatment*. New York, NY: Wiley.

Carroll, K. M. *et al.* (2000), "A general system for evaluating therapist adherence and competence in psychotherapy research in the addictions." *Drug and Alcohol Dependence 57*, 225–238.

Carroll, K. M., Rounsaville, B. J., & Keller, D. S. (1991), "Relapse prevention strategies for the treatment of cocaine abuse." *American Journal of Drug and Alcohol Abuse 17*(3), 249–265.

Casey, R. J., & Berman, J. S. (1985), "The outcome of psychotherapy with children." *Psychological Bulletin 98*, 388–400.

Center for Substance Abuse Treatment (1998). *Adolescent Substance Abuse: Assessment and treatment (CSAT Treatment Improvement Protocol Series)*. Rockville, MD: SAMSHA.

Chambless, D. L. (1996), "In defense of dissemination of empirically supported psychological interventions." *Clinical Psychology: Science and Practice 3*, 230–235.

Chambless, D. L., & Hollon, S. D. (1998), "Defining empirically supported therapies." *Journal of Consulting and Clinical Psychology 66*, 7–18.

Clarke, G. N. (1995), "Improving the transition from basic efficacy research to effectiveness studies: Methodological issues and procedures." *Journal of Consulting and Clinical Psychology 63*, 718–725.

Concannon, C., McMahon, B., & Parker, K. P. (1989), "Peer group treatment for adolescent drug abuse." Unpublished manual, University of California, San Francisco.

Coombs, R. H., & Paulson, M. J. (1988), "Contrasting family patterns of adolescent drug users and nonusers." In R. H. Coombs (ed.), *The Family Context of Adolescent Drug Use.* New York: Haworth Press, 59–72.

Coombs, R. H., Paulson, M. J., & Palley, R. (1988), "The institutionalization of drug use in America: Hazardous adolescence, challenging parenthood." In R. H. Coombs (ed.), *The family context of adolescent drug use.* New York, NY: The Haworth Press, 9–37.

Crits-Christoph, P. (1996), "The dissemination of efficacious psychological treatments." *Clinical Psychology: Science and Practice 3(3)*, 260–263.

Dakof, G. A. (2000), "Understanding gender differences in adolescent drug abuse: Issues of comorbidity and family functioning." *Journal of Psychoactive Drugs 32*, 25–32.

Davison, G. C., & Lazarus, A. A. (1994), "Clinical innovation and evaluation: Integrating practice with inquiry." *Clinical Psychology: Science and Practice 1(2)*, 157–168.

Dembo, R., Farrow, D., Des Jarlais, D. C., Burgos, W., & Schmeidler, J. (1981), "Examining a casual model of early drug involvement among inner-city junior high school youths." *Human Relations 34(3)*, 169–193.

Dennis, M. L. *et al.* (2000), *The Cannabis Youth Treatment (CYT) Experiment: Preliminary findings.* A report to H. Westley Clark, Director Center for Substance Abuse Treatment, Substance Abuse and Mental Health Services Administration, Department of Health and Human Services.

Dennis, M. L. *et al.* (in press), "The Cannabis Youth Treatment (CYT) Experiment: A multi-site study of five approaches to outpatient treatment for adolescents." *Addiction.*

Diamond, G. M., & Liddle, H. A. (1996), "Resolving a therapeutic impasse between parents and adolescents in Multidimensional Family Therapy." *Journal of Consulting and Clinical Psychology 64(3)*, 481–488.

Diamond, G. M., Liddle, H. A., Hogue, A., & Dakof, G. A. (1999), "Alliance building interventions with adolescents in family therapy: A process study." *Psychotherapy 36(4)*, 355–368.

Diamond, G. S., & Diamond, G. M. (in press), "Studying core mechanisms of change: An agenda for family based process research." In H. A. Liddle, D. Santisteban, R. Levant & J. Bray (eds), *Family Psychology Intervention Science.* Washington, DC: American Psychological Association.

Diamond, G. S., & Liddle, H. A. (1999), "Transforming negative parent–adolescent interactions: From impasse to dialogue." *Family Process 38*, 5–26.

DiGiuseppe, R., Linscott, J., & Jilton, R. (1996), "Developing the therapeutic alliance in child–adolescent psychotherapy." *Applied and Preventive Psychology 5(2)*, 85–100.

Dishion, T. J., & Andrews, D. W. (1995), "Preventing escalation in problem behaviors with high-risk young adolescents: Immediate and 1-year outcomes." *Journal of Consulting and Clinical Psychology 63*, 538–548.

Dishion, T. J., Capaldi, D., Spracklen, K. M., & Li, F. (1995), "Peer ecology of male adolescent drug use." [Special issue: Developmental processes in peer relations and psychopathology.] *Developmental Psychopathology 7*, 803–824.

Durlak, J. A., Wells, A. M., Cotten, J. K., & Johnson, S. (1995), "Analysis of selected methodological issues in child psychotherapy research." *Journal of Clinical Child Psychology 24*, 141–148.

Elkin, I., Pilkonis, P., Docherty, J., & Sotsky, S. (1988), "Conceptual and methodological issues in comparative studies of psychotherapy and pharmacotherapy, I: Active ingredients and mechanisms of change." *American Journal of Psychiatry 145*, 909–917.

Ferrari, J. R., & Olivette, M. J. (1993), "Perceptions of parental control and the development of indecision among late adolescent females." *Adolescence 28*, 963–970.

Forehand, R. (1990), "Families with a conduct problem child." In G. H. Brody & I. E. Sigel (eds), *Methods of Family Research: Biographies of research projects: Vol. 2. Clinical populations.* Hillsdale, NJ: Lawrence Erlbaum Associates, Inc, 1–30.

French, M. T. *et al.* (in press), "The economic cost of outpatient marijuana treatment for adolescents: Findings from a multisite field experiment." *Journal of Substance Abuse Treatment.*

Fruzetti, A., & Linehan, M. (in press), *Dialectical Behavior Therapy for Couples and Families.* New York: Guilford Press.

Fuligni, A. J., & Eccles, J. S. (1993), "Perceived parent–child relationships and early adolescents' orientation toward peers." *Developmental Psychology 29*, 622–632.

Garfield, S. L. (1996), "Some problems associated with 'validated' forms of psychotherapy." *Clinical Psychology: Science and Practice 3*, 218–229.

Garmezy, N., Masten, A. S., & Tellegen, A. (1984), "The study of stress and competence in children: A building block for developmental psychopathology." *Child Development 55*, 97–111.

Gerstein, D. R., & Johnson, R. A. (1999), *Adolescent and Young Adults in the National Treatment Improvement Evaluation Study* (National Evaluation Data Services Report). Rockville, MD: Center for Substance Abuse Treatment.

Gottfredson, D. C., & Koper, C. S. (1996), "Race and sex differences in the prediction of drug use." *Journal of Consulting and Clinical Psychology 64*(2), 305–313.

Greenberg, M. T., Speltz, M. L., & DeKlyen, M. (1993), "The role of attachment in the early development of disruptive behavior problems." *Development and Psychopathology 5*, 191–213.

Griest, D. L., & Forehand, R. (1982), "How can I get any parent training done with all these other problems going on?: The role of family variables in child behavior therapy." *Child and Family Behavior Therapy 4*, 73–80.

Hawkins, J. D., Arthur, M. W., & Catalano, R. F. (1995), "Preventing substance abuse." In M. Tonry & D. P. Farrington (eds), *Building a Safer Society: Strategic approaches to crime prevention. Crime and Justice: A review of the research.* Chicago: University of Chicago Press, Vol. 19, 343–427.

Hawkins, J. D., Catalano, R. F., & Miller, J. Y. (1992), "Risk and protective factors for alcohol and other drug problems in adolescence and early adulthood: Implications for substance abuse prevention." *Psychological Bulletin 112*, 64–105.

Hayes, A .M., Castonguay, L. G., & Goldfried, M. R. (1996), "The study of change in psychotherapy: A reexamination of the process–outcome correlation paradigm. Comment on Stiles and Shapiro (1994)." *Journal of Consulting and Clinical Psychology 64*, 909–914.

Heinicke, C. M. (1990), "Toward generic principles of treating parents and children: Integrating psychotherapy with the school-aged child and early family intervention." *Journal of Consulting and Clinical Psychology 58*, 713–719.

Henggeler, S. W. *et al.* (1998), "Effects of multisystemic therapy on drug use and abuse in serious juvenile offenders: A progress report from two outcome studies." *Family Dynamics Addiction Quarterly 1*, 40–51.

Hill, C. E. (1994), "From an experimental to an exploratory naturalistic approach to studying psychotherapy process." In R. L. Russell (ed.), *Reassessing psychotherapy research.* New York: Guilford Press, 144–165.

Hill, J. P., & Holmbeck, G. N. (1986), "Attachment and autonomy during adolescence." In G. J. Whitehurst (ed.), *Annals of Child Development.* Greenwich, CT: JAI, Vol. 3, 145–189.

Hoagwood, K., Hibbs, E., Brent, D., & Jensen, P. (1995), "Introduction to the Special Section: Efficacy and effectiveness in studies of child and adolescent psychotherapy." *Journal of Consulting and Clinical Psychology 63*, 683–687.

Hogue, A., & Liddle, H. A. (1999), "Family-based preventive intervention: An approach to preventing substance use and antisocial behavior." *American Journal of Orthopsychiatry 69*(3), 278–293.

Hogue, A., & Liddle, H. A. (in press), "Multidimensional family prevention for at-risk adolescents." In T. Patterson (ed.), *Handbook of Psychotherapy* (Volume on Cognitive and Behavioral Therapies). New York: John Wiley & Sons.

Hogue, A., Liddle, H. A., Becker, D., & Johnson-Leckrone, J. (in press), "Family-based prevention counseling for high-risk young adolescents: Immediate outcomes." *Journal of Community Psychology*.

Hogue, A., Liddle, H. A., & Rowe, C. (1996), "Treatment adherence process research in family therapy: A rationale and some practical guidelines." *Psychotherapy 33*(2), 332–345.

Hogue, A. *et al.* (1998), "Treatment adherence and differentiation in individual versus family therapy for adolescent substance abuse." *Journal of Counseling Psychology 45*, 104–114.

Jackson-Gilfort, A., & Liddle, H. A. (in press), "Family therapy engagement and culturally relevant theme content for African-American adolescent males." *American Journal of Orthopsychiatry.*

Jackson-Gilfort, A., Liddle, H. A., Dakof, G., & Tejeda, M. (in press), "Facilitating engagement of African-American male adolescents in family therapy: A cultural theme process study." *Journal of Black Psychology*.

Jessor, R. (1993), "Successful adolescent development among youth in high risk settings." *American Psychologist 48*, 117–126.

Jessor, R., Van Den Bos, J., Vanderryn, J., Costa, F. M., & Turbin, M. S. (1995), "Protective factors in adolescent problem behavior: Moderator effects and developmental change." *Developmental Psychology 31*, 923–933.

Kandel, D., & Andrews, K. (1987), "Process of adolescent socialization by parents and peers." *International Journal of the Addictions 22*, 319–342.

Kazdin, A. E. (1986), "Comparative outcome studies of psychotherapy: Methodological issues and strategies." *Journal of Consulting and Clinical Psychology 54*(1), 95–105.

Kazdin, A. E. (1991), "Effectiveness of psychotherapy with children and adolescents." *Journal of Consulting and Clinical Psychology 59*, 785–798.

Kazdin, A. E. (1994), "Psychotherapy for children and adolescents." In A. Bergin & S. Garfield (eds), *Handbook of Psychotherapy and Behavior Change* (4th edn). New York: Wiley, 543–594.

Kazdin, A. E. (1999), "Current (lack of) status of theory in child and adolescent psychotherapy research." *Journal of Clinical Child Psychology 28*, 533–543.

Kazdin, A. E., Bass, D., Ayers, W. A., & Rodgers, A. (1990), "Empirical and clinical focus of child and adolescent psychotherapy research." *Journal of Consulting and Clinical Psychology 58*, 729–740.

Kazdin, A. E., & Kagan, J. (1994), "Models of dysfunction in the developmental psychopathology." *Clinical Psychology: Science and Practice 1*, 35–52.

Kazdin, A. E., & Weiss, J. R. (1998), "Identifying and developing empirically supported child and adolescent treatments." *Journal of Consulting and Clinical Psychology 66*, 19–36.

Kumpfer, G. P., Molgaard, V., & Spoth, R. (1996), "The Strengthening Families Program for the prevention of delinquency and drug use." In R. D. Peters & R. J. McMahon (eds), *Preventing Childhood Disorders, Substance Abuse, and Delinquency*. Thousand Oaks, CA: Sage, 241–267.

Kumpfer, K. L., & Alvarado, R. (1995), "Strengthening families to prevent drug use in multiethnic youth." In G. J. Botvin, S. Schinke & M. A. Orlandi (eds), *Drug abuse prevention with multiethnic youth*. Thousand Oaks, CA: Sage, 255–294.

Lebow, J. L., & Gurman, A. S. (1995), "Research assessing couple and family therapy." *Annual Review of Psychology 46*, 27–57.

Lerner, R. M., & Spanier, G. B. (1978), "A dynamic interactional view of child and family development." In R. M. Lerner & G. B. Spanier (eds), *Child Influences on Marital and Family Interaction: A life-span perspective*. New York: Academic Press, Inc., 1–22.

Liddle, H. A. (1982), "On the problems of eclecticism: A call for epistemologic clarification and human scale theories." *Family Process 21*, 243–250.

Liddle, H. A. (1991), "Empirical values and the culture of family therapy." *Journal of Marital and Family Therapy 17*(4), 327–348.

Liddle, H. A. (1995), "Conceptual and clinical dimensions of a multidimensional, multisystems engagement strategy in family-based adolescent treatment." *Psychotherapy 32*, 39–58.

Liddle, H. A. (1999), "Theory development in a family-based treatment for adolescent drug abuse." *Journal of Clinical Child Psychology 28*(4), 521–532.

Liddle, H. A. (2000), *Multidimensional Family Therapy Treatment (MDFT) for the Adolescent Cannabis Users. (Volume 5 of the Cannabis Youth Treatment (CYT) manual series.)* Rockville, MD: Center for Substance Abuse Treatment, Substance Abuse and Mental Health Services Administration. (http://www.samhsa.gov/csat/csat.htm).

Liddle, H. A., Becker, D., & Diamond, G. M. (1997), "Family therapy supervision." In C. Watkins (ed.), *Psychotherapy Supervision.* New York: Wiley Publishers, 400–418.

Liddle, H. A., & Dakof, G. A. (1995), "Family-based treatments for adolescent drug abuse: State of the Science." In E. Rahdert & D. Czechowicz (eds), *Adolescent Drug Abuse: Clinical assessment and therapeutic interventions.* [NIDA Research Monograph 156, NIH Publication No. 95-3908.] Rockville, MD: National Institute on Drug Abuse, 218–254.

Liddle, H. A., Dakof, G. A., & Diamond, G. (1991), "Adolescent substance abuse: Multidimensional family therapy in action." In E. Kaufman & P. Kaufman (eds), *Family Therapy of Drug and Alcohol Abuse.* Boston, MA: Allyn and Bacon, 120–171.

Liddle, H. A. *et al.* (in press), "Multidimensional family therapy for adolescent substance abuse: Results of a randomized clinical trial." *American Journal of Drug and Alcohol Abuse.*

Liddle, H.A., & Diamond, G. (1991), "Adolescent substance abusers in family therapy: The critical initial phase of treatment." *Family Dynamics of Addictions Quarterly 1*, 55–68.

Liddle, H. A. *et al.* (1992), "The adolescent module in multidimensional family therapy." In G. Lawson & A. Lawson (eds), *Family Therapy in Adolescent Drug Abusers.* Rockville, MD: Aspen, 165–186.

Liddle, H. A., & Hogue, A. (2000), "A developmental, family-based, ecological preventive intervention for antisocial behavior in high-risk adolescents." *Journal of Marital and Family Therapy 26*, 265–279.

Liddle, H. A., Rowe, C. L., Dakof, G., & Lyke, J. (1998), "Translating parenting research into clinical interventions for families of adolescents." *Clinical Child Psychology and Psychiatry 3*, 419–443.

Liddle, H. A. *et al.* (2000), "Towards a developmental family therapy: The clinical utility of adolescent development research." *Journal of Marital and Family Therapy 26*, 491–506.

Luster, T., & Okagaki, L. (1993), "Multiple influences on parenting: Ecological and life-course perspectives." In T. Luster & L. Okagaki (eds), *Parenting: An ecological perspective.* Hillsdale, NJ: Lawrence Erlbaum, 227–250.

Mann, B. J., Borduin, C. M., Henggeler, S. W., & Blaske, D. M. (1990), "An investigation of systemic conceptualizations of parent–child coalitions and symptoms change." *Journal of Consulting and Clinical Psychology 58*, 336–344.

McMahon, R. J., Slough, N. M., & Conduct Problems Prevention Research Group (1996), "Family-based intervention in the Fast Track Program." In R. D. Peters & R. J. McMahon (eds), *Preventing Childhood Disorders, Substance Abuse, and Delinquency.* Thousand Oaks, CA: Sage, 90–110.

Miklowitz, D., & Goldstein, M. (1998), *Bipolar Disorder: A family-centered treatment approach.* New York: Guilford.

Miller, G. E., & Prinz, R. J. (1990), "Enhancement of social learning family interventions for childhood conduct disorder." *Psychological Bulletin 108*, 291–307.

Minuchin, S., & Fishman, H. C. (1981), *Family Therapy Techniques*. Cambridge, MA: Harvard University Press.

Moncher, F. J., & Prinz, R. J. (1991), "Treatment fidelity in outcome studies." *Clinical Psychology Review 11,* 247–266.

National Institute on Drug Abuse (1999), "Multidimensional family therapy for adolescents." In *Principles of drug addiction treatment: A research-based guide*. Rockville, MD: NIDA, 40–41.

Newcomb, M. D. (1992), "Understanding the multidimensional nature of drug use and abuse: The role of consumption, risk factors and protective factors." In M. Glantz & R. Pickens (eds), *Vulnerability to Drug Abuse*. Washington, DC: American Psychological Association, 255–297.

Newcomb, M. D., & Bentler, P. M. (1988), *Consequences of Adolescent Drug Use: Impact on the lives of young adults*. Newbury Park, CA: Sage Publications.

Newcomb, M. D., & Bentler, P. M. (1989), "Substance use and abuse among children and teenagers." *American Psychologist 44*(2), 242–248.

Newcomb, M. D., & Felix-Ortiz, M. (1992), "Multiple protective and risk factors for drug use and abuse: Cross-sectional and prospective findings." *Journal of Personality and Social Psychology 63*(2), 280–296.

Newcomb, M. D., Maddahian, E., & Bentler, P. M. (1986), "Risk factors for drug use among adolescents: Concurrent longitudinal analysis." *American Journal of Public Health 76,* 525–531.

Nichols, M. P., & Schwartz, R. C. (1998), *Family Therapy: Concepts and methods*. Needham Heights, MA: Allyn & Bacon.

O'Donnell, J., Hawkins, J. D., & Abbott, R. D. (1995), "Predicting serious delinquency and substance use among aggressive boys." *Journal of Consulting and Clinical Psychology 63*(4), 529–537.

O'Leary, K. D. (in press), "Challenges in a 30-year program of research: Conduct disorders/ADHD, the marital discord/depression link, and partner abuse." In H. A. Liddle, D. Santisteban, D. F. Levant, & J. H. Bray (eds), *Family Psychology: Science based interventions*. Washington, DC: American Psychological Association.

Omer, H., & Dar, R. (1992), "Changing trends in three decades of psychotherapy research: The flight from theory into pragmatics." *Journal of Consulting and Clinical Psychology 60*(1), 88–93.

Ozechowski, T. J., & Liddle, H. A. (2000), "Family-based therapy for adolescent drug abuse: Knowns and unknowns." *Clinical Child and Family Psychology Review 3*(4), 269–298.

Pardeck, J. A., & Pardeck, J. T. (1990), "Family factors related to adolescent autonomy." *Adolescence 25,* 311–319.

Patterson, G. R., Reid, J. B., & Dishion, T. J. (1992), *A Social-Interactional Approach, Vol. 4: Antisocial boys*. Eugene, OR: Castalia.

Patterson, G. R., & Stouthamer-Loeber, M. (1984), "The correlation of family management practices and delinquency." *Child Development 55,* 1299–1307.

Persons, J. B. (1991), "Psychotherapy outcome studies do not accurately represent current models of psychotherapy: A proposed remedy." *American Psychologist 46,* 99–106.

Petraitis, J., Flay, B. R., & Miller, T. Q. (1995), "Reviewing theories of adolescent substance use: Organizing pieces in the puzzle." *Psychological Bulletin 117*(1), 67–86.

Pickens, R. W., & Svikis, D. S. (1991), "Prevention of drug abuse: Targeting risk factors." In L. Donohew, & H. E. Sypher (eds), *Persuasive Communication and Drug Abuse Prevention. Communication*. Hillsdale, NJ: Lawrence Erlbaum, 35–49.

Pompi, K. F. (1994), "Adolescents in therapeutic communities: Retention and posttreatment outcome." In F. M. Tims, G. De Leon & N. Jainchill (eds), *Therapeutic Community: Advances in research and application* (NIDA Research Monograph edn). Rockville, MD: National Institute on Drug Abuse, Vol. 144, 128–161.

Prinz, R. J., & Miller, G. E. (1991), "Issues in understanding and treating childhood conduct problems in disadvantaged populations." *Journal of Clinical Child Psychology 20*, 379–385.

Prinz, R. J., & Miller, G. E. (1996), "Parental engagement in interventions for children at risk for conduct disorder." In R. D. Peters & R. J. McMahon (eds), *Preventing Childhood Disorders, Substance Abuse, and Delinquency*. Thousand Oaks, CA: Sage, 161–183.

Reid, J. B. (1993), "Prevention of conduct disorder before and after school entry: Relating interventions to developmental findings." *Development and Psychopathology 5*, 243–262.

Resnick, M. D. *et al.* (1997), "Protecting adolescents from harm: Findings from the National Longitudinal Study on Adolescent Health." *Journal of the American Medical Association 278*(10), 823–831.

Robbins, M. S., Alexander, J. F., Newell, R., & Turner, C. W. (1996), "The immediate effect of reframing on client attitude in family therapy." *Journal of Family Psychology 10*(1), 28–34.

Robinson, N. S., & Garber, J. (1995), "Social support and psychopathology across the lifespan." In D. Cicchetti & D. J. Cohen (eds), *Developmental Ppsychopathology, Vol. 2: Risk, disorder, and adaptation*. New York: Wiley, 162–209.

Rowe, C. L., Liddle, H. A., & Dakof, G. A. (in press), "Classifying adolescent substance abusers by level of externalizing and internalizing symptoms." *American Journal of Child and Adolescent Psychiatry*.

Rutter, M. (1987), "Psychosocial resilience and protective mechanisms." *American Journal of Orthopsychiatry 57*, 316–331.

Sameroff, A. J. (1975), "Early influences on development: Fact or fancy?" *Merrill Palmer Quarterly 21*, 267–294.

Schmidt, S., Liddle, H. A., & Dakof, G. A. (1996), "Multidimensional family therapy: Parenting practices and symptom reduction in adolescent drug abuse." *Journal of Family Psychology 10*, 12–27.

Sechrest, L. (1994), "Recipes for psychotherapy." *Journal of Consulting and Clinical Psychology 62*, 952–954.

Selekman, M. D., & Todd, T. C. (1991), "Major issues from family therapy research and theory: Implications for the future." In T. Todd & M. Selekman (eds), *Family Therapy with Adolescent Substance Abusers*. Boston, MA: Allyn and Bacon, 311–325.

Seligman, M. E. P. (1996), "The effectiveness of psychotherapy: The Consumer Reports study." *American Psychologist 50*, 965–974.

Shilts, L. (1991), "The relationship of early adolescent substance use to extracurricular activities, peer influence, and personal attitudes." *Adolescence 26*, 613–617.

Shoham-Salomon, V. (1990), "Interrelating research processes of process research." *Journal of Consulting and Clinical Psychology 58*, 295–303.

Spoth, R., Redmond, C., & Shin, C. (1998), "Direct and indirect latent-variable parenting outcomes of two universal family-focused preventive interventions: Extending a public health-oriented research base." *Journal of Consulting and Clinical Psychology 66*, 385–399.

Sroufe, L. A., & Rutter, M. (1984), "The domain of developmental psychopathology." *Child Development 55*, 17–29.

Stanton, M. D., & Shadish, W. R. (1997), "Outcome, attrition, and family-couples treatment for drug abuse: A meta-analysis and review of the controlled, comparative studies." *Psychological Bulletin 122*(2), 170–191.

Steinberg, L. (1990), "Autonomy, conflict, and harmony in the family relationship." In S. S. Feldman & G. R. Elliott (eds), *At the Threshold — The developing adolescent*. Cambridge, MA: Harvard University Press, 255–276.

Steinberg, L. (1991), "Adolescent transitions and alcohol and other drug use prevention." In E. N. Goplerud (ed.), *Preventing Adolescent Drug Use: From theory to practice*. OSAP Prevention Monograph-8. Rockville, MD: DHHS.

Steinberg, L., Elmen, J. D., & Mounts, N. S. (1989), "Authoritative parenting, psychosocial maturity, and academic success among adolescents." *Child Development 60*, 1424–1436.

Steinberg, L., Fletcher, A., & Darling, N. (1994), "Parental monitoring and peer influences on adolescent substance use." *Pediatrics 93*, 1060–1064.

Stewart, D. G., & Brown, S. A. (1994, August), "Antisocial behavior and long-term outcome of adolescent substance abuse treatment." In S. A. Brown (chair), "Long-term outcome among adolescents following alcohol and drug treatment." Symposium presented at the annual convention of the American Psychological Association, Los Angeles.

Szapocznik, J., Perez-Vidal, A., Hervis, O. E., Brickman, A. L., & Kurtines, W. M. (1989), "Innovations in family therapy: Strategies for overcoming resistance to treatment." In R. A. Wells & V. J. Giannetti (eds.), *Handbook of Brief Psycho-therapies*. New York, NY: Plenum Press, 93–114.

Task Force on Promotion and Dissemination of Psychological Procedures, Division of Clinical Psychology, American Psychological Association (1995), "Training in and dissemination of empirically-validated psychological treatments: Report and recommendations." *The Clinical Psychologist 48*, 3–23.

Taylor, T., Adelman, H. S., & Kaser-Boyd, N. (1985), "Exploring minors' reluctance and dissatisfaction with psychotherapy." *Professional Psychology: Research and Practice 16*(3), 418–425.

Tolan, P. H. (1996), "Characteristics shared by exemplary child clinical interventions for indicated populations." In M. C. Roberts (ed.), *Model Programs in Child and Family Mental Health*. Hillsdale, NJ: Lawrence Erlbaum, 91–108.

Tolan, P. H., Guerra, N., & Kendall, P. C. (1995), "A developmental–ecological perspective on antisocial behavior in children and adolescents: Toward a unified risk and intervention framework." *Journal of Consulting and Clinical Psychology 63*(4), 579–584.

Tolan, P. H., & McKay, M. M. (1996), "Preventing serious antisocial behavior in inner-city children." *Family Relations 45*, 148–155.

Turner, R. M. (1992), "Launching cognitive-behavioral therapy for adolescent depression & drug abuse." In S. Budman, M. Hoyt & S. Friedman (eds), *Casebook of Brief Therapy*. New York: Guilford Press, 135–156.

Turner, R. M. (1993), "Dynamic cognitive-behavioral therapy." In T. Giles (ed.), *Handbook of Effective Psychotherapy*. New York: Plenum Press, 437–454.

Volk, R. J., Edwards, D. W., Lewis, R. A., Sprenkle, D. H., Piercy, F. P. (1989), "Family systems of adolescent substance abusers." *Family Relations 38*, 266–272.

Waldron, H. B. (1997), "Adolescent substance abuse and family therapy outcome: A review of randomized trials." In T. H. Ollendick & R. J. Prinz (eds), *Advances in Clinical Child Psychology*. New York: Plenum Press, Vol. 19, 199–234.

Waltz, J., Addis, M. E., Koerner, K., & Jacobson, N. S. (1993), "Testing the integrity of a psychotherapy protocol: Assessment of adherence and competence." *Journal of Consulting and Clinical Psychology 61*, 620–630.

Webster-Stratton, C., & Herbert, M. (1993), "What really happens in parent training?" *Behavior Modification 17*, 407–456.

Weinberg, N. Z., Rahdert, E., Colliver, J. D., & Glantz, M. D. (1998), "Adolescent substance abuse: A review of the past 10 years." *Journal of American Child Adolescent Psychiatry 37*(3), 252–261.

Weiss, J. R., Weisz, B., Alicke, M. D., & Klotz, M. L. (1987), "Effectiveness of psychotherapy with children and adolescents: A meta-analysis for clinicians." *Journal of Consulting and Clinical Psychology 55*, 542–549.

Weiss, J. R., Weisz, B., Han, S. S., Granger, D. A., & Morton, T. (1995), "Effects of psychotherapy with children and adolescents revisited: A meta-analysis of treatment outcome studies." *Psychological Bulletin 117*, 450–468.

Williams, R. J., & Chang, S. Y. (2000), "A comprehensive and comparative review of adolescent substance abuse treatment outcome." *Clinical Psychology: Science and Practice 7*(2), 138–166.

Wills, T. A. (1990), "Multiple networks and substance use." *Journal of Social and Clinical Psychology 9*(1), 78–90.

Winters, K. C., Latimer, W. L., & Stinchfield, R. D. (1999), "Adolescent treatment for alcohol and other drug abuse." In T. Tarter, R. T. Ammerman & P. J. Ott (eds), *Sourcebook on Substance Abuse: Etiology, methodology, and intervention*. New York: Allyn and Bacon, 350–361.

Yeaton, W. H., & Sechrest, L. (1981), "Critical dimensions in the choice and maintenance of successful treatments: Strength, integrity, and effectiveness." *Journal of Consulting and Clinical Psychology 49*, 156–167.

Chapter 12

Cigarette Smoking Treatment for Substance-Abusing Adolescents

Mark G. Myers*

Theoretical Background and Rationale

Over the past 25 years there have been substantial declines in the overall prevalence of cigarette smoking in the United States. However, youth smoking rates have been increasing since 1992 (National Institute on Drug Abuse, 1996). The substantial persistence of adolescent smoking into adulthood (Johnston, O'Malley & Bachman, 1992; Pierce & Gilpin, 1996) suggests that many of today's adolescent smokers are at risk for a variety of cigarette-related health problems. Research on smoking among substance-abusing youth reveals that this a particularly heavy smoking group, that their cigarette use persists into early adulthood, and that smoking-related health problems appear during adolescence (Myers & Brown, 1994, 1997). Nevertheless, relatively few intervention and research efforts have targeted smoking cessation among youth in general, with even less known regarding smoking treatment for substance-abusing adolescents (Henningfield, Michaelides & Sussmann, 2000; Wagner, 2000). Although a substantial body of research exists regarding smoking cessation for adults, studies on adolescent samples are sparse. Furthermore, the few published reports on adolescent smoking cessation report little or no success in effecting cessation (cf. Sussman, Lichtman, Ritt & Pallonen, in press).

Because of the dearth of specific empirical evidence, various sources and issues were considered in the design of this smoking cessation intervention for substance-abusing adolescents: (a) naturalistic studies describing youth smoking cessation efforts; (b) adolescent development; (c) motivation for behavior change; (d) strategies from the adult smoking cessation literature; and (e) considerations specific to substance-abusing adolescents.

Intervention design was based on a biobehavioral model, within which addiction is viewed as a process involving both biological (e.g., physical dependence, pharmacological

The preparation of this chapter was supported by grants from the National Institute on Alcohol Abuse and Alcoholism and from the University of California Tobacco Related Disease Research Program.

*Correspondence regarding this chapter should be addressed to Mark Myers, Ph.D., University of California, San Diego, Veterans Affairs San Diego Healthcare System Psychology 116B, V.A. Medical Center, 3350 La Jolla Village Dr., San Diego, CA 92161, (619) 552-8585 x3436, electronic mail may be sent to mgmyers@ucsd.edu.

Innovations in Adolescent Substance Abuse Interventions, pages 263–283.
Copyright © 2001 by Elsevier Science Ltd.
ISBN: 0-08-043577-7

reinforcement) and social–behavioral factors (environmental influences, learning history, cognitions and attitudes, etc.) (Donovan, 1988). An emerging literature suggests important differences between adolescents and adults in the process of addiction across a wide range of substances including nicotine (Brown, Vik & Creamer, 1989; Kassel, 2000; Myers & Brown, 1996). These findings indicate the importance of developmental considerations and adolescent-specific risk factors in the design of adolescent addiction research and treatment. A modified biobehavioral model of addiction forms the conceptual basis of the current smoking which employs cognitive and behavioral strategies to address both biological (e.g., nicotine dependence) and psychosocial factors (e.g., peer influences). As such, the intervention described below centers on identifying the role of cigarette use in the life of the adolescent, and provides strategies and techniques by which to reduce nicotine dependence and alter smoking behaviors.

Correlates and Predictors of Adolescent Smoking Cessation

A large literature exists on the etiology of cigarette smoking, and findings to date suggest that factors influencing smoking initiation differ from those related to smoking cessation (Ary & Biglan, 1988; Leventhal & Cleary, 1980). Studies consistently find that many adolescents desire to stop smoking (Karle et al., 1994; Sargent, Mott & Stevens, 1998), frequently self-initiate smoking cessation attempts (Ershler, Leventhal, Fleming & Glynn, 1989; McNeill, West, Jarvis, Jackson & Bryant, 1986), yet generally fail to maintain abstinence (Ershler et al., 1989; Hansen, 1983). Correlates of adolescent smoking cessation and relapse identified in naturalistic studies are valuable as indicators of factors to assess and modify during treatment. A review of existing research on adolescent smoking cessation provides information on the roles of nicotine dependence (Ary & Biglan, 1988; Hansen, 1983), psychosocial factors (e.g., peer influences [Chassin, Presson & Sherman, 1984; Ershler et al., 1989]), and smoking-related attitudes and cognitions (Chassin, Presson & Sherman, 1984; Hansen, Collins, Johnson & Graham, 1985) in adolescent smoking cessation.

Developmental Considerations

A critical issue when working with adolescent smokers is that of peer group influence, an integral part of adolescent development. Adolescent smokers, even those with substance use problems, consume cigarettes at rates that are significantly lower than typical for adult smokers (often ten cigarettes or fewer per day; Myers & Brown, 1994). Although it is important to address the physical dependence on tobacco, peer issues may be equally important. The role of peers in adolescent smoking is best understood within the context of adolescent social identity (Eiser & van der Pligt, 1985; Leventhal, Keeshan, Baker & Wetter, 1991). In particular, cigarettes provide adolescents a means for meeting and interacting with others, and thus play a role in the process of developing an independent identity. Because smoking is normative among substance-abusing adolescents, attitudes regarding the social-identity role of cigarettes and skills for refusing temptations to smoke may prove to represent critical factors in the process of smoking cessation for these youth.

Motivation for Behavior Change

Motivation has been identified as a critical influence in changing addictive behaviors (e.g., Miller & Rollnick, 1991; Prochaska, DiClemente & Norcross, 1992). Motivational issues may be especially important for adolescent smokers, as suggested by the difficulty in engaging adolescents in smoking cessation efforts (e.g., Peltier, Telch & Coates, 1982). Adolescents may be less motivated to change their smoking behavior because they typically will have experienced fewer negative consequences from smoking than adult smokers (Flay, 1993). Substance-abusing teens are particularly likely to perceive cigarette smoking as normative since they tend to be exposed to high levels of smoking in their environment (e.g., associating with other abusers or with youth in recovery). Motivation enhancement techniques are therefore likely to be particularly important when intervening with substance-abusing teens, especially for those who have little initial desire to change their smoking behavior. Thus, identifying obstacles to initial participation and including techniques to enhance and maintain motivation for change are important components of a smoking cessation intervention for this population.

Adult Smoking Cessation Strategies

The adult smoking cessation literature is a valuable source for identifying potential techniques to be incorporated as part of smoking cessation treatment for substance-abusing adolescents. The efficacy of behavioral smoking cessation interventions for adults is supported by a substantial research literature (Baillie, Mattick, Hall & Webster, 1994). Adult smoking cessation treatment typically includes components focused on reducing nicotine dependence, behavioral habit control techniques, and relapse prevention strategies (Brown & Emmons, 1991). At this time, it is not known which particular components are the efficacious ingredients in multicomponent smoking cessation programs (Hajek, 1994). Therefore, it appears appropriate to incorporate multiple components at this early stage of treatment development for substance-abusing adolescent smokers.

The value of employing nicotine reduction techniques (e.g., gradual reduction in cigarette consumption) or nicotine replacement is consonant with evidence that greater tobacco involvement predicts teen smoking persistence (e.g., Ary & Biglan, 1988; Ershler *et al.*, 1989; Hansen, 1983). Compared to adult smokers, adolescents have a relatively brief history of tobacco use, generally smoke fewer cigarettes per day, and as a result may be less physically dependent on nicotine (Kassel, 2000). However, existing research finds that adolescents do experience physical withdrawals when attempting cessation (e.g., Ershler *et al.*, 1989), suggesting the utility of nicotine reduction and/or replacement strategies (Patten, 2000).

Youth smoke in a variety of places and situations (e.g., at home, watching TV, talking with friends) (Biglan, McConnell, Severson, Bavry & Ary, 1984), suggesting that adolescents may benefit from behavioral stimulus control strategies aimed at breaking associations between certain situations/events and cigarette smoking. Techniques for managing and controlling urges or cravings are also likely to be important in the process of adolescent smoking cessation. Moreover, the high rates of adolescent relapse following smoking cessation attempts (Ershler *et al.*, 1989; Hansen, 1983; Sussman *et al.*, 1999) indicate a need for relapse prevention techniques.

Substance Abuse Issues

Concerns regarding possible detrimental effects of quitting smoking on recovery from alcohol and other drug use problems represent a potential obstacle to smoking cessation treatment for substance abusers (Bobo & Gilchrist, 1983; Bobo, Gilchrist, Schilling, Noach & Schinke, 1987). Studies investigating smoking cessation among drug and alcohol abusers have found no influence of cessation efforts on relapse to alcohol and drug use (Hughes, 1993; Martin *et al.*, 1997; Sees & Clark, 1993). In fact, several studies have found that successful quitters have very low rates of alcohol and drug relapse (Bobo *et al.*, 1987; Martin *et al.*, 1997). Furthermore, one study found that persistent smoking following treatment for adolescent substance abuse is associated with higher levels of subsequent alcohol and drug involvement (Myers & Brown, 1997). Taken together, these results imply that cigarette smoking cessation does not have a deleterious effect on alcohol and other drug use abstinence. However, it is important for clinicians to be aware of such concerns and address them directly if they arise.

Description of the Intervention

Assessment

A biobehavioral view of addictive behaviors requires a broad-based assessment (Donovan, 1988), and cigarette smoking should similarly be viewed as occurring in a broad context. The primary goals of assessment are to gain an understanding of the factors that maintain the smoking behavior (nicotine dependence, social cues, and mood management) and identify obstacles to behavior change. Domains to be evaluated include nicotine dependence, smoking-related cues, the various contexts in which smoking occurs, cognitions regarding the anticipated effects from smoking, and perceived positive and negative consequences of smoking. While an ideal assessment incorporates multiple sources of data, the limitations of clinical practice typically dictate reliance on adolescent reports. Adolescent self-report of smoking behaviors is typically reliable (Barnea, Rahav & Teichman, 1987) and can be supplemented by self-monitoring data and biochemical verification when feasible.

Assessment of cigarette smoking can be accomplished relatively briefly, and serves to provide baseline information for monitoring progress, and to enhance motivation for engaging in behavior change (Miller & Rollnick, 1991). Because of the range of cigarette involvement observed among youth, information regarding history of smoking and current smoking pattern is useful for assessing the stage of tobacco use development for each teen. Smoking-specific data that should be collected include: age at which first smoked a cigarette; age when regular (weekly) smoking began; age of daily smoking onset; number of previous cessation efforts; and length of abstinence during previous cessation attempts. A careful assessment of cigarette-smoking pattern (e.g., self-monitoring for one week) is particularly important for adolescents because of the variability typically observed in daily cigarette use during the course of a week.

It should be noted that few measures of tobacco use and smoking have been subjected to psychometric evaluation for adolescents. Moreover, since no established treatment guidelines exist for teen smoking cessation, diagnostic assessment of nicotine dependence may be of limited utility with adolescents. However, because the extent of tobacco involvement is a predictor of successful cessation in naturalistic studies (Sussman, Lichtman, Pitt & Pallonen, in press), assessment of adolescent nicotine dependence in a continuous fashion is recommended. Although limited psychometric data are available for adolescent smokers, preliminary evidence exists for the utility of an adolescent-specific revision of the Fagerstrom Tolerance Questionnaire (see Prokhorov, Pallonen, Fava, Lin & Niaura, 1996). This instrument is a brief self-report questionnaire (seven items) that provides dependence scores ranging from 0 to 9.

Treatment Overview

The program described below was designed for adolescents receiving treatment for alcohol and other drug abuse. However, this comprehensive intervention can be employed independently from substance abuse treatment. Based on previous experience, the intervention is best delivered in a group modality; however, content can be adapted for individual treatment.

Session Structure

Sessions begin with review and discussion of previous material and practice activities; new material is introduced; new skills and techniques are practiced; practice activities are selected. Key points are written on a blackboard or dry erase board as each session progresses.

Because adolescence is characterized by efforts to establish independence and autonomy, it is important to solicit feedback from group members regarding the perceived helpfulness and relevance of material discussed in session. Comprehension of session content and adherence to practice activities must be assessed in order to anticipate and identify barriers to compliance. A collaborative approach is important so as to reduce resistance and assist in matching the intervention to the ability and motivation of each participant.

Prior to the introduction of a new topic a rationale that conforms to the biobehavioral framework of the intervention is discussed. In order to enhance comprehension and acceptance of each topic, examples relevant to each adolescent's own experience are elicited and/

or provided. Handouts that outline each topic area and provide detailed and specific examples can help reinforce intervention content and facilitate practice activities.

Behavior modification and skill enhancement activities assist in facilitating cigarette use reduction and provide an opportunity for rehearsing skills for maintaining gains. Adolescent input is important in deciding the details and extent of the practice activity assignments. In order to minimize problems with compliance, it is best to limit the quantity of practice activities since these may be perceived as school-like. It is especially important to select activities that will be successfully completed so as to enhance self-efficacy.

Session Content

The intervention consists of six primary topic areas, each of which roughly corresponds with a single session (in our study, the treatment consists of six sessions). However, the amount of time devoted to any particular topic should be determined by the needs, abilities, and motivation level of the adolescent participants.

Introduction and Treatment Philosophy

At the outset of treatment, the rationale and philosophy of the intervention is discussed with group members. It is emphasized that participation does not *mandate* smoking cessation. Rather, the group is designed to explore each adolescent's experiences and thoughts regarding cigarette use, to provide information regarding nicotine addiction and cigarette smoking, and each participant is responsible for setting his or her own goals for behavior change. This introduction is intended to reduce resistance and facilitate engagement in treatment. Next, members are invited to share their own experiences with cigarette use. This discussion is initiated by asking each adolescent to describe their first experience with cigarettes (What was going on? Why did you try it the first time?) and their impressions of that experience (How was it? What did you like or dislike about it?). Participants are invited to describe the progression of their cigarette use (How long was it until you were smoking regularly/weekly and then daily?). Finally, group members are asked to share previous attempts at smoking cessation (Have you tried to quit before? How many times? How did you go about it? What was it like for you? What caused you to go back to smoking?). After group members have described their experiences, the clinician summarizes the responses, pointing out similarities and differences among individuals. Information from this discussion is useful for understanding individual experiences of group members and provides useful material for future sessions.

Topic 1: Motivational Enhancement and Goal Setting

Once the introductory discussion has been concluded, the session shifts to examination of individual positive and negative consequences of smoking. The goal is to enhance motivation for behavior change by generating ambivalence regarding cigarette use. This topic is introduced by stating that group members must be getting benefits from cigarette use and asking them to generate positive aspects of the behavior (which are listed on the board). The object of this exercise is to generate a comprehensive list of reinforcers. After listing positive aspects, participants are next asked to describe aspects of cigarette use that they do not enjoy. Identifying negative aspects of use is helpful in increasing motivation for change by generating ambivalence about smoking. Domains of negative aspects of smoking include health, financial issues, social sanction, and addiction. Specific and personal examples are generated for each domain (e.g., specific health concerns such as: "It's harder for me to breathe", "I have asthma"). Negative consequences that are personal and real are more likely to be effective in generating ambivalence in contrast to global statements such as "It's bad for me." After a complete list has been generated, participants are asked to identify which negative consequences are seen as most bothersome or undesirable.

After reviewing adolescent-generated benefits and costs of cigarette use, information is provided regarding youth cigarette use through a series of questions designed to highlight negatives or common misperceptions:

1. For how long do you expect to keep smoking/when do you think you might quit?
After participants have responded, research-based information is provided from studies on the persistence of smoking: e.g., the median age at cessation for those who begin smoking during adolescence (Pierce & Gilpin, 1996); 80 percent of adolescents receiving substance abuse treatment persist in smoking four years following treatment, and the continuing smokers are more likely to be abusing alcohol and drugs than those who have stopped smoking (Myers & Brown, 1997).

2. What proportion of students at your school smoke cigarettes?
Age and gender-appropriate normative information regarding smoking rates is provided as a contrast to the overestimates of peer smoking typically generated by adolescents who smoke (this information can be derived from national surveys, e.g., National Institute on Drug Abuse, 1996, although it is better to provide local data if available). If they come to perceive their use as significantly above that of their peers, they may be more likely to consider reducing or ending their use of cigarettes.

3. How much do you think it costs the tobacco companies to produce a pack of cigarettes?
Estimates provided by the American Cancer Society suggest it costs approximately six cents to produce a pack of cigarettes (not considering advertising costs, etc.). Participants are invited to comment on the discrepancy between cost to the companies and cost to them.

Goal Setting

Participants are asked to select their goals for treatment. Personal responsibility is emphasized ("What you get out of this group is up to you"). A range of possible goals is provided, with participation in group sessions and learning about cigarette use and cessation techniques at one end of the spectrum, and smoking cessation at the other end. Each adolescent is asked to specify their goal in a contract which is signed by the adolescent and clinician.

Suggested practice activities. Before the end of the first session, participants are asked if they are interested in learning more about their own cigarette use. Self-monitoring is suggested as an activity for accomplishing this. Adolescents are instructed to monitor smoking with "wrap sheets," which are small monitoring forms that fit around or inside a pack of cigarettes on which adolescents note the time of day before they light a cigarette ("Write before you light").

Topic 2: Nicotine

This topic is introduced by inviting participants to share their views on nicotine as an addictive drug. Group members are asked whether they perceive nicotine as an addictive drug, and if so, why? Participants also are asked to define "addiction" and describe why nicotine does or does not fit that definition. Comparisons are elicited between nicotine and other drugs of abuse familiar to the adolescents. Discussion focuses on factors common to addictive substances: reinforcing effects; tolerance and withdrawal; and the difficulty of cessation (relapse).

The drug effects of nicotine are discussed. For example: "Nicotine is considered a drug because of its effects: nicotine acts as a stimulant and can make people feel more awake or alert. Smokers describe positive effects including feelings of pleasure, and reduced anxiety and tension." When discussing the reinforcing effects of nicotine, examples previously generated by group members should be used. The broad range of nicotine effects is discussed, noting that although it is primarily a stimulant drug, nicotine is often used to manage stress and anxiety, and some believe it helps feelings such as depression and boredom. The point is that one drug, nicotine, can have many different effects.

The concepts of tolerance and withdrawal are discussed next. Because substance-abusing teens have extensive experience with alcohol and other drugs, they are asked to share their understanding of these concepts. Tolerance is defined as "the body getting used to a substance so that more is needed to get the same effect." After providing a definition, group members are asked whether they have experienced tolerance. An effective example of tolerance is to contrast the physical effects experienced when they first smoked a cigarette (typically dizziness and/or nausea), with current effects from smoking. The primary point is that as use increases, more nicotine is needed to get the same effects.

When discussing withdrawal effects, participants are asked to describe what happens after long periods (at least several hours) without smoking (e.g., during previous cessation attempts, when in smoke-free environments for an extended time, etc.). A list of withdrawal effects that has relevance to the participants then can be generated. Typical nicotine withdrawal effects include strong urges or cravings, fatigue, difficulty concentrating, and irritability or anxiety. After the discussion of tolerance and withdrawal, it is useful to inform group members that research studies show that people, without realizing it, seem to regulate their smoking to keep a certain level of nicotine in the body. This can help adolescent smokers better understand the physiological processes that may undermine attempts to quit smoking.

Relapse following smoking cessation attempts is then reviewed. Discussion of relapse begins with group members sharing their experiences with cessation attempts. Participant opinions can be elicited as to whether it is more or less difficult to quit smoking than to stop using alcohol or other drugs. A useful illustration of the difficulty of smoking cessation is to compare rates of alcohol and drug relapse with smoking relapse following treatment. Rates are compared by drawing on the board a relapse curve for alcohol, then asking group members to estimate what the relapse curve for a drug such as heroin looks like, drawing that curve, and then asking the adolescents to guess where the smoking cessation relapse curve falls (in reality, each curve is very similar, Hunt, Barnett & Branch, 1971). This exercise helps adolescents understand similarities in the addictive process across seemingly different drugs.

The topic is summarized by reiterating the notion that the drug effects of nicotine play an important role in maintaining cigarette smoking and make it difficult to stop.

Reducing Nicotine Intake

The rationale for reducing nicotine intake is that cutting down on nicotine use *before* quitting smoking can make cessation easier by reducing withdrawal and cravings: "The less dependent one is on nicotine, the easier it is to stop smoking." The methods described below are introduced in the context of reducing nicotine intake, but also serve other functions in the process of smoking cessation. For example, each strategy includes behavioral components which facilitate the process of behavior change (e.g., changing brands can alter stimulus characteristics of the behavior; smoking on a fixed schedule can serve to break conditioned cues and provides practice with managing urges). In addition, providing several options gives participants a choice of strategies. Finally, success with these relatively simple strategies can serve to increase momentum and motivation for change.

The methods for reducing nicotine intake before attempting cessation are introduced, explained, and adolescents are given written materials outlining the procedures.

Brand Fading

The rationale for brand fading (Prue, Krapfl & Martin, 1981) rests on the idea that switching to lower nicotine content brands will help the adolescent get used to taking in less of the drug. The idea is that those who employ this technique will be less dependent on nicotine at the time of cessation since they will be smoking a very low nicotine-yield cigarette.

Instructions for brand changing:

A. (1) A switch to a new brand of cigarettes is done each week or two.
   (2) Decrease nicotine content by about 0.2–0.3 mg. at each switch (the Federal Trade Commission publishes a list of nicotine content for popular brands).

B. Brand changing is most successful when these rules are followed closely.
    (1) If you don't like the first brand you smoke, try one of the other brands in the selected range of nicotine content.
    (2) Each brand change should be considered a "clean break." Don't smoke any of your old cigarettes after you switch to a new brand. Finish all your old brand of cigarettes, and then make the brand change. Don't smoke higher nicotine cigarettes offered to you by friends.
    (3) Commit yourself to smoking your new brand. Once you decide on a brand to smoke, if you can, buy the number of packs needed to last you for a week. By buying the right number of cigarettes you won't run out of your new brand.
    (4) Give yourself time to adjust to your new brand. Your body will usually take a few days to adjust to the lower nicotine level. It will adjust after three or four days — just give it time.

Decreasing the Number of Cigarettes Smoked

The goal of this strategy is to gradually reduce the number of cigarettes smoked. A 15–20 percent reduction is usually recommended over a one-week period. The idea is to eliminate "less important" cigarettes rather than "favorite" cigarettes. It is often helpful to count out a daily cigarette supply at the beginning of each day, and carry that number in the pack. This strategy makes it easier to adhere to the limit and may reduce the temptation to smoke more. Self-monitoring using "wrap sheets" also helps keep track of the number of cigarettes consumed.

Smoking on a Fixed Interval

This technique involves setting a minimum interval between successive cigarettes (Cinciripini, Welter, & McClure, 1997). The initial interval is determined based on the average number of cigarettes smoked daily. For example, an adolescent who smokes ten cigarettes per day can begin on a 45-minute schedule.

Instructions for smoking on a fixed interval:

1. Start out smoking once every 45 minutes (where you wait 45 minutes between each cigarette you smoke).
2. Try to smoke only one cigarette each time.
3. Increase the time between cigarettes by 15 minutes after a few days when you're comfortable with the schedule. Increase the time between cigarettes *when you feel ready to do so.*
4. This method will work only if you stick to the schedule. It's OK to go longer without smoking, but don't smoke more often than your schedule.
5. If you slip, go back to the schedule, or drop back to a more frequent schedule but don't go back to smoking whenever you want!

Suggested practice activity. Ask participants whether they would like to try one of the reduction techniques, and have each select a strategy to pursue. For those who select cigarette reduction, review daily smoking pattern and decide which cigarette(s) to eliminate. For brand fading, a readily available brand should be selected; also determine that the teen will be able to acquire the chosen cigarettes. For smoking on an interval, the starting schedule should match current smoking pattern.

Topic 3: Smoking is a Learned Habit

A discussion of reasons for smoking other than the drug effects of nicotine serves as an introduction to the idea of smoking as a learned habit. Group members generate a list of all the different smoking situations they have experienced. This list is used to illustrate that smoking is a powerful habit, a behavior that is repeated frequently in similar situations so that it becomes virtually automatic. A useful example for demonstrating the frequency of this behavior is to estimate the number of puffs taken over the course of a year: the average number of puffs or drags on a cigarette (ten) is multiplied by average cigarettes per day and then by the number of days in the year. The resulting number serves to emphasize the high frequency of smoking behavior.

Next, the concept of triggers is discussed. Broadly defined, a trigger is something that increases the likelihood of smoking: any event, person, place or thing that is associated with smoking (the previously generated list of smoking situations serves as a list of triggers). A simplified behavior chain is helpful for illustrating this concept: Triggers lead to urges, and urges then lead to the behavior of smoking (see Figure 1). The behavior chain is used to convey the following points: (1) triggers are learned through repeated association with smoking; (2) triggers are one of the reasons that it is difficult to stop smoking — they serve as reminders to smoke; and (3) just as triggers are learned over time, they can be unlearned. The behavior chain is an important tool for demonstrating methods for "unlearning" the smoking habit.

Breaking Triggers (Stimulus Control)

The initial method discussed for changing the association between triggers and smoking is the strategy of stimulus control, or limiting smoking to fewer situations. The rationale for this strategy derives from the behavior chain: avoiding smoking in response to a trigger will lead to weakening and then breaking the association. The "smoking place" is a strategy for unlearning triggers: a single location is selected for smoking, thereby reducing associations with the regular triggers. The "smoking place" strategy is usually implemented at home with adolescents, and later implemented at school or work if applicable and feasible.

Figure 1: Behavior chain for smoking.

Instructions for choosing a "smoking place":

1. Pick a place at home where you *usually don't* smoke.
2. Pick a place where you don't usually do other things like socialize, talk on the phone, eat, watch TV, read mail, etc.
3. This should be a place where the *only thing* you'll do there is smoke. The idea is that you won't associate smoking in this place with any other kind of activity or situation, so don't pick your favorite place in the house.
4. Don't pick a place that's so uncomfortable that you'll end up smoking in other places.
5. If you forget and smoke somewhere else, go to your smoking place or put the cigarette out until you can go to your designated smoking place.

Suggested practice activity. Determine which group members would like to select a smoking place, and have each identify a specific location at home that will be their "smoking place." The criteria for selecting a smoking place are reviewed with an emphasis on the importance of not engaging in other behaviors (i.e., no socializing, etc.) while smoking there.

Topic 4: Managing Urges

Strategies for managing or controlling urges are introduced by reviewing the behavior chain and discussing the "urge" link. The rationale for urge control centers on the notion that *not* smoking in response to an urge or craving weakens the association between trigger and smoking behavior, thus leading to "unlearning" the smoking habit. To illustrate this point, participants are engaged in a discussion regarding their experiences with urges and cravings for use of alcohol or other drugs. How do you get through urges? How long do urges last? Are the urges different now than when you first stopped using? Participant responses during this discussion are used to illustrate that: (1) urges tend to come and go: smoking urges typically last 10–15 minutes before they weaken; (2) urges become less frequent and less powerful over time as a result of breaking the association; and, (3) group members have been successful managing urges for alcohol and other drug use.

Discussion continues with reviewing strategies for coping with urges. Group members are invited to share strategies used for combating alcohol and drug urges and to comment on whether these would help with smoking urges (adolescents often feel cigarette urges are more difficult because smoking is common in their environment). Urge control strategies ("DEADS" — Martin, 1994) are introduced and discussed:

- D   Delay
- E   Escape
- A   Avoid
- D   Distract
- S   Substitute

Delay. The simplest strategy for managing an urge is to wait it out. Urges fade after ten to 15 minutes, even without smoking. It helps to have a positive attitude about the urge disappearing: thoughts such as "This won't last, the urge will go away," or "I would like a cigarette, but I'm not going to have one, because I don't need one" can help. The most important thing to remember is that an urge will go away with time.

Escape. Another technique for dealing with an urge is to leave or escape the trigger that led to the urge. An example is getting up and leaving a place where others are smoking.

Avoid. Some situations that lead to a temptation for smoking can be avoided. For example, places where people frequently smoke, such as coffee shops, are best avoided when trying to cut down or quit smoking. This strategy is especially important in the initial days and weeks after quitting.

Distract. Another way to control urges is to remain occupied with the activity going on when the urge started or to get busy with something. There are many activities that can keep one's mind off smoking: reading a book or magazine, watching TV, listening to music, walking, or taking a shower. Sports and exercise are excellent forms of distraction.

Substitute. Substituting something else for a cigarette is an effective way to control urges. For example, sugarless candy or sugarless gum, fruit, or a drink can be consumed in place of smoking. Healthy substitutes are important for those concerned with weight gain following smoking cessation. Straws or toothpicks can be chewed to help by "keeping your mouth busy." The trick is to come up with something that can be readily substituted for a cigarette. This is particularly important in situations that are difficult to avoid (e.g., socializing with friends, going to NA/AA meetings).

Each strategy is reviewed and specific examples are elicited from group members. As an exercise, the adolescents are asked to describe a common trigger situation and determine which of the DEADS strategies would be useful in that particular circumstance.

A parallel is drawn between smoking cessation and successful recovery from alcohol and drug abuse in that learning how to get through urges or cravings is one of the keys to success. The DEADS strategies represent tools to be used in the process of smoking cessation, and a well-stocked "tool box" will increase chances at success. It is important to emphasize that each individual must try various strategies to find out what works best for him or her.

Suggested practice activity. A relatively easy urge control exercise is to attempt to delay one urge each day for 15 minutes. Have each group member describe a situation or trigger for which they will practice urge control and which strategies they will employ. Urge control practice following later sessions can be accomplished by incrementally increasing the time between urge and smoking (e.g., start with 15 minutes, and add ten- or 15-minute increments each week), as well as trying urge control in response to different triggers.

Instructions for urge control practice:

1. From the time you feel the urge or craving, wait it out for 15 minutes.
2. Use different kinds of DEADS strategies to find out what works for you.
3. Start out by selecting a relatively easy urge (don't start with one that will be difficult such as the first cigarette of the day).

Topic 5: Social Support and Refusal Skills

This topic is introduced by reviewing social situations that trigger smoking. Discussion focuses on perceptions of the role of smoking in these situations. Specifically, group members are asked whether they perceive smoking cigarettes as a behavior that facilitates meeting new people, helps them feel more comfortable around peers, or provides them a common bond with other adolescents. Invite participants to imagine what it would be like for them in such situations if they did not smoke: how would others react, how might they feel differently? In addressing these issues, it is helpful to have adolescents take a different perspective and discuss how they view non-smokers or friends who are trying to quit smoking. The discussion is summarized by reflecting back to group members the potential difficulties of being a non-smoker in peer and social settings.

Discussion of the social role of smoking is followed by introducing skills for enlisting social support and refusing offers of cigarettes. The topic of the importance of social support for successful abstinence from alcohol and drugs is raised, and adolescents are asked how they manage social pressures to use alcohol and drugs. When discussing strategies for enlisting support for quitting smoking, specific examples must be elicited of who will provide support and how these persons might be helpful (e.g., "My best friend will support me by not smoking around me and not giving me a cigarette even if I ask"). It is important to convey that people who care about the adolescent will want to help and be supportive.

Similarly, behaviors by peers and family members that make it more difficult to quit smoking should be identified (e.g., smoking around the adolescent; offers of cigarettes; deriding their ability to quit). Group members are asked to consider how others may be unhelpful and discuss how they would manage these situations. Refusal strategies are then introduced in the context of assertive skills. Discussion of assertiveness begins with adolescents describing their understanding of the concept. Assertiveness is contrasted with aggressive and passive behaviors:

1. The assertive person has respect for the rights of others and her or his own rights.
2. The passive person respects others' rights at the expense of her or his own rights.
3. The aggressive person respects her or his own rights at the expense of the rights of other people.

After clarifying the concept of assertiveness, concrete examples of each type of behavior are provided. Next, guidelines for assertive behavior are reviewed, using behaviors previously identified as unhelpful as examples.

1. You can only control your own behavior, not that of others. You can ask others to change their behavior, but they have the right to refuse.
2. It is important to know in advance what you want to get out of a particular situation or circumstance.
3. Communicate clearly and specifically what it is you want.
4. Pay attention to body language; avoid presenting a passive or aggressive posture.
5. The timing of attempts at assertive behavior is important. In particular, make sure you're calm and composed when making a request or having a discussion with someone.
6. It is important to use "I" statements, and avoid words such as "should" and "never."
7. When criticizing someone, address the *behavior* you don't like rather than characteristics of the *person*.
8. To provide constructive feedback, use the "sandwich" technique: start with something positive about the issue/person, follow this with criticism/feedback, then end with a positive comment.

After reviewing the assertive guidelines, a specific example is discussed in detail, contrasting the consequences that follow from passive, aggressive, and assertive behaviors. Role plays of assertive refusal behaviors are conducted, based on scenarios previously generated by the group members. Role plays are conducted with pairs of adolescents successively playing roles, with corrective feedback provided as needed.

Suggested practice activity. It is critical that skills for eliciting support are practiced in situations that engender success. To this end, initial practice should be recommended in non-threatening situations for which success is highly likely (e.g., asking close friends and family for support with changing their smoking behaviors). Over time, adolescents are encouraged to continue practicing refusal strategies so as to improve the likelihood of later employing these strategies upon quitting smoking.

Topic 6: Cessation and Relapse Prevention

This topic represents the final module in the intervention. It is likely that some group members may not yet be ready to attempt cessation. The purpose of presenting relapse prevention issues is to prepare adolescents for eventual cessation attempts and help them anticipate the associated difficulties. Discussion begins with reviewing group members' prior experiences with smoking cessation and describing what was easy, what was difficult, and what led to relapse. Based on group-generated examples, difficulties associated with the process of smoking cessation are highlighted. The message to group members is to expect some degree of difficulty when quitting and to set aside sufficient time and energy for attempting cessation.

The distinction between quitting and maintenance is defined. Quitting and maintenance are two different parts of becoming a non-smoker. Quitting refers to the first few days and weeks after stopping smoking. Quitting is the time when people experience withdrawal symptoms from nicotine and the strongest urges and cravings. During this time adolescents must remain on guard in the face of triggers for smoking. Attention must be directed at anticipating and preparing for difficult situations. This is accomplished by identifying triggers that will become high risk for relapse situations and determining ahead of time which urge control strategies will be most useful. Frequently occurring triggers for smoking that are part of daily routine represent the primary high-risk situations for the quitting phase. The role of social support during the quitting phase is emphasized, and strategies for enlisting social support and refusing offers of cigarettes are reviewed.

The maintenance phase refers to the period when urges and withdrawals become weaker. At this point it is no longer necessary to be constantly on guard and fewer adjustments are needed in daily routine. In this phase it is important to anticipate difficult triggers and less frequent situations that are likely to present risk for relapse. Emotions and stressful situations are important triggers for which coping strategies must be identified.

Commonly employed elements for planning a smoking cessation attempt from adult-derived behavioral smoking cessation programs are outlined. An important first step is setting a quit date and sticking to it. After the date has been set, a plan for eliminating cigarette smoking-related cues is devised: making sure no cigarettes are readily available at home, disposing of lighters and ashtrays etc.; and cleaning/deodorizing smoking areas (e.g., rooms and cars). During the quitting phase it is helpful to alter daily routine in order to avoid or disrupt usual triggers (this will be familiar since most adolescents will have already worked on putting off urges and reducing cigarette consumption). Minimizing nicotine withdrawals is another important issue during the quitting phase. While few data exist with respect to adolescent smokers, nicotine replacement products (patch and gum) significantly increase cessation success for adult smokers (Patten, 2000). Nicotine replacement is discussed, with an emphasis that these products are not a cure-all, and must be combined with behavior change strategies to be most effective. Information should be provided regarding the advantages of nicotine replacement and caution regarding side effects and the danger of smoking while using the patch or nicotine gum.

At this time there are no accepted guidelines for use of the nicotine patch or gum with adolescents (Patten, 2000). This topic must be approached with particular caution because of the wide range of smoking behavior found among teens. A rule of thumb adopted by researchers working with adolescent smokers is that nicotine replacement may not be appropriate for those who smoke fewer than ten cigarettes per day (R. Brown, personal communication). Adolescents are given written information regarding nicotine patch and gum, and told that the decision to use these products must be made together with their parents. It may be helpful to contact parents directly to discuss issues related to use of nicotine replacement products.

Relapse prevention is the final topic discussed. High-risk situations are explained using the behavior chain. Those triggers that produce strong urges to smoke after cessation are high-risk situations. Group members then identify personal high-risk situations and are assisted in generating urge control strategies for specific triggers. Discussion includes review of urge control strategies currently employed by group members, and identification of strategies most likely to be effective in high-risk situations. At this stage it is important to promote self-efficacy by highlighting adolescent successes in changing their smoking behaviors. Stress and anger are common smoking triggers for substance-abusing adolescents. The following is a brief list of stress and anger management strategies:

Instructions for dealing with stress or anger/frustration:

(1) Take a "time out." Get out of the situation, walk away, cool off, take a deep breath, count slowly to ten, think of something fun you've done recently or would like to do or will be doing.
(2) Change how you're thinking! Changing the way you think about a situation can help make it less stressful. Try the following steps:
   (a) Figure out what is triggering the urge or craving: *Ask yourself:* "Why do I want to smoke?"
   (b) Figure out what's going on in the situation. *Ask yourself:* "What's really going on here? How will smoking a cigarette help me? What do I really think would help me deal with this?"
   (c) Figure out a different way to think about and understand what's going on. *Get some perspective on the situation* so you can see it in a more positive way. *Ask yourself:* "Is this really such a big deal? Are things really that bad?"
(3) Talk to yourself! Say things to yourself that will help you get through an urge. Think about your reasons for quitting: the good things about being a non-smoker, or remember the bad things about smoking. Think about how hard you've worked to quit smoking.
(4) Get physical! Physical activity is a great way to deal with stress and fight urges! It can be anything: taking a walk, skateboarding, jogging, aerobics, pick-up games (basketball, softball, volleyball), even doing household chores or cleaning will work!

Empirical Studies

Results from the intervention development study suggest the utility of this smoking intervention in producing decreases in cigarette smoking and motivating cessation attempts (Myers, Brown, Kelly & Tapert, 1997; Myers, Brown & Kelly, 2000). Thirty-five adolescents, ages 13 to 18 (40 percent female), participated in the treatment development study and were followed for three months' post treatment. Although only two participants had stopped smoking by the end of treatment, six adolescents were abstinent at the three-month follow-up. Over half of the participants (n = 17) attempted cessation during the three-month post-treatment period. Those attempting cessation reported an average of almost 30 smoke-free days, and several engaged in multiple smoking cessation attempts. Thus, participants made substantial efforts at changing their smoking behavior after completing the intervention. Findings from the study suggest no negative effect on alcohol and other drug abstinence from smoking cessation efforts. Although not statistically significant, the proportion of alcohol and drug relapses was lower among those attempting smoking cessation compared with adolescents who did not attempt to quit smoking (13 versus 33 percent respectively). Similarly, no differences were found on number of days abstinent from alcohol and drugs between those who did and did not attempt smoking. These data provide preliminary evidence that smoking cessation intervention in the context of adolescent addiction treatment poses no risk to substance use outcome.

In the absence of a control group, conclusions cannot be drawn regarding the efficacy of this intervention. However, the data support the feasibility of intervening with cigarette use among adolescents treated for alcohol and other drug abuse, and indicate that the present intervention shows promise in effecting smoking cessation attempts. The findings to date must, however, be interpreted with caution since they are based on a small sample for which no comparison group is available.

Prescriptive/Matching Issues

At this time, specific prescriptive and matching guidelines for smoking cessation treatment development for this population are premature. Two issues to be considered include status of alcohol and other drug recovery and psychiatric comorbidity.

Teens in Early Recovery

Teens who are struggling with their alcohol and other drug use are unlikely to succeed with smoking cessation because of the strong associations between tobacco, alcohol, and other drug use. However, this should not preclude participation in the current intervention. One advantage of the intervention design is that it accommodates a wide range of readiness for changing cigarette smoking behaviors. In addition, many of the strategies and techniques imparted are relevant to changing alcohol and drug use behaviors, and thus may serve to reinforce other aspects of treatment. Also, preliminary evidence does not indicate any detrimental effect on recovery from smoking cessation attempts. As such, this intervention is considered appropriate for adolescents in the early stages of recovery.

Comorbidity

Comorbid psychopathology is common among substance-abusing youth, yet little is known regarding optimal smoking cessation treatment for individuals with concurrent psychiatric disorders. For example, adults with a history of major depression are at increased risk for a depressive episode following smoking cessation (Glassman, 1993). This suggests that changes in depressive symptoms should be monitored throughout the process of smoking reduction and cessation. It may also be advisable to discourage smoking cessation efforts by an adolescent experiencing significant depression. As with adults, adolescents often report stress as a trigger for smoking. Therefore, stress management (relaxation techniques, self-hypnosis, etc.) may represent a useful adjunct to smoking intervention, particularly for anxiety-prone adolescents. Physical exercise can also be a positive strategy for managing negative affective symptoms among substance abusing youth attempting smoking reduction or cessation.

Future Directions

The field of adolescent smoking cessation treatment is currently in its infancy. While preliminary evidence suggests the utility of the present intervention for effecting smoking cessation attempts, additional research is needed to confirm these findings. To this end, a controlled treatment outcome study is currently under way to formally evaluate the efficacy of the intervention described above. Our research indicates that adolescent participants frequently attempt cessation following the intervention, suggesting that continued support for cessation may enhance outcomes. Studies of adolescent substance abuse treatment outcome demonstrate that aftercare attendance corresponds with better substance use outcomes (Brown, 1993). Borrowing from this model, continued support in the form of additional voluntary sessions following the completion of the formal intervention or by promoting the formation of an adolescent support group for smoking cessation may serve to improve smoking cessation rates. Future studies are needed to inform as to the optimal methods for supporting continued and successful smoking cessation efforts among substance-abusing youth.

Summary

Results from the treatment development study from which this intervention was derived demonstrate that substance-abusing adolescents can be engaged in efforts to change their cigarette-smoking behaviors. This finding is particularly important given the poor outcome reported by most adolescent smoking cessation studies published to date. Some of the strategies adopted in the course of the intervention development study may have contributed to the observed outcomes. In particular, addressing tobacco use in the context of substance abuse treatment overcomes recruitment difficulties common to adolescent smoking cessation efforts. By incorporating tobacco intervention as part of addiction treatment, all adolescent smokers can be educated regarding nicotine dependence and receive training in skills relevant to smoking cessation. An important aspect of addressing tobacco use in the context of substance abuse treatment is that a more consistent message is delivered regarding addiction, an approach that avoids the problem of labeling certain substances as more "dangerous" than others. Finally, the finding that smoking cessation efforts do not detrimentally influence substance use outcomes commends the standard inclusion of tobacco interventions when treating adolescent substance abuse.

References

Ary, D. V., & Biglan, A. (1988), "Longitudinal changes in adolescent smoking behavior: Onset and cessation." *Journal of Behavioral Medicine 11*, 361–382.

Baillie, A. J., Mattick, R. P., Hall, W., & Webster, P. (1994), "Meta-analytic review of the efficacy of smoking cessation interventions." *Drug & Alcohol Review 13*, 57–170.

Barnea Z., Rahav G., & Teichman M. (1987), "The reliability and consistency of self-reports on substance use in a longitudinal study." *British Journal of Addiction 82*, 891–898.

Biglan, A., McConnell, S., Severson, H. H., Bavry, J., & Ary, D. V. (1984), "A situational analysis of adolescent smoking." *Journal of Behavioral Medicine 7*, 109–114.

Bobo, J. K., & Gilchrist, L. D. (1983), "Urging the alcoholic client to quit smoking cigarettes." *Addictive Behaviors 8*, 297–305.

Bobo, J. K., Gilchrist, L. D., Schilling, R. F., Noach, B., & Schinke, S. P. (1987), "Cigarette smoking cessation attempts by recovering alcoholics." *Addictive Behaviors 13*, 209–215.

Brown, R. (1998), personal communication, May 25.

Brown, R. A., & Emmons, K. M. (1991), "Behavioral treatment of cigarette dependence." In J. A. Cocores (ed.), *The Clinical Management of Nicotine Dependence*. New York: Springer-Verlag.

Brown, S. A. (1993), "Recovery patterns in adolescent substance abuse." In J. S. Baer, G. A. Marlatt, & R. J. McMahon (eds), *Addictive Behaviors Across The Lifespan: Prevention, Treatment and Policy Issues*. Beverly Hills, CA: Sage Publications, 161–183.

Brown, S. A., Vik, P. W., & Creamer, V. A. (1989), "Characteristics of relapse following adolescent substance abuse treatment." *Addictive Behaviors 14*, 291–300.

Chassin, L., Presson, C. C., & Sherman, S. J. (1984), "Cognitive and social influence factors in adolescent smoking cessation." *Addictive Behaviors 9*, 383–390.

Cinciripini, P. M., Wetler, D. W., & McClure, J. B. (1997), Scheduled reduced smoking: Effects on smoking abstinence and potential mechanisms of action. *Addictive Behaviors 22*, 759–767.

Donovan, D. M. (1988), "Assessment of addictive behaviors: Implications of an emerging biopsychosocial model." In D. M. Donovan & G. A. Marlatt (eds), *Assessment of Addictive Behaviors*. New York: Guilford Press, 3–50.

Eiser, J. R., & van der Pligt, J. (1985), "Attitudinal and social factors in adolescent smoking: In search of peer group influence." *Journal of Applied Social Psychology 14*, 348–363.

Ershler, J., Leventhal, H., Fleming, R., & Glynn, K. (1989), "The quitting experience for smokers in sixth through twelfth grades." *Addictive Behaviors 14*, 365–378.

Flay, B. R. (1993), "Youth tobacco use: Risks, patterns, and control." In C. T. Orleans & J. D. Slade (eds), *Nicotine addiction: Principles and management*. New York: Oxford University Press, 365–384.

Glassman, A. H. (1993), "Cigarette smoking: Implications for psychiatric illness." *American Journal of Psychiatry 150*, 546–553.

Hajek, P. (1994), "Treatments for smokers." *Addiction 89*, 1543–1549.

Hansen, W. B. (1983), "Behavioral predictors of abstinence: Early indicators of a dependence on tobacco among adolescents." *International Journal of the Addictions 18*, 913–920.

Hansen, W. B., Collins, L. M., Johnson, C. A., & Graham, J. W. (1985), "Self-initiated smoking cessation among high school students." *Addictive Behaviors 10*, 265–271.

Henningfield, J., Michaelides, T., & Sussman, S. (2000), "Developing treatment for tobacco addicted youth — issues and challenges." *Journal of Child and Adolescent Substance Abuse 9*(4), 5–26.

Hughes, J. R. (1993), "Treatment of smoking cessation in smokers with past alcohol/drug problems." *Journal of Substance Abuse Treatment 10*, 181–187.

Hunt, W. A., Barnett, L. W., & Branch, L. G. (1971), "Relapse rates in addiction programs." *Journal of Clinical Psychology 27*, 455–456.

Johnston, L. D., O'Malley, P. M., & Bachman, J. G. (1992), *Smoking, Drinking, and Illicit Drug Use Among American Secondary School Students, College Students, and Young Adults, 1975–1991: Volume I, Secondary school students*. US Department of Health and Human Service, Public Health Service, National Institutes of Health, National Institute on Drug Abuse. Bethesda, MD: NIH Publication No. 93-3480.

Karle, H. *et al.* (1994), "Tobacco control for high-risk youth: Tracking and evaluation issues." *Family and Community Health 16*, 10–17.

Kassel, J. D. (2000), "Are adolescent smokers addicted to nicotine? The suitability of the nicotine dependence construct as applied to adolescents." *Journal of Child and Adolescent Substance Abuse 9*(4), 27–50.

Leventhal, H., Keeshan, P., Baker, T., & Wetter, D. (1991), "Smoking prevention: Towards a process approach." *British Journal of Addiction 86*, 583–587.

Leventhal, H., & Cleary, P. D. (1980), "The smoking problem: A review of research and theory in behavioral risk modification." *Psychological Bulletin 88*, 370–405.

Martin, J. E. (1994), "Project Scrap Treatment Manual." San Diego State University.

Martin, J. E. *et al.* (1997), "Prospective evaluation of three smoking interventions in 205 recovering alcoholics: One-year results of Project SCRAP-Tobacco." *Journal of Consulting and Clinical Psychology 65*, 190–194.

McNeill, A. D., West, R. J., Jarvis, M., Jackson P., & Bryant A. (1986), "Cigarette withdrawal symptoms in adolescent smokers." *Psychopharmacology 90*, 533–536.

Miller, W. R., & Rollnick, S. (1991), "What motivates people to change?" In W. R. Miller & S. Rollnick (eds), *Motivational Interviewing*. New York: Guilford Press, 14–29.

Myers, M. G., & Brown, S. A. (1994), "Smoking and health in substance abusing adolescents: A two year follow-up." *Pediatrics 93*, 561–566.

Myers, M. G., & Brown, S. A. (1996), "The Adolescent Relapse Coping Questionnaire: Psychometric validation." *Journal of Studies on Alcohol 57*, 40–46.

Myers, M. G., & Brown, S. A. (1997), "Cigarette smoking four years following treatment for adolescent substance abuse." *Journal of Child and Adolescent Substance Abuse 7*, 1–15.

Myers, M. G., Brown, S. A., Kelly, J. F., & Tapert, S. F. (1997), "A cigarette smoking intervention for substance abusing adolescents: Preliminary findings." Symposium paper presented at the Association for Advancement of Behavior Therapy Annual Meeting, Miami Beach, FL, November.

Myers, M. G., Brown, S. A., & Kelly, J. F. (2000), "A smoking intervention for substance abusing adolescents: Outcomes, predictors of cessation attempts, and post-treatment substance use." *Journal of Child and Adolescent Substance Abuse 9*(4), 77–91.

National Institute on Drug Abuse (1996), *National Survey Results on Drug Use from the Monitoring the Future Study, 1975–1995* (NIH Publication No. 96-4139). Washington, DC: US Government Printing Office.

Patten, C. (2000), "A critical evaluation of nicotine replacement therapy for teenage smokers." *Journal of Child and Adolescent Substance Abuse 9*(4), 51–76.

Peltier, B., Telch, M. J., & Coates, T. J. (1982), "Smoking cessation with adolescents: A comparison of recruitment strategies." *Addictive Behaviors 7*, 71–73.

Pierce, J. P., & Gilpin, E. (1996), "How long will today's new adolescent smoker be addicted to cigarettes?" *American Journal of Public Health 86*, 253–256.

Prochaska, J. O., DiClemente, C. C., & Norcross, J. C. (1992), "In search of how people change: Applications to addictive behaviors." *American Psychologist 47*, 1102–1114.

Prokhorov, V. A., Pallonen, U. E., Fava, J. L, Lin, D., & Niaura, R. (1996), "Measuring nicotine dependence among high risk adolescent smokers." *Addictive Behaviors 21*(1), 117–127.

Prue, D. M., Krapfl, J. M, & Martin, J. E. (1981), "Brand fading: The effects of gradual changes to low tar and nicotine cigarettes on smoking rate, carbon monoxide, and thiocyanate." *Behavior Therapy 12*, 400–416.

Sargent, J. D., Mott, L. A., & Stevens, M. (1998), "Predictors of smoking cessation in Adolescents." *Archives of Pediatrics and Adolescent Medicine 152*(4), 388–393.

Sees, K. L., & Clark, H. W. (1993), "When to begin smoking cessation in substance abusers." *Journal of Substance Abuse Treatment 10*, 189–195.

Sussman, S., Lichtman, K., Ritt, A., & Pallonen, U. (1999). "Effects of thirty four adolescent tobacco use cessation and prevention trials on regular users of tobacco products." *Substance Use and Misuse 34*, 1469–1503.

Wagner, E. F. (2000), "Introduction" to special issue on nicotine addiction among adolescents. *Journal of Child and Adolescent Substance Abuse 9*(4), 1–4.

Chapter 13

Psychopharmacological Therapy

Yifrah Kaminer*

Relative to research evaluating the efficacy of psychosocial interventions for adolescent substance use problems, research evaluating the efficacy of pharmacotherapeutic interventions for teen substance abuse has been neglected (Kaminer, 1995). Yet, the largest subgroup of adolescents with substance-related disorders (SRD) presenting in clinical settings are those with both substance use and other psychiatric disorders. This particular subgroup may stand to benefit most from effective pharmacotherapies for SRDs (Kaminer, 1994a). In an attempt to move forward research and clinical practice in regard to pharmacotherapeutic interventions for substance-abusing teens, the objectives of this chapter are fourfold: (1) to clarify the reasons behind the scarcity of publications on and research of pharmacological interventions for SRD in adolescents; (2) to review present knowledge concerning pharmacotherapy for substance-abusing adolescents with and without psychiatric comorbidity; (3) to highlight the importance of a comprehensive treatment of adolescents with SRD, in particular combining psychosocial and pharmacological interventions; and (4) to outline suggestions for future directions for the development of pharmacotherapies for SRDs for this age group.

Difficulties in the Development of Pharmacotherapy for Adolescents with SRD

In contrast to the increased acceptance of pharmacotherapy for adults with SRD, there has been little systematic research evaluating the safety and efficacy of psychotropic medications in the treatment of adolescents with SRD. This lack of attention poses a major challenge to the development of psychopharmacology for substance-abusing teens. Models for the pharmacotherapy of SRDs (with or without psychiatric comorbidity) among adults derive largely from the disease model of addiction. This model has been very influential in the addiction field since the 1930s, but may have limited applicability to adolescent substance abuse since it does not incorporate the type of

*Correspondence concerning this chapter should be addressed to: Yifrah Kaminer, M.D., Alcohol Research Center, Department of Psychiatry, The University of Connecticut Health Center, Farmington, CT, USA.

Innovations in Adolescent Substance Abuse Interventions, pages 285–311.
ISBN: 0-08-043577-7

developmental perspective that appears critical to understanding teen substance use problems.

Other challenges of providing pharmacological treatment for adolescents with SRD are embedded in philosophical, conceptual and economic factors which have limited the scope of clinical research and treatment (Hoffmann, Sonis & Halikas, 1987). Certainly, the issue of the potential risks and benefits of pharmacotherapy for individuals who have not reached adulthood remains hotly debated (Biederman, 1992). A related controversy concerns the prescribing of potentially abusable medications to individuals already struggling with addiction. Many parents also face the dilemma of whether their offspring's potential to outgrow early onset psychiatric disorder without pharmacological intervention is a realistic expectation, or merely a form of denial and rationalization which may have profound negative consequences by leaving a potentially treatable disorder untreated. In addition, unfavorable public perceptions of pediatric psychopharmacology may be related to outdated beliefs that medications represent "chemical restraints" to be used with the chronically mentally ill.

Moreover, psychopharmacological approaches also may be inconsistent with some perspectives on recovery from substance use problems. For example, Hoffmann *et al.* (1987) note that twelve-step self-help groups such as Alcoholics Anonymous (AA) do not acknowledge the importance of accurate medical and psychiatric diagnoses, which are a necessary component of psychopharmacotherapy. Furthermore, twelve-step sponsors of dually diagnosed adolescents participating in self-help groups may have a strong objection to any medication, even those without known abuse potential (i.e. lithium, neuroleptics), given the perspective's general orientation toward abstinence from alcohol and other drugs. This perspective can have the negative consequence of exposing the dually diagnosed adolescent to increased risk for relapse to substance use and/or other disorders (Kaminer, 1994a).

Drug-Specific Pharmacotherapy

In a review of the pharmacological treatment of adolescent SRD, Kaminer (1995) referred to four drug-specific pharmacological strategies that are commonly utilized for the treatment of SRD: (1) make psychoactive substance administration aversive (e.g. disulfiram for alcohol dependence); (2) substitute for the psychoactive substance (e.g. methadone for heroin dependence); (3) block the reinforcing effects of the psychoactive substance (e.g. naltrexone for opioids abuse); and (4) relieve craving/withdrawal (e.g. clonidine for heroin dependence; desipramine for cocaine dependence). A fifth strategy often added to this list pertains to the pharmacotherapy of comorbid psychiatric disorders.

Detoxification from opioids, alcohol, barbiturates, benzodiazepines, and other psychoactive agents needs to follow rigorous procedures in a timely fashion. There have been no empirical studies on detoxification of adolescents with SRD; however, clinical experience suggests that there is no reason to assume that this therapeutic process should be any different from that of adults with SRD, as long as legal consent is obtained. Thus, it is recommended that detoxification for adolescents follow clinically accepted practice for detoxification for adults.

Across the next several pages, pharmacotherapy for the abuse and dependence of nicotine, alcohol, cocaine, and opioids will be reviewed with special emphasis on adolescents' needs. Other drugs are not discussed in this review (e.g., marijuana, hallucinogens, inhalants) due to lack of empirical data on their pharmacotherapy. Also, no scientific information on the pharmacotherapy of polysubstance abuse in adolescents currently is available. Finally, the topic of interactions between psychoactive drugs and psychotropic medications is of significant importance, but is beyond the scope of the current chapter (the interested reader is referred to Ciraulo, Shader, Greenblatt & Creelman, 1995).

Nicotine

The primary pharmacotherapy for nicotine dependence involves the strategy of finding a substitute and more controllable mode of administration for nicotine. The invention of self-administered agents such nicotine gum, the nicotine transdermal patch, and nicotine nasal spray was a breakthrough in the treatment of nicotine dependence among adults. The efficacy of these agents doubled success rates of treatment programs for adults from about 15 percent (validated long-term abstinence) to about 30 percent (West, 1992). Furthermore, their success in treating nicotine dependence and promoting smoking cessation improved even more when behavioral or cognitive therapy sessions were added to a comprehensive treatment plan (Lichtenstein & Glasgow, 1992). To date, the appropriateness of these intervention strategies for adolescent smoking remains debatable, and almost no research has examined their efficacy in treating nicotine dependence among teens (Patten, 2000).

Only one study of the effectiveness of nicotine gum for treating smoking included adolescents (i.e., 15- to 18-year-olds), although the actual number of teens among the sample of 612 smokers was not reported (Johnson, Stevens, Hollis & Woodson, 1992). No special reference was made regarding the characteristics and treatment outcome of these adolescents in the outpatient clinic sample studied. Moreover, there have been no published studies of the effectiveness of the nicotine patch or nasal spray with adolescents.

Side effects of nicotine gum include bad taste and sore mouth and jaws because it is hard to chew. The patch may increase nicotine toxicity, particularly if the person continues to smoke. It can irritate the user's skin and disrupt sleep if left on for 24 hours. The nicotine spray can cause irritation to the user's mucous membranes. Moreover, some people find it difficult to wean themselves off these nicotine replacement therapies (Lichtenstein & Glasgow, 1992), and none of these therapies should be used by active smokers.

No specific contraindications for the use of the nicotine replacement strategies by adolescents with nicotine dependence are known. It appears that any therapeutic trial should start as a carefully designed case study for consenting adolescents with severe nicotine dependence. It is noteworthy that recent reports show an association between nicotine dependence and major depressive disorder (Breslau, Kilbey & Andreski, 1993), some of which have focused on adolescent populations (Goodman & Capitman, 2000).

Alcohol

The most common unidimensional pharmacotherapy to prevent alcohol consumption is aversive therapy with disulfiram. This antidipsotropic agent produces a reaction with ethanol by inhibiting the liver enzyme aldehyde dehydrogenase which catalyzes the oxidation of aldehyde (the major metabolic product of ethanol to acetate). The resulting accumulation of acetaldehyde is responsible for the aversive symptoms from disulfiram. With experience, these aversive symptoms become paired with ethanol consumption, and thus decrease the likelihood that alcohol will be consumed. The success of this controversial pharmacotherapy has been mediocre at best (Alterman, O'Brien & McLellan, 1991).

Aversive therapy in children and adolescents has always been controversial, and standard clinical practice has been to use it only in extreme cases of violent behavior or severe self-injurious behavior among the mentally retarded, and only after other treatment modalities have failed (Council on Scientific Affairs, 1987). It appears unlikely that aversive pharmacotherapy for adolescents with alcohol dependence will be commonly accepted until the following three pivotal questions are answered: Which treatments are effective for alcohol abuse/dependence among adolescents? What are the targeted symptom behaviors for adolescent alcohol problems? For whom are the treatments effective? The present consensus in the literature on these questions is as follows: because of the inherent complexity of alcoholism and the heterogeneity of patient characteristics, no single treatment method can work for all patients, and patient–treatment matching might enhance treatment effectiveness.

Although disulfiram has been available for several decades, its efficacy has not been firmly established despite nearly 100 studies reporting on its oral administration (Fuller, Branchey & Brightwell, 1986). Voluntary self-administration of disulfiram has been shown to help reduce drinking frequency in a very limited number of controlled clinical trials. However, the medication does not enhance counseling in aiding alcoholic patients to sustain continuous abstinence or delay the resumption of drinking (American College of Physicians, 1989). In other words, there is no evidence that prescription of disulfiram will have any beneficial effect without concurrent therapy and rehabilitation. Finally, patients who are compliant and who live a relatively stable lifestyle are candidates for a more successful treatment outcome with disulfiram (Schuckit, 1985). A recent report of two adolescent males with alcohol dependence who were prescribed disulfiram showed a limited short-term benefit for only one of the teens (Myers, Donahue & Goldstein, 1994).

Findings regarding the pharmacotherapy of alcoholism generated interest in the impact of alcohol consumption on opioid receptors and the potential utility of an opioid antagonist such as naltrexone to block the reinforcing properties of alcohol. Naltrexone has been found to be safe and effective in reducing rates of relapse, levels of craving, and number of drinking days among adult heavy drinkers and alcoholics, both as a stand-alone treatment (Volpicelli, Alterman, Hayashida & O'Brien, 1992) and with adjunctive psychotherapy (O'Malley *et al.*, 1992). In a case report, Wold and Kaminer (1997) reported on the successful short-term treatment of an alcohol-dependent adolescent with a daily oral dose of 50 mg of naltrexone.

Acamprosate is a compound that acts on the central nervous system, with a diversity of actions in several neurotransmitter systems affected by chronic ethanol intake. Acamprosate has been shown to interfere with excitatory amino acids transmission, primarily glutamate, and to modulate positively GABA transport in different brain areas.

Recent studies showed statistically significant differences in cumulative abstinence for patients who received acamprosate versus placebo (Sass, Soyka, Mann & Zieglgansberger, 1996; Whitworth, Fischer & Lesch, 1996). No studies on the treatment of adolescents with acamprosate have been reported.

Finally, the serotonergic system appears to play a role in the pathophysiology of alcohol dependence. Selective serotonin reuptake inhibitors (SSRIs) have been shown to have a limited clinical utility in reducing alcohol consumption among adults with no more than moderate severity of depression (Kranzler, Burleson, Korner & DelBoca, 1995a). However, SSRIs may be an effective treatment in reducing depressive symptoms and alcohol consumption among adult alcoholic patients with severe depression (Cornelius *et al.*, 1997). A small double-blind placebo-controlled study utilizing an SSRI in adolescents conducted by Deas, Randall & Roberts (1998) showed no significant improvement in alcohol consumption or depression scores for those who received active medication.

Cocaine

Research has implicated the neurotransmitter dopamine as the leading catecholamine responsible for the specific reinforcing effects of cocaine and craving/withdrawal symptoms among cocaine users (Kosten, 1990). Neuroleptics were hypothesized to block the cocaine-induced euphoria initiated by mesolimbic and mesocortical neuroanatomic reward pathways, leading to attenuation of cocaine self-administration by animals (Gawin, Allen & Humblestone, 1989a). However, neuroleptics are known to produce anhedonia and extrapyramidal side effects among humans, and medication compliance has been problematic. Flufenthixol decanoate is a neuroleptic agent that was reported in an open trial to rapidly decrease cocaine craving and use, and increase the average time retained in treatment (Gawin, Allen & Humblestone, 1989a). It has been postulated that compliance with this medication would be satisfactory, especially compared with other neuroleptic agents, due to its lack of anhedonic effects.

Sporadic case reports about the capacity of lithium to block cocaine-induced euphoria have not been confirmed, even among adult cocaine abusers with bipolar spectrum disorders (Nunes, McGrath, Steven & Quitkin, 1990). The primary pharmacological treatment strategy for cocaine abuse has been focused mainly on the reduction/elimination of cocaine abstinence-related craving, rather than blocking the drug's reinforcing properties. The reduction of craving is essential to improve relapse prevention rates by decreasing attrition from treatment and enabling the introduction of additional therapeutic interventions.

Based on the theory that chronic stimulant use results in depletion of dopamine and reduction in dopaminergic activity, it was hypothesized that craving for cocaine would be reduced by increasing dopaminergic stimulation (Meyer, 1992). There is sparse evidence to support the depletion theory. However, the following direct and indirect dopaminergic agents have shown some efficacy for addressing cocaine abuse in open trials in adults: L-dopa, carbidopa, bromocriptine, amantadine, methylphenidate, and mazindol (Meyer, 1992).

Another theory that appears to have neurobiological support suggests that craving is mediated by supersensitivity of presynaptic-inhibiting dopaminergic autoreceptors. The tricyclic antidepressant desipramine was found to desensitize these receptors and facilitate cocaine abstinence by attenuating craving for seven to 14 days from the onset of therapy. Gawin *et al.* (1989b) reported a six-week double-blind random assignment study of desipramine treatment for cocaine craving in adults. The treated outpatient adult cocaine abusers were more frequently abstinent, were abstinent for longer periods, and had less craving for cocaine compared with lithium- and placebo-treated patients. Kosten *et al.* (1992) presented six-month follow-up data on 43 of the 72 patients originally reported by Gawin *et al.* (1989b). It was found that self-reported cocaine abstinence during the six-month period was significantly greater in patients treated with desipramine (44 percent) than in those treated with lithium (19 percent) or placebo (27 percent).

There has been only one detailed case study supporting the use of desipramine for treatment of cocaine use by an adolescent (Kaminer, 1992a). A six-month follow-up utilizing the Teen Addiction Severity Index (T-ASI) (Kaminer, Bukstein & Tarter, 1991; Kaminer, Wagner, Plummer & Seifer, 1993) confirmed continued abstinence and progress in other life domains. In this case, desipramine treatment (200 mg/d, plasma level stabilized around 130 g/L) was instituted for the treatment of three psychiatric disorders simultaneously (i.e., cocaine dependence, major depressive disorder, and attention deficit hyperactivity disorder), thus preventing polypharmacy.

Other research has found that the intensity of cocaine craving is independent of depression during the first week of abstinence among newly abstinent chronic cocaine abusers (Ho, Cambor & Bodner, 1991). This finding suggests that withdrawal-related dysphoria during the first week of abstinence will not respond to the antidepressant properties of desipramine, and may be alleviated earlier than the depressive symptomatology of a patient diagnosed as cocaine dependent with MDD (major depressive disorder). This may also differentiate a cocaine-dependent adolescent from a dually diagnosed one. It is recommended that the results from a single case study be viewed with caution until such findings are replicated in other studies. The Kaminer (1992a) case study did not confirm the three-phase model of cocaine abstinence (i.e. crash, withdrawal, extinction) suggested by Gawin and Kleber (1986). Instead, a two-stage process of cocaine craving response to treatment by desipramine (i.e., a period of gradual improvement followed by a significant improvement) characterized this case. Weddington *et al.* (1990) describe findings similar to Kaminer (1992a) in a study of twelve adult cocaine addicts.

Two other cases in which cocaine-dependent adolescents were treated with desipramine had less positive outcomes (Kaminer, 1994b). For one adolescent, the clinical symptoms responded favorably to desipramine for about 30 days, at which time the patient dropped out of treatment. The second adolescent, who had abused amitriptyline prior to treatment, developed postural hypotension following the introduction of desipramine. As a result, the medication was discontinued.

Dopamine system dysregulation is probably not the only mechanism underlying cocaine addiction. The serotonin system has been implicated as well, although small open-label studies of serotoninergic agents showed conflicting results in the treatment of cocaine abuse (Kosten & McCance, 1996). Another recent development in the pharmacological treatment of cocaine dependence is the use of carbamazepine. The theoretical rationale for this intervention is that the agent blocks cocaine-induced kindling and increases dopamine concentration. However, double-blind trials using carbamazepine have not supported this theory (Kranzler, Bauer, Hersh & Klinghoffer, 1995b; Montoya, Levin, Fudala & Gorelick, 1994).

Stimulants have proven to be useful for the treatment of children and adolescents diagnosed with ADHD (attention deficit hyperactivity disorder). The pharmacokinetic similarities between an illegal stimulant such as cocaine and therapeutic stimulants such as methylphenidate, magnesium pemoline, and dextroamphetamine have led to the assumption that they might be useful for the treatment of cocaine abuse. Also, it has been suggested that adult abuse of cocaine could be attributed to a residual type of ADD (Weiss, Pope & Mirin, 1985). A review of the literature did not support these assumptions (Kaminer, 1992b), and a recent double-blind, placebo-controlled study of methylphenidate for cocaine abuse offered little support for this treatment (Grabowski *et al.*, 1997).

Opiates

Four maintenance pharmacotherapies are currently used in the United States for treatment of opiate abuse: methadone, naltrexone, LAAM (Levo-alpha-Acetylmethadol), and buprenorphine (Kosten & McCance, 1996). LAAM and buprenorphine address some limitations of methadone and naltrexone, including illicit diversion of take-home methadone doses, difficulties with detoxification from methadone maintenance to a drug-free state, polydrug abuse, and poor compliance on naltrexone.

Methadone maintenance (MM) is a common form of opiate substitution therapy and is usually reserved for the treatment of adult heroin addicts. The desired response from MM is threefold: (1) to prevent the onset of opioid abstinence syndrome; (2) to eliminate drug hunger or craving; and (3) to block the euphoric effects of any illicitly self-administered opioids. As a general rule, patients who have not been dependent on opioids for at least one year or who have not previously made any attempt at withdrawal are not appropriate candidates for prolonged opioid maintenance (Jaffe, 1986).

Methadone maintenance should not rely on methadone administration alone, even in adequate daily dosage, as a "magic bullet" for curing heroin addiction. McLellan *et al.* (1993) reported that patients in an MM program who also received a psychosocial-services package fared better than two other groups of patients who received counseling in addition to MM, or MM only.

No person under 18 years of age may be admitted to an MM treatment program unless an authorized adult signs an official consent form (FDA-2635 consent for methadone maintenance treatment). Patients under age 18 are required to have two documented attempts at short-term detoxification or drug-free treatment to be eligible for MM. A one-week waiting list period is required after a detoxification attempt. However, before an attempt is repeated, the program physician has to document in the minor's record that the patient continues to be or is again physiologically dependent on narcotic drugs (Parrino, 1992). Methadone maintenance, and not opioid detoxification, is the treatment of choice for pregnant adolescents who abuse heroin. This daily pharmacotherapy eliminates the danger of contracting Acquired Immunodeficiency Syndrome (AIDS) from a contaminated needle. It also assures a relatively stable plasma level of methadone which reduces the fetus's risk of developing intrauterine distress, as compared to heroin, which has a short half-life and causes abrupt changes in plasma level (Finnegan & Kandall, 1992).

LAAM (Levo-alpha-Acetylmethadol) is an agent that is quite similar to methadone in its pharmacological actions, and it has been approved for treatment of opioid dependence. It is converted into active metabolites that have longer biological half-lives than methadone. Opioid withdrawal symptoms are not experienced for 72 to 96 hours after last oral dose; therefore LAAM need be given only three times per week. LAAM has been shown to have equivalent effects to methadone in terms of suppressing illicit opioid abuse and encouraging a more productive lifestyle (Jaffe, 1986).

Buprenorphine is a partial opioid agonist–antagonist, and also is used as an analgesic due to its ability to produce morphine-like effects at low doses. This agent relieves opiate withdrawal, diminishes craving, and does not produce euphoria. It is more difficult to overdose on buprenorphine than on methadone because of its opiate antagonist effects in high doses (Rosen & Kosten, 1991).

Many heroin addicts also abuse cocaine, which "speeds" the rush from heroin injected alone (i.e. a speed ball). Methadone maintenance treatment does not reduce cocaine abuse for many patients. Buprenorphine may reduce cocaine use in opiate addicts (Kosten, Kleber & Morgan, 1989), but additional research is needed.

Advances in Pharmacotherapy for Adults with SRD

Recent developments in the pharmacological treatment of nicotine and cocaine, and the increased acceptance of auricular acupuncture as a therapeutic procedure for addictions are noteworthy.

Nicotine

New developments in the nicotine substitute field include nicotine inhalers, nicotine sprays, and sustained-release (SR) buproprion (Tonnesen, Norregaard, Mikkelsen, Jorgensen & Nilsson, 1993). The nicotine devices offer the person the choice of when and where to use them (similar to cigarette smoking), but a potential concern could be that it would be difficult to quit using the device. In a recent article, Patten (2000) review the benefits and risks of employing nicotine replacement strategies with adolescents. Buproprion is an antidepressant that in combination with the nicotine patch may be better than either medication alone. The recommended dose of buproprion SR should not exceed 300 mg/day because of its increased association with seizures. It is not advisable to take this medication during pregnancy. There has not been enough experience to judge the safety of buproprion or nocotine replacement therapy with other new antidepressants such as SSRIs, venlafaxine, and nefazodone.

Cocaine

It has been suggested that a potentially viable treatment for cocaine abuse would be one that interrupts the delivery process of cocaine to cocaine receptors. This alternative to traditional pharmacotherapeutic approaches has attracted considerable attention. Antibodies which may catalyze degradation of cocaine to an inactive form, release the inactive products, and retain the ability for further binding to cocaine receptors could provide a treatment for cocaine dependence that works primarily through the blunting of reinforcement (Landry, Zhao, Yang, Glickman & Georgiadis, 1993). This form of passive immunization by an artificial enzyme could provide a new avenue for treatment.

Acupuncture

The use of acupuncture for the treatment of drug addiction was discovered serendipitously (Wen, 1979). Over the last 20 years, several reports regarding the benefits of acupuncture for the treatment of various addictions have been published. The drugs investigated included opiates, tobacco, and alcohol (for a review, see Margolin, Avants, Chang & Kosten, 1993). Most investigations of acupuncture for the treatment of substance use disorders suffer from problems of design and assessment; however, a few well-designed studies have appeared in the literature.

Smith and Khan (1988) reported that 40 percent of adult patients dependent on cocaine gave a series of clean urine tests after several weeks of treatment by auricular acupuncture. Margolin, Avants, Chang & Kosten (1993) studied the effectiveness of acupuncture versus various pharmacotherapies for cocaine dependence in methadone-maintained patients. These investigators found a higher abstinence rate for acupuncture (44 percent) in comparison to amantadine (15 percent) or placebo (13 percent), but not in comparison with desipramine (26 percent). Thus, it appears that acupuncture warrants further investigation as a treatment for substance use problems among different populations, including adolescents.

Pharmacotherapy of Comorbid Psychiatric Disorders

Psychiatric comorbidity is not uncommon among children and adolescents with psychiatric disorders (Anderson, Williams, McGee & Silva, 1987). Psychiatric comorbidity in the form of dual and triple diagnosis is common among clinical populations of adolescents with SRD (Bukstein, Brent & Kaminer, 1989). The most common psychiatric diagnoses among teens with SRDs are depressive disorders and/or conduct disorder. Other diagnoses frequently reported in this population include: bipolar mood disorders; anxiety disorders; ADHD; and eating disorders. Also, cluster B DSM-IV Axis II diagnoses (American Psychiatric Association, 1994), which include antisocial, borderline, histrionic, and narcissistic personality disorders, are common among adolescent substance abusers (Grilo *et al.*, 1995).

It is often unclear whether an SRD patient's presenting psychiatric symptoms are a consequence of substance abuse, or are indicative of a comorbid psychiatric disorder. Among such patients, the sequelae of psychoactive substance intoxication and/or withdrawal are often difficult to distinguish from the signs and symptoms of comorbid psychiatric disorder. When comorbidity does exist, childhood-onset psychiatric disorders typically precede SRD (Christie *et al.*, 1988). Moreover, it is important to reemphasize that dual diagnosis is a term limited to the relation between different disorders only, and not to the relation among different symptoms associated with SRD.

From a treatment perspective, reliable and valid diagnosis of comorbid psychiatric disorders is of great significance. The misdiagnosis of comorbidity and the precocious introduction of medications may lead to life-threatening errors in treatment. To help ensure reliable and valid comorbidity diagnosis, a substance-free washout period of at least two weeks is recommended. Pharmacotherapy should not be initiated prior to this washout period. This is especially true for antidepressants, since approximately 25 percent of all children and adolescents initially diagnosed with major depressive disorder demonstrate spontaneous syndromatic recovery within two weeks (Ambrosini, Bianchi, Rabinovich & Elia, 1993).

Major Depressive Disorder

Conceptual difficulties regarding the validity of depression as a distinct diagnostic entity in children and adolescents remain. Substantial uncertainty still exists regarding what factors best represent depression among children and adolescents: individual symptoms, regularly occurring syndromes, or constitutionally based disorders. It is also unclear which mental status variables should be examined in depressed youth when evaluating treatment effects. Adolescents who are diagnosed with major depressive disorders (MDD) are commonly treated with either TCAs such as imipramine and amitriptyline or by selective serotonin reuptake inhibitors (SSRIs) such as fluoxetine, sertraline, paroxetine, and fluvoxamine.

Empirical data do not support the efficacy of TCAs in child and adolescent MDD (Birmaher *et al.*, 1998), although these medications have proven effective for the treatment of adult MDD. With a samples of adolescents, Geller, Cooper & Graham (1990) and Ryan, Puig-Antich, Cooper, *et al.* (1986) tried to replicate the findings from studies of the treatment of adult MDD, which have reported that TCA steady-state plasma levels of more than 125 micrograms per liter (pg/L) predict response (Nelson, Mazure & Quinlan, 1984). No relation was found between plasma levels of imipramine or desipramine and clinical response in adolescents with MDD. Ambrosini *et al.* (1993) reviewed treatment studies of children and adolescents that focused on TCAs. They concluded that although these medications' superiority to placebo has not been proven, more than half of the subjects treated openly do respond, and they suggested that the maximal benefits from antidepressants most likely emerge after eight to ten weeks of treatment when plasma levels of TCAs are maintained in the 200 nanograms per milliliter (ng/mL) range. Moreover, they recommended that maintenance treatment should be continued for up to six months after remission.

Several other pharmacologic treatment approaches for MDD have been tested with adolescents as well. A recent a double-blind placebo-controlled study using an SSRI (fluoxetine) for the treatment of children and adolescents with depression concluded that fluoxetine was superior to placebo in the acute phase of MDD (Emslie, Rush & Weinberg, 1997). Lithium and electro-convulsive therapy (ECT) augmentation in refractory adolescent MDD and monoamine oxidaze inhibitor (MAOI) treatment of adolescent atypical depression were reported in open-design studies (Ryan, Meyer, Dachille, Mazzie & Puigh-Antich, 1988a; Ryan *et al.*, 1988b). These reports suggest the potential use of these agents in the management of refractory MDD in adolescents, but await further confirmation in more rigorous studies.

Side Effects

In general, antidepressant medications produce similar side effects in adolescents and adults. These include the anticholinergic effects of TCAs, usually correlated with plasma levels, such as dry mouth, drowsiness, nausea, constipation, urinary retention, tremor, flushed face, and excessive sweating. Neurotoxic effects of antidepressants include seizures, behavioral changes, and delirium. Data concerning tricyclic neurotoxicity in adolescents is limited to sporadic case reports. TCAs may induce behavioral precipitation or induction of rapid cycling of manic symptoms (Strober & Carlson, 1982). The TCAs may be lethal in overdose, primarily because of cardiovascular toxicity (Ambrosini *et al.*, 1993).

Depressed patients commonly attempt suicide by overdosing on TCAs because the ratio between an effective and lethal dosage is relatively low. The suspected pathophysiological mechanism is that TCAs, and desipramine in particular, may increase noradrenergic neurotransmission, which leads to increased cardiac sympathetic tone and could predispose vulnerable persons to ventricular tachyarrhythmias, syncope, and sudden death. Several case studies of children and adolescents indicated that fatalities could occur even when a medically acceptable dosage for the treatment of depression is being prescribed (Werry, 1995). Current experience suggests that a baseline electrocardiogram (EKG) needs to be done before initiating TCA treatment. A physical examination and medical history should emphasize the cardiovascular system of the patient and family members in order to detect any cardiac vulnerability. Resting pulse should not exceed 130 beats per minute, and blood pressure should not exceed 140/90 mm Hg. Prolongation of the P–R interval on the EKG should not exceed 0.21 seconds, the QRS complex should not be prolonged by more than 30 percent over baseline, and the QTc interval in particular should be within normal limits.[1] It is noteworthy that abuse of the TCA amitriptyline for its sedative effects was reported by an adolescent and adults with psychoactive substance use disorders (Kaminer, 1994b). Finally, abrupt discontinuation of TCAs may produce withdrawal symptoms, the most common of which are cholinergic effects.

In comparison to TCAs, SSRIs produce fewer anticholinergic effects, less sedation, less weight gain, and fewer ECG changes. The most common side effects of SSRIs are gastrointestinal, neuropsychiatric, and behavioral. Among adolescents, these side effects

---

[1] QT interval represents the time required for ventricular electrical systole. It varies with heart rate, and one can estimate QTc (corrected QT) interval normally less than 0.42 second in males and 0.43 second in females by the formula QTc = QT/R–R interval.

include (in order of decreasing frequency): dry mouth, somnolence, dizziness, fatigue, tremor, headache, constipation, anorexia, dyspepsia, and stomach aches (Leonard, March, Rickler & Allen, 1997). It also should be noted that mania was among the side effects reported in the treatment of five adolescents for depression with the SSRI fluoxetine (Venkataraman, Naylor & King, 1992). Finally, coadministration of SSRIs with TCAs or within a few weeks following discontinuation of TCAs is contraindicated because of potentially significant drug interactions that may raise the plasma level of these agents to a toxic level.

Suicidal risk is an important concern in the pharmacologic treatment of adolescents with both SRDs and depression. In comparison to TCAs, SSRIs are less cardiotoxic with over-doses, and they lack sedative potentiation with alcohol. Therefore, the use of SSRIs is preferable for MDD in impulsive or suicidal adolescents. Early reports regarding paradox-ical increases in suicidality were not supported. Furthermore, reduction of suicidal behavior in adults treated with an SSRI was reported in a double-blind placebo-controlled study (Verkes et al., 1998). However, further study of the safety and efficacy of SSRIs in youth is still necessary. Finally, Worthington, Fava & Alpert (1996a) reported that ongoing SRD is a negative predictor of response to treatment with an SSRI of depressive disorders among adults, and particularly women. However, McGrath, Nunes & Stewart (1996) reported that that imipramine treatment of adult alcoholics with primary depression was safe and improved depression. Additional studies on the pharmacotherapy of comorbid SRD and depressive disorders are needed.

Bipolar Disorder

The core phenomenology of bipolar disorder is similar regardless of age. However, as in the treatment of depressive disorders, it is unclear whether age of onset influences treat-ment response. Lithium is the pharmacotherapy of choice for bipolar disorder, although there are no large-scale, systematic studies in children and adolescents (Carlson, 1990). A recent double-blind placebo-controlled study of lithium for adolescent bipolar disorders with secondary SRD concluded that the medication was an efficacious treatment for both disorders (Geller, Cooper & Sun, 1998).

The following indications for the initiation of lithium treatment for adolescents were noted by Carlson (1990, p. 32):

> presence or history of disabling episodes of mania and depression; episode(s) of severe depression with a possible history of hypomania; pres-ence of an acute severe depression characterized by psychomotor retardation, hypersomnia, and psychosis; positive family history for a bipolar disorder (these adolescents are at risk for developing a manic episode when treated with antidepressants and may develop a rapid cycling course); an acute psychotic disorder with affective features; and behavior disorders characterized by severe emotional lability and aggression when there is a positive family history of major mood or bipolar disorder or lithium responsiveness.

DeLong and Aldershof (1987) reported that of 59 bipolar child and adolescent patients studied, two-thirds were considered favorable responders to lithium therapy. Poor responders consisted of subjects with ADHD, conduct disorder, or both. Indeed, children misdiagnosed with ADHD have been shown actually to suffer from bipolar mood disorder (Isaac, 1991). Lithium's efficacy in treatment of acute symptomatology and long-term management of bipolar disorder in adults is well established and extensively documented in the literature; however, the failure rate for lithium in prevention of bipolar disorder is approximately 33 percent (Prien & Gelenberg, 1989)

Side effects of lithium in adolescents are similar to those manifested in adults; tremor, urinary frequency, nausea, and diarrhea are the most common. Contraindications for the use of lithium include heart and kidney disease, diuretic use, chronic diarrhea, and electrolyte imbalance. Baseline assessments before initiating lithium therapy include blood electrolytes, urea and nitrogen levels, blood count with differential, thyroid function tests, and pregnancy test due to the potential teratogenic effects of lithium. The recommended therapeutic blood level is within the therapeutic range of 0.7 to 1.2 millequivalents per liter (mEq/L). A level of more than 1.4 mEq/L should not be exceeded due to a risk of toxicity. Signs of toxicity include severe neurobehavioral and gastrointestinal symptoms.

Anticonvulsants such as carbamazepine and valproic acid serve as second-tier medications for bipolar disorder. Combinations of these medications have been reported to have a synergistic effect in adult patients resistant to lithium monotherapy. The recommended blood levels for anticonvulsants, contraindications, and side effects are similar across age groups. Compared to lithium, monitoring of fluid and electrolyte intake is not required, and the risk of toxicity is lower should serum levels exceed the recommended therapeutic range. In some cases, bipolar disorder may be refractory to all of these agents. Two new anticonvulsants, gabapentin and iamotrigine, appear useful as mood stabilizers in the treatment of bipolar disorders in adults (Pollack & Scott, 1997).

Another alternative, verapamil (a calcium channel antagonist), has been used without clear effectiveness in the treatment of adults with a bipolar disorder. In addition, verapamil is associated with depression (Barton & Gitlin, 1987). However, successful combined use of verapamil and valproic acid in the treatment of prolonged mania in an adolescent has been reported (Kastner & Friedman, 1992). Finally, it should be noted that adolescents with SRD and a comorbid bipolar disorder are at very high risk for suicidal or aggressive behavior and should be followed carefully.

Anxiety Disorders

Most disorders from the anxiety disorders spectrum such as panic disorder, post-traumatic stress disorder, and obsessive–compulsive disorder (OCD) in youth share phenomenological similarities with the adult patterns. However, some anxiety disorders, such as separation anxiety and school phobia, are unique to children and adolescents. The median age for the onset of anxiety disorders is 15 years of age (Christie *et al.*, 1988). The use of anti-anxiety medications with addictive properties and withdrawal symptoms upon tapering off, such as benzodiazepines, is not recommended for adolescents with comorbid SRD. Sedation, drowsiness, decreased mental acuity, and behavioral disinhibition have been reported as side effects, and should be monitored carefully. Furthermore, benzodiazepines such as alprazolam, which are commonly used among adults with anxiety disorders, have not been unequivocally proven to be more efficacious than TCAs or SSRIs for the treatment of anxiety disorders among teens.

A review of the literature on the relationship between alcohol dependence and anxiety disorders concluded that children of alcoholics are more likely to develop anxiety disorders than comparison populations (Schuckit & Hesselbrock, 1994). This suggests some degree of heritable association between the two classes of disorders. Also, the high rates of comorbidity in some studies reflect a mixture of true anxiety disorders among subjects with alcohol abuse along with temporary, but at times severe, substance-induced anxiety syndromes.

Panic Disorder

Panic disorder is uncommon before puberty, and it may manifest itself with or without agoraphobia. No studies regarding the pharmacological treatment of panic disorder in adolescents have yet been reported. A recent study of adults with panic disorder reported that both the benzodiazepine alprazolam and the TCA imipramine demonstrated efficacy during acute treatment of panic disorder on most measures of panic and non-panic anxiety, as well as on measures of phobic avoidance and panic-related social disability (Schweizer, Rickels, Weiss & Zavodnick, 1993). These clinical benefits were achieved without any concomitant behavioral therapy or psychotherapy and were sustained throughout an eight-month course of maintenance therapy without any dose escalation. The same research group studied short- and long-term outcome after drug taper (Rickels, Schweizer, Weiss & Zavodnick, 1993). The authors concluded that "over the long term, patients originally treated with imipramine or placebo did as well at follow-up as patients treated with alprazolam, without the problems of physical dependence and discontinuation that any long-term alprazolam therapy entails" (Rickels, Schweizer, Weiss & Zavodnick, 1993, p. 67). Cognitive behavioral therapy alone for panic disorder showed better outcome than a combined CBT and imipramine. It appears that this result can be attributed to the discontinuation of the medication. Adult panic disorder patients with comorbid SRD responded less favorably to an SSRI in a naturalistic, longitudinal study of panic disorder (Worthington, Pollack & Otto, 1996b). The investigators concluded that SRD is a negative predictor of response to the treatment of panic disorder.

Separation Anxiety and School Phobia

These disorders have been studied for more than 20 years. In contrast to an early report regarding a positive response to imipramine compared to placebo (Gittelman & Klein, 1971), recent studies have failed to show superiority of TCAs (e.g., imipramine, clomipramine) to placebo in the treatment of separation anxiety (Bernstein, 1990; Klein, Koplewicz & Kanner, 1992). It is noteworthy that these disorders were found to be associated with adult forms of panic and depressive disorders, and thus may long-term impacts if left untreated (Gittelman & Klein, 1984; Weissman, Jarrett & Rush, 1987).

Overanxious and Avoidant Disorders

A study of the effects of alprazolam on children and adolescents with these disorders was reported by Simeon *et al.* (1992). They failed to show efficacy of alprazolam in comparison to placebo. This finding stands in marked contrast to the favorable effects reported in studies with adults, and Simeon *et al.* intend to increase the dosage of alprazolam and the length of pharmacotherapy in a future study. The authors did not discuss the implications of the addictive potential of alprazolam in this study.

Buspirone hydrochloride is an anxiolytic drug pharmacologically different from the benzodiazepines. This agent has been marketed as a less sedative anxiolytic that does not potentiate alcohol effects and has a low abuse potential. Buspirone has been used successfully to treat an adolescent with overanxious disorder who did not tolerate treatment with desipramine (Kranzler, 1988). Buspirone therapy was associated with reduced anxiety among anxious alcoholic adults as compared to placebo. This medication may be useful in clinical treatment of teens with SRD and anxiety symptoms.

Post-traumatic Stress Disorder

To date, there is little evidence that drug treatment has a central role in the treatment of PTSD. The primary treatment has been cognitive behavioral therapy designed to help patients to regain control over their anxiety, feelings, and sense of helplessness. Intrusive experiences of PTSD have proved to be the symptom cluster that responds best to pharmacotherapy using TCAs, MAOI, clonidine, and SSRIs (Katz, Fleisher & Kjernisted, 1996). The overlap between PTSD and other anxiety and depressive disorders creates a difficulty in the assessment of treatment outcomes. Clonidine was administered in an open-label trial to preschoolers with PTSD (Harmon & Riggs, 1996). Target symptoms of PTSD were improved in most children. Benzodiazepines, TCAs, and SSRIs may be useful as adjunctives to psychosocial treatment in youth (Werry & Aman, 1993). No pharmacological studies on adolescents with SRD and comorbid PTSD have been reported.

Obsessive–Compulsive Disorder

The psychopharmacological treatment of OCD has been extensively studied. This disorder is relatively uncommon among substance abusers. Antianxiety agents appear to be ineffective, but the tricyclic antidepressant clomipramine was reported to have significant superiority over placebo in lessening OCD symptoms in children and adolescents (DeVeaugh-Geiss *et al.*, 1992). Clomipramine appears to have better results than desipramine, but this conclusion remains to be tested in future studies. Placebo-controlled studies with SSRIs such as fluvoxamine (Luvox) (Riddle, 1998), and fluoxetine (Prozac) (Jenike, Baer, Minichiello, Rauch & Buttolph, 1997) support their effectiveness in adolescent OCD. The studies reviewed may have significant importance for the development of pharmacotherapies for the treatment of adolescents with SRD and comorbid anxiety disorders.

Eating Disorders

Anorexia and bulimia nervosa are psychiatric disorders predominantly diagnosed in females. A phenomenon of "crossover" from anorexia to bulimia is common during the five-year period following the onset of anorexia nervosa (Sullivan, Bulik, Fear & Pickering, 1998). In terms of comorbidity with SRDs, bulimia is more commonly diagnosed among substance abusers than anorexia nervosa. Anorexia nervosa is less commonly comorbid with SRD (Sullivan *et al.*, 1998), and no effective pharmacotherapy for anorexia nervosa has been reported in a double-blind, placebo-controlled trial. Only a limited number of open-label trials with the SSRI fluoxetine noted some short-term improvement.

One of the diagnostic criteria for bulimia nervosa according to DSM-IV (American Psychiatric Association, 1994) is the use of laxatives or diuretics in order to prevent weight gain. The misuse of medications without an addictive potential and in the "service of the disorder" does not meet the criteria for SRD. However, females in general, and bulimic patients in particular, tend to use diet pills. Indeed, Johnston, Bachman & O'Malley (1998) reported that female and male high school seniors used stimulants with equal frequency, and females used diet pills more often. The abuse of medications with addictive potential (e.g., stimulants sold over the counter), and the somewhat trendy use of cocaine reported in the media in order to lose weight, create a nosological dilemma in determining whether the eating-disordered patient qualifies for the diagnosis of SRD, particularly when the person is bulimic.

Since the mid-1980s, pharmacological trials in adult patients have demonstrated the short-term efficacy of several antidepressants in diminishing bingeing frequencies in bulimic patients. These include imipramine, desipramine, and phenelzine (an MAOI), as well as several new-generation antidepressants including trazodone, bupropion, and fluoxetine (Kennedy & Garfinkel, 1992). The bulimic symptomatology improved even in the absence of coexistent depression and was not correlated with pretreatment severity or plasma medication levels. These findings do not support early studies linking the etiology of mood disorders and eating disorders based on epidemiological and family studies (Hudson, Pope & Jonas, 1983). Lithium carbonate was reported to reduce bulimic episodes in open-label studies (Hsu, 1984).

Schizophrenia

No studies on the comorbidity of SRD and schizophrenia have been reported among adolescents. However, there are no data from adult patients to suggest that there should be any difference between the pharmacotherapy of schizophrenic patients with or without accompanying SRD. Therefore, until reported otherwise, neuroleptics remain the category of medications of choice for adolescents with comorbid SRD and schizophrenia.

Conduct Disorder

Conduct disorder (CD), ADHD, and oppositional defiant disorder (ODD) represent the largest group of child and adolescent psychiatric referrals. Comorbidity among these disorders is very common, and the debate whether ODD is a mild variant or a precursor of CD is still inconclusive (Abikoff & Klein, 1992). In child and adolescent psychiatry, aggression is most commonly associated with a diagnosis of CD. Also, impulsivity, irritability, and mood lability are often the targets of pharmacological treatment as part of a comprehensive treatment plan that also includes psychosocial and behavioral interventions (Stewart, Myers & Burket, 1990). Neuroleptics have been used for the treatment of aggressive behavior with and without CD in adolescents since the 1960s with mixed results accompanied by severe side effects (Campbell, 1992). Lithium, anticonvulsants, and the beta blocker propranolol have been used clinically, but the results have been ambiguous (Campbell, 1992; Kuperman & Stewart, 1987; Lavin & Rifkin, 1993). Treatment of violent children and adolescents aged five to 15 years with clonidine was reported in an open-label study (Kemph, DeVane & Levin, 1993). Aggression decreased, with minimal side effects in most children. The most impressive results on the clinical efficacy of a medication in CD with and without ADHD was reported by Klein *et al.* (1997). A randomized placebo-controlled study of methylphenidate with six- to 15-year-old subjects, two-thirds of whom had ADHD, revealed that key aspects of antisocial adjustment appear to be treatment responsive. The effect was independent of severity of the children's initial ADHD symptoms.

The SSRI fluoxetine was reported to improve impulsive aggressive behavior better than placebo in adults with personality disorders who did not have mood disorders or schizophrenia (Coccaro & Kavoussi, 1997). The anticonvulsant divalproex sodium was administered in an open-label study to a small group of conduct-disordered adolescent marijuana users (Donovan, Susser & Nunes, 1996). The investigators examined the hypothesized link between epileptoid activity and explosiveness as suggested by Monroe (1970). Marijuana may have an anti-epileptoid activity and may be used in a subgroup of CD adolescents to "calm down" (i.e., self-medication). Therefore, an anticonvulsant medication may substitute the self-medication effect of marijuana. Most subjects showed marked improvement in temper and mood in response to divalproex sodium. More studies are necessary to improve the pharmacotherapy of adolescent CD with or without comorbid RSD.

The best case for medication can be made for the management of the frequently diagnosed comorbid disorders with CD, such as ADHD with stimulants, and symptomatic relief of depressive or anxiety disorders by selective pharmacotherapy with antidepressants. Riggs, Thompson, Mikulich, Whitmore & Crowly (1996), and Riggs, Leon & Mikulich (1998) reported in two small-scale open-label studies that pemoline and buproprion improved ADHD symptomatology in delinquent adolescents with SRD. Also, Riggs, Mikulich & Coffman (1997) reported that fluoxetine improved depression in a similar population.

Attention Deficit Hyperactivity Disorder

ADHD is an early onset (age less than seven years) disorder by definition, characterized by inattention and/or hyperactivity with impulsivity. Its prevalence in the general pediatric population is estimated between three and five percent in elementary-school children. The rate of ADHD in a given age group appears to decline by 50 percent approximately every five years (Hill & Schoener, 1996). A considerable segment of the patients with ADHD have developmental disorders such as learning disabilities, as well as psychiatric disorders such as mood, anxiety, and conduct disorders. Conduct disorder is considered to be a necessary mediator for the development of SRD in ADHD patients (Biederman *et al.*, 1997).

The effectiveness of the primary psychopharmacological agents used to treat this disorder (i.e., stimulant therapy) has been extensively documented (Spencer *et al.*, 1996). The pharmacological agents include: methylphenidate (Ritalin), dextroamphetamine (Dexedrine), magnesium pemoline (Cylert), and mixed salts of amphetamines (Adderal). These stimulants improve classroom behavior, academic performance, interpersonal interactions, oppositional and conduct behavior. If an adolescent does not improve after receiving an appropriate dosage of one of the stimulants, a trial of one of the other stimulants is recommended.

Adverse effects include decreased appetite, weight loss, insomnia, possible mood lability, and a potentially reversible growth suppression once the medication is discontinued. Recent case reports about the uncommon but robust association between pemoline and irreversible liver damage raise concerns whether this medication should continue to be used. Abuse of therapeutic stimulants by adults or by adolescents with ADHD is uncommon. Intravenous abuse of methylphenidate was reported in adults (Parran & Jasinski, 1991), and intranasal abuse of methylphenidate in adolescents was reported in case reports by Garland (1998) and Jaffe (1991). Clinicians should be aware that peers, siblings, and parents may abuse the medication, particularly if they have SRD (Kaminer, 1992b).

Tricyclic antidepressants have also been found to be effective in the treatment of ADHD symptomatology (Wilens, Biederman & Geist, 1993). Desipramine and other TCAs may serve as alternate pharmacotherapy to stimulants. However, these antidepressants should be used primarily when an ADHD patient is manifesting a comorbid anxiety or depressive disorder. Side effects of TCAs (reviewed earlier), in particular cardiotoxicity and the increasing knowledge regarding the new generations of antidepressants such as SSRIs, should be considered prior to treatment with TCAs. It is noteworthy that adverse effects of smoking marijuana while receiving TCAs for ADHD were reported (Wilens, Biederman & Spencer, 1997). These included transient cognitive changes, delirium, and tachycardia.

The clinical impact of the antidepressant buproprion has been attributed to its noradrenergic effect. Both dopaminergic and noradrenergic mechanisms have been postulated in ADHD. Buproprion was reported in a single-blind trial to produce moderate to marked improvement in global behavioral measures among adolescents with ADHD or CD (Simeon, Ferguson, Van Wyck & Fleet, 1986). Conners *et al.* (1996) reported similar results in a double-blind placebo-controlled trial with ADHD-diagnosed children. A comparative drug trial with methylphenidate showed similar overall efficacy (Barrickman *et al.*, 1995).

Clonidine, an alpha-2 adrenergic receptor agonist, is increasingly being used for the treatment of ADHD. It is used alone or as a supplementary treatment to stimulants (Hunt, Capper & O'Connell, 1990). Clonidine has also been used for sleep disturbances associated with ADHD (Prince, Wilens, Biederman, Spencer & Wozniak, 1996), and in patients with comorbid tic disorders (Steingard, Biederman, Spencer, Wilens & Gonzalez, 1993). In most instances, the comorbidity of tic disorders is not a contraindication for the use of stimulants. Adjunct treatment of the tics with other medications (e.g., clonidine, neuroleptics) is usually effective. Neuroleptics, carbamazepine, lithium, and valproic acid are not recommended as treatments for ADHD due to equivocal efficacy, at best, and serious side effects. In summary, for adolescents with SRD and comorbid ADHD, the concomitant treatment of both disorders is recommended. Medications with low abuse potential such as pemoline or buproprion are preferred (Riggs, 1998).

Combination of Psychosocial and Pharmacological Treatments

The emerging consensus among treatment researchers is that a biopsychosocial, multidimensional, problem-oriented approach is necessary to meet the needs of adolescent substance abusers. Carroll (1997) advocated for the concomitant provision of some form of psychosocial treatment with pharmacotherapy in the treatment of SRDs. She argued that this approach will particularly foster replicability of findings and address several common problems in clinical trials (e.g., attrition, medication non-compliance, reduction of error variance, and ethical issues associated with placebo controls). In her own words, "Careful selection and standardization of the psychosocial context in which medications are delivered will improve the validity, precision, and power of pharmacotherapy efficacy research" (Carroll, 1997, p. 923).

No empirical data regarding the combination of pharmacotherapy (of either psychiatric comorbidity or substance abuse) and psychosocial interventions in adolescent substance abuse are available. However, clinicians and clinical researchers may want to consider that a combined pharmacotherapy and psychotherapy intervention model may have, in any given case, additive, interactive, or independent effects, or may be less effective than either modality alone. Clearly, more research is needed in this area.

Future Directions for Pharmacotherapy with Adolescents

Eichelman (1988) described four important principles for the pharmacologic treatment of adults: (1) treat the primary illness; (2) use the most benign interventions when treating; (3) have some quantifiable means of assessing efficacy; and (4) institute drug trials systematically. These principles are even more important with younger patients. Ethical principles must govern clinical research and treatment in adolescent SRD and comorbid psychiatric disorders (Munir & Earls, 1992). Improved communication with and education of the public, and especially parents of patients, regarding the nature of SRD and the efficacy of pharmacotherapy is necessary. Patients who would like to maintain their motivation to comply with the medication regime should join or develop self-help groups for patients with SRD and comorbid psychiatric disorders. Parents and therapists in the treatment facility may be instrumental in helping them succeed in this effort.

A study by McLellan *et al.* (1993), reviewed previously in the section on opiates, confirms empirically a cumulative effect of treatment modalities in their adult patients. Pharmacotherapy alone cannot deal with polysubstance abuse and the various domains that the

adolescent with SRD struggles with in the recovery process. However, no single psychosocial strategy appears to be superior to others in dealing with adolescents SRD (Catalano,
Hawkins, Wells, Miller & Brewer, 1990–91). The initial pharmacotherapy may be needed to
attain short-term abstinence and ensure treatment retention, while concurrent or sequential
psychosocial interventions can lead to more sustained abstinence and longer-term improvement. This treatment orientation to adolescent SRDs is similar the treatment of depression
(Weissman, Jarrett & Rush, 1987) and substance abuse in adults (Kranzler *et al.*, 1995a).

In summary, continued development of pharmacotherapy for the treatment of adolescents with SRD is warranted, and may ultimately improve treatment options and outcomes
for substance-abusing teens. Future research must include the systematic study of new
therapeutic agents, maintenance of strict ethical principles in treatment and research,
improved communication with families and the media, and understanding and promoting
the concept that pharmacotherapy may be an important component of a comprehensive
multimodal (i.e., biopsychosocial) treatment package.

References

Abikoff, H., & Klein, R. G. (1992), "Attention deficit hyperactivity and conduct disorder; comorbidity
and implications for treatment." *Journal of Consulting and Clinical Psychology 60*, 881–892.

Alterman, A. I., O'Brien, C. P., & McLellan, A. T. (1991), "Differential therapeutics for substance
abuse." In R. J. Frances and S. I. Miller (eds), *Clinical Textbook of Addictive Disorders*. New
York: Guilford Press, 369–390.

Ambrosini, P. J., Bianchi, M. D., Rabinovich, H., & Elia, J. (1993), "Antidepressant treatments in
children and adolescents: I. Affective disorders." *Journal of the American Academy of Child and
Adolescent Psychiatry 32*, 1–6.

American College of Physicians (1989), "Disulfiram treatment of alcoholism." *Annals of Internal
Medicine 111*, 943–945.

American Psychiatric Association (1987), *Diagnostic and Statistical Manual of Mental Disorders*
(3rd edn rev.) Washington, DC: American Psychiatric Association.

American Psychiatric Association (1994), *Diagnostic and Statistical Manual of Mental Disorders*
(4th edn). Washington, DC: American Psychiatric Association.

Anderson, J. C., Williams, S., McGee, R., & Silva, P. A. (1987), "DSM-III disorders in preadoles-
cent children." *Archives of General Psychiatry 44*, 69–76.

Babor, T. F., DelBoca F. K., McLaney, M. A., & Higgins-Biddle, J. (1991), "Just say Y.E.S.:
Matching adolescents to appropriate interventions for alcohol and other drug-related problems."
Alcohol Health & Research World 15, 77–86.

Barrickman, L. L. *et al.* (1995), "Bupropion versus methylphenidate in the treatment of attention-
deficit hyperactivity disorder." *Journal of the American Academy of Child and Adolescent Psychiatry 34*, 649–657.

Barton, B., & Gitlin, M. J. (1987), "Verapamil in treatment-resistant mania: An open-label study."
Journal of Clinical Psychopharmacology 7, 101–103.

Berman, E., & Wolpert, E. A. (1987), "Intractable manic-depressive psychosis with rapid cycling in
an 18-year-old depressed adolescent successfully treated with electroconvulsive therapy." *Journal
of Nervous and Mental Disease 175*, 236–239.

Bernstein, G. A. (1990), "Anxiety disorders." In B. D. Garfinkel, G. A. Carlson, & E. B. Weller (eds),
Psychiatric Disorders in Children and Adolescents. Philadelphia, PA: W. B. Saunders, 64–83.

Biederman, J. (1992), "New developments in pediatric psychopharmacology." *Journal of the American Academy of Child and Adolescent Psychiatry 31*, 14–15.

Biederman, J. *et al.* (1997), "Is ADHD a risk factor for psychoactive substance use disorders? Findings from a four-year prospective follow-up study." *Journal of the American Academy of Child and Adolescent Psychiatry 36*, 21–29.

Birmaher, B. *et al.* (1998), "Randomized, controlled trial of amitriptyline versus placebo for adolescents with treatment resistant major depression." *Journal of the American Academy of Child and Adolescent Psychiatry 37*, 527–535.

Breslau, N., Kilbey, M., & Andreski, P. (1993), "Nicotine dependence and major depression: New evidence from a prospective investigation." *Archives of General Psychiatry 50*, 31–35.

Bukstein, O. G., Brent, D., & Kaminer, Y. (1989), "Comorbidity of substance abuse and other psychiatric disorders in adolescents." *American Journal of Psychiatry 146*, 1131–1141.

Campbell, M. (1992), "The pharmacological treatment of conduct disorders and rage outbursts." *Psychiatric Clinics of North America 15*, 69–85.

Carlson, G. A. (1990), "Bipolar disorders in children and adolescents". In B. D. Garfinkel, G. A. Carlson, & E. B. Weller (eds), *Psychiatric Disorders in Children and Adolescents*. Philadelphia, PA: W.B. Saunders, 21–36.

Carroll, K. M. (1997), "Manual-guided psychosocial treatment: A new virtual requirement for pharmacotherapy trials." *Archives of General Psychiatry 54*, 923–928.

Catalano, R. F., Hawkins, J. D., Wells, E. A., Miller, J., & Brewer, D. (1990–91), "Evaluation of the effectiveness of adolescent drug abuse treatment, assessment of risks for relapse, and promising approaches for relapse prevention." *International Journal of Addiction 25*, 1085–1140.

Christie, K. A. *et al.* (1988), "Epidemiologic evidence for early onset of mental disorders and higher risk of drug abuse in young adults." *American Journal of Psychiatry 145*, 971–975.

Ciraulo, D. A., Shader, R. I., Greenblatt, D. J., & Creelman, W. (eds) (1995), *Drug Interactions in Psychiatry,* (2nd edn) Baltimore, MD: Williams and Wilkins.

Coccaro, E. F., & Kavoussi, M. D. (1997), "Fluoxetine and impulsive aggressive behavior in personality-disordered subjects." *Archives of General Psychiatry 54*, 1081–1088.

Conners, C. K. *et al.* (1996), "Buproprion hydrochloride in attention deficit disorder with hyperactivity." *Journal of the American Academy of Child and Adolescent Psychiatry 35*, 1314–1321.

Cornelius, J. R. *et al.* (1997), "Fluoxetine in depressed alcoholics: A double-blind placebo-controlled trial." *Archives of General Psychiatry 54*, 700–705.

Council on Scientific Affairs (1987), "Aversion therapy." *Journal of the American Medical Association 258*, 2562–2566.

Deas, D., Randall, C., & Roberts, J. (1998), "Sertraline treatment of depressed adolescent alcoholics." Scientific Meeting of the Research Society on Alcoholism, Hilton Head, SC.

Delong, G. R., & Aldershof, A. L. (1987), "Long-term experience with lithium treatment in childhood: correlation with clinical diagnoses." *Journal of the American Academy of Child and Adolescent Psychiatry 26*, 389–394.

DeVeaugh-Geiss, J. *et al.* (1992), "Clomipramine hydrochloride in childhood and adolescent obsessive–compulsive disorder: A multicenter trial." *Journal of the American Academy of Child and Adolescent Psychiatry 31*, 45–49.

Donovan, S. J., Susser, E. S., & Nunes, E. V. (1996), "Divalproex sodium for use with conduct-disordered adolescent marijuana users." *American Journal on Addictions 5*, 181.

Eichelman, B. (1988), "Toward a rational pharmacotherapy for aggressive and violent behavior." *Hospital and Community Psychiatry 39*, 31–39.

Emslie, G. J., Rush, A. J., & Weinberg, W. A. (1997), "A double-blind randomized placebo-controlled trial of fluoxetine in children and adolescents with depression." *Archives of General Psychiatry 54*, 1031–1037.

Finnegan, L. P., & Kandall, S. R. (1992), "Maternal and neonatal effects of alcohol and drugs." In J. H. Lowinson, P. Ruiz, R. B. Millman, & J. G. Langrod (eds), *Substance Abuse Comprehensive Textbook*. Baltimore, MD: Williams & Williams, 628–656.

Fuller, R. K., Branchey, M. H., & Brightwell, D. R. (1986), "Disulfiram treatment of alcoholism." *Journal of the American Medical Association 256*, 1449–1455.

Garland, E. J. (1998), "Intranasal abuse of prescribed methylphenidate." *Journal of the American Academy of Child and Adolescent Psychiatry 37*, 573–574.

Gawin, F. H., & Kleber, H. D. (1986), "Abstinence symptomatology and psychiatric diagnosis in cocaine abusers." *Archives of General Psychiatry 43*, 107–113.

Gawin, F. H., Allen, D., & Humblestone, B. (1989a), "Outpatient treatment of crack cocaine smoking with flufenthixol decanoate." *Archives of General Psychiatry 46*, 322–325.

Gawin, F. H., *et al.* (1989b), "Desipramine facilitation of initial cocaine abstinence." *Archives of General Psychiatry 46*, 117–121.

Geller, B., Cooper, T. B., & Graham, D. L. (1990), "Double-blind placebo-controlled study of nortriptyline in depressed adolescents using a 'fixed plasma level' design." *Psychopharmacology Bulletin 26*, 85–90.

Geller, B., Cooper, T. B., & Sun, K. (1998), "Double-blind and placebo-controlled study of lithium for adolescent bipolar disorders with secondary substance dependency." *Journal of the American Academy of Child and Adolescent Psychiatry 37*, 171–178.

Gerrard, D. L., & Saenger, G. (1966), *Outpatient Treatment of Alcoholism*. Toronto: University of Toronto Press.

Gittelman, K. R., & Klein, D. F. (1971), "Controlled imipramine treatment of school phobia." *Archives of General Psychiatry 25*, 204–207.

Gittelman, K. R., & Klein, D. F. (1984), "Relationship between separation anxiety and panic and agoraphobic disorders." *Psychopathology Supplement 17*, 56–65.

Goodman, E., & Capitman, J. (2000), "Depressive symptoms and cigarette smoking among teens." *Pediatrics 106*, 748–755.

Grabowski, J et al. (1997), "Replacement modication for cocaine dependence: Methylphenidate." *Journal of Clinical Psychopharmacology 17*, 485–488.

Grilo, C. M. *et al.* (1995), "Psychiatric comorbidity in adolescent inpatients with substance use disorders." *Journal of the American Academy of Child and Adolescent Psychiatry 34*, 1085–1091.

Harmon, R. J., & Riggs, P. D. (1996), "Clonidine for posttraumatic stress disorder in preschool children." *Journal of the American Academy of Child and Adolescent Psychiatry 35*, 1247–1249.

Hill, J. C., & Schoener, E. P. (1996), "Age-dependent decline of attention deficit hyperactivity disorder." *American Journal of Psychiatry 153*, 1143–1146.

Ho, A., Cambor, R., & Bodner, G. (1991), "Intensity of craving is independent of depression in newly abstinent chronic cocaine abusers." Presented at the 53rd annual scientific meeting of the Committee on Problems of Drug Dependence, Palm Beach, FL.

Hoffmann, N. G., Sonis, W. A., & Halikas, J. A. (1987), "Issues in the evaluation of chemical dependency treatment programs for adolescents." *Pediatric Clinics of North America 34*, 449–459.

Hsu, L. K. G. (1984), "Treatment of bulimia with lithium." *American Journal of Psychiatry 141*, 1260–1262.

Hudson, J. I., Pope, H. G., & Jonas, J. M. (1983), "Phenomenologic relationship of eating disorders to major affective disorder." *Psychological Research 9*, 345–354.

Hunt, R. D., Capper, L., & O'Connell, P. (1990), "Clonidine in child and adolescent psychiatry." *Journal of Child and Adolescent Psychopharmacology 1*, 87–101.

Isaac, G. (1991), "Bipolar disorder in prepubertal children in special education setting: Is it rare?" *Journal of Clinical Psychiatry 52*, 165–168.

Jaffe, J. H. (1986), "Opioids." In A. I. Frances, & R. E. Hales, (eds), *Annual Review*, Vol. 5. Washington, DC: American Psychiatric Press, 137–159.

Jaffe, S. L. (1991), "Intranasal abuse of prescribed methylphenidate by an alcohol and drug abusing adolescent with ADHD." *Journal of the American Academy of Child and Adolescent Psychiatry 30*, 774–775.

Jenike, M. A., Baer, L., Minichiello, W. E., Rauch, S. L., & Buttolph, M. L. (1997), "Placebo-controlled trial of fluoxetine and phenelzine for obsessive–compulsive disorder." *American Journal of Psychiatry 154*, 1261–1264.

Johnson, R. E., Stevens, V. J., Hollis, J. F., & Woodson, G. T. (1992), "Nicotine chewing gum use in the outpatient care setting." *Journal of Family Practice 34*, 61–65.

Johnston, L., Bachman, J. G., & O'Malley, R. M. (1998), *Details of Annual Drug Survey*. Ann Arbor: University of Michigan News and Information Services.

Kaminer, Y. (1992a), "Desipramine facilitation of cocaine abstinence in an adolescent." *Journal of the American Academy of Child and Adolescent Psychiatry 31*, 312–317.

Kaminer, Y. (1992b), "Clinical implications of the relationship between attention-deficit hyperactivity disorder and psychoactive substance use disorders." *American Journal on Addictions 1*, 257–264.

Kaminer, Y. (1994a), *Adolescent Substance Abuse: A Comprehensive Guide to Theory & Practice*. New York: Plenum Press.

Kaminer, Y. (1994b), "Tricyclic antidepressants: Therapeutic use for cocaine craving and potential for abuse." *Journal of the American Academy of Child and Adolescent Psychiatry 33*, 592.

Kaminer, Y. (1995), "Issues in the pharmacological treatment of adolescent substance abuse." *Journal of Child and Adolescent Psychopharmacology 5*, 93–106.

Kaminer, Y., Bukstein, O. G., & Tarter, R. E. (1991), "The Teen Addiction Severity Index (T-ASI): Rationale and reliability." *The International Journal of the Addictions 26*, 219–226.

Kaminer, Y., Tarter, R. E., Bukstein, O. G., & Kabene, M. (1992a), "Staff, treatment completers', and noncompleters' perceptions of the value of treatment variables." *American Journal on Addictions 1*, 115–120.

Kaminer, Y., Tarter, R. E., Bukstein, O. G., & Kabene, M. (1992b), "Comparison between treatment completers and noncompleters among dually diagnosed substance-abusing adolescents." *Journal of the American Academy of Child and Adolescent Psychiatry 31*, 1046–1049.

Kaminer, Y., Wagner, E., Plummer, B., & Seifer, R. (1993), "Validation of the Teen Addiction Severity Index (T-ASI)." *American Journal on Addictions 2*, 250–254.

Kastner, T., & Friedman, D. L. (1992), "Verapamil and valproic acid treatment of prolonged mania." *Journal of the American Academy of Child and Adolescent Psychiatry 31*, 271–275.

Katz, L., Fleisher, W., & Kjernisted, K. (1996), "A review of psychobiology and pharmacotherapy of posttraumatic stress disorder." *Canadian Journal of Psychiatry 41*, 233–238.

Kemph, J. P., DeVane, C. L., & Levin, G. M. (1993), "Treatment of aggressive children with clonidine: Results of an open pilot study." *Journal of the American Academy of Child and Adolescent Psychiatry 32*, 577–581.

Kennedy, S. H., & Garfinkel, P. (1992), "Advances in diagnosis and treatment of anorexia nervosa and bulimia nervosa." *Canadian Journal of Psychiatry 37*, 309–315.

Klein, R. G., Koplewicz, H. S., & Kanner, A. (1992), "Imipramine treatment of children with separation anxiety disorder." *Journal of the American Academy of Child and Adolescent Psychiatry 31*, 21–28.

Klein, R. G. *et al.* (1997), "Clinical efficacy of methylphenidate in conduct disorder with and without attention deficit hyperactivity disorder." *Archives of General Psychiatry 54*, 1073–1080.

Kosten, T. R. (1990), "Neurobiology of abused drugs: Opioids and stimulants." *Journal of Nervous and Mental Disease 178*, 217–227.

Kosten, T. R., & McCance, E. (1996), "A review of pharmacotherapies for substance abuse." *American Journal on Addictions 5*, 58–65.

Kosten, T. R., Kleber, H. D., & Morgan, C. (1989), "Treatment of cocaine abuse with buprenorphine." *Biological Psychiatry 26*, 637–639.

Kosten, T. R., Gawin, F. H., Kosten, T. A., Morgan, A., Rounsaville, B. J., Schottenfeld, R., & Kleber, H. D. (1992), "Six month follow-up of short-term pharmacotherapy for cocaine dependence." *American Journal on Addictions 1*, 40–49.

Kranzler, H. R. (1988), "Use of buspirone in an adolescent with overanxious disorder." *Journal of the American Academy of Child and Adolescent Psychiatry 27*, 789–790.

Kranzler, H. R., Burleson, J. A., Korner, P., & DelBoca, F. K. (1995a), "Placebo-controlled trial of fluoxetine as an adjunct to relapse prevention in alcoholics." *American Journal of Psychiatry 152*, 391–397.

Kranzler, H. R., Bauer, L. O., Hersh, D., & Klinghoffer, V. (1995b), "Carbamazepine treatment of cocaine dependence: A placebo-controlled trial." *Drug and Alcohol Dependence 38*, 203–211.

Kuperman, S., & Stewart, M. A. (1987), "Use of propranolol to decrease aggressive outbursts in younger patients." *Psychosomatics 28*, 315–319.

Landry, D. W., Zhao, K., Yang, X. Q., Glickman, M., & Georgiadis, T. M. (1993), "Antibody-catalyzed degradation of cocaine." *Science 259*, 1899–1901.

Lavin, M., & Rifkin, A. (1993), "Diagnosis and pharmacotherapy of conduct disorder." *Biological Psychiatry 17*, 875–885.

Leonard, H. I., March, J., Rickler, K. C., & Allen, A. J. (1997), "Pharmacology of the selective serotonin reuptake inhibitors in children and adolescents." *Journal of the American Academy of Child and Adolescent Psychiatry 36*, 725–736.

Lichtenstein, E., & Glasgow, R. E. (1992), "Smoking cessation: What have we learned over the past decade?" *Journal of Consulting and Clinical Psychology 60*, 518–527.

Margolin, A., Avants, S. K., Chang, P., & Kosten, T. R. (1993), "Acupuncture for the treatment of cocaine dependence in methadone maintained patients." *American Journal on Addictions 2*, 194–201.

McGrath, P. J., Nunes, E. V., & Stewart, J. W. (1996), "Imipramine treatment of alcoholics with primary depression." *Archives of General Psychiatry 53*, 232–240.

McLellan, A. T., Arndt, I. O., Metzger, D. S., Woody, G. E., & O'Brien, C. P. (1993), "The effects of psychosocial services in substance abuse treatment." *Journal of the American Medical Association 269*, 1953–1959.

Meyer, R. E. (1992), "New pharmacotherapies for cocaine dependence revisited." *Archives of General Psychiatry 49*, 900–904.

Miller, W. R. (1985), "Motivation for treatment: A review with special emphasis on alcoholism." *Psychology Bulletin 98*, 84–107.

Monroe, R. R. (1970), *Episodic Behavior Disorders: A Psychodynamic and Neurophysiologic Analysis.* Cambridge, MA: Harvard University Press.

Montoya, I. D., Levin, F. R., Fudala, P., & Gorelick, D. A. (1994), "A double blind comparison of carbamazepine and placebo for the treatment of cocaine dependence." In L. S. Harris (ed.), *Problems of Drug Dependence 1993,* Rockville, MD: NIDA Research Monograph 141 (Vol. 2), 435.

Munir, K., & Earls, F. (1992), "Ethical principles governing research in child and adolescent psychiatry." *Journal of the American Academy of Child and Adolescent Psychiatry 31*, 408–414.

Myers, W. C., Donahue, J. E., & Goldstein, M. R. (1994), "Disulfiram for alcohol use disorders in adolescents." *Journal of the American Academy of Child and Adolescent Psychiatry 33*, 484–489.

Nelson, C., Mazure, C., & Quinlan, P. M. (1984), "Drug responsive symptoms in melancholia." *Archives of General Psychiatry 41*, 663–668.

Nunes, E. V., McGrath, P. J., Steven, W., & Quitkin, F. M. (1990), "Lithium treatment for cocaine abusers with bipolar spectrum disorders." *American Journal of Psychiatry 147*, 655–657.

O'Malley, S. S. *et al.* (1992), "Naltrexone and coping skills therapy for alcohol dependence." *Archives of General Psychiatry 49*, 881–887.

Parran, T. V., & Jasinski, T. R. (1991), "Intravenous methylphenidate abuse: prototype for prescription drug abuse." *Archives of Internal Medicine 151*, 781–783.

Parrino, M. W. (1992), *State Methadone Maintenance Treatment Guidelines*. Rockville, MD: US Department of Health and Human Services.

Patten, C. A. (2000), "A critical evaluation of nicotine replacement therapy for teenage smokers." *Journal of Child & Adolescent Substance Abuse 9*, 51–75.

Pollack, M. H., & Scott, E. L. (1997), "Gabapentin and lamotrigine: Novel treatments for mood and anxiety disorders." *CNS Spectrums 2*, 56–61.

Prien, R. E., & Gelenberg, A. J. (1989), "Alternative to lithium for preventive treatment of bipolar disorder." *American Journal of Psychiatry 146*, 840–848.

Prince, J. B., Wilens, T. E., Biederman, J., Spencer, T. J., & Wozniak, J. R. (1996), "Clonidine for sleep disturbances associated with ADHD." *Journal of the American Academy of Child and Adolescent Psychiatry 35*, 599–605.

Rey, J. M. (1993), "Oppositional defiant disorder." *American Journal of Psychiatry 150*, 1769–1778.

Rickels, K., Schweizer, E., Weiss, S., & Zavodnick, S. (1993), "Maintenance drug treatment for panic disorder. Short and long-term outcome after drug taper." *Archives of General Psychiatry 50*, 61–68.

Riddle, M. A. (1998), "Obsessive–compulsive disorder in children and adolescents." *CNS Spectrums 3* (suppl. 1), 21–23.

Riggs, P. D., Thompson, L. I., Mikulich, S. K., Whitmore, E. A., & Crowly, T. J. (1996), "An open trial of pemoline in drug-dependent delinquents with ADHD." *Journal of the American Academy of Child and Adolescent Psychiatry 35*, 1018–1024.

Riggs, P. D., Mikulich, S. K., & Coffman, L. M. (1997), "Fluoxetine in drug-dependent delinquents with major depression: An open trial." *Journal of Child and Adolescent Psychopharmacology 7*, 87–95.

Riggs, P. D. (1998), "Clinical approach to treatment of ADHD in adolescents with substance use disorders and conduct disorder." *Journal of the American Academy of Child and Adolescent Psychiatry 37*, 331–332.

Riggs, P. D., Leon, S. L., & Mikulich, S. K. (1998), "An open trial of buproprion for ADHD in adolescents with substance use disorders and conduct disorder." *Journal of the American Academy of Child and Adolescent Psychiatry 37*, 1271–1278.

Rosen, M. I., & Kosten, T. R. (1991), "Buprenorphine: Beyond methadone." *Hospital and Community Psychiatry 42*, 347–349.

Ryan, N. *et al.* (1986), "Imipramine in adolescent major depression: Plasma level and clinical response." *Acta Psychiatrica Scandinavica 73*, 275–288.

Ryan, N., Meyer, V., Dachille, S., Mazzie, D., & Puigh-Antich, J. (1988a), "Lithium antidepressant augmentation in TCA-refractory depression in adolescents." *Journal of the American Academy of Child and Adolescent Psychiatry 27*, 371–376.

Ryan, N. et al., (1988b), "MAOI in adolescent major depression unresponsive to tricyclic antidepressants." *Journal of the American Academy of Child and Adolescent Psychiatry 27*, 755–758.

Sass, H., Soyka, M., Mann, K., & Zieglgansberger, W. (1996), "Relapse prevention by acamprosate: Results from a placebo-controlled study on alcohol dependence." *Archives of General Psychiatry 53*, 673–680.

Schuckit, M. A. (1985), "A one year follow-up of men alcoholics given disulfiram." *Journal on Studies of Alcohol 46*, 309–312.

Schuckit, M. A., & Hesselbrock, V. (1994), "Alcohol dependence and anxiety disorders: What is the relationship?" *American Journal of Psychiatry 151*, 1723–1734.

Schweizer, E., Rickels, K., Weiss, S., & Zavodnick, S. (1993), "Maintenance drug treatment of panic disorder results of a prospective, placebo controlled comparison of alprazolam and imipramine." *Archives of General Psychiatry 50*, 51–60.

Simeon, J., Ferguson, H. B., Van Wyck, Y., & Fleet, J. (1986), "Buproprion hydrochloride in attention deficit disorder with hyperactivity in adolescents." *Canadian Journal of Psychiatry 31*, 581–585.

Simeon, J. *et al.* (1992), "Clinical, cognitive, and neurophysiological effects of alprazolam in children and adolescents with overanxious and avoidant disorders." *Journal of the American Academy of Child and Adolescent Psychiatry 31*, 29–33.

Smart, R. G., & Gray, G. (1978), "Multiple predictors of dropout from alcoholism treatment." *Archives of General Psychiatry 35*, 363–367.

Smith, M. O., & Khan, I. (1988), "An acupuncture program for the treatment of drug addicted persons." *Bulletin Narcotics 40*, 35–41.

Spencer, T. *et al.* (1996), "Pharmacotherapy of attention-deficit hyperactivity disorder across the life cycle." *Journal of the American Academy of Child and Adolescent Psychiatry 35*, 409–432.

Steingard, R., Biederman, J., Spencer, T., Wilens, T., & Gonzalez, A. (1993), "Comparison of clonidine response in the treatment of ADHD with and without comorbid tick disorders." *Journal of the American Academy of Child and Adolescent Psychiatry 32*, 350–353.

Stewart, J. T., Myers, W. C., & Burket, R. C. (1990), "A review of the pharmacotherapy of aggression in children and adolescents." *Journal of the American Academy of Child and Adolescent Psychiatry 29*, 269–277.

Strober, M., & Carlson, G. (1982), "Bipolar illness in adolescents with major depression, clinical, genetic, and psychopharmacologic predictions in a three-to-four year prospective follow-up investigation." *Archives of General Psychiatry 39*, 549–555.

Sullivan, P. F., Bulik, C. M., Fear, J. L., & Pickering, A. (1998), "Outcome of anorexia nervosa: A case-control study." *American Journal of Psychiatry 155*, 939–946.

Tonnesen, P., Norregaard, J., Mikkelsen, K., Jorgensen, S., & Nilsson, F. (1993), "A double-blind trial of a nicotine inhaler for smoking cessation." *Journal of the American Medical Association 269*, 1268–1271.

Venkataraman, S., Naylor, M. W., & King, C. A. (1992), "Mania associated with fluoxetine treatment in adolescents." *Journal of the American Academy of Child and Adolescent Psychiatry 31*, 276–281.

Verkes, R. J *et al.* (1998), "Reduction by paroxetine of suicidal behavior in patients with repeated suicide attempts but not major depression." *American Journal of Psychiatry 155*, 543–547.

Volpicelli, J. R., Alterman, A., Hayashida, M., & O'Brien, C. P. (1992), "Naltrexone in the treatment of alcohol dependence." *Archives of General Psychiatry 49*, 876–880.

Weddington, W. W. *et al.* (1990), "Changes in mood, craving and sleep during short-term abstinence reported by male cocaine addicts: A controlled residential study." *Archives of General Psychiatry 47*, 861–868.

Weiss, R. D., Pope, H. G., & Mirin, S. M. (1985), "Treatment of chronic cocaine abuse and attention deficit disorder residual type, with magnesium pemoline." *Drug and Alcohol Dependence 15*, 69–72.

Weissman, M. M., Jarrett, R. B., & Rush, J. A. (1987), "Psychotherapy and its relevance to the pharmacotherapy of major depression: A decade later (1976–1985)." In H. Y. Meltzer (ed.), *Psychopharmacology: The Third Generation of Progress*. New York: Raven Press, 1059–1069.

Wen, H. L. (1979), "Acupuncture and electrical stimulation (AES) outpatient detoxification." *Modern Medicine in Asia 11*, 23–24.

Werry, J. S. (1995), "Cardiac arrhythmias make desipramine an unacceptable choice in children." *Journal of the American Academy of Child and Adolescent Psychiatry 34*, 1239–1241.

Werry, J. S., & Aman, M. G. (eds) (1993), *Practitioner's Guide to Psychoactive Drugs for Children and Adolescents*. New York: Plenum Press.

West, R. (1992), "The 'nicotine replacement paradox' in smoking cessation: How does nicotine gum really work?" *British Journal of Addiction 87*, 165–167.

Whitworth, A., Fischer, F., & Lesch, O. M. (1996), "Comparison of acamprosate and placebo in long-term treatment of alcohol dependence." *Lancet 347*, 1438–1442.

Wilens, T. E., Biederman, J., & Geist, D. E. (1993), "Nortriptyline in the treatment of ADHD: A chart review of 58 cases." *Journal of the American Academy of Child and Adolescent Psychiatry 32*, 343–349.

Wilens, T. E., Biederman, J., & Spencer, T. J. (1997), "Adverse effects of smoking marijuana while receiving tricyclic anti depressants." *Journal of the American Academy of Child and Adolescent Psychiatry 36*, 45–48.

Wold, M., & Kaminer, Y. (1997), "Naltrexone for alcohol abuse." *Journal of the American Academy of Child and Adolescent Psychiatry 36*, 6–7.

Worthington, J., Fava, M., & Alpert, J. (1996a), "Relationship of lifetime history of alcohol or substance abuse/dependence to antidepressant treatment response." Presented at the 36th annual meeting of the New Clinical Drug Evaluation Unit Program, Boca Raton, FL.

Worthington, J., Pollack, M. H., & Otto, M. W. (1996b), "Effect of lifetime history of alcohol or substance dependence on severity and treatment of panic disorder." Presented at the 36th annual meeting of the New Clinical Drug Evaluation Unit Program, Boca Raton, FL.

Zweben, A., & Li, S. (1981), "The efficacy of role induction in preventing early dropout from outpatient treatment of drug dependency." *American Journal of Drug and Alcohol Abuse 8*, 171–183.

Chapter 14

The Assertive Aftercare Protocol for Adolescent Substance Abusers

Susan Harrington Godley, Mark D. Godley, and Michael L. Dennis*

Youth with substance abuse and dependence problems enter treatment with varying levels of abuse/dependence severity. Treatment systems have developed in most areas in the United States that offer multiple levels of care to address these different severity levels. The Center for Substance Abuse Treatment (1993) has provided guidelines for the treatment of alcohol- and other drug-abusing adolescents and described three levels of outpatient treatment and six types of inpatient treatment or residential care options. Similarly, the American Society of Addiction Medicine (ASAM) (1996) has identified five levels of services for adolescents: (1) early intervention; (2) outpatient treatment; (3) intensive outpatient treatment; (4) medically monitored inpatient treatment; and (5) medically managed intensive inpatient treatment. A review of the history of substance abuse treatment reveals a rapid expansion of inpatient and residential adolescent treatment options in the 1970s and1980s, and then a decline of such programs in the 1990s. This decline was caused by the advent of managed care and a closer scrutiny of these programs by both public and third-party purchasers (Bukstein, 1995; Norbett & McMenamy, 1996; White, 1998). Still, in most locales residential treatment programs for adolescent substance abusers remain available. For example, a review of a 1995 case management resource guide for Midwestern states (Center for Healthcare Information, 1996) confirmed 24 hospital-based inpatient and 25 additional residential treatment programs providing substance abuse treatment for adolescents in five Midwestern states.

It has become common practice for adolescents with the most severe problems to be referred to residential programs (Bukstein, 1995), as several states now mandate the use of ASAM (1996) guidelines for making treatment placement decisions. Following residential treatment, it is also standard practice for an aftercare plan to be developed that includes a goal for continued treatment with an outpatient provider. In actuality, however, many adolescents do not participate or participate only minimally in aftercare treatment (Alford,

*This work was supported by the National Institute on Alcohol Abuse and Alcoholism grant no. RO1 AA10368. The interpretations and conclusions are solely those of the authors and do not represent the position of NIAAA or the National Institutes of Health.

We wish to thank Colleen Colby, Rod Funk, Melissa Kehart, Lora Passetti, and Matt Orndorff for their assistance in helping prepare the manuscript.

Koehler, & Leonard, 1991; Dennis, Scott, Godley, & Funk, 1998; Hoffman & Kaplan, 1991). One reason this might occur is that residential facilities often serve large geographic areas; thus when an adolescent returns to his or her home community it is necessary to link with a service provider different from the residential treatment provider. The adolescent may find the transition to a new service provider difficult, especially when motivation to engage in treatment is low, as is often the case with teenagers. Another potential reason the linkage to aftercare services is difficult is the magnitude of concomitant problems these adolescents have, including families with multiple problems that present barriers to accessing further treatment. The Assertive Aftercare Protocol (AAP) described in this chapter is designed specifically for adolescents whose problems warrant residential treatment and for whom the likelihood of following through with aftercare recommendations is low.

Theoretical Background and Rationale

The Assertive Aftercare Protocol is an integrated approach to providing aftercare to adolescents who have been in residential treatment with the goals of (a) increasing their contact with aftercare treatment and (b) increasing the overall effectiveness of substance abuse treatment. The protocol was based on: (1) the characteristics of the target population; (2) techniques that would enhance aftercare treatment contact and access to other needed treatment (e.g., telephone outreach and home visits); and (3) promising techniques from the literature that appeared to fit the characteristics and needs of these adolescents. This population is characterized by multiple and severe problems, and they have high rates of relapse following residential treatment. They often return to an environment that includes adults in the home with multiple problems and/or substance-using peers.

   Promising techniques that have been identified for use with this population include (a) increasing the adolescent's involvement in aftercare treatment, (b) teaching, practicing, and reinforcing skills needed in the natural environment to solve problems, communicate, deal with anger, and prevent relapse, and (c) working with parents and others in the home environment to support continued abstinence. The Community Reinforcement Approach (Azrin, 1976; Azrin, Sisson, Meyers, & Godley, 1982; Meyers and Smith, 1995) involves such techniques, and seeks to alter the youth's social environment to support and reinforce abstinence from alcohol and other drugs. In addition, because substance-abusing adolescents often have multiple problems and are involved in multiple service systems, it is necessary to help the adolescent link with other needed/mandated services and advocate for the adolescent within complicated service systems. For example, clients may need to be linked with a mental health center to address psychiatric problems, or the adolescent may be involved with a probation officer who does not fully understand other services needed by the client. Linkage and advocacy activities draw upon case management techniques that include home-based work (Godley, Godley, Pratt, & Wallace, 1994, Godley, 1995; Siegal & Rapp, 1996; Willenbring, Ridgely, Stinchfield, & Rose, 1991).

   The first part of this chapter provides an in-depth overview and background information related to the characteristics of the population and promising evidence-based strategies for

working with this population. The second part of this chapter provides an o
AAP as it is presently being tested in a randomized field experiment.

Characteristics of Substance-abusing Adolescents

There is ample evidence suggesting that many adolescents with substance abuse problems, especially those admitted to residential treatment, have multiple problems including: involvement with the criminal justice system (Alford, Koehler, & Leonard, 1991; CSAT, 1993; Schiff & Cavaiola, 1990; Winters, 1998); a history of victimization (Schiff & Cavaiola, 1990); symptoms of PTSD (Deykin & Buka, 1997); symptoms of ADHD and/or conduct disorders (Adams & Wallace, 1994; Brown, Gleghorn, Schuckit, Myers, & Mott, 1995; Bukstein, 1995; Moss & Kirisci, 1995); a peer group of close friends who use alcohol and marijuana (Alford, Koehler, & Leonard, 1991); other mental health problems including mood disorders, anxiety disorders, eating disorders, suicidal behavior, and serious mental illness (Bukstein, 1995; Clark *et al.*, 1995; Fleisch, 1993; Schiff & Cavaiola, 1990); and involvement with child protective services (Dennis *et al.*, 1998). In addition, these youth often engage in risky sexual behaviors (Martin, Kaczynski, Maisto, Bukstein, & Moss, 1995; Schiff & Cavaiola, 1990), and at least one study suggests that there are more health problems among inpatient adolescent alcohol abusers such as appetite changes, weight loss, eczema, headaches, and episodes of loss of consciousness (Arria, Dohey, Mezzich, Bukstein, & Van Thiel, 1995).

Family functioning has also been linked to substance abuse among adolescents (Brook, Brook, Gordon, Whiteman, & Cohen, 1990; Dishion, Patterson, & Reid, 1988; Hawkins, Catalano, & Miller, 1992; Hops, Tildesley, Lichtenstein, Ary, & Sherman, 1990). In a review of studies that examined potential family factors related to adolescent substance use problems, Bukstein (1995) identifies parental substance use or abuse, poor parent–child relationships, low perceived parental support, low emotional bonding, and poor parent management techniques. For example, Schiff and Caviola (1990) found that parental substance abuse and parental psychiatric treatment history were higher among a group of adolescents with substance abuse problems than among a group without alcohol or drug problems. Cumes-Rayner *et al.* (1992) found that sons were more likely to drink heavily if their fathers drank heavily. This group of researchers also found that boys who were heavy drinkers were more likely to report that their families had difficulty settling disagreements and that they spent less time at home than boys who were light drinkers. These findings suggest that disharmony in the home may play a role in adolescent substance abuse.

Severity of Adolescents Admitted to Residential Treatment

Recently, Dennis and colleagues (Dennis, Scott *et al.*, 1998) analyzed data from 271 adolescents admitted to either outpatient or residential treatment to assess differences between groups based on the level of care to which they were admitted. At treatment intake, all adolescents completed the Global Assessment of Individual Needs–Initial (GAIN–I) (Dennis, Webber, White, Senay *et al.*, 1996). The GAIN is divided into eight areas: background and treatment arrangements; substance use; physical health; risk behaviors;

mental health; environment; legal; and vocational. In each area, the questions check for major problem areas and the recency of such problems. If a given problem occurred in the past year, additional symptom-based questions (e.g., criteria for alcohol dependence) are asked for the past year. If a problem occurred in the past 90 days, detailed behavioral counts are collected (e.g., days of alcohol use, days of drinking over five drinks per day, etc.). The GAIN also asks detailed questions about lifetime and current (past 90 days) service utilization, as well as changes in the client's cognitive state (e.g., self-efficacy to resist alcohol/drug use, resistance to treatment, motivation to be in treatment, and what services the client currently wants from treatment). Interested readers are referred to www.chestnut.org/LI/gain for more information regarding the psychometrics of this instrument.

A comparison of adolescents admitted to outpatient treatment with those admitted to residential treatment revealed no significant differences on demographic variables (see Table 1) and several significant differences on clinical variables (see Table 2). Adolescents admitted to residential were more likely to report two or more prior substance abuse treatment episodes (17 percent vs. 44 percent), weekly alcohol use (four percent vs. 33 percent), and weekly (primarily marijuana) drug use (46 percent vs. 66 percent). Adolescents admitted to residential were more likely to report symptoms of physiological dependence on alcohol (15 percent vs. 38 percent) or drugs (39 percent vs. 64 percent), and less likely to only report symptoms of abuse (52 percent vs. 36 percent) or substance use (32 percent vs. 19 percent). There were no significant differences with regard to sexual risk in the past 90 days; both groups reported behaviors that put them at risk with 33 percent reporting one sexual partner, 37 percent reporting multiple sexual partners, and 46 percent reporting having sex without any type of protection within the past 90 days. Also, there were no significant differences with regard to PTSD and ADHD between the two groups, although a high percentage in both groups reported these symptoms. When the means of the 22 GAIN–I indices of problem severity are standardized to t-scores across

Table 1: Demographic characteristics of adolescents admitted to outpatient and residential substance abuse treatment programs.

Demographic	Outpatient N=54	Residential N=217	Total N=271	χ^2
Female	26%	37%	35%	2.46
Non-white	24%	32%	30%	1.22
Single-parent family	44%	42%	42%	0.11
DCFS ward	7%	8%	8%	0.05
Employed/in school	61%	59%	59%	0.08
Current criminal justice involvement	74%	73%	73%	0.04
Ever homeless	19%	18%	18%	0.01
Alcohol used weekly in home	20%	25%	24%	0.48
Drugs used weekly in home	6%	15%	13%	3.24
Been victimized	65%	73%	72%	1.52

Table 2: Percentage of adolescents reporting symptoms of severity by their level of care.

Symptoms of severity	Outpatient N=54	Residential N=217	Total N=271	χ^2
Prior substance abuse treatment episodes				26.61*
None	59%	24%	31%	
One	24%	32%	31%	
2 + episodes	17%	44%	38%	
Drug use (past 90 days)				
Weekly alcohol use	4%	33%	27%	18.50*
Weekly marijuana use	41%	64%	59%	9.34*
Weekly crack/cocaine use	2%	11%	9%	4.38*
Weekly heroin/opioid use	2%	5%	4%	1.06
Weekly other drug use	6%	16%	14%	4.01*
Alcohol severity				16.56*
No use	2%	1%	2%	
Use	32%	19%	21%	
Abuse	52%	36%	39%	
Dependence	0%	6%	5%	
Physiological dependence	15%	38%	34%	
Drug use severity				31.02*
No use	0%	1%	1%	
Use	24%	4%	8%	
Abuse	33%	24%	26%	
Dependence	4%	8%	7%	
Physiological dependence	39%	64%	59%	
Mental health[1]				
General mental distress	28%	49%	45%	7.77*
PTSD[2]	43%	54%	51%	2.14
ADHD[2]	55%	56%	56%	0.01
Conduct disorder[2]	35%	59%	53%	8.87*
Sexual risk (past 90 days)				4.41
No sexual partners	39%	27%	30%	
One sexual partner	35%	33%	33%	
Multiple sexual partners	26%	40%	37%	
Unprotected sex	41%	47%	46%	

[1]Percent of clents that scored in the Clinical and Acute ranges of the corresponding scales.
[2]N=187 for these measures.
*$p < 0.05$.

adolescents and graphed, it is easy to see the differences between these two groups, with youths admitted to residential treatment proving to have the most severe problems on all but two of the indices (see Figure 1).

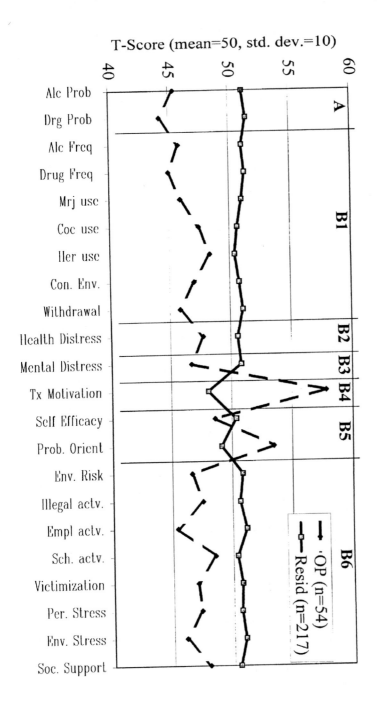

Figure 1: Comparison of mean standardized GAIN–1 scale scores of adolescents admitted to residential and outpatient substance abuse treatment.

Indices are listed by ASAM criteria: A — Diagnosis, B1 — Intoxication/withdrawal, B2 — Biomedical, B3 — Psychological, B4 — Treatment acceptance/resistance, B5 — Relapse potential, B6 — Recovery environment, other. Scores normalized to a mean of 50 with a standard deviation of 10; thus a difference of 5 points is the equivalent of an effect size of 0.5, 10 points is the equivalent of an effect size of 1.0.

Treatment Outcomes after Residential Treatment

Considering the severity of the problems of these adolescents, it is not surprising that the existing studies reveal high levels of relapse for adolescents. Moreover, while many programs seem to have some success in reducing adolescent drug use, they are not as successful in reducing alcohol and marijuana use, the drugs most commonly used by adolescents in the United States (Catalano, Hawkins, Wells, & Miller, 1991). Brown, Vik, & Creamer (1989) found that 60 percent of adolescent substance abusers experienced a relapse within the first three months after discharge from residential treatment, and nearly 80 percent relapsed in the first twelve months. They also found that a majority of adolescent relapses occurred when there was social pressure from peers to drink. Kennedy and Minami (1993) found that 47 percent of adolescents who participated in a three-day hospitalization and a 22-day wilderness-treatment program reported abstinence from alcohol and other drugs for the first year post-treatment. For their sample, relapses were most likely during the first three months post-discharge. In addition, individuals who did not attend Alcoholics Anonymous/Narcotics Anonymous after treatment were more likely to relapse.

Hoffman and Kaplan (1991) provided post-discharge data on a select group of over 800 adolescents who participated in residential treatment. Youth in their study attended treatment programs that used a private client follow-up service. Most of these adolescents came from middle-class families where at least one parent was employed. The researchers found dramatic differences in post-treatment abstinence rates depending on the extent to which clients participated in aftercare activities. For example, the best results were found among clients who took part in such activities two or more times per week throughout the first year after treatment. Parental attendance at support groups and the degree of substance abuse in the post-treatment peer group of the adolescents were also strongly related to sustained abstinence. Notably, among this group, only 25 percent attended support groups or aftercare activities at least twice per week for the entire year following treatment. These data suggest that even with a group of relatively affluent adolescents, compliance with aftercare recommendations is poor.

Alford, Koehler, and Leonard (1991) studied the outcomes of 157 adolescents who attended an inpatient treatment program based primarily on an AA/NA twelve-step approach. At six months follow-up, the percentage of participants who were abstinent or essentially abstinent (three or fewer slips) ranged from 30 percent to 79 percent, with female completers reporting the best outcomes. The ranges of abstinence did not change much at one year (28 percent to 70 percent) or at two years (27 percent to 61 percent), but there were large differences within certain groups. For example, 71 percent of the males met the criteria for abstinence or essentially abstinent at six months, but only 48 percent met the criteria at one year follow-up. Another finding was that those participants who regularly attended AA/NA were more likely to be abstinent or essentially abstinent at the two-year follow-up.

Norbert and McMenamy (1996) report outcome data based on 108 admissions one year after discharge from a 45-day adolescent inpatient chemical dependency unit with an aftercare program. Outcome data were based on parents' reports of adolescent behavior, with questionnaires being administered in an aftercare group or by telephone interview. Based on parent report, the authors report that 57 percent of the youth had not used alcohol or drugs six months after discharge and that 82 percent had not used in the past month. However, potential problems that may have compromised the validity of these data include the use of parental reports (rather than adolescent reports) and asking sensitive questions in a group treatment situation.

Dennis, Scott, Godley, and Funk (1998) administered the follow-up version of the GAIN (Dennis, Webber *et al.*, 1996) at three months with 177 youth discharged from residential treatment after stays ranging from one to 34 weeks. Substance abuse outcomes were classified into five categories: stable in the community; in outpatient treatment; in inpatient treatment, incarcerated; or relapsed and needing readmission. Sixty percent were in the relapse category and appeared to need readmission to treatment based on meeting one or more of the following criteria: (1) reported alcohol or drug use 13 or more days in the past 90 days; (2) reported drinking most of the day or having five or more drinks in one day in the last 90; (3) reported alcohol or drugs were interfering with responsibilities at home, work or school one or more days of the last 90; (4) any drinking or drug use in the past week; (5) using drugs for most of the day or more than five times in one day in the last 90 days; (6) any physical symptoms when trying to cut down; or (7) any combination of 12 or more of 22 DSM-IV symptoms of withdrawal during the past week. Fourteen percent of the adolescents were in a controlled environment at follow-up, two percent were in a substance abuse inpatient facility, one percent were participating in substance abuse outpatient treatment, and 24 percent were stable at the time of follow-up. Even though all adolescents were routinely referred to aftercare, only 36 percent reported attending one or more aftercare sessions, and only 28 percent reported attending two or more aftercare sessions.

Treatment Techniques Related to Preventing Relapse

Catalano *et al.* (1991) reviewed studies that examined pretreatment, during-treatment, and post-treatment factors related to relapse. Results from pre- and during-treatment studies suggested that those with extensive criminal histories may need more intensive and longer treatment, and that programs that targeted education, leisure, exposure to prosocial groups, and recreation yielded positive results. Participation of parents during treatment was positively related to treatment completion and fewer problems during treatment. Programs with staff who favor practical, problem-oriented approaches over psychoanalytic or confrontation therapies were more successful. Although it is widely suspected that post-treatment factors may account for most of the variance in drug treatment outcomes, only one study reviewed by Catalano and his colleagues examined the effect of post-treatment factors. This study suggested the need to address educational issues and provide behavioral and cognitive skills training to help reduce cravings and increase social skills. These skills were considered tools for clients to establish non-drug-using social contacts in work and school settings.

Recently, a number of studies have attempted to identify factors related to adolescent relapse and how these factors may differ from those associated with adult relapse. Myers,

Brown, and Mott (1993) found that coping skills assessed during treatment are predictive of six-month post-treatment outcome and may play a large role in negotiating high-risk relapse situations. Other work has suggested the importance of social support and problem-focused coping when facing a high-risk relapse situation (Myers & Brown, 1990; Richter, Mott, & Brown 1992; Vik, Grizzle, & Brown, 1992). What is clear from the research is that youth are faced with situations in which relapse is often likely to occur and that there are procedures that may help reduce relapse. Researchers have hypothesized that relapse can be prevented or attenuated by higher involvement of youth in aftercare programs (Alford, Koehler, & Leonard, 1991; Catalano *et al.*, 1991; Fertman, 1991; Fertman & Toca, 1989).

Family involvement in treatment also appears related to reducing adolescent relapse. Numerous models of family treatment have been implemented with adolescent substance abusers including multidimensional family therapy (MDFT) (Liddle, 1992; Liddle & Dakof, 1995; Diamond & Liddle, 1996; Schmidt, Liddle, & Dakof, 1996), Functional Family Therapy (FFT) (Waldron & Slesnick, 1998; Waldron, Slesnick, Brody, Turner, & Peterson, 2000), and behavioral methods including contingency-contracting and problem-solving techniques (Azrin, Donohue, Besalel, Kogan, & Acierno, 1994; Bry, Conboy, & Bisgay, 1986; Bry, 1988). Research to date suggests that family-based treatments can engage and retain adolescents with serious drug abuse and their families in treatment (Liddle, Dakof, & Diamond, 1991; Santisteban *et al.*, 1996), significantly reduce adolescent drug use and related comorbid symptoms in a relatively short time (Joanning, Quinn, Thomas, & Mullen, 1992; Lewis, Piercy, Sprenkle, & Trepper, 1990; Bry *et al.*, 1986; Friedman, 1989; Henggeler, Borduin, Melton *et al.*, 1991), and sustain these gains at follow-ups of six months to one year (Liddle *et al.*, 1991; Szapocznik, Murray, Scopetta *et al.*, 1989). At the point of entering aftercare, adolescents are reintegrating into the family situation after a period of separation that was the result of residential treatment and/or other situations (e.g., juvenile detention). Reintegration can be difficult for both the adolescent and the parent, who may have welcomed the respite from one another. Given the evidence for the efficacy of family treatment with this population and the obvious issues surrounding family reintegration after a period of residential treatment, family involvement is likely a critical component of aftercare interventions.

There have been consistent calls for strong aftercare components by researchers in the adolescent treatment field (Alford, Koehler, & Leonard, 1991; Catalano *et al.*, 1991; Catalano, Wells, Jenson, & Hawkins, 1989; Fertman, 1991; Fertman & Toca, 1989). Bukstein (1995) also seems to make a strong case for an assertive aftercare intervention when he describes several guidelines for treatment. He advocates for treatment that is: (1) intense and of sufficient duration; (2) comprehensive in that it targets multiple domains of adolescent lives; (3) sensitive to the cultural and socioeconomic realities of the adolescent; (4) encouraging of family involvement; (5) encouraging of compliance with a wide range of social services, such as juvenile justice, child welfare, attendance at self-help groups; and 6) extended to include an aftercare component that reinforces changes that have been achieved during primary treatment. The Assertive Aftercare Protocol represents an attempt to manualize an integrated aftercare approach that can be replicated and studied.

Overview of the Assertive Aftercare Protocol (AAP)

AAP is currently being tested with youth admitted to a residential facility from an eleven-county area that covers 7477 square miles in central Illinois. Adolescents may be eligible for the AAP intervention if they complete a minimum of one week of residential treatment, regardless of whether or not they successfully completed residential treatment. Presently, the AAP is available to adolescents and their caregivers for 12 to 14 weeks after discharge.

During the assertive aftercare intervention, the case manager works with the adolescent for approximately ten sessions, the caregiver(s) for two sessions, both the caregiver and the adolescent for two sessions, and other community resources (e.g., school, probation, child welfare, psychiatric services) as needed. AAP case managers conduct most of their sessions with participants and their caregivers in the home. The home setting is believed to promote engagement, especially since the large geographic area served by the residential treatment facility makes it impractical for clients to travel back to the residential treatment facility for appointments. Moreover, research suggests that most will not link to traditional aftercare when it is delivered in the traditional facility-based outpatient model. In addition to face-to-face sessions with youth and their families, case managers may make telephone calls to clients between sessions or send greeting cards for encouragement, and may take them to a restaurant or recreational activity to enhance social recreational skills.

Sessions with the Adolescent

While AAP case managers encourage the adolescent to attend whatever aftercare treatment has been recommended in their discharge plan, the case manager provides the manualized AAP intervention regardless of compliance with other aftercare recommendations. Depending on the length of residential treatment, adolescents will have received at least some training in a number of skill areas (e.g., problem solving, communication, and relapse prevention), but their aftercare challenge is to apply these skills in the natural environment. As needed, the AAP case manager draws upon a number of manualized Adolescent Community Reinforcement procedures (Godley *et al.*, in press) including: (1) Functional Analysis of Substance Using Behaviors; (2) Functional Analysis of Pro-social Behaviors; (3) use of the Happiness Scale and Goals of Counseling to help the adolescent set goals; (4) communication skills; (5) problem-solving skills; (6) social/recreational counseling; (7) relationship counseling with family/peers; (8) job finding; and (9) relapse prevention (Meyers & Smith, 1995). Throughout the sessions, the case manager constantly works with the client to identify reinforcers, help them establish goals in their own words, and find prosocial activities that the client enjoys to replace substance-using behavior. To facilitate engagement, the case manager approaches the adolescent with a positive, non-judgmental attitude, communicating to the adolescent that if they use the skills and become substance-free, the quality of their life will improve and they will have a brighter future. The goals of the individual sessions with adolescents include:

1. *Promoting continued abstinence from alcohol and drugs.* Most adolescents will have been substance-free during their residential stay and then return to an environment in which they used substances before. In order to promote continued abstinence, the Functional Analysis of Substance Using Behavior, that may have been completed in residential treatment, is reviewed or initiated to help the adolescent identify potential trigger situations and plan alternate activities. The case manager also encourages attendance at regular aftercare sessions and, if available, twelve-step group sessions. Another procedure used to promote abstinence is monthly urine testing. Results of urine testing are not used punitively. Rather, negative urine tests provide the opportunity for reinforcement and positive urine tests provide the opportunity to redirect the client to a review of relapse prevention procedures, the negative consequences of continued use, and the positive consequences of a substance-free lifestyle. If the adolescent relapses, the goal is to terminate the relapse or to minimize continued use.
2. *Promote positive social support.* Through the Functional Analysis of Pro-social Behaviors, the case manager helps the adolescent identify areas of interest, explore community activities not related to drug use, and identify peers that are not involved in substance-using behaviors. Communication and problem-solving training with both the adolescent and the parent help to promote positive relationships in the home and in other settings.
3. *Minimizing distress.* While AAP work is primarily concerned with reducing alcohol and drug use, case managers have a very broad focus. The Happiness Scale assesses how the adolescent feels about eleven life areas and is used to set goals that are most important to the adolescent, with the assumption that if they feel positive about other areas of their lives (school, relationships, work, criminal justice involvement, money management) then the density of environmental reinforcers increases the probability of abstinence from alcohol and other drugs.

Sequencing of Adolescent Sessions and Content

The goals of the initial sessions are to establish rapport and complete or review the Functional Analysis for Substance Using and for Pro-social Behaviors. Later sessions are similar in that the case manager constantly assesses the need for reviewing procedures, searches for client reinforcers, and takes advantage of teaching opportunities to reinforce the skills. Typical case manager activities during a session include: (1) asking if relapse occurred and reviewing relapse prevention procedures; (2) listening for opportunities to incorporate skills training procedures with 'real-life' problems and issues (e.g., problem-solving, communication, anger management, job-seeking); (3) asking about attendance at aftercare sessions and encouraging attendance; (4) asking about social activities and encourage social activities; and (5) agreeing upon simple "homework" to practice and reinforce skills and increase opportunities for prosocial activities.

Sessions with the Caregiver

The purpose for the caregiver sessions is to ease the transition from residential treatment for the adolescent and family and provide the caregiver with information and skills to support his or her adolescent's recovery. It can be assumed that the newly discharged adolescent, as well as his or her caregiver(s), will experience significant readjustments after the adolescent returns home. There may or may not be some ongoing parental engagement in their adolescent's treatment, depending on the residential treatment experience. Most of the time, caregivers have attended group family education sessions while their child was in treatment and learned new communication techniques during those sessions. The case manager contacts with caregivers provide the opportunity to build on what the caregiver learned while participating in these family sessions. In working with the caregiver, the AAP case manager works to enlist the caregiver as a supportive person in the adolescent's recovery while providing additional information and opportunities to practice important parenting skills like positive communication and problem-solving. While the caregiver may contribute to problems of the adolescent, through their own substance use or poor parenting skills, the AAP case manager approaches them in a non-confrontive and supportive manner. The goals of the caregiver sessions include:

1. *Educating the parents about the most important things they can do to help prevent relapse.* Most adolescents will have been substance-free during their residential stay and then return to an environment in which they used substances before. AAP case managers provide the parents with information about four research-supported parenting behaviors/skills that can support their child's recovery. The first involves being a good role model with regard to their own substance use in front of their children. Increasing positive communication within the family (i.e., engaging in more positive than critical communications) and monitoring their child's activities (i.e., knowing who they are with and where they are) also are encouraged. Parents also are directed to get actively involved in the adolescent's life outside of the home. Parents can support prosocial activities by providing transportation or helping the adolescent enroll for recreational activities available in their communities (Bry, 1998, January; Catalano, 1998, Hops, 1998).
2. *Improving positive communication in the family.* Most families can benefit from learning positive communication techniques — but these families have often experienced a very negative period due to behavior that led to residential treatment. Therefore, positive communication techniques are taught and reinforced during sessions with the goal of having them generalize to other communication between the adolescent and caregiver.
3. *Assess when additional referrals are necessary.* Some families may have significant problems with parental substance abuse, family violence, or mental health issues. Part of the case manager's role is to assess when it is appropriate to help families locate additional services for these serious issues.

Sequencing of Caregiver Sessions and Content

During the first session with the caregiver, the AAP case manager works to establish rapport and reviews the AAP process. Techniques for improving communication and problem-solving are reviewed and practiced in the second session. Optimally, the caregiver and adolescent will both be present for the third and fourth caregiver sessions. During these sessions, both have an opportunity to identify areas of their relationship they need to work on through the completion of caregiver–adolescent versions of the Happiness Scales, and practice communication and problem-solving skills by role-playing real-life situations together.

Case Management Activities

Because of the high rate of co-occurring problems for this population, case management activities are an important part of AAP (Godley, Godley, Karvinen, & Slown, 2001). As previously discussed, high percentages are engaged in the criminal justice system and many have school problems (if they are still in school), mental health problems, and family problems. These multiple problems lead to involvement with multiple agencies. Often, clients are on probation at the time they enter residential treatment, and when they return home they are mandated to attend outpatient substance abuse treatment. Clients also may have mental health problems requiring psychiatric services. Determining when additional referrals are needed for these additional problems is a central activity for the AAP case manager. Linkages to community-based services are not easily made by most of these adolescent clients despite legal prescriptions for attendance. AAP case managers facilitate their clients' participation in community-based programs by monitoring and providing assistance to assure attendance. This may include assisting the adolescent in obtaining transportation and needed medical, dental, mental health, educational, recreational, vocation, and social services. This work often leads to opportunities to apply other procedures such as problem-solving or communication skills. Case managers also engage in extensive discussions with other service providers or attend staffing meetings at other agencies. The AAP case manager often has a unique view of the client because of their home visits and work with caregivers, which enhances their effectiveness as a client advocate. The case manager attempts to assist adolescents and their families in obtaining appropriate services and benefits to which they are entitled. This may include interagency resource brokering to facilitate service provision, assisting individuals in negotiating with governmental bureaucracies, and helping individuals understand their rights.

Pilot Work

A randomized field trial currently under way is the first examination of the efficacy of AAP. A quasi-experimental pilot study compared a group who received a type of case management services with a group of clients who did not have case management (Godley *et al.*, 1994). Subjects were 58 adolescents who had undergone residential treatment who volunteered to participate and were available at their three-month post-discharge date. With an average age of 15.5 years, the majority of the sample were male (78 percent) and non-Hispanic Whites (85 percent; eleven percent African-American, and three percent Hispanic). Twenty-four percent were on probation at intake, 83 percent had been arrested at least once in the last twelve months, and 25 percent had been jailed at least once. The mean age of the onset of alcohol and drug use was 12.3 years. Alcohol was the drug of first or second choice for 88 percent of the sample. A high percentage (85 percent) also used marijuana. Fifty-five percent reported using alcohol weekly; 14 percent used it daily. Twenty-two percent reported using marijuana weekly; 36 percent used it daily.

Consistent with literature previously reviewed, approximately 64 percent of the clients used alcohol on one or more days in the three months following discharge. The case management group had fewer days of alcohol use than the non-case-managed group (5.15 vs. 9.00; effect size d = 2.406). The rates of use, however, varied considerably. Clients used alcohol a mean of 6.48 days (S.D. = 13.67), with 15 adolescents using just one day, nine using two to six days, five using seven to 16 days, and seven using 30 or more days. This revealed at least three patterns of use/relapse during the three-month follow-up: Major Relapse (12.69 percent), which was defined as six or more days of alcohol use; Minor Relapse (52.6 percent), which was defined as one to five days of alcohol use; or Abstinent (34.72 percent), which was defined as no days of use. A recognizable difference was observed in the distribution of relapse days between the two treatment groups, depending in part on the severity of relapse. The differences in days of substance use for clients receiving case management were much larger among those with major relapses (case management group M = 12.3 vs. non-case-management group M = 24.8 days; d = 2.5) than those with only a few lapses (case management group M = 1.56 vs. non-case-management group M = 2.17 days; d = 0.0381). This suggests that case management might be particularly effective for the major relapsers. Another difference between the two groups was that the case management group was more likely to have gone to AA or some other self-help meeting (3.52 vs. 2.32; d = 0.496). Although this pilot study was severely limited by the lack of randomization and small sample size, it suggests the potential for a post-discharge case management intervention. Also of note is that the case management procedures used in this pilot study were only one part of what constitutes the AAP intervention and did not include Adolescent Community Reinforcement Approach procedures.

Future Directions

The first randomized field study of AAP is currently under way. Should this work prove promising, the procedures would need to be replicated and evaluated in other locations to test the model's generalizability. Further studies could examine if modifications of the model work better in different settings (for example, large urban settings). Also, while AAP is designed to address those with severe substance abuse and concomitant problems, it may work better with certain sub-populations within that target population. For example, one subgroup that presents problems for AAP are adolescents who attend residential treatment while on administrative leave from the Department of Corrections. We are finding that the current practice is to send these youth back to the correctional facilities either at the time of discharge or shortly thereafter if they are unsuccessfully discharged from residential treatment. AAP might best be initiated after their release from the correctional facility.

Another important area to study is the cost-effectiveness of this intervention. The use of home visits may make it an expensive intervention. Aftercare services of this type typically are not reimbursed by third-party payers, and data regarding the cost-effectiveness of this approach, relative to more traditional aftercare approaches, would be a critical evaluation component.

Summary

This chapter describes an Assertive Aftercare Procedure which has been specifically designed for adolescents whose substance abuse and other problems are severe enough to warrant residential treatment. AAP is a manualized intervention being tested in a randomized field study. The intervention was developed to address the clinical characteristics of adolescents treated in residential facilities, which include a higher severity of problems than seen in adolescents treated in an outpatient setting, multiple problems, poor compliance with aftercare treatment recommendations, and a high probability of relapse after treatment. AAP is based on operationalizing techniques that researchers have found promising for preventing relapse, which include problem-focused strategies, strategies aimed at increasing social support and prosocial activities, and family involvement in treatment. These procedures are framed in a community reinforcement approach adapted for use with adolescents and their caregivers. A case management component is integral to AAP to aid in accessing treatment and other services needed by these multi-problem adolescents who already tend to be involved in multiple service systems (e.g., probation, child welfare). AAP case managers typically work with adolescents and their caregivers in their homes to enhance treatment engagement and compliance.

The current study will be completed in 2002, and results should provide useful information to drug treatment providers regarding the effectiveness of this approach. Should the approach prove more effective than *status quo* aftercare, further studies should address the generalizability of this approach, compare its effectiveness to other aftercare approaches, examine its cost-effectiveness, and study its effectiveness with different subpopulations.

References

Adams, L., & Wallace, J.L. (1994), "Residential treatment for the ADHD adolescent substance abuser." *Journal of Child & Adolescent Substance Abuse 4*, 35–44.

Alexander, J. F., Waldron, H. B., Newberry, A. M., & Liddle, N. (1990), "The functional family therapy model." In A. S. Friedman & S. Granick (eds), *Family Therapy for Adolescent Drug Abuse*. Lexington, MA: Lexington Books, 183–200.

Alford, G. S., Koehler, R. A., & Leonard, J. (1991), "Alcoholics Anonymous–Narcotics Anonymous model inpatient treatment of chemically dependent adolescents: A 2-year outcome study." *Journal of Studies on Alcohol 52*, 118–126.

American Society of Addiction Medicine (1996), *Patient Placement Criteria for the Treatment of Psychoactive Substance Use Disorders* (2nd edn). Chevy Chase, MD: ASAM.

Arria, A., Dohey, M. A., Mezzich, A. C., Bukstein, O. G., & Van Thiel, D. H. (1995), "Self-reported health problems and physical symptomatology in adolescent alcohol abusers." *Journal of Adolescent Health 16*, 226–231.

Azrin, N. H. (1976), "Improvements in the community reinforcement approach to alcoholism." *Behaviour Research and Therapy 14*, 339–348.

Azrin, N. H., Donohue, B., Besalel, V. A., Kogan, E. S., & Acierno, R. (1994), "Youth drug abuse treatment: A controlled outcome study." *Journal of Child & Adolescent Substance Abuse 3*, 1–16.

Azrin, H. H., Sisson, W., Meyers, R., & Godley, M. (1982), "Alcoholism treatment by disulfiram and community reinforcement therapy." *Journal of Behavior Therapy and Experimental Psychiatry 13*, 105–112.

Brook, J. S., Brook, D. W., Gordon, A. S., Whiteman, M., & Cohen, P. (1990), "The psychosocial etiology of adolescent drug use: A family interactional approach." *Genetic, Social, and General Psychology Monographs 116*, 111–267.

Brown, S. A., Gleghorn, A., Schuckit, M. A., Myers, M. G., & Mott, M. A. (1995), "Conduct disorders among adolescent alcohol and drug abusers." *Journal of Studies on Alcohol 57*, 314–324.

Brown, S. A., Vik, P. W., & Creamer, V. A. (1989), "Characteristics of relapse following adolescent substance abuse treatment." *Addictive Behaviors 14*, 291–300.

Bry, B. H. (1988), "Family-based approaches to reducing adolescent substance use: Theories, techniques and findings." In E. R. Radhert & J. Grabowski (eds), *Adolescent Drug Abuse: Analyses of Treatment Research.* Washington, DC: US Government Printing Office.

Bry, B. H. (1998, January), "The targeted adolescent family and multisystems intervention, (TAFMI): Prevention intervention with youths at risk for substance abuse." Workshop presented at the meeting of the Eighth International Conference on Treatment of Addictive Behaviors, Santa Fe, NM.

Bry, B. H., Conboy, C., & Bisgay, K. (1986), "Decreasing adolescent drug use and school failure: Long-term effects of targeted family problem-solving training." *Child and Family Behavior Therapy 8*, 43–59.

Bukstein, O. G. (1995), *Adolescent Substance Abuse: Assessment, Prevention and Treatment.* New York: John Wiley & Sons, Inc.

Catalano, R. (1998, January), "The importance of the family to the prevention and treatment of substance abuse." Keynote address presented at the meeting of the Eighth International Conference on Treatment of Addictive Behaviors, Santa Fe, NM.

Catalano, R. F., Hawkins, J. D., Wells, E. A., Miller, J., & Brewer, D. (1991), "Evaluation of the effectiveness of adolescent drug abuse treatment, assessment of risks for relapse, and promising approaches for relapse prevention." *The International Journal of the Addictions 25*, 1085–1140.

Catalano, R. F., Wells, E. A., Jenson, J. M., & Hawkins, J. D. (1989), "Aftercare services for drug-using institutionalized delinquents." *Social Service Review 63*, 553–577.

Center for Healthcare Information (1996), *Case Management Resource Guide: 1996 Edition. Volume 3: Midwestern U.S.* Irvine, CA: CHI.

Center for Substance Abuse Treatment (1993), *Guidelines for the Treatment of Alcohol- and other Drug-abusing Adolescents* (DHHS Publication No. (SMA) 93-2010). Rockville, MD: Substance Abuse and Mental Health Services Administration.

Clark, D. B. *et al.* (1995), "Identifying anxiety disorders in hospitalized adolescents with alcohol abuse or dependence." *Psychiatric Services 46*, 618–620.

Cumes-Rayner, D. P. *et al.* (1992), "A high-risk community study of paternal alcohol consumption and adolescents' psychosocial characteristics." *Journal of Studies on Alcohol 53*, 626–635.

Dennis, M. L. *et al.* (1998), "Towards better placement and case mix adjustments in adolescent and adult substance abuse treatment systems." Presentation at the Eighth International Conference on Treatment of Addictive Behavior, Sante Fe, NM, January 10–15.

Dennis, M. L., Scott, C. K., Godley, M. D., & Funk, R. (1998), "Analyzing and Using Data from Outcome Monitoring in Substance Abuse Treatment." Panel Presentation at the American Evaluation Association Conference, Chicago IL, November 4–7.

Dennis, M. L. *et al.* (1996), *Global Appraisal of Individual Needs (GAIN): Version 12/96.* Bloomington, IL: Lighthouse Institute, Chestnut Health Systems.

Deykin, E.Y., & Buka, S. L. (1997), "Prevalence and risk factors for posttraumatic stress disorder among chemically dependent adolescents." *The American Journal of Psychiatry 154,* 752–757.

Diamond, G. S., & Liddle, H. A. (1996), "Resolving a therapeutic impasse between parents and adolescents in multidimensional family therapy." *Journal of Consulting and Clinical Psychology 64*(3), 481–488.

Dishion, T. J., Patterson, G. R., & Reid, J. R. (1988), "Parent and peer factors associated with drug sampling in early adolescence: Implications for treatment." In E. R. Rahdert & J. Grabowski (eds), *Adolescent Drug Abuse: Analyses of treatment research.* National Institute on Drug Abuse Research Monograph 77. Rockville, MD: National Institutes of Health, 69–93.

Fertman, C. I. (1991), "Aftercare for teenagers: Matching services and needs." *Journal of Alcohol and Drug Education 36,* 1–11.

Fertman, C. L. & Toca, O. A. (1989), "A drug and alcohol aftercare service: Linking adolescents, families, and schools." *Journal of Alcohol and Drug Education 34*(2), 46–53.

Fleisch, B. (1993). *Approaches in the Treatment of Adolescents with Emotional and Substance Abuse Problems* (DHHS Publication No. (SMA) 93-1744), Rockville, MD: Substance Abuse and Mental Health Services Administration.

Friedman, A. S. (1989), "Family therapy vs. parent groups: Effects on adolescent drug abusers." *The American Journal of Family Therapy 17*(4), 335–347.

Godley, S. H. (1995), *A Case Manager's Manual for Working with Adolescent Substance Abusers.* Bloomington, IL: Lighthouse Institute.

Godley, S. H., Godley, M. D., Karvinen, T., & Slown, L. L. (2001), The Assertive Aftercare Protocol: A case manager's manual for working with adolescents after residential treatment of alcohol and other substance use disorders. Bloomington, IL: Lighthouse Institute.

Godley, S. H., Godley, M. D., Pratt, A., & Wallace, J. L. (1994), "Case management services for adolescent substance abusers: A program description." *Journal of Substance Abuse Treatment 11,* 309–317.

Godley, S. H., Meyers, R. J., Smith, J. E., Godley, M. D., Titus, J. M., Karvinen, T., Dent, G., Passetti, L., & Kelberg, P. (in press), *The Adolescent Community Reinforcement Approach for Adolescent Cannabis Users, Cannabis Youth Treatment (CYT) Series, Volume 4.* Rockville, MD: Center for Substance Abuse Treatment, Substance Abuse and Mental Health Services Administration.

Hawkins, J. D., Catalano, R. F., & Miller, J. Y. (1992), Risk and protective factors for alcohol and other drug problems in adolescent and early adulthood: Implications for substance abuse prevention. *Psychological Bulletin 112,* 64–105.

Henggeler, S. W. *et al.* (1991), "Effects of multi systemic therapy on drug use and abuse in serious juvenile offenders: A progress report from two outcome studies." *Family Dynamics of Addiction Quarterly 1,* 40–51.

Hoffman, N. G., & Kaplan, R. A. (1991), *One-year Outcome Results for Adolescents: Key correlates and benefits of recovery.* St Paul, MN: CATOR/New Standards.

Hops, H. (1998, January), "From adolescence to adulthood: A 10-year family perspective on substance use and abuse." Keynote address presented at the meeting of the Eighth International Conference on Treatment of Addictive Behaviors, Santa Fe, NM.

Hops, H., Tildesley, E., Lichtenstein, E., Ary, D., & Sherman, L. (1990), "Parent–adolescent problem-solving interactions and drug use." *American Journal of Drug and Alcohol Abuse 16,* 239–258.

Joanning, H., Quinn, W., Thomas, F., & Mullen, R. (1992), "Treating adolescent drug abuse: A comparison of family systems therapy, group therapy, and family drug education." *Journal of Marital and Family Therapy 18,* 345–356.

Kennedy, B. P. & Minami, M. (1993), "The Beech Hill Hospital/Outward Bound adolescent chemical dependency treatment program." *Journal of Substance Abuse Treatment 10*, 395–406.

Lewis, R. A., Piercy, F. P., Sprenkle, D. H., & Trepper, T. S. (1990), "Family-based interventions for helping drug-abusing adolescents." *Journal of Adolescent Research 5*(1), 82–95.

Liddle, H. A. (1992), "A multidimensional model for the adolescent who is abusing drugs and alcohol." In W. Snyder & T. Ooms (eds), *Empowering Families, Helping Adolescents: Family-centered treatment of adolescents with alcohol, drug abuse, and other mental health problems*. US Department of Health and Human Services, Office for Treatment Improvement, ADAMHA, Washington, DC: United States Public Health Service, US Government Printing Office.

Liddle, H. A., & Dakof, G. A. (1995), "Efficacy of family therapy for drug abuse: Promising but not definitive." *Journal of Marital and Family Therapy 21*(4), 511–544.

Liddle, H. A., Dakof, G. A., & Diamond, G. (1991), "Adolescent substance abuse: Multidimensional family therapy in action." In E. Kaufman & P. Kaufman (eds), *Family Therapy of Drug and Alcohol Abuse*. Boston, MA: Allyn and Bacon, 120–171.

Martin, C. S., Kaczynski, N. A., Maisto, S. A., Bukstein, O. M., & Moss, H. B. (1995), "Patterns of DSM-IV alcohol abuse and dependence symptoms in adolescent drinkers." *Journal of Studies on Alcohol 56*, 672–680.

Meyers, R. J., & Smith, J. E. (1995), *Clinical Guide to Alcohol Treatment: The community reinforcement approach*. New York: Guilford Press.

Moss, H. B., & Kirisci, L. (1995). "Aggressivity in adolescent alcohol abusers: relationship with conduct disorder." *Alcoholism: Clinical and Experimental Research 19*, 642–646.

Myers, M. G. & Brown, S. A. (1990), "Coping and appraisal in relapse risk situations among adolescent substance abusers following treatment." *Journal of Adolescent Chemical Dependency 1*, 95–115.

Myers, M. G., Brown, S. A., & Mott, M. A. (1993), "Coping as a predictor of adolescent substance abuse treatment outcome." *5*, 15–29.

Norbert, R., & McMenamy, C. (1996), "Treatment outcomes in an adolescent chemical dependency program." *Adolescence 31*, 91–107.

Richter, S. S., Mott, M. A., & Brown, S. A. (1992), "The impact of social support and self-esteem on adolescent substance abuse treatment outcome." *Journal of Substance Abuse 3*, 371–386.

Santisteban, D. A., Szapocznik, J., Perez-Vidal, A., Kurtines, W. M., Murray, E. J., & LaPerriere, A. (1996), "Efficacy of interventions for engaging youth/families into treatment and some factors that may contribute to differential effectiveness." *Journal of Family Psychology 10*, 35–44.

Schiff, M. M. & Cavaiola, A. A. (1990), "Teenage chemical dependence and the prevalence of psychiatric disorders: Issues for prevention." *Journal of Adolescent Chemical Dependency 1*, 35–46.

Schmidt, S. E., Liddle, H. A., & Dakof, G. A. (1996), "Changes in parenting practices and adolescent drug abuse during multidimensional family therapy." *Journal of Family Psychology 10*(1), 12–27.

Siegal, H. A., & Rapp, R. C. (eds) (1996), *Case Management and Substance Abuse Treatment: Practice and experience*. New York: Springer Publishing Company.

Szapocznik, J. *et al.* (1989), Structural family versus psychodynamic child therapy for problematic Hispanic boys." *Journal of Consulting and Clinical Psychology 57*(5), 571–578.

Vik, R. W., Grizzle, K. L., Brown, S. A. (1992), "Social resource characteristics and adolescent substance abuse relapse." *Journal of Adolescent Chemical Dependency 2*, 59–74.

Waldron, H. B., & Slesnick, N. (1998), "Treating the family." In W. R. Miller & N. Heather (eds), *Treating Addictive Behaviors: Processes of change* (2nd edn). New York: Plenum Press, 271–285.

Waldron, H. R., Slesnick, N., Brody, J. L., Turner, C. W., & Peterson, T. R. (2000), "Four- and seven-month treatment outcomes for substance-abusing youth." Manuscript submitted for publication.

White, W. L. (1998), *Slaying the Dragon: The history of addiction treatment and recovery in America*. Bloomington, IL: Lighthouse Institute.

Willenbring, M. L., Ridgely, M. S., Stinchfield, R., & Rose, M. (1991), *Application of Case Management in Alcohol and Drug Dependence: Matching techniques and populations*. Washington, DC: National Institute on Alcohol Abuse and Alcoholism.

Winters, K. C. (1998), "Kids and drugs: treatment recognizes link between delinquency and substance abuse." *Corrections Today* 60, 118–121, 163–166.

Chapter 15

Twelve-Step-Based Interventions for Adolescents

Jon D. Kassel* and Shannon I. Jackson

Introduction

Epidemiological studies repeatedly have confirmed that the majority of American adolescents experiment with both licit and illicit drugs, and that the use of drugs by most teens appears to be predominantly experimental and episodic in nature. Nonetheless, a significant proportion of adolescents do progress to heavier, more regular use, and ultimately will experience significant problems because of their alcohol or other drug involvement. The demand for interventions to address substance abuse problems among adolescents has led to the development of numerous primary, secondary, and tertiary prevention programs, many of which lack both a firm theoretical base and demonstrated effectiveness (see Wagner, Brown, Monti, Myers, & Waldron, 1999). Of the extant programs designed to treat adolescent drug problems, there is strong reason to believe that the overwhelming majority are steeped within the influential Twelve-step orientation of Alcoholics Anonymous (Lawson, 1992). As such, the goal of this chapter is to provide an overview of the Twelve-step approach to the treatment of adolescent substance abuse, as well as to examine the philosophical, theoretical, and empirical bases upon which such programs rest.

Theoretical Background and Rationale

As a first step in understanding Twelve-step approaches to the treatment of substance use disorders, several terms need clarification. First, Twelve-step programs derive from the twelve steps of Alcoholics Anonymous (AA). As depicted in Table 1, these steps are viewed as integral to the process of recovery from alcohol dependence, and, as such, all members of AA are encouraged to proceed through the steps in a fairly linear fashion. It is important to note that AA ideology and organizational functioning have been adopted by

Preparation of this chapter was supported by Grant No. 1R29AA12240-01 to Jon D. Kassel from the National Institute on Alcohol Abuse and Alcoholism.

*Correspondence concerning this chapter should be addressed to: Jon D. Kassel, Ph.D., Department of Psychology, University of Illinois at Chicago. Shannon I. Jackson, M.A., Department of Clinical and Health Psychology, University of Florida.

Innovations in Adolescent Substance Abuse Interventions, pages 333–351.
Copyright © 2001 by Elsevier Science Ltd.
ISBN: 0-08-043577-7

Table 1: The Twelve Steps of Alcoholics Anonymous.

Step 1	We admitted we were powerless over alcohol — that our lives had become unmanageable.
Step 2	Came to believe that a power greater than ourselves could restore us to sanity.
Step 3	Made a decision to turn our will and our lives over to the care of God *as we understood Him.*
Step 4	Made a searching and fearless moral inventory of ourselves.
Step 5	Admitted to God, to ourselves and to another human being the exact nature of our wrongs.
Step 6	Were entirely ready to have God remove all these defects of character.
Step 7	Humbly asked Him to remove our shortcomings.
Step 8	Made a list of all persons we had harmed, and became willing to make amends to them all.
Step 9	Made direct amends to such people wherever possible, except when to do so would injure them or others.
Step 10	Continued to take personal inventory and when we were wrong promptly admitted it.
Step 11	Sought through prayer and meditation to improve our conscious contact with God *as we understood Him,* praying only for knowledge of his will for us and the power to carry that out.
Step 12	Having had a spiritual awakening as the result of these steps, we tried to carry this message to alcoholics and to practice these principles in all our affairs.

other self-help groups for a wide range of problem behaviors including nicotine dependence (Lichtenstein, 1999), narcotics dependence (Chappel, 1992), compulsive gambling (Rosenthal, 1992), eating disorders (Johnson & Sansone, 1993), and post-traumatic stress (Brende, 1993). Moreover, Twelve-step programs have been conceived to help family and friends of the identified patient as well (i.e., Al-Anon, Alateen, Gam-Anon). Thus, whereas all of these respective programs utilize Twelve-step approaches, the steps vary according to specific aspects of the presenting problem. Put simply, although AA is but one of many Twelve-step programs, its ideological framework is at the core of the many fellowships and programs designed to help individuals suffering from problems with addictive behaviors.

Alcoholics Anonymous

Alcoholics Anonymous (AA) has been variously defined as a treatment for alcoholism, a social movement (Wallace, 1983), a religious organization (Ellis & Schoenfeld, 1990), an ideology (Tournier, 1979), and even a cult (Bufe, 1991). AA's inception can be traced to Akron, Ohio, where in 1935, two chronic alcoholics met and shared their interest in helping individuals with drinking problems achieve and maintain sobriety (see Kurtz,

1979, for a detailed history of AA). Borrowing from William James's pragmatism, Christian fundamentalist ideology as practiced by the Oxford Group, and Carl Jung's concept of religious conversion, Bill Wilson, "Dr. Bob," and other early AA founders formulated the Twelve Steps of AA (Alcoholics Anonymous, 1984). These steps, along with the AA "Big Book," constitute the content and philosophy out of which AA predicates its program of recovery.

AA views alcoholism as a disease, comprising physical, emotional, and spiritual factors (Alcoholics Anonymous, 1976). At its core, AA regards the disease as having a single etiology and a progressive course that only can be arrested through abstinence. Although physical and psychological symptoms are believed to result from alcoholism, they are not thought to play a central role in the etiology of the disorder. At the same time, much emphasis is placed on confronting one's "character defects," the central focus of which is often self-centeredness. Thus, according to AA, fundamental components involved in recovery include: admitting that one is powerless over alcohol; the belief in a "higher power;" writing and expressing a "fearless moral inventory;" making amends to all those harmed by the alcoholic; and the "passing on" of the AA message to other alcoholics. The AA principles clearly contain a strong spiritual emphasis, with the concept of a higher power noted in step 2, unambiguously replaced by "God" in steps 3, 5, 6, 7, and 11. Reconstruction of relationships with other people is emphasized through the use of confession and restitution, as noted in steps 8 and 9. Moreover, the recovering alcoholic is urged to help other alcoholics, as emphasized in step 12. Of course, as its namesake implies, anonymity is central to AA philosophy. A tenet of AA is that members ought never publicly divulge their affiliation with AA. Correspondingly, the policy of "what is said in these rooms, stays in these rooms" presumably provides a safe and supportive atmosphere in which members can honestly share their experiences.

Although AA has never been exclusionary regarding its membership (e.g., "The only requirement for AA membership is a desire to stop drinking"), its primary function has been to help alcohol-dependent individuals, as defined by the presence of tolerance and withdrawal, live a sober life. As such, its original membership was comprised almost entirely of male alcoholics, almost all of whom were middle-aged or older. Moreover, "Many [of the original members] tended to doubt the ability of women to get sober — and some told young people to go out and come back when they'd had enough to drink" (Alcoholics Anonymous, 1999, p. 1). Although the makeup of membership in AA has certainly changed over the last 65 years — as of 1998, 34 percent of members were women, two percent were under 21, and nine percent under 30 — the question of whether AA is appropriate for adolescent substance abusers is an important one that continues to be asked. We will revisit this issue later in this chapter.

The Minnesota Model, while subsuming the basic tenets and philosophy of AA, offers a more comprehensive approach to the treatment of alcohol and drug abuse (McElrath, 1997). Cook (1988a) ascribes four key tenets to the Minnesota Model philosophy. The first is the belief that substance-dependent individuals can modify and change their beliefs, attitudes, and behavior. As such, it is believed that feelings of hopelessness and despair can be overcome through a process of increased self-efficacy. Second, the goals of treatment include abstinence from all mood-altering chemicals and a general improvement in lifestyle. Implicit in this view is the notion of *chemical dependency*, that is, individuals who are dependent on one particular drug or class of drugs should abstain from all drug use, lest they risk relapse to their drug of choice, or transfer their addiction to another substance. Third, the approach endorses the *disease model* of substance dependence, which represents an explanatory concept encompassing social, psychological, spiritual, but predominantly biological dimensions of alcohol and drug dependence (see Sheehan & Owen, 1999). Indeed, from the disease model perspective, the hallmark of substance dependence is loss of control over use, coupled with the belief that drug dependence is a chronic and progressive condition, usually resulting in death if left untreated (Morrison & Smith, 1987). Finally, Cook (1988a) notes that the following components are also integral to Minnesota Model programs: (1) group therapy; (2) didactic lectures; (3) use of recovering addicts as primary counselors; (4) use of a multidimensional staff, often comprising social workers, psychologists, clergy, physicians, and recovering addicts; (5) a therapeutic milieu; (6) work assignments (i.e., laundry, maintenance); (7) family counseling; (8) AA attendance; (9) daily readings from the AA "Big Book;" (10) sharing of one's life history; (11) "working" the first five steps of AA; and (12) recreational and physical activity. In sum, the Minnesota Model emphasizes lifestyle change organized around AA philosophy and utilizes a continuum-of-care approach to the treatment of substance dependence.

Description of the Intervention

Clinic-based AA oriented interventions for substance abusers primarily have taken the form of the Minnesota Model approach. Thus, characteristic chemical dependency treatment facilities offer multidimensional programs that are steeped in an AA orientation and philosophy. The typical inpatient treatment for adolescent patients consists of attending daily AA or NA meetings, individual and group therapy, and educational lectures on problem areas or one of the twelve steps (Lawson, 1992). The pervasiveness of the Twelve-step approach may be due, in part, to the observation that many programs are founded and run by alcoholics or drug-dependent individuals who gained sobriety through participation in a Twelve-step program (Selekman & Todd, 1991). Moreover, the Twelve-step model tends to be viewed by treatment providers as one that is flexible and easily implemented.

Recent estimates suggest that there are about 100,000 AA groups worldwide, comprising almost two million members (Alcoholics Anonymous, 1999). In addition to the Twelve steps, AA also boasts Twelve traditions reflecting "the means by which AA maintains its unity and relates itself to the world about it, the way it lives and grows" (p. 15; Alcoholics Anonymous, 1976). These traditions stress the importance of: (1) unity; (2) a "loving God;" (3) group autonomy; (4) carrying the message to other alcoholics; (5) a public policy based on attraction rather than promotion; and (6) remaining non-professional (i.e., meetings run only by recovering members) and self-supporting.

Although AA meetings are intended to be autonomous, they generally take one of several forms. In a Step Meeting, perhaps the most common format, members discuss one of the Twelve steps of AA, sharing their experience with that step, how the step has helped them grow, and any struggles they might still be having with the step. A Discussion Meeting is a more open-ended forum in which members are asked at the meeting's outset if there are any particular issues they would like to share and discuss with the group. As in the Step Meeting, members are then free to speak or not. Finally, the Speaker Meeting, which itself has several variants, generally offers a less interactive format during which one or more AA members shares their stories of "what it was like, what happened, and what it is like now" with the group (Bean, 1975).

An important element of the AA approach is the Sponsor, an "expert" senior member to whom initiates can turn for advice during the course of recovery. The Sponsor is usually a person who has been a member of AA for quite some time, has worked a successful "program of recovery," and is of the same sex as the initiate. In fact, previous research has demonstrated that across a variety of group contexts, sponsors help to facilitate the process of socialization to the group (Alibrandi, 1985; Moreland & Levine, 1989). A second aspect of AA is the extent to which individual members engage in AA-related social activities (Bean, 1975). Newer members are encouraged to arrive at meetings early, help make coffee, and, most importantly, befriend their fellow group members. Research has suggested that role-taking within the group, such as volunteering to be squad leader or steering committee representative, may also be instrumental in initiating and maintaining change (Bohnice & Orensteen, 1950; Kammeier & Anderson, 1976; Patton, 1979). Social interaction with other members often extends beyond the confines of the meeting as well, and may play an important role in members' recovery.

Several studies suggest that AA members share certain psychological characteristics. For instance, Trice and Roman (1970) found that "full-fledged" AA affiliates exhibited strong affiliative needs, had been intensively labeled by both themselves and other "mandated societal agents" as alcoholic, and, relative to those who chose not to affiliate with AA, had fewer physical sequelae and had been more prone to guilt prior to entry in AA. Others have suggested that AA members exhibit greater alcohol dependence (Ogborne & Glasser, 1981; Vaillant, 1983), use more external controls to stop drinking (O'Leary *et al.*, 1980), and have better childhood emotional environments (Vaillant, 1983) than do alcoholics not in AA. Emrick (1987), on the other hand, has argued that the most striking finding concerning AA affiliates is the absence of specific commonalities. In an extensive review of the literature, Emrick found that demographic variables including education, socioeconomic status, employment status, legal status, adult social competence, social stability, and religion appear to be unrelated to AA membership.

Although there has been a great deal of armchair speculation as to what makes AA "work," very few studies have systematically attempted to delineate the processes of change associated with success in AA. Morgenstern, Labouvie, McCrady, Kahler, and Frey (1997) examined the therapeutic effects and mechanisms of action of affiliation with AA after attending a Minnesota Model treatment facility. Results indicated that increased affiliation with AA predicted better outcomes, and that these effects were mediated by a set of common change factors, including maintenance of self-efficacy and increased active coping efforts. Interestingly, Fiorentine and Hillhouse (2000) found that substance abuse treatment participants with pretreatment Twelve-step involvement stayed in treatment longer and were more likely to complete the 24-week program. Moreover, both pretreatment Twelve-step involvement and duration of participation in drug treatment were associated with subsequent Twelve-step involvement. Finally, Snow, Prochaska, and Rossi (1994) reported a positive relationship between the use of behaviorally oriented change processes (e.g., stimulus control, behavior management) and increased involvement in AA.

Taken together, these findings are consistent with the observation that many behavioral principles are actually inherent to the AA program (McCrady, 1994; Wagner & Kassel, 1995), including: (1) stimulus control (avoid drinking environments, develop interests and habits incompatible with drinking/drug use); (2) behavioral coping ("don't drink, go to meetings," call your sponsor); (3) cognitive coping (recite the "serenity prayer," tell yourself to take it "one day at a time"); (4) covert sensitization (remember the consequences of your drinking, tell your "story" at meetings); (5) self-management (stress delayed reinforcers versus immediate reinforcers despite initial punishments); (6) expanding behavioral repertoire (learn social skills, establish social support, implement new reinforcers); and (7) modeling (watch and learn from successful AA members). Thus, behavioral strategies clearly complement, and may be essential to, a Twelve-step approach.

Attempting to better understand the processes of change at work in AA, Kassel and Wagner (1993) reviewed several diverse literatures relevant to AA and proposed that several possible mechanisms of change are worthy of further empirical scrutiny. First, they noted that since AA comprises groups of people, mechanisms of change known to be operative in both professionally led group therapy and peer-led self-help groups may similarly be operative within AA. Potential change mechanisms of this sort include supportive techniques (e.g., empathy, instillation of hope), expressive techniques (e.g., catharsis, telling one's "story"), and insight-oriented techniques (e.g., explanation, checking in with the group). Second, as a group's ideology is known to exert a strong persuasive influence on group members (Antze, 1979; Zurcher & Snow, 1981), it is conceivable that AA's rich ideological framework, as expressed in the Twelve Steps, the Big Book, and other pamphlets and literature, contributes to recovery. Indeed, recent work suggests that commitment to Twelve-step ideology, specifically the notion that controlled drug use is not possible, predicted abstinence independent of Twelve-step participation and other potentially mediating variables (Fiorentine & Hillhouse, 2000). Finally, based on the assumption that AA also can be viewed as a social order or movement (e.g., Room, 1993), several processes of commitment generation to social orders (e.g., sacrifice, investment, renunciation, communion, mortification, and transcendence; see Kanter, 1968) may be relevant to understanding how initiates become and remain committed to AA and its principles (Donovan, 1984; Rudy, 1986).

In summary, AA is clearly a complex and multifaceted program of recovery. Possessing a rich ideological framework, AA has consistently grown in size since its inception over 65 years ago, and has been incorporated into the treatment program offered by most addiction treatment facilities. At the same time, it is important to remember that little is known with respect to how AA facilitates change in adult, let alone adolescent, substance abusers.

Empirical Studies

In spite of its pervasive influence, AA remains one of the most controversial and least understood interventions for the treatment of alcohol problems. The controversy surrounding AA stems, in large part, from the paucity of sound empirical research concerning its efficacy. Indeed, the inherent difficulties in conducting research on AA are well known, and include lack of membership "criteria," anonymity as a central philosophical tenet, self-selection biases, absence of control groups, little long-term follow-up, and variability in content and process both within and across AA groups (Montgomery, Miller, & Tonigan, 1993; Tonigan, Ashcroft, & Miller, 1995). Thus, methodological shortcomings often render empirical studies of AA efficacy equivocal at best.

Acknowledging these limitations, several reviews have provided summaries of the empirical literature on the efficacy of both the Minnesota Model (e.g., Cook, 1988b) and, more specifically, AA among adult substance abusers (Emrick, Tonigan, Montgomery, & Little, 1993; Hoffman & Miller, 1992; Kownacki & Shadish, 1999). Findings offer modest support for the Minnesota Model (Collins, 1995; Winters, Latimer, & Stinchfield, 1999), but are undermined by the many methodological shortcomings of the studies. Regarding AA, Kownacki & Shadish (1999) concluded that severe selection biases compromised all quasi-experimental studies, while randomized studies actually yielded worse results for AA than non-randomized studies and were biased by selection of coerced subjects. Indeed, according to their review: (a) attending conventional AA meetings was associated with worse outcomes relative to no-treatment or alternative treatments; (b) residential AA-modeled treatments performed similarly to various alternative interventions; and (c) several components of AA, including the use of recovering alcoholics as therapists, peer-led self-help therapy groups, teaching the Twelve-step process, and conducting an honest personal inventory, appeared to be associated with positive outcomes.

Several recent well-designed studies have yielded findings strongly supporting the efficacy of Twelve-step oriented programs (Ouimette, Finney, & Moos, 1997; Moos, Finney, Ouimette, & Suchinsky, 1999; Project MATCH Research Group, 1993). Interestingly, several reports suggest that mere attendance at AA may not be particularly beneficial in and of itself; rather, the degree to which one embraces the program and truly becomes affiliated with AA appears more predictive of positive outcome (Caldwell & Cutter, 1998; Montgomery, Miller, & Tonigan, 1995).

Turning to the adolescent literature, it is disheartening to observe that very few studies have examined the efficacy of AA and Minnesota Model programs among young substance abusers. Hazelden, one of the first facilities to implement the Minnesota Model approach, has published several reports indicating extremely positive outcomes among adolescents treated for substance abuse. One such study claimed that of 480 teens who completed treatment, 46 percent of those contacted at a one-year follow-up reported no use of alcohol, and 68 percent indicated no use of other drugs during the follow-up period (Keskinen, 1986). Although initially encouraging, these findings must be tempered by the fact that only 53 percent of the original sample were contacted at follow-up. In a review of programs based on the Minnesota Model, Harrison and Hoffman (1989) observed that 42 percent of treated adolescents reported total abstinence during the one-year follow-up period, while another 23 percent used alcohol and other drugs on a less-than-monthly basis. Again, however, as these follow-up data represent only 49 percent of the original sample, caution must be taken in interpreting such findings.

Alford, Koehler, and Leonard (1991) examined substance use in 157 male and female chemically dependent adolescents at six, twelve, and 24 months after leaving an inpatient treatment program based almost entirely on the Twelve-step approach. Results revealed that both treatment completers and non-completers (i.e., those who left treatment prematurely against professional advice) demonstrated less drug use after treatment than before. However, although a significant percentage of completers were reportedly abstinent at six months post-treatment, abstinence rates declined precipitously by one and two years after treatment. Moreover, in the absence of a comparison group, it is difficult to draw any definitive conclusions regarding the efficacy of such an approach. Interestingly, the authors also reported that 17 percent of treatment completers were found, at two-year follow-up, to have returned to relatively frequent use of one or more psychoactive substances, yet also appeared to be functioning rather successfully in the context of social and civil behavior. The authors noted that this finding is particularly interesting in light of the commitment to abstinence stressed in Twelve-step-oriented programs. In addition, they asserted that abstinence was clearly associated with more successful, adaptive functioning. Nevertheless, these findings raise the question of whether some adolescents may respond better to moderation-management-based approaches relative to abstinence-based approaches typically endorsed by Twelve-step models.

Kennedy and Masahiko (1993) followed 74 male and 17 female adolescents with substance abuse disorders for one year post-treatment at an inpatient treatment facility whose program involved a 22-day wilderness phase. Results suggested that participation in AA, as well as severity of drug use and psychopathology, were associated with relapse risk. Specifically, subjects with severe psychopathology and greater substance use involvement who were not attending AA were 4.5 times more likely to relapse than subjects with less psychopathology and prior drug use who attended AA. These findings suggest that participation in a Twelve-step program, in conjunction with other treatment methods, increases the likelihood of successful recovery for adolescent drug abusers.

Kelly and Myers (1997) examined the impact of Twelve-step group involvement on adolescents in relation to outcome three months after completing an inpatient substance abuse program. They found more frequent attendance at Twelve-step groups was associated with less post-treatment substance involvement. Among teens who attended meetings, abstainers attended significantly more meetings and tended to affiliate with meetings targeted for adolescents. Kelly and Myers (1998) further reported that being female and highly motivated to remain abstinent were significant predictors of Twelve-step attendance. Finally, Kelly, Myers, and Brown (1999) noted that the positive effects of Twelve-step attendance appear to be mediated through common processes of change, specifically enhancement of both self-efficacy and motivation for abstinence.

More recently, Winters, Stinchfield, Opland, Weller, and Latimer (2000) examined the effectiveness of a Minnesota Model approach with adolescent substance abusers. They reported that adolescents who completed treatment demonstrated far superior outcomes than those who did not complete treatment or those who received no treatment. Fifty-three percent of treatment completers reported either abstinence or a minor lapse for the twelve months following treatment compared to 15 percent of treatment non-completers and 28 percent of teens on a treatment waiting-list. Indeed, several other studies have reported comparable success rates, ranging from 50 percent to 60 percent at one-year post-treatment, for adolescents who participated in Twelve-step-oriented treatment (e.g., Brown,

Vik, & Creamer, 1989; Knapp, Templer, Cannon, & Dobson, 1991; Richter, Brown, & Mott, 1991).

Overall, the few empirical studies investigating the effectiveness of the Twelve-step model with adolescent drug abuse treatment offer tentative support for the approach. Nevertheless, studies comparing the effectiveness of AA with other treatment alternatives for adolescents are rare. Moreover, the comparison of Twelve-step models of treatment with no-treatment controls is generally precluded by ethical considerations. The extent to which there is a need for greater attention to developmental issues unique to adolescence and their impact on the effectiveness of Twelve-step models also has received little attention. Moreover, although a few studies have addressed the issue of treatment-matching, far more work needs to be done in this critical area. These issues are addressed in the following sections.

Prescriptive and Matching Issues

Although a host of psychological and psychiatric treatments has been attempted with adult alcohol abusers (Donovan *et al.*, 1994; Kassel, Wagner, & Unrod, 1999), few treatments have demonstrated differential effectiveness when evaluated with heterogeneous groups of alcoholics (Miller & Hester, 1986). As such, evidence suggests that there is no single treatment approach that is effective for all persons with alcohol-related problems. Indeed, a number of years ago the Institute of Medicine (1990) concluded the questions "Does treatment work?" or "Which treatment works best?" may no longer be appropriate. Instead, "What kinds of individuals, with what kinds of alcohol problems, are likely to respond to what kinds of treatments, by achieving what kinds of goals, when delivered by what kinds of practitioners?" is the question researchers and practitioners should be pursuing. The "matching" hypothesis underlying this important and complex question assumes that prescribing specific types of treatments based on individual characteristics will improve treatment outcomes (Donovan & Mattson, 1994).

In recent years, there has been considerable interest in determining the potential benefits of treatment-matching. There are at least three interests that drive patient-matching research (Longabaugh, Wirtz, DiClemente, & Litt, 1994). First, it is important to maximize the effectiveness of a particular treatment. Second, interest lies in focusing on specific client variables, as well as determining how clients with certain characteristics might be treated more effectively. Third, the idea that matching particular types of patients to particular types of treatments should enhance the overall effectiveness of the interventions is of critical importance.

Project MATCH (Matching Alcoholism Treatment to Client Heterogeneity), a large, multisite trial funded by the National Institute of Alcohol Abuse and Alcoholism, has received much attention for its attempt to examine interactions between patient characteristics and different treatment types (Twelve-step facilitation, cognitive behavioral coping skills training, and motivational enhancement). Although often misinterpreted (see Marlatt, 1999), the findings from this ambitious study essentially suggest that, when randomly assigned to the respective treatments, clients (all of whom were alcohol-dependent) fared equally well, regardless of specific patient characteristics, including severity of alcohol involvement, cognitive impairment, client conceptual level, gender, meaning seeking, motivational readiness to change, psychiatric severity, social support for drinking versus abstinence, sociopathy, and drinking pattern typology (Project MATCH Research Group, 1997, 1998). Thus, "Matching clients with identified attributes to these treatment modalities did not appreciably enhance treatment effectiveness on our primary drinking outcome measures" (Project MATCH Research Group, 1997, p. 23).

Although few of Project MATCH's a priori matching hypotheses were supported, some have suggested that the study supports the efficacy of the Twelve-step approach in that subjects in the Twelve-step condition fared as well as those in the cognitive behavioral and motivational enhancement interventions. However, it is important to note that the Twelve-step facilitation treatment differs substantially from mere Alcoholics Anonymous meeting attendance. Although patients were encouraged to attend AA meetings and "work" the Twelve Steps, the effects of AA affiliation itself cannot be separated from the effects of the intense, individual intervention. Moreover, AA attendance was not controlled in the study. Finally, it is important to remember that Project MATCH was never intended to be a treatment efficacy study. Thus, the conclusions that can be drawn regarding the efficacy of any of its particular interventions are limited.

Analogous to the adult substance abuse literature, research on adolescent drug treatment reveals no evidence to support the superiority of any one general or specific approach (Catalano, Hawkins, Wells, Miller, & Brewer, 1991). Perhaps not surprisingly, little attention has been paid to the issue of treatment-matching for adolescent substance abusers, particularly in the context of Twelve-step programs. Hohman and LeCroy (1996) investigated the characteristics of treated adolescents who affiliated with AA versus those that do not. Results suggested that affiliators were more likely to have had prior treatment, had friends who did not use drugs, had less parental involvement while in treatment, and had more feelings of hopelessness. Thus, in the spirit of treatment-matching, these data offer a first step toward delineating characteristics of substance-abusing adolescents that may predispose to AA affiliation. Clearly, however, much more theory-driven research is needed to address this issue.

Several studies have examined whether certain pretreatment characteristics are predictive of outcome for adolescents treated in Twelve-step-oriented programs. For example, Knapp *et al.* (1991) reported that better outcomes (e.g., drug and alcohol use, grades, family adjustment) were associated with being female, having fewer legal difficulties, fewer neurological risk factors, less pathological MMPI scores, higher Verbal IQ, and lower Performance IQ. Adams and Wallace (1994) observed that, although adolescent substance abusers with a diagnosis of attention deficit hyperactivity disorder had equally desirable treatment outcomes, their stay in residential treatment was significantly shorter than that of non-diagnosed clients. Cady, Winters, Jordan, Solberg, and Stinchfield (1996) investigated the role of pre-treatment readiness to change (motivation) as a predictor of outcome. Results indicated that those adolescents who were more motivated to change fared better subsequent to treatment.

In sum, we know very little about the characteristics of adolescents who do well in Twelve-step-oriented treatments. Most of the studies conducted in this area have been exploratory in nature and, as such, have not been particularly informative. Replication of such findings is clearly needed. We believe that this is a critical area for future study given the current reality that the majority of adolescent substance abuse facilities are steeped in the Twelve-step orientation and philosophy. Furthering our knowledge of who benefits from these programs, as well as who does not, is crucial to the provision of adequate treatment.

Future Directions

Several critical issues emerge from our discussion of AA-oriented treatment of adolescent substance abusers. First, the lack of standardized and widely accepted diagnostic criteria for adolescent substance abuse has resulted in disparate and often atheoretical attempts to assess and treat substance abuse problems among adolescents (Leccese & Waldron, 1994; Wagner & Kassel, 1995; Winters, 1990). Indeed, most adolescent substance abuse treatment programs have based their services primarily on their own specific philosophical orientation using procedures extrapolated from adult substance abuse treatment models. In most instances, this has clearly been the case for Twelve-step, AA-oriented treatment of adolescents. Moreover, as originally conceived, AA was a program geared to facilitate abstinence and life change among chronic alcoholics who were both middle-aged and male. Thus, the extent to which AA may be developmentally inappropriate for adolescents must still be questioned.

Acknowledging the importance of valid assessment of adolescent substance abusers, Martin, Kaczynski, Maisto, Bukstein, and Moss (1995) reported that several diagnostic criteria (e.g., withdrawal, physical problems) of the *Diagnostic and Statistical Manual of Mental Disorders*, Version 4 (DSM-IV; American Psychiatric Association, 1994) did not apply well among even the heaviest adolescent drinkers. Moreover, the presence of tolerance — historically one of the hallmarks of drug dependence — did not differentiate problem from non-problem drinkers, whereas alcohol-related blackouts, craving, and risky sexual behavior — none of which are DSM-IV criteria — were common in adolescents with DSM-IV alcohol dependence and abuse diagnoses. Thus, there is strong reason to believe DSM-IV criteria for substance abuse and dependence disorders have significant limitations when applied to adolescents (Martin & Winters, 1998).

Second, it is common practice to label adolescents with alcohol and drugs problems as "alcoholic" or "drug addict." Indeed, adolescent patients who refuse to acknowledge that they are "addicts" are often perceived as being in a state of denial (Selekman & Todd, 1991). And yet acceptance of these labels is crucial to the very foundation of most Twelve-step programs. Lawson (1992) observes, "Most 12-Step programs spend whatever time is necessary to cajole new patients into admitting that they are alcoholics or addicts" (p. 225). In this context, it is important to remember that over time as many as one-third of alcoholics "mature out" of problem drinking into more moderate forms of consumption or complete abstinence. Among those without a formal diagnosis of alcoholism, the rate of "spontaneous recovery" is even higher (Fillmore, 1988). Moreover, drinking among younger individuals has been found to be less consistent and predictable over time than drinking among adults (Fillmore, 1987). Thus, once again, the extent to which valid diagnoses are made among adolescents presenting with drug problems must be seriously questioned and addressed (see Tarter, 1990).

The impact of such potentially pejorative labels has not been empirically evaluated in adolescent populations. It is conceivable that, in accepting the label of alcoholic or addict, adolescents with substance abuse problems may continue to take drugs or drink because they incorporate "addict" into their sense of self. This may have important long-range implications for teenagers, in that one of the primary developmental tasks of adolescence is identity formation. On the other hand, substance-abusing adolescents who do not come to identify themselves as having substance use problems may not take steps to address these concerns. Regardless, the impact of labels, and the identification of oneself as an "addict," remain important and underresearched areas in the treatment of substance use problems among youth.

Third, there remains debate about what actually constitutes problematic drug use among adolescents. As noted earlier, most adolescents engage in drug use of one kind or another. One study even suggests that normative, experimental use of drugs and alcohol among adolescents is associated with better psychological health relative to both those who abuse substances *and* those who refrain from any use (Shedler & Block, 1990). Indeed, as Baer, MacLean, & Marlatt (1998) asserted, "Many of the problems associated with substance use do not come from those who are addicted in a traditional sense, but rather from those who intermittently use heavily. The label 'alcoholic' or 'addict' does not apply to such individuals, who most likely do not feel that their lives have become unmanageable because of substance use" (p. 205). Thus, the difficult but critical task of teasing apart genuine abuse and dependence problems from those stemming from intermittent lapses in judgment or age-appropriate experimentation deserves further attention.

Fourth, the appropriateness of the Twelve-step model for adolescents may be called into question when one considers developmental and diagnostic issues unique to this age group. For example, Ehrlich (1987) described several critical developmental issues in treating adolescents versus adults. Specifically, adults generally have a well-formed identity prior to becoming a drug or alcohol abuser, and can recall this identity in treatment and work toward regaining losses that resulted from their addiction. Adolescents, however, often develop their sense of identity around the addiction, and thus possess no established, integrated sense of self prior to the onset of their drug use. Moreover, adolescents who are truly drug dependent likely have developed their coping repertoire in the context of drug use. Thus, they are often asked to make a profound identity shift from someone who uses drugs to someone who does not in the absence of alternative coping strategies.

The typical manner in which adolescents use alcohol and drugs is different from that of adults (Bailey & Rachal, 1993; Baer *et al.*, 1998). For example, adolescents generally drink and use more episodically than adults do, and the negative consequences of adolescent substance use/abuse differ from those seen in adult substance use/abuse. Moreover, adolescents with substance use problems may be more likely to present with co-occurring problems such as depressive symptoms, family disruption, academic problems, problem behaviors, deviance, low levels of conventionality, and peer drug use (Deykin, Buka, & Zeena, 1992; Hawkins, Catalano, & Miller, 1992). Indeed, given AA's tendency to focus predominantly on alcohol and drug use, it is conceivable that other problems that accompany substance abuse among teens may go unheeded.

Sixth, influential work in recent years has emphasized the importance of understanding the client's level of motivation, or readiness to change, in treatment planning (e.g.,

Prochaska, Diclemente, & Norcross, 1992). The basic premise of the stages of change model is that people typically progress through five stages — precontemplation, contemplation, preparation, action, and maintenance — when engaged in efforts to modify behavior. An important implication of this model is that a treatment plan should ideally take into account the client's location on this continuum of change. From this perspective, it makes sense to treat someone who does not want to change their behavior (precontemplation) differently from someone who is highly motivated to change (preparation). It could be argued that AA and other Twelve-step-oriented treatments frequently do not take into account individual differences in motivation. In fact, AA states that the only requirement for membership is a desire to stop drinking. As noted earlier, Twelve-step-oriented treatments often invoke the construct of "denial" to explain insufficient motivation to change. In the context of adolescent substance abusers, it is not uncommon to see clients who are mandated to treatment, or at relatively early stages in the onset of substance use problems. This in part explains Anderson's (1992) observation that adolescent substance abusers are often non-compliant with treatment recommendations. The extent to which Twelve-step programs can accommodate the needs of such less motivated clients needs to be assessed.

Finally, as discussed earlier, AA rests on a firm and relatively inflexible ideological base concerning how recovery can and will occur (Kassel & Wagner, 1993). This ideology, particularly as reflected in the Twelve Steps, might act as a deterrent to some adolescents. Notions of powerlessness, belief in a higher power, sharing a personal "fearless moral inventory" with another person, and passing on the AA message to others may be concepts most adolescents are not prepared to accept. An important question is whether adolescents who reject certain aspects of AA philosophy are "in denial" or are responding in a developmentally appropriate and honest manner. Relatedly, as AA and Twelve-step programs view abstinence as the only acceptable outcome for treatment, one wonders whether other possible outcomes (e.g., reduced substance involvement, controlled drinking as an adult) should be considered for at least some substance-abusing teenagers (e.g., those with less severe substance use problems).

Summary

To review, although there is some evidence to suggest that the Minnesota Model and other Twelve-step approaches are successful for adults, far less is known about their effectiveness for adolescents. Most studies have been hampered by methodological limitations, and little is known about the processes that govern change among those who derive benefit from Twelve-step treatments. Moreover, the characteristic emphasis on substance abuse as a primary disease in Twelve-step programs may result in insufficient attention to other problem areas that may accompany substance use problems in adolescence. Inherent in AA philosophy is the belief in relative homogeneity among substance-abusing individuals: they abuse alcohol and drugs because they have an incurable disease. As a result, it becomes difficult to match a client's specific needs to an appropriate intervention when all clients, regardless of age or co-occurring problems, are believed to have the same needs.

As noted by Tucker and King (1999), the Twelve-step approach can be contrasted in several important ways with what is known about help-seeking and behavior change processes. Thus, in opposition to some of the core tenets of Twelve-step treatments, (a) both the development and resolution of substance abuse problems vary across individuals; (b) changes in environmental contexts often influence the initiation, maintenance, and resolution of addictive behaviors; (c) recovery can occur through a number of pathways, and treatment is neither a necessary nor sufficient condition for its occurrence; (d) the functional value of treatment varies across individuals; (e) problems resulting from substance abuse frequently motivate help-seeking behavior; and (f) social forces can influence help-seeking behavior and processes. These issues are particularly pressing with respect to the treatment of adolescent substance abusers.

At the same time, we do believe that for *some adolescents*, AA and its derivative programs will work quite well. Indeed, AA clearly has been of tremendous value and help to thousands of individuals, including some teenagers, over the past 65 years. In all likelihood, certain aspects of Twelve-step programs are attractive to adolescents (e.g., peer-led groups, flexibility in meeting times, no cost to attend meetings, provision of social support). Questions remain, however, about for whom Twelve-step approaches are most effective, and whether the approach can accommodate the developmental vicissitudes of adolescence. In sum, given both the importance of developing effective interventions for adolescent substance abusers and the dearth of research in this area, it is incumbent upon future researchers of AA and Twelve-step-oriented programs to properly assess the efficacy of this approach for younger populations.

References

Adams, L., & Wallace, J. L. (1994), "Residential-treatment for the ADHD adolescent substance-abuser." *Journal of Child and Adolescent Substance Abuse 4*, 35–44.

Alcoholics Anonymous (1976), Alcoholics Anonymous: The story of how many thousands of men and women have recovered from alcoholism. New York: Alcoholics Anonymous World Services.

Alcoholics Anonymous (1984), *Twelve Steps and Twelve Traditions*. New York: Alcoholics Anonymous World Services.

Alcoholics Anonymous (1999), "1998 membership survey: A snapshot of A.A. membership." *About AA: A Newsletter for Professionals, Summer 1999*, 1–4.

Alford, G. S., Koehler, R. A., & Leonard, J. (1991), "Alcoholics Anonymous–Narcotics Anonymous model inpatient treatment of chemically dependent adolescents: A 2-year outcome study." *Journal of Studies on Alcohol 52*, 118–126.

Alibrandi, L. A. (1985), "The folk psychotherapy of Alcoholics Anonymous." In S. Zimberg, J. Wallace, & S. B. Blume (eds), *Practical Approaches to Alcoholism Psychotherapy* (2nd edn). New York: Plenum Press, 239–256.

American Psychiatric Association (1994), *Diagnostic and Statistical Manual of Mental Disorders (DSM-IV): fourth edition*. Washington, DC: American Psychiatric Association.

Anderson, L. P. (1992), "Differential treatment effects". In L. L'Abate, Ferrer, J., & Serritella, D.A. (eds), *Handbook of Differential Treatments for Addictions*. Boston: Allyn & Bacon, 23–40.

Antze, P. (1979), "Role of ideologies in peer psychotherapy groups." In M. A. Lieberman & L. D. Borman (eds), *Self-help Groups for Coping with Crisis*. San Francisco: Jossey-Bass.

Baer, J. S., MacLean, M. G., & Marlatt, G. A. (1998), "Linking etiology and treatment for adolescent substance abuse: Toward a better match." In R. Jessor (ed.), *New Perspectives on Adolescent Risk Behavior*. New York: Cambridge University Press, 182–220.

Bailey, S. L., & Rachal, J. V. (1993), "Dimensions of adolescent problem drinking." *Journal of Studies on Alcohol 54*, 555–565.

Bean, M. (1975), "Alcoholics Anonymous: Chapter 1: Principles and methods." *Psychiatric Annals 5*, 7–21.

Bohnice, E. A., & Orensteen, A. C. (1950), "An evaluation of the services and program of the Minneapolis chapter of Alcoholics Anonymous." Unpublished Master's Thesis, University of Minnesota, Minneapolis, MN.

Brende, J. O. (1993), "A 12-step recovery program for victims of traumatic events." In J. P. Wilson & B. Raphael (eds), *International Handbook of Traumatic Stress Syndromes*. New York: Plenum Press, 867–877.

Brown, S. A., Vik, P. W., & Creamer, V. A. (1989), "Characteristics of relapse following adolescent substance abuse treatment." *Addictive Behaviors 14*, 291–300.

Bufe, C. (1991). *Alcoholics Anonymous: Cult or cure?* San Francisco, CA: See Sharp Press.

Cady, M. E., Winters, K. C., Jordan, D. A., Solberg, K. B., & Stinchfield, R. D. (1996), "Motivation to change as a predictor of treatment outcome for adolescent substance abusers." *Journal of Child and Adolescent Substance Abuse 5*, 73–91.

Caldwell, P. E., & Cutter, H. S. G. (1998), "Alcoholics Anonymous affiliation during early recovery." *Journal of Substance Abuse Treatment 15*, 221–228.

Catalano, R. F., Hawkins, J. D., Wells, E. A., Miller, J., & Brewer, D. (1991), "Evaluation of the effectiveness of adolescent drug abuse treatment, assessment of risks for relapse, and promising approaches for relapse prevention." *International Journal of the Addictions 25*, 1085–1140.

Chappel, J. H. (1992), "Effective use of Alcoholics Anonymous and Narcotics Anonymous in treating patients." *Psychiatric Annals 22*, 409–418.

Collins, G. B. (1995), "Why treatment for alcohol dependence is changing." *Alcoholism Treatment Quarterly 12*, 23–39.

Cook, C. C. H. (1988a), "The Minnesota Model in the management of drug and alcohol dependency: miracle, method or myth? Part I. The philosophy and the programme." *British Journal of Addiction 83*, 625–634.

Cook, C. C. H. (1988b), "The Minnesota Model in the management of drug and alcohol dependency: miracle, method or myth? Part II. Evidence and conclusions." *British Journal of Addiction 83*, 735–748.

Deykin, E. Y., Buka, S. L., & Zeena, T. H. (1992), "Depressive illness among chemically dependent adolescents." *American Journal of Psychiatry 149*, 1341–1347.

Donovan, D. M. *et al.* (1994), "Issues in the selection and development of therapies in alcoholism treatment matching research." *Journal of Studies on Alcohol Supplement 12*, 138–148.

Donovan, D. M., & Mattson, M. E. (1994), "Alcoholism treatment matching research: Methodological and clinical issues." *Journal of Studies on Alcohol Supplement 12*, 5–14.

Donovan, M. E. (1984), "A sociological analysis of commitment generation in Alcoholics Anonymous." *British Journal of Addiction 79*, 411–418.

Ehrlich, P. (1987), "12-Step principles and adolescent chemical dependence treatment." *Journal of Psychoactive Drugs 19*, 311–317.

Ellis, A., & Schoenfeld, E. (1990), "Divine intervention and the treatment of chemical dependency." *Journal of Substance Abuse 2*, 459–468.

Emrick, C. D. (1987), "Alcoholics Anonymous: Affiliation processes and effectiveness as treatment." *Alcoholism: Clinical and Experimental Research 11*, 416–423.

Emrick, C. D., Tonigan, J. S., Montgomery, H., & Little, L. (1993), "Alcoholics Anonymous: what is currently known?" In B. S. McCrady & W. R. Miller (eds), *Research on Alcoholics Anonymous: Opportunities and alternatives.* New Brunswick, NJ: Rutgers Center of Alcohol Studies, 41–76.

Fillmore, K. M. (1987), "Prevalence, incidence and chronicity of drinking patterns and problems among men as a function of age: A longitudinal and cohort analysis." *British Journal of Addiction 82*, 77–83.

Fillmore, K. M. (1988), *Evaluating Recovery Outcomes.* San Diego: University of California Press.

Fiorentine, R., & Hillhouse, M. P. (2000). "Drug treatment and 12-step program participation: The additive effects of integrated recovery activities." *Journal of Substance Abuse Treatment 18,* 65–74.

Fiorentine, R., & Hillhouse, M. P. (2000), "Exploring the additive effects of drug misuse treatment and twelve-step involvement: Does twelve-step ideology matter?" *Substance Use and Misuse 35,* 367–397.

Harrison, P. A., & Hoffmann, N. (1989), "CATOR report: adolescent treatment completers one year later." St Paul, MN: CATOR.

Hawkins, J. D., Catalano, R. F., & Miller, J. Y. (1992), "Risk and protective factors for alcohol and other drug problems in adolescence and early adulthood: Implications for substance abuse prevention." *Psychological Bulletin 112,* 64–105.

Hoffman, N. G., & Miller, N. S. (1992), "Treatment outcomes for abstinence-based programs." *Psychiatric Annals 22,* 402–408.

Hohman, M., & LeCroy, C. W. (1996), "Predictors of adolescent A.A. affiliation." *Adolescence 31,* 339–352.

Institute of Medicine (1990), *Broadening the Base of Treatment for Alcohol Problems.* Washington, DC: National Academy Press.

Johnson, C. L., & Sansone, R. A. (1993), "Integrating the twelve-step approach with traditional psychotherapy for the treatment of eating disorders." *International Journal of Eating Disorders 14,* 121–134.

Kammeier, M. L., & Anderson, P. O. (1976), "Two years later: Post-treatment participation in AA by 1970 Hazelden patients." Presented at the meeting of the 27th annual meeting of the Alcohol and Drugs Problems Association. New Orleans, LA.

Kanter, R. M. (1968), "Commitment and social organization: A study of commitment mechanisms in utopian communities." *American Sociological Review 33,* 499–517.

Kassel, J. D., & Wagner, E. F. (1993), "Processes of change in Alcoholics Anonymous: A review of possible mechanisms." *Psychotherapy 30,* 222–234.

Kassel, J. D., Wagner, E. F., & Unrod, M. (1999), "Alcoholism-Behavior Therapy." In M. Hersen & A. S. Bellack (eds), *Handbook of Comparative Interventions for Adult Disorders.* New York: John Wiley and Sons, 626–651.

Kelly, J. F., & Myers, M. G. (July, 1997), "Adolescent treatment outcome in relation to 12-step group attendance." Poster presented at the Research Society on Alcoholism Annual Conference Proceedings. San Francisco, CA.

Kelly, J. F., & Myers, M. G. (November, 1998), "Predictors of adolescent 12-step group attendance following inpatient substance abuse treatment." Poster presented at the Association for the Advancement of Behavior Therapy Annual Proceedings. Washington, DC.

Kelly, J. F., Myers, M. G., & Brown, S. A. (November, 1999), "The effects of 12-step group attendance on common processes of change following inpatient substance abuse treatment: Analysis of a mediational model." Poster presented at the Association for Advancement of Behavior Therapy Annual Proceedings. Toronto, Canada.

Kennedy, B. P., & Masahiko, M. (1993), "The Beech Hill Hospital/Outward Bound adolescent chemical dependency treatment program." *Journal of Substance Abuse Treatment 10,* 395–406.

Keskinen, S. (1986), *Hazelden Pioneer House, 1984 profile, six-month and twelve-month outcomes.* Center City, MN: Hazelden Foundation.

Knapp, J., Templer, D., Cannon, W. G., & Dobson, S. (1991), "Variables associated with success in an adolescent drug treatment program." *Adolescence 26*, 305–317.

Kownacki, R. J., & Shadish, W. R. (1999), "Does Alcoholics Anonymous work? The results from a meta-analysis of controlled experiments." *Substance Use and Misuse 34*, 1897–1916.

Kurtz, E. (1979), *Not-God: A history of Alcoholics Anonymous*. Center City, MN: Hazelden.

Lawson, G. W. (1992), "Twelve-step programs and the treatment of adolescent substance abuse." In G. W. Lawson & A. W. Lawson (eds), *Adolescent Substance Abuse: Etiology, treatment, and prevention*. Gaithersburg, MD: Aspen Publishers, Inc., 219–229.

Leccese, M., & Waldron, H. B. (1994), "Assessing adolescent substance use: A critique of current measurement instruments." *Journal of Substance Abuse Treatment 11*, 553–563.

Lichtenstein, E. (1999), "Nicotine Anonymous: Community resource and research implications." *Psychology of Addictive Behaviors 13*, 60–68.

Longabaugh, R., Wirtz, P. W., DiClemente, C. C., & Litt, M. (1994), "Issues in the development of client–treatment matching hypotheses." *Journal of Studies on Alcohol 12*, 46–59.

Marlatt, G. A. (1996), "Harm reduction: Come as you are." *Addictive Behaviors 21*, 779–788.

Marlatt, G. A. (1999), "From hindsight to foresight: A commentary on Project MATCH." In M. A. Tucker, D. M. Donovan, & G. A. Marlatt (eds), *Changing Addictive Behavior: Bridging clinical and public health strategies*. New York: Guilford Press, 45–66.

Martin, C. S., Kaczynski, N. A., Maisto, S. A., Bukstein, O. M., & Moss, H. B. (1995), "Patterns of DSM-IV alcohol abuse and dependence symptoms in adolescent drinkers." *Journal of Studies on Alcohol 56*, 672–680.

Martin, C. S., & Winters, K. C. (1998), "Diagnosis and assessment of alcohol use disorders among adolescents." *Alcohol Health and Research World 22*, 95–105.

McCrady, B. S. (1994), "Alcoholics Anonymous and behavior therapy: Can habits be treated as diseases? Can diseases be treated as habits?" *Journal of Consulting and Clinical Psychology 62*, 1159–1166.

McElrath, D. (1997), "The Minnesota Model." *Journal of Psychoactive Drugs 29*, 141–144.

Miller, W. R., & Hester, R. K. (1986), "The effectiveness of alcoholism treatment: What research reveals." In W. R. Miller & N. Heather (eds), *Treating Addictive Behaviors: Processes of change*. New York: Plenum Press, 121–174.

Montgomery, H. A., Miller, W. R., & Tonigan, J. S. (1993), "Differences among AA groups: Implications for research." *Journal of Studies on Alcohol 54*, 502–504.

Montgomery, H. A., Miller, W. R., & Tonigan, J. S. (1995), "Does Alcoholics Anonymous involvement predict treatment outcome?" *Journal of Substance Abuse Treatment 12*, 241–246.

Moos, R. H., Finney, J. W., Ouimette, P. C., & Suchinsky, R. T. (1999), "A comparative evaluation of substance abuse treatment: 1. Treatment orientation, amount of care, and 1-year outcomes." *Alcoholism: Clinical and Experimental Research 23*, 529–536.

Moreland, R. L., & Levine, J. M. (1989), "Newcomers and oldtimers in small groups." In P. B. Paulus (ed.), *Psychology of Group Influence* (2nd edn). Hillsdale, NJ: Lawrence Erlbaum.

Morgenstern, J., Labouvie, E., McCrady, B. S., Kahler, C. W., & Frey, R. M. (1997), "Affiliation with Alcoholics Anonymous after treatment: A study of its therapeutic effects and mechanisms of action." *Journal of Consulting and Clinical Psychology 65*, 768–777.

Morrison, M. A., & Smith, Q. T. (1987), "Psychiatric issues of adolescent chemical dependence." *Pediatric Clinics of North America 34*, 461–480.

Ogborne, A. C., & Glaser, F. B. (1981), "Characteristics of affiliates of Alcoholics Anonymous: A review of the literature." *Journal of Studies on Alcohol 42*, 661–675.

O'Leary, D. E. *et al.* (1980), "Alcohol use patterns and Alcoholics Anonymous affiliation as predictors of alcoholism treatment outcome." *Research Communications on Substance Abuse 1*, 197–209.

Ouimette, P. C., Finney, J. W., & Moos, R. H. (1997), "Twelve-step and cognitive-behavioral treatment for substance abuse: A comparison of treatment effectiveness." *Journal of Consulting and Clinical Psychology 65*, 230–240.

Patton, M. (1979), "The outcomes of treatment: A study of patients admitted to Hazelden in 1976." Center City, MN: Hazelden Foundation.

Prochaska, J. O., DiClemente, C. C., & Norcross, J. C. (1992). "In search of how people change: Applications to addictive behaviors." *American Psychologist 47*, 1102–1114.

Project MATCH Research Group (1993), "Project MATCH: Rationale and methods for a multisite clinical trial-matching patients to alcoholism treatment." *Alcoholism: Clinical and Experimental Research 17*, 1130–1145.

Project MATCH Research Group (1997), "Matching alcoholism treatment to client heterogeneity: Project MATCH posttreatment drinking outcomes." *Journal of Studies on Alcohol 58*, 7–29.

Project MATCH Research Group (1998), "Matching alcoholism treatments to client heterogeneity: Project MATCH three-year drinking outcomes." *Alcoholism: Clinical and Experimental Research 22*, 1300–1311.

Richter, S., Brown, S., & Mott, M. (1991), "The impact of social support and self-esteem on adolescent substance abuse treatment outcome." *Journal of Substance Abuse 3*, 371–385.

Room, R. (1993), "Alcoholics Anonymous as a social movement." In B. S. McCrady & W. R. Miller (eds), *Research on Alcoholics Anonymous: Opportunities and alternatives*. New Brunswick, NJ: Rutgers Center of Alcohol Studies, 167–187.

Rosenthal, R. J. (1992), "Pathological gambling." *Psychiatric Annals 22*, 72–78.

Rudy, D. R. (1986), *Becoming Alcoholic: Alcoholics Anonymous and the reality of alcoholism*. Carbondale, IL: Southern Illinois University Press.

Selekman, M., & Todd, T. C. (1991), "Crucial issues in the treatment of adolescent substance abusers and their families." In T. C. Todd & M. Selekman (eds), *Family Therapy Approaches with Adolescent Substance Abusers*. Boston, MA: Allyn and Bacon, 3–19.

Shedler, J., & Block, J. (1990), "Adolescent drug use and psychological health: A longitudinal inquiry." *American Psychologist 45*, 612–630.

Sheehan, T., & Owen, P. (1999), "The disease model." In B. S. McCrady & E. E. Epstein (eds), *Addictions: A comprehensive guidebook*. New York: Oxford University Press, 268–286.

Snow, M. G., Prochaska, J. O., & Rossi, J. S. (1994), "Processes of change in Alcoholics Anonymous: maintenance factors in long-term sobriety." *Journal of Studies on Alcohol 55*, 362–371.

Tarter, R. E. (1990), "Decision-tree for adolescent assessment and treatment planning." *American Journal of Drug and Alcohol Abuse 16*, 1–46.

Tonigan, J. S., Ashcroft, F., & Miller, W. R. (1995), "AA group dynamics and 12-step activity." *Journal of Studies on Alcohol 56*, 616–621.

Tournier, R. E. (1979), "Alcoholics Anonymous as treatment and as ideology." *Journal of Studies on Alcohol 40*, 230–239.

Trice, H. M., & Roman, P. M. (1970), "Sociopsychological predictors of affiliation with Alcoholics Anonymous: A longitudinal study of 'treatment success'." *Social Psychiatry 5*, 51–59.

Tucker, J. A., & King, M. P. (1999), "Resolving alcohol and drug problems: influences on addictive behavior change and help-seeking processes." In J. A. Tucker, D. M. Donovan, & G. A. Marlatt (eds), *Changing Addictive Behavior: Bridging clinical and public health strategies*. New York: Guilford Press.

Vaillant, G. (1983), *The Natural History of Alcoholism: Courses, patterns and paths to recovery*. Cambridge, MA: Harvard University Press.

Wagner, E. F., Brown, S. A., Monti, P. M., Myers, M. G., & Waldron, H. B. (1999), "Innovations in adolescent substance abuse intervention." *Alcoholism: Clinical and Experimental Research 23*, 236–249.

Wagner, E. F., & Kassel, J. D. (1995), "Substance use and abuse." In R. T. Ammerman & M. Hersen (eds), *Handbook of Child Behavior Therapy in the Psychiatric Setting*. New York: John Wiley, 367–388.

Wallace, J. (1983), "Ideology, belief, and behavior: Alcoholics Anonymous as a social movement." In E. Gottheil, K. A. Druley, T. E. Skoloda, & H. M. Waxman (eds), *Etiologic Aspects of Alcohol and Drug Abuse*. Springfield, IL: Charles C. Thomas.

Winters, K. C., Latimer, W. L., & Stinchfield, R. D. (1999), "Adolescent treatment." In P. J. Ott & R. E. Tarter (eds), *Sourcebook on Substance Abuse: Etiology, epidemiology, assessment, and treatment*. Boston, MA: Allyn and Bacon, 350–361.

Winters, K. C., Stinchfield, R. D., Opland, E., Weller, C., & Latimer, W. W. (2000), "The effectiveness of the Minnesota Model approach in the treatment of adolescent drug abusers." *Addiction 95*, 601–612.

Winters, K. D. (1990), "The need for improved assessment of adolescent substance use involvement." *Journal of Drug Issues 20*, 487–502.

Zurcher, L. A., & Snow, D. A. (1981), "Collective behavior: social movements." In M. Rosenberg & R. Turner (eds), *Social Psychology: Sociological Perspectives*. New York: Bass, 447–482.

Chapter 16

Substance Abuse Interventions with Latino Adolescents: A Cultural Framework

Andres G. Gil, Jonathan G. Tubman, and Eric F. Wagner*

This chapter presents a cultural framework for the development of effective substance abuse interventions for Latino youth. The conceptual background and rationale for interventions with Latino youth are presented, and cultural factors relevant to the implementation of interventions are discussed. We conclude with a description of a brief intervention for alcohol and drug abuse for use with juvenile justice populations and tailored to meet the specific needs and life circumstances of Latino adolescents and their families.

Two essential issues must be addressed as a preamble to this chapter. First, it is widely recognized that the Latino population of the United States is not a monolithic entity. Rather, it is composed of numerous groups that are heterogeneous in terms of a wide range of factors including their geographical location, national origin, and immigration history. Inherent in any discussion of substance abuse interventions for Latinos are challenges related to accounting for similarities and differences among the various Latino groups in the United States, both in terms of putative risk factors and amenability to treatment factors.

A second key issue concerns overarching strategies to pursue in the development of interventions tailored to the needs of specific ethnic or cultural groups. One approach is to develop interventions that apply equally to all populations, regardless of racial/ethnic background. Another strategy is to develop interventions that are tailored to specific racial/ethnic groups. The perspective that guides this chapter assumes there are similarities in the etiology of drug use across racial/ethnic groups. However, a growing body of research also indicates there are risk factors for substance use and abuse specific to Latino youth based on their unique migration and assimilation experiences. Furthermore, despite similarities in the etiology of drug use, racial/ethnic groups present with idiosyncratic cultural characteristics and values that may require attention to unique factors in the "process" of intervention. Based on these common and unique factors, some researchers have proposed that treatment approaches should be formulated for specific racial/ethnic and cultural groups (e.g., James & Moore, 1997), while others have suggested placing less emphasis on race or ethnicity while attending more to common social or environmental influences (Howard, LaVeist & McCaughrin, 1996).

*Preparation of this chapter was supported by National Institute on Alcohol Abuse and Alcoholism Grant AA12180 to the authors.

Innovations in Adolescent Substance Abuse Interventions, pages 353–378.

Latino Populations in the United States

The scope of this chapter does not permit an exhaustive description of Latinos in the United States. We present information that is pertinent to our approach to the adaptation of substance abuse interventions to the needs of Latino youth and their families. The Latino population of the United States has expanded rapidly due to higher fertility rates and recent immigration patterns and numbered in excess of 35 million people in 2000, or 12.5 per cent of the total US population (US Census Bureau, 2000). It is estimated that Latinos will account for 42 percent of new population growth in the US between 1990 and 2010 (Vega & Gil, 1998). By the year 2050, the Latino population in the US is projected to consist of 25 percent of the entire national population (Spencer & Hollmann, 1998). The current US Latino population is composed of groups with diverse origins including Mexican (58.5 percent), Central and South American (8.8 percent), Puerto Rican (9.6%), and Cuban (3.5 percent), with the remaining 19.6 percent derived from a mix of Latino national origins. In addition, the Latino population in the US is significantly younger (by an average of ten years) that the Non-Hispanic White African-American, and Asian populations (US Census Bureau, 1999).

Within US Latino communities, there are disagreements about the designation "Latino" or "Hispanic." The debate centers on the differential acceptability of labels that artificially agglomerate different peoples with varied cultural traditions versus those that are more culturally and racially neutral (Hayes-Bautista & Chapa, 1987; Nieves-Squires, 1991). In the context of this chapter, we will use these terms interchangeably. More important, however, than how to label different racial/ethnic groups are the different migration histories and socio-demographic characteristics of various Latino subgroups (Portes & Rumbaut, 1990). For example, Mexican Americans have a long history in the US, including the experiences of recent immigrants alongside the experiences of families who have spent multiple generations in California, New Mexico, and Texas, even prior to the time these territories became part of the US.

In contrast, many recent Central American and Cuban immigrants entered the US only after changes in immigration laws enacted in 1965. This highlights how the shifting nature of legal and illegal immigration serves as a constant source of change in the composition of Latino populations in the US. Latino populations in the State of California and Miami-Dade County, Florida, are good examples of how immigration patterns are shaped in large part by key historical events in countries of origin. During the 1960s, most of the Latino population in California of Mexican origin was born in the US. By the early 1990s, a new influx of immigrants changed the population distribution such that more than 50 percent were born in Mexico (Vega & Gil, 1998). The Latino population of Miami-Dade County, which was primarily of Cuban origin from the 1960s through the early 1980s, has become more diverse due to the increasing immigration of people from Nicaragua, El Salvador, and other Central American and Caribbean countries, including Mexico (Vega & Gil, 1998), and now less than half of the population is Cuban (44.9%) (U.S. Census, 2000).

In addition to differences among Latinos related to the country of origin, there are important variations based on geographic location within the US (Portes & Rumbaut, 1990; Marin & Marin, 1991). Therefore, it is not surprising that population samples of

Latino adolescents demonstrate differences in drug use among national subgroups (Gil and Vega, 2001; Warheit, Vega, Elfenbein, Gil & Zimmerman, 1996). Circumstances in the East, West, and Midwest are different for all US populations, including Latinos. With such diversity, a pertinent issue is whether it is possible to develop interventions that apply to all Latino groups. Our view is that cultural relevancy is a dynamic tension in all community-based interventions given the increasing diversity of adolescent and adult Latino populations in the US. Any researcher or practitioner implementing substance use/abuse interventions will need to be cognizant of variables that impact program effectiveness, regardless of the race or ethnicity of the target population. We propose that there are core elements that need to be addressed in the development of interventions for Latino youth. These elements must be adjusted to meet the needs of specific Latino groups, their location, and historical time. We present these core components using a theoretical framework that accounts for the key elements of the formative immigration experiences of Latino youth and their families.

Theoretical Background and Rationale for Interventions with Latino Youth

Ethnicity and acculturation are likely to impact multiple aspects of the alcohol and other drugs (AOD) treatment process (Collins, 1993). The contrast between commonplace drug use in contemporary America and significantly lower rates of use in Latin America highlights the importance of social and cultural factors for explaining differences in drug use among racial/ethnic groups in the US (Vega, Gil & Wagner, 1998). Vega and Gil (1999) presented a model to explain drug use behaviors among Latino adolescents. This model provides a compelling theoretical framework for specifying substance abuse interventions for Latino youth. It provides a logical, theoretically grounded approach for linking Latino adolescents and their parents to the social environments in which they live, and it describes the contingencies of social psychological adaptation that occur within these environments. This model utilizes elements of the work of other researchers who have studied drug use and adaptation among Latino youth. Researchers whose work has informed this model include: Szapocznik and colleagues, who have developed structural family interventions that address family acculturation factors contributing to Latino adolescent drug use; Felix-Ortiz and others, who have addressed the influence of cultural identity on substance use; and Portes and Rumbaut, who have attempted to explain social and environmental factors that affect the assimilation of Latino youth in the US.

The Vega and Gil model for the explanation of drug use behavior among Latino teens has an ecological focus. One working assumption is that drug use among immigrant and US-born Latino adolescents is influenced significantly by the socialization experiences of the adolescents and their families. National survey data, such as those in the Monitoring the Future Study, show that rates of substance use among Latino youth fall between the higher rates of Non-Hispanic White and lower rates of African-American adolescents (Johnston, O'Malley & Bachman, 2000). Empirical studies that have included Latino subgroups of immigrant and US-born youth have found lower levels of drug use among immigrant Latino youth than among US-born Latino youth, and drug use increases among immigrants as the length of residence in the US increases (Vega & Gil, 1998).

Much of the literature describing models of mental health and substance use interventions for Latino populations are non-empirical in nature. Practice guidelines often have been formulated regarding appropriate strategies for the treatment of Latino populations based on anthropological and social–psychological knowledge about Latino cultures. This literature identifies important facets of Latino culture that can influence treatment effectiveness, highlighting the need for sociocultural interventions that are intended to supplement models of AOD treatment (Gloria & Peregoy, 1996). Key facets of Latino culture include cultural values and attitudes in the areas of familism (Marin & Marin, 1991), personal preferences such as personalism (Comas-Diaz, 1994), traditional gender roles (Arredondo, Weddige, Justice & Fritz, 1987; Marin & Marin, 1991), and spiritualism (Koss-Chioino, 1995).

These overlapping cultural factors have resulted in the recommendation that treatment begin with a "slow" process of establishing trust, given the Latino cultural preference for establishing "personal" relationships (Gloria & Peregoy, 1996). Other recommendations underscore the important role of the family, both as a source of social support that should be used in the treatment process, and as an impediment to disclosure due to the value attached to family loyalty. Such cultural factors are important and should always be viewed within the context of level of acculturation of the target Latino population. The approach of this chapter is to present a theoretical framework that acknowledges these cultural elements, but moves one step further in demonstrating one particular treatment approach that has been adapted to fit the experiences and needs of a Latino population.

We begin with a theoretical framework explaining patterns of substance use among Latino youth. The components of this framework include: (a) the context of exit from country of origin; (b) the immigration experience entering the US; (c) acculturation processes; (d) segmented assimilation; (e) acculturation stress; and (f) family stress (see Figure 1). All of these factors, together with other social or biological influences, form an integrative set of circumstances that are uniquely pertinent to the explanation of substance use and abuse among Latino adolescents. As such, these factors include elements that are specific to the development of substance abuse interventions for Latino youth. In addition to these ethnic-specific elements, however, there are other factors that are common to developmental processes promoting substance use in other social groups. Based on this understanding, our view is that the development of interventions with Latino youth and their families can and should use techniques that are known to be effective with a range of populations. The minimum requirement should be alertness to factors unique to the circumstances, experiences, and cultural traditions of Latino adolescents and their families. In essence, we advocate for Latino-focused interventions that modify and supplement existing interventions, so that unique influences upon substance use among Latino adolescents are addressed in the interventions.

In this section, we will review each of the six components of this framework, examining current knowledge in each domain concerning substance use and abuse and relating current knowledge to the development of effective substance abuse interventions. First, we present mechanisms by which these elements can influence the adaptation and functioning

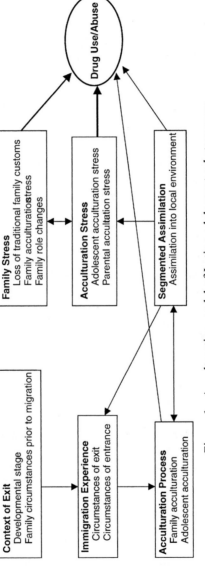

Figure 1: Acculturative model of Latino adolescent substance use.

of Latino youth. Second, we apply these factors in an intervention currently being implemented with Latino youth in South Florida.

Context of Exit

Rumbaut (1996) emphasized the importance of the context of exit for immigrants in their ongoing adaptation to the migration experience. Economic and political forces that "push" migrants from their country of origin can drive immigration into the US. Many Latino immigrants to the US have been driven from their country of origin by traumatic experiences including devastating civil wars (e.g., in Nicaragua or El Salvador), as well as other political and economic pressures (e.g., from Cuba, Mexico). Circumstances of exit influence adolescents and their families via stressful experiences including finding the means to leave their country of origin and the difficulties of separating from extended family networks. For example, researchers working with immigrant families have highlighted long separations between parents and children as a common stressor (Santisteban *et al.*, 1997). These separations occur when parents come to the US and bring the rest of their family later, or when children arrive, but one or both parents remain behind. Critical issues in such separations include the reestablishment of preexisting family relations and structures or accommodating changes that have occurred in the interim. Given the strong reliance upon and importance of the family among Latinos (Marin & Marin, 1991; Vega, 1990), it is not surprising that disruptions within the family have been identified as early sources of emotional and behavioral problems for Latino youth (Gloria & Peregoy, 1996; Santisteban & Szapocznik, 1982).

A moderating factor related to context of exit from country of origin is the developmental stage of children or adolescents at the time of immigration. The developmental implications of migration for middle and late adolescents are very different than those for younger children. For example, growing up within a relatively consistent sociocultural context in the country of origin may allow older immigrant children to develop a cohesive sense of identity before entering the US environment (Vega, Gil & Wagner, 1998). Second-generation and very young immigrant children may be reared in an environment rife with social and cultural conflicts and competition between the traditional values of their parents and those of their peers in the new society (Portes & Rumbaut, 1990; Rumbaut, 1995, 1996).

Context of Entrance

The context of entrance comprises the continuation of characteristics associated with the context of exit from the country of origin. Most historical evidence suggests that the majority of immigrants successfully adjust to relocation. Therefore, care must be taken not to present immigration as maladaptive. Yet, there is ample evidence that some families and adolescents experience a great deal of stress and conflict as they attempt to adjust to social norms in the US, and these difficulties often are expressed among adolescents in the form of substance use and delinquency. Difficulties significantly associated with circumstances of exit and of entrance have been described in recent epidemiological studies, including higher levels of psychiatric and substance abuse/dependence disorders among US-born Latinos than among foreign-born Latinos (Vega, Alderete, Kolody & Aguilar-Gaziola, 1998). Similarly, the work of Szapocznik and colleagues has demonstrated significant difficulties encountered by families as they address acculturation differences between immigrant parents and their children (e.g., Szapocznik *et al.*, 1988; Szapocznik & Kurtines, 1980).

Acculturation Factors

Drug use, delinquency, and other problem behaviors among Latino youth are influenced by socialization experiences and the experiences of their families in their new environments. This process is known as acculturation. A core assumption is that acculturation simultaneously evolves in several critical areas, including the contexts of exit from the country of origin and entrance into the US described above (Fabrega, 1989). Experiences involving adjustment to a new cultural setting can threaten the functioning of families, and in particular, relationships among family members. Acculturation is a discontinuous and idiosyncratic process, rather than a monolithic one. In the framework presented above, the family plays many important roles (e.g., as a source of multiple stressors, as well as a system of buffers that can reduce risk for delinquency and adolescent AOD use/abuse).

The process of acculturation is one that creates intergenerational transitions from the culture of origin to the development of bicultural capabilities among family members, typically the younger generation. This produces stress for the acculturating individual and the broader family system (Ruiz & Casas, 1981). Within the family, this produces a "cultural shift," a dynamic tension that may increase stress (Mendoza & Martinez, 1981), and exacerbate normative intergenerational conflicts. The work of Szapocznik and colleagues (e.g., Szapocznik *et al.*, 1988; Szapocznik & Kurtines, 1980) illustrates the potential for the acculturation process to produce stress and conflict in the family as adolescents become more acculturated into the values and behaviors of American society, and parents in turn become more authoritarian as they attempt to stop what they see as a downward progression into inappropriately liberal attitudes and behaviors.

Nearly every study describing the influence of acculturation upon adolescent problem behavior has documented significant direct relations, both cross-sectionally and longitudinally. While findings differ across studies in exactly how acculturation may be related to maladjustment, there are important factors subsumed by the acculturation process that need to be considered in the development of prevention programs that involve Latino youth and their families. For example, social psychologists have struggled to describe how acculturation operates at the individual level. There are several overlapping approaches to conceptualizing and measuring acculturation in American social psychology, including linear acculturation models (e.g., Rogler, Cortes & Malgady, 1991), cultural identity (e.g., Felix-Ortiz & Newcomb, 1995), multidimensional models (e.g., Keefe & Padilla, 1987; Padilla, 1980; Szapocznik, Scopetta, Kurtines & Arnalde, 1978), and orthogonal models (Oetting, 1993). It is universally acknowledged that acculturation is a product of multiple ongoing processes that are idiosyncratic, dynamic, and complex. The varying ways in which acculturation has been conceptualized have produced a series of lenses through which researchers have looked at the influence of acculturation on the behavior and adjustment of Latino youth and their families.

Acculturation influences adolescent substance use and abuse through its interactions with other risk and protective factors. For example, modeling and other elements of social learning are relevant to the process of acculturation since immigrant children and adolescents are exposed to prevalent attitudes, norms, and behaviors in contemporary American society, including those related to substance use and experimentation. There are also influences related to the stressors that the acculturation process imposes on immigrant families. These stressors are sociocultural in nature, and include economic factors, as well as cultural conflicts within and outside the family. These elements are integral to the development of substance use/abuse interventions with Latino youth. However, the influence of acculturation must be considered in the developmental context of broader individual, social, and socioeconomic factors that affect all youth, regardless of ethnic background or level of acculturation.

Segmented Assimilation

Contemporary sociological studies have produced models for explaining different mechanisms by which recent immigrants are incorporated both socially and economically into their new country. These models include elements such as the circumstances and conditions that precipitated immigration, and the social and cultural compatibility between immigrants and the societies that they enter (i.e., contexts of exit and entrance [Portes & Rumbaut, 1990]). Another element is the influence of "local" communities on the assimilation of immigrant children and adolescents. Ethnic enclaves where large numbers of immigrants establish and maintain communities influence the process of acculturation. Researchers have reported that when enclaves are highly developed and stable, lower rates of mental health problems are found (Kuo, 1976).

This concept of segmented assimilation is salient for understanding individual and group adaptation among Latino immigrants (Portes, 1993). Segmented assimilation is predicated on the distinctive socialization experiences of groups, and the existence of distinctive pathways into American society for individuals. The integration and underclass assimilation models require implicitly extensive deculturation. The integration model requires social integration into dominant ethnic groups, while the underclass model requires social integration into the street culture of disorganized inner-city ghettos. Both of these alternative models assume intergenerational conflicts between immigrant parents and children who were either born in the US or immigrated when they were very young. Rumbaut (1995) refers to this type of individual adjustment as "subtractive" because it operates as a zero-sum gain (i.e., you must give up cultural knowledge and associated practices to acquire new ones). This is, in fact, the fundamental assumption of the linear gradient acculturation model. Over time, all immigrants become Americanized to some mythical standard cultural form. The segmented assimilation concept emphasizes a second form of cultural incorporation, a bicultural option of integration into ethnic enclaves. This requires an assimilation process very similar to what Gibson (1995) calls "additive acculturation," which entails maintaining the core of cultural knowledge and practices, but adding instrumental knowledge and skills of exogenous, and potentially dominant, cultural groups.

Cultural contact and socialization among Latino adolescents is heavily influenced by the cultural settings in which they occur. The identities and cultural memberships selected by adolescents, although not totally volitional, have important ramifications for adherence to conventional behavior over the life course, including delinquency and drug use. With regard to immigrants, the more they conserve their culture of origin, the less likely they are to be influenced by American underclass culture, or by integration into middle-class American culture, both of which feature much higher levels of adolescent drug use than is found in their own culture. Nevertheless, culture is dynamic rather than static, and some degree of acculturation is inevitable. We can expect that adolescents who immigrate early in their lives will attain a higher level of acculturation simply as a function of ongoing maturational processes, developmental processes, and length of exposure. The salient question of segmented assimilation is "To which American culture do immigrant adolescents acculturate?" The answer is shaped by the influences of local environment and ethnic enclaves. Therefore, it is necessary to adjust substance abuse interventions implemented in specific Latino ethnic enclaves to local circumstances.

Acculturation Stress

At present, relations between cultural orientation and drug use among Latino adults have been directly or indirectly tested in three large epidemiological surveys (Amaro, Whitaker, Coffman & Heeren, 1990; Burnam, Hough, Karno, Escobar & Tebles, 1987; Vega, Kolody, Hwang & Noble, 1993). The results are consistent. High acculturation is associated with significantly higher drug use, and in particular, illicit drug use. Furthermore, biculturalism was not found to be a protective factor for drug use (Burnam *et al.*, 1987), and individuals with low levels of acculturation had much lower rates of drug use than bicultural individuals (Amaro *et al.*, 1990). It is important to note, however, that acculturation measures are broad indicators of knowledge acquisition and behavioral practices, but do not actually assess group-level processes or their relation to individual adaptation. For example, acculturation measures do not directly assess the effects of limited economic opportunities, language barriers, or satisfactory social adjustment. Moreover, with regard to children and adolescents, there is evidence that immigrant children are influenced by acculturation in ways fundamentally different from their US-born Hispanic counterparts (Gil, Vega & Dimas, 1994; Gil, Wagner & Vega, 2000; Vega & Gil, 1998).

A more basic issue concerns the extent of, and the ways in which, the process of acculturation creates stress and conflict for families and individuals, as well as how such difficulties influence adolescent problem behaviors. This alternative approach to Latino adolescent adjustment and delinquency is reflected in the early work of Szapocznik *et al.* (1978, 1980) with Cuban American families. These researchers found that acculturation occurs more quickly among immigrant children than among their parents, and that boys acculturate faster than girls. In clinical studies, these investigators reported that this differential rate of acculturation led to differences in intergenerational behavioral expectations. Immigrant parents, already struggling to reestablish their lives and to develop an adequate economic base, were bewildered and frustrated by their children, who quickly learned and emulated American cultural norms for demeanor, entertainment preferences, dress, and personal etiquette. This often led to conflicts over appropriate behavior. Parents were sensitive to losing control of their children in this new cultural setting, and often attempted to impose additional structure upon adolescent conduct, resulting in further deterioration in parent–child communication and increases in association with delinquent peers, delinquent behavior, and experimental drug use.

Other researchers have described the distribution and the effects of acculturative stress among Hispanic adolescents (e.g., Gil & Vega, 1996; Gil, Vega & Biafora, 1998; Gil, Vega & Dimas, 1994; Vega, Gil & Wagner, 1998). In comparisons of Hispanic youth attending South Florida middle schools, these researchers have documented greater total acculturation stress and difficulties among immigrant Hispanic teens, but stronger effects of acculturation stress on adjustment among US-born Hispanic teens. The findings from these studies confirm the impression that Latino adolescents born in the US are more susceptible to internalization of minority status, and that behavioral outcomes of this process, including delinquent behavior, will be exhibited in school settings.

Much of the impact of acculturation factors, however, appears to involve "third-variable" influences (e.g., Vega, Zimmerman, Warheit, Apospori & Gil, 1993a). For example, in a study on the effects of acculturation and family protective factors on delinquent behavior among Cuban adolescents, acculturation factors, family factors, and the interaction of acculturation and family factors each independently predicted delinquent behavior. The salience of acculturation stress to intervention strategies will be addressed later in the following domains: (a) familism, Hispanic family values, traditions, and attitudes as risk and resilience factors for Latino youth; (b) individual differences in acculturation stress among immigrant and US-born Latino youth; (c) differences in intergenerational acculturation in client families; (d) the influence of cultural values on help-seeking and service utilization; and (e) health belief systems within Hispanic cultures.

Family Stress

Family adjustment is a critical domain in which acculturation and acculturation stress can influence problem behavior among immigrant adolescents. Moreover, family influences on problem behavior may be particularly salient for Latino youth. The family and family processes are key elements of Hispanic culture (Marin & Marin, 1991; Vega, 1990). The term "familism" has been used to describe the propensity in Hispanic cultures for individuals to maintain strong feelings of loyalty, reciprocity, and solidarity toward the family (Marin & Marin, 1991). The influence of the family and the totality of social, instrumental, and emotional support exchanged among family members have been used to explain the relatively good health outlook of Latinos in the US, despite their lower socioeconomic status and low health care access and utilization (Vega & Amaro, 1994).

There are significant cultural variations in family rules and the monitoring of children with regard to problem behaviors (Catalano, Hawkins, Krenz *et al.*, 1993; Vega & Gil, 1998). Many Latinos have a strong preference for residing in close proximity to other family members (Mindle, 1980), favoring frequent face-to-face contact with extended family members (Keefe, 1984; Vega, 1990). There is growing evidence that traditional familistic values serve a protective function against adolescent maladjustment (Vega *et al.*, 1993c). In addition, Vega, Gil, and Wagner (1998) have shown that the loss of familism and parental respect, which accompany greater acculturation among Latino adolescents, increases predisposition toward deviant behaviors and alcohol use. Other researchers (e.g., Rodriguez & Zayas, 1990) have found that norms concerning parental respect and family loyalty attenuate criminal behavior among Latino youth. Given these findings, disruptions of family living arrangements and emotional ties, often precipitated by emigration from the country of origin, constitute important elements to consider in the design and implementation interventions with Latino youth (Rumbaut & Rumbaut, 1976).

Changes in traditional attitudes about the family and in family structures may increase ongoing stress for Latino adolescents. Research conducted among Latino adolescents in South Florida has shown that immigrant adolescents are more susceptible to personal problems as a result of changes in family structure than adolescents from other racial/ethnic backgrounds (Gil, Vega & Biafora, 1998). Research also has demonstrated that immigrants are less likely than US-born Latinos, African Americans, or Whites to experience low levels of familism and family cohesion (Vega *et al.*, 1993a), and that familism is inversely related to acculturation among immigrants but not among US-born Latinos (Gil, Vega & Dimas, 1994). Therefore, acculturation (among immigrants) and US nativity reduce familism and increase acculturation conflicts, with both of these factors associated with subsequent drug use behaviors (Vega & Gil, 1998). It is evident that familism is especially important in mediating the effects of various risk factors on adolescent delinquency and drug use (Vega & Gil, 1998; Vega, Gil & Wagner, 1998). Therefore, there is compelling evidence for connections between the decline of traditional familistic values among more acculturated Latinos, problems associated with acculturation gaps between parents and children, and increases in family conflicts. Current research evidence suggests the family is a key protective factor among Latinos for outcomes related to health (Vega & Amaro, 1994), juvenile delinquency, and drug use (Gil, Vega & Biafora, 1998; Vega, 1990).

Cultural Factors Relevant to Interventions

Thus far, we have presented a general theoretical framework that has addressed both cultural and acculturative factors salient to adaptation among Latino youth in the US. In this section, we describe the salience of these factors for the development of alcohol and drug use interventions specifically targeting Latino adolescents. At present, knowledge about the effective treatment of drug use/abuse among ethnic minorities is scant. Regarding Latinos, we know little about how factors such as nativity, acculturation, and national origin influence the effectiveness of available treatments. Based on existing epidemiological literature, we believe that acculturation, acculturation stress, acculturation gaps, nativity, and family factors are critical variables to be considered in the implementation of treatments, and in the evaluation of their effectiveness. Furthermore, the literature suggests that familiarity with a target group's cultural values and attitudes is essential in order for treatment programs to be culturally appropriate. There is a critical need to empirically evaluate the influence of these variables on treatment effectiveness. In the intervention project we present below, we address these ethnic-specific factors as amenability to treatment factors. That is, these variables are conceptualized as potential moderators of treatment effectiveness within the context of an intervention that is applicable to broader populations of adolescents.

Acculturation and Acculturation Stress

Available research on acculturation, acculturation stress, health beliefs, and health utilization informs intervention efforts with Latinos. Levels of acculturation and acculturation stress are salient aspects in the lives of Latino youth and their families that interact with other elements of their social environment. Research findings illustrate that US-born and immigrant Latino youth present with different needs and strengths, and treatment programs should be attuned to these differences. Moreover, cultural belief systems, and the life circumstances of Latino groups in the US, support the efficacy of brief interventions, as well as program delivery formats that are based in the communities where clients live and that include some level of family involvement.

One form of brief intervention that has proven effective with Latino families has been Brief Strategic/Structural Family Therapy (BSFT) (e.g., Santisteban *et al.*, 1997). These researchers have used this form of family intervention to address youth substance use by targeting child behavioral problems, as well as ongoing family functioning. The premise of this therapy is that reductions in problem behaviors in children and adolescents, accompanied by improvements in family functioning, will reduce and prevent substance abuse. This premise is based upon research demonstrating that children exhibiting conduct and antisocial behaviors are at risk for substance use and abuse, and that poor family functioning can serve as a risk factor for adolescent substance abuse.

Family Acculturation Gaps

One important area that affects immigrant families, regardless of racial, ethnic, or national background, is acculturation differences between parents and children resulting from children adopting values and behaviors of American society more rapidly than their parents. As stated earlier, these acculturation differentials become sources of stress by exacerbating developmentally normative intergenerational differences and conflicts (Santisteban *et al.*, 1997). Clinical and epidemiological studies have demonstrated the existence of family acculturation gaps among Latino families (e.g., Santisteban *et al.*, 1997; Szapocznik *et al.*, 1978; Szapocznik *et al.*, 1988; Vega & Gil, 1998). This correlate of family conflict would have to be addressed in interventions that include the participation of family members. An effective approach may involve helping the family to bridge acculturation gaps by fostering improved communication and better understanding of the various cultural perspectives that evolve within immigrant families.

Familism and Traditional Family Values

The ways in which the family manifests itself in the lives of Latinos leads to specific strategies for involving family members in the treatment of adolescents. With regard to substance use, we know that the family can serve as a protective factor in preventing substance use. However, it is equally important to recognize that family conflicts and the parenting efforts of Latinos may have unintended negative effects. For example, the close contact and support often found in Latino families may unintentionally "enable" youth who develop substance use problems, particularly male adolescents who are often treated differently from their female counterparts. These family influences may be addressed in several ways. The most basic avenue is to be cognizant of the important role played by the family, and to assess the level of functioning of families involved in treatment. Given the significance accorded to maintaining family solidarity, and the interdependent functioning within the family, therapists engaging Latino populations must understand that the responsibility of each family member to the greater family whole will be a key constraint on any intervention strategy (Gloria & Peregory, 1996). Therefore, the family unit needs to be included in the various tactics comprising an intervention. This is not easy when dealing with substance abuse issues in which a great deal of family conflict may have already occurred by entry into treatment. At the very least, however, "key" family member(s) should be involved in the intervention.

In addition, the importance of the family within Latino cultures is reflected by the literature emphasizing family therapy as a treatment of choice for ethnic substance users (Gloria, Trainor, Beasley & Robinson-Kurpius, 1996; Ho, 1987; Santisteban *et al.*, 1997; Thurman, Swaim & Plested, 1995). In specific terms, researchers have emphasized that family interventions that respect and recognize the preferred hierarchical structures of Latino families (Santisteban *et al.*, 1997), and the role and responsibility of each family member to the greater family whole (Gloria & Peregoy, 1996), are likely to be more acceptable to Latino clients. However, it is important to note that Hispanic adolescents with substance use problems, when given the choice between individual and family intervention, typically choose individual treatment (Wagner, Gil & Tubman, 1999). Moreover, preliminary data suggest that for Hispanic youth with substance use problems attendance rates are lower and dropout rates are higher for those assigned to family intervention versus individual intervention (Wagner, 2000). The implication of these findings is that individual interventions may be a viable alternative to family intervention, especially when the goal is to reach as many youth as possible in an optimally engaging manner.

An additional point concerns the need to assess how acculturation levels may influence family interactions and social norms or expectations. While many acculturated adolescents may express disdain for the "old" or "antiquated" ways of their Latino parents, therapists and researchers must pay attention to how these expressed attitudes manifest themselves in terms of ongoing behavior patterns. This sounds simpler than it actually is, given the fact that the behaviors and attitudes of Latino youth *vis-à-vis* their families are influenced by concurrent developmental processes and a wide range of contextual factors.

Finally, long separations between parents and their children are a common source of stress in Hispanic families (Santisteban *et al.*, 1997). Obvious issues of concern in these separations relate to the reestablishment of stable family relations and structures. Given the importance of the family in Latino culture, disruptions within the family have been identified as early sources of problems for Hispanic youth (Gloria & Peregoy, 1996; Santisteban & Szapocznik, 1982). Thus, researchers developing family interventions for use with Latino youth should consider the potential impact of family separations on family functioning.

Contexts of Exit and Entrance

Earlier in this chapter, we discussed how contexts of entrance and exit affect the adaptation and experiences of immigrant families and their members. These factors are relevant for treatment approaches given the potential influence of immigration experiences on individual and family functioning. For example, immigrant youth who arrive in the US during their adolescent years may have very different experiences from those who arrived at younger ages. Older immigrant adolescents are more likely to have direct experience with the stressors that precipitated the family's decision to emigrate. In addition, older immigrant adolescents are more likely to have had childhood social environments characterized by congruence between the family's values and those of the general society. In these ways, when and how immigrant adolescent arrive in the US may have implications for treatment.

Problem Orientation

Brief interventions that address multiple problems, and have the goal of early and concrete improvements, are more likely to be relevant to the "problem orientation" of Latinos (Santisteban *et al.*, 1997). This is not to suggest that Latinos are not interested in long-term, future-oriented solutions for individual and family problems. It indicates, however, that the views and attitudes of Latinos with regard to psychosocial interventions are that interventions must address what the clients perceive as the current problem situation. Thus brief, problem-focused interventions may be best for engaging Latino clients in treatment.

Barriers to Participation

Researchers have observed that "the help seeking behavior of Latinos in the US is framed by a paradox" (Vega & Kolody, in press). Low rates of mental health service utilization among Latinos have been reported for decades (e.g., Jimenez, Alegria, Pena & Vera, 1997), while for ethnic groups such as Mexican Americans, minority status and stressful social and economic conditions should result in higher prevalence rates for mental health problems (Vega & Rumbaut, 1991). Recent studies confirm that Latinos are at least as likely as Non-Hispanic Whites to demonstrate mental health problems, yet Latinos continue to have lower utilization of mental health services (Giachello, 1994; Molina & Aguirre-Molina, 1994; Vega & Kolody, in press).

Several factors have contributed to lower rates of service utilization including: cultural values; shortages of bilingual and bicultural health providers; language barriers; and institutional barriers that undermine the Hispanic cultural emphasis on social ties (Giachello, 1994). For example, researchers have reported that Hispanic men and women are more likely to delay substance abuse treatment because of a reluctance to acknowledge their addictions and their discomfort at being separated from family for treatment (Kline, 1996). A broader problem is that most interventions were not originally developed with Latino groups in mind, and have been applied to Hispanics without modification. The procedures, techniques, and methods of these treatments emerge from Anglo-American cultural viewpoints. For example, conventional Anglo-American referral strategies ignore how important social ties are to Hispanic cultures (Smart & Smart, 1995). Moreover, Hispanic cultural values of avoiding interpersonal conflicts and de-emphasizing negative behaviors that occur in such conflicts (e.g., Trandis, Marin & Betancourt, 1984) have caused Hispanic families to drop out of interventions that do not consider these values. Latinos tend to need strong interpersonal connections with therapists, service providers, and institutions for successful interfaces with the health care system (Gloria & Peregoy, 1996). Lack of attention to these issues and low cultural competence have been identified as reasons for the underutilization of, and early termination from, intervention programs (Sue & Sue, 1990).

Despite evidence of low rates of service utilization, recent research has shown improvement in retention in interventions once Latinos reach service providers (O'Sullivan, Peterson, Cox & Kirkeby, 1989; Hu, Snowden, Jerrell & Nguyen, 1991). Furthermore, the matching of Latino clients with culturally competent therapists and with other Latinos in treatment has resulted in lower dropout rates (O'Sullivan & Lasso, 1992). Perhaps more importantly, knowing where to seek treatment, and having more information about available programs and services, have been shown to increase the likelihood of service utilization, nearly five-fold in one study (Vega & Kolody, in press). Therefore, the recruitment and retention of Latino participants in intervention programs will require efforts that specifically address the barriers that this population is likely to encounter as they seek help or access services.

Available literature emphasizes the importance of delivering information to Hispanic families regarding the availability and nature of services. In addition, retention of participants is more likely when there is ethnic and language matching between client and service provider. Finally, it is important for service providers to assess the degree of acculturation of clients participating in specific programs and their adherence to the traditional values of Latinos (Comas-Diaz, 1989). This information provides a basis for understanding the degree to which the Latino clients more or less adhere to traditional Hispanic cultural values, and should inform the approach the therapist takes with the clients in treatment.

Program Evaluation

Historically, little attention has been paid to the difficulties and challenges of evaluating programs and interventions for culturally and linguistically distinct groups. In general, there is agreement that understanding cultural factors is important for the development, implementation, and evaluation of interventions for Latino groups (Cervantes & Pena, 1998). The ability of evaluators to incorporate cultural factors such as language, acculturation, family values, and community attitudes has been labeled "cultural competence" (Orlandi, 1992). While this term, somewhat overused in the literature, has been argued to have political overtones, the fact is that evaluators must incorporate cultural factors into their evaluation plan to provide the most appropriate evaluation of a given program or intervention. For example, the effectiveness of an intervention for Latino families may be greater for less acculturated, recent immigrants than for those who have lived in the US all their lives. Evaluations that are not culturally competent may miss this by failing to measure the immigration history and level of acculturation of the Latino participants. Moreover, while specific interventions may be equally effective with different ethnic groups, it is likely that there will be "process" variables that differentially influence treatment outcome among different groups of clients. Inasmuch as there are practical limitations on the number of variables to be included in an evaluation, it is a major challenge to identify the most salient cultural factors critical to evaluation (Wagner, Swensen & Henggeler, 2000).

Given the limitations of available research, it is difficult to find empirical evidence that alcohol and substance use interventions have been successful with Hispanic/Latino populations (Casas, 1992), or which interventions are more or less appropriate for individuals who are more or less acculturated. Nonetheless, the use of culturally relevant assessment instruments is critical, and factors that should be measured include: (a) level of acculturation; (b) acculturation stress; (c) family acculturation conflicts; (d) language preferences; (e) migration history; (f) family functioning (e.g., familism, cohesion, communication); (g) cultural identity; and (h) generational level.

While a range of factors specific to Latino populations must be considered in the implementation of outcome evaluations, an additional factor needs to be addressed in conducting process evaluations. Often interventions are designed for other populations and modified subsequently for Latino participants. It is essential to capture changes in the delivery of the intervention as staff make necessary adjustments to meet the needs of the new client population. A proper evaluation needs to include systematic documentation of adjustments made during program implementation.

An Intervention for Latino Youth: Alcohol Treatment Targeting Adolescents in Need (ATTAIN)

We conclude by presenting an ongoing project which illustrates several of the basic elements we have discussed. We describe the basic tenets of the intervention model, and then address how this intervention program has been modified and implemented with Latino adolescents. The project is entitled Alcohol Treatment Targeting Adolescents in Need (ATTAIN) (Wagner, Gil & Tubman, 2000), and is funded by the National Institute on Alcohol Abuse and Alcoholism.

Description of the Intervention Model

Guided Self-Change (GSC) treatment (Sobell & Sobell, 1998) is a brief cognitive-behavioral, motivational intervention designed for use with individuals with alcohol and other drug (AOD) problems. Originally, this treatment was developed for problem drinkers, a group not severely dependent on alcohol but still demonstrating alcohol problems. The focus on problem drinking derived from research showing that this type of alcohol problem is more prevalent than more severe drinking problems (Cahalan & Room, 1974; Institute of Medicine, 1990) and does not necessarily progress to become more severe (Pattison, Sobell & Sobell, 1977; Sobell & Sobell, 1987, 1993). Another major influence on the development of GSC treatment was the finding that one session of advice and counseling was more effective in addressing alcohol problems of mild to moderate severity than more traditional and intensive treatment (Edwards *et al.*, 1977; Orford, Oppenheimer & Edwards, 1976). Additional influences included research documenting recovery from AOD problems without treatment or help (Saunders & Kershaw, 1979; Tuchfeld, 1976; Waldorf & Biernacki, 1982), the importance of client's motivation to change in determining treatment outcome (DiClemente & Prochaska, 1982; Miller, 1983, 1985; Prochaska, 1983), and the social-learning premise that allowing goal choice (e.g., abstinence from alcohol vs. moderation) increases an individual's commitment to a goal (Sobell & Sobell, 1995).

GSC treatment can be used individually, with couples, or with groups, with minor variations in format and materials. Individual GSC treatment (GSC-I) represents the prototype and has been standardized and manualized for clinical and research applications (Sobell & Sobell, 1993). An initial study compared the effectiveness of GSC treatment with and without a relapse prevention component (Sobell & Sobell, 1993). The two approaches proved equally effective, with a total reduction in reported alcohol consumption of 53.8 percent compared to the year preceding treatment, a near doubling of abstinence rates from the year prior to treatment to the one-year post-treatment follow-up, and very high consumer satisfaction ratings.

A second study examined the effectiveness of GSC treatment involving adult clients and their spouses drinking (Sobell, Sobell & Leo, 1993). In one treatment condition, the spouse intervention focused only on providing an understanding of the clients' treatment program and a realistic perspective for viewing recovery from alcohol problems. A second treatment condition also included explicit instructions to spouses about how to be supportive of partners' attempts to change their drinking. In both treatment conditions the clients received standard GSC individual treatment (GSC-I). Clients in both groups improved equally, and an interesting interaction effect was observed. Clients lacking confidence in their own ability to recover did better when treatment included explicit spousal instruction in how to be supportive.

Additional studies have found GSC-I treatment to be highly effective in managed-care settings (Breslin, Sobell, Sobell, Cunningham & Kwan, 1995) and with Spanish-speaking clients (Ayala-Velazquez, Echeverria, Sobell & Sobell, 1997). It is worth noting that group GSC treatment has been attempted with Spanish-speaking clients but was unsuccessful due to cultural proscriptions against the personal disclosure to strangers of weaknesses, emotional vulnerability, and failures (Ayala-Velazquez, personal communication, October 21, 1997).

Rationale for Using Guided Self-change (GSC) Treatment with Adolescents

GSC treatment may be particularly well suited for adolescents exhibiting a range of problem behaviors (i.e., multi-problem youth) given its format, the underlying change producing procedures, its flexibility, and ease of use. GSC initially was developed for problem drinkers and not for individuals severely dependent on alcohol. Adolescents with substance use problems have a relatively brief history of substance involvement and typically demonstrate episodic alcohol and other drug consumption. Thus, the vast majority of substance-abusing teens have problems of mild to moderate severity and do not demonstrate dependency (Wagner & Kassel, 1995). In addition, GSC is heavily reliant on cognitive-behavioral techniques, which have been shown to be more effective than non-behavioral approaches in reducing problem behaviors (including substance use problems) among adolescents (Garrett, 1985; Mulvey, Arthur & Reppucci, 1993).

This intervention can be administered in a flexible manner, in individual, family, or group formats. Family therapies have yielded some positive effects in treatment studies with multi-problem antisocial youth (Garrett, 1985; Mulvey, Arthur & Reppucci, 1993), and GSC offers a means to compare the same intervention administered in individual versus family-involved formats. Moreover, this intervention, by design, promotes the type of treatment atmosphere (e.g., therapeutic genuineness, active and direct communication, the ability to withstand limit testing, converting action into words) thought to be optimally effective for youth with conduct problems (Richards & Sullivan, 1996). In addition, motivational interventions like GSC appear to be particularly effective for clients at earlier stages of change or who demonstrate high levels of anger (Heather, Rollnick, Bell & Richmond, 1996; Waldron & Miller, in press). Many adolescent populations (e.g., teenagers with substance use problems, juvenile offenders) are known to have low levels of motivation for change and high levels of anger (Garrett, 1985; Mulvey, Arthur & Reppucci, 1993). This intervention also is a short-term, cost-effective therapy. This may be a particularly efficient way of treating vulnerable adolescent populations who are difficult to engage. As evidence grows supporting the effectiveness of this treatment, GSC treatments ultimately may be very feasible approaches for addressing substance use problems among underserved adolescent populations, such as Latinos, either as a stand-alone substance abuse treatment or as the substance abuse component of broader interventions.

Modification of Guided Self-change to Latino Adolescents

There are several elements of project ATTAIN developed to address specific treatment "process" factors related to the implementation of GSC with Latino adolescents. First, the intervention is being implemented and delivered geographically in the communities in which the target adolescents and their families reside. This feature of the project increases sensitivity to several of the issues discussed earlier related to the accessibility of interventions for members of Latino communities. Second, several "process" variables specific to implementation of GSC among Latino adolescents are being addressed as amenability to treatment factors. These are discussed more fully below.

The family long has been recognized as a primary source of influence in the theoretical and empirical literatures concerning the development and maintenance of adolescent substance use problems (see Hawkins, Catalano & Miller, 1992; Hops, Tildesley, Lichtenstein, Ary & Sherman, 1990; Petraitis, Flay & Miller, 1995). The treatment literature has documented that the family can play a major role in influencing an adolescents' motivation to change their patterns of substance use (Brown, Myers, Mott & Vik, 1994; Waldron, 1997) in particular, when adolescents are of Latino descent (e.g., Szapocznik & Kurtines, 1980; Szapocznik *et al.*, 1988). For example, there are important ethnic variations in family rules and monitoring of children with relation to AOD use (Catalano, Hawkins, Krenz *et al.*, 1993; Vega & Gil, 1998).

As we have documented earlier in this chapter, the structure of family relations and emotional ties is disrupted by emigration from the country of origin (e.g., Rumbaut & Rumbaut, 1976). Traditionally, Latinos have a strong preference for residing in close proximity to other family members (Mindle, 1980) and favor face-to-face contact with extended family members (Keefe, 1984; Vega, 1990). As such, Hispanic culture has been described as highly familistic, and there is evidence that these traditional familistic values can serve as a protective factor for adolescent maladjustment (Vega, 1990; Gil & Vega, 1996). Given the prominence of the family as a focus of Hispanic culture, a major modification to GSC in project ATTAIN has been the emphasis on a family-involved format.

While individual-format behavior therapy and family therapy are two common modalities for adolescent psychotherapy, individual-format behavior therapies have received a great deal of empirical support and are used widely. In contrast, family-based psychotherapies, despite a strong rationale based on the assumption that families are a key context for adolescent development, have much less empirical support despite their wide clinical usage (Kendall & Morris, 1991). Kendall & Morris (1991) suggest the comparison of individual therapy with family-involved therapy as a necessary first step toward understanding what are the most effective interventions for specific adolescent problems. Project ATTAIN follows the suggestion of Kendall & Morris by comparing the efficacy of individual-format GSC treatment to that of family-involved GSC treatment for juvenile offenders who have alcohol or other drug problems.

Family-involved GSC is implemented in such a way that one or more family member(s) is (are) actively involved in the intervention with the target adolescent. They are recruited to participate in the intervention so that they are available to serve as additional sources of support for the behavioral changes called for by GSC. The involvement of family members in the intervention will be done in a manner that respects traditional family hierarchies; this is congruent with the Latino cultural values about the nature and the role of the family. This format for implementing GSC attempts to use highly valued elements of Latino culture to create an additional, culturally appropriate structure to develop and maintain motivation for behavioral change among substance-abusing adolescents. Therefore, the family-involved format for GSC builds upon the unique strengths and cultural traditions in Latino families to facilitate the therapeutic objectives of GSC, significant reductions in adolescents' alcohol and other drug use.

As described earlier, brief, cognitive-behavioral interventions appear to be more congruent with the cultural values and attitudes of Latino populations. GSC focuses on concrete problem behaviors at the present moment and provides clearly identified techniques for assisting adolescents to develop skills directly relevant to reductions of drug and alcohol use. These features of GSC are particularly appropriate for Latino teens and families because of their tendency to access treatment and services for specific problems that are perceived as needing immediate attention, and because of their expectations that professionals will provide concrete, knowledge-based techniques. With reference to the issue of acculturation, there are several factors that are considered treatment moderator or "amenability to treatment" variables in ATTAIN. These include nativity, length of time living in the US, and level of acculturation. We have developed several hypotheses using these variables that are being tested to determine the generalizability of GSC across different Hispanic subgroups and levels of acculturation.

The preceding overview of ATTAIN serves to illustrate how adolescent substance abuse treatment may be developed and evaluated in a manner that is culturally competent. The project is documenting the influence of cultural-specific factors on treatment outcomes for GSC. These objectives address the need to move beyond the deductive approach traditionally used when implementing substance use/abuse interventions among Latino populations to the empirical testing of hypotheses that will serve as the foundation for the future development of ethnically sensitive intervention programs.

Summary

The Latino population in the US is heterogeneous and growing rapidly. With regard to Latino adolescents' substance use, studies have described significant differences in the prevalence of, and risk factors associated with, substance use patterns based on level of acculturation and nativity. There is a paucity of studies evaluating the effectiveness of intervention strategies for Latino youth with substance use problems. This chapter has described a theoretical framework that can be used to develop and evaluate effective interventions for Latino populations. There are, however, important areas that deserve further attention. To date, research on Latinos receiving substance abuse intervention lacks detail in terms of client characteristics, treatment services, and the effectiveness of treatment. There is a need to empirically test approaches that incorporate culturally relevant elements (e.g., familism, personalism). In order to establish whether and how these variables influence treatment effectiveness, interventions must be developed in which hypotheses related to these factors are tested with Latino populations.

References

Amaro, H., Whitaker, R., Coffman, G., & Heeren, T. (1990), "Acculturation and marijuana and cocaine use: Findings from HHANES 1982–84." *American Journal of Public Health 80*, 54–60.

Arredondo, R., Weddige, R. L., Justice, C. L., & Fritz, J. (1987), "Alcoholism in Mexican-Americans: Intervention and treatment." *Hospital and Community Psychiatry 38*, 180–183.

Ayala-Velazquez, H. E., Echeverria, L. S., Sobell, M., & Sobell, L. (1997), "Auto Control Dirigido: Intervencioines breves para bebedores problema en Mexico." *Revista Mexicana de Psicologia (Mexican Journal of Psychology) 14*, 113–127.

Breslin, F. C., Sobell, L. C., Sobell, M. B., Cunningham, J. C., & Kwan, E. (1995), "Prognostic markers for a stepped care approach: The utility of within treatment drinking variables." Paper presented at the 29th Annual Meeting of the Association for Advancement of Behavior Therapy, Washington, DC, November.

Brown, S. A., Myers, M. G., Mott, M. A., & Vik, P. W. (1994), "Correlates of success following treatment for adolescent substance abuse." *Applied and Preventive Psychology 3*, 61–73.

Burnam, A., Hough, R., Karno, M., Escobar, J., & Telles, C. (1987), "Acculturation and lifetime prevalence of psychiatric disorders among Mexican Americans in Los Angeles." *Journal of Health and Social Behavior 28*, 89–102.

Cahalan, D., & Room, R. (1974), *Problem Drinking among American Men.* New Brunswick, NJ: Rutgers Center of Alcohol Studies.

Casas, J. M. (1992), "A culturally sensitive model for evaluating alcohol and other drug abuse prevention programs: A Hispanic perspective." In M. A. Orlandi & R. Weston (eds), *Cultural Competence for Evaluators: A guide for alcohol and other drug abuse prevention practitioners working with ethnic/racial communities. OSAP cultural competence series 1.* US Department of Health & Human Services, Rockville, MD, 75–116.

Catalano, R. F. *et al.* (1993), "Using research to guide culturally appropriate drug use prevention." *Journal of Consulting and Clinical Psychology 61*, 804–811.

Cervantes, R. C., & Pena, C. (1998), "Evaluating Hispanic/Latino programs: Ensuring cultural competence." *Alcoholism Treatment Quarterly 16*(1–2), 109–131.

Collins, L. R. (1993), "Sociocultural aspects of alcohol use and abuse: Ethnicity and gender." *Drugs and Society 8*, 89–116.

Comas-Diaz, L. (1989), "Culturally relevant issues and treatment implications for Hispanics." In D. R. Koslow & E. P. Salett (eds), *Crossing Cultures in Mental Health.* Washington, DC: Sietar International, 31–48.

Comas-Diaz, L. (1994), "An integrative approach." In L. Comas-Diaz & B. Greene (eds), *Women of Color: Integrating ethnic identities and gender in psychotherapy.* New York: Guilford Press, 287–318.

DiClemente, C. C., & Prochaska, J. O. (1982), "Self-change and therapy change of smoking behavior: A comparison of processes of change in cessation and maintenance." *Addictive Behaviors 7*, 133–142.

Edwards, G. *et al.* (1977), "Alcoholism: A controlled trial of 'treatment' and 'advice.'" *Journal of Studies on Alcohol 38*, 1004–1031.

Fabrega, H. (1989), "Cultural relativism and psychiatric illness." *Journal of Nervous and Mental Disease 177*, 415–425.

Felix-Ortiz, M., & Newcomb, M. D. (1995), "Cultural identity and drug use among Latino and Latina adolescents." In G. J. Botvin, S. Schinke & M. A. Orlandi (eds), *Drug Use Prevention with Multiethnic Youth.* Thousand Oaks, CA: Sage Publications, 147–165.

Garrett, C. (1985), "Effects of residential treatment on adjudicated delinquents: A meta-analysis." *Journal of Research in Crime and Delinquency 22*, 287–308.

Giachello, A. L. M. (1994), "Issues of access and use." In C. W. Molina & M. Aguirre-Molina (eds), *Latino Health in the US: A growing challenge.* Washington, DC: American Public Health Association, 83–111.

Gibson, M. A. (1995), "Additive acculturation as a strategy for school improvement." In R. G. Rumbaut & W. A. Cornelius (eds), *California's Immigrant Children: Theory, research, and implications for educational policy.* San Diego, CA: Center for US–Mexican Studies, University of California, San Diego, 77–106.

Gil, A. G., & Vega, W. A. (1996), "Two different worlds: Acculturation stress and adaptation among Cuban and Nicaraguan families." *Journal of Social and Personal Relationships 13*(3), 435–456.

Gil, A. G., & Vega, W. A. (2001), "Latino drug use: Scope, risk factors, and reduction strategies." In M. Aguirre-Molina, C. W. Molina & R. E. Zambrana (eds), *Health issues in the Latn community.* NY: Jossey-Bass.

Gil, A. G., Vega, W. A., & Biafora, F. (1998), "Temporal influences of family structure and family risk factors on drug use initiation in a multiethnic sample of adolescent boys." *Journal of Youth and Adolescence 27*, 373–393.

Gil, A. G., Vega, W. A., & Dimas, J. (1994), "Acculturative stress and personal adjustment among Hispanic adolescent boys." *Journal of Community Psychology 22*, 43–54.

Gil, A. G., Wagner, E. F., & Vega, W. A. (2000), "Acculturation, familism, and alcohol use among Latino adolescent males: Longitudinal relations." *Journal of Community Psychology 28*(4), 443–458.

Gloria, A. M., & Peregoy, J. J. (1996), "Counseling Latino alcohol and other substance users/ abusers." *Journal of Substance Abuse Treatment 13*, 119–126.

Gloria, A. M., Trainor, C. M., Beasley, J. A., & Robinson-Kurpius, S. E. (1996), "Where have we been? Where are we? Where are we going? Issues in adolescent substance use." In D. Gross & D. Capuzzi (eds), *Adolescent Substance Use Prevention and Intervention: A guide for counselors, teachers and parents*. Alexandria, VA: American Counseling Association, 307–333.

Hawkins, J. D., Catalano, R. F., & Miller, J. Y. (1992), "Risk and protective factors for alcohol and other drug abuse problems in adolescence and early adulthood: Implications for substance abuse prevention." *Psychological Bulletin 112*, 64–105.

Hayes-Bautista, D. E., & Chapa, J. (1987), "Latino terminology: Conceptual bases for standardized terminology." *American Journal of Public Health 77*, 61–68.

Heather, N., Rollnick, S., Bell, A., & Richmond, R. (1996), "Effects of brief counseling among male heavy drinkers identified in general hospital wards." *Drug and Alcohol Review 15*, 29–38.

Ho, M. K. (1987), *Famly therapy with ethnic minorities*. Beverley Hills, CA: Sage Publications.

Hops, H., Tildesley, E., Lichtenstein, E., Ary, D., & Sherman, L. (1990), "Parent–adolescent problem-solving interactions and drug use." *American Journal of Drug and Alcohol Abuse 16*, 239–258.

Howard, D. L., LaVeist, T. A., & McCaughrin, W. C. (1996), "The effect of social environment on treatment outcomes in outpatient substance misuse treatment organizations: Does race really matter?" *Substance Use & Misuse 31*(5), 617–638.

Hu, T. W., Snowden, L. R., Jerrell, J. M., & Nguyen, T. D. (1991), "Ethnic populations in public mental health services: Services choice and level of use." *American Journal of Public Health 81*, 1429–1434.

Institute of Medicine (1990), *Broadening the Base of Treatment for Alcohol Problems*. Washington, DC: National Academy Press.

James, W. H., & Moore, D. D. (1997), "Screening for substance use among ethnic minority adolescents: Patterns and prevention approaches." *Substance Abuse 18*(2), 57–66.

Jimenez, A. L., Alegria, M., Pena, M., & Vera, M (1997), "Mental health utilization in women with symptoms of depression." *Women and Health 25*, 1–21.

Johnston, L. D., O'Malley, P. M., & Bachman, J. G. (1999), *National Survey Results on Drug Use from the Monitoring the Future Study, 1975–1998*. Washington, DC: US Department of Health and Human Services, National Institute on Drug Abuse, NIH Publication No. 99-4660.

Keefe, S. E. (1984), "Real and ideal extended families among Mexican Americans and Anglo Americans: On the meaning of close family ties." *Human Organization 43*, 65–70.

Keefe, S. E., & Padilla, A. M. (1987), *Chicano Ethnicity*. Albuquerque, NM: University of New Mexico Press.

Kendall, P. C., & Morris, R. J. (1991), "Child therapy: Issues and recommendations." *Journal of Consulting and Clinical Psychology 59*(6), 777–784.

Kline, A. (1996), "Pathways into drug user treatment: The influence of gender and racial/ethnic identity." *Substance Use & Misuse 31*(3), 323–342.

Koss-Chioino, J. D. (1995), "Traditional and folk approaches among ethnic minorities." In J. F. Aponte, R. Y. Rivers & J. Wohl (eds), *Psychological Interventions and Cultural Diversity*. Boston: Allyn & Bacon, 145–163.

Kuo, W. H. (1976), "Theories of migration and mental health: An empirical testing on Chinese-Americans." *Social Science Medicine 10*, 297–306.

Marin, G., & Marin, B. V. (1991), *Research with Hispanic Populations*. Newbury Park, CA: Sage Publications.

Mendoza, R. J., & Martinez, J. L. (1981), "The measurement of acculturation." In A. Baron Jr. (ed.), *Exploration in Chicano psychology* (pp. 71–82). NY: Praeger Publishers.

Miller, W. R. (1983), "Motivational interviewing with problem drinkers." *Behavioural Psychotherapy 11*, 147–172.

Miller, W. R. (1985), "Motivation for treatment: A review with special emphasis on alcoholism." *Psychological Bulletin 98*, 84–107.

Mindle, C. H. (1980), "Extended familism among urban Mexican-Americans, Anglos and Blacks." *Hispanic Journal of Behavioral Sciences 2*, 21–34.

Molina, C. W., & Aguirre-Molina, M. (1994), *Latino health in the U.S.: A growing challenge*. Washington, D.C.: American Public Health Association.

Mulvey, E. P., Arthur, M. W., & Reppucci, N. D. (1993), "The prevention and treatment of juvenile delinquency: A review of the research." *Clinical Psychology Review 13*, 133–167.

Nieves-Squires, S. (1991), "Hispanic women: Making their presence in campus less tenuous." *Project on the Status and Education of Women*. Washington, DC: Association of American Colleges.

Oetting, E. R. (1993), "Orthogonal cultural identification: Theoretical links between cultural identification and substance use." In M. R. De La Rosa & J. L. Recio Adrados (eds), *Drug Abuse Among Minority Youth: Methodological issues and recent research advances*. Washington DC: National Institute on Drug Abuse, NIH Publication No. 93-3479, 32–56.

Orford, J., Oppenheimer, E., & Edwards, G. (1976), "Abstinence or control: The outcome for excessive drinkers two years after consultation." *Behaviour Research and Therapy 14*, 409–418.

Orlandi, M. A. (1992), "The challenge of evaluating community-based prevention programs: A cross-cultural perspective." In M. A. Orlandi & R. Weston (eds), *Cultural Competence for Evaluators: A guide for alcohol and other drug abuse prevention practitioners working with ethnic/racial communities. OSAP cultural competence series 1*. US Department of Health & Human Services, Rockville, MD, 1–22.

O'Sullivan, M. J., & Lasso, B. (1992), "Community mental health services for Hispanics: A test of the culture compatibility hypothesis." *Hispanic Journal of Behavioral Sciences 14*(4), 455–468.

O'Sullivan, M., Peterson, P. D., Cox, G. B., & Kirkeby, J. (1989), "Ethnic populations: Community mental health services ten years later." *American Journal of Community Psychology 17*, 17–30.

Padilla, A. M. (1980), *Acculturation Theory, Models and Some New Findings*. Boulder, CO: Westview.

Pattison, E. M., Sobell, M. B., & Sobell, L. C. (1977), *Emerging Concepts of Alcohol Dependence*. New York: Springer.

Petraitis, J., Flay, B. R., & Miller, T. Q. (1995), "Reviewing theories of adolescent substance use: Organizing pieces of the puzzle." *Psychological Bulletin 117*(1), 67–86.

Portes, A. (1993), "Segmented assimilation among new immigrant youth: A conceptual framework." In R. G. Rumbaut & W. A. Cornelius (eds), *California's Immigrant Children: Theory, research, and implications for educational policy*. San Diego, CA: Center for US–Mexican Studies, University of California, San Diego, 71–76.

Portes, A., & Rumbaut, R. G. (1990), *Immigrant America: A portrait*. Berkeley, CA: University of California Press.

Prochaska, J. O. (1983), "Self-changers versus therapy versus Schachter" (Letter to the editor). *American Psychologist 38*, 853–854.

Richards, I., & Sullivan, A. (1996), "Psychotherapy for delinquents?" *Journal of Adolescence 19*, 63–73.

Rodriguez, O., & Zayas, L. H. (1990), "Hispanic adolescents and antisocial behavior: Sociocultural factors and treatment implications." In A. R. Stiffman & L. E. Davis (eds), *Ethnic Issues in Adolescent Mental Health.* Newbury Park, CA: Sage, 147–171.

Rogler, L., Cortes, D., & Malgady, R. (1991), "Acculturation and mental health status among Hispanics." *American Psychologist 6*, 585–597.

Ruiz, R. A., & Casas, J. M. (1981), "Culturally relevant behavioristic counseling for Chicano college students." In P. B. Pedersen, J. G. Draguns, W. J. Lonner, & J. E. Trimble (eds), *Counseling across cultures* (pp. 181–202). Honolulu, Hawaii: University of Hawaii Press.

Rumbaut, R. G. (1995), "New Californians: Comparative research findings on the educational progress of immigrant children." In Center for US–Mexico Studies, *California's Immigrant Children: Theory, research, and implications for educational policy.* San Diego, CA: University of California, San Diego, 16–69.

Rumbaut, R. G. (1996), "The crucible within: Ethnic identity, self-esteem, and segmented assimilation among children of immigrants." *International Migration Review 18*, 748–794.

Rumbaut, R. D., & Rumbaut, R. G. (1976), "The family in exile: Cuban expatriates in the United States." *American Journal of Psychiatry 133*, 395–399.

Santisteban, D. *et al.* (1997), "Brief structural/strategic family therapy with African American and Hispanic high-risk youth." *Journal of Community Psychology 25*(5), 453–471.

Santisteban, D., & Szapocznik, J. (1982), "Substance abuse disorders among Hispanics: A focus on prevention." In R. M. Becerra, M. Karno & J. Escobar (eds), *Mental Health and Hispanic Americans: Clinical Perspectives.* New York: Grune and Straton, 83–100.

Saunders, W. M., & Kershaw, P. W. (1979), "Spontaneous remission from alcoholism: A community study." *British Journal of Addiction 74*, 251–265.

Smart, J. F., & Smart, D. W. (1995), "Acculturative stress of Hispanics: Loss and challenge." *Journal of Counseling & Development 73*, 390–396.

Sobell, M. B., & Sobell, L. C. (eds) (1987), *Conceptual Issues Regarding Goals in the Treatment of Alcohol Problems.* New York: Hayworth Press.

Sobell, M. B., & Sobell, L. C. (1993), *Problem Drinkers: Guided self-change treatment.* New York: Guilford Press.

Sobell, L. C., & Sobell, M. B. (1995), *Alcohol Timeline Followback* (TLFB) Computer Software. Toronto, Canada: Addiction Research Foundation.

Sobell, M. B., & Sobell, L. C. (1998), "Guiding Self-Change." In W. R. Miller & N. Heather (eds), *Treating Addictive Behaviors: Processes of Change*, 2nd edn. New York: Plenum Press.

Sobell, L. C., Sobell, M. B., & Leo, G. I. (1993), "Spousal social support: A motivational intervention for alcohol abusers." Paper presented at the Annual Meeting of the Association for Advancement of Behavior Therapy, Atlanta, GA, November.

Spencer, G., & Hollmann, F. W. (1998), "National population projections." In US Census Bureau, *Population Profile of the United States, 1997.*

Sue, D. W., & Sue, D. (1990), *Counseling the Culturally Different: Theory and practice.* New York: John Wiley.

Szapocznik, J., & Kurtines, W. (1980), "Acculturation, biculturalism and adjustment among Cuban Americans." In A. Padilla (ed.), *Psychological Dimensions on the Acculturation Process: Theory, models and some new findings.* Boulder, CO: Westview Press, 56–78.

Szapocznik, J. *et al.* (1988), "Engaging adolescent drug abusers and their families in treatment: A strategic structural systems approach." *Journal of Consulting and Clinical Psychology 56*(4), 552–557.

Szapocznik, J., Scopetta, M., Kurtines, W. & Arnalde, M. (1978), "Theory and measurement of acculturation." *Interamerican Journal of Psychology 12*, 113–130.

Thurman, P. J., Swain, R., & Plested, B. (1995), "Intervention and treatment of ethnic minority substance abusers." In J. F. Aponte, R. Y. Rivers & J. Whol (eds), *Psychological Intervention and Cultural Diversity*. Boston, MA: Allyn and Bacon, 215–233.

Trandis, H. C., Marin, G., & Betancourt, H. (1984), "Simpatia as a cultural script of Hispanics." *Journal of Personality and Social Psychology 47*, 1363–1375.

Tuchfeld, B. S. (1976), *Changes in Patterns of Alcohol Use Without the Aid of Formal Treatment: An exploratory study of former problem drinkers*. Research Triangle Park, North Carolina: Research Triangle Institute.

US Census Bureau (1999), *Population estimates program*, December 23.

US Census (2000), Profiles of general population characteristics: 2000 Census of population and housing, United States. U.S. Department of Commerce, Economics, and Statistics Administration, U.S. Census Bureau.

Vega, W. A. (1990), "Hispanic families in the 1980s: A decade of research." *Journal of Marriage and the Family 52*, 1015–1024.

Vega, W. A., Alderete, E., Kolody, B., & Aguilar-Gaxiola, S. (1998), "Illicit drug use among Mexican and Mexican Americans in California: The effects of gender and acculturation." *Addiction 93*, 1839–1850.

Vega, W. A., & Amaro, H. (1994), "Latino Outlook: Good Health, Uncertain Prognosis." *Annual Review of Public Health 15*, 39–67.

Vega. W. A., & Gil, A. G. (1998), *Drug Use and Ethnicity in Early Adolescence*. New York: Plenum Press.

Vega, W. A., & Gil, A. G. (1999), "A Model for Explaining Drug Use Behavior Among Hispanic Adolescents." *Drugs and Society 14*, 55–73.

Vega, W. A., Gil, A. G., & Wagner, E. (1998), "Cultural adjustment and Hispanic adolescent drug use." In W. A. Vega & A. G. Gil (eds), *Drug Use and Ethnicity in Early Adolescence*. New York: Plenum Press, 125–148.

Vega, W. A., Gil, A. G., Warheit, G. J., Zimmerman, R. S., & Apospori, E. (1993), "Acculturation and delinquent behavior among Cuban American adolescents: Toward an empirical model." *American Journal of Community Psychology 21*, 113–125.

Vega, W. A., & Kolody, B. (in press), "Research gaps and disparities in mental health services to Hispanics." *Psychiatric Services*.

Vega, W. A., Kolody, B., Hwang, J., & Noble, A. (1993), "Prevalence and magnitude of perinatal substance exposures in California." *New England Journal of Medicine 32*, 850–854.

Vega, W. A., & Rumbaut, R. (1991), "Ethnic minorities and mental health." *Annual Review of Sociology 17*, 351–383.

Vega, W. A., Zimmerman, R. S., Warheit, G. J., Apospori, E., & Gil, A. G. (1993), "Risk factors for early adolescent drug use in four racial/ethnic groups." *American Journal of Public Health 83*, 185–189.

Wagner, E. F. (Principal Investigator) (2000), "Alcohol treatment targeting adolescents in need (ATTAIN)." National Institute on Alcohol Abuse and Alcoholism grant R01-AA12180.

Wagner, E. F., Gil, A. G., & Tubman, J. G. (1999), "Pilot data on juvenile offenders' preferences for individual versus family therapy for substance use problems." Unpublished manuscript.

Wagner, E. F., Swensen, C. C., & Henggeler, S. W. (2000), "Practical and methodological challenges in community-based interventions." *Children's Services: Social Policy, Research, and Practice 3*, 211–231.

Wagner, E. F., & Kassel, J. D. (1995), "Substance use and abuse." In R. T. Ammerman & M. Hersen (eds), *Handbook of Child Behavior Therapy in the Psychiatric Setting*. New York: John Wiley and Sons.

Waldorf, D., & Biernacki, P. (eds) (1982), *Natural Recovery from Heroin Addiction: A review of the incidence literature*. New York: Human Science.

Waldron, H. B. (1997), "Adolescent substance abuse and family therapy outcome: A review of randomized trials." In T. H. Ollendick & R. J. Prinz (eds), *Advances in Clinical Child Psychology*. New York: Plenum Press, 199–234.

Waldron, H. B., & Miller, W. R. (in press), "Client anger as a predictor of differential response to treatment." In R. Longabaugh (ed.), *Client–Treatment Matching*. Rockville, MD: NIAAA Monograph.

Warheit, G. J, Vega, W. A., Elfenbein, P. R., Gil, A. G., & Zimmerman, R. S. (1996), "A comparative analysis of cigarette, alcohol, and illicit drug use among an ethnically diverse sample of young adolescents." *Journal of Drug Issues 26*, 901–922.

Index